"A historical triumph! Here is the high drama of the most dangerous moment of the Cold War played out in the transcribed words of a small band of men groping their way toward a peaceful resolution. This remarkable book is an unprecedented illumination of the anguish of policy-making—and powerful proof of the cool and careful leadership of John F. Kennedy."

—Arthur Schlesinger, Jr.

"*The Kennedy Tapes* is a splendid achievement, as powerful and exciting a book as one is likely to read this year. . . . For all the thousands of pages on the missile crisis, these tapes possess an immediacy, a 'What would you do?' quality, that no historical account can match. . . . As with any good book about a great event, this one has a little of everything—suspense, humor, pathos, even darkest-before-the-dawn melodrama."

—Barry Gewen, *New York Times Book Review*

"These transcripts are at once the most important document of the crisis (and arguably, the entire Cold War period) and an unsurpassed look at White House and foreign policy decision-making. Even so, perhaps the greatest accomplishment of the book is to put a human face on that moment at which the superpowers stood closest to the brink of nuclear war. . . . To read it is to be in the White House in those fateful days of October, 1962. . . . *The Kennedy Tapes* is a must-read, not only for the student of history or international affairs, but for citizens of any country who hold out the hope that the Earth will never face such a crisis again."

—James Baker, *The Observer* [UK]

"These tapes re-create for those of us who lived through the Cuban Missile Crisis the tension and emotion of men deliberating a life and death decision for a world seemingly gone mad—a world which, it is now clear, was even more dangerous than we understood at the time."

—Robert McNamara

"[T]he transcripts . . . capture the power and drama of the moment. They show just how raw things were in the White House. They let readers hear leaders thinking out loud about what to do to force the Soviets to withdraw the missiles. They raise ideas about nuclear weapons, political power and civilian control of the military that remain vital today. . . . The tapes show men mulling over a global chess game in which the wrong move kills millions."   —Tim Weiner, *New York Times*

"The result is gripping history, as Kennedy and his advisors—the so-called Executive Committee, or "ExComm" of the National Security Council—react to the news that the Soviet Union, despite repeated public assurances to the contrary, had placed nuclear missiles in Cuba. The editing and annotations are understated; the concluding analysis is compelling."   —Richard J. Tofel, *Wall Street Journal*

"*The Kennedy Tapes* is an unremitting white-knuckle ride through the 14 crucial days in which the world seemed to be hurtling towards nuclear wipeout. . . . [It] gives an extraordinary insight into high-level decision-making at a time of unprecedented crisis."
                    —Adam Newey, *The Independent* [UK]

"No previous work has conveyed more clearly the sometimes chilling, sometimes heated, sometimes foggy atmosphere in that room during the Cold War's most dangerous fortnight. . . . Read the book."
                    —Theodore C. Sorensen, *Washington Monthly*

"This book is as extraordinary and illuminating as it is fun to read: an immensely vivid portrait of the President and his advisers steering their way, day by day, through the first nuclear confrontation. You won't be able to put the book down! It will transform your understanding of our government in crisis and of President Kennedy. Here is dispassionate intelligence performing at its very best."
                    —Richard E. Neustadt, Harvard University

THE KENNEDY TAPES

INSIDE THE WHITE HOUSE DURING THE CUBAN MISSILE CRISIS

→→→ *THE CONCISE EDITION* ←←←

Edited by
Ernest May and Philip Zelikow

David Coleman
George Eliades
Francis Gavin
Max Holland
Erin Mahan
Timothy Naftali
David Shreve
Associate Editors

Patricia Dunn
Assistant Editor

W. W. NORTON & COMPANY
NEW YORK • LONDON

Copyright © 2002, 2001 by The Miller Center of Public Affairs

Portions of this edition were previously published in *THE PRESIDENTIAL RECORDINGS:
John F. Kennedy, The Great Crises*, Volumes One, Two, and Three

Previous edition published by Harvard University Press as *The Kennedy Tapes: Inside the
White House During the Cuban Missile Crisis* by Philip D. Zelikow and Ernest R. May.
Copyright © 1997 by the President and Fellows of Harvard College

For information about permission to reproduce selections from this book, write to
Permissions, W. W. Norton & Company, Inc., 500 Fifth Avenue, New York, NY 10110

The text and display of this book are composed in Bell
Composition by Tom Ernst
Manufacturing by the Haddon Craftsmen, Inc.
Production manager: Amanda Morrison

Library of Congress Cataloging-in-Publication Data

The Kennedy tapes : inside the White House during the Cuban missile crisis / edited by
Ernest May and Philip Zelikow.—Concise ed.
p. cm.
Includes bibliographical references and index.
ISBN 0-393-32259-9 (pbk.)
1. Cuban Missile Crisis, 1962—Sources. 2. Kennedy, John F. (John Fitzgerald),
1917–1963—Archives. I. May, Ernest R. II. Zelikow, Philip, 1954–
E841 .K4655 2002
973.922—dc21   2001044484

W. W. Norton & Company, Inc., 500 Fifth Avenue, New York, N.Y. 10110
www.wwnorton.com

W. W. Norton & Company Ltd., Castle House, 75/76 Wells Street, London W1T 3QT

1 2 3 4 5 6 7 8 9 0

Contents

Preface to the Concise Edition

By mid-October 1962, the Cold War had intensified in unforeseen ways. Cuba, long a virtual colony of United States, had moved into the Soviet orbit. In late August, U. S. newspapers had begun reporting shipments of Soviet weapons to Cuba. President John F. Kennedy told the U.S. public that, to the best of his knowledge these weapons were defensive, not offensive. Soviet Premier Nikita Khrushchev had given him absolute assurances that this was the case. "Were it to be otherwise," Kennedy said, "the gravest issues would arise."

Shortly before 9:00 A.M. on Tuesday, October 16, Kennedy's assistant for national security affairs, McGeorge Bundy, brought to his bedroom photographs showing that the "gravest issues" had indeed arisen. Taken from very high altitude by a U-2 reconnaissance plane, these photographs showed the Soviets in Cuba setting up ballistic missiles targeted on cities in the continental United States.

For Kennedy, the presence of these missiles was intolerable. During the next 13 days, Kennedy and a circle of advisers debated how to cope with the challenge, knowing that one possible outcome was nuclear war. Throughout the crisis, U.S. decision making centered in the White House, and there, unknown to any of those present except President Kennedy and possibly his brother Robert, hidden tape recorders were capturing the deliberations, word for word. The resultant recordings provide a record of crisis decision making without parallel at any other time or place in history.

Before and after becoming president, Kennedy had made use of a recording device called a Dictaphone, mostly for dictating letters or notes. In the summer of 1962 he asked Secret Service Agent Robert Bouck to conceal recording devices in the Cabinet Room, the Oval Office, and a study/library in the Mansion. Without explaining why, Bouck obtained Tandberg reel-to-reel tape recorders, high-quality machines for the period, from the U.S. Army Signal Corps. He placed two of these machines in the basement of the West Wing of the White House in a room reserved for storing private presidential files. He placed another in the basement of the Executive Mansion.

The West Wing machines were connected by wire to two micro-

phones in the Cabinet Room and two in the Oval Office. Those in the
Cabinet Room were on the outside wall, placed in two spots covered by
drapes where once there had been wall fixtures. They were activated by
a switch at the President's place at the Cabinet table, easily mistaken for
a buzzer press. Of the microphones in the Oval Office, one was in the
kneehole of the President's desk, the other concealed in a coffee table
across the room. Each could be turned on or off with a single push on an
inconspicuous button.

We do not know where the microphone in the study of the Mansion
was located. In any case, Bouck, who had chief responsibility for the system, said in 1976, in an oral history interview, that President Kennedy
"did almost no recording in the Mansion." Of the machine in the basement of the Mansion, he said: "Except for one or two short recordings, I
don't think it was ever used."

President Kennedy also had a Dictaphone hooked up to a telephone
in the Oval Office and possibly also to a telephone in his bedroom. He
could activate it, and so could his private secretary, Evelyn Lincoln, who
knew of the secret microphones, often made sure that they were turned
off if the President had forgotten to do so, and took charge of finished
reels of tape when they were brought to her by Bouck or Bouck's assistant, Agent Chester Miller.

The most plausible explanation for Kennedy's making secret tape
recordings is that he wanted material to be used later in writing a memoir. Since he seems neither to have had transcripts made (with two minor
exceptions in 1963) nor to have listened to any of the tapes, it is unlikely
that he wanted them for current business. He had himself written histo-
ries and was by most accounts prone to asking historians' questions:
How did this situation develop? What had previous administrations
done? He knew how hard it was to answer such questions from surviving documentary records. And he faced the apparent likelihood that,
even if reelected in 1964, he would be an out-of-work ex-president when
not quite 51 years old.

Those who have spent much time with the tapes and those who have
compared the tapes to their own experience working with Kennedy find
no evidence that he taped only self-flattering moments. He often made
statements or discussed ideas that would have greatly damaged him had
they become public. Early in the missile crisis, for example, he mused
about his own possible responsibility for having brought it on. "Last
month I said we weren't going to [allow it]," he said. "Last month I
should have said that we don't care." He never seemed to make speeches
during a meeting for the benefit of future listeners. His occasional taped

monologues were private dictation about something that had happened or what he was thinking, obviously for his own later reference.

Two other points apply. First, he had no reason to suppose that the tapes would ever be heard by anyone other than himself unless he chose to make them available. They were completely secret. Second, he could hardly have known just what statements or positions would look good to posterity, for neither he nor his colleagues could know how the stories would turn out.

The tapes of missile crisis debates establish far more clearly than any other records the reasons why Kennedy thought Soviet missiles in Cuba so dangerous and important. They make abundantly clear that his preoccupation was not with Cuba or the immediate threat to the United States. He feared that, if he did not insist on removal of the missiles, Soviet Premier Nikita Khrushchev would be emboldened to try to take over West Berlin, in which case he—Kennedy—would have only two choices. He would either have to abandon the two and a half million West Berliners theretofore protected by the United States, or he would have to use nuclear weapons against the Soviet Union, for there was no imaginable way of defending West Berlin with conventional military forces. The Soviet missiles in Cuba would then be a "thing in our guts" constraining the U.S. nuclear threats to save Berlin.

This concise edition of *The Kennedy Tapes* contains material that has come to light since 1997, when the book first appeared. The material from the September conversations is new, including excerpts from important transcripts revealing the thinking behind Kennedy's public warning of "gravest consequences" and his puzzlement about Soviet motivations before the crisis erupted. This edition also includes transcripts of some taped telephone conversations that were not placed in the collection of the John F. Kennedy Library until 1998.

When we prepared the original transcripts, we worked with the analog cassettes released to the public by the Kennedy Library. With both of us listening to these again and again and again, we managed to make out a large part of what was said and to identify which words were those of Kennedy or of other major participants with distinctive voices. For this version, we were able to obtain from the Kennedy Library Digital Audio Tape (DAT) copies of the original reels. We, and this volume, are also now part of the large Presidential Recordings Project that has been established by the Miller Center of Public Affairs at the University of Virginia. That project has enabled us to take advantage of some added technology, especially high-end headphone amplifiers. Most importantly, we were able to draw on the Miller Center team that was assembled for preparing the complete reference volumes of Kennedy's presidential recordings, the first three of which are being published in 2001. The project scholars who helped us perfect the transcripts are listed on the title page as associate editors. We are especially grateful for the contribution of Timothy Naftali, who directs the Miller Center's Presidential Recordings Project. He is one of the world's leading scholars on the Cuban missile crisis and was the principal transcriber of the September 1962 conversations included in this volume.

In the transcripts presented in this volume (and which can be found without any abridgement in Volumes 2 and 3 of the John F. Kennedy reference series), we have been able to make out many words and phrases that were previously incomprehensible. Our speaker identifications have become more certain, particularly in the cases of individuals who either spoke infrequently or had voices without distinctive accents. In some instances, we heard meaning that we had missed before.

We are grateful to Drake McFeely and W. W. Norton for making it possible to put in the hands of readers this updated, concise version of a unique body of source material concerning what was probably the most dangerous crisis in the history of humankind.

ERNEST R. MAY   PHILIP D. ZELIKOW

A Note on Sources

In addition to the various memoirs and other writings cited as sources in our footnotes, we have relied on the relevant archival holdings for the White House and the various agencies of the U.S. government, held mainly in the John F. Kennedy Library in Boston and the National Archives, Washington, D.C. We have also relied on the less formal holdings of that useful private institute, the National Security Archive, Washington, D.C.

Each footnote appearing for the first time in a chapter is fully cited on first reference. The one exception made was for the many footnotes citing the U.S. Department of State, *Foreign Relations of the United States 1961–63* (Washington, DC: Government Printing Office). Footnotes that include references to *Foreign Relations of the United States* are abbreviated as *FRUS* and include the volume number and page numbers. For *FRUS* references other than those from 1961 to 1963, the appropriate years are included.

Introduction

On the morning when he first saw photographs of Soviet missiles in Cuba, John Fitzgerald Kennedy was 4 months and 18 days past his forty-fifth birthday. During the 13 days of crisis that followed, he would ask advice from some men older than he and from a few who were younger. All had been molded by World War II and the Cold War. *Munich, Pearl Harbor,* the *iron curtain, containment,* the *Berlin blockade, Korea, McCarthyism, Suez-Hungary, Sputnik,* and other such shorthand references to recent history called up shared memories and shared beliefs. A reader for whom those terms have only faint associations may misunderstand some of the dialogue recorded here. This introductory chapter aims at providing such a reader a sense of the framework of experience within which Kennedy and his advisers interpreted the crisis.

Munich captured a world of meaning, especially for Kennedy. His father had played a role in the drama. He himself had published a book analyzing it. *Munich,* of course, referred not to a single event but to a series of events and to their supposed lesson or lessons. The Munich conference of 1938 capped efforts by Britain to appease Nazi Germany, arguably making up for too-harsh peace treaties imposed after World War I. Czechoslovakia had been created by those treaties. At Munich, Britain compelled Czechoslovakia to cede to Germany borderlands populated by German speakers. When the Nazi dictator Adolf Hitler subsequently seized non-German Czechoslovakia and invaded Poland, Britain changed policy. World War II commenced. *Munich* and *appeasement* became synonyms for wishful weakness in the face of aggression.

Kennedy's father, Joseph Patrick Kennedy, a famous stock speculator and one of the few millionaires openly to back Franklin Roosevelt, was Roosevelt's ambassador to Britain at the time of the Munich conference.[1] Both in cables to the State Department and in public speeches and interviews, Joe Kennedy backed Britain's appeasement of Germany. He continued to do so. Well into World War II, he argued that Britain had been right to conciliate Hitler and that the best interests of the world would be served by a compromise peace. Joe Kennedy also spoke out against any action by his own government that might embroil the United States in the war. He thus marked himself as both an appeaser and an isolationist. (In his 1992 novel, *Fatherland*, Robert Harris imagines the world as it might have been had Britain come to terms with Hitler. One plot line concerns a visit to Europe in the 1960s by President Kennedy. But the President is Joe Kennedy, not John.)

John Kennedy was 21 and a third-year undergraduate at Harvard at the time of the Munich Conference.[2] During the conference, he seemed to agree with his father; the coming of war gave him second thoughts. Previously a desultory student, preoccupied with games and girls, he turned in his final college year to writing a long honors thesis, with the laborious title, "Appeasement at Munich (the Inevitable Result of the Slowness of Conversion of the British Democracy to Change from a Disarmament Policy to a Rearmament Policy)." Family friends helped him polish the manuscript and publish it under the improved title *Why England Slept*. Appearing in 1940, only weeks after the fall of France, it became a surprise best-seller. It did not entirely contradict his father's position. Indeed, Joe Kennedy read and approved the final draft. But the book struck a different stance. Declaring appeasement a weak policy forced on British governments by British public opinion, it called on the United States to arm so as not to have to follow a similar policy if challenged by totalitarianism.

All his life, Kennedy would carry the burden of being Joe Kennedy's son. Robert Lovett, Truman's secretary of defense and one of the elder statesmen whom Kennedy would consult during the missile crisis, voted against Kennedy in 1960 because Joe Kennedy was his father.[3] George Ball, who would be under secretary of state and a regular member of Kennedy's missile crisis circle, writes in his memoirs that he joined the Kennedy administration only after assuaging doubts similar to Lovett's: "I had long despised the elder Kennedy, who represented everything I disliked and mistrusted. He had been a buccaneer on Wall Street, an opportunist in politics, and a debilitating influence when our civilization was fighting for its life; now we were once more engaged against an enemy with the same face of tyranny. Before I could wholeheartedly support the new President, I had to satisfy myself that he was free of his father's views and influence. Just after the election I had carefully analyzed his writings and speeches—and had found reassurance that the father's noxious views had not infected the son."[4] So, for Kennedy, *Munich* and *appeasement* connoted not only past events and their supposed lessons but also his own need continually to prove that his views were not his father's.

Another member of the missile crisis circle in whose words one can hear echoes of the 1930s is Secretary of State Dean Rusk. Eight years older than Kennedy, Rusk had grown up in circumstances that Kennedy could scarcely imagine. The son of a poor Georgia farmer, he could remember running through the cold night to reach an outdoor privy and wearing underwear stitched from flour sacks. But he had managed to go to Davidson College in North Carolina. From there he had gone on to a Rhodes Scholarship. Studying at Oxford from 1931 to 1934 and spending several months in Germany, he had seen at firsthand not only Hitler's dictatorship but an event highlighted in *Why England Slept*—an Oxford Union debate of February 1933 that resulted in a 275-to-153 vote in favor of the resolution "This House will in no circumstances fight for King and Country." Rusk remembered ruefully how he himself, back in the United States teaching at a women's college in northern California, had argued for giving Hitler some leeway. His subsequent conversion was so complete that tears could come to his eyes when he pleaded with students not to be seduced by appeasement and isolationism.[5]

Pearl Harbor was another historical reference point for Kennedy and his advisers. Practically all Americans had been shocked to learn on December 7, 1941, that Japanese planes had bombed the U.S. naval base at Pearl Harbor and sunk or severely damaged the warships anchored there. Most could recall ever afterward exactly where they were when they heard this news. Kennedy and a friend with whom he shared an apartment in the District of Columbia had just finished a pickup game of touch football on the grounds near the Washington Monument. They heard the first bulletins on their car radio while driving home.[6]

On Kennedy himself, the Pearl Harbor attack had no immediate effect. During the previous year, as the nation moved further and further away from isolationism, the armed forces had expanded. Concealing chronic ailments that should have exempted him, Kennedy had wangled a commission in the naval reserve. As one team of biographers comments, "Thus, a young man who could certainly not have qualified for the Sea Scouts on [the basis of] his physical condition, entered the U.S. Navy."[7] He was serving as an ensign in the Office of Naval Intelligence when the Pearl Harbor attack occurred.

Rusk, having been in ROTC and remained in the reserve, had been called to active duty in 1940. He was a captain in the Army, also in Washington, serving in Army intelligence. And in the same building with Kennedy was Adlai E. Stevenson, who would be Kennedy's ambassador to the United Nations in October 1962. Eight years older than Rusk and 17 years older than Kennedy, Stevenson was a prominent Chicago lawyer serving as a civilian assistant to the secretary of the Navy. In Chicago, he had been a conspicuous critic of the positions espoused by Joe Kennedy. Ironically, he would be the person in Kennedy's missile crisis circle regarded as most nearly an advocate of appeasement.[8]

President Roosevelt's address to Congress on Pearl Harbor had breathed moral outrage. He declared December 7, 1941, "a date which will live in infamy," remembered for an "unprovoked and dastardly attack." The two members of Kennedy's missile crisis circle whose references to Pearl Harbor would echo some of Roosevelt's indignation were two not then in uniform or in government service—George Ball and Kennedy's younger brother, Robert Francis (or Bobby), who would be his attorney general. Ball, approximately the same age as Rusk, was a wealthy Chicago lawyer, friendly with Stevenson. He had worked in the Treasury Department during the early New Deal but then returned to private practice. Though he had been, if anything, more critical than Stevenson of the isolationism identified with Joe Kennedy, he had stayed away from Washington, and he would continue to do so until the spring of 1942. Robert Kennedy, at the time of Pearl Harbor, was barely 16 years old and a third-year student at a Rhode Island preparatory school, struggling for passing grades.[9]

In the debates recorded on Kennedy's tapes, Pearl Harbor has a presence as pervasive as Munich. Recollections of Pearl Harbor had helped to make worst-case worry about surprise attack a guiding theme for post-war U.S. military planning and procurement. Absent Pearl Harbor, the whole debate about the Soviet missiles in Cuba might have been different, for supposed lessons from the Pearl Harbor attack shaped the intelligence collection apparatus that informed Kennedy of the missiles and kept him and his advisers abreast of day-to-day developments. Most important of all, Pearl Harbor served as a conclusive example of the proposition that a secretive government might pursue its ambitions, or relieve its frustrations, by adopting courses of action that objectively seemed irrational or even suicidal. This proposition haunts the discussions of Soviet motives and possible Soviet reactions during the missile crisis.

Though Kennedy and his advisers carried away from World War II itself memories that influenced their thinking in October 1962, the memories were not counterparts to Munich or Pearl Harbor. They were individual, not collective. Kennedy, continuing to hide his ailments, was assigned combat duty as the skipper of a 12-man patrol torpedo boat in the southwest Pacific. When the boat was rammed by a Japanese destroyer, Kennedy managed to save most of his crew. He towed one man ashore by keeping his teeth clenched on the man's lifejacket strings. Graphically recounted in a *New Yorker* article by writer John Hersey (and later in a book by Robert Donovan), the story of PT 109 made young Kennedy famous once again. The experience may also, however, have contributed to the caution he would exercise during the missile crisis. He wrote to his father at the time: "When I read that we will fight the Japs for years if necessary and will sacrifice hundreds of thousands if we must—I always like to check from where he is talking—it's seldom out here. People get so used to talking about billions of dollars and millions of soldiers that thousands of dead sounds like drops in the bucket. But if those thousands want to live as much as the ten I saw—they should measure their words with great, great care."[10]

Invalided out after his return from the Pacific, Kennedy did a brief stint as a newspaper reporter. He covered the San Francisco conference of April 1945, from which came the final Charter of the United Nations organization. Adlai Stevenson, who was there as a senior adviser to the U.S. delegation, had responsibility for press relations. "It was all a little ridiculous," Stevenson remarked later, "me interpreting developments play by play in a secret room at the Fairmont Hotel, whose number was known to not less than 50–75 U.S. correspondents."[11] Kennedy, one of the 50 to 75, wrote for his newspaper, in the vein of his earlier, private letter:

> The average GI on the street . . . doesn't seem to have a very clear-cut conception of what this meeting is about. But one bemedaled marine sergeant gave the general reaction when he said: "I don't know much about what's going on—but if they just fix it so that we don't have to fight any more—they can count me in."
>
> "Me, too, sarge."[12]

The Pacific War that had commenced at Pearl Harbor ended with Japan's surrender in August 1945. Two other men who would be around Kennedy during the missile crisis had also seen service in that war. Curtis LeMay, who would be chief of staff of the Air Force in October 1962, and Kennedy's most hawkish adviser, had been transferred from the European theater to take over the 20th Air Force, based on Guam. Slightly older than Rusk, he had joined the Army Air Corps in 1928, leaving Ohio State University without a degree. The mission of LeMay's command was strategic bombing of the Japanese home islands. After analyzing the command's operations, LeMay ordered a complete change in tactics. The B-29s had been flying at high altitude in order to be safe from antiaircraft fire. LeMay calculated that at much lower altitudes, there might be somewhat greater loss of aircraft but that this disadvantage would be more than offset by increases in bomb loads and in bombing accuracy. Experience seemed to prove him right. In a low-level attack on Tokyo in March 1945, his 325-plane force lost only 14 aircraft and hit a much higher than usual percentage of its targets.

An admiring observer of LeMay's management of the 20th Air Force was Army Air Forces Lieutenant Colonel Robert S. McNamara, who would later be Kennedy's secretary of defense and LeMay's civilian boss. McNamara was less than a year older than Kennedy. He, too, came of Irish immigrants but his forbears had taken the Panama route to California. Although his parents were never as poor as Rusk's and he grew up in a city rather than on a farm, he remembered money's being scarce in his family. While attending the University of California at Berkeley, he had had to live at home in Oakland, and he and a classmate would drive to school, hoarding gas by coasting downhill whenever possible.[13] He majored in economics, had a superb record, and graduated at 21 but, to his lasting vexation, failed to win a Rhodes Scholarship. He went on instead to Harvard Business School. During the period of the Munich conference and *Why England Slept*, McNamara was studying management just across the Charles River from Kennedy. After graduation, he was one of a group kept on at the Business School to teach the new subject of financial control. Early in 1942, the Air Forces appropriated the entire group and gave McNamara a commission. He served in Europe until late in 1944, urging on commanders exactly the type of benefit-versus-cost calculation that he saw exemplified by LeMay.

McNamara and LeMay were not to see eye to eye during the missile crisis. Indeed, they may not have seen eye to eye in 1945, when LeMay was clearly gratified not only by the cost-effectiveness of his operations but by their consequences. Of the March 1945 raid, LeMay boasted later: "We burned up nearly sixteen square miles of Tokyo," then quoted the official report from the time: "There were more casualties than in any other military action in the history of the world."[14] LeMay had also had command responsibility for the special bomber group that attacked Hiroshima and Nagasaki, and his attitude toward the first atomic bombs was dismissive. He rejected the notion that they were somehow special, morally or otherwise. "The assumption seems to be," he wrote, "that it is much more wicked to kill people with a nuclear bomb, than to kill people by busting their heads with rocks."[15] At least in later years, McNamara would argue vehemently that nuclear weapons were special and ought never to be used.

During the final year of World War II and the early postwar years, Kennedy and the men who would surround him during the missile crisis moved into the era of the Cold War.[16] The syndicated columnist, Walter

Lippmann, popularized that term as early as 1946. Winston Churchill contributed another enduring one when he declared, also in 1946, "From Stettin in the Baltic to Trieste in the Adriatic, an *iron curtain* has descended across the continent" (editors' emphasis).[17] Yet another new term—*containment*—came into wide use in 1947. George Kennan, a professional diplomat, later an eminent historian, gave *containment* currency through an article published in 1947 under the pseudonym X in the quarterly *Foreign Affairs*. He called for "a long-term, patient but firm and vigilant containment of Russian expansive tendencies," particularly through "adroit and vigilant application of counter-force at a series of constantly shifting geographical and political points, corresponding to the shifts and maneuvers of Soviet policy."

Kennedy's attitudes evolved much as those of most other Americans did. When reporting on the San Francisco conference and its aftermath, he had expressed some wariness about the future. Explaining to the editor of the *Atlantic Monthly* why he could not complete a projected article in favor of arms limitation, Kennedy wrote: "The Russians . . . have demonstrated a suspicion and lack of faith in Britain and the United States which, while understandable in the light of recent history, nevertheless indicates that in the next few years it will be prudent to be strong."[18] These comments from the 1940s foreshadow the wary empathy with which he would approach the Soviet Union as president.

Kennedy ran successfully for Congress in 1946. There he supported President Harry Truman's efforts to put containment into practice by giving aid to European countries threatened either by the Soviet Union or by domestic Communist Parties. While his father spoke out publicly against wasting money or running risks on behalf of foreigners unable to solve their own problems, Kennedy made a well-publicized speech in the House, declaring that the United States had a duty not only "to prevent Europe and Asia from becoming dominated by one great military power" but to prevent "the suffering people of Europe and Asia from succumbing to the soporific ideology of Red totalitarianism."[19]

As the language of Kennedy's speech attests, Americans had come increasingly to see Soviet totalitarianism as a threat comparable to that of Nazi totalitarianism. One seeming lesson of the 1930s was that the United States should not do what it had done then. The U.S. government should instead make clear that, in case of aggression in any way resembling Hitler's, the United States would be in the front line from the very first day.

In 1948 the Truman administration set an example. Berlin, the former German capital, lay well inside eastern Germany, occupied by the

Soviets under wartime agreements. Berlin itself, however, had American, British, and French sectors too, creating a populous Western island within the Soviet zone. In June, the Soviets suddenly imposed a blockade, stopping all rail and road traffic from the West into Berlin. After reflecting on alternatives, President Truman ordered a round-the-clock airlift to deliver food and supplies to the city. If the Soviets interfered, the result could well have been war. The Soviets let the planes go through. After some months, they suspended the blockade. From then on, Berlin stood as a symbol of U.S. determination to put U.S. lives on the line to defend against forceful Soviet takeover of any part of Europe.

In 1949, the United States signed the North Atlantic Treaty with Canada, Britain, and various West European states. The Senate as well as the executive branch thus committed the United States to the principle that an attack on any European signatory would be treated by the United States as an attack on itself. At the time, the commitments to Berlin and to the North Atlantic Treaty were made easier by the U.S. monopoly on nuclear weapons and by misplaced confidence that that monopoly would last.

Despite the vigor of his initial support for containment, Kennedy seemed a mere observer of these events. Others who would be around him in October 1962 were, however, deeply engaged. Robert Lovett was under secretary of state and a key adviser to Truman and Secretary of State George Marshall on the Berlin blockade. Rusk, who had become a colonel during the war and ended up on Marshall's Pentagon staff, had followed Marshall to the State Department and was assistant secretary for U.N. affairs. LeMay, a three-star general in the newly independent Air Force, was commander of U.S. Air Forces in Europe. He thus organized and ran the airlift, and did so with the same driving efficiency he had shown in the Pacific.

Time and again during the missile crisis debates, one person or another would make reference to the blockade and airlift. For some reason, they tended to misdate it, placing it in 1947–48 instead of 1948–49. But Kennedy and Rusk, in particular, would mention the blockade as the one example in the past of a direct Soviet challenge to the West. And Kennedy would cite the episode as one in which the United States had been free to use nuclear weapons and had chosen not to do so.[20]

After the Berlin blockade crisis, the Cold War intensified. In 1949 the Soviets surprised the West by testing an atomic bomb. It became clear that Soviet dictator Joseph Stalin, instead of giving priority to repairing war damage, was pouring resources into military modernization. In late June 1950 came the Korean War. Soviet-backed North Korea suddenly launched a major offensive against U.S.-backed South Korea. Interpreting this as a challenge to the principles of the U.N. Charter and possibly as a rehearsal for a similar offensive in divided Germany, Truman immediately sent in U.S. military forces. Before the year was out, North Korea had been defeated, but Communist China had intervened and pushed the battle line back to the preconflict boundary.

The commander of U.S. and U.N. forces, General Douglas MacArthur, declared that China's intervention created a "new war." He proposed various operations against China proper. When the Truman administration remained adamant against extending the war beyond the Korean peninsula, MacArthur appealed for support from Truman's political opponents in Congress and elsewhere. Truman relieved MacArthur of his command. MacArthur then came home, greeted by huge crowds in city after city and received with a standing ovation by a joint session of Congress. Protracted hearings followed, calling into question the wisdom of Truman's policy and creating speculation about Truman's possible impeachment. Passions eventually died down but only after a parade of other World War II military leaders joined in testifying that MacArthur's position was unsound. Meanwhile, the Soviets had initiated truce talks, and eventually all parties accepted an armistice, leaving the country divided very much as previously.

This long and decidedly unpopular war was another important landmark for men in Kennedy's missile crisis circle. Shortly before the 1950 North Korean offensive, Rusk voluntarily left his job as deputy under secretary of state to assume the lower-ranking post of assistant secretary for Far Eastern affairs. The Communists' success in the Chinese Civil War had stirred domestic furor; many in Congress and elsewhere alleged that the United States had "lost" China, possibly because of Communist subversives within the U.S. government. (One of the attackers was Congressman John Kennedy, who declared in 1949 that the United States's China policy had "reaped the whirlwind. . . . What our young men had saved, our diplomats and our President have frittered away."[21]) The Far Eastern Bureau thus became the hottest spot in the department, if not in the executive branch, and hence a challenge to Rusk's strong sense of duty. Looking back, Rusk took pride in having fended off such charges and especially for having been one who counseled patience and restraint during the Korean War.

LeMay's retrospect on the Korean War was exactly the opposite of Rusk's. After initiating the Berlin airlift, LeMay had returned to the United States to take over the U.S. Strategic Air Command (SAC). Technically a unified command directly under the Joint Chiefs of Staff

(JCS), it was, for practical purposes, an all–Air Force command with the mission of preparing to destroy the Soviet homeland. LeMay made it one of the most efficient and dedicated organizations in military history. When the Korean War opened, LeMay urged that SAC attack North Korea "immediately with incendiaries and delete four or five of their largest towns."[22] He remained ever afterward angry that his proposal was rejected. He also favored bombing China once the Chinese had intervened, and he argued gruffly that they never would have intervened had they been presented with a credible threat that the result would be incendiary raids on their cities.

Maxwell Taylor, who would be Chairman of the Joint Chiefs of Staff during the missile crisis, also had a part in the Korean War.[23] About the same age as Adlai Stevenson, Taylor was a Missouri-born West Pointer. A linguist who had gone back to the academy to teach French and Spanish and served a tour in Asia as a Japanese language officer, he had been on General Marshall's staff in Washington early in World War II, then been a distinguished paratroop commander in Europe. Analyzing the Korean War for the Army staff, he concluded that the war's military objectives had been poorly defined. Shortly before a final truce agreement was reached, Taylor assumed the principal U.S. military command in Korea. From this experience as a whole, he concluded that the U.S. government had made a mistake in treating diplomatic negotiations and military pressures as alternatives rather than as complementary courses of action, best pursued simultaneously. As to whether the United States had been right or wrong to keep the war so limited, he remained of two minds—not of Rusk's but also decidedly not of LeMay's. These lessons—and this past ambivalence—would influence his thinking when he sat with Kennedy in October 1962 and interpreted for him the advice of LeMay and the other chiefs of staff.

Apart from its particular lessons for individuals, the Korean War had lasting effects on U.S. policymaking. Until World War II, the military establishment had had almost no voice in foreign policy decisions. After the war, Congress made provision for a National Security Council (NSC), intending it to ensure that presidents would not totally ignore military considerations when making decisions about international relations. Besides the President, the principal members were the Secretary of State and the civilian Secretary of Defense. The Chairman of the Joint Chiefs of Staff was later designated as an adviser to, but not a member of, the NSC. Until the Korean War, the Secretary of State remained the pivotal member of the NSC and the principal framer of foreign policy.

During and after the Korean War, the military establishment gained a much stronger voice.[24] Dwight Eisenhower, who succeeded Truman, had the advantage of being himself a five-star general and a hero of World War II. He sought to reduce the influence of the uniformed military largely because of concern that they might use that influence to increase military spending. Despite his background and the force of his personality, he was only partially successful. Military leaders who criticized his policies found ready supporters on Capitol Hill and in the press. Kennedy was among them.

During the missile crisis, Kennedy would hold only one formal meeting with the Joint Chiefs of Staff. He and the others would usually rely on Taylor to report their views. But that did not make their views any less weighty. Kennedy and his civilian advisers recognized that it would be inadvisable—to say no more—to adopt a line of action that leaders in the uniformed military would unite in opposing. During the spring of 1962, Kennedy's light reading would include a novel by Fletcher Knebel and Charles Bailey, *Seven Days in May,* in which military leaders engineer a coup against a president who seems to them too pacifistic. Asked by a friend whether something of the sort could actually happen, Kennedy said he thought it could.[25] The fact that such a contingency did not seem totally unrealistic in 1962 traced in large part to the Korean War and the MacArthur affair.

The period of the Korean War had also been the high phase of McCarthyism.[26] The label came from Joe McCarthy, a loutish Senator from Wisconsin, who had taken to its outer limit the tactic of detecting domestic U.S. Communists and Communist sympathizers as the chief sources of trouble both in the United States and in the world. But McCarthy's success in capturing headlines and terrorizing individuals and agencies reflected widespread public anxiety fed by, among other things, proof that prominent officials of the Roosevelt administration had been secret Soviet agents. Alger Hiss, Rusk's immediate predecessor in managing U.N. affairs in the State Department, had gone to the penitentiary.

To assuage public anxiety, the executive branch, Congress, and officials in state and local governments and in private bodies such as colleges and churches established rules and procedures that did in fact resemble earlier efforts to find witches or to punish heretics. Many rules and procedures inhibiting if not barring free speech remained commonplace in 1962.

Kennedy's father was a strong and an unrepentant supporter of McCarthy. Kennedy, who moved from the House to the Senate after the election of 1952, was on good terms with McCarthy. Robert Kennedy went to work on McCarthy's staff. After finishing Harvard during

World War II, he had served briefly in the Navy as an enlisted man and had just graduated from the University of Virginia Law School. After a row with McCarthy's chief staffer, Roy Cohn, he quit. He later worked with senators who were critical of McCarthy and Cohn and helped draft a report that led to formal Senate censure of McCarthy in 1954, a censure that effectively ended McCarthy's career.

John Kennedy did not vote for or against the McCarthy censure. He was in a hospital undergoing a series of life-threatening operations to arrest one of his disabilities—spinal degeneration that kept him in constant and increasing pain. He could, of course, have recorded a position by pairing with another senator. He was the only Democrat not to do so. This fact, together with Bobby's work for McCarthy, helped to keep alive suspicion of John Kennedy—like father, like son, like brother.

By October 1962 McCarthyism itself would seem far in the past. Memories of its virulence, however, persisted. So did public anxiety. A hit film of 1962, John Frankenheimer's *The Manchurian Candidate*, starring Kennedy's friend Frank Sinatra, was based on the premise that Communists could manipulate U.S. political processes through their own mind-controlled puppets. When Kennedy and his advisers talked at the White House about possible public reactions to one option or another, many of them had in the backs of their minds hysteria such as that which had risen during the first decade of the Cold War. This in turn would increase their sensitivity to opinions such as those of LeMay.

During the 1950s, the careers of Kennedy and Stevenson had intersected again. After World War II, Stevenson had gone back to his home state of Illinois to practice law, oversee a small town newspaper, and manage a farm in the village of Libertyville. (His friend George Ball observed: "He had the normal equipment of any good farmer of the area: a tennis court, a swimming pool, a horse or two, and a few sheep.")[27] In 1948 the Illinois Democratic machine enlisted Stevenson as its clean-government candidate for governor. Eloquent, obviously sincere, and running against a Republican tarred by scandal, he swept the state. Though Stevenson wanted to seek a second term as governor, Truman and others talked him into becoming the presidential nominee. Again, he was eloquent and obviously sincere. All the Kennedys supported him. He garnered many more votes than Truman had in 1948, but not enough to avoid being overrun by Eisenhower.

Four years later, Stevenson was again the candidate against Eisenhower. Prior to the Democratic convention, Kennedy decided to seek the vice presidential nomination. He had in the meantime again achieved celebrity through a book. Titled *Profiles in Courage*, it sketched biographies of senators, from the early republic on, who had risked their careers for unpopular principles. Kennedy's work on it had kept him occupied while recuperating from back surgery. It not only became a best-seller; it won a Pulitzer Prize. Given his failure to vote on the McCarthy censure, his book title provoked from the Democratic left a rebuke that he needed less profile and more courage. (Eleanor Roosevelt was usually the person credited.)

For the vice-presidential nomination, Kennedy's chief opponent was Senator Estes Kefauver, who had unsuccessfully opposed Stevenson in the presidential primaries. Stevenson disappointed Kennedy by deciding to support neither candidate but to let the delegates make their own choice, and Kefauver won. Robert Kennedy joined Stevenson's campaign train and suffered even greater disappointment by watching the candidate in action. "Stevenson just did not seem to be able to make any kind of decision," he commented later.[28]

At some point after Stevenson's second defeat, Kennedy decided that he would try himself to be the Democratic presidential nominee in 1960. This effort would preoccupy him and his brother from then until the 1960 election.

In the course of seeking the presidency, Kennedy confronted three clusters of issues that would become central concerns for him after being elected and that would bear critically on his management of the missile crisis. Their catch terms were *strategic balance, European security*, and *Third World.*

Strategic balance referred to the relationship between U.S. and Soviet nuclear arsenals.[29] The years between Hiroshima and Kennedy's swearing-in as president saw dizzying advances in nuclear weapons and related military technologies. Having cracked the secret of making bombs based on nuclear fission, scientists and engineers in both the West and the Soviet Union turned successfully to exploiting the vastly greater potential energy of nuclear fusion. The blast of an atomic bomb, a fission weapon, had been calculated in kilotons, each kiloton equivalent to 1,000 tons of TNT. The blast of a hydrogen bomb, a fusion weapon, was calculated in megatons, each equivalent to 1,000 kilotons, or 1 million tons, of TNT.

Before long, both Soviet and Western weapons laboratories became able to mass-produce both fission and fusion weapons and to increase explosive power while reducing both size and weight. The bombs used against Hiroshima and Nagasaki had been huge, hand-crafted devices, so delicate and so difficult to engineer that it had been hard to imagine their ever existing in large numbers. The Hiroshima bomb had been 10 feet long, weighed almost 5 tons, and, to be loaded in an airplane and armed to explode, required a crew of experts, working several days. By the time of the missile crisis, bombs 20 times more powerful were 3 feet long, shaped like ordinary TNT bombs, and easily slapped onto the wing of a ground-based or carrrier-based fighter bomber.[30]

During the 1950s, both camps succeeded in increasing the range, speed, and accuracy with which they could deliver nuclear weapons. In 1957 Soviet Sputnik rockets put objects in space orbit, demonstrating an apparent capability for intercontinental ballistic missiles (ICBMs), which would be in flight only about 30 minutes to reach the United States and against which there was no known defense.

The Sputnik flights sparked panicky debate in the United States about an impending missile gap. Democrats, with Kennedy one of the leaders, charged that Eisenhower administration penny-pinching had allowed the Soviets to gain a lead that not only compromised containment but also possibly jeopardized national survival.

To appease critics, the Eisenhower administration stepped up work on high-thrust rockets and large capacity reentry vehicles. It was for the same purpose and also to placate allies that the administration arranged to place intermediate-range ballistic missiles (IRBMs) abroad—Thors in Britain, Jupiters in Italy and Turkey. By the time of the 1960 presidential election, the Eisenhower administration had moved far along in the development of several models of ICBMs, with a solid-fueled Minuteman the most promising. It was also well along on Polaris, a missile of intermediate range but classified as a submarine-launched ballistic missile (SLBM) rather than an IRBM.

As of 1960 the actual nuclear arsenal of the United States was enormous. That of the Soviet Union, according to calculations by the U.S. intelligence community, was smaller but also huge. With competition spurred by the Sputniks, the arsenals grew almost by the day. When Eisenhower yielded the presidency to Kennedy, the United States would have around 18,000 nuclear weapons. The most powerful were 10-megaton bombs carried by intercontinental bombers (B-52s). The least powerful were tactical weapons that could be fired from 8-inch guns or even from jeep-mounted mortars. The gross yield of all these weapons probably equaled 1 million times that of the bomb that had obliterated Hiroshima, dry-roasted most of its 85,000 people, and irradiated tens of thousands more. Though U.S. intelligence analysts doubted that the total Soviet arsenal yet matched the United States's, they had no question that the Soviets, too, possessed what critics already decried as overkill. To generals and admirals who talked of nuclear victory over the

Soviet Union, President Eisenhower, according to notes of one White House meeting, "expressed his concern that there just might be nothing left of the Northern Hemisphere."[31]

The rationale for continuing to accumulate new and improved nuclear weapons resided in another watch term of the Cold War: *second strike*. During the 1950s some of the best minds in the world tried to untangle the logic of using nuclear weapons to defend territory despite the likelihood that their actual use would obliterate the territory and be suicidal for the defender. One early insight was that a nuclear arsenal might not achieve any deterrent effect—indeed might encourage both aggression and nuclear war—if it could be destroyed in a disarming first strike, for a state might be tempted to rid itself at once of both resistance to its aggression and any danger of its own annihilation. It followed that a nuclear arsenal served as an effective deterrent if configured so that significant forces would survive any attempt at a disarming first strike. This second strike capability would guarantee the attacker's devastation, no matter what.

From the concept of second strike came arguments for large and diversified nuclear forces and for comparatively invulnerable nuclear weapons delivery systems. Hence came routines under which the U.S. Strategic Air Command, when put on alert, as in October 1962, would keep approximately 180 bombers in the air at all times. Fully loaded with thermonuclear bombs, these bombers would go a preassigned line a certain distance from the Soviet Union and then, unless ordered to proceed, would turn around and fly back. (Two of the decade's biggest movies, *Fail Safe* and *Dr. Strangelove*, end with such a plane not turning back.) Hence came also a crash effort to produce nuclear-powered submarines able to carry and fire SLBMs. Moving silently near the ocean floor, they probably could not be targeted for a disarming first strike. Hence, too, came programs for putting ground-based missiles in underground silos, surrounded by thick concrete, where they would be vulnerable only to enemy missiles of extraordinary power and accuracy. On the missile crisis tapes, the language of nuclear strategic debates rarely appears. Kennedy and many of those around him had, however, steeped themselves in those debates. The inherent dilemmas which many had studied but which no one had resolved can be heard in insistent undertone in what they said to each other during the Cuban crisis. "Do they really believe that they can cow us into not using our nuclear weapons?" they are often asking implicitly about the Soviets. "Are we willing to take actions that could set in train a nuclear war?" they are continually asking of themselves. And one cannot fully comprehend their debates without awareness of these unspoken questions and of their perception that hundreds of millions of lives hung on the answers.

Though there was evident public support for racing the Russians in building missiles and accumulating nuclear weapons, there was also evident public enthusiasm for possibly turning the arms race around. During the mid-1950s the public learned that radioactive fallout from nuclear weapons tests could affect areas far from the test sites. Strontium-90 generated by tests in Nevada showed up in milk in New Jersey. *Newsweek* in 1957 devoted a special section to "this insidiously invisible powder" of which "a concentrated teaspoonful could kill 30 million people."[32] All over the country, schoolchildren had already become accustomed to crouching under desks or running for fallout shelters in nuclear attack drills. Pressure from scientists and concerned parents caused the Eisenhower administration to enter negotiations with the Soviets about a possible test-ban treaty. At the end of Eisenhower's presidency, these negotiations had gone far enough to offer at least faint promise of an agreement that might conceivably be a first step toward slowing the nuclear arms competition.

Public attitudes in the United States toward nuclear weapons loom large in the background of the missile crisis. These attitudes were clearly ambivalent. The public wanted the United States to be number one in nuclear weapons as in other spheres. Kennedy struck fire with audiences during the 1960 campaign by declaring: "Our defense policy can be summed up in one word: first. I do not mean first if. I do not mean first but; I mean first—period."[33] At the same time, there was a sense of despair, probably best caught in the hugely popular 1959 film *On the Beach*. Based on a best-selling novel by Nevil Shute, directed by Stanley Kramer, the film starred Gregory Peck as a U.S. submarine commander. Peck's boat surfaces in Australia after a U.S.-Soviet nuclear war. There is no communication with the rest of the planet. The Australians understand that they are doomed by a slowly approaching radioactive cloud. No one can explain the war. People line up for suicide pills. Peck sails his submarine back to the California coast to see if anything survives. Nothing does. What seems a sign of life turns out to be an empty Coca-Cola bottle dangling among telephone wires.

The second key issue complex—European security—was linked inseparably with the strategic balance. The United States had become engaged in the Cold War primarily from concern that the Soviet Union might expand into Western Europe. Increased concern, fueled by evidence of the Soviet arms buildup and especially by the Korean War, caused the United States in the 1950s to station U.S. military forces in

Europe and to press successfully for West German membership in NATO and for West Germany to provide troops and other forces for NATO.

Always anxious as to whether the Americans would actually live up to their promises of military support, given the history of the two world wars, Europeans became newly nervous as they observed the accelerating nuclear arms race. On the one hand, they feared that the Americans would decide to save themselves and let Europe go—would refuse, as the phrase went, to trade Chicago for Bonn. On the other hand, Europeans feared that the United States might either take some rash action that would precipitate a Soviet attack on Europe or, trying to protect the U.S. homeland while at the same time sticking by the commitment to Europe, would make a war for the rescue of Europe a nonnuclear war, the result of which could be a replay of World War II. While Americans made their calculations chiefly about future wars, Europeans remembered the tens of millions lost between 1914 and 1945. For many of them, a 1-in-1,000 chance of a nuclear war that would kill 500 million looked better than a 1-in-100 chance of a war that killed only 50 million.

For Europeans, the Suez crisis of 1956 provided the strongest evidence that the United States might put its own national and global interests ahead of the interests of its NATO allies. This crisis, which would be cited repeatedly in missile crisis debates, originated with Egypt's nationalization of the Suez Canal. Ignoring advice to the contrary from Eisenhower, the British and French conspired with the Israelis and commenced military operations that surprised Washington no less than Cairo. Through ruthless use of diplomatic and economic pressure, Eisenhower forced the British and French to desist. Meanwhile, the Soviets sent tanks into Hungary to suppress a rebellion that had briefly offered promise of that country's liberation from tight Soviet control. *Suez-Hungary* in missile crisis debates implied that the Soviets might use a crisis over Cuba to achieve an objective somewhere else, possibly in Berlin. For Europeans, *Suez* stood for the moment when they had been shocked into awareness of how much inferior in power they were to the United States, and how dependent on that power.

From that time onward, the U.S. government had increasing difficulty coping with the question of how credibly to assure Europeans that it would actually defend them and would do so without bringing on their ruin. As the Soviets acquired more and more capacity for attacking the continental United States, Americans searched for strategies that would continue to reassure Europeans but that would reduce the risk of nuclear cataclysm. For the Eisenhower administration, NATO ground forces constituted a trip wire. If the Soviets moved against them, the next event would be a U.S. nuclear strike on the Soviet Union. Especially after the Sputnik shots, Americans cast about for possible intermediate steps such as a period of nonnuclear combat or of use only of tactical nuclear weapons. Under the label "flexible response," the introduction of plans for such intermediate stages would be a central element in the Kennedy administration's revamping of U.S. strategic planning.

At the same time, U.S. officials remained sensitive to European concerns and eager to allay them. General Lauris Norstad, who commanded NATO forces at the end of the Eisenhower administration and well into the Kennedy administration, proposed the creation of a European nuclear force, the object being to assure the West Europeans—and caution the Russians—that a Soviet attack on Europe could bring nuclear retaliation regardless of U.S. concern about the safety of the continental United States. Variants of this idea were to be debated throughout the Kennedy administration.

The U.S. positioning of IRBMs in Britain, Italy, and Turkey was part of this effort to allay European fears of being left in the lurch. But so fast was the evolution both of missile technology and of thinking about nuclear weapons that the Thors and Jupiters were to seem obsolete before they became operational. In part, this was because more accurate, longer-range missiles came along. In larger part, it was because of second strike reasoning. Maxwell Taylor had become chief of staff of the Army after his Korean tour. He had been a dissenter within the Eisenhower administration, criticizing overreliance on strategic nuclear weapons. After retiring in 1959, he made his dissent public in *The Uncertain Trumpet,* a book that caught Kennedy's attention. In this book, Taylor described the Jupiter missiles as "a sterile asset" because, being "fixed and without mobility," they became "stationary bulls-eyes."[34] After the British had arranged for the Thors to be replaced by less vulnerable systems, members of the Kennedy administration would discuss among themselves removing the Jupiters from Italy and Turkey and perhaps replacing them with Mediterranean-based Polaris SLBMs. But Norstad and the Turks themselves counseled against such action and the Jupiters went in, at least until something better was arranged. During the missile crisis, analogies would often be made between U.S. IRBMs in Turkey and Soviet IRBMs in Cuba.

From the late 1950s into the early 1960s, the key pressure point testing the firmness of U.S. guarantees to Europe was, as early in the Cold War, Berlin. Stalin's successor, Nikita Khrushchev, threatened in 1958 to sign a separate peace treaty with East Germany, turn over to the East Germans control of Berlin, and declare that, so far as he was concerned, westerners no longer had any legal rights within the city. Meeting unbending opposition from Eisenhower, Khrushchev postponed action. He revived the threat during 1960, then let it be known that he would hold off action until the United States had a new president. Kennedy would therefore take office under warning that difficulties over Berlin, possibly a crisis, loomed ahead.

The term *Third World* came into use to describe those countries which had not aligned themselves with either the Soviet Union or the West. Since most were comparatively poor and a number were new countries, previously European colonies, *Third World* often applied to countries that *were* aligned but that happened to be poor, as for example, those in Latin America.

The so-called Third World had by 1960 become a major theater of East-West competition. Khrushchev spoke of sponsoring "wars of national liberation." The Eisenhower administration had countered with modest programs of economic aid for non-Communist states and, on occasion, with covert action aimed at overturning regimes believed to be aligning themselves with the Soviets. At the same time that they took the administration to task for the "missile gap," Democrats criticized the scale and direction of its competition for the Third World.

This criticism became stronger and attracted wider attention within the United States because of several developments late in the 1950s. One was a civil war in the former Belgian Congo, where one faction sought and obtained Soviet aid while others obtained U.S. aid. Though the Soviet-backed faction lost, the contest went on for some time, and the durability of the victory by the U.S.-backed faction remained in doubt. A second development was a civil war of sorts in the landlocked kingdom of Laos. Because the Communist North Vietnamese supported the Pathet Lao faction and the Soviets airlifted some supplies to the Pathet Lao, the contest was interpreted in the United States as one where Khrushchev aimed at winning one of his wars of national liberation.

A third development, of signal importance for understanding the debates recorded here, was the revolution in Cuba.[35] It originated with a relatively small band of guerrillas operating from mountain bases in eastern Cuba. The existing Cuban government, headed by Fulgencio Batista, had become more and more corrupt, partly as a result of alliances with U.S. gangsters who operated casinos in Havana. Whatever popular support Batista had once possessed he lost. Though his regime had been generally incompetent, his police had been relatively successful in rooting out all organized opposition other than that of the guerrillas and of underground factions such as the Cuban Communist Party. The result was that the Cuban populace had no one to whom to turn as an alternative to Batista other than the flamboyant guerrilla leader Fidel Castro.

When Batista's regime collapsed at the very end of 1958, Castro easily took control of Havana. At the time, many Cubans and many Americans looked on Castro as essentially a radical reformer but not necessarily anti-U.S. or pro-Soviet. Some of the most prominent U.S. news correspondents in Cuba encouraged such a view. As a result, for a year or more Castro had some support in the United States. At one point he gave a talk at Harvard University, where he was welcomed by the then dean, McGeorge Bundy, and applauded by a throng of faculty and students.

By mid-1959, if not earlier, U.S. feeling toward Castro had cooled. He was not only expropriating U.S. property without compensation; he was also taking property from and jailing Cubans who criticized him. He had developed a working alliance with the now largely aboveground Communist Party, and the very long speeches to which he was prone became increasingly critical of the United States. During the following year, he began openly to align himself with the Soviet Union and to accept Soviet aid. The Eisenhower administration retaliated with economic sanctions. Ports in the United States, particularly in Florida, received streams of refugees, mostly members of the middle class and intellectuals whom Castro had either dispossessed or silenced. Castro's Cuba came increasingly to be characterized in the United States as a base for Communist subversion in the hemisphere.

Latin Americans, long envious of the extent of U.S. support for and attention to Europe, clamored for aid from Washington to help them combat Cuban propaganda and avoid acquiring Castros of their own. The Rio Treaty of 1947 had set a precedent for the North Atlantic Treaty. It committed the United States and other independent states of the Americas to one-for-all, all-for-one mutual defense, coordinated through an Organization of American States (OAS). Subsequently, in the global Cold War, the United States had seemed to forget about the Western Hemisphere. The success of Castro in Cuba revived Washington's interest in the Americas. It made Latin American states honorary members of the Third World.

The emergence of the loosely defined Third World as a major arena of East-West competition revived some conditions of the early Cold War. Back then, many Americans had seen the contest with the Soviets as something like a holy war. In 1950 Truman's advisers composed a statement of basic U.S. national security policy—number 68 in a series of

National Security Council papers; hence NSC 68. Formally endorsed by Truman, this document pronounced the issues of the Cold War to be "momentous, involving the fulfillment or destruction not only of this Republic but of civilization itself" and declared the Cold War to be "in fact a real war in which the survival of the free world is at stake."[36] (The chief drafters of NSC 68 were Secretary of State Dean G. Acheson and the chief of his Policy Planning Staff, Paul H. Nitze, both of whom would be advisers to Kennedy during the missile crisis.) A decade of a nuclear arms race and other experiences had produced a calmer outlook, reflected by Kennedy in his inaugural address, when he spoke of the sound of a trumpet "not as a call to battle . . . but a call to bear the burdens of a long twilight struggle."

With regard to the Third World, U.S. rhetoric could return to the level of the era of NSC 68. Kennedy devoted three paragraphs of his inaugural address to "those new states whom we welcome to the ranks of the free," to "those peoples in the huts and villages of half the globe struggling to break the bonds of mass misery," and to "our sister republics south of our border." To the last he offered "a new alliance for progress—to assist free men and free governments in casting off the chains of poverty." He complemented that offer with a vow "to oppose aggression or subversion anywhere in the Americas." The Third World seemed at the time to be a theater for replaying containment. The risk that the Congo or Laos or Cuba would become the tinderbox for a nuclear war seemed small—until October 1962.

Kennedy won the Democratic nomination in July 1960 and went on to win the presidency in November. Four facts about that campaign year testify to peculiarities of the period and hence illuminate the crisis that occurred less than two years later. First, both Kennedy and his opponent, Vice President Richard Nixon, were in their forties. As Kennedy would say in his inaugural, the torch had passed to a new generation. Truman, Eisenhower, and those around them had been molded by the Progressive Era, World War I, and the 1920s. For Kennedy and Nixon alike, remembered history began with the 1930s and World War II. Second, Kennedy won nomination and election despite strong opposition on the ground of his being a Roman Catholic. His success indicated the ebbing strength of the religious bigotry that had previously been a strong strain in American culture. Third, Kennedy's thin margin of success over Nixon— fewer than 120,000 votes out of more than 68 million—was widely attributed to his successful use of television, particularly in face-to-face debates staged by the networks. The 1960 election helped to seal the primacy of television as the key medium of communication between presidents and would-be presidents and the public.

Lastly, and most importantly for the context of the missile crisis, the 1960 election was a referendum on nuances of the Cold War. Neither candidate talked about much else. When Kennedy promised pocketbook benefits, he did so on the ground that faster economic growth would enable the United States more successfully to compete with the Soviet Union, to demonstrate the superiority of capitalism over communism, and to prevail in the arms race. Kennedy and Nixon vied to prove which would be better able to stand up against Khrushchev. For example, Kennedy (or at least his campaign staff) attacked Nixon and the administration of which he was part for failing to support exile "freedom fighters" seeking to return to Cuba and overturn Fidel Castro. At the same time, Kennedy and Nixon vied for the mantle of prudent guardian of nuclear peace. Both men called insistently for somehow limiting what Kennedy would describe in his inaugural as "the steady spread of the deadly atom."

Kennedy's inauguration on January 20, 1961, can be seen as portending the crisis recorded in this book. On the preceding day, Washington was hit with one of the heaviest snowfalls in its history. The only surface traces of highways leading into the city were columns of abandoned cars and trucks. But inauguration morning, while still more than freezing cold, came with glittering sunshine. Not long before, the nation had heard from Eisenhower a gloomy farewell warning, including a caution about a "military-industrial complex" emerging in control of society. Now, people saw on television a new president, young, topcoatless, bareheaded, asserting that energy, faith, and devotion "will light our country and all who serve it—and the glow from that fire can truly light the world."

By that day, Kennedy had assembled most of the circle that would surround him during the missile crisis. Despite predictable outrage and ridicule, he made his 35-year-old brother Bobby attorney general. He brought into the White House as all-purpose aide and chief speechwriter his longtime Capitol Hill assistant, Theodore Sorensen. Even younger than Robert Kennedy, Sorensen was a Nebraska liberal, originally interested only in domestic issues. He had developed such rapport with Kennedy that he could speak as well as write in Kennedy's natural cadences.

Most of the others were comparative strangers to Kennedy at the beginning of his administration. Kennedy complained to his transition adviser, Richard Neustadt, "I don't know any people. I only know voters."[37] To complement Sorensen, Kennedy picked as staff aide for national security affairs Harvard dean McGeorge Bundy. Two years younger than Kennedy, Bundy had been an academic star at Yale, served in the Navy in the European theater during World War II, and afterward coauthored a book with Henry L. Stimson, who had been Roosevelt's (and William Howard Taft's) secretary of war and Herbert Hoover's secretary of state. Bundy's bloodline was Republican, and he did campaign work for Republican candidates in both national and state elections. He and Kennedy had become acquainted after Kennedy was elected to the Harvard Board of Overseers in 1956. They matched each other in quickness of mind and taste for irony, and Kennedy gambled that they could work well together in the intimacy of the White House.

Kennedy asked Robert Lovett to take a cabinet post, but Lovett pleaded ill health. He did, however, nominate the men whom Kennedy eventually chose as secretary of state and secretary of defense—Rusk and McNamara.

Kennedy had known that he did not want Stevenson as secretary of state. Not only had he and Bobby developed qualms about Stevenson during the 1956 campaign; both were angry at Stevenson for having taken himself out of the 1960 race but then allowed the anti-Kennedy left, led by Eleanor Roosevelt, to try to draft him. Kennedy used flattery to induce Stevenson to accept the post of ambassador to the United Nations. Kennedy's own preference for State was Senator J. William Fulbright of Arkansas, a Rhodes Scholar and former university president, with whom Kennedy had been close on Capitol Hill, but Fulbright's advocacy of racial segregation made him too vulnerable. So Kennedy turned to the stranger suggested by Lovett, and Rusk, who had been president of the Rockefeller Foundation since leaving the State Department in 1953, accepted without condition.

McNamara, Lovett's nominee for Defense, was president of the Ford Motor Company, where he had gone after World War II. At Ford he had achieved several design and production successes and had stanched losses due to the spectacular failure of the Edsel. Though he was a nonconformist among Ford executives, living in Ann Arbor instead of Grosse Pointe and skiing instead of golfing, McNamara lived in a cocooned, nonpolitical world. He had become attuned to the Cold War, he testified in 1961, by reading some quotations from Stalin published in *Foreign Affairs* in 1949. The Korean War intruded on his life by disrupting Ford's production schedule. His only known public allusion to McCarthyism was elliptical and occurred a year after McCarthy's censure. Overriding objections from company headquarters, McNamara spoke at the University of Alabama, condemning the current "grave pressure to conformity." When Kennedy interviewed him, liked him, and offered him a cabinet post, McNamara not only hesitated but, unlike Rusk, set conditions. Chiefly, McNamara asked for a guarantee that he would control appointments in his department. Though surprised, Kennedy acceded.[38]

For secretary of the Treasury, Kennedy chose C. Douglas Dillon, who had been a fellow Harvard overseer. The son of a financier who had been as much a buccaneer as Joe Kennedy, Dillon had headed his father's firm, Dillon Read. Though 32 at the time of Pearl Harbor, he had become a Navy flier and won an Air Medal in the southwest Pacific. He had served Eisenhower in various diplomatic posts, ending up as under secretary of state. His being an unregenerate Republican was an asset because it offered reassurance to the financial community and also, more broadly, symbolized continuity. Kennedy hesitated only because his father expressed skepticism as to whether Dillon really understood money. What probably tipped the scale was Dillon's evident fit with the likes of Bundy and McNamara. Both Dillon and Bundy had both gone to the exclusive Groton preparatory school where, school legend had it, the headmaster's reports on Dillon always said "Can do better," even when Dillon's grades were A-pluses.

On the day before inauguration, Kennedy and his prospective national security team met with Eisenhower and members of the outgoing administration. Though Eisenhower had deliberately built an image as an aloof, grandfatherly president who exercised authority reluctantly and only when necessary and though he had aged in office, no one long in his company failed to see the steeliness, shrewdness, and sheer brain power that had made him the most effective commander of allied armies in the entirety of history. Kennedy and his entourage went away from this meeting having heard from Eisenhower warnings that war could be ignited in any of a number of places around the globe, especially Berlin. Kennedy said to Bobby afterward that he was shaken by the "equanimity" with which Eisenhower spoke of the nuclear arsenal.[39]

However much they might discount voices from the past, Kennedy and the others could not ignore what they heard from Eisenhower. Eisenhower's views would continue to carry weight with a large part of the public, and the new administration would often need his support or at least his silence. During the missile crisis, Kennedy would keep in regular touch with Eisenhower. And readers of these tape transcripts should bear in mind that an often unspoken question in Kennedy's mind regarding recommendations before him must have been, "If I do this, will General Eisenhower back me?"

The first crisis of the Kennedy administration concerned Cuba. It was the Bay of Pigs affair.[40] When Kennedy charged that the Eisenhower administration was doing too little for Cuban exile "freedom fighters," he did so in ignorance that the Central Intelligence Agency, with active encouragement from Vice President Nixon, was arming and training Cuban exiles for an effort to unseat Castro. (Nixon never believed that Kennedy did not know this; he died convinced that Democrats in the CIA had let Kennedy in on the secret and that Kennedy was taking advantage of Nixon's being honor bound to guard the secret.) After being elected, Kennedy received a briefing on the plan. After becoming president, he learned that the plan had been expanded. Originally envisioning only the establishment of a guerrilla base in the Cuban highlands, it now called for a brigade-sized amphibious landing and a march toward Havana in expectation of internal upheaval.

Kennedy approved the expanded CIA plan, but with misgivings. The Alliance for Progress announced in his inaugural address aimed at helping non-Marxists gain the initiative in Latin American reform movements. He feared that evident U.S. intervention in Cuba would revive denunciation of Yankee imperialism and frustrate the Alliance. Also, he feared that U.S. military engagement in Cuba might encourage Khrushchev to make a move somewhere else, perhaps against Laos or Berlin. The director of central intelligence, Allen Dulles, had, however, an impressive reputation as an engineer of covert action. The actual man in charge was Richard Bissell, whom Kennedy knew as creator and manager of the program for U-2 reconnaissance and with whom Bundy had studied economics as an undergraduate at Yale. After repeatedly saying to Dulles and Bissell that he wanted the noise level kept down and that he would in no circumstances commit U.S. military forces, Kennedy gave a final go-ahead.

On April 17, 1961, 1,400 Cubans arrived off the south coast of Cuba and embarked in small boats for the nearby beach around the Bay of Pigs. Everything that could go wrong had already started to go wrong. The B-26 aircraft that bombed Cuban airfields landed in Miami, with the pilots' claiming to be defectors from the Cuban Air Force. Their story came apart almost at the moment reporters began to quiz them. They and their planes were identified as belonging to the CIA. In Cuba, they had missed most of their targets. Much of Castro's air strength survived. His planes strafed the landing parties and sank two of the exiles' four freighters, including the one with most of their communications equipment. Castro's land forces meanwhile arrived in the area in overwhelming force. And the rest of Cuba remained free of any uprisings. The 1,000 survivors soon surrendered.

Even though U.S. sponsorship of the landing had been effectively proven by the unmasking of the pilots, Kennedy stuck to the position he had taken earlier. He rejected pleas from Bissell and others that he order U.S. Navy and Air Force units into action to support the exiles. When asked at a press conference, he declined to criticize the CIA. "There's an old saying that victory has a hundred fathers and defeat is an orphan," he replied. "I am the responsible officer of this government." Later he told Dulles and Bissell that, after a decent interval, they would have to leave. "In a parliamentary system I would resign," he said. "In our system the President can't and doesn't. So you . . . must go."[41]

The Bay of Pigs affair had many consequences important for the subsequent missile crisis. First of all, it damaged severely Kennedy's standing among groups previously attracted to him by his father's reputation and by the fact that he had not voted to censure McCarthy. Hard-line Cuban exiles never came close to forgiving him. Nor did Americans who were as much old-fashioned nationalists as anti-Communists. For them, Cuba was as American as apple pie. Its being Communist was intolerable. In their eyes, Kennedy was a gutless appeaser. In varying degrees, this was also a common verdict among senior military officers, particularly in the Navy and Air Force, and in the CIA's Clandestine Service. Awareness of anger and contempt carrying over from the Bay of Pigs affair would affect Kennedy and others during the crisis of October 1962.

A second, closely related consequence of the affair was the development within Kennedy's inner circle of personal animus against Castro. Kennedy, and his brother even more, longed for some redeeming opportunity. They organized a new set of covert operations, code-named Mongoose, to stir up trouble in Cuba and, if opportunity offered, to bring down Castro. Some looked to assassination of Castro. The governing directive, issued in November 1961, said that the United States would "help the people of Cuba overthrow the Communist regime from within Cuba and institute a new government with which the United States can live at peace." An update of March 14, 1962, added: "The U.S. will make use of indigenous resources, internal and external, but recognizes that final success will require decisive U.S. military intervention." Under constant badgering from the younger Kennedy, the CIA came up with a number of what veteran intelligence officer Richard Helms later termed "nutty schemes."[42]

Anxious to be ready in case anything came of Mongoose, the President and the Attorney General saw to it that the military services prepared for possible intervention. As a result, the JCS put on a first-priority basis the drafting of contingency plans. The Tactical Air Command,

which had the responsibility for providing air support for ground operations, drew up specifications for an air campaign designed to precede
amphibious landings. LeMay, as chief of staff of the Air Force, approved
it. On October 6, 1962, his government agitated by shipments of Soviet
arms to Cuba, the Commander in Chief of U.S. forces in the Atlantic
(CINCLANT), Admiral Robert L. Dennison, ordered urgent preparations
to carry out the landings themselves.[43] Thus, when Kennedy and his
advisers considered the invasion of Cuba, it was an option that the military services were much better prepared to carry out than might have
been the case, absent the earlier Bay of Pigs affair.

The Bay of Pigs affair affected the missile crisis in another way: It
made Kennedy sharply aware of shortcomings in his decision-making
processes. Kennedy concluded, for one thing, that he should not make
decisions about national security issues by relying exclusively on advisers with national security portfolios. Thereafter, he almost always consulted Sorensen and Bobby and sometimes others whose primary loyalty
was to him and who would think above all of his interests.

Kennedy also came to recognize that native brain power did not
entirely make up for lack of experience. He had relied on the presumed
expertise of Dulles and Bissell. When he took the precaution of checking
their plan with the Joint Chiefs of Staff, he had been assured that it had
"a fair chance of success." Only through *post hoc* review did Kennedy discover that Dulles and Bissell had shut out many of their CIA colleagues,
thus keeping him from learning that many others in the agency had had
doubts, especially about the premise that the exiles' landing would spark
a popular uprising. Only then did he learn that the JCS response had
been a dodge to avoid taking issue with the CIA. Among themselves, he
was told, the JCS interpreted "fair chance" to mean three-to-one against.

When Kennedy effected the removal of Dulles and Bissell, he
replaced Dulles with John McCone. A 58-year-old steel industry veteran, McCone had served in the Defense Department in the Truman
administration and become head of the Atomic Energy Commission
under Eisenhower. Since McCone was a Republican personally close to
Eisenhower, Kennedy had no reason to expect personal loyalty. When in
the Senate, however, he had observed and applauded the firmness with
which McCone had controlled the supersecret nuclear weapons bureau-
cracies and the candor with which he had answered questions about sen-
sitve test-ban issues. He could trust McCone not deliberately to mislead
him. Meanwhile, Bundy added some CIA veterans to his White House
staff and began in other ways to reach directly into the intelligence community. By the time of the missile crisis, Kennedy and Bundy and others

in the circle would have an understanding of intelligence not only far beyond what they had had in 1961 but well beyond that of most subsequent administrations.

Kennedy also made changes in his relationship with the military establishment. The behavior of the JCS regarding the Bay of Pigs affair enraged him. Alluding to the rows of ribbons that decorated their uniforms, he exclaimed, "Those sons-of-bitches with all the fruit salad just sat there nodding, saying it would work."[44] Kennedy was particularly angry at the JCS Chairman, Army General Lyman Lemnitzer. He added Maxwell Taylor to his White House staff as someone to interpret for him communications from the Chiefs. As soon as Lemnitzer's term ran out, Kennedy made Taylor JCS Chairman. During the missile crisis, Kennedy could know that what he heard about the view of military leaders came from a man whom he had chosen and whom he had calibrated.

The Bay of Pigs affair had effects also on Kennedy's style of decision making. Afterward, he recognized that he had not only listened to too few advisers but that he had given the issues too little time. Eisenhower, before giving him the public backing that he sorely needed, subjected him to a staff school quiz. "Mr. President," Eisenhower asked, "before you approved this plan did you have everybody in front of you debating the thing so that you could get the pros and cons yourself and then made the decision . . . ?" Kennedy had to confess that he had not. Bundy, whose offer to resign Kennedy rejected, also counseled that he become much more deliberative.[45]

When the missile crisis arrived, Kennedy applied the lessons taught him by the Bay of Pigs affair. From the outset, he assembled a comparatively large circle of advisers, not all of whom were obvious choices. He included Treasury Secretary Dillon. He brought in State Department experts on both the Soviet Union and Latin America. To be sure that knowledge and wisdom from the past were not ignored, he also brought in Dean Acheson, Robert A. Lovett, and John J. McCloy, key figures from the Truman administration. And, as the records in this volume testify, he squeezed from these advisers everything they could say about the options open to him. If there were flaws in Kennedy's decision making during the missile crisis, they are the exact opposite of those in the Bay of Pigs affair. The reader of these records may conclude that, if anything, he listened to too many people and listened to some of them too long.

Other events of the Kennedy presidency prior to the missile crisis also bore on the deliberations documented here. All during the spring of 1961, both before and after the Bay of Pigs affair, Kennedy dealt with the problem that had headed Eisenhower's agenda during the preinaugural conference—Laos. After acquiring some detailed knowledge about that isolated, sparsely settled kingdom, Kennedy concluded that it was not a good place in which to draw a hard and fixed line.

To act on this conclusion without compromising his residual credentials as a hard-line Cold Warrior, Kennedy engaged in sleight of hand. He made tough speeches about stopping the spread of Communism in Southeast Asia, and he deployed warships and troops so as to create an impression that he was prepared to make Laos a theater of war. Subtly in his speeches, and more explicitly in secret communications to Moscow, Kennedy meanwhile indicated that, though he was not prepared publicly to abandon Laos to Communist rule, he would not be averse to a deal that made Laos neutral, with its pro-Communist faction participating in a coalition government.

Time magazine took Kennedy to task at one point. Predicting that Laos would soon disappear behind an iron curtain, the magazine's editors wrote: "Kennedy declared he would 'pay any price' to assure the survival and success of liberty. But the price in Laos seemed too high."[46] In the end, however, Kennedy got his way. He managed to seem uncompromising while in reality seeking and obtaining an accommodation that averted a genuine crisis.

In June 1961 Kennedy traveled to Vienna for a summit meeting with Khrushchev. Eisenhower had held a summit meeting soon after the death of Stalin. He had met with Khrushchev in the United States in 1959 and had planned to meet him in Paris in 1960. Just before the latter meeting was to take place, a U.S. U-2 disappeared over the Soviet Union. Since the very existence of the U-2 was then a carefully kept secret, Eisenhower denied Soviet charges that he had sent a "spy plane" over their territory. Khrushchev then triumphantly produced not only wreckage of the plane but the living pilot, Gary Powers. A Soviet SA-2 SAM had shot it down, and Powers had ejected safely instead of taking the cyanide capsule he was supposed to have taken. This U-2 affair destroyed the projected Paris summit. It also made U.S. diplomats thereafter very sensitive about intelligence overflights, a fact that would affect the timing of the missile crisis.[47]

Kennedy had wanted an early meeting with Khrushchev, hoping to resume the progress toward detente that had been broken by the U-2 affair. He jumped at Khrushchev's indication that he, too, wanted such a meeting. As the time for it arrived, however, Kennedy was of two minds. He worried, on the one hand, that it might be too soon after the Bay of Pigs affair and that Khrushchev, thinking him weak, would make impossible demands. On the other hand, he thought that only through a face-to-face encounter could he convince Khrushchev that he was tough but not intransigent. At Vienna, Kennedy spent many hours with Khrushchev. He had already, before inauguration, set up a secret channel for personal correspondence. There would eventually be enough material that, when finally released and published in 1996, it filled more than 300 printed pages. But Kennedy's image of Khrushchev was probably shaped by the Vienna meeting more than by anything he later saw on paper or heard from his Soviet experts. Though that image would become more nuanced later, it never entirely ceased to be what Kennedy described to British prime minister Harold Macmillan in a London stopover on the way home. "The President," noted Macmillan, "was completely overwhelmed by the ruthlessness and barbarity of the Russian Chairman. It reminded me in a way of Lord Halifax or Neville Chamberlain trying to hold a conversation with Herr Hitler."[48]

At Vienna, Khrushchev revived his earlier threat to sign a separate peace treaty with East Germany and thus to call into question the legitimacy and perhaps the survival of West Berlin. Kennedy did his utmost to convince Khrushchev that his position on Berlin was not comparable to his position on Laos. He said specifically: "Here, we are not talking about Laos. . . . [I]f we were to accept the Soviet proposal US commitments would be regarded as a mere scrap of paper. Western Europe is vital to our national security. . . . If we were to leave West Berlin, Europe would be abandoned as well. . . . We cannot accept that."[49] Kennedy returned to Washington, however, unsure that Khrushchev had absorbed the message, fearful that he had not convinced the Soviet leader that he was not the weakling of the Bay of Pigs affair, and hence anxious about the future.

During the summer of 1961, the possibility of a major Berlin crisis preoccupied the Kennedy administration. Kennedy and his advisers reviewed innumerable proposals and plans, most of which sketched scenarios that ended in nuclear war. The scenarios differed chiefly in the numbers of intermediate steps envisioned between a Soviet challenge and a presidential order releasing nuclear weapons for operational use. One of the more ingenious, emanating from Harvard economist Thomas C. Schelling, called for replying to a Soviet move against Berlin with a demonstration nuclear drop on a Hiroshima-sized Soviet city.[50]

Applying lessons from the Bay of Pigs affair and acting somewhat as he would in the missile crisis, Kennedy searched widely for advice, insisted on going over and over alternative courses of action, and pressed for imagination to expand the menu. For a July 1961 meeting that Bundy characterized as perhaps the most important yet held, Kennedy called in no fewer than 25 people.[51]

Even though Kennedy meant what he said to Khrushchev about Berlin's being qualitatively different from Laos, his tactics were not altogether unlike those applied to Laos. He and his advisers came gradually to recognize that the most immediate problem for Khrushchev was a huge outflow of the best-educated and most highly skilled East Germans. They simply walked or took a street car from East to West Berlin and from there went on to West Germany.

By word and act, Kennedy tried to erase from Khrushchev's mind any doubt that the United States would risk its own existence if necessary to protect West Berlin. In a televised address to the nation on July 25, Kennedy said, "We have given our word that an attack upon that city will be regarded as an attack upon us all. . . . [I]f war begins, it will have begun in Moscow, not Berlin." He asked and obtained additional money and authority to call up reservists. But in his speeches and in diplomatic communications, Kennedy was careful to speak of West Berlin and not, as had been customary earlier, simply of Berlin. It sent a calculated signal that the United States would not necessarily feel compelled to act if the Soviets or East Germans were to do something in the portion of Berlin already under their control.

On August 13, the East Germans suddenly put up a barbed wire barrier, effectively penning East Berliners in their sector of the city. Soon afterward, with Soviet help, they added back of the barbed wire a concrete wall with watchtowers overlooking an intervening area that machine guns and guard dogs made into a killing ground. This Berlin Wall would stand for the next 28 years as a grotesque monument of the Cold War.

As the Wall went up, Kennedy and other Western leaders repeated in stronger and stronger language their determination to stand by the people of West Berlin. Neither Kennedy nor any other responsible leader seriously suggested acting to reverse the closing off of East Berlin. Gradually, the atmosphere of crisis lightened. But no one in the West regarded the erection of the Wall as a culmination or even a caesura in the long-building Berlin crisis. It was a common assumption that the Wall was a temporizing device and that Khrushchev would soon resume an effort to take possession of West Berlin. Kennedy administration officials continued to work out elaborate plans for countering possible Soviet moves. They were to be especially surprised by the Cuban crisis because, on its eve, they were seeing indications that another serious Berlin crisis might be about to break.

After the Berlin crisis of 1961 and before the missile crisis, three developments changed the light in which Kennedy and his advisers perceived U.S.-Soviet relations. The first was the complete disappearance of

the "missile gap," with the Kennedy administration's becoming certain—
and advertising to the Soviets—that, far from being at a disadvantage,
the United States held an enormous lead in capacity to deliver nuclear
weapons at intercontinental range, and in a second strike no less than in
a first. The second, which was closely correlated, was a surge within the
administration of hope for some kind of detente with the Soviets, which
would reduce the danger of nuclear war. The third was nagging reemer-
gence, in connection with the congressional elections of 1962, of public
debate about the role of Cuba in the global Cold War.

From the beginning, there had been doubts about the "missile gap."
Photography from U-2s had never found ICBM launchers in numbers
corresponding to Khrushchev's boasts. Because the capabilities of the U-
2 remained secret even after the May 1960 affair, Eisenhower could only
hint that he had evidence calling the missile gap thesis into question.
Kennedy and other Democrats paid no attention. Moreover, some insid-
ers supported them. Air Force intelligence estimates discounted U-2
imagery, pointing out that it covered only a fraction of the Soviet Union,
noting that Soviet radar had detected every U-2 flight from the first one
on, and arguing that the Soviets would therefore base their ICBMs
where clouds would ordinarily mask them.

Kennedy and his principal aides learned soon after taking office that
most of the intelligence community apart from the Air Force doubted
the existence of a wide missile gap. Coping with competing service
budgetary claims, the new administration also found itself in need, like
its predecessor, of questioning service estimates of the Soviet threat.
Hence, Kennedy, McNamara, and others increasingly moderated their
language about U.S.-Soviet competition in long-range missiles. They did
sponsor and obtain congressional approval for substantial increases in
strategic and other defense programs. They did not, however, agree to
anything like the ICBM deployments advocated by the Air Force.
LeMay's protégé and successor as head of the Strategic Air Command,
General Thomas Power, urged acquiring 10,000 Minuteman ICBMs.
White House analysts concluded that a few hundred would be ample.
McNamara set a ceiling of 1,000, acknowledging that the extra hundreds would go primarily to appeasing Air Force friends on Capitol Hill.

From 1957 on, the CIA had attempted to top its accomplishments with
the U-2 by putting up a satellite that would take pictures of the Soviet
Union from space. This effort, code-named CORONA, suffered 13 succes-
sive failures. In the summer of 1961, it finally scored the first of what
would be an extraordinary series of successes. The very first imagery
recovered from a CORONA reentry vehicle provided more photographic

coverage of a greater area than had all the U-2 flights combined. While it showed the Soviets hard at work on new versions of an ICBM, it provided convincing evidence that their existing ICBM arsenal was meager.

By coincidence, the CIA's human intelligence collectors had meanwhile acquired a prime agent high in the Soviet military bureaucracy. Colonel Oleg Penkovsky smuggled to them microfilm of numerous Soviet Defense Ministry documents. He also told his handlers in great detail about what he heard and saw by virtue of his status as a senior officer well connected not only in the Strategic Rocket Forces but in Soviet military intelligence.[52] All this jibed neatly with what appeared in U-2 and CORONA imagery.

Although the intelligence community phrased its conclusions in characteristically guarded language, these conclusions were much more reassuring than earlier ones. A year later, in July 1962, a National Intelligence Estimate would say: "By the mid-1960s, the USSR will have acquired a substantial missile capability to deliver nuclear weapons against the US. . . . [H]owever, the Soviets could still not expect to destroy the growing numbers of US hardened, airborne, seaborne, and fast reaction nuclear delivery vehicles."[53] In other words, second-strike capability seemed assured for a long time to come.

Kennedy notified the Soviets of his new knowledge. To keep the notification in low key, he had it put into a speech by Deputy Secretary of Defense Roswell Gilpatric. This presumably ensured its being read attentively in Moscow without being front page news at home. Gilpatric said: "The fact is that this nation has nuclear retaliatory force of such power that an enemy move which brought it into play would be an act of self-destruction. . . . Our forces are so deployed and protected that a sneak attack could not effectively disarm us. . . . In short, we have a second strike capability which is at least as extensive as what the Soviets can deliver by striking first."[54]

Armed with this knowledge about the favorable strategic balance, Kennedy and his advisers became modestly hopeful that the Soviets would perceive how far behind they were, calculate how much it would cost them to catch up, and conclude that their best interests would be served by arms control arrangements that put a stop to or at least braked the nuclear arms race. Just before the missile crisis, Kennedy and Khrushchev exchanged messages about a possible meeting in November, when Khrushchev planned to come to New York for the opening of the U.N. General Assembly. Kennedy wrote that he thought they might be "within striking distance of a test-ban agreement" which might be a harbinger of greater accomplishments to come.[55]

Troubling Kennedy also were continuing questions about Cuba. Robert Kennedy, who had learned about the Bay of Pigs plan only at the last moment, expressed concern immediately afterward lest the fiasco have wider effects on the Cold War. He wrote his brother, "If we don't want Russia to set up missile bases in Cuba, we had better decide now what we are willing to do to stop it."[56] This concern, as well as anger on his brother's behalf, probably had something to do with his zeal in promoting Mongoose. But Khrushchev had long before denied that he had any such intention. He did so again in a private letter to President Kennedy, upbraiding him for having supported the exiles' operation and asserting vehemently that the United States had no cause for trying to unseat Castro. He wrote, "We have stated on many occasions, and I now state again, that our Government does not seek any advantages or privileges in Cuba. We have no bases in Cuba, and we do not intend to establish any."[57]

By early 1962, Kennedy's own feelings about Castro and Cuba seemed to have cooled. At the very beginning of the year, his brother was pushing Mongoose with undiminished energy. The overthrow of Castro had "top priority," Robert Kennedy reportedly told the Mongoose team; "No time, money, effort—or manpower is to be spared."[58] But the operating head of the team, General Edward Lansdale, complained not long afterward that there had been no high-level decision for follow-on military intervention. By the beginning of March, Lansdale understood that he was to cut back to a program of limited action not inconsistent with stated U.S. policy, which denied any intention of going beyond isolating Cuba and limiting Cuban influence.[59] At the end of April, Kennedy held a meeting—the last of 1962, so far as we know—with Cuban exile leaders who were supposed to have formed a government, had the Bay of Pigs landing succeeded. They went away frustrated, because Kennedy refused either to set up training camps for a new landing attempt or to say a word encouraging hope that he would eventually approve an armed invasion.[60]

The probable reason for Kennedy's lessened interest in Cuba was rising concern about Berlin. In mid-February 1962 he had a difficult conversation with the German ambassador, Wilhelm Grewe. Parts of the memorandum for the record deserve quotation because they show Kennedy's personal views on the problem of European security discussed earlier and frequently central in the missile crisis debates:

> The President stated that the situation which might develop over Berlin deserved serious thought. We wanted to convince the Soviets, in the event of a major confrontation, that the US was prepared to go all out and that this deserved a last thought on their part. No one

expected to fight a conventional war in Europe, which we could not do without being overwhelmed. . . . [I]f we face a major defeat in Europe, then nuclear weapons will be used, but we must exhaust the full battery of other possibilities before pressing the button. . . . The US took this question quite seriously. We felt our survival was tied up with that of Western Europe.[61]

Speaking soon afterward with congressional leaders, Kennedy confessed his puzzlement about Khrushchev. "We are not convinced," he said, "that the Soviets themselves are sure of what course of action they are going to follow. . . . We just don't know."[62]

In March 1962 Khrushchev returned to the attack, telling Kennedy in a private communication that, in his view, Berlin had to become a demilitarized free city. State Department experts told the President that they thought Khrushchev had given up hope of negotiating satisfactory terms for Berlin. In July, Kennedy received another private letter from Khrushchev, in which the Soviet leader rambled on about possibly replacing Western military forces in Berlin with U.N. police units. The U.S. ambassador in Moscow and experts in the State Department voiced worry, as did European leaders.[63]

Kennedy answered Khrushchev with public releases. He allowed reporter Stewart Alsop to interview him for a feature article in the *Saturday Evening Post*. On the basis of what Kennedy said, Alsop wrote: "Khrushchev must not be certain that, where its vital interests are threatened, the United States will never strike first."[64]

In August, Kennedy's attention was pulled back to Cuba. On New Year's Day 1962, when Castro paraded his military forces, U.S. informants in Havana had reported that he displayed Soviet-built MiG fighters, mostly of comparatively out-of-date design. They saw no other weaponry worth special comment. In July, however, Cuba's defense minister, Castro's brother, Raul, spent two weeks in Moscow. Not long afterward, the CIA reported Soviet freighters steaming for Cuba with what appeared to be military cargo on board. And CIA human sources in Cuba relayed numerous reports of military equipment arriving at Cuban ports and moving to interior areas under Soviet guard.[65]

Noting that the reports from human sources were scattered and contradictory, CIA analysts offered a cautious judgment that the Soviet shipments were probably surface-to-air air defense missiles (SAMs) and that some of the other equipment reaching Cuba consisted of radar and electronic gear associated with such missiles. McCone, the Director of Central Intelligence (DCI), nevertheless began to send Kennedy, Rusk, and others a stream of communications stating his personal opinion that the Soviets might be planning to base medium-range ballistic missiles (MRBMs) in Cuba. He made the point that the longest range Soviet SAMs, the SA-2s, were indistinguishable from MRBMs with a 350-mile range. McCone's telegraphic-style notes on a meeting at the White House on August 23, attended by Kennedy, Rusk, McNamara, Taylor, and Bundy, show early indications of thoughts that would become better articulated when the missile crisis broke:

3. President requested analysis of the danger to the United States and the effect on Latin America of missile installations. . . .
4. President raised the question of whether we should make a statement in advance of our position, should the Soviets install missiles and the alternative actions open to us in such event. In the course of the discussion, apparent many in the room related action in Cuba to Soviet actions in Turkey, Greece, Berlin, Far East and elsewhere. McCone questioned value of Jupiter missiles in Turkey and Italy. McNamara agreed they were useless but difficult politically to remove them. . . .
5. President raised question of what we should do against Soviet missile sites in Cuba. Could we take them out by air or would a ground offensive be necessary. . . .
6. President raised question of what we should do in Cuba if Soviets precipitated a Berlin crisis.[66]

Even if Kennedy felt as much concern about Cuba as McCone's memorandum suggests, that concern was probably short lived. Two contemporaneous reports dampened whatever residual enthusiasm he might have had for Mongoose; independently, a CIA group and an operational group headed by Taylor concluded that there was no real hope of Castro's being overthrown, absent large-scale U.S. military intervention. As for the possibility broached by McCone—that the Soviets were preparing to put surface-to-surface missiles in Cuba—Kennedy learned that U-2 flights over Cuba had discerned nothing except work on SAM sites and emplacements of short-range cruise missiles (or pilotless aircraft) designed for shore defense. Intelligence data thus reinforced the earlier assurances from Khrushchev. And these assurances were repeated by the amiable Soviet ambassador, Anatoly Dobrynin, who spoke with Robert Kennedy and soon afterward with U.S. ambassador to the United Nations Adlai Stevenson, saying flatly to each that the Soviet government had no intention whatever of using Cuba as an offensive military base. What Dobrynin said privately was then said publicly out of Moscow by the official TASS news service.[67]

Although the true crisis would commence in October, when Soviet missiles were sighted in Cuba, Kennedy and some of his advisers reviewed many of the relevant issues in a series of meetings on September 4, from which issued Kennedy's warning that offensive weapons could create the "gravest issues." The President had his tape recorder running, and excerpts from conversations that day and later in September appear here as part of the essential record of U.S. crisis decision making.

In the Cabinet Room, now and during the crisis proper, President Kennedy would sit at the head of a long oblong table, tall windows to his back and book alcoves on the wall opposite. The hidden microphones were so positioned as to catch his voice better than those of others. Also, though he would often use a word, then check himself and substitute another, and frequently leave sentences unfinished, he was usually both precise and clear. On the tapes, his accent and cadence can be recognized by anyone who has ever heard a sound recording of one of this speeches.

Kennedy was, of course, almost two years older than when he took office, promising "to bear any burden." He had the same bush of brown hair, the same calm, ruddy face, the same penetrating blue eyes. In his voice, a listener can hear surviving traces of his earlier personae, even of the 23-year-old author of *Why England Slept*. But the shadows around his eyes had darkened, and the lines there and at the corners of his mouth were more deeply etched. A listener can detect on the tapes some of the wariness induced by the Bay of Pigs experience; the combination of puzzlement and fear carried over from Vienna, the Berlin Wall, and other dealings with the Soviets; and, above all, a sense of the responsibility symbolized by the military aides, always within a 90-second hail, who handed off to one another every eight hours the black vinyl satchel known as "the football," which contained the codes that the President alone had authority to use and that, if used, would unleash a rain of nuclear bombs and missiles.

On the President's right sat the team from the State Department: Secretary Rusk, Under Secretary Ball, and, in due course, Edwin Martin, the assistant secretary for American Republics affairs; U. Alexis Johnson, the under secretary for political affairs; and Llewellyn "Tommy" Thompson, who had recently been U.S. ambassador to Moscow.

Tall, portly, and almost completely bald, Rusk had an impassive face. He resembled distantly a statue of Buddha. His manner conveyed both authority and insecurity. More experienced than most others at the table, he sometimes spoke as if coaching amateurs. But he also spoke as someone who had never achieved as much independence as some of the others or as much rapport with the President. Unlike McNamara, he had set no conditions for taking his post. As a result, he had had one unwanted assistant after another pushed on him by the White House. He had recently pulled Martin out of Economic Affairs to take over the American Republics Bureau so that Martin could sit on a former White House staffer, Richard Goodwin, sent over to ramrod the Alliance for Progress. Other White House staffers made fun of Rusk for his formality and his reluctance or inability to act as a McNamara-like manager, and Rusk almost certainly knew that this was so.

In the missile crisis debates, Kennedy addresses McNamara as Bob and Dillon, Rusk's near contemporary, as Doug, but Rusk is always "Mr. Secretary"; rarely would anyone say *Dean*. Though Rusk's interventions are often lengthy and appear well organized and well prepared, his soft Georgia accent, with a slight overlay of Oxford drawl, is not always easy to understand, and he often gropes for words.

Ball, by contrast, was more assertive than is always apparent to a reader. His interventions were often well organized—briefs prepared by a skilled litigator—and Ball often spoke with table-thumping emphasis and not a trace of inner uncertainty. But Ball lacked experience comparable to Rusk's, for he had dealt mostly with economic issues. Also, he had the disability of having been, and seeming still, more identified with Stevenson than with Kennedy.

Martin is a minor figure in the debates. So is Alexis Johnson. Thompson, by contrast, is one whom Kennedy continually consults and heeds. He is the one person around the table who has known and studied Khrushchev. About the same age as Rusk, he had grown up on a ranch in Colorado, graduated from the state university, and entered the Foreign Service. He was sent to the Soviet Union in World War II after a rush course in Russian (which he never spoke with the facility of old Russia hands like Kennan). Although he was away from Soviet affairs for much of the time between the war and 1957, when he went back to Moscow as ambassador, he established closer relationships with Soviet leaders than had any of his predecessors, and especially with Khrushchev.[68] When interpreting or predicting Soviet actions, Thompson does not hesitate to contradict anyone, including the President. Nor does he draw back from saying what he thinks Kennedy should do. When Thompson's slow, dry voice is heard on the tapes, one can be sure that everyone else at the table was paying attention.

On the President's left sat the Defense team: McNamara, Deputy Secretary of Defense Roswell Gilpatric, Joint Chiefs Chairman Taylor, and Assistant Secretary of Defense for International Security Affairs Paul Nitze. Though not as tall or heavy as Rusk, McNamara gave the impression of being the larger of the two. Lanky, loose limbed, like a high-power generator in human form, with slicked-down black hair parted in the middle, wearing rimless glasses, McNamara dominated physically almost any group he joined. On the tapes, one can almost hear him keeping impatience barely under control, then barging in to catalogue his own points. "Number one . . . , number two . . . , number three . . . ," he would say, slapping first one bony finger, then another against the palm of his right hand. Though his intensity seldom lightened, associates remembered one occasion when he reached "number six . . ." and laughed at discovering that he was out of fingers.[69]

Unlike Rusk, McNamara had gained confidence from experience in office. (And he had not lacked confidence when he started.) He had won most of his battles in the Pentagon and on Capitol Hill. He was conscious of having the complete trust of the President and respect, if not awe, from all the others who would be in the missile crisis circle. McNamara's voice, in contrast to that of Rusk, was always more forceful than may be evident to someone reading the transcripts but not hearing the tapes.

Gilpatric, a studious Wall Street lawyer, commanded respect when he spoke, but rarely spoke. While Taylor entered the discussion frequently, he did so less often as the President's personal friend and former staff aide than as spokesman for the Joint Chiefs. Someone listening to the tapes, unaware of the past relationship between Kennedy and Taylor, might be inclined to discount Taylor's interventions in part because they so often summarize what the chiefs have been saying or what they are likely to say. Also, a slight lisp and a tendency to fumble for words cause Taylor to seem less articulate than many of the others. But the reader should bear in mind that, when Taylor speaks, he conveys to those in the room a sense not only of what the Chiefs say but of what they could conceivably say—eventually—to Congress and the public.

Nitze brought to the Pentagon team experience that almost matched Rusk's.[70] A Wall Street financier who had shifted to public service during World War II, Nitze had headed the Policy Planning Staff in the State Department during the Korean War. But Nitze made most of his contribution to missile crisis decision making in small groups working outside the White House, chiefly on Berlin contingencies. He is seldom heard on Kennedy's tapes.

Across the table from the President sat, from his left to his right, his two key assistants, Sorensen and Bundy, Secretary of the Treasury Dillon, the Attorney General, and the Vice President. On the tapes, while Sorensen speaks only occasionally, he is a constant presence because he is usually the last crafter of words that the President is going to voice or include in a letter or cable. Bundy speaks more often but always briefly and crisply. He never offers extended analyses in the manner of Rusk or McNamara. As a rule, the rest of the table quietens for both Sorensen and Bundy, for, except for Robert Kennedy, Sorensen is the person there who best knows the President's mind and habits of thought, while Bundy is the clarifier—the person who frames in precise language the issue that the President must decide. In Sorensen's voice one can still hear a touch of the onetime University of Nebraska debater, in Bundy's the patrician intellectual who would cut off fellow professors and finish their sentences in language more clear than their own.

Dillon's speaking style is very much like Kennedy's, though the accent is upper-class New York, faintly reminiscent of Franklin Roosevelt. Like Kennedy, Dillon leaves sentences unfinished if his meaning is clear; he does not use ten words where eight will do. And his customary lead-in has no trace of diffidence. A reader of the transcripts should be aware that he says "it seems to *me-e*," conveying the impression that he believes it must seem so to anyone.

Bobby's voice is like his brother's but more crisp, more urgent, more combative. And Lyndon Johnson's is in his small-group style, not in the flat, wooden, somewhat unctuous tones of his public addresses, where the microphone or camera seems to make him self-conscious about having grown up poor, gone to Southwest Texas State Teachers College, and never learned the manners of the eastern elite. On Kennedy's tapes, one hears the former Senate majority leader with the legendary capacity for personal persuasion. When the Kennedys are out of the room, Johnson takes command. Sometimes he even asserts himself when one or both are there.

Often, DCI McCone is present. His voice is flat, confident, occasionally opinionated or quarrelsome. Adlai Stevenson sometimes comes down from New York. Mostly, however, he is present by virtue of what he writes or says over the phone. Senators, congressmen, and service chiefs, including LeMay, show up for cameo appearances. However, their reactions, and possible reactions around the country, weigh on the minds of Kennedy and his advisers much more frequently than their words acknowledge. For all of their being kept secret by Kennedy and kept under lock and key by the government for almost 35 years, these tapes record the decision making of a democracy.

THE KENNEDY TAPES

Tuesday, September 4, 1962

12:35 P.M.

Meeting on Soviet Arms Shipments to Cuba

Congressmen, especially Senator Kenneth Keating of New York, had begun to question the White House's handling of the obvious buildup of Soviet weapons in Cuba. There were rumors of the installation of Russian missiles, certainly conventionally armed surface-to-air missiles (SAMs), but possibly even surface-to-surface nuclear rockets. Indeed, photography from a secret U-2 flight flown over the island on August 29 had just confirmed for Kennedy the existence of eight SAM sites. Assuming that word about the Soviet SAMs in Cuba would soon leak, Kennedy thought he needed a public statement of policy to answer the Republican charges that he was just letting the Soviet Union turn Cuba into a dangerous military base. He asked Secretary of State Dean Rusk to draft such a statement. He then gathered his advisers on the afternoon of September 4 to review the draft. He found that several, including Robert Kennedy, were quite worried about the Soviet arms buildup on the island.

Although there was as yet no firm evidence of nuclear missiles, some in Kennedy's inner circle thought that it was only a matter of time before Khrushchev decided to install that kind of force in Cuba. This group, led by Attorney General Robert F. Kennedy, viewed the impending public statement as a golden opportunity to send a clear warning to Khrushchev that the United States would never countenance a Soviet nuclear base in Castro's Cuba. Kennedy was worried. On August 31, he had told General Marshall Carter, who was running the CIA in John McCone's absence, to put the readout from the August 29 flight "in the box and nail it shut."[1] A freeze on sharing this information with anyone but the top foreign policy-makers and analysts remained in effect. However, it was not going to last forever with interest so high on Capitol Hill and in the media.

Rusk voiced the opinion that "any placing by the Soviets of a significant offensive capability in the hands of this self-announced aggressive regime in Cuba would be a direct and major challenge to this hemi-sphere and would warrant immediate and appropriate action." Though Kennedy's national security assistant McGeorge Bundy said, "We don't want to get into the position of being frightened by this group," Secretary of Defense Robert McNamara replied that the deliveries of MiG fighter aircraft were cause for concern. He then continued.

.   .   .

Robert McNamara: . . . I further feel that they'll be adding to what could be interpreted as offensive strength in the months ahead.

President Kennedy: The missiles really are what are significant?

McGeorge Bundy: Surface-to-surface missiles are the turning point.

.   .   .

McNamara: They can, they may well put surface-to-surface missiles or missile launchers, artillery or missile launchers in there. They have that equipment in their own force. In the first place, it will be a question: Do they have it or don't they have it? We won't be sure. Is it equipped with a nuclear warhead or isn't it equipped with a nuclear warhead? Is it substantial or isn't it substantial? I just worry about the President hav-ing made a statement which can be used as a lever by elements of the Congress and of the public, unless we know exactly what we're going to do under those circumstances. If we have a plan, we know what it is and we're are all agreed on it, then I think a firm statement is excellent. But unless we have . . . it seems to me we could cause great [*unclear*].

Bundy: Our preliminary analysis of the consequences for us, Bob, of the establishment of a surface-to-surface nuclear capability gives me at least the feeling that we wouldn't have to act.

Dean Rusk: I think we'd have to act, Bob, exactly how and by what stages we'd . . . for example, I would suppose that if you're going to take on a bloodbath in Cuba, you'd precede it by a systematic blockade to weaken Cuba before you actually go to put anybody ashore.

McNamara: See I wonder why we . . . if we do it then, why wouldn't we do it today? This is one of the actions that we can consider today as a matter of fact. There's no question the Soviets are shipping arms to Cuba; that's clear. They've said so. Now, we can—

President Kennedy: The reason we don't is that, is because we figure that they may try to blockade Berlin and we would then try to blockade Cuba. But I think that the reason we don't today is the [*unclear*] is that it wouldn't do them that much harm for quite a while—

Rusk: [*Unclear.*]

President Kennedy: —and then Berlin would be the obvious response—

Rusk: [*Unclear.*] The configuration in Cuba still is defensive.

. . .

McNamara: There is a related point: You have asked, Mr. President, on two or three occasions whether we believe it would be wise to ask for authority from Congress to call up reserve and guard forces while they're out of session, if international events make that desirable. I personally believe it would be wise to ask for that authority, assuming that we could achieve it without controversy. It relates to Cuba, in one respect, that the forces that we would require could be required for Berlin, Southeast Asia, or Cuba.

Rusk: Mr. President, I think I would agree with the Secretary of Defense on that. I think we . . . it would be very helpful for us to have it but I think it would more effective if we could do it quickly and quietly. The Soviets would get the message.

McNamara: Yes. Yes—

Rusk: But, if we're going to have a great turmoil—

McNamara: Yes.

Rusk: —and hullaballoo about it, then it would be better to have that in connection with a specific action taken—

McNamara: Exactly—

Rusk: —[*unclear*] call the Congress back in special session.

McNamara: Exactly; but I mention it now because if the leadership wants to act in relation to Cuba, one of the best actions I can think of is exactly this.

President Kennedy: Well, now—if we, let's say we get them down here at five this afternoon, on an off-the-record basis we give them more or less what we know about these things and tell them when this information is to become available and the number of people that are there . . . and any other question they want. In the meanwhile we're going to go over this statement. At least we're going to have something to say about this. It's going to get out . . . so that I can say to Pierre to put it out at six.[2] Whatever he's going to put out, he's going to put out the information about these sites and any other statement we've got [*unclear*] worked out.

Bundy: I would suggest that we be very careful, Mr. President, about going with that full statement today simply because the issues involved are very grave and—

President Kennedy: That's right but I think what we've got to do is . . . we can't permit somebody to break this story before we do.

Bundy: The SAM site business can be broken promptly. That doesn't—
Bundy and the President start talking over each other.

President Kennedy: But everyone's going to want to know what we're going to do about it.

Bundy: We don't have to put all these statements out at once. They don't—

Robert Kennedy: Can I raise a—

President Kennedy: Yeah.

Robert Kennedy: I think that [*unclear*] that while you were out that I don't think that this is just a question about what we are going to do about this. I think it's a question about Cuba in the future. And then I think that it's the judgment of everybody around this table that this is only one step—we've seen it being built up for the last six months or eight months, whatever it might be—that this is going [to] continue. There's going to be . . . three months from now, there's going to be something else going on, six months from now . . . That eventually it's very likely that they'll establish a naval base there for submarines perhaps, or that they'll put surface-to-surface missiles in.

And what steps, we—what position will we be in at that time, if we consider that surface-to-surface missiles, and I think maybe we should reach a determination on that, that surface-to-surface missiles in Cuba would be so harmful that we would have to undertake an invasion of Cuba, or a blockade which eventually would lead to an invasion and the Marines going in, and the airborne, et cetera. Then, whether . . . Or even a naval base or some of these other things. That in this kind of a statement, that you traced the history of Cuba and even mention the Monroe Doctrine and say, point out that this was captured in a different way and the Monroe Doctrine doesn't apply as it did in the past; but we still have our responsibilities to national security, that, making some of these points that were made in Secretary Rusk's statement, and then also say that there're certain things that would violate our national security. And we would then have to take appropriate action and such things would be the establishment of surface-to-surface missiles or the putting of, of, of a nuclear weapons base.

Now, my point is, I think that it's much more difficult for them to take steps like that after you've made that statement. . . .

. . . [T]his gives us a reason to put out a statement as to what really is going to be our policy, not just on the surface-to-air missiles, but what is our . . . going to be our policy as far as Cuba in the future is concerned. I think that's—

Rusk: The great problem, the great difficulty, of course, as we all know [*unclear*] . . . I think that, looking at Cuba, I think that it would be fairly easy to come to answers to the questions that are posed at the present time. But the United States has such a worldwide confrontation with the Soviet Union that when the time comes to act, the President will have to take into account how that action relates to the worldwide confrontation and what the situation is everywhere else at the same time because his problems are total and comprehensive. I mean, if we were relatively isolated in the world, which we were before World War II, we could concentrate on Cuba and say, "If this in Cuba, then that follows." But we've got a million men overseas in confrontation with the Soviet bloc and this is a part of that confrontation. This is the thing that makes it so agonizingly difficult.

Robert Kennedy: Yeah. I understand that. So, therefore, I think that you really have to reach a determination of whether putting surface-to-surface missiles in Cuba would be where you'd really have to face up to it, and figure that you are going to have to take your chances on something like that. Everything you do, whether you do it in Southeast Asia, or Berlin or Cuba or wherever is going to have some effect on the Soviet Union elsewhere. And whether there are certain things that they do that—

. . .

McNamara: No, I don't mean to overemphasize the offensive capability of them. But they're going to continue to increase whatever offensive capability they have—

Bundy: I think that really is a question, Bob. It seems to me that everything they have put in so far, really is, insofar as you can make these distinctions, a defensive weapon. Fighters are defensive aircraft for use against bombers and photographic reconnaissance. The SAMs are the same thing, surface-to-air missiles don't go . . . are a stupid way of reaching Florida.

Robert Kennedy: Well, Mac, that's what you do, I mean, at the present juncture, if you were them—

Bundy: No, I'm only saying that the other step seems to me a much larger step than the development of the kind of thing we've seen over the last year and a half which is fully consistent with their behavior in a lot of other countries.

Robert Kennedy: I just . . . I think we can all assume that they are going to take those steps eventually.

. . .

President Kennedy: What is it you suggest that we announce today, aside from this statement, which is rather long? What is it, in short, you think we ought to announce as far as what our future action should be towards Cuba? Aside from consultations, or aside from Guantánamo?

What Bobby, I guess, is saying is that we should announce today that if they put in ground-to-ground missiles, we will—

Robert Kennedy: They take certain [*unclear*]—I think, no I think some study should go on—

Rusk: Well, if we designated ground-to-ground missiles or we specified the nuclear weapon, I think we would create a kind of panic that the facts themselves don't now justify.

Bundy: That's correct.

Rusk: And that this could heat the matter up much faster than if we could get some general language, then, take account of the point that Bob McNamara made. . . . It would be better to get a warning to the Soviets in more general terms so that we do not create for them a major prestige problem in not moving down that trail and then make it very clear to our friends in the hemisphere—

President Kennedy: This is . . . the key sentence is, "Any placing by the Soviets of a significant offensive capability in the hands of this self-announced . . . would be a direct and major challenge . . . would warrant immediate—"

Rusk: —"appropriate action."

. . .

President Kennedy: Well, I think, that we can shorten this thing, boil it down. The key thing you need right now are these missiles, also put them into proportion: We are in much more danger from the Soviet Union than we are from Cuba.

McNamara: Sure.

. . .

President Kennedy: OK. Now you can work on this. So that part's all right. I don't—there's nothing particularly . . . I think you can just say you got it and describe what it is to them. By then we will have this statement in order and then I think at that time the Secretary can say we want to keep some proportion. We've got Berlin and the big danger's it would—They don't have offensive capability against us and they also, they don't have an ability to, in the final analysis, to prevent us from doing what we think needs to be done. But the big problem is the fact of these other obligations. So, if we lock them in, that takes care of really the big [*unclear*] physically.

. . .

4:00 P.M.

Drafting Meeting on the Press Statement

In the three hours since this group last met, Robert Kennedy had been very busy. Besides drafting a new version of the statement on Cuba for the President, the Attorney General met with Soviet ambassador Anatoly Dobrynin at the Soviet Embassy. The Attorney General had made use of the meeting to mention Cuba, but the Soviet ambassador said nothing to deter Kennedy from his belief that it was only a matter of time before Moscow put nuclear missiles on the island.[3]

The group was larger for this second Cuban meeting of the day. Among the new participants were the Treasury secretary, Douglas Dillon; the assistant secretary of state for inter-American affairs, Edwin Martin; and the Air Force Chief of Staff, General Curtis LeMay. Kennedy was widening the circle to confirm the instincts of his key advisers and to tighten the statement before it went out. Discussion now centered on the new Robert Kennedy draft. In the struggle over whether to use the evening's statement to send a warning to the Soviets, Robert Kennedy had scored a victory.

The President and his key advisers considered how much of the intelligence data at hand on the Soviet buildup should be revealed in this statement. Then they turned to broader policy concerns.

· · ·

C. Douglas Dillon: The only thing I think you want to be careful of is . . . making a threat to do something if they get some particular weapon in Cuba. If you make your threat that you'll never let it come out of Cuba, which is still the key; but the other thing means that you're—

President Kennedy: Well, I would say ground-to-ground missiles, you'd—

Dillon: Well, that's . . . if you want to put it on that maybe—

President Kennedy: Yeah.

Dillon: —that's a strong enough one to put it on, but just saying "offensive weapons," I don't know what an offensive weapon is. They'd argue. Might say tanks are but I don't know.

McGeorge Bundy: That's a substantive question. I mean how far—it's clear that we want to make a statement that makes it plain that they will be confined and not make a . . . head for the rest of the hemisphere with this stuff.

Dean Rusk: Well, what about this then? "To date, bloc assistance has been limited to weapons normally associated with defense. Were it to be otherwise the greatest questions would arise."

. . .

President Kennedy: What we are doing is, first we're going to give the details of what assistance they've sent to Cuba.

Bundy: That's right . . . what they have not.

President Kennedy: Secondly, we have . . . And what they have not. Then secondly we are going to give a unilateral guarantee against the use of any of these forces against anyone in the hemisphere.

Bundy: Against anybody else.

President Kennedy: Third, we're going to say that the [*unclear*] indirect methods of taking steps against them [*unclear*] direct. Then I think we ought to say something about, at the end, that we have to keep in mind for those who are . . . This is a dangerous world and we have to keep in mind . . . don't want to use the word *totality* again, but all of the dangers we live with. The fact of the matter is the major danger is the Soviet Union with missiles and nuclear warheads, not Cuba. We don't want to get everybody so fixed on Cuba that they regard . . . So in some way or other we want to suggest that at the end. This is a matter of [*unclear*] danger, as is Berlin as is Southeast Asia as are a great many areas which are—

Bundy: I think there is a question, Mr. President, whether you want to do that in this statement or whether that's something we make clear as we go along.

President Kennedy: Well, I know, I think we've got to say something about that otherwise you don't want everybody to blow on this, you get everybody so mesmerized here that all these other places which are also—

Rusk: I think, perhaps [*unclear*]—

President Kennedy: This is not an aggressive danger to us except indirectly.

Bundy: As it now stands.

President Kennedy: Compared with these other places. Now somewhere we've got to get that in, it seems to me, right from the beginning. Give some guidance.

. . .

President Kennedy: Oh about the . . . I'd like to ask General [Curtis] LeMay a little about what these SAM sites could mean if we were going to carry out an attack on Cuba. What hazard would this present to you?

Curtis LeMay: Well, it would mean you'd have to get, of course, your force in there to knock them out so that the rest of the attacking forces would be free to take on the other targets. That'd be the first thing we'd do. We'd have to go in low level and get them.

President Kennedy: OK.

LeMay: These missiles have no low-level capability so you go in low and take them out.

President Kennedy: You'd have to go hit the radar?

LeMay: And the missiles, too.

Unidentified: [*Unclear.*]

President Kennedy: Would that be a difficult operation?

LeMay: No, sir.

Rusk: They would probably have low-level, smaller antiaircraft guns.

LeMay: Lose our tactical fighters going in low, uh, huh.

Rusk: Yeah.

President Kennedy: You mean they would use antiaircraft [guns]?

Rusk: They would use 20 mm [*unclear*]—

LeMay: Well, they would probably not see us until we got within a few miles of the coastline.

Rusk: Yeah.

LeMay: And you'd put part of your force on those missiles to knock them out.

Rusk: Right.

LeMay: Of course, you've got to get the airfields very quick too.

Rusk: Sure.

LeMay: But this complicates any assault plans you might have. It's another target you've got to worry about.

President Kennedy: Yeah. How about . . . let's see . . . how are we now . . . are we going to continue our observation of the island?

Unidentified: [*Unclear.*]

Marshall Carter: We have not yet faced that problem, sir. We have a bird ready to go tomorrow morning and we would like to send it to cover that portion which was obstructed by clouds on the [August] 29th mission. We could go in across the Isle of Pines—hit the two— [*pointing to a map*] hit right there on the first of the green sites and then cover the island down and back, avoiding the present area. We don't need any more coverage of that area now.[4]

President Kennedy: This would be about 75,000 feet, would it, depending?

LeMay: Sixty-five [thousand], 70,000 feet, yes sir.

Carter: I think that's a safe operation. But I think also it's safe for the entire island now, but next week it may not be and it might not be now.

President Kennedy: He has to go over land doesn't he, to get this thing, these [*unclear*]?

Carter: Yes sir, these are verticals.[5]

LeMay: Well, once these things become operational they have the capability of shooting a U-2 down, of course. We can go to the low altitude 101s, but [*unclear*].[6]

President Kennedy: You can't get much, can you?

LeMay: You can't hide them very well.

. . .

5:00 P.M.

Meeting with Congressional Leadership

As planned, Kennedy met with congressional leaders to prepare them for his forthcoming public statement on the Soviet weapons buildup in Cuba. The meeting opened with the deputy director of central intelligence, General Marshall Carter, providing a briefing on the buildup. (The director of central intelligence, John McCone, was honeymooning with his new bride.)

Before a large map of Cuba, Carter used a pointer to indicate the positions of 8 known sites for SA-2 SAMs, each with a horizontal range of up to 30 miles and vertical range of up to 100,000 feet, and 8 torpedo boats carrying conventionally armed missiles with ranges of up to 17 miles. He reported that the number of MiG fighters was now up to 60 but still included no high-performance MiG 21s. Though Carter commented on the continuing heavy flow of Soviet dry cargo ships toward Cuba, he answered a question from Republican House Minority Leader Charles Halleck by saying, "There are no indications of any offensive weapons right now, sir. These weapons are defensive." General Curtis LeMay, the chief of staff of the Air Force, confirmed this appraisal, and Kennedy can be heard on the tape whispering pleasedly to someone at his side, "Did he just say 'defensive'?"

The meeting continued with interrogations from Republican senators Alexander Wiley of Wisconsin, Bourke Hickenlooper of Iowa, and Everett Dirksen of Illinois and from Democratic senators Richard Russell of Georgia, J. William Fulbright of Arkansas, and Mike Mansfield of Montana.

. . .

Alexander Wiley: Mr. President, may I ask a question? How do you define the question of missile sites? I understood you to say that they were defensive instead of offensive, is that right?

Marshall Carter: Yes, sir. These are designed for shooting down aircraft and that's all.

Wiley: Well, now then, the next question is, what is our policy in relation to Cuba? I'm just back from the hinterland and everybody is inquiring about it and I said I'll have to talk to the executive who spearheads foreign policy or the Secretary of State. What is to be our policy? Just to sit still and let Cuba carry on?

President Kennedy: [*Unclear statement.*] On this matter we are going to make an announcement in regard to the existence of these sites today.

We're also going to state that the United States would prevent the use of any of these military weapons, any of this force against any neighboring country, but that this . . . which I have never thought a very likely prospect but at least it has been discussed. Any concern that this buildup, military buildup would be used against another country, another neighbor would be . . . We will indicate that if that were done, the United States would intervene under its Rio Treaty and the Monroe Doctrine and all the rest.

As to whether the United States would intervene in Cuba in order to . . . at this point, I would think it would be a mistake. We're talking about—we have to keep some proportion—we're talking about 60 MiGs, we're talking about some ground-to-air missiles which from the island, which do not threaten the United States. We are not talking about nuclear warheads. We've got a very difficult situation in Berlin. We've got a difficult situation in Southeast Asia and a lot of other places. So that if I were asked, I would say that I could not see, under present conditions, the United States intervening. It would be a major military operation. General LeMay can describe it in more detail. It would be a major military operation.

Wiley: Blockading [*unclear*].[7]

President Kennedy: Well, a blockade is a major military operation, too. It's an act of war. We could blockade . . . there's no evidence that that would bring down Castro for many, many months. You'd have a food situation in which you'd have people starving and all the rest. In addition, Berlin obviously would be blockaded also. And if Berlin were blockaded one of our reprisals obviously could be the actions of various kinds against Cuba. But I would say today . . . listen I think Berlin is coming to some kind of a climax this fall, one way or another, before Christmas. And I think that today I would think it would be a mistake for us to talk about military action or a blockade [against Cuba]. Blockades are very difficult. It's a big island and you have to stop ships of the Soviet Union and other ships. And it would be regarded as a belligerent act; and it would be regarded as a warlike act. I would think we would have to assume that there would be actions taken against countries. . . . I think that we therefore should not do that. I don't see that the Soviet . . .

This is annoying and it's a danger. I think the dangers to this hemisphere [*unclear*] by Cuba is by subversion and example. There's obviously no military threat, as yet, to the United States. The military threat quite obviously is still the Soviet Union which has missiles and hydrogen bombs.

So that, in answer to your question, I would . . . even though I know a lot of people want to invade Cuba, I would be opposed to it today. So I think we ought to keep very close surveillance on Cuba which we are doing and keep well informed and make it very clear that the placing in Cuba of missiles which could reach the United States would change the nature of the . . . buildup and therefore would change the nature of our response.

·   ·   ·

Mike Mansfield: Well, Mr. President, I'd hate for you to lie down, but I think it ought it to be understood that when you issue a statement, and give these facts and figures, that the reaction may well be a call for action of some kind or another. I would hope that this would not be used for the purpose of creating a situation which would tend to undermine your authority and your responsibility. I would hope that we would move with caution and we will not be carried away by these figures and facts that you have given us this afternoon. I think we would have to expect that there will be a certain reaction which may not be very satisfactory.

President Kennedy: Oh, I expect that, but as I say, [*short, unclear aside to someone else*]. All right, as I say we're talking about 58 MiGs, we're talking about some ground-to-air missiles. That really isn't comparable to the threats we face all around. So that I think that's just the perspective we have to keep it in, even though no one would desire more to see Castro thrown out of there; but throwing Castro out of there is a major military operation. It's just a question of when we decide that that's the proper action for us to take. It is an operation which has to be mounted over a period of time and we could anticipate that there would be reactions in other parts of the world, by the Communist bloc against other vulnerable areas as we carve out Cuba. So I think we just have to try to keep all that in perspective.

Mansfield: Well, that's the point—

President Kennedy: There's no easy aspect to throwing Castro out. If we had it, we'd do it. Except an outright military action which involves a great many divisions—a number of divisions—and a great deal of our military power and I think we've got Berlin, we've got Turkey and Iran . . . We've got southeast Asia, so I—

Unidentified: Formosa also.

J. William Fulbright: Do you think?

President Kennedy: And Formosa.

Fulbright: Do you think, Mr. President, if we did decide to take some firm action about Cuba, that this would turn the pancake over, that this would start Russia off here, there, somewhere else?

Rusk: I think this will lead to a very very severe crisis indeed. I couldn't predict exactly what the Soviets would do but I would think that they would almost certainly make a major move on Berlin of some sort. You remember, the unfortunate combination of Hungary and Suez in 1955 and '6. Now, if on the other side, as the President indicated, the Soviets made a move on Berlin, this opens up some possibilities with Cuba with world support, that we would not have if we at the moment took initiative against Cuba because of circumstances.

Fulbright: This is the other side of the pancake.

Rusk: See, that's the other side of the pancake. Because this is a part of the worldwide confrontation of the free world and the Soviet Union. We have a million men outside the United States as part of this confrontation. All right, this has to be thought of in relation to the whole because you can't deal with these simply as little isolated [*unclear*] instances but the total situation.

Richard Russell: That's undoubtedly true, but Senator Mansfield is right about . . . it may cause a great deal of reaction because this Cuban thing—

President Kennedy: That's right.

Russell: —is in the nature of an offense to the national pride, [*chuckling*] and there's something personal about it too. It's so close down there that . . . a man wouldn't get ruffled about something that happened in Berlin, much less Hungary or some other part of the world, but he would get upset about Cuba.

Unidentified: [*Unclear.*] [*Short pause.*]

President Kennedy: Well, this statement will be out and it won't have any reference to our meeting here but it will be a statement of fact and you've heard the facts as they come along, we'll make available to you. And I would think that if we ever get any information about ground-to-ground missiles then the situation would then be quite changed and we would have to [*unclear*].

Unidentified: Well, thank you, Mr. President.

. . .

At the end of the meeting with the congressional leadership, Robert McNamara, it seems, gathered a few of the congressmen for a short separate meeting with the President to discuss the need for a special grant of standby authority to permit the administration to call up 150,000 reservists. Kennedy had been considering a call-up in August as a response to the increasingly tense situation in West Berlin. His advisers had discouraged him. Now, it seemed that recent events in Cuba could provide another argument for the reserve call-up that Kennedy wanted.

5:55 P.M.

Meeting on the Congressional Resolution

For the second time in twenty months, President Kennedy intended to seek congressional authority for special reserve mobilization powers. In mid-1961, following the dramatic Kennedy-Khrushchev summit in Vienna, where the mercurial Soviet leader had vowed to solve once and for all the Berlin problem, Congress approved a call-up as part of a program of expanding defense spending. Now it was the specter of twin crises, in and around Cuba and Berlin, combined with the fact that Congress was about to recess for the midterm elections, that prompted the administration's request.

The recording begins with McNamara's reporting on the results of the 1961 U.S. military buildup and the reasons why more was needed now.

Robert McNamara: The authority that was granted last summer has expired. As you know it covered authority to call up 250,000 men during a period of 11 months and that authority expired with the 1st of July.

Since that authority was granted, we have added about 300,000 men to the regular forces: roughly 40[,000] to 50,000 men to the Navy, about the same number to the Air Force, and 110[,000] to 120,000 men to the Army. All of the forces are in substantially better shape today than they were on June 30th of last year.

The Army has been expanded in terms of combat-ready divisions by about 45 percent. There were then 11 combat-ready divisions. There are today 16 combat-ready divisions.

The Air Force has had a very substantial expansion in its tactical air strength. A portion of that tactical air strength that has been added, however, is not yet combat ready and won't be combat ready for six to nine months.

The Navy has been expanded by the addition of a large number of amphibious craft as well as logistical support ships.

So, we are much stronger today than we were 13 or 14 months ago when we asked for authority to call up Reserve and Guard personnel.

On the other hand, there are both military and political and psychological reasons why it would be desirable, we believe, to have authority to call up between 150[,000] and 250,000 personnel during the period that Congress is out of session, say roughly from the 1st of October to the end of February. We've been considering that. I just mentioned it briefly, a moment ago, to Chairman [Carl] Vinson and Chairman [Richard] Russell.[8] They mentioned that the House would meet on Friday—

Unidentified: On Thursday.

McNamara: Rather Thursday. We have a draft resolution, essentially the same as the resolution passed a year ago. I think we're all agreed, all of us who have considered this problem, that if there is to be any controversy, any debate, any argument over whether this is a wise move or not, it would be undesirable to submit it to—[*Tape cuts off briefly.*]

President Kennedy: Then [*unclear*] the numbers revised [by] General [Burgess]?

McNamara: Yes, sir. We would.

President Kennedy: But it seems to me quite possible that you would have to call up some air units before the end of the year, if not earlier. Because I think they would be the most likely units we'd call.

We don't have any plans to call up any [National] Guard divisions?

McNamara: No, sir. They . . . If—

President Kennedy: That's why I think the 150 is enough. When it gets beyond that, then we're [*unclear*] crisis more, and after that we draft a [*unclear*].

. . .

Everett Dirksen: Mr. Secretary, how are we going to avoid acrimonies today in view of the gripes that obtained in the last call-up of reserves . . . ?

President Kennedy: Sir, that's why we're talking to you now.

Dirksen: Yeah, [*unclear*].

Now, I think there is probably one way to pour some sugar on that department and achieve that tactic, if in any kind of a statement you were going to particularly mention . . . definitely say "in view of the developments in Cuba" . . . people understand that . . . and a few other things, put 'em in . . . have no doubt in their minds as to why this is needed. You [*unclear*]. Now, Mr. President, I was [*unclear*] yesterday, I was the guest of the Winnebago Labor Day, on Labor Day.[9] The only thing they wanted to talk about, those that talked to me, wanted to talk about Cuba . . . in Cuba. So this is very much in the average person's mind and you'll have to lay it right on the line in any statement you make; otherwise they'll be hell-a-poppin for one and we won't have any good answers for them, unless you give us the answers.

. . .

At the end of the day Pierre Salinger, the White House press secretary, read the final text of the President's statement to reporters. Its language provided the pivot for the crisis that would erupt nearly six weeks later. It read:

> All Americans, as well as all of our friends in this hemisphere, have been concerned over the recent moves of the Soviet Union to bolster the military power of the Castro regime in Cuba. Information has reached this Government in the last four days from a variety of sources which establishes without doubt that the Soviets have provided the Cuban Government with a number of antiaircraft defense missiles with a slant range of 25 miles which are similar to early models of our Nike. Along with these missiles, the Soviets are apparently providing the extensive radar and other electronic equipment which is required for their operation. We can also confirm the presence of several Soviet-made motor torpedo boats carrying ship-to-ship guided missiles having a range of 15 miles. The number of Soviet military technicians now known to be in Cuba or en route—approximately 3,500—is consistent with assistance in setting up and learning to use this equipment. As I stated last week, we shall continue to make information available as fast as it is obtained and properly verified.
>
> There is no evidence of any organized combat force in Cuba from any Soviet bloc country, of military bases provided to Russia, of a violation of the 1934 treaty relating to Guantánamo, of the presence of offensive ground-to-ground missiles, or of other significant offen-

sive capability either in Cuban hands or under Soviet direction and guidance. Were it to be otherwise, the gravest issues would arise.

The Cuban question must be considered as a part of the worldwide challenge posed by Communist threats to the peace. It must be dealt with as a part of that larger issue as well as in the context of the special relationships which have long characterized the inter-American system.

It continues to be the policy of the United States that the Castro regime will not be allowed to export its aggressive purposes by force or by the threat of force. It will be prevented by whatever means may be necessary from taking action against any part of the Western Hemisphere. The United States, in conjunction with other hemisphere countries, will make sure that while increased Cuban armaments will be a heavy burden to the unhappy people of Cuba themselves, they will be nothing more.

His official day at an end, the President went for his evening swim at 7:35 P.M.

Saturday, September 29, 1962

11:00 A.M.

Meeting on the Soviet Union

With Republicans remaining on the offensive, Kennedy had felt obliged to make yet another statement. Bundy outlined a formula but said it would be unsuitable if the President intended to invade Cuba. In fact, Kennedy followed Bundy's cues. He said to the press on September 13 regarding Cuba, "Unilateral military intervention on the part of the United States cannot currently be either required or justified." Underscoring what he had said earlier, he added, however, that if Cuba "should ever . . . become an offensive military base of significant capacity for the Soviet Union, then this country will do whatever must be done to protect its own security and that of its allies."[1]

Largely at the urging of Republican senators Kenneth Keating of New York and Homer Capehart of Indiana, the Senate on September 20 passed by 86 to 1 a resolution authorizing use of force against Cuba "to prevent the creation or use of an externally supported offensive military capability endangering the security of the U.S." Kennedy continued to think such a contingency remote and now had from the CIA's top analytic group, its Board of Estimates, a Special National Intelligence Estimate which said that use of Cuba by the Soviet Union as a base for offensive ballistic missiles "would be incompatible with Soviet practice to date and with Soviet policy as we presently estimate it. It would indicate a far greater willingness to increase the level of risk in US-Soviet relations than the USSR has displayed thus far. . . ."[2]

But a letter from Khrushchev dated September 28 had brought Kennedy potentially ominous news about Berlin. In it, Khrushchev said, "The abnormal situation in Berlin should be done away with. . . . And under present circumstances we do not see any other way out but to sign a German peace treaty." Moreover, Khrushchev commented angrily on agitation in the United States for action against Cuba. The congressional resolution, he said, "gives ground to draw a conclusion that the U.S. is evidently ready to assume responsibility for unleashing nuclear war." Khrushchev asserted that he would not force the Berlin issue until after the U.S. congressional elections, but he seemed to say that, by the second half of November, time would run out.[3]

Other members of the administration were alarmed about Berlin. Defense Secretary McNamara returned from a trip to Europe and said at a press conference on September 28 that conditions in Berlin were as tense as any since those in Korea during the Korean War. He added bite to the by then well-worn assertion of U.S. interest in Berlin by saying that the United States would "utilize whatever weapons are needed to preserve our vital interests" and then saying, "Quite clearly, we consider access to Berlin a vital interest."[4]

To Kennedy and members of his circle Khrushchev remained a mystifying figure. In early 1962, they knew, Khrushchev had suffered domestic setbacks. He had had to admit to shortfalls in his announced goals for increased food production and, indeed, to raise state-controlled food prices. He had also backed away from previously announced plans to reduce spending on traditional branches of the armed forces in order to strengthen the new Strategic Rocket Forces.[5] This evidence suggested that Khrushchev might need an offsetting foreign policy success. Other evidence suggested that he might not have taken at full value U.S. efforts to demonstrate determination not to yield on Berlin.

Just recently, Khrushchev had granted long interviews to two Americans. In early September he had invited Kennedy's interior secretary, Stewart Udall, to visit him at Petsunda in Georgia. Perhaps assuming that Udall's functions resembled those of interior ministers in Soviet states, who usually had large police and internal security functions, Khrushchev harangued him about Berlin, saying that he intended to put Kennedy in a position in which he would have to settle the Berlin problem: "We will give him a choice—go to war or sign a peace treaty." Delivering his own counterpart to the Gilpatric speech, in his own vernacular, Khrushchev said: "It's been a long time since you could spank us like a little boy—now we can swat your ass." He assured Udall that he would not act until after the U.S. congressional elections. "Then," he said, "we shall see whether you bring us to the brink of war."[6]

More disturbingly, Khrushchev had told the poet Robert Frost on September 7 that he believed the United States and Western Europe to be weak and worn out. He invoked Tolstoy's comment to Maxim Gorky about old age and sex: "The desire is the same; it's the performance that's different." As Frost cleaned this up when answering questions from U.S.

reporters, it came out: "He said we were too liberal to fight." This was how Kennedy first heard it, and it infuriated him, not least because it provided fodder for Republicans in the congressional campaign.[7]

To try better to understand Khrushchev, Kennedy called in the State Department's two leading Soviet experts, Charles (Chip) Bohlen, who had been ambassador in Moscow in the mid-1950s, and Llewellyn Thompson, who had succeeded Bohlen and had left the post only weeks earlier. (Foy Kohler had been designated to replace Thompson but had not yet left Washington.) The President and the former ambassadors had been discussing other parts of Khrushchev's long letter when Bohlen shifted focus to the paragraphs on Berlin.

· · ·

Charles Bohlen: Well, Mr. President, I think this letter gives you a vehicle to make a response, speaking now of the Berlin section of it, which can I say, I feel quite strongly is necessary in some form or other. Now, there are three or four different ways that you can get this over that the regularity with which he [Khrushchev] has been telling everybody that the United States is too liberal, et cetera, et cetera, to fight. And I must say the general feeling, I think is that, among the demonologists, is chances are he believes this. And now the question is how can you convey—

President Kennedy: Why would he say it? What is the argument for his saying it?

Bohlen: Well, he believes—if you take it from his own military point of view—that the local military situation [that] makes the correlation of forces is all in their favor and he probably thinks that in view of public opinion and [unclear] of the horrors of a nuclear war that the United States would not . . . would back away from that point. Therefore he's got a situation with all the advantage on his side where he can proceed. And there'll be a great whooping and yelling around but that nothing will happen. But the thing he's interested in, which is the only thing you worry about, is a nuclear war. And this is cockeyed, I think. Although, I don't know, if you read some of Joe's articles, [unclear] old Alsop's articles about de Gaulle's view and all this other stuff.

President Kennedy: But de Gaulle . . . that's why I think de Gaulle . . . I think de Gaulle would like to start to get out of Berlin and [unclear] blame the United States. Because, if they could only get Berlin eliminated, then they could really have a . . . Europe which would be in pretty good shape.

· · ·

Bohlen: And I think that de Gaulle's chief mistake about the Russian thing is that he attributes the present structure of Russian power to be identical with the time of Stalin. And he never can forget that he stood up to Stalin and said, "Nuts to you," and Stalin came around. And he doesn't realize that this guy, and I think Tommy would—I'd like to know what Tommy thinks about this—operates in a very different power circumstance from Stalin.[8] Stalin could change anything like that himself, whereas this guy has pressures and tendencies that he has to take cognizance of, if he . . . and this limits his personal sphere of maneuver.

But the question is, Mr. President, and this obviously is a subject we're not supposed to ask you. [*He laughs.*] But . . . this is your business and not ours. That it seems to me very important to halt this sort of progress that the Russians are doing in Berlin, building up this enormous record of saying that the West is not going to do it [fight for Berlin].

. . .

Llewellyn Thompson: The other thing it might be is that—
Bohlen: —what in God's name—?
Thompson: The other reason why he might make these remarks is that he wants to, he wants to—
Bohlen: To show those to some of the others.
Thompson: Yeah, to provoke us into a strong reply, which he can use to ease [*unclear*] policy. In either case it would argue for going back at him.
President Kennedy: I mean for us to, for us to—do you want some orange juice?
Thompson: No, thanks.
President Kennedy: For us to . . . for him to tell Americans and other people that the Americans aren't going to fight . . . that doesn't seem to me to . . . what would be the log[ic] . . . as you say unless he wants us to, [*unclear*] first [*unclear*] to fight but I don't ever—if that's his opinion you don't really announce it, because that's really rubbing our face in it. Do you think therefore—it could be—He doesn't have to have a reason for everything. If he's telling what he actually thinks—
Thompson: Yeah.
Bohlen: Agreed.
Thompson: He's capable of doing it.

. . .

President Kennedy: What do you think is the reason that they are going ahead with Cuba in this massive way? They must know that it . . . I thought one reason why they [*unclear*] Berlin because we'd take a reprisal against Cuba . . . they want to make it as difficult as possible. What other reason can there be? Because they began this buildup in June. In late June there was no indication of an invasion by the United States at this time, so [*unclear*].

Thompson: Well, I would suspect that Castro is nervous about what might be going on and the pressure has been pretty—

President Kennedy: Sorry?

Thompson: —within the bloc, the Communist bloc, this is a good step for him; he's helping this country defend itself against U.S. imperialism and . . .

Bohlen: This is the satellite bond that you get. The Poles and stuff like that . . .

President Kennedy: Yeah.

Bohlen: They think that Castro was planning it. They sent a guy over there, Che Guevara, you know, to try and persuade the Russians to let them join the Warsaw Pact, to give them formal coverage and Soviet protection.[9] And the Russians refused to do this. And then this is what they did. And also, as Tommy mentioned, he said from the point of view of the Communist world, it is very important for him to be out in front, showing that he is militant, pushing for the great cause.

President Kennedy: Why do you think they refused to put him in the Warsaw Pact?

Bohlen: Oh, because this is too much for the Russians because then they're not sure what the United States might do—

President Kennedy: Right.

Bohlen: —and they don't want to be committed to go to war over Cuba, [*Kennedy mumbles assent*] if there is an American attack. Oh, I think this has been very clear all the way going back to '60 when he first began to rattle the rockets about Cuba, then he made a statement before anyone would call him on that thing, he made a statement saying, "It's just symbolic." And they haven't gone beyond that and this latest one, which he refers to here; the September 11th one seems to me to have been primarily issued in order to tack on the rider about not doing anything about Berlin.

Thompson: I think, in general, he's, he has very much in mind that meeting you and that, I think, if he can settle Berlin, then—

Bohlen: Well this is what bothers me . . . the hell out of me. He's coming over here in the end of November and this letter is really pitched to the . . . twice he refers to the resumption of the dialogue . . . and then in the last paragraph he talks about the: "Of great importance for finding the ways to solve both this problem . . . are personal contacts of statesmen on the highest level." Well that means between you and him. But, the question is: What in God's name could be the best solution to the Berlin thing if you did meet?

President Kennedy: [*Unclear*] I don't—unless he wants to demonstrate that he's doing every possible—

Bohlen: Well, I mean, this still leaves the situation as it was. I think, from your point of view, [*unclear*] don't see that [there's] anything very much to negotiate about as long as he is insisting on the removal of certain troops.

Thompson: Well, I think, Chip [Bohlen], that if he, I think he's, first of all, that he is in a position where he has . . . he feels he has got to go ahead and sign this treaty.

Bohlen: Yes, I think everybody—

Thompson: And I don't think he wants to play Russian roulette with that and just toss a coin and see whether there's war or not. If he wants to . . . he could get us to accept the East German . . . Solution C approach, where we would accept East Germans deployed at the checkpoint.[10] Each of us maintain a [*unclear*] position [*unclear*] would be acceptable [*unclear*] his treaty.

. . .

Bohlen: Of course this question as to why the Russians are pushing this thing [Berlin] so hard is one that I have [*unclear*] almost four years and I don't think that anybody [is] clear why. . . . And de Gaulle may not care if the United States takes the blame for any sort of a sellout, or whatever you want to call it, in Berlin.

But on the other hand most of the fellows in the French Foreign Office particularly feel that Khrushchev is doing this because of the whole effect on West Germany and on the alliance. In other words, he is seeking larger aims than just Berlin.

I must say, I don't think that. I think that Berlin is a . . . these are the kind of repercussions and results [on] which he would naturally capitalize if they happened. But I don't think he's playing these moves on Berlin with this in view. I don't know what you feel about the alliance.

Thompson: Well, I think he's hooked personally on . . . He's always boasted that this was his solution, that he dreamed this whole thing up.

Bohlen: Yeah.

Thompson: He got way out and he's gotten further out since.

. . .

President Kennedy: Well, why would they build up Cuba? Why would . . . I mean he must . . . if he calculates correctly, he must realize that what's happened in Cuba this summer makes it much more difficult for us to accept any, to engage ourselves now to have a deal over Berlin. I mean, that's just not been—

Bohlen: [*Unclear.*] This is one thing that I'm convinced of, is that the Russian mind does not have the foggiest comprehension of the American political process. They really believe that you are sort of the dictator of the United States and can do any damn thing you want, and that . . . This just comes through the doctrine. You see, they consider that the capitalist system, that democracy in a capitalist system is just a part of flimflam and [is] a disguise for the control by Wall Street and all this other . . . Look at the way he keeps talking about Dean Rusk being a tool of the Rockefellers because he was head of the thing.[11] I think he genuinely believes in it. So that all this stuff that you—

Thompson: The Pentagon and Wall Street. [*Unclear.*]

Bohlen: Yeah. It's a very complicated sort of process. But I think the conclusion that they reach is that public opinion doesn't—

President Kennedy: Really count.

Bohlen: —really have any real effect and [*unclear*] enormous pressure this can put on a presidency.

President Kennedy: And I suppose we don't . . . we over . . . we underestimate the pressures that go on him, not from public opinion but from other [*unclear*].

Bohlen: Well, I think you can describe public opinion in the Soviet Union the same way that a good general pays great attention to the morale of his troops. In other words, he doesn't let troop morale dictate his course of action, because then he wouldn't be worth a damn as a general. He is very conscious of the fact that they rely on the morale. I mean this just . . . but this doesn't mean any—

President Kennedy: But you don't think that he would calculate what they're doing in Cuba as a broad sort of traditional position and so on would [*unclear*] really intensify the feeling here greatly, and make it much more difficult to do anything about Berlin?

Bohlen: No, sir, I think this is probably something that's just a complete blank page in his mind. I think that—what Tommy said—I think he did Berlin because here it was something they had engaged in about this regime, and then the Cubans got very scared and panicky for fear there was going to be another, sort of, Bay of Pigs, something like this. Which they would probably have lost.

President Kennedy: [*Comments indistinctly.*]

Bohlen: And went to the Russians and said, "My goodness, my goodness, you've got to help us." Their first idea was to put them in a treaty, and then the Russians put these arms in there; and then also the effect of his standing in the Communist world because the Chinese have been constantly attacking Khrushchev from the left, which is the first time in Bolshevik history that this has ever happened. Heretofore they have always been the extreme left—denouncing yellow Soviet so-and-so as the opportunist and everything like it. The Chinese now come and say, "You are scared of the thing." Now there is one factor that underlies [*unclear*] that I don't know anything about. Tommy may have some ideas about it.

Thompson: History [*unclear*] points their way [*unclear*] move is to keep the Chinese from doing it—

Bohlen: This is what I mean.

Thompson: —[*taking*] the Chinese with it.

Bohlen: Well, the Chinese are not in much shape to give very much help.

Thompson: [*Unclear*] I think it doesn't.

Bohlen: Yeah, I think it is more in the psychological field, of his leadership in there, [*Thompson murmurs assent*] the other factor may be in there. But the one question that perhaps may underlie this is that we know now that all this flap about the missile gap is just for the birds because they didn't put their main effort on ICBMs and our estimate now of the correlation of military forces is heavily in our favor [*someone mumbles assent*] and not in their[s]. Now, if you go back to the history of the Sino-Soviet dispute, you will see the Chinese undoubtedly believe, completely literally, the Soviet claims which they were making in '57 and '58 of having . . . the balance having shifted in their . . . point. And I just wonder whether or not in the Soviet hierarchy how much real understanding there is of the actual correlation of military force or whether they are not operating on their previous, sort of, at least, announced estimate that they had sort of passed us. And their policy would be much more intelligible if they believed that; because if they believed that they had the nuclear, sort of, equality, or even superiority, then their lines of action would be quite continuous, I mean, quite consistent. But it is not consistent if it's viewed in the light of what our estimate of the two forces are.

President Kennedy: We are taking a look at a contingency plan for sort of building up a staging area in Florida for . . . in case we ever have to go into Cuba. This would be impossible, I suppose, to keep this completely—we'll look at this next week—to keep it completely submerged. But obviously there is no sense in having about a four months' gap between the time we've decided to do something about Cuba and have to wait. So, we want to begin to build up down there. Now, I suppose that will surface. . . . What effect does that have?

Bohlen: Well, they'll pick it up with all of this stuff, [*unclear*] calling up this . . . Getting the authorization to call up 150,000 reservists and state this in Congress. They'll make a big thing out of it. And I think this inevitably will . . .

President Kennedy: Do you see any reason not to do it?

Bohlen: I don't. Although the question is—I'll tell you one thing, Mr. President, that I do think is that if you ever come to do any action against Cuba, it would almost have to be on the basis of a declaration of war. I mean serious action, that is—

President Kennedy: Yeah.

. . .

Thompson: I think . . . I had the impression, that at the start of the Cuban thing, that the Russians thought it wasn't going to last and they were very reluctant to get too committed, to put too much in there.

President Kennedy: Of course, if we had gone in a year ago—and it was much easier in April after the Bay of Pigs—and you had that become the regular United States invasion . . . I have always thought that they would—of course you can't tell what they would do, a year ago. Now . . . but it always seemed to me they would just grab West Berlin, don't you think?

Bohlen: Well, they might have, Mr. President, and this might have led to general war. But I think the situation is getting to the point where there are so many places, there are many instances where if we take certain kinds of forcible actions, the Russians can retaliate. I think we tend [*unclear*] to let the Berlin situation dominate our whole action [*unclear*]. But this is what the Russians are clearly trying to do. [*Unclear.*]

. . .

Bohlen: Their play is . . . the Russian game has always traditionally been this way with the non-Communist power . . . is to push, pull, to feel around and then judge, make their next move based upon their estimate of the reaction to what people do. There is a phrase of Lenin in which he said there are certain situations which you control with bayonets: if you run into mush, you go forward; if you run into steel, you withdraw. And since anything that Lenin said is enshrined in letters—

President Kennedy: That's right.

Bohlen: —in gold and scarlet, I still think that Khrushchev's attitude on Berlin is in one sense to test us.

. . .

Thompson: Generally speaking, I think, Khrushchev has felt, at least up until recently, that things are going his way and he needn't take any risks, that he is playing for the big stakes and not the small. In places like Iran and others, where he could have done a lot of things, but if he did, he'd [*unclear*] make it more difficult to spread further later on. And he's been . . . in Laos the same way and there are other complicating factors there, but. . . . In general, I don't think he wants to really run a real risk of war at this time.

Bohlen: I wouldn't think so.

Thompson: [*Unclear.*]

Bohlen: But then you come back to what is their estimate of the general correlation of military forces?

Thompson: Well, it certainly isn't something that can be deliberately calculated in this period. A wise thing to do . . .

. . .

Bohlen: The only question is do they realize to what extent we cover their installations and therefore we know what ICBM rockets they have and what we have, which is growing every month here, I think?

President Kennedy: I think he thinks they've got enough to cause such damage to us, that we wouldn't want to accept that damage unless the provocation was extreme. But, of course, those are all calculations he has to make about what we are going to do, and what the French will do and what the British will do. And I suppose it just comes back to what you . . . we were originally saying, that it's just a question of how do we convince him that the risk is there. And that raises whether we ought to go with this letter or not. Or whether we just choose to ignore this and just let this thing drop until he comes over here in November.[12]

. . .

Tuesday, October 16, 1962

During the first part of October, President Kennedy received intelligence on the unceasing stream of Soviet military equipment reaching Cuba. The CIA informed him that MiG forces in Cuba now included the latest models, MiG-21s, which were capable of carrying nuclear bombs or nuclear-armed air-to-surface missiles. On October 9, a U.S. Navy reconnaissance plane brought back evidence of Soviet cargo ships carrying crated IL-28 bombers.[1] Twin-engine jets with a range of about 750 miles, IL-28s were known to carry nuclear as well as conventional bombs. Since they were of old design and being phased out of the Soviet air force, they were not necessarily the "offensive weapons" against which Kennedy had warned in his public statements of September 4 and September 13. When drafting the first warning, he and his advisers had agreed that, as McGeorge Bundy put it, surface-to-surface missiles would bring the "turning point."

News about the IL-28s did, however, cause Kennedy to authorize a U-2 reconnaissance flight over Cuba. For nearly a month, Director of Central Intelligence John McCone had pressed for such a flight. Secretary of State Dean Rusk and others had resisted, fearing that the U-2 would be detected or even shot down, as over the Soviet Union in 1960, with consequent diplomatic embarrassment, given the U.S. claim to concern regarding the sovereignty and territorial integrity of other states. Kennedy now ruled in McCone's favor, and a U-2 streaked across Cuba on October 14 just as, on ABC's news program *Issues and Answers*, presidential national security assistant McGeorge Bundy was denying the presence of Soviet missiles on the island.

During October 15, experts at the CIA's National Photographic Intelligence Center (NPIC), in a nondescript building at 5th and K Streets in Washington, pored over photos from that October 14 U-2 flight over Cuba. Seeing images of missiles much longer than SAMs, they leafed through files of photos from the Soviet Union and technical data microfilmed by Soviet officer (and Anglo-American spy) Oleg Penkovsky. They came up with a perfect match. These were medium-range ballistic missiles (MRBMs) of the SS-4 family. At about 5:30 in the afternoon, Arthur Lundahl, the head of NPIC, passed the news to CIA headquarters out in Langley, Virginia.[2]

In ignorance of what was in progress at NPIC, McNamara had met that afternoon with the Joint Chiefs of Staff and dozens of lower-level officials. Although McNamara explained that Kennedy had decided not to take any military action against Cuba during the next three months, the group reviewed plans for a massive air strike on Cuba and for an invasion.

That evening, Bundy and his wife gave a small dinner at their home on Foxhall Road for Charles (Chip) and Avis Bohlen. Chip Bohlen was going off to be U.S. ambassador to France. Called away to the telephone, Bundy heard CIA deputy director for intelligence Ray Cline say cryptically, "Those things we've been worrying about—it looks as though we've really got something." "It was a hell of a secret," Bundy wrote later. Though he considered immediately calling Kennedy, he concluded that a few hours made no difference. The President had been in New York State, speaking for Democratic congressional candidates, and had gotten back to Washington in the early hours of the morning. Bundy, as he also wrote later, "decided that a quiet evening and a night of sleep were the best preparation" the President could have for what lay ahead of him. Kennedy never reproached Bundy for giving him that extra rest.[3]

Bundy brought his news to the private quarters of the White House at about 9:00 A.M. on Tuesday, October 16. In the major morning papers, the President had seen one front-page story about Cuba. The *Washington Post* reported that "Communist sources" were floating a rumor of a possible trade—the West to make concessions on Berlin in return for a slowdown in the Soviet buildup of Cuba. State Department spokesman Lincoln White denied seeing any such proposal and said, "It would have been kicked out the window so fast it would have made your head swim." The *Post*'s front page and that of the *New York Times* featured a Boston address by Eisenhower, attacking the Kennedy administration's "dreary foreign record." In his administration, Eisenhower said, "No walls were built. No threatening foreign bases were established."

President Kennedy told Bundy to round up officials—secretly—for a meeting later that morning. He phoned his brother Robert and asked him to come to the White House, where they briefly discussed the sensational news. At 9:25 President Kennedy began his regular schedule, meeting astronaut Walter Schirra and his family. In a brief break, just before 10:00, the President went to Kenny O'Donnell's office and, as O'Donnell later recalled, said, "You still think the fuss about Cuba is unimportant?"

"Absolutely," O'Donnell answered. "The voters won't give a damn about Cuba."

Kennedy then gave O'Donnell the news. "I don't believe it," O'Donnell replied. "You better believe it," Kennedy said and added drily, "Ken Keating will probably be the next President of the United States."[4]

After two more routine meetings that morning, Kennedy was able to open up about the missiles again for about half an hour with Bohlen, who was paying a previously scheduled farewell call as he prepared to depart for Paris. Kennedy finished his meeting with Bohlen and went on to the Cabinet Room.

11:50 A.M.

Meeting on the Cuban Missile Crisis

Kennedy was in the Cabinet Room with his five-year-old daughter, Caroline, when his advisers filed into the Cabinet Room, accompanied by Lundahl and other experts from NPIC who set up photograph displays on easels. As Caroline was taken back to the residence and the meeting began, Kennedy turned on the tape recorder. With McCone again absent from Washington, this time for a family funeral, his deputy, General Marshall (Pat) Carter, led the intelligence briefing.

Marshall Carter: This is the result of the photography taken Sunday, sir. There's a medium-range ballistic missile launch site and two new military encampments on the southern edge of the Sierra del Rosario in west-central Cuba.

President Kennedy: Where would that be?

Carter: West-central, sir. That's . . .

Arthur Lundahl: South of Havana. [*quieter, as an aside*] I think this [*unclear*] represents these three dots we're talking about.

Carter: Have you got the big pictures?

Lundahl: Yes, sir.

Carter: The President would like to see those.

The launch site at one of the encampments contains a total of at least 14 canvas-covered missile trailers measuring 67 feet in length, 9 feet in width. The overall length of the trailers plus the tow bars is approximately 80 feet. The other encampment contains vehicles and tents but with no missile trailers.

Lundahl: [*quietly to President Kennedy*] These are the launchers here. Each of these are places we discussed. In this instance the missile trailer is backing up to the launching point. The launch point of this particular vehicle is here. This canvas-covered [*unclear*] is 67 feet long.

Carter: The site that you have there contains at least eight canvas-covered missile trailers. Four deployed probable missile erector launchers. These are unrevetted.[5] The probable launch positions as indicated are approximately 850 feet, 700 feet, 450 feet—for a total distance of about 2,000 feet.

In Area Two, there are at least 6 canvas-covered missile trailers, about 75 vehicles, and about 18 tents. And in Area Number Three we have 35 vehicles, 15 large tents, 8 small tents, 7 buildings, and 1 building under construction. The critical one—do you see what I mean?—is this one.

Lundahl: [*quietly to President Kennedy*] There is a launcher right there, sir. The missile trailer is backing up to it at the moment. [*Unclear.*] And the missile trailer is here. Seven more have been enlarged here. Those canvas-covered objects on the trailers are 67 feet long, and there's a small building between the two of them. The eighth one is the one that's not on a particular trailer. [*Unclear*] backs up. That looks like the most-advanced one. And the other area is about 5 miles away. There are no launcher erectors on there, just missiles.

. . .

President Kennedy: How do you know this is a medium-range ballistic missile?

Lundahl: The length, sir.

President Kennedy: The what? The length?

Lundahl: The length of it, yes.

President Kennedy: The length of the missile? Which part? I mean which . . . ?

Lundahl: The length of the missile, sir, is—

President Kennedy: Which one is that?

Lundahl: This will show it, sir.

President Kennedy: That?

Lundahl: Yes. Mr. Graybeal, our missile man, has some pictures of the equivalent Soviet equipment that has been dragged through the streets of Moscow that can give you some feel for it, sir.

Sidney Graybeal: There are two missiles involved. One of them is our [designation] SS-3, which is 630 mile [range] and on up to near 700. It's 68 feet long. These missiles measure out to be 67 foot long. The other missile, the 1,100 [mile range] one is 73 foot long.

The question we have in the photography is the nose itself. If the nose cone is not on that missile it measures 67 feet—the nose cone would be 4 to 5 feet longer, sir—and with this extra length we could have a missile that'd have a range of 1,100 miles. The missiles that were known through the Moscow parade—we've got the data on that [unclear] on the pictures.

President Kennedy: Is this ready to be fired?

Graybeal: No, sir.

President Kennedy: How long . . . ? We can't tell that can we, how long before it can be fired?

Graybeal: No, sir. That depends on how ready the GSC [ground support for the missile] [is], how—

President Kennedy: Where does it have to be fired from?

Graybeal: It would have to be fired from a stable, hard surface. This could be packed earth. It could be concrete, or asphalt. The surface has to be hard. Then you put a flame deflector plate on that to direct the missile.

Robert McNamara: Would you care to comment on the position of nuclear warheads? This is in relation to the question from the President—when can these be fired?

Graybeal: Sir, we've looked very hard. We can find nothing that would spell nuclear warhead in terms of any isolated area or unique security in this particular area. The mating of the nuclear warhead to the missile—from some of the other short-range missile data—[it] would take about a couple of hours to do this.

McNamara: This is not fenced, I believe, at the moment?

Lundahl: Not yet, sir.

McNamara: This is important, as it relates to whether these, today, are ready to fire, Mr. President. It seems almost impossible to me that they would be ready to fire with nuclear warheads on the site without even a fence around it. It may not take long to place them there, to erect a fence. But at least at the moment there is some reason to believe the warheads aren't present and hence they are not ready to fire.

Graybeal: Yes, sir. We do not believe they are ready to fire.

Maxwell Taylor: However, there is no feeling that they can't fire from this kind of field position very quickly: isn't that true? It's not a question of waiting for extensive concrete pads and that sort of thing.

Graybeal: The unknown factor here, sir, is the degree to which the equipment has been checked out after it's been shipped from the Soviet Union here. It's the readiness of the equipment. If the equipment is checked out, the site has to be accurately surveyed—the position has to be known. Once this is known, then you're talking a matter of hours.

Taylor: Well, could this be an operational site except perhaps for the fact that at this point there are no fences? Could this be operational now?

Graybeal: There is only one missile there, sir, and it's at the actual, apparently, launching area. It would take them—if everything were checked out—it would still take them in the order of two to three hours before they could get that one missile up and ready to go, sir.

· · ·

Lundahl: May I report, sir, that two additional SAC [U-2] missions were executed yesterday. They were taken to the Washington area last night. They're currently being chemically processed at the Naval Center in Suitland and they're due to reach us at the National PI Center around 8:00 tonight.[6] Both of these missions go from one end of Cuba to the other, one along the north coast and one along the south. So additional data on activities, or these storage sites which we consider critical, may be in our grasp, if we can find them.

· · ·

McGeorge Bundy: [*Unclear*], Mr. President. Because the weather won't have been clear all along the island. So we can't claim that we will have been—certainly we surely do not have up-to-date photographic coverage on the whole island. I should think one of our first questions is to—

President Kennedy: Authorize more flights.

Bundy: —consider whether we should not authorize more flights on the basis of COMOR priorities.[7]

There's a specific question of whether we want a closer and sharper look at this area. That, however, I think should be looked at in the context of the question of whether we wish to give tactical warning and any other possible activities.

Robert McNamara: I would recommend, Mr. President, that you authorize such flights as are considered necessary to obtain complete coverage of the island. Now this seems to be ill defined. But I purposely define it that way because we're running into cloud cover on some of these flights and I would suggest that we simply repeat the flight if we have cloud cover and repeat it sufficiently often to obtain the coverage we require.

President Kennedy: General Carter, can you go do that?

Carter: Yes, sir.

McNamara: Now this is U-2 flying.

Carter: U-2, sir.

McNamara: This specifically excludes the question that Mac [Bundy] raised of low-level flying, which I think we ought to take up later, after our further discussions of the possibilities here.[8]

. . .

President Kennedy: Mr. Rusk?

Dean Rusk: Mr. President this is, of course, a very serious development. It's one that we, all of us, had not really believed the Soviets could carry this far. They seemed to be denying that they were going to establish bases of their own [in Cuba] and this one that we're looking at is a Soviet base. It doesn't do anything essential from a Cuban point of view. The Cubans couldn't do anything with it anyhow at this stage.

Now, I do think we have to set in motion a chain of events that will eliminate this base. I don't think we can sit still. The question then becomes whether we do it by a sudden, unannounced strike of some sort or we build up the crisis to the point where the other side has to consider very seriously about giving in, or even the Cubans themselves take some action on this.

The thing that I'm, of course, very conscious of is that there is no such thing, I think, as unilateral action by the United States. It's so intimately involved with 42 allies and confrontation in many places that any action that we take will greatly increase the risks of a direct action involving our other alliances and our other forces in other parts of the world.

So I think we have to think very hard about *two* major courses of action as alternatives. One is the quick strike. The point where we think there is the overwhelming, overriding necessity to take all the risks that are involved in doing that. I don't think this in itself would require an invasion of Cuba. You could do it with or without such an invasion—in other words, if we make it clear that what we're doing is eliminating this particular base or any other such base that is established. We ourselves are not moved to general war. We're simply doing what we said we would do if they took certain action. Or we're going to decide that this is the time to eliminate the Cuban problem by action [unclear] the island.

The *other* would be, if we have a few days from the military point of view, if we have a little time, then I would think that there would be another course of action, a combination of things, that we might wish to consider. First, that we stimulate the OAS procedure immediately for prompt action to make it quite clear that the entire hemisphere considers that the Rio Pact has been violated, and [unclear] over the next few days, under the terms of the Rio Pact.[9] The OAS could constitute itself as an organ of consultation promptly, although maybe it may take two or three days to get instructions from governments and things of that sort. The OAS could, I suppose, at any moment take action to insist to the Cubans that an OAS inspection team be permitted to come and itself look directly at these sites, provide assurances to the hemisphere. That will undoubtedly be turned down, but it will be another step in building up our position.

I think also that we ought to consider getting some word to Castro, perhaps through the Canadian ambassador in Havana or through his representative at the U.N. I think perhaps the Canadian ambassador would be the best, the better channel to get to Castro, get him apart privately and tell him that this is no longer support for Cuba, that Cuba is being victimized here, and that the Soviets are preparing Cuba for destruction, or *betrayal.* You saw the [*New York*] *Times* story yesterday morning that high Soviet officials were saying, "We'll trade Cuba for Berlin." This ought to be brought to Castro's attention. It ought to be said to Castro that this kind of a base is intolerable and not acceptable. The time has now come when he must, in the interests of the Cuban people, must now break clearly with the Soviet Union and prevent this missile base from becoming operational.

And I think there are certain military actions that we might well want to take straight away. First, to call up highly selected units, up to 150,000, unless we feel that it's better, more desirable, to go to a general national emergency so that we have complete freedom of action. If we announce, at the time that we announce this development—and I think we do have to announce this development some time this week—we announce that we are conducting a surveillance of Cuba, over Cuba, and we will enforce our right to do so. We reject the condition of secrecy in this hemisphere in a matter of this sort.

We reinforce our forces in Guantánamo. We reinforce our forces in the southeastern part of the United States, whatever is necessary from the military point of view, to be able to give, clearly, an overwhelming strike at any of these installations, including the SAM sites. And also to take care of any MiGs or bombers that might make a pass at Miami or at the United States. Build up heavy forces, if those are not already in position.

We then would move more openly and vigorously into the guerrilla field and create maximum confusion on the island [of Cuba]. We won't be too squeamish at this point about the overt/covert character of what is being done. . . .

I think it would be important for you to consider calling in General Eisenhower, giving him a full briefing before a public announcement is made as to the situation and the courses of action which you might determine upon.

But I think that, by and large, there are these two broad alternatives: One, the quick strike.

The other, to alert our allies and Mr. Khrushchev that there is an utterly serious crisis in the making here, and that Mr. Khrushchev may not himself really understand that or believe that at this point.

I think then we'll be facing a situation that could well lead to general war. Now with that we have an obligation to do what has to be done, but to do it in a way that gives everybody a chance to pull away from it before it gets too hard.

Those are my reactions of this morning, Mr. President. I naturally need to think about this very hard for the next several hours, what I and my colleagues at the State Department can do about it.

McNamara: Mr. President, there are a number of unknowns in this situation I want to comment upon and, in relation to them, I would like to outline very briefly some possible military alternatives and ask General Taylor to expand upon them.

But before commenting on either the unknowns or outlining some military alternatives, there are two propositions I would suggest that we ought to accept as foundations for our further thinking. My first is that if we are to conduct an air strike against these installations, or against any part of Cuba, we must agree now that we will schedule that prior to the time these missile sites become operational. I'm not prepared to say when that will be. But I think it is extremely important that our talk and our discussion be founded on this premise: that any air strike will be planned to take place prior to the time they become operational. Because, *if* they become operational *before* the air strike, I do not believe we can state we can knock them out before they can be launched. And if they're launched there is almost certain to be chaos in part of the East Coast or the area in a radius of 600 to 1,000 miles from Cuba.

Secondly, I would submit the proposition that any air strike must be directed not solely against the missile sites, but against the missile sites plus the airfields, plus the aircraft which may not be on the airfields but hidden by that time, plus all potential nuclear storage sites. Now this is a fairly extensive air strike. It is not just a strike against the missile sites, and there would be associated with it potential casualties of Cubans, not of U.S. citizens, but potential casualties of Cubans in, at least, in the hundreds, more likely in the low thousands—say two or three thousand. It seems to me these two propositions should underlie our discussion.

Now, what kinds of military action are we capable of carrying out and what may be some of the consequences? We could carry out an air strike within a matter of days. We would be ready for the start of such an air strike within a matter of days. If it were absolutely essential, it could be done almost literally within a matter of hours. I believe the Chiefs would prefer that it be deferred for a matter of days. But we are prepared for that quickly.

The air strike could continue for a matter of days following the initial day, if necessary. Presumably there would be some political discussions taking place either just before the air strike or both before and during.

In any event, we would be prepared, following the air strike, for an invasion, both by air and by sea. Approximately seven days after the start of the air strike that would be possible, if the political environment made it desirable or necessary at that time.

Fine. Associated with this air strike undoubtedly should be some degree of mobilization. I would think of the mobilization coming not before the air strike but either concurrently with or somewhat following, say possibly five days afterwards, depending upon the possible invasion requirements. The character of the mobilization would be such that it could be carried out in its first phase at least within the limits of the authority granted by Congress. There might have to be a second phase, and then it would require a declaration of a national emergency.

Now this is very sketchily, the military capabilities, and I think you may wish to hear General Taylor outline his.

Taylor: We're impressed, Mr. President, with the great importance of getting a strike with all the benefit of surprise, which would mean *ideally* that we would have all the missiles that are in Cuba above ground, where we can take them out.

That desire runs counter to the strong point the Secretary made, if the other optimum would be to get every missile before it could become operational. Practically, I think, our knowledge of the timing of the readiness is going to be so difficult that we'll never have the exact, perfect timing. What we'd like to do is to look at this new photography, I think, and take any additional, and try to get the layout of the targets in as near an optimum position as possible, and then take them out without any warning whatsoever.

That does not preclude, I don't think Mr. Secretary, some of the things that you've been talking about. It's a little hard to say in terms of time, how much I've discussed. But we must do a good job the first time we go in there, pushing a hundred percent just as far, as closely, as we can with our strike. I'm having all the responsible planners in this afternoon, Mr. President, at 4:00, to talk this out with them and get their best judgment.

I would also mention among the military actions we should take, that once we have destroyed as many of these offensive weapons as possible, we should prevent any more coming in, which means a naval blockade. So I suppose that, and also, a reinforcement of Guantánamo and evacuation of dependents.

So really, in point of time, I'm thinking in terms of *three* phases.

One, an initial pause of some sort while we get completely ready and get the right posture on the part of the target, so we can do the best job.

Then, virtually concurrently, an air strike against, as the Secretary said, missiles, airfields, and nuclear sites that we know of. At the same time, naval blockade. At the same time, reinforce Guantánamo and evacuate the dependents. I'd then start this continuous reconnaissance, the list that you have is connected, continuing over Cuba.

Then the decision can be made as we're mobilizing, with the air strike, as to whether we invade or not. I think that's the hardest question militarily in the whole business, and one which we should look at very closely before we get our feet in that deep mud in Cuba.

Rusk: There are certainly one or two other things, Mr. President. [Soviet foreign minister Andrei] Gromyko asked to see you Thursday [October 18]. It may be of some interest to know what he says about this, if he says anything. He may be bringing a message on this subject. I just want to remind you that you are seeing him and that may be relevant to this topic. I might say, incidentally, sir, that you can delay anything else you have to do at this point.

Secondly, I don't believe, myself, that the critical question is whether you get a particular missile before it goes off because if they shoot those missiles we are in general nuclear war. In other words, the Soviet Union has got quite a different decision to make if they shoot those missiles, want to shoot them off before they get knocked out by aircraft. So I'm not sure that this is necessarily the precise element, Bob.

McNamara: Well, I would strongly emphasize that I think our planning should be based on the assumption it is, Dean. We don't know what kinds of communications the Soviets have with those sites. We don't know what kinds of control they have over those warheads.

If we saw a warhead on the site and we knew that that launcher was capable of launching that warhead I would, frankly, I would strongly urge against the air attack, to be quite frank about it, because I think the danger to this country in relation to the gain that would accrue would be excessive. This is why I suggest that if we're talking about an air attack I believe we should consider it *only* on the assumption that we can carry it off before these become operational.

President Kennedy: What is the advantage? There must be some major reason for the Russians to set this up. It must be that they're not satisfied with their ICBMs. What'd be the reason that they would . . . ?

Taylor: What it'd give them is, primarily, it makes a launching base for short-range missiles against the United States to supplement their rather defective ICBM system, for example. That's one reason.

President Kennedy: Of course, I don't see how we could prevent further ones from coming in by submarine. I mean, if we let them blockade the thing, they come in by submarine.

McNamara: Well, I think the only way to prevent them coming in, quite frankly, is to say you'll take them out the moment they come in. You'll take them out and you'll carry on open surveillance. And you'll have a policy to take them out if they come in.

I think it's really rather unrealistic to think that we could carry out an air attack of the kind we're talking about. We're talking about an air attack of several hundred sorties because we don't know where these [Soviet] airplanes are.[10]

Bundy: Are you absolutely clear on your premise that an air strike must go to the whole air complex?

McNamara: Well, we are, Mac, because we are fearful of these MiG-21s. We don't know where they are. We don't know what they're capable of. If there are nuclear warheads associated with the launchers, you must assume there will be nuclear warheads associated with aircraft. Even if there are not nuclear warheads associated with aircraft, you must assume that those aircraft have high-explosive potential.

We have a serious air defense problem. We're not prepared to report to you exactly what the Cuban air force is capable of; but I think we must assume that the Cuban air force is definitely capable of penetrating, in small numbers, our coastal air defense by coming in low over the water. And I would think that we would not dare go in against the missile sites, knock those out, leaving intact Castro's air force, and run the risk that he would use part or all of that air force against our coastal areas—either with or without nuclear weapons. It would be a very heavy price to pay in U.S. lives for the damage we did to Cuba.

Rusk: Mr. President, about why the Soviets are doing this, Mr. McCone suggested some weeks ago that one thing Mr. Khrushchev may have in mind is that he knows that we have a substantial nuclear superiority, but he also knows that we don't really live under fear of his nuclear weapons to the extent that he has to live under fear of ours.

Also, we have nuclear weapons nearby, in Turkey and places like that.

President Kennedy: How many weapons do we have in Turkey?

Taylor: We have the Jupiter missiles.

Bundy: We have how many?

McNamara: About 15, I believe to be the figure.

Bundy: I think that's right. I think that's right.

Rusk: But then there are also delivery vehicles that could easily be moved through the air.

McNamara: Aircraft.

Rusk: Aircraft and so forth, route them through Turkey.

And Mr. McCone expressed the view that Khrushchev may feel that it's important for us to learn about living under medium-range missiles, and he's doing that to sort of balance that political, psychological flank.

I think also that Berlin is very much involved in this. For the first time, I'm beginning really to wonder whether maybe Mr. Khrushchev is entirely rational about Berlin. [Acting U.N. secretary-general] U Thant has talked about his obsession with it. And I think we have to keep our eye on that element.

But they may be thinking that they can either bargain Berlin and Cuba against each other, or that they could provoke us into a kind of action in Cuba which would give an umbrella for them to take action with respect to Berlin. In other words, like the Suez-Hungary combination [in 1956]. If they could provoke us into taking the first overt action, then the world would be confused and they would have what they would consider to be justification for making a move somewhere else.

But I must say I don't really see the rationality of the Soviets pushing it this far unless they grossly misunderstand the importance of Cuba to this country.

Bundy: It's important, I think, to recognize that they did make this decision, as far as our estimates now go, in early summer, and that this has been happening since August. Their TASS statement of September 12 [actually 11] which the experts, I think, attribute very strongly to Khrushchev himself, is all mixed up on this point. It has a rather explicit statement: "The harmless military equipment sent to Cuba designed exclusively for defense, defensive purposes. The president of the United States and the American military, the military of any country, know what means of defense are. How can these means threaten the United States?"

Now *there*. It's very hard to reconcile that with what has happened. The rest, as the Secretary says, has many comparisons between Cuba and Italy, Turkey, and Japan. We have other evidence that Khrushchev honestly believes, or at least affects to believe, that we have nuclear weapons in Japan. That combination . . .

Rusk: Gromyko stated that in his press conference the other day, too.

Bundy: Yeah. They may mean Okinawa.

McNamara: It's unlikely, but it's conceivable the nuclear warheads for these launchers are not yet on Cuban soil.

Bundy: Now it seems to me that it is perfectly possible that they are in that sense a bluff. That doesn't make them any less offensive to us, because we can't have proof about it.

McNamara: No. But it does possibly indicate a different course of action. And therefore, while I'm not suggesting how we should handle this, I think this is one of the most important actions we should take: to ascertain the location of the nuclear warheads for these missiles. Later in the discussion we can revert back to this. There are several alternative ways of approaching it.

President Kennedy: Doug, do you have any . . . ?

C. Douglas Dillon: No. The only thing I would say is that this alternative course of warning, and getting public opinion, and OAS action, and telling people in NATO and everything like that. It would appear to me to have the danger of getting us wide out in the open and forcing the Russians, the Soviets, to take a position that if anything was done they would have to retaliate.

Whereas a quick action, with a statement at the same time saying this is all there is to it, might give them a chance to back off and not do anything. Meanwhile, you've got to think that the chance of getting through this thing without a Russian reaction is greater under a quick strike than building the whole thing up to a climax, and then going through with what will be a lot of debate on it.

Rusk: That is, of course, a possibility, but . . .

Bundy: The difficulties. I share the Secretary of the Treasury's [Dillon's] feeling a little bit. The difficulties of organizing the OAS and NATO. The amount of noise we would get from our allies saying that if they can live with Soviet MRBMs, why can't we? The division in the alliance. The certainty that the Germans would feel that we *were* jeopardizing Berlin because of our concern over Cuba. The prospect of that pattern is not an appetizing one.

Rusk: Yes, but you see, everything turns crucially on what happens.

Bundy: I agree, Mr. Secretary.

Rusk: And if we go with the quick strike, then, in fact, they do back it up, then you have exposed all of your allies and ourselves to all these great dangers without the slightest consultation, or warning, or preparation.

Bundy: You get all these noises again.

President Kennedy: But, of course, warning them, it seems to me, is warning everybody. And obviously you can't sort of announce that in four days from now you're going to take them out. They may announce within three days that they're going to have warheads on them. If we come and attack, they're going to fire them. So then what'll we do? Then we don't take them out. Of course, we then announce: "Well, if they do that, then we're going to attack with nuclear weapons."

Dillon: Yes, sir. That's the question that nobody—I didn't understand—nobody had mentioned is whether this takeout, this mission, was going to be able to deal with it with high explosives?

President Kennedy: How effective can the takeout be, do they think?

Taylor: It'll never be a hundred percent, Mr. President, we know. We hope to take out a vast majority in the first strike. But this is not just one thing, one strike—one day, but continuous air attack for whenever necessary, whenever we discover a target.

Bundy: You are now talking about taking out the air force as well, I think, speaking in those terms.

I do raise again the question whether we [*unclear*] the military problem. But there is, I would think, a substantial political advantage in limiting the strike in surgical terms to the thing that is in fact the cause of action.

U. Alexis Johnson: I suggest, Mr. President, that if you're involved in several hundred strikes, and against airfields, this is what you would do: Preinvasion. And it would be very difficult to convince anybody that this was not a preinvasion strike.

I think also, once you get into this volume of attack, that public opinion reaction to this, as distinct from the reaction to an invasion—there's very little difference. And from both standpoints it would seem to me that if you're talking about a general air attack program, you might as well think about whether we can eradicate the whole problem by an invasion just as simply, with as little chance of reaction.

Taylor: Well, I would think we should be in a position to invade at any time, if we so decide. Hence that, in this preliminary, we should be thinking that it's all bonus if we are indeed taking out weapons.

President Kennedy: Well, let's say we just take out the missile bases. Then they have some more there. Obviously they can get them in by submarine and so on. I don't know whether you just can't keep high strikes on.

Taylor: I suspect, Mr. President, that we'd have to take out the surface-to-air missiles in order to get in. To get in, take some of them out. Maybe [*unclear*].

President Kennedy: How long do we estimate this will remain secure, this information, until people have it?

Bundy: In terms of the tightness of our intelligence control, Mr.

President, I think we are in unusually and fortunately good position. We set up a new security classification governing precisely the field of offensive capability in Cuba just five days ago, four days ago, under General Carter. That limits this to people who have an immediate, operational necessity in intelligence terms to work on the data, and the people who have—

President Kennedy: How many would that be, about?

Bundy: Oh that will be a very large number, but that's not generally where leaks come from. And the more important limitation is that only officers with a policy responsibility for advice directly to you receive this.

President Kennedy: How many would get it over in the Defense Department, General, with your meeting this afternoon?

Taylor: Well, I was going to mention that. We'd have to ask for relaxation of the ground rules that Mac has just enunciated, so that I can give it to the senior commanders who are involved in the plans.

President Kennedy: Would that be about 50?

Taylor: No, sir. I would say that, at this stage, 10 more.

McNamara: Mr. President, I think, to be realistic, we should assume that this will become fairly widely known, if not in the newspapers, at least by political representatives of both parties within, I would say, I'm just picking a figure, I'd say a week. And I say that because we have taken action already that is raising questions in people's minds.

Normally when a U-2 comes back, we duplicate the films. The duplicated copies go to a series of commands. A copy goes to SAC. A copy goes to CINCLANT.[11] A copy goes to CIA. And normally the photo interpreters and the operational officers in these commands are looking forward to these. We have stopped all that, and this type of information is going on throughout the department.

And I doubt very much that we can keep this out of the hands of members of Congress, for example, for more than a week.

Rusk: Well, Senator Keating has already, in effect, announced it on the floor of the Senate.

Bundy: [*speaking over Rusk*] Senator Keating said this on the floor of the Senate on the 10th of October: "Construction has begun on at least a half-dozen launching sites for intermediate-range tactical missiles."

Rusk: That's correct. That's exactly the point. Well, I suppose we'll have to count on announcing it not later than Thursday or Friday of this week.

Carter: There is a refugee who's a major source of intelligence on this, of course, who has described one of these missiles in terms which we can recognize, who is now in this country.

President Kennedy: Is he the one who's giving Keating his stuff?

Carter: We don't know.[12]

Bundy: My question, Mr. President, is whether, as a matter of tactics, we ought not to interview Senator Keating and check out his data. It seems to me that that ought to be done in a routine sort of way by an open officer of the intelligence agency.

Carter: I think that's right.

President Kennedy: You have any thoughts, Mr. Vice President?

Vice President Johnson: I agree with Mac that *that* ought to be done. I think that we're committed at any time that we feel that there's a buildup that in any way endangers, to take whatever action we must take to assure our security. I would think that the Secretary's evaluation of this thing being around all over the lot is a pretty accurate one. I wouldn't think it'd take a week to do it. I think they ought to [*unclear*] before then.

I would like to hear what the responsible commanders have to say this afternoon. I think the question we face is whether we take it out or whether we talk about it. And, of course, either alternative is a very distressing one. But, of the two, I would take it out—assuming that the commanders felt that way.

I'm fearful if we . . . I spent the weekend with the ambassadors of the Organization of American States. I think this organization is fine. But I don't think, I don't rely on them much for any strength in anything like this.

And I think that we're talking about our other allies, I take the position that Mr. Bundy says: "Well we've lived all these years [with missiles]. Why can't you? Why get your blood pressure up?" But the fact is the country's blood pressure *is* up, and they are fearful, and they're insecure, and we're getting divided, and I don't think that . . .

I take this little *State Department Bulletin* that you sent out to all the congressmen. One of the points you make: that any time the buildup endangers or threatens our security in any way, we're going to do whatever must be done immediately to protect our own security. And when you say that, why, they give unanimous support.

People are really concerned about this, in my opinion. I think we have to be prudent and cautious, talk to the commanders and see what they say. I'm not much for circularizing it over the Hill or with our allies, even though I realize it's a breach of faith, not to confer with them. We're not going to get much help out of them.

Bundy: There is an intermediate position. There are perhaps two or three of our principal allies or heads of government we could communicate with, at least on a 24-hour notice basis—

Vice President Johnson: I certainly—

Bundy: —ease the . . .

Vice President Johnson: Tell the alliance we've got to try to stop the planes, stop the ships, stop the submarines and everything else they're [the Soviets] sending. Just not going to permit it. And then—

Bundy: Stop them from coming in there.

Vice President Johnson: Yeah.

President Kennedy: Well this is really talking about are two or three different potential operations.

One is the strike just on these three bases.

The second is the broader one that Secretary McNamara was talking about, which is on the airfields and on the SAM sites and on anything else connected with missiles.

Third is doing both of those things and also at the same time launching a blockade, which requires, really, the third and which is a larger step.

And then, as I take it, the fourth question is the degree of consultation. I don't know how much use consulting with the British . . . I expect they'll just object. Just have to decide to do it. Probably ought to tell them, though, the night before.

Robert Kennedy: Mr. President?

President Kennedy: Yes?

Robert Kennedy: We have the fifth one, really, which is the invasion. I would say that you're dropping bombs all over Cuba if you do the second, air and the airports, knocking out their planes, dropping it on all their missiles. You're covering most of Cuba. You're going to kill an awful lot of people, and we're going to take an awful lot of heat on it. And then— you know the heat. Because you're going to announce the reason that you're doing it is because they're sending in these kind of missiles.

Well, I would think it's almost incumbent upon the Russians then, to say, "Well, we're going to send them in again. And if you do it again, we're going to do the same thing to Turkey. And we're going to do the same thing to Iran."

President Kennedy: I don't believe it takes us, at least . . . How long does it take to get in a position where we can invade Cuba? Almost a month? Two months?

McNamara: No, sir. No, sir. It's a bare seven days after the air strike, assuming the air strike starts the first of next week. Now, if the air strike were to start today, it wouldn't necessarily be seven days after today, but I think you can basically consider seven days after the air strike.

President Kennedy: You could get six divisions or seven divisions into Cuba in seven days?

Taylor: No, sir. There are two plans we have. One is to go at maximum speed, which is the one referred to you by Secretary McNamara, about seven days after the strike. We put in 90,000 men in 11 days.

If you have time, if you can give us more time, so we can get all the advance preparation and prepositioning, we'd put the same 90,000 in, in five days. We really have the choice of those two plans.

President Kennedy: How would you get them in? By ship or by air?

McNamara: By air.

Several: Airdrop and ship.

McNamara: Simultaneous airdrop and ship.

President Kennedy: Do you think 90,000 is enough?

Taylor: At least it's enough to start the thing going. And I would say it would be, ought to be, enough.

McNamara: Particularly if it isn't directed initially at Havana, the Havana area. This is a variant. General Taylor and . . .

President Kennedy: We haven't any real report on what the state of the popular reaction would be to all this, do we? We don't know whether . . .

Taylor: They'd be greatly confused, don't you think?

President Kennedy: What?

Taylor: Great, great confusion and panic, don't you think? It's very hard to evaluate the effect from what the military consequences might be.

McNamara: Sometime today, I think, at the State Department, we will want to consider that. There's a real possibility you'd *have* to invade. If you carried out an air strike, this might lead to an uprising, such that in order to prevent the slaughter of the free Cubans, we would have to invade to reintroduce order into the country. And we would be prepared to do that.

Rusk: I would rather think if there were a complete air strike against all air forces, you might as well do it. Do the whole job.

President Kennedy: Well, now, let's decide what we ought to be doing.

Robert Kennedy: Could I raise one more question?

President Kennedy: Yeah.

Robert Kennedy: Is it absolutely essential that you wait seven days after you have an air strike? I would think that seven days, that's what you're going to have all—

Taylor: If you give less, you run the risk of giving up surprise. If you start moving your troops around in order to reduce that.

Robert Kennedy: Yeah. The only thing is, there's been so much attention on Berlin in the last . . . Would you have to move them so that everybody would know it was Cuba?

Taylor: Well, it's troops, plus shipping even more so, you know. You're going to have to assemble the ships necessary, and that will be very very overt, and we can think of no way to cover that up.

McNamara: May I suggest, Max, that we mention this other plan we talked about. We should be prepared for a series of eventualities after the air strike starts. I think it's not probable, but it's conceivable that the air strike would trigger a nationwide uprising. And if there was strong opposition among the dissident groups, and if the air strike were highly successful, it's conceivable that some U.S. troops could be put in in less than seven days.

Taylor: That's correct. At first our air, our airdrops, and our Marines. Well, the airdrop at least, beginning in five days. That might do the trick if this is really a national upheaval.

McNamara: So we should have a series of alternative plans is all I'm suggesting, other than the seven days.

Robert Kennedy: I just think that five days, even a five-day period—the United States is going to be under such pressure by everybody not to do anything. And there's going to be also pressure on the Russians to do something against us.

If you could get it in, get it started so that there wasn't any turning back, they couldn't . . .

President Kennedy: But I mean the problem is, as I understand it . . . you've got two problems.

One is how much time we've got on these particular missiles before they're ready to go. Do we have two weeks? If we had two weeks, we could lay on all this and have it all ready to go. But the question really is whether we can wait two weeks.

Bundy: Yeah.

. . .

Taylor: I think our point of view may change somewhat with a tactical adjustment here, a decision that would take out only the known missile sites and not the airfields. There is a great danger of a quick dispersal of all the interesting aircraft. You'd be giving up surprise. There's no [*unclear*] attack. Missiles can't run off quite as readily.

President Kennedy: The advantage of taking out these airplanes would be to protect us against a reprisal by them?

Taylor: Yes.

President Kennedy: I would think you'd have to assume they'd be using iron bombs and not nuclear weapons. Because, obviously, why would the Soviets permit nuclear war to begin under that sort of half-assed way?

McNamara: I think that's reasonable.

. . .

President Kennedy: Well, now, what is it we have, what is it we want to, need to, do in the next 24 hours to prepare for any of these three? It seems to me that we want to do more or less the same things, no matter what we finally decide.

. . .

President Kennedy: I think, what we ought to do is, after this meeting this afternoon, we ought to meet tonight again at six, consider these various proposals.

In the meanwhile, we'll go ahead with this maximum, whatever is needed, from the flights. And, in addition, we will . . .

I don't think we've got much time on these missiles. They may be . . . So it may be that we just have to . . . We can't wait two weeks while we're getting ready to roll. Maybe we just have to just take them out, and continue our other preparations if we decide to do that. That may be where we end up.

I think we ought to, beginning right now, be preparing to present what we're going to do *anyway*. We're certainly going to do [option] number one. We're going to take out these missiles.

The questions will be whether, what I would describe as number two, which would be a general air strike. That we're not ready to say, but we should be in preparation for it.

The third is the general invasion. At least we're going to do number one. So it seems to me that we don't have to wait very long. We ought to be making *those* preparations.

Bundy: You want to be clear, Mr. President, whether we have definitely decided *against* a political track. I, myself, think we ought to work out a contingency on that.

Rusk: We'll develop both tracks.

President Kennedy: I don't think we ought to do the OAS. I think that's a waste of time. I don't think we ought to do NATO.

We ought to just decide who we talk to, and how long ahead, and how many people, really, in the government. There's going to be a difference between those who know that—this will leak out in the next few days—there are these bases. Until we say, or the Pentagon or State, won't be hard. We've already said it on the . . . So let's say we've got two or three days.

Bundy: Well, let's play it, shall we, play it still harder and simply say that there is no evidence. I mean, we have to [*unclear*] be liars.

President Kennedy: We ought to stick with that until we want to do something. Otherwise we give ourselves away, so let's—

Bundy: May I make one other cover plan suggestion, Mr. President?

President Kennedy: Yes.

Bundy: There will be meetings in the White House. I think the best we can do is to keep the people with a specific Latin American business black and describe the rest as intensive budget review sessions.[13] But I haven't been able to think of any other.

President Kennedy: Nobody, it seems to me, in the State Department. I discussed the matter with Bohlen of the Soviet part and told him he could talk to [Llewellyn] Thompson. So that's those two. It seems to me that there's no one else in the State Department that ought to be talked to about it in any level at all until we know a little more.

And then, as I say, in Defense we've got to keep it as tight as possible, particularly what we're going to do about it. Maybe a lot of people know about what's there. But what we're going to do about it really ought to be, you know, the tightest of all because [*unclear*] we bitch it up.

McNamara: Mr. President, may I suggest that we come back this afternoon prepared to answer three questions.

First, should we surface our surveillance? I think this is a very important question at the moment. We ought to try to decide today either yes or no.

President Kennedy: By "surface our"?

McNamara: I mean, should we state publicly that, that you have stated we will act to take out any offensive weapons. In order to be certain as to whether there are or are not offensive weapons, we are scheduling U-2 flights or other surveillance—

Bundy: [*chuckling*] This is covert reconnaissance.

McNamara: Well, all right, or reconnaissance flights to obtain this information. We'll make the information public.

President Kennedy: That'd be one. All right, why not?

McNamara: This is one question. A second question is: Should we precede the military action with political action? If so, on what timing?

I would think the answer is almost certainly yes. And I would think particularly of the contacts with Khrushchev. And I would think that if these are to be done, they must be scheduled, in terms of time, very, very carefully in relation to a potential military action. There must be a very, very precise series of contacts with him, and indications of what we'll do at certain times following that.

And, thirdly, we should be prepared to answer your questions regarding the effect of these strikes and the time required to carry them off. I think—

President Kennedy: How long it would take to get them organized.

McNamara: Exactly. We'll be prepared—

President Kennedy: In other words, how many days from tomorrow morning would it . . . How many mornings from tomorrow morning would it take to get the, to take out just these missile sites, which we need to know now. How long before we get the information about the rest of the island, do you figure, General?

Bundy: It could take weeks, Mr. President.

President Kennedy: Weeks?

Bundy: For complete coverage of a cloud-covered island.

Unidentified: Well, depending on the weather.

Taylor: Well, we've got about 80 percent now, don't we?

Carter: Yes, sir. It depends much on what we get out of yesterday's flight, sir. They won't be—

Bundy: There are clouded areas, Mr. President, as I understand it. And there are areas that are going to be very substantially in permanent, or nearly permanent, cloud cover.

Carter: We'll have preliminaries by six tomorrow morning.

President Kennedy: Well, there is the part of the island that isn't covered by this flight we're [expecting to learn about] by tomorrow morning. What about doing that tomorrow, plus the clouded part, doing low level? Have we got a plane that goes—

Bundy: We can certainly go low level, and we have been reluctant to do that.

The one thing to worry about on low level is that that will create a sense of tactical alert in the island. And I'm not sure we want to do that. Our guess is that the high-level ones have not, in fact, been detected.

Taylor: I think that's correct.

Bundy: No reactions.

President Kennedy: I would think that if we are going to go in and take out this, and any others we find, that we would at the same time do a general low-level photographic reconnaissance.

Bundy: You could at the same time do a low level of all that we have not seen. That would certainly be sensible.

President Kennedy: Then we would be prepared, almost any day, to take those out.

Bundy: As a matter of fact, for evidentiary purposes, someone has made the point this morning that if we go in on a quick strike, we ought to have a photographic plane take shots of the sites.

President Kennedy: All right. Well, now, I think we've got to watch out for this, for us to be doing anything quickly and quietly and completely. That's what we've got to be doing the next two or three days. So, we'll meet at 6:00?

Robert Kennedy: How long? Excuse me. I just wondered how long it would take, if you took it and had an invasion.

Taylor: To mount an invasion?

Robert Kennedy: No. How long would it take to take over the island? *Bundy carries on a side conversation about how to describe this meeting to the press.*

Taylor: Very hard to estimate, Bobby. But I would say that in five or six days the main resistance ought to be overcome. We might then be in there for months thereafter, cleaning that up.

McNamara: Five or seven days of air, plus five days of invasion, plus—

President Kennedy: I wonder if CIA could give us the state . . . the latest on his popular . . . so we get some idea about our reception there.

I just hate to even waste these six hours. So it may be that we will want to be doing some movements in the next six hours.

. . .

The meeting now begins to break up. Various separate conversations begin as some people leave. President Kennedy's next appointment was for a formal lunch with the crown prince of Libya.

. . .

6:30 P.M.

Meeting on the Cuban Missile Crisis

The morning meeting had ended with an understanding that the Pentagon team would analyze possibilities for a quick air strike, possibly followed by an invasion. Rusk and others at State would study how the administration could act promptly and effectively against the missiles without surprising allies in the hemisphere and Europe and possibly losing their support.

While this went on, Kennedy kept to his announced schedule. He presided over a formal lunch for the crown prince of Libya. Adlai Stevenson was present. After lunch, Kennedy invited Stevenson to the family quarters. Showing Stevenson the U-2 photos, Kennedy said, "I suppose the alternatives are to go in by air and wipe them out or to take other steps to render the weapons inoperable." Stevenson's position was: "Let's not go into an air strike until we have explored the possibilities of a peaceful solution."

During the afternoon, Stevenson took part in the meetings at the State Department. So did Soviet experts Bohlen and Thompson and the assistant secretary for Latin America, Edwin Martin.

At Justice, Robert Kennedy had meanwhile held in his own office a meeting of those involved in Operation Mongoose. Describing the "general dissatisfaction" of the President with progress thus far, the Attorney General focused discussion on a new and more active program of sabotage that had just been prepared by the CIA. Pressed by the CIA representative (Richard Helms) to explain the ultimate objective of the operation and what to promise the Cuban exiles, Robert Kennedy hinted the President might be becoming less averse to overt U.S. military action. He wondered aloud how many Cubans would defend Castro's regime if the country were invaded. After discussing the possibility of having Cuban émigrés attack the missile sites, he and the rest of the group seemed to agree this was not feasible.

At the Pentagon, the Joint Chiefs of Staff conferred with CIN-CLANT, the commanders of SAC and the Tactical Air Command (TAC), and the general commanding the 18th Airborne Corps. McNamara joined later. Presuming that the Soviets would not initiate a nuclear war against the United States, the JCS favored an attack, regardless of whether the missiles were operational. They nevertheless approved several prudential steps to increase U.S. readiness for nuclear war. After McNamara left, the JCS agreed that they did not favor use of low-level reconnaissance flights over Cuba, fearing that they would "tip our hand." They also agreed they would rather do nothing than limit an air strike only to MRBMs.[14] In the last 40 minutes before returning to the White House, McNamara and Gilpatric worked out an outline of three alternative courses of action, which McNamara would present at the meeting.

From 4:00 on, Kennedy himself had been occupied with his regular schedule. He was able to return to the missile problem only as his advisers gathered in the Cabinet Room at 6:30. Taylor arrived a bit late, after the meeting began. President Kennedy activated the tape recorder as the meeting opened with the intelligence briefing.

President Kennedy: Find anything new?

Marshall Carter: Nothing on the additional film, sir. We have a much better readout on what we had initially.

· · ·

President Kennedy: There isn't any question in your mind, however, that it is an intermediate-range [actually medium-range] missile?

Carter: No. There's no question in our minds at all. These are all the characteristics that we have seen with live ones.

Dean Rusk: You've seen actual missiles themselves and not just the boxes, have you?

Carter: No, we've seen . . . in the picture there is an actual missile.

Rusk: Yeah. Sure there is [*tone is serious, not sarcastic*].

Carter: Yes. There's no question in our mind, sir. And they are genuine. They are not a camouflage or covert attempt to fool us.

McGeorge Bundy: How much do we know, Pat? I don't mean to go behind your judgment here, except that there's one thing that would be really catastrophic, [which] would be to make a judgment here on a bad guess as to whether these things are . . . We mustn't do that.

How do we really know what these missiles are, and what their range is?

Carter: Only that from the readout that we have now, and in the judgment of our analysts, and of the Guided Missile and Astronautics Committee which has been convening all afternoon, these signatures are identical with those that we have clearly earmarked in the Soviet Union, and have fully verified.[15]

Bundy: What made the verification? That's really my question. How do we know what a given Soviet missile will do?

Carter: We know something from the range firings that we have vetted for the past two years. And we know also from comparison with the characteristics of our own missiles as to size and length and diameter. As to these particular missiles, we have a family of Soviet missiles for which we have all accepted the specifications.

Bundy: I know that we have accepted them, and I know that we've had these things in charts for years. But I don't know how we know.

Carter: Well, we know from a number of sources, including our IRONBARK sources, as well as from range firings which we have been vetting for several years, as to the capabilities.[16] But I would have to get the analysts in here to give you the play-by-play account.

Rusk: Pat, we don't know of any 65-foot Soviet missile that has a range of, say, 15 miles, do we?

Carter: Fifteen miles? No, we certainly don't.

Rusk: In other words, if they are missiles this size, they are missiles of considerable range, I think.

Robert McNamara: I tried to prove today—I am satisfied—that these were not MRBMs. And I worked long on it. I got our experts out, and I could not find evidence that would support any conclusion *other* than that they are MRBMs. Now, whether they're 1,100 miles, 600 miles,

900 miles is still a guess in my opinion. But that they are MRBMs seems the most probable assumption at the moment.

Bundy: I would apparently agree, given the weight of it.

At Rusk's request, Assistant Secretary Edwin Martin outlined a possible private appeal to Castro to break with the Soviet Union.

. . .

Rusk: The disadvantage in that is, of course, the advance notice if he judges that . . . We would not, in this approach here, say exactly what we would do. But it might, of course, lead him to bring up mobile antiaircraft weapons around these missiles themselves, or take some other action that will make the strike there more difficult. But there is that move.

There are two other problems that we are concerned about. If we strike these missiles, we would expect, I think, maximum Communist reaction in Latin America. In the case of about six of those governments, unless the heads of government had some intimation requiring some preparatory steps from the security point of view, one or another of those governments could easily be overthrown. I'm thinking of Venezuela, for example, or Guatemala, Bolivia, Chile, possibly even Mexico. And therefore the question will arise as to whether we should not somehow indicate to them, in some way, the seriousness of the situation so they can take precautionary steps, whether we tell them exactly what we have in mind, or not.

The other is the NATO problem. We would estimate that the Soviets would almost certainly take some kind of action somewhere. For us to take an action of this sort without letting our closer allies know of a matter which could subject them to very great danger is a very far reaching decision to make. And we could find ourselves isolated, and the alliance crumbling, very much as it did for a period during the Suez affair, but at a moment of much greater danger over an issue of much greater danger than the Suez affair for the alliance.

I think that these are matters that we'll be working on very hard this evening. But I think I ought to mention them because it's necessarily a part of this problem.

President Kennedy: Can we get a little idea about what the military thing is? Well, of course, [number] one, is to suggest taking these out.

McNamara: Yes, Mr. President. General Taylor has just been with the Chiefs, and the unified commanders went through this in detail.

To take out only the missiles, or to take out the missiles and the MiG aircraft and the associated nuclear storage facilities, if we locate them, could be done in 24 hours warning. That is to say, 24 hours between the time of decision and the time of strike, starting with a time of decision no earlier than this coming Friday [October 19] and with the strike therefore on Saturday [October 20], or anytime thereafter with 24 hours between the decision and the time of strike.

General Taylor will wish to comment on this, but the Chiefs are strong in their recommendation *against* that kind of an attack, believing that it would leave too great a capability in Cuba undestroyed. The specific number of sorties required to accomplish this end has not been worked out in detail. The capability is for something in excess of 700 sorties per day. It seems highly unlikely that that number would be required to carry out that limited an objective, but at least that capability is available in the Air Force alone, and the Navy sorties would rise on top of that number. The Chiefs have also considered other alternatives extending into the full invasion. You may wish to discuss [that] later. But that's the answer to your first question.

President Kennedy: That would be taking out these three missile sites, plus all the MiGs?

McNamara: Well, you can go from the three missile sites, to the three missile sites plus the MiGs, to the three missile sites plus MiGs plus nuclear storage plus airfields, and so on up through the potential offensive.

President Kennedy: Just the three missiles [sites], however, would be—

McNamara: Could be done with 24-hours notice, and would require a relatively small number of sorties. Less than a day's air attack, in other words.

President Kennedy: Of course, all you'd really get there would be . . . what would you get there? You'd get the, probably, you'd get the missiles themselves that have to be on the . . .

McNamara: You'd get the launchers and the missiles on the—

President Kennedy: The launchers are just what? They're not much, are they?

McNamara: No. They're simply a mobile launch device.

Maxwell Taylor: This is a point target, Mr. President. You're never sure of having, absolutely, getting everything down there. We can certainly do a great deal of damage because we can whip [*unclear*]. But, as the secretary says here, there was unanimity among all the commanders involved in the Joint Chiefs that, in our judgment, it would be a mistake to take this very narrow, selective target because it invited reprisal attacks and it may be detrimental.

Now if the Soviets have been willing to give nuclear warheads to these missiles, there is just as good reason for them to give a nuclear capability to these bases. We don't think we'd ever have a chance to take them again, so that we'd lose this first strike surprise capability.

Our recommendation would be to get complete intelligence, get all the photography we need, the next two or three days—no hurry in our book. Then look at this target system. If it really threatens the United States, then take it right out with one hard crack.

President Kennedy: That would be taking out some of those fighters, bombers, and—

Taylor: Fighters, the bombers. IL-28s may turn up in this photography. It's not at all unlikely there are some there.

President Kennedy: Think you could do that in one day?

Taylor: We think that [in] the first strike we'd get a great majority of this. We'll never get it all, Mr. President. But we then have to come back day after day, for several days. We said five days, perhaps, to do the complete job. Meanwhile we could then be making up our mind as to whether or not to go ahead and invade the island. . . .

McNamara: Mr. President, could I outline three courses of action we have considered and speak very briefly on each one?

The first is what I would call the political course of action, in which we follow some of the possibilities that Secretary Rusk mentioned this morning by approaching Castro, by approaching Khrushchev, by discussing with our allies. An overt and open approach politically to the problem, attempting to solve it. This seemed to me likely to lead to no satisfactory result, and it almost stops subsequent military action. Because the danger of starting military action *after* they acquire a nuclear capability is so great, I believe we would decide against it, particularly if that nuclear capability included aircraft as well as missiles, as it well might at that point.

A second course of action we haven't discussed, but lies in between the military course we began discussing a moment ago and the political course of action, is a course of action that would involve declaration of open surveillance: A statement that we would immediately impose a blockade against offensive weapons entering Cuba in the future and an indication that, with our open surveillance reconnaissance which we would plan to maintain indefinitely into the future, we would be prepared to immediately attack the Soviet Union in the event that Cuba made any offensive move against this country.

Bundy: Attack who?

McNamara: The Soviet Union. In the event that Cuba made *any* offensive move against this country. Now this lies short of military action against Cuba, direct military action against Cuba. It has some major defects.

But the third course of action is any one of these variants of military action directed against Cuba, starting with an air attack against the missiles. The Chiefs are strongly opposed to so limited an air attack. But even so limited an air attack is a very extensive air attack. It is not 20 sorties or 50 sorties or 100 sorties, but probably several hundred sorties. We haven't worked out the details. It's very difficult to do so when we lack certain intelligence that we hope to have tomorrow or the next day. But it's a substantial air attack. And to move from that into the more extensive air attacks against the MiGs, against the airfields, against the potential nuclear storage sites, against the radar installations, against the SAM sites, means—as Max suggested—possibly 700 to 1,000 sorties per day for five days. This is the very, very rough plan that the Chiefs have outlined, and it is their judgment that that is the type of air attack that should be carried out.

To move beyond that, into an invasion following the air attack, means the application of tens of thousands, between 90 and over 150,000 men, to the invasion forces.

It seems to me almost certain that any one of these forms of direct military action will lead to a Soviet military response of some type, some place in the world. It may well be worth the price. Perhaps we should pay that. But I think we should recognize that possibility and, moreover, we must recognize it in a variety of ways.

We must recognize it by trying to deter it, which means we probably should alert SAC, probably put on an airborne alert, perhaps take other alert measures. These bring risks of their own associated with them.

It means we should recognize that by mobilization. Almost certainly, we should accompany the initial air strike with at least a partial mobilization. We should accompany an invasion following an air strike with a large-scale mobilization, a very large-scale mobilization, certainly exceeding the limits of the authority we have from Congress, requiring a declaration therefore of a national emergency.

We should be prepared, in the event of even a small air strike and certainly in the event of a larger air strike, for the possibility of a Cuban uprising, which would force our hand in some way. [It] either forces us to accept an unsatisfactory uprising, with all of the adverse comment that would result, or would force an invasion to support the uprising.

. . .

President Kennedy: I think the difficulty, it seems to me, is . . . I completely agree that there isn't any doubt that if we announced that there were MRBM sites going up that that would change . . . we would secure a good deal of political support after my statement. And that the fact that we indicated our desire to restrain, this really would put the burden on the Soviets.

On the other hand, the very fact of doing that makes the military . . . we lose all the advantages of our strike. Because if we announce that it's there, then it's quite obvious to them that we're gonna probably do something about it, I would *assume.*

Now, I don't know that. It seems to me what we ought to be thinking about tonight is: If we made an announcement that the intelligence has revealed that there are . . . If we did the note, message, to Khrushchev . . . I don't think that Castro has to know we've been paying much attention to it, any more than . . . Over a period of time it might have some effect, [but] he's not going to suddenly back down, change. I don't think he plays it that way.

So having a note to Khrushchev. It seems to me my press statement was so *clear* about how we *wouldn't* do anything under these conditions, and under the conditions that we *would.* He must know that we're going to find out. So it seems to me he just . . .

Bundy: That's, of course, why he's been very, very explicit with us in communications to us about how dangerous this is—

President Kennedy: That's right.

Bundy: —in the [September 11] TASS statement and his other messages.

President Kennedy: But he's initiated the danger, really, hasn't he? He's the one that's playing God, not us.

. . .

Rusk: I would not think that they would use a nuclear weapon unless they're prepared for general nuclear war. I just don't see that possibility.

Bundy: I would agree.

Rusk: That would mean that—you know we could be just utterly wrong—but we've never really believed that Khrushchev would take on a general nuclear war over Cuba.

Bundy: May I ask a question in that context?

President Kennedy: We certainly have been wrong about what he's trying to do in Cuba. There isn't any doubt about that. Not many of us thought that he was going to put MRBMs on Cuba.

Bundy: No. Except John McCone.

Carter: Mr. McCone.

President Kennedy: Yeah.

Bundy: But the question that I would like to ask is, quite aside from what we've said and we're very hard locked on to it, I know: What is the strategic impact on the position of the United States of MRBMs in Cuba? How gravely does this change the strategic balance?

McNamara: Mac, I asked the Chiefs that this afternoon, in effect. They said: "Substantially." My own personal view is: Not at all.

Bundy: Not so much.

McNamara: And I think this is an important element here. But it's all very . . .

Carter: The reason our estimators didn't think that they'd put them in there, is because of—[17]

Bundy: That's what they said themselves in [the] TASS statement.

Carter: That's what they said themselves. But then, going behind that—

President Kennedy: But why? Didn't they think they'd be valuable enough?

Bundy: Doesn't improve anything in the strategic balance.

Carter: Doesn't improve anything. That was what the estimators felt, and that the Soviets would not take the risk.[18]

Mr. McCone's reasoning, however, was: If this is so, then what possible reason have they got for going into Cuba in the manner in which they are, with surface-to-air missiles and cruise-type missiles? He just couldn't understand *why* the Soviets were so heavily bolstering Cuba's defensive posture. There must be something behind it. Which led him *then* to the belief that they must be coming in with MRBMs.

Taylor: I think from a cold-blooded point of view, Mr. President, you're quite right in saying that these are just a few more missiles targeted on the United States. However, they can become a very, rather important, adjunct and reinforcement to the strike capability of the Soviet Union. We have no idea how far they will go.

But more than that, these are, to our nation it means a great deal more, as we all are aware, if they have them in Cuba and not over in the Soviet Union.

Bundy: Oh, I ask the question with an awareness of the political . . . [*chuckles*].

President Kennedy: Well, let's say . . . I understand, but let's just say that they get these in there. And then you can't . . . They get sufficient capacity, so we can't . . . with warheads. Then you don't want to knock them out because that's too much of a gamble.

Then they just begin to build up those air bases there, and then put more and more. I suppose they really . . . Then they start getting ready to squeeze us in Berlin. Doesn't that . . . ?

You may say it doesn't make any difference if you get blown up by an ICBM flying from the Soviet Union or one from 90 miles away. Geography doesn't mean that much. . . .

Taylor: We would have to target them with our missiles and have the same kind of pistol pointed at the head situation as they have in the Soviet Union at the present time.

Bundy: No question. If this thing goes on, an attack on Cuba becomes general war. And that's really the question: Whether . . .

President Kennedy: That's why it shows the Bay of Pigs was really right. If we had done it right. That was [a choice between] better and better, and worse and worse.

Taylor: I'm impressed with this, Mr. President. We have a war plan over there for you. [It] calls for a quarter of a million American soldiers, marines, and airmen to take an island we launched 1,800 Cubans against, a year and a half ago. We've changed our evaluations about it.

.   .   .

President Kennedy: I said we weren't going to [allow it].

Bundy: That's something we could manage.

President Kennedy: Last month I said we weren't going to [allow it]. Last month I should have said that we don't care. But when we said we're *not* going to, and then they go ahead and do it, and then we do nothing, then I would think that our risks increase.

I agree, what difference does it make? They've got enough to blow us up now anyway. I think it's just a question of . . . After all, this is a political struggle as much as military.

Well, so where are we now? Where is the . . . ? I don't think the message to Castro's got much in it.

Let's just try to get an answer to this question: How much . . . ? It's quite obviously to our advantage to surface this thing to a degree before . . . first to inform these governments in Latin America, as the Secretary suggests. Secondly, let the NATO people who have the right to some warning: Macmillan, de Gaulle. How much does this diminish . . . ? Not [telling them] that we're going to do anything, but the existence of them, without any say about what we're gonna do.

Let's say, 24 hours ahead of our doing something about it, we inform Macmillan. We make a public statement that these have been found on the island. That would be a notification, in a sense, of their existence and everybody could draw whatever conclusion they wanted to.

Edwin Martin: I would say this, Mr. President. That I would . . . that if you've made a public statement, you've got to move immediately, or you're going to have a [*unclear*] in *this* country.

President Kennedy: Oh, I understand *that*. We'll be talking about . . . Say we're going to move on a Saturday. And we would say on a Friday that these MRBMs, that the existence of this, presents the gravest threat to our security and that appropriate action must be taken.

. . .

C. Douglas Dillon: What is the advantage of the announcement earlier? Because it's to build up sympathy, or something, for doing it. But you get the simultaneous announcement of what was there, and why you struck, with pictures and all—I believe would serve the same [purpose].

George Ball: Well, the only advantage is it's a kind of ultimatum in which there is an opportunity of a response which would preclude it [the strike]. I mean it's more for the appearance than for the reality. Because obviously you're not going to get that kind of response.

. . .

President Kennedy: I'm not completely . . . I don't think we ought to abandon just knocking out these missile bases, as opposed to . . . That's a much more defensible [and] explicable, politically, or satisfactory in every way, action than the general strike which takes us into the city of Havana, and it is plain to me, takes us into much more hazardous . . . shot down . . .

Now, I know the Chiefs say: "Well, that means their bombers can take off against us." But . . .

Bundy: Their bombers take off against us. Then *they* have made a general war against Cuba of it, which then becomes much more their decision.

We move this way and the political advantages are *very* strong, it seems to me, of the small strike. It corresponds to "the punishment fits the crime" in political terms. We are doing only what we warned repeatedly and publicly we would have to do. We are not generalizing the attack. The things that we've already recognized and said that we have not found it necessary to attack, and said we would not find it necessary to attack . . .

President Kennedy: Well, here's . . . Let's look, tonight. It seems to me we ought to go on the assumption that we're going to have the general, number two we would call it, course number two, which would be a general strike and that you ought to be in position to do that, then, if you decide you'd like to do number one.

Bundy: I agree.

Robert Kennedy: Does that encompass an invasion?

President Kennedy: No. I'd say that's the third course.

Let's first start with, I'd just like to first find out, the air, so that I would think that we ought to be in position to do [options] one and two, which would be:

One would be just taking out these missiles and whatever others we'd find in the next 24 hours.

Number two would be to take out all the airplanes.

And number three is to invade.

Dillon: Well, they'd have to take out the SAM sites also, Mr. President.

President Kennedy: OK, but that would be in two, included in number two. Of course, that's a terrifically difficult—

Dillon: Well, that may be [option] three and invasion [is option] four.

. . .

President Kennedy: Right. Well, now, what is it, in the next 24 hours, what is it we need to do in order, if we're going to do, let's first say, one and two by Saturday or Sunday? You're doing everything that is . . .

McNamara: Mr. President, we need to do two things, it seems to me.

First, we need to develop a specific strike plan limited to the missiles and the nuclear storage sites, which we have not done. This would be a part of the broader plan, but I think we ought to estimate the minimum number of sorties. Since you have indicated some interest in that possibility, we ought to provide you that option. We haven't done this.

President Kennedy: OK.

McNamara: But that's an easy job to do.

The second thing we ought to do, it seems to me, as a government, is to consider the consequences. I don't believe we have considered the consequences of any of these actions satisfactorily. And because we haven't considered the consequences, I'm not sure we're taking all the action we ought to take now to minimize those.

I don't know quite what kind of a world we live in after we have struck Cuba, and we've started it. We've put, let's say, 100 sorties in, just for purposes of illustration. I don't think you dare start with less than 100. You have 24 objects. Well, you 24 vehicles, plus 16 launchers, plus a possible nuclear storage site. Now that's the absolute minimum that you would wish to kill. And you couldn't possibly go in after those with less than, I would think, 50 to 100 sorties.

Taylor: And you'll miss some.

McNamara: And you'll miss some. That's right.

Now after we've launched 50 to 100 sorties, what kind of a world do we live in? How do we stop at that point? I don't know the answer to this. I think tonight State and we ought to work on the consequences of any one of these courses of actions, consequences which I don't believe are entirely clear to any of us.

Ball: At any place in the world.

McNamara: At any place in the world, George. That's right. I agree with you.

Taylor: Mr. President, I should say that the Chiefs and the commanders feel so strongly about the dangers inherent in the limited strike that they would prefer taking *no* military action rather than to take that limited first strike. They feel that it's opening up the United States to attacks which they can't prevent, if we don't take advantage of surprise.

President Kennedy: Yeah. But I think the only thing is, the chances of it becoming a much broader struggle are increased as you step up the . . . Talk about the dangers to the United States, once you get into beginning to shoot up those airports. Then you get into a lot of antiaircraft. And you got a lot of . . . I mean you're running a much more major operation, therefore the dangers of the worldwide effects, which are substantial to the United States, are increased. That's the only argument for it [the limited strike].

I quite agree that, if you're just thinking about Cuba, the best thing to do is to be bold, if you're thinking about trying to get this thing under some degree of control.

· · ·

President Kennedy: Let's not let the Chiefs knock us out on this one, General, because I think that what we've got to be thinking about is: If you go into Cuba in the way we're talking about, and taking all the planes and all the rest, then you really haven't got much of an argument against invading it.

· · ·

Taylor: Well, I would be . . . personally Mr. President, my inclination is all against the invasion, but nonetheless trying to eliminate as effectively as possible every weapon that can strike the United States.

President Kennedy: But you're not for the invasion?

Taylor: I would not be, at this moment. No, sir. We don't want to get committed to the degree that shackles us with him in Berlin.

McNamara: This is why I say I think we have to think of the consequences here. I would think a forced invasion [an invasion forced on the United States], associated with assisting an uprising following an extensive air strike, is a highly probable set of circumstances. I don't know whether you could carry out an extensive air strike of, let's say, the kind we were talking about a moment ago—700 sorties a day for five days—without an uprising in Cuba. I really—

U. Alexis Johnson: Based on this morning's discussion we went into this, talked to some of your people, I believe, a little bit. And we felt an air strike, even of several days, addressed to military targets primarily, would not result in any substantial unrest. People would just stay home and try to keep out of trouble.

McNamara: Well, when you're talking about military targets, we have 700 targets here we're talking about. This is a very damned expensive target system.

Taylor: That was in that number [*unclear*], Mr. Secretary. But that's not the one I recommended.

McNamara: Well, *neither* is the one I'd recommend.

· · ·

Robert Kennedy: Mr. President, while we're considering this problem tonight, I think that we should also consider what Cuba's going to be a year from now, or two years from now. Assume that we go in and knock these sites out. I don't know what's gonna stop them from saying: "We're going to build the sites six months from now, and bring them in [again]."

Taylor: Nothing permanent about it.

Robert Kennedy: Where are we six months from now? Or that we're in any better position? Or aren't we in a worse position if we go in and knock them out, and say: "Don't do it"? I mean, *obviously*, they're gonna have to do it then.

McNamara: You have to put a blockade in following any limited action.

Robert Kennedy: Then we're going to have to sink Russian ships. Then we're going to have to sink Russian submarines.

Taylor: Right. Right.

Robert Kennedy: Now, [think] whether it wouldn't be the argument, if you're going to get into it at all, whether we should just get into it, and get it over with, and take our losses. And if he wants to get into a war over this . . .

Hell, if it's war that's gonna come on this thing, he sticks those kinds of missiles in after the warning, then he's gonna get into a war over six months from now, or a year from now on something.

McNamara: Mr. President, this is why I think tonight we ought to put on paper the alternative plans and the probable, and possible consequences thereof, in a way that State and Defense could agree on. Even if we disagree, then put in both views. Because the consequences of these actions have not been thought through clearly. The one that the Attorney General just mentioned is illustrative of that.

President Kennedy: If it doesn't increase very much their strategic strength, why is it—can any Russian expert tell us—why they . . . ? After all Khrushchev demonstrated a sense of caution over Laos. Berlin, he's been cautious—I mean, he hasn't been . . .

Ball: Several possibilities, Mr. President. One of them is that he has given us word now that he's coming over in November to the U.N. He may be proceeding on the assumption, and this lack of a sense of apparent urgency would seem to support this, that this isn't going to be discovered at the moment and that, when he comes over, this is something he can do, a ploy—that here is Cuba armed against the United States.

Or possibly use it to try to trade something in Berlin, saying he'll disarm Cuba if we'll yield some of our interests in Berlin and some arrangement for it. I mean that—it's a trading ploy.

Bundy: I would think one thing that I would still cling to is that he's not likely to give Fidel Castro nuclear warheads. I don't believe that has happened or is likely to happen.

President Kennedy: Why does he put these in there, though?

Bundy: Soviet-controlled nuclear warheads.

President Kennedy: That's right. But what is the advantage of that? It's just as if we suddenly began to put a major number of MRBMs in Turkey. Now that'd be goddamn dangerous, I would think.

Bundy: Well, we did, Mr. President.

Alexis Johnson: We did it. We did it in England.

President Kennedy: Yeah, but that was five years ago.[19]

Alexis Johnson: That's when we were short. We put them in England too when we were short of ICBMs.

President Kennedy: But that was during a different period then.

Alexis Johnson: But doesn't he realize he has a deficiency of ICBMs vis-à-vis our capacity perhaps? In view of that he's got lots of MRBMs and this is a way to balance it out a bit.

Bundy: I'm sure his generals have been telling him for a year and a half that he was missing a golden opportunity to add to his strategic capability.

Ball: Yes. I think you look at this possibility that this is an attempt to add to his strategic capabilities.

A second consideration is that it is simply a trading ploy, that he wants this in so that he can—

Alexis Johnson: It's not inconsistent. If he can't trade then he's still got the other.

Various speakers begin talking simultaneously.

Bundy: —political impact in Latin America.

Carter: We are now considering these, then, Soviet missiles, a Soviet offensive capability.

Ball: You have to consider them Soviet missiles.

Carter: It seems to me that if we go in there lock, stock, and barrel, we can consider them entirely Cuban.

Bundy: Ah, well, what we say for political purposes and what we think are not identical here.

Ball: But, I mean, any rational approach to this must be that they are Soviet missiles, because I think Khrushchev himself would never, would never, risk a major war on a fellow as obviously erratic and foolish as Castro.

Taylor: His second lieutenant.

Robert Kennedy: Well, I want to say, can I say that one other thing is whether we should also think of whether there is some other way we can get involved in this, through Guantánamo Bay or something. Or whether there's some ship that . . . you know, sink the *Maine* again or something.[20]

· · ·

President Kennedy: Well, what about my . . . the question would be therefore what I might say to Gromyko about this matter, if you want me to just get in the record, by asking him whether they plan to do it.

Bundy: Putting it the other way around, saying that we are putting great weight upon the assurance of his.

Ball: Well, I think what you get is to call their attention to the statement that you've made on this. And that this is your public commitment and you are going to have to abide by this, and you just want assurances from him that they're living up to what they've said, that they're not going to . . .

President Kennedy: Well, let's say he said: "Well, we're not planning to."

Bundy: [*reading from TASS statement of September 11*] "The government of the Soviet Union also authorized TASS to state that there is no need for the Soviet Union to shift its weapons for the repulsion of aggression for a retaliatory blow to any other country, for instance, Cuba. Our nuclear weapons are so powerful in their explosive force, the Soviet Union has so powerful rockets to carry these nuclear warheads, that there is no need to search for sites for them beyond the boundaries of the Soviet Union."

President Kennedy: What date was that?

Bundy: September 11th.

Dillon: When they were all there.

Carter: Or certainly on the way.

. . .

President Kennedy: Well it's a goddamn mystery to me. I don't know enough about the Soviet Union, but if anybody can tell me any other time since the Berlin blockade where the Russians have given us so clear a provocation, I don't know when it's been. Because they've been awfully cautious, really. The Russians . . . I've never . . .

Now, maybe our mistake was in not saying some time before this summer, that if they do this we're going to act. Maybe they'd gone in so far that it's . . .

Robert Kennedy: Yeah, but then why did they put that [TASS] statement in?

President Kennedy: This was following my statement, wasn't it?

Robert Kennedy: September 11th.

President Kennedy: When was my statement?

. . .

Ball: No, this [TASS statement] is two days before your statement [*but seven days after the White House statement of September 4*].

. . .

President Kennedy leaves the Cabinet Room. The recording machine is still running as McNamara, Bundy, Ball, and a few others begin their own informal discussion of the crisis issues.

. . .

Bundy: What I would suggest is that someone be deputied to do a piece of paper which really is: What happens?

I think the margin is between whether we [do the] take out the missiles only strike, or take a lot of air bases. This is tactical, within a decision to take military action. It doesn't overwhelmingly, it may substantially, but it doesn't overwhelmingly change the world.

I think any military action *does* change the world. And I think *not* taking action changes the world. And I think these are the two worlds that we need to look at.

. . .

McNamara: Now, the second alternative, I'd like to discuss just a second because we haven't discussed it fully today, and I alluded to it a moment ago.

I'll be quite frank. I don't think there *is* a military problem there. This is my answer to Mac's question—

Bundy: That's my honest [opinion?] too.

McNamara: —and therefore, and I've gone through this today, and I asked myself: "Well, what is it then if it isn't a military problem?"

Well, it's just exactly this problem: that if Cuba should possess a capacity to carry out offensive actions against the U.S., the U.S. would act.

Unidentified: That's right.

Unidentified: You can't get around that one.

McNamara: Now it's that problem. This is a domestic political problem. In the announcement we didn't say we'd go in and not [that] we'd kill them. We said we'd act. Well, how will we act? Well, we want to act to prevent their use. That's really the [*unclear*].

Now, how do we act to prevent their use? Well, first place, we carry out open surveillance, so we know what they're doing. At all times. Twenty-four hours a day from now and forever, in a sense, indefinitely.

What else do we do? We prevent any further offensive weapons coming in. In other words, we blockade offensive weapons.

Bundy: How do we do that?

McNamara: We search every ship.

Ball: There are two kinds of blockade: a blockade which stops ships from coming in; and simply a seizure—I mean simply a search.

McNamara: A search, that's right.

Ball: Yeah.

Martin: Well, it would be the search and removal, if found.

Bundy: You have to make the guy stop to search him. And if he won't stop, you have to shoot, right?

Martin: And you have to remove what you're looking for if you find it.

McNamara: Absolutely. Absolutely. And then an ultimatum. I call it an ultimatum. Associated with these two actions is a statement to the world, particularly to Khrushchev, that we have located these offensive weapons. We're maintaining a constant surveillance over them. If there is ever any indication that they're to be launched against this country, we will respond not *only* against Cuba, but we will respond directly against the Soviet Union with a full nuclear strike.

Now this alternative doesn't seem to be a very acceptable one. But wait until you work on the others.

Bundy: That's right. [*Laughter.*]

.   .   .

McNamara: And really, what I tried to do was develop a little package that meets the action requirement of that paragraph I read. Because, as I suggested, I don't believe it's primarily a military problem. It's primarily a domestic political problem.

Carter: Well, as far as the American people are concerned, action means military action, period.

McNamara: Well, we have a blockade. Search and removal of offensive weapons entering Cuba. Mac again, I don't want to argue for this because I don't—

Carter: No. I think it's an alternative.

McNamara: —think it's a perfect solution by any means. I just want to . . .

.   .   .

Carter: It's a series of single, unrelated acts, not by surprise. This coming in there, on a Pearl Harbor [kind of surprise attack], just frightens the hell out of me as to what goes beyond. The Board of National Estimates have been working on this ever since . . .

Bundy: What goes beyond what?

Carter: What happens beyond that. You go in there with a surprise attack. You put out all the missiles. This isn't the end. This is the *beginning*, I think. There's a whole hell of a lot of things . . .

McNamara: Well, that then takes me into the third category of action. I'd lump them all in the third category. I call it overt military action of varying degrees of intensity, ranging . . .

And if you feel there's any difference in them, in the kind of a world we have after the varying degrees of intensity, you have to divide category three into subcategories by intensity, and probable effect on the world thereafter. And I think there is, at least in the sense of the Cuban uprising, which I happen to believe is a most important element of category three. It applies to some elements, some categories in category three, but not all.

But, in any event, what kind of a world do we live in? In Cuba what action do we take? What do we expect Castro will be doing after you attack these missiles? Does he survive as a political leader? Is he overthrown? Is he stronger, weaker? How will he react?

How will the Soviets react? What can . . . How could Khrushchev afford to accept this action without some kind of rebuttal? I don't think he can accept it without some rebuttal. It may not be a substantial rebuttal, but it's gonna have to be some. Where? How do we react in relation to it?

What happens if we do mobilize? How does this affect our allies' support of us in relation to Berlin? Well, you know far better than I the problems. But it would seem to me if we could lay this out tonight, and then meet at a reasonable time in the morning to go over a tentative draft, discuss it, and then have another draft for some time in the afternoon . . .

. . .

Everyone was still trying to conceal the start of the crisis by appearing to maintain their known schedules. President Kennedy went to another farewell dinner for Bohlen, hosted by columnist Joseph Alsop. At the dinner he drew Bohlen aside and they had a long, animated, private conversation. Kennedy reportedly asked Bohlen if he could stay, but Bohlen feared that delaying his long-planned departure for Paris might arouse unwanted notice and comment.

Meetings resumed that evening at the State Department, winding up in Rusk's office at about 11:00 P.M. McNamara slept at the Pentagon that night. McCone returned to Washington.

As arranged on Tuesday, Kennedy's advisers met at 8:30 Wednesday morning, October 17, in a conference room on the seventh floor of the State Department. McCone, now back in Washington, joined them. There, Ball reiterated his opposition to any military action, expressing doubt that the Soviet leaders really understood what they had done. Thompson argued that Khrushchev knew what he was doing and wanted a showdown on Berlin. In this view, Khrushchev thought the missiles in Cuba armed him for that confrontation. Taylor and McCone sided with Thompson. After less than an hour, McCone and Bundy left for the White House.

Arriving at about 9:30 A.M., McCone briefed President Kennedy. The CIA director came away with the impression that Kennedy, too, leaned toward prompt military action. Kennedy asked McCone to go to Gettysburg and give Eisenhower a full briefing. McCone then drove off to Pennsylvania and reported back later that Eisenhower thought the situation was intolerable. The former president said he would support any decisive military action.

Thursday, October 18, 1962

President Kennedy had spent most of the previous day on a scheduled campaign trip to Connecticut. After his return the previous evening, he was still concealing the crisis from the press and public by keeping to his regular schedule as much as he could. That schedule began on October 18 at 9:30 A.M. with an awards ceremony, followed by a Cabinet meeting to discuss the budget.

11:10 A.M.

Meeting on the Cuban Missile Crisis

Sometime during the previous day, possibly before he left the White House for his scheduled political trip to Connecticut, Kennedy received a memo from Adlai Stevenson urging that Kennedy send personal emissaries to Khrushchev and Castro instead of taking any military action. Stevenson warned that any U.S. military action could lead to reprisals in Turkey or Berlin and could then escalate. "To start or risk starting a nuclear war is bound to be divisive at best," he wrote, "and the judgments of history seldom coincide with the tempers of the moment." While he said that he understood Kennedy's dilemma, he wrote with underscoring: *"the means adopted have such incalculable consequences that I feel you should have made it clear that the existence of nuclear missile bases anywhere is negotiable before we start anything."*[1] Stevenson then returned to his duties at the United Nations in New York.

That same morning of October 17 the Joint Chiefs of Staff reconvened to plan just the military action that Stevenson so abhorred. The Joint Staff had worked through the night to come up with plans for air strikes against five different sets of targets. Identified by Roman numerals I to V, these alternative plans were frequently discussed in the following days. They are given here, with associated numbers of sorties; the estimated sortie numbers continued to climb as planning continued.[2] The initial numbers were:

I. Missile and nuclear storage sites only	52
II. Same as above plus IL-28s, MiG-21s	104
III. Same as above plus other aircraft, SAMs, cruise msls, and msl boats	194
IV. All military targets but tanks	474
V. All military targets; prelude to invasion	2,002

The Chiefs still opposed any strike limited only to the missile sites. They continued also to view any blockade as merely a complement to, not an alternative for, an air strike. They assumed, in addition, that a blockade would require a formal declaration of war.

About 15 senior officials had met again for several hours the afternoon of October 17.[3] Almost all leaned toward taking some political action before launching an air strike. They reviewed a large number of possible courses of action and speculated about imaginable Soviet responses. McNamara and Taylor worried that any diplomatic efforts would alert the Soviets and thwart an effective strike. McNamara and Gilpatric belittled the significance of the Soviet MRBM deployments for the overall strategic balance. McCone and Taylor argued that the MRBMs did, indeed, change the balance. But this difference of opinion did not prevent general agreement that the United States could not allow the Soviet deployment to stand.

It was in this context that Kennedy's advisers, for the first time, discussed in detail the pros and cons of a blockade. Bohlen and Thompson continued to insist that Khrushchev's aim was to achieve something with regard to Berlin and that the U.S. government ought not to be diverted from that by concentrating its attention exclusively on Cuba.

Kennedy had invited former Secretary of State Dean Acheson to join his circle of advisers. Formidably self-assured and gifted not only with cutting wit but also with great ability in advocacy, Acheson participated in these Wednesday meetings, calling for a prompt air strike with no attempt at prior negotiation. Before adjourning for dinner, the conferees had also reviewed the possibility of a blockade coupled with a declaration of war against Cuba.

During the dinner break Robert Kennedy and Sorensen drove to the airport to meet the President, returning from Connecticut. Sorensen gave him a written summary of the day's discussions, emphasizing how fluid matters remained. (It included a list of around twenty questions as yet unresolved.) President Kennedy decided to stay out of the discussions until the next day. Robert Kennedy and Sorensen then returned to the State Department. The meeting resumed at 10:00 P.M. and went until nearly midnight.

During this late-hour meeting, Rusk had endorsed and elaborated on the alternative of a strike against the missile sites with no prior negotiation. Taylor and McCone supported him, with McCone's mentioning Eisenhower's views. Bohlen still urged that an ultimatum be given before an attack. Thompson, Martin, and Gilpatric preferred a complete blockade with the declaration of war.

At the end of this meeting, Robert Kennedy summarized the major options that had been aired. They apparently were:

> An ultimatum to Khrushchev followed by a strike
> A limited strike without prior warning or negotiation, but with notifying key allies
> A political warning followed by a naval blockade and readiness for other actions
> A large-scale strike after some political preparation
> Proceeding directly to an invasion.

Sorensen's earlier note for Kennedy had a similar list. Various forms of political action and messages to Khrushchev were considered, as well as various kinds of strikes. Many questions were identified for further analysis, especially about likely Soviet responses.

During the night of October 17–18, a few officials wrote brief papers for the President summarizing their personal beliefs. Douglas Dillon submitted a memo stating opposition to negotiations of any kind with Khrushchev. He recommended a blockade coupled with intensive surveillance of Cuba and a demand that Cuba begin removal of the weapons forthwith. If the Cubans refused or the military pronounced the blockade infeasible, Dillon favored an immediate air strike. He said that the Soviet Union had "initiated a test of our intentions that can determine the future course of world events for many years to come." He continued, "I . . . believe that the survival of our nation demands the prompt elimination of the offensive weapons now in Cuba."[4]

George Ball wrote a passionate memo arguing that the MRBMs made little strategic difference. Noting that "we tried Japanese as war criminals because of the sneak attack on Pearl Harbor," Ball argued that a surprise strike, "far from establishing our moral strength . . . would, in fact, alienate a great part of the civilized world by behaving in a manner wholly contrary to our traditions, by pursuing a course of action that would cut directly athwart everything we have stood for during our national history, and condemn us as hypocrites in the opinion of the world." Ball recommended a blockade that might ultimately cripple and bring down the Castro government.[5]

Bohlen, preparing to depart for Paris, also wrote a memo for Rusk, concisely explaining his preference for giving the Soviets an ultimatum before launching a strike. Though he had taken a different view, Rusk was impressed and apparently persuaded by Bohlen's memo and decided to share it with his colleagues and President Kennedy when they next gathered at the White House.[6]

On the morning of October 18, Sorensen noted for Kennedy that "two big questions must be answered, and in conjunction with each other." One was which kind of military action to choose, and the other was whether political action, such as a letter to Khrushchev, should precede any military move. The Rusk approach, he said, was for a strike without warning. The Bohlen approach was to approach Khrushchev first.[7]

Meanwhile, intelligence analysts had pored over photos from the earlier U-2 flights. They found something new—evidence of fixed IRBM sites in addition to the MRBM sites that had already been identified. With twice the range of MRBMs (2,200 miles instead of 1,100) and warheads of roughly twice as much yield (up to 5 megatons), these missiles could menace all parts of the continental United States except the Pacific Northwest.

As officials received this new information on the morning of October 18, their attitudes hardened. McNamara called McCone to say that he now thought prompt and decisive action necessary. Taylor told the Joint Chiefs that the news tipped him toward supporting the maximum option—full invasion of Cuba. This then became the unanimous position of the JCS. These early-morning discussions of the new intelligence set the mood as officials filed into the Cabinet Room.

·   ·   ·

John McCone: We think we got the entire island. What we didn't get because of clouds, we won't know until after we develop them.

I think you should know that these six missions involve 28,000 linear feet of film. And when this is enlarged, it means the Center [NPIC] has to examine a strip of film 100 miles long, 20 feet wide. Quite a job.

Go ahead, Art.

Arthur Lundahl: Yes, sir. Mr. President, gentlemen, the first and most important item I would seek to call to your attention is a new area hitherto never seen by us, some 21 miles to the southwest of Havana, which we have at the moment labeled a probable MRBM/IRBM launch complex. The name of the town nearest is this [Guanajay]. It is there. . . .

The orientation of the axis of the pads, 315 [degrees], which will bring you into the central massif of the United States. We call it M/IRBM, sir. We have never identified, irrevocably, the signature of the Soviet intermediate range ballistic missile which is estimatedly a 2,000-mile missile. But the elongation of the pads and the location of the control bunkers, between each pair of pads, has been the thing that has suggested to our hearts, if not our minds, the kind of thing that might accompany an IRBM.

· · ·

President Kennedy: If an unsophisticated observer . . . If we wanted to ever release these pictures to demonstrate that there were missiles there, it would not be possible to demonstrate this to the satisfaction of an untrained observer, would it?

Lundahl: I think it would be difficult, sir. By some eight years of experience in looking at the evolution in the Soviet Union, the signature emerges very clearly to us. I think the uninitiated would like to see the missile and the tube that it fits in.

· · ·

Dean Rusk: Mr. President, I think this changes my thinking on the matter if you have to [*unclear*] from the point of view of U.S. [*unclear*]. The first question we ought to answer is: Is it necessary to take action? And I suppose that there is compelling reason to take action here. For if no action is taken, it looks now as though Cuba is not going to be just an incidental base for a few of these things, but, basically an [*unclear*] with MRBMs, and IRBMs, and that sort of thing. Cuba could become a formidable military problem in any contest we would have with the Soviet Union over a threat in any other part of the world. I think our colleagues in Defense will want to comment on that very carefully because that's a very important point. But I do think that when the full scope of this becomes known, that no action would undermine our alliances all over the world very promptly.

On September 4th you said, "There is no evidence of any organized combat force in Cuba from any Soviet bloc country, or of military bases provided by Russia, in violation of the '34 treaty relating to Guantánamo, or of the presence of offensive ground-to-ground missiles; or other significant offensive capability either in Cuban hands or under Soviet direction and guidance. Were it to be otherwise the gravest issues would arise."

Now that statement was not made lightly at that time. These elements that were mentioned were pointing our fingers to things that were very fundamental to us. And it was intended as a clear warning to the Soviet Union that these are matters that we will take with the utmost seriousness. When you talk about the gravest issues, in the general language of international exchange, that means something very serious.

I think also we have to think of the effect on the Soviets if we were to do nothing. I would suppose that they would consider this a major backdown and that this would free their hands for almost any kind of adventure they might want to try out in other parts of the world. If we are unable to face up to a situation like Cuba against this kind of threat, then I think they would be greatly encouraged to go adventuring and would feel that they've had it made as far as intimidation of the United States is concerned.

I think also that we have an almost unmanageable problem in this country getting any support for the foreign policy that we would need to pursue, if we are going to sustain the cause of independence of states and freedom in all parts of the world. We've got a million men in uniform outside the United States. We've got foreign aid programs. We've got a major effort we're making in every continent. And it seems to me that inaction in this situation would undermine and undercut the enormous support that we need for the kind of foreign policy that will eventually ensure our survival.

Now action involves very high risks indeed, and I think that this additional information, if anything, increases the risk because the challenge is much more serious and the counteraction, I would suppose, would have to be heavier than we have, in fact, been talking about. But we can expect you would have to have in the back of your own mind, with whatever decision you take, the possibility—if not the likelihood—of a Soviet reaction somewhere else running all the way from Berlin right around to Korea, and the possibility of a reaction against the United States itself. I don't think that you can make your decision under any assumption that this is a free ride, or easier, or anything of that sort.

I would suppose that with those first missiles that we were talking about, that a quick strike with quick success in the matter of a couple hours' time—with 50 to 60 sorties, that sort of thing, where it's obvious then that the matter is over and finished and that was the purpose of our engagement—that that would have a much more reduced risk of a military response on the other side. But getting these other installations and getting involved in various parts of the island, I think would increase the risk of a military response down there.

The action also has to be thought of in connection with alliance solidarity. There we're faced with conflicting elements. Unless we're in a situation where it is clear that the alliance is with us and understands the problem, then an unannounced, or unconsulted, quick action on our part could well lead to a kind of allied disunity that the Soviets could capitalize upon very strongly.

It's one thing for Britain and France to get themselves isolated within the alliance over Suez. But it's quite another thing for the alliance if the United States should get itself in the same position because we are the central bone structure of the alliance. I think this is a different kind of problem that we have to think very hard about.

Now, I think that, as far as I'm concerned, I would have to say to you that if we enter upon this path of challenging the Soviets, the Soviets who themselves have embarked upon this fantastically dangerous course, that no one can surely foresee the outcome.

I was prepared to say when I came over here, before when I got this information, that even the 50-sortie strike would very probably move by specific steps into much more general action, at least as far as Cuba is concerned, and possibly in other situations.

Now, there is another fact, Mr. President, that bothers me considerably. I think the American people will willingly undertake great danger and, if necessary, great suffering, if they have a deep feeling that we've done everything that was reasonably possible to determine whether this trip was necessary. Also that they have a clear conscience and a good theory of the case.

The first point, whether this trip is necessary. We all, of course, remember the guns of August where certain events brought about a general situation in which at the time none of the governments involved really wanted.[8] And this precedent, I think, is something that is pretty important.

We had a clear conscience in World War II, the Pearl Harbor attack up against the background of Hitler's conduct resolved that problem. In the case of Korea, we had an organized large-scale aggression from North Korea, and we were doing it as part of a general United Nations commitment. Even with that start, the Korean aspect of it—the Korean war—got out of control as far as the general support of the American people were concerned, before it was over.

Now, these considerations that I've just mentioned would militate in favor of a consultation with Khrushchev and an implication that we will act because, in the first instance, there is the possibility, only a possibility, that Mr. Khrushchev might realize that he's got to back down on this. We can't be . . . I have no reason to expect that. This looks like a very serious and major commitment on his part. But at least it will take that point out of the way for the historical record, and just might have in it the seeds of prevention of a great conflict.

The Rio Pact is, I think clearly, our strongest legal basis for whatever action we need to take. The other possibility is a straight, is a straight declaration of war, which carries with it many legal privileges as a belligerent that would be extremely useful for us to have. But there is plenty of room in the Rio Pact for meeting this kind of threat, and I would suppose—Mr. Martin will have to comment on this—I would suppose there would be no real difficulty in getting a two-thirds vote in favor of necessary action.

But if we made the effort and failed to get the two-thirds vote at the time, which I would doubt would be the result, then at least we will have tried. And as far as the American people are concerned, we'd have done our very best on that.

Now, it seems to me, that the further information we have about the bases, other bases in other parts of the island, the buildup generally throughout Cuba, does raise the question as to whether a declaration of a national emergency and, if necessary, a declaration of war on Cuba may not be the necessary step here rather than spotty single strikes here and there around about the island. Because this could become a cops and robbers game, each strike becoming not only more difficult from a military point of view, but more difficult from your, from a political point of view, and it looks as though we have a larger problem to solve. And we may have to solve it in a larger way.

Now the principal alternative to that is, of course, to put in the short strikes, the brief strikes, and try our hand at getting it over with promptly as far as these particular installations are concerned. But these other bases, I think, create larger problems. Casualties go up a great deal and the challenge goes up a great deal. I think that the question is whether—I'd like to hear my colleagues comment on this—whether the action we would take, would have to take even in the most limited sense, would have to be large enough to involve the greatest risks in any event. Therefore we might as well solve the problem.

I would like to . . . Mr. Bohlen left a note last night after our meeting, wrote it out at about midnight or early this morning, just before he left. And I would like to read you certain paragraphs of this. He said:

> The existence of Soviet MRBM bases in Cuba cannot be tolerated. The objective therefore is their elimination by whatever means may be necessary.

There are two means in essence: by diplomatic action or by military action.

No one can guarantee that this can be achieved by diplomatic action, but it seems to me essential that this channel should be tested out before military action is employed. If our decision is firm (and it must be) I can see no danger in communication with Khrushchev privately, worded in such a way that he realizes that we mean business.

This I consider an essential first step no matter what military course we determine on if the reply is unsatisfactory. The tone and tenor of his reply will tell us something, but I don't believe that a threat of general nuclear war should deter us. If he means it, he would have so reacted even if the strike should come first.

My chief concern about a strike without any diplomatic effort is that it will eventually, that it will immediately, lead to war with Cuba and would not be the neat quick disposal of the bases, as was suggested. Furthermore, I am reasonably certain that the allied reaction would be dead against us, especially if the Soviet Union retaliated locally (in Turkey or Italy or in Berlin).

A communication with Khrushchev would be very useful for the record in establishing our case for action.

In general I feel that a declaration of war would be valuable since it would open up every avenue of military action: air strikes, invasion or blockade. But we would have to make a case before our allies to justify such a declaration of war. If we acted first and sought to justify it later we would be in a spat of great consequence.

Finally, I feel very strongly that the belief in a limited, quick action is an illusion and would lead us into a total war with Cuba on a step-by-step basis which would greatly increase the probability of general war.

That best course would be, he says, a carefully worded and serious letter to Khrushchev, before we take the action, the steps, and then followed by a declaration of war. We were talking about this last night. I think it is in this range of problems that we need to concentrate our attention, Mr. President. Otherwise we just . . . how we see the nature of the threat. I think our Defense colleagues ought to talk a moment about the actual military aspect of the threat itself.

Robert McNamara: Mr. President, here is listed . . . there are a series of alternative plans ranging from Roman numeral I was about 50 sorties, directed solely against the known MRBMs, known as of last night, to Roman numeral V, which covers the alternative invasion plan.

All of these plans are based on one very important assumption: That we would attack, with conventional weapons, against an enemy who is not equipped with operational nuclear weapons. If there's any possibility that the enemy is equipped with operational nuclear weapons, I'm certain the plans would have to be changed.

Last evening we were discussing the relative merits of these forms of military action, assuming that at some point military action was required. It has been the view of the Chiefs, based on discussions within the last two days, and it was certainly my view, that either Roman numeral I or Roman numeral II, very limited air strikes against very limited targets, would be quite inconclusive, very risky, and almost certainly lead to further military action prior to which we would have paid an unnecessary price for the gains we achieved.

And therefore the Chiefs and I would certainly have recommended last night, and I would recommend more strongly today, that we not consider undertaking either Roman numeral I, or Roman numeral II. In other words, we consider nothing short of a full invasion as applicable military action. And this only on the assumption that we're operating against a force that does not possess operational nuclear weapons.

President Kennedy: Why do you change . . . why has this information changed the recommendation?

McNamara: Last evening, it was my personal belief that there were more targets than we knew of, and it was probable there would be more targets than we could know of at the start of any one of these strikes. The information of this morning, I think, simply demonstrates the validity of that conclusion of last evening.

Secondly, when we're talking of Roman numeral I, it's a very limited strike against MRBMs only, and it leaves in existence IL-28s with nuclear weapon-carrying capability, and a number of other aircraft with nuclear weapon-carrying capability, and aircraft with strike capability that could be exercised during our attack, or immediately following our attack on the MRBMs, with great possible risk of loss to either Guantánamo and/or the eastern coast of the U.S.

I say great loss, I'm not thinking in terms of tens of thousands, but I'm thinking in terms of sporadic attacks against our civilian population, which would lead to losses, I think, we would find it hard to justify in relation to the alternative courses open to us, and in relation to the very limited accomplishment of our limited number of strikes.

Robert Kennedy: Bob, what about alternative number II, on the basis that you're going against offensive weapons? You're going to go against the missiles, and you're going to go against their planes. What are the arguments against that? I mean that would prevent them knocking our population.

McNamara: It is much to be preferred over number I, in my opinion. It would have to be larger than is shown now because of the additional number of targets required, and it gets very close to alternative III, in terms of number of sorties. Number II [strike] was prepared before we had the additional information, of last night's [photo] interpretation. We showed a hundred sorties. I think it more likely that number II, with the information we now have, and the information we're likely to have today and tomorrow, would merge into number III, which is a 200-sortie strike. I doubt very much we could stop there.

Maxwell Taylor: I would agree with that statement of the Secretary's, that really II is hardly possible now. We're really talking about III, you realize, because you'll have to take the SAM sites out, if you're going to go for all the airfield strikes. We're probably going out to the point where you're going to have to take other targets related to affecting [*unclear*].

. . .

President Kennedy: Let me ask you this, Bob, what we're talking about is III versus V, isn't it?

McNamara: Yes, sir.

President Kennedy: Then the advantage of III is that you would hope to do it in a day.

McNamara: Yes, and it could be done in a day.

President Kennedy: And invasion V, would be seven, eight, or nine days, with all the consequences. . . .

McNamara: That is correct.

President Kennedy: The increase in tension.

Now, if we did III, we would assume that by the end of the day their ability to use planes against us, after all they don't have that much range, so they'd have to come back to the field and organized it right.

McNamara: Yes. You would assume, by the end of the day, their air force could be nearly destroyed. I say nearly because there might be a few sporadic weapons around.

Taylor: Yes, I would stress the point, Mr. President, that we'll never be guaranteeing 100 percent.

McNamara: That's right. That's right.

President Kennedy: But at least as far as their . . . except with nuclear. I would think you would have to go on the assumption that they are not going to permit nuclear weapons to be used against the

United States from Cuba unless they're going to be using them from everyplace.

McNamara: Well, they could . . . I'm not sure they can stop it. This is why I emphasized the point I did. I don't believe the Soviets would authorize their use against the U.S., but they might nonetheless be used.

And, therefore, I underline this assumption, that all of these cases are premised on the assumption there are no operational nuclear weapons there. If there's any possibility of that I would strongly recommend that these plans be modified substantially.

Now I would go back just one second. I evaded the question Secretary Rusk asked me, and I evaded it because I wanted this information discussed first. The question he asked me was: How does—in effect—how does the introduction of these weapons to Cuba change the military equation, the military position of the U.S. versus the U.S.S.R.?

And, speaking strictly in military terms, really in terms of weapons, it doesn't change it at all, in my personal opinion. My personal views are not shared by the Chiefs. They are not shared by many others in the department. However, I feel very strongly on this point and I think I could argue a case, a strong case, in defense of my position.

This doesn't really have any bearing on the issue, in my opinion, because it is not a military problem that we're facing. It's a political problem. It's a problem of holding the alliance together. It's a problem of properly conditioning Khrushchev for our future moves. And the problem of holding the alliance together, the problem of conditioning Khrushchev for our future moves, the problem of dealing with our domestic public, all requires action that, in my opinion, the shift in military balance does not require.

President Kennedy: On holding the alliance. Which is going to strain the alliance more: This attack by us on Cuba, which most allies regard as a fixation of the United States and not a serious military threat? I mean, you'd have to . . . an awful lot of conditioning would have to go in before they would accept, support our action against Cuba, because they think that we're slightly demented on this subject.

So there isn't any doubt that whatever actions we take against Cuba, no matter how good our films are, are going to cause [problems] in Latin America. A lot of, a lot of people would regard this as a mad act by the United States, which is due to a loss of nerve because they will argue that, taken at its worst, the presence of these missiles really doesn't change the . . . If you think that, they're going to, certainly. With all the incentives to think the other way, viewing this as you do as an American, what's everybody else going to think who isn't under this gun?

McNamara: Aren't the others going to think exactly as I do?

Taylor: May I comment, Mr. President?

With regard to what we've just seen in intelligence, it seems to me three things stand out. The first is the very rapid . . . the energy with which they are developing the mobile missiles. In the course of 24 hours since Sunday [October 14, the day of the U-2 flight that first photographed the MRBM sites]. They are moving very fast to make those weapons operational.

Whether they're operational today? I would agree with the Secretary that probably not, but I don't think anyone can assure you. At any time at least one or more of these missiles will become operational.

Now, number two, the IL-28s. We've been expecting this. But now they've turned up in a very plausible location, I would say, and they're lying there inviting attack—an ideal time to take them out.

Now third, the IRBMs really put a new factor in, as I look at it. Yesterday, when we looked at this we had only a few of the mobile type [MRBMs]. I was far from convinced that the big showdown would be required. Today we're getting new pictures, and the vision of an island that's going to be a forward base, can become a forward base, of major importance to the Soviets.

Also, the targets that we're seeing, however, the kind of air attack we're talking about means nothing. We can't take this threat out by actions from the air. So that we have argued more and more that if, indeed, you're going to prevent that kind of thing, invasion is going to be required.

McGeorge Bundy: But you don't mean that you can't prevent it in the sense of stopping it from happening the next day. You mean that for the long pull you're going to have to take the island.

Taylor: Yes, you can't destroy a hole in the ground. We can't prevent this construction going ahead by any air actions. Conceivably diplomatic action might stop it, but only diplomatic action, or occupation as far as I can see, can prevent this kind of threat from building up.

Now, if those statements are roughly correct, then what does it mean in terms of time? Well, it means that, insofar as getting the mobile missiles out, time is of the essence. But the faster the better, if it's not already too late. And I would say that, again, we're not sure that it is not too late, with respect to one or more of the missiles.

. . .

President Kennedy: The question is really whether the Soviet reaction, and who knows this, would be measurably different if they were presented with an accomplished fact days after, I mean one day, not the invasion [*unclear*] just the accomplished fact. [The question is] whether their reaction would be different than it would be if they were given a chance to pull them out.

If we said to Khrushchev that: "We have to take action against it. But if you begin to pull them out, we'll take ours out of Turkey." Whether he would then send back: "If you take these out, we're going to take Berlin" or "We're going to do something else." And then we'd be . . .

Llewellyn Thompson: An important factor there is, if you do this first strike, you'd have killed a lot of Russians and that doesn't . . . inevitable reaction. On the other hand, if you do give him notice, the thing I would fear the most is a threat to Turkey and Italy to take action, which would cause us considerable difficulty [*unclear*].

President Kennedy: You mean if . . .

Bundy: What is your preference, Tommy?

Thompson: My preference is this blockade plan. I think this declaration of war and these steps leading up to it. I think it's very highly doubtful that the Russians would resist a blockade against military weapons, particularly offensive ones, if that's the way we pitched it before the world.

President Kennedy: What do we do with the weapons already there?

Thompson: Demand they're dismantled, and say that we're going to maintain constant surveillance, and if they are armed, we would then take them out. And then maybe do it.

I think we should be under no illusions; this would probably in the end lead to the same thing. But we do it in an entirely different posture and background and much less danger of getting up into the big war.

The Russians have a curious faculty of wanting a legal basis despite all of the outrageous things they've done. They attach a lot of importance to this. The fact that you have a declaration of war. They would be running a military blockade legally established. I think it would greatly deter them.

·   ·   ·

President Kennedy: In other words, under this plan however, we would not take these missiles that they now have out, or the planes they now have out.

Thompson: Not in the first stage. I think it would be useful to say that if they were made operational we might, or would—

President Kennedy: Of course then he would say that: "Well, if you do that, then we will . . ."

Thompson: As Chip [Bohlen] says, I agree with him, that if they're prepared to say: "All right, if you do this, then this is nuclear world war," then they would do that anyway. I think he [Khrushchev] would make a lot of threatening language but in very vague terms in keeping his—

President Kennedy: Yeah. I would think it more likely he would just grab Berlin. That's the more likely.

Thompson: I think that or, if we just made the first strike, then I think his answer would be, very probably, to take out one of our bases in Turkey, and make it quick too and then say that: "Now I want to talk."

I think the whole purpose of this exercise is to build up to talks with you, in which we try to negotiate out the bases. There are a lot of things that point to that.

One thing that struck me very much is, if it's so easy to camouflage these things or to hide them in the woods, why didn't they do it in the first place? They surely expected us to see them at some stage. That, it seems, would point to the fact their purpose was for preparation of negotiations.[9]

.   .   .

U. Alexis Johnson: Now, of course, Mr. President, there are obvious counters to the blockade. The obvious one being in Berlin.

President Kennedy: Yes.

Robert Kennedy: And also the argument against the blockade is that it's a very slow death. And it builds up, and it goes over a period of months, and during that period of time you've got all these people yelling and screaming about it, you've got the examination of Russian ships and the shooting down the Russian planes that try to land there. You have to do all those things.

.   .   .

Thompson: I think Khrushchev will deny that these are Soviet bases. [*Unclear.*] I think that what he'd say is: "What are you getting so excited about? The Cubans asked us for some missiles to deal with these emigre bases that are threatening, have attacked and are threatening attack." And that: "These are not missiles other than defensive. They're much less offensive than your weapons in Turkey. You've got these armed with nuclear warheads. We haven't given any nuclear weapons to them. These are simply to deal with the threat to Cuba." That would be his general line.

Rusk: Well, that would be patently false on its face because of the nature of the weapons. [*Mixed voices.*]

Bundy: If we act, they'd better be Cuban missiles, surely.

Rusk: I think our action is aimed at Cuba just as much as possible in this situation.

Thompson: You want to make it, if you do any of these steps, make it as easy as possible for him to back down.

I think almost certainly it leads to . . . his answer would be also: "This is so serious, I'm prepared to talk to you about it." We could scarcely refuse then. That's if you have world war being threatened. So I think you'd just immediately assume the next step. That's why I think that the Attorney General's point, while certainly valid, is somewhat weakened in that during this period you would be negotiating out this thing.

Rusk: But if he were to say: "Let's talk." Then you'd have to say to him: "Stop immediately all activities on such and such fields, sites and so forth."

Thompson: I'd impose a blockade while you do it.

President Kennedy: The blockade wouldn't be sufficient. Because he could go on developing what he's got there. We don't know how much he's got there.

Alexis Johnson: Yeah. But he would—You impose the blockade on Cuba, and he imposes the blockade on Berlin. And then you start to talk. And he would trade these two off.

Rusk: That's what he would figure.

Alexis Johnson: That's what he would figure, yes.

Thompson: Seems to me that one point on this—there are a lot of little signs—but I was always curious as to why he [Khrushchev] said he would defer this [a renewed confrontation over Berlin] until after the election. It seems to me it is all related to this.

McCone: I'm sure he was waiting for Berlin to ask.

Mr. President, you might be interested in General Eisenhower's reaction to this. I talked to him at your request.

I briefed him, showed him the photography and all the rest of this. He was careful, I think, not to take a position, because I had no position and I was very careful not to indicate to him your position, as agreed in our telephone conversation.

However, I can report that the thrust of his comments would indicate that he felt first that the existence of offensive capabilities in Cuba was intolerable from the standpoint of this country.

Secondly, I think he felt that limited actions such as strafing, as anticipated in I, or II, or even III, in this paper, would *not* be satisfactory. It would cause the greatest fear and concern with our allies and in all areas of the world where the Soviets might take similar action against installations—the United States installations that were in jeopardy with others such as Turkey or Pakistan or elsewhere.

He felt really that if a move was made—and I think if I pinned him down he would recommend that—it should be an all out military action. He talked of conceiving it to go right to the jugular first, not an invasion that involves landing on the beach and working slowly across the island. But a concentrated attack right on Havana first and taking the heart of the government out. And he felt if this was done, probably the thing would be in disarray, so it could be done with a minimum loss of life and time.

· · ·

C. Douglas Dillon: Mr. President, what is the whole idea, I'm not quite clear, of talking to Khrushchev ahead of time? What could he do that would remove this danger that we have from these MRBMs that are present and already there? What could he do that would satisfy us? It seems to me very difficult to see any action you can take that he might say: "Sure, I'll take them out sometime," and then do the opposite their old way.

I can't quite understand how we achieve anything. We may achieve something in sort of . . . for history in showing we've done something. But that's a different argument than the argument of really trying to achieve anything. I don't see how we really achieve anything with them.

Rusk: Yes, sir. There are the two alternatives. In general, he might reduce his involvement. He might step it up in his reply.

Dillon: But you can't believe his reply, whatever it is.

Rusk: But you can check his reply.

Thompson: I think the most he'd do in the way of concession would be to say that he will not take any further action while these talks go on. Meantime, we've said that we were going to keep an eye on him, and the problem is that if they become operational, they might be turned to the Cubans. [*Unclear.*] But I don't think he'd ever just back down.

· · ·

McCone: I don't think he can believe that we don't know all about this. It's done in a semiovert way. These convoys have moved. People have observed them. We've got refugee reports, gossip of all kinds. All that we know doesn't come from our aerial photography, by any manner or means.

I'm inclined to think that if we were . . . I think the board studying this would agree that there would be a . . . that Khrushchev would engage us in some type of a negotiation, that we'd be locked into [it] and couldn't move.[10] I don't think there would be an answer that would be so negative that it would give us freedom of action. Hence, it would be somewhat like the Geneva test suspension business. We got into it and we couldn't get out of it!

President Kennedy: The only, to me—

McCone: The [*unclear*] thing would be built up right under our—

President Kennedy: The only offer we would make, it seems to me, that would have any sense, according to him, would be the . . . giving him some out, would be our Turkey missiles.

Bundy: I believe, Mr. President, that that is equally valid if we make the sudden strike. Now, I think it may well be important to have a message in Khrushchev's hands *at that moment*, saying that we, among other things, all the wicked things that have led to this, but also that we understand this base problem and that we do expect to dismantle our Turkish base. That has one small advantage, which is that if he strikes back, we will have at least given him a peaceful out on that.

President Kennedy: You see, Berlin is—

Bundy: I don't think we can keep that Turkish base in this counter [-move].

Dillon: I think you get your same point by doing this thing simultaneously. That way as you do by the other thing [*unclear*].

Rusk: A direct exchange though that seems to be a Cuba-Turkey exchange, would be quite serious. Now it's true that we have talked with the Turks a year ago about getting those, taking the Jupiters out of there for other reasons.[11]

Bundy: No, no, I don't . . . to advance it is good, but as simply one way of reducing your costs and controlling your dangers.

Alexis Johnson: What you want is to talk to the Turks as if you were going to put a Polaris or two in those waters.[12]

Bundy: Yeah. Which should make everyone feel better. We have Soviet submarines are going to be in the Caribbean. I mean this is a political not a military problem.

McNamara: If there is a strike without a preliminary discussion with Khrushchev, how many Soviet citizens will be killed? I don't know. It'd be several hundred at absolute minimum.

Bundy: Killed, as in casualties?

McNamara: Killed. Absolutely. We're using napalm, 750-pound bombs. This is an extensive strike we're talking about.

Bundy: Well, I hope it is.

McNamara: I think we must assume we'll kill several hundred Soviet citizens. Having killed several hundred Soviet citizens, what kind of response does Khrushchev have open to him?

It seems to me that it just *must* be a strong response, and I think we should expect that. And, therefore, the question really is are we willing to pay some kind of a rather substantial price to eliminate these missiles? I think the price is going to be high. It may still be worth paying to eliminate the missiles. But I think we must assume it's going to be high—the very *least* it will be will be to remove the missiles in Italy and Turkey. I doubt we could settle [the problem] for that.

Dillon: Well, I think they'll take Berlin.

George Ball: Mr. President, I think that it's easy sitting here to, to underestimate the kind of sense of affront that you would have in the allied countries within—even perhaps in Latin America, if we act without warning, without giving Khrushchev some way out. Even though it may be illusory, I think we still have to do it because I think that the impact on the opinion and the reaction would be very much different.

A course of action where we strike without warning is like Pearl Harbor. It's the kind of conduct that one might expect of the Soviet Union. It is not conduct that one expects of the United States. And I have a feeling that this 24 hours [warning] to Khrushchev is really indispensable.

President Kennedy: And then if he says: "Well if you do that, we're going to grab Berlin." The point is, he's probably going to grab Berlin anyway.

Ball: Sure. We go ahead.

President Kennedy: He's going to take Berlin anyway.

Alexis Johnson: We pay that price.

McNamara: I suspect the price we pay to Khrushchev will be about the same, whether we give him the advance warning or don't give him the advance warning. The advance warning has the advantage of *possibly* giving him an out that would reduce the requirement that we enter with military force. That's a bare possibility, not great. It has the advantage George has mentioned of causing less friction with the rest of the world.

It has some disadvantages: a reduction of military surprise, but the disadvantage of that is not very great.

It carries with it, however, I believe, the great disadvantage that once you start down that course he outmaneuvers you.

Dillon: Well, the only advantage I see to it is the one you say, George, and that is that if you decide to do this, and you want to put yourself in the right position with the world, you [do this] as part of a [military] program that never stops. You have 24-hour notice. But you're under no illusion that anything he says is going to stop you.

You go ahead and do it [the strike]. You're not doing it for the purpose of getting him to come up and do something. What you're doing is to set the stage. That makes some sense.

Alexis Johnson: If you go the blockade route, you could take more time in these steps; on the other hand, you hold the danger of his outmaneuvering you.

President Kennedy: If he grabs Berlin, of course. Then everybody would feel we lost Berlin, because of these missiles, which as I say, do not bother them.

Thompson: My guess is that he would not immediately attack Berlin, but he would precipitate the real crisis at first, in order to try to sap our morale and—

Dillon: The difference is that in Cuba we've shown that we will take action, at a point which nobody knows. That's the great danger, now, to us; they think we will never take action. So I think our position has [unclear] possibility [unclear].

Bundy: I think he [Thompson] and I agree. I think the precipitation of a Berlin crisis is just as bad, if we've let this happen to us, against all our promises to ourselves.

Dillon: Worse.

President Kennedy: You mean, in other words, in late November when he [Khrushchev] grabs Berlin?

Robert Kennedy: What do we do when he moves into Berlin?

Bundy: If we could trade off Berlin, and not have it our fault. [Chuckles.]

Dillon: Well, that's the danger. To have already acted in Cuba and—

McNamara: Well, when we're talking about taking Berlin, what do we mean exactly? Does he take it with Soviet troops?

President Kennedy: That's what it would seem to me.

McNamara: Then we have . . . I think there's a real possibility. We have U.S. troops there. What do they do?

Taylor: They fight.

McNamara: They fight. I think that's perfectly clear.

President Kennedy: And they get overrun.

McNamara: Yes, they get overrun, exactly.

Unidentified: Well, you have a direct confrontation.

Robert Kennedy: Then what do we do?

Taylor: Go to general war, if it's in the interest of ours.

Unidentified: It's then general war. Consider the use of . . .

President Kennedy: You mean nuclear exchange? [Brief pause.]

Taylor: Guess you have to.

Bundy: I do see your . . . If you go in at the same time that you do this [attack on Cuba] and you'll say to him: "Berlin still means general war." I don't think he will do it that way.

Unidentified: I doubt whether he would . . . I don't think he'd [*unclear*].

Rusk: You'd have to start at least with tactical nuclear weapons if he tried to attack Berlin [*unclear*] a blockade.

Taylor: I think they'd use East German forces, rather than bringing their own troops in.

President Kennedy: Let me ask you. It seems to me we have been talking about the alliance, you've got two problems. One would be the problem of the alliance when we say to them that the presence of these missiles requires a military action by us. There's no doubt that they will oppose that, because they'll feel that their risks increase, and this is a risk to us. They'll argue what is Secretary McNamara's point.

If we don't take any action, then of course there will be a more gradual deterioration, I suppose. Isn't that the argument?

Rusk: I think that will be very fast.

Dillon: Very rapidly.

Bundy: Very rapid.

Dillon: Very rapid.

President Kennedy: After my statement, and then, I mean . . . Somehow we've got to take some action because we couldn't . . . Because the alliance would disintegrate.

Now, the question really is to what action we take which lessens the chances of a nuclear exchange, which obviously is the final failure. That's the obvious direction. . . . so that . . . And at the same time, maintain some degree of solidarity with our allies. Now, if you want that to be the course, then it would seem to me that II might [*unclear*].

Dillon: From the point of view of our allies, they think that certainly this strong setup in Cuba, this sort of weakens our ability to help them everywhere. So it is in the interest of the alliance to have this thing eliminated even though it does create some dangers.

President Kennedy: Now, to get a blockade on Cuba, would we have to declare war on Cuba with a blockade?

Bundy: Yes, we do.

．　．　．

President Kennedy: I think we shouldn't assume we have to declare war. The declaration of a state of war is a . . . Because it seems to me if you're going to do that, you really—it doesn't make any sense not to invade. I think we ought to consider whether we do need the . . .

At least let's just think with this a minute. We do the message to Khrushchev and tell him that if work continues, etcetera, etcetera. We at the same time launch the blockade. If the work continues, that we go in and take them out.

We don't declare war. It doesn't seem to me that a declaration of war . . . Then I think you have to get into an invasion. What do you do—when he—?

Ball: The great difficulty of a blockade without a declaration of war is that it is an illegal blockade, that it will be very difficult—

Bundy: It is an act of aggression against everybody else.

Ball: Everybody. Including our allies.

Rusk: What? You could have a blockade imposed under Article 8 of the Rio Treaty. After all, this is within the territorial framework of the Rio—

. . .

President Kennedy: Now, obviously, knowing the Soviets and the way Khrushchev reacts always, I don't think that we could assume that he's going to stop working.

I'm not sure exactly what we get out of this particular course of action, except that it doesn't go quite—it doesn't raise it [the escalation] immediately as high as it would be under ordinary, other conditions.

Ball: Mr. President, I would like to suggest that if you have a blockade, without some kind of ultimatum, that work must stop on the missile sites or you take them out. That you'll have an impossible position with the country, because they will not sit still while work goes on making these things operational. And I think this is one of the real problems of the blockade, is that it's a rather a slow agony and you build up all kinds of fears and doubts in the minds of people here.

Now on the question of the blockade, I think that it is Tommy's view that even the Soviet Union would be influenced by the question as to whether there was a declaration of war or not.

Thompson: Yes, I think so. You might be able to frame it in such a way that if your world postures were going to prevent this threat to us from these offensive weapons, and therefore, you were surveilling properly, if they . . . if work goes on, then we will stop any further supplies coming in. And for that reason, and to that extent, we are in a state of war with Cuba. It's a little different from saying we're going to war to destroy them. That's really the thing to make you . . . At least your world posture isn't [unclear].

Bundy: It seems to me that's your whole posture. Even if you go in with a strike, your posture is simply that this man has got entangled in the notion of doing unacceptable things, from the point of view of the security of the hemisphere. That has to be your posture. And if those stop, we're not concerned with what there is, the freedom of Cuba.

You will, in fact, get into the invasion before you're through, I'm sure. Either way.

Thompson: Well, I think you probably will the other way too, in the end, very likely.

.   .   .

Thompson: I don't think he'd want to take military action around Cuba. He's too much at a disadvantage there. It would be more dangerous than somewhere else. That's why I think he might respect it, or maybe he takes the big action in Berlin which is this gamble which he's shown for four years he's reluctant to take.

I think he's building up now to, and probing to see whether or not he could do it [Berlin]. The strongest argument to me for a strike, is that that would be very convincing and dangerous to him in Berlin.

Rusk: I think that this is the other part of the coin. He may feel he has to respond. But he knows that he's dealing with people [the American government] who are going to respond to him. [Khrushchev thinks:] Or maybe he's a little crazy and you can't trust them.

Taylor: I would think the credibility of our response in Berlin is enhanced by taking action in Cuba, rather than being diminished.

Bundy: I think this could be right. [*Mixed voices murmuring agreement.*]

Taylor: If he's going to blockade Berlin, he'll do it regardless of the . . .

President Kennedy: Let's say the situation was reversed, and he had made the statement about these missiles similar to the ones I made about [Cuba]. Similar to the ones about our putting missiles in Turkey. And he had made the statement saying that serious action could result if we put them in, and then we went ahead and put them in. Then he took them out [attacked them] some day.

To me, there's some advantages of that if it's all over. Hungary.[13] It's over so quick, supposedly, then really . . . almost the next move is up to him. Now, he may take these moves, but . . .

.   .   .

Taylor: I think sooner or later, we'll be—

President Kennedy: Well, that's what I meant. We go ahead. Let's just say this is a prospective course of action.

And tomorrow afternoon [Friday, October 19] I'd announce these [*unclear*] and the existence of these missiles, and say that we're calling Congress back, and when we consider this Saturday morning, so everybody knows about it. It isn't Pearl Harbor in that sense. We've told everybody.

Then we go ahead Saturday [October 20] and we take them out, and announce that they've been taken out. And if any more are put in, we're going to take those out.

Bundy: And the air force.

President Kennedy: And the air force. And that we don't want any war, and so on and so forth, but we're not going to permit this, in view of the fact that—

Taylor: We would take the air force out tomorrow, too? I mean, that's a little too fast for us—

President Kennedy: On Saturday.

Taylor: On the 21st [Sunday] we could get this [attack] out.

President Kennedy: Sunday has historic disadvantages [*referring to memories of Pearl Harbor*]. [*Bundy laughs.*]

· · ·

Robert Kennedy: I think George Ball has a hell of a good point.

President Kennedy: What?

Robert Kennedy: I think just the whole question of, you know, assuming that you do survive all this, we don't have, the fact that we're not . . . what kind of a country we are. The fact that you just don't [*unclear*].

Rusk: This business of carrying the mark of Cain on your brow for the rest of your lives is something [*unclear*].

Robert Kennedy: The fact that they'll be mad. We did this against Cuba. We've talked for 15 years that the Russians being [planning for] the first strike against us, and we'd never do that. Now, in the interest of time, we do that to a small country. I think it's a hell of a burden to carry.

Thompson: By far the strongest argument against this is that, killing the Russians, which to my mind means you are going to end up the whole way, and [*unclear*].

McNamara: Yes, this is why I don't believe we can stop with a large air strike. If we've killed Russians, we're going to have to go in. They can't stop. That's the main reason we have to go on.

President Kennedy: Let's just say, wait a second Bob, but if we make this announcement. Say, the afternoon before we send a message to Khrushchev, saying that: "We said that we'd have to do it. We're going to have to do it, and you ought to get the Russians out of there within the next 12 hours."

Now that . . . we lose a good deal of advantage as far as surprise. But what, of course, we are trying to do is to get these missiles. I'm not so worried about the air. If they [the aircraft] have got atomic bombs, they can get a couple of them over on us anyway, but at least the air you can take out, can't you? After all they don't maintain their position over that island each time a plane takes off. There are not that many, after all.

· · ·

Rusk: If the military situation doesn't require it, if you took just a little more time before you actually hit, and you let the several public opinions know about this in Cuba, as well as in the Soviet Union. It would be more difficult in the Soviet Union to get really informed. But if people realize that this is a major thing coming, then something may crack.

Thompson: There's one important related point to that, on which we have the first varied information. That is that Khrushchev got himself into this aggressive posture in Berlin and everything on his own. I mean, he's taken credit for it time and time again.

And the advantage that hasn't been mentioned about the notification to him is that he would have to show it to his colleagues, and there is a possibility of restraint there. I think there was some indication that in the abortive Paris summit meeting, that he was under strict instructions to break that up because they were afraid to go down the course he was following.[14] There is some chance that this could happen.

I mean we haven't had any solid information on this. But I can cite very minor things that happened at the time of the U-2 [shoot-down] where the military, who normally never talk to me, came over and tried to calm me down, that sort of thing, and showing that they were concerned that Khrushchev was being impetuous and running risks.

Although there are advantages and disadvantages, I feel strongly about some notification to him.

· · ·

Thompson: Well I think that's worth a little bit of discussion if there is the possibility, and I don't know about a deal for the bases for Turkey. And we substitute Polaris for the missiles we've got there. It seems to me in negotiations this isn't entirely to be rejected. Negotiations with him over this whole broad complex of questions. We've got to have it eventually or else have war.

And there's some advantage even in our proposing it. Say: "This won't wait for your trip in November, come on over."

Because these other paths, it seems to me, you're playing Russian roulette. You're flipping a coin as to whether you end up with world war or not.

President Kennedy: The only question is whether, giving him the time, whether he makes a guarantee. Now, as I say, he's not going to be any more happy about this than we are, I assume. Though the only thing is, he seems to be happier with the fact that he's taking much more of a risk than perhaps we would have taken.

But . . . if he responds, giving us an ultimatum in a sense, the question really is whether we're worse off then. There is an argument that we are worse off, if . . . in that . . .

He might accept something when it's accomplished, just like we might. [As] in the case of Hungary. He wouldn't accept it perhaps so much in advance.

Thompson: I think Mr. McCone's right. If you approach him, you are almost certainly going to have to get into negotiations.

Rusk: Well you may have a negotiation proposal, that doesn't mean that you have to get into it. Because the condition of it might be: You stop this work on these missiles—

Thompson: But if this is accompanied with this notification that we are going to bomb Cuba if the work goes on in this. And if it's accompanied with the blockade on any further supplies of this sort, this is a strong action.

President Kennedy: No, I feel that there's a difference in our action, and therefore in their response, between our knocking out these missiles and planes, and invading Cuba.

Thompson: I think there is.

President Kennedy: Obviously, if he knocked out our missiles . . . If he had said that he that was going to knock out our missile sites, and went and did it one afternoon in Turkey, it would be different than if the Russian army started to invade Turkey. Face it: there's a ten-day period of shootings.

And nobody knows what kind of success we're going to have with this invasion. Invasions are tough, hazardous. They've got a lot of equipment. A lot of—thousands of—Americans get killed in Cuba, and I think you're in much more of a mess than you are if you take out these . . .

I mean, this is all presumption, but I would think that if he invades Iran, it takes ten days and there's a lot of fighting in Iran. We're in a much more difficult position [with an invasion] than if he takes out those bases out there. It may be that his response would be the same, nobody can guess that, but by stretching it out you increase the . . .

Robert Kennedy: I don't think you have to make up your mind if you're going to invade. Even in the first 24 hours, 48 hours—

Taylor: We can't invade that fast, Mr. President. It will take at least seven days, unless we have some advance preparations that we can't make now.

President Kennedy: Why is that? Why? You mean, getting these people into there?

Taylor: Getting in position. We're now not making any moves that could give away our intentions.

Robert Kennedy: So I think you can always hold that out.

. . .

President Kennedy: What does that do for us though, Tommy? I mean, do you think that there's a chance that he might—do what with the . . .

Thompson: What Khrushchev will do?

Bundy: Khrushchev will call for a summit.

Thompson: I think that's almost certain.

I think it's quite possible that he would say that: "I'm prepared to take no further action in Cuba pending these talks." And in the meantime if we made this announcement there, would then make the announcement: That we will knock these things off; if there were any further work done on them. And stop any others from coming in.

In the meantime, the military makes their moves in preparation for an invasion. So I don't think [*unclear*]. The Russians would know this, and this is a strong warning to them. In some ways . . .

President Kennedy: Well, if we ever get to a summit, then he's going to be talking about Berlin.

Dillon: Well the only point in talking to them is the point originally that George made, [which] is that it gives us a better position with our allies. Not perhaps with Khrushchev but with the world.

Ball: I think the history too would give us a better position.

Dillon: That's it. For history, or to the world, we've done it. But that's what we're doing it for. We're not doing it to the . . . and if he does have other [*unclear*].

McCone: [*Unclear*] a demand on him right away. For instance, there are quite a number of ships, in transit. You demand that they would be turned around.

Thompson: If he does have trouble at this point—

McCone: And demand that this work stop at once.

Bundy: How much better are you off before history if you ask him 24 hours ahead of time, if he says: "I want a summit," and you say, "Nuts."

Rusk: [*Unclear.*] It's what has to happen in Cuba. Before there can be a summit.

Theodore Sorensen: And before we would call off—

Bundy: You can have that in the first message. It's very likely he would propose that we meet. But we can't meet unless we can have agreement on these things.

Taylor: Doesn't the Gromyko call this afternoon have some advantages from the possibility that we can get him to lie that he doesn't have them—

Rusk: Well I was going to suggest that the President consider expressing to Gromyko our deep disturbance about all this provocation in Cuba. Read to him from this paragraph of this statement of September 4th and see what Gromyko says. See if he will lie about it, because Ambassador Dobrynin said there are no offensive weapons there and so forth, but Dobrynin might not know.

Robert Kennedy: Well, what if he says there are? Then what do you do?

Rusk: I don't think the President ought to disclose to Gromyko what we have in mind, until we get an actual message to him [Khrushchev].

Robert Kennedy: What if he says to you: "We've just got the same kind of weapons you've got in Turkey. Because they're no more offensive than your weapons in Turkey"? Then what do you do? What do you do?

Rusk: He's talking about [a Turkish and NATO deployment decision made] five years ago and that's not relevant. Well, first the Rio Treaty.

Second, that we have here in this postwar era a rough status quo. When they took strong action against Hungary, on the ground that this was on their side of that status quo. Now they're penetrating into this hemisphere which violates not only modern obligations but historic well-known policies of the United States toward this hemisphere.

In fact, in any event NATO was itself built as a direct response to Soviet aggression, fully registered on the agenda of the U.N. In 1946 we didn't have any allies. There was no Rio Pact or NATO or CENTO or SEATO. The only allies that we had were those that were the disappearing allies that fought together during World War II. And these things came into being as a result of Stalin's policies. It makes all the difference in the world in this situation.

President Kennedy: How many missiles do we have in Turkey?

Bundy: Fifteen.

Plus nuclear-equipped aircraft?

McNamara: Yes.[15]

·   ·   ·

Taylor: One point we haven't mentioned, Mr. President, is the fact we still haven't all the intelligence. I'm impressed with how our minds have changed on this in 24 hours based upon this last intelligence. I think before we really commit ourselves we ought to get the full picture of this island.

Bundy: I agree.

Roswell Gilpatric: That's why Monday [October 22], I think, is better than Saturday [October 20].

Taylor: I think so, very much so.

President Kennedy: Monday?

Taylor: As long as you think you can hold it.

McCone: I think, tomorrow morning at this time we could have a quite a good deal more information, from the photography we ran yesterday.

I'm worried about this getting out. I think it's remarkable that it's been held this week. For that reason I feel that we mustn't delay too long.

President Kennedy: We haven't much time.

McNamara: Mr. President, I think we can hold it, however, till Monday [October 22]. I think the thing that is lacking is not more intelligence, although that will modify our position somewhat. What's lacking here is a real well thought out course of action, or alternative courses of action.

I think we ought to go back this afternoon and split up into a couple of groups and assign one group one course of action, another group another course of action and work them out in great detail. My guess is that both of these courses of action—really there are only two we're talking about.

I would call one a rapid introduction to military action. The other is a slow introduction to military action. Those are really the only two courses of action that we are talking about.

The slow introduction is a political statement followed, or accompanied, by a blockade. The rapid introduction is a brief notice to Khrushchev followed by a strike.

Now those are basically the only two alternatives we've discussed with you. We ought to take both of those and follow them through and find out what the prices are likely to be and how to minimize those prices.

President Kennedy: Well, let me ask you this. Is there anyone here who doesn't think that we ought to do something about them? I guess there's only . . .

McNamara: I, for one, am not clear however which of these two courses we should follow.

President Kennedy: Well, we've got so many different alternatives as far as the military action. As I say, we have the blockade without a declaration of war. We've got a blockade with a declaration of war. We've got strikes I, II, and III. We've got invasion. We've got notification to Khrushchev and what that notification ought to consist of.

Robert Kennedy: In other words, it's not really that bad though. Because if you have the strike, you don't have to make up your mind about the invasion. I mean, that's not going to come for three or four days—

President Kennedy: A blockade—

Bundy: In one sense you have to make up your mind to face it if you have to.

Robert Kennedy: Yeah. I think everybody's [*unclear*]. So all you have really, as Bob says, all you have is really the two courses of action.

And I think that as long as it really has come down to this after talking about this for 48 hours . . .

. . .

President Kennedy: But now, what have we . . . ? What is this group going to do as far as meeting? Trying to get some more final judgments on all these questions which we turned around?

Sorensen: Well, can I make a suggestion there, Mr. President?

It seems to me that the various military courses have been outlined here as the Secretary says. They need to be developed in more detail, step by step, and so on. But there has also been general though not unanimous agreement that you are likely to be making some kind of representation to Khrushchev ahead of time, maybe very shortly ahead of time. And I think that you ought to have, in great detail, drawn up what that representation would consist of. Were it a letter, what will be a satisfactory answer? And soon.

President Kennedy: Yes. Well, we have to have . . . certainly to do the Khrushchev. We have to decide in advance we'd do it, or whether I would make the public statement that we really had talked about the afternoon before.

These are some of the questions now. How do we want to function?

Rusk: Well, I think that we ought to draw the group together except for those who are going to be needed on military assignments.

McNamara: I don't believe the military problem, the military plans, need much elaboration. That isn't really what I was thinking about.

What I was really thinking about is this give-and-take here.

Bundy: That's very true.

McNamara: Which we haven't gone through. I think the price of any one of these actions is going to be very very high. I can visualize a whole series of actions that the Russians are going to take. And it seems to me we ought to lay those down. And then we ought to consider, how can we reduce that price?

And I would suggest, therefore, that under the guidance of State, because this is primarily an international political problem, we develop two groups here. And that we have Defense and State people in those two groups, and we take two or three hours this afternoon to let those two groups take these two basic alternatives. They can derive any number of variations they wish to.

But one is a minimum military action, a blockade approach, with a slow buildup to subsequent action. And the other is a very forceful military action with a series of variants as to how you enter it. And consider how the Soviets are going to respond. This is what we haven't done.

Dillon: Well, not only the Soviet response but what the response to the response will be.

McNamara: [*Mixed voices.*] I think that's it, exactly. So then, how we respond to these responses.

. . .

President Kennedy then leaves the meeting, and it begins to break up. A few participants stay behind and continue to talk in mixed conversations.

. . .

McNamara: I think you have to look to the end of the other course to really see the potential of a blockade. The end to the other course, the end to the other course is the missiles out of Cuba and some kind of a price. Now the minimum price are missiles out of Turkey and Italy, it seems to me.

Edwin Martin: With Castro still there?

McNamara: Pardon me?

Martin: Castro's still there.

Bundy: No, Castro goes out on either of these roads in my judgment, at the end of the road.

McNamara: He may or may not. This is something to think about.

But, in any case, the minimum price you pay under the military course of action is missiles out of Turkey and Italy. And they *may* be out by *physical* means. Because of the Russians moving against them. And you have a serious potential division in the alliance. Now it seems to me that's the *best* possible situation you could be in as a result of the military course. I can visualize many worse situations.

Under the blockade, [*tapes changing, material repeated*] the best possible situation—

Bundy: The other thing you can do with a blockade is consult. That's clear. You can consult with everybody.

McNamara: The best possible conclusion of a blockade, it seems to me, is that the alliance is not divided. You have agreed to take your missiles out of Turkey and Italy, and the Soviets have agreed either to take them out of Cuba or impose some kind of control comparable to your control over the missiles in Turkey and Italy. Now that's the *best* possible solution. There are many worse solutions.

Taylor: Now, I thought we were hoping last night that we would get the collapse of Castro.

McNamara: Well you might get that.

Martin: I think so, too. [*Unclear*] best, I think—

Bundy: I believe that Castro is not going to sit still for a blockade and that that's to our advantage. I'm convinced myself that Castro has to go. I always thought . . . It never occurred to [me before], I just think, his [Castro's] demon is self-destruction and we have to help him do that.

McNamara: Well, then you're going to pay a bigger price. Because—

Bundy: Later.

McNamara: Later. And I think that's a possibility. But the price is going to be larger. I really think we've got to think these problems through more than we have.

At the moment I lean to the blockade because I think it reduces the very serious risk of large-scale military action from which this country cannot benefit under what I call program two [surprise strike].

Bundy: Russian roulette and a broken alliance.

McNamara: Russian roulette, exactly so, and a broken alliance.

Robert Kennedy: Can I say this? What are the chances of . . . You've got to say to him, "They can't continue to build these missiles. All right then, so you're going to have people flying over all the time." Well, at night it looks a little different than it did the next morning.

McNamara: Oh, he's not going to stop building. He's going to continue to build.

Robert Kennedy: But not if you knock them out though, Bob?

McNamara: I think this goes back to what you say, at the time of blockade. I'm not sure you can say that.

Robert Kennedy: Are you going to let him continue to build the missiles?

McNamara: This goes back to what you begin to negotiate. He says: "I'm not going to stop building. You have them in Turkey." At the time you've acted by putting the blockade on. That's done.

Robert Kennedy: All right. Then you let them build the missiles? And you let them—

McNamara: Then you talk.

Thompson: Is your assumption that he would run the blockade?

McNamara: No, no. But they have goods inside that they use to carry on construction.

Robert Kennedy: We tell them they can build as many missiles as they want?

McNamara: Oh, no. No, what we say is: "We are going to blockade you. This is a danger to us. We insist that we talk this out and the danger be removed."

Robert Kennedy: Right. Now, but they're going to go ahead and build the missiles.

McNamara: That's right.

[*responding to an interjection*] Overflights, definitely.

So they—

Robert Kennedy: They put the missiles in place and then they announce they've got atomic weapons.

McNamara: Sure. And we say we have them in Turkey. And we're not going to tolerate this.

Sorensen: What is the relationship then between the blockade and the danger?

McNamara: Well, all this time Castro is being strangled.

Thompson: Why wouldn't you say that if construction goes on, you would strike?

McNamara: Well, I might, I might. But that is a more dangerous form of the blockade.

· · ·

President Kennedy went to his scheduled meeting with the Japanese minister for trade and industry, Eisaku Sato, and then had lunch in the Mansion.

Near Midnight

Kennedy Summarizes a Late-Night Meeting

After lunch and a brief swim, while still in the Mansion, President Kennedy met with former secretary of state Dean Acheson. Acheson outlined his views in favor of an immediate air strike without prior warning to the Soviets.

At 3:30 P.M. Rusk and McNamara came back over to the White House from their meetings at the State Department and reported on their progress. At 4:30 Rusk again returned to the White House, this time with Thompson, to prepare President Kennedy for his meeting with Soviet foreign minister Andrei Gromyko. That meeting began at 5:00. Meanwhile Bundy, as planned, briefed and talked with former secretary of defense Robert Lovett. McNamara and McCone also spoke to Lovett.

The meeting with Gromyko lasted until about 7:15. Gromyko emphasized the need to settle the Berlin issue. Though he repeated the promise that the Soviets would do nothing before the November elections in the United States, he warned that later in that month the Soviet government would bring the Berlin problem to conclusion. If there was no understanding, Gromyko said that "the Soviet government would be compelled, and Mr. Gromyko wished to emphasize the word *compelled*," to take steps to end the Western presence in Berlin. Gromyko described the Western military presence in Berlin as a "rotten tooth which must be pulled out."

Gromyko also complained about U.S. threats against Cuba. The Soviet Union was only training Cubans in the use of defensive weapons. President Kennedy said that "there was no intention to invade Cuba" and that he would have been glad to give Khrushchev assurances to that effect, if asked. Yet Soviet shipments of arms to Cuba were an extremely serious matter, as a result of which the two countries faced "the most dangerous situation since the end of the war [World War II]. "

Returning to Cuban fears, Gromyko referred to the Bay of Pigs invasion attempt of 1961. Kennedy cut in to say that he'd already admitted that this had been a mistake. He repeated that he "would have given assurances that there would be no further invasion, either by refugees or by U.S. forces." But since the Soviet shipments of arms had begun in July, the situation had changed.

Kennedy then read from his September 4 and 13 public statements, looking for a reaction. None was evident. The two leaders also discussed the ongoing negotiations to restrict nuclear testing and Kennedy agreed to see Khrushchev when the Soviet leader came to the United States for the U.N. meeting in November.[16]

After Gromyko left, Rusk and Thompson stayed and President Kennedy asked Lovett and Bundy to join them.

President Kennedy returned to his residential quarters for dinner at about 8:20. Meanwhile, at the State Department, meetings had continued with people coming and going. State's acting legal adviser, Leonard Meeker, had been brought into the deliberations to do a legal analysis of blockade options. Meeker suggested the term *defensive quarantine* instead of *blockade*.

At about 9:15 P.M. Kennedy called the group of advisers back to the White House. Since the meeting was after hours, he dared not hold it in the West Wing of the White House for fear that reporters would notice and wonder. So the meeting was held in the Oval Room on the second floor of the Executive Mansion. Therefore the session could not be tape-recorded.

After the others left, President Kennedy went to the Oval Office, possibly accompanied by his brother. Aware that he had been unable to record the meeting, President Kennedy turned on the recording machine there in the Oval Office and began to dictate.

President Kennedy: [*Unclear*], Secretary [Robert] McNamara, Deputy Secretary [Roswell] Gilpatric, General [Maxwell] Taylor, Attorney General [Robert Kennedy], George Ball, Alexis Johnson, Ed Martin, McGeorge Bundy, Ted Sorensen.[17] During the course of the day, opinions had obviously switched from the advantages of a first strike on the missile sites and on Cuban aviation to a blockade.

Dean Acheson, with whom I talked this afternoon, stated that while he was uncertain about any of the courses, favored the first strike as being most likely to achieve our result and less likely to cause an extreme Soviet reaction. That strike would take place just against the missile sites.

When I saw Robert Lovett, later after talking to Gromyko, he was not convinced that any action was desirable. He felt that the missile strike, the first strike, would be very destructive to our alliances. The Soviets would inevitably bring about a reprisal; that we would be blamed for it—particularly if the reprisal was to seize Berlin. And that we'd be regarded as having brought about the loss of Berlin with inadequate provocation, they having lived with these intermediate-range ballistic missiles for years.

Bundy continued to argue against any action on the grounds that there would be, inevitably, a Soviet reprisal against Berlin and that this would divide our alliance and that we would bear that responsibility. He felt we would be better off to merely take note of the existence of these missiles, and to wait until the crunch comes in Berlin, and not play what he thought might be the Soviet game.

Everyone else felt that for us to fail to respond would throw into question our willingness to respond over Berlin, [and] would divide our allies and our country. [They felt] that we would be faced with a crunch over Berlin in two or three months and that by that time the Soviets would have a large missile arsenal in the Western Hemisphere which would weaken our whole position in this hemisphere and cause us, and face us with the same problems we're going to have in Berlin anyway.

The consensus was that we should go ahead with the blockade beginning on Sunday night. Originally we should begin by blockading Soviets against the shipment of additional offensive capacity, [and] that we could tighten the blockade as the situation requires. I was most anxious that we not have to announce a state of war existing, because it would obviously be bad to have the word go out that we were having a war rather than that it was a limited blockade for a limited purpose.

It was determined that I should go ahead with my speeches so that we don't take the cover off this, and come back Saturday night [October 20].

President Kennedy then turned off the tape recorder.

Friday, October 19, 1962

To the press and public, this was a day on which the President was scheduled to fly to Cleveland, Ohio, and then on to Illinois for speeches and activities in Springfield and Chicago. But before leaving town, Kennedy wanted to confer secretly and directly with his military leaders.

9:45 A.M.

Meeting with the Joint Chiefs of Staff

Continuing their analysis of earlier U-2 photography, National Photographic Interpretation Center analysts confirmed that the two MRBM sites near San Cristobal each had a regiment with eight SS-4s on launchers and eight more at hand for a second salvo. They pronounced both sites already operational. They had found another regiment of SS-4s east of Havana near Sagua La Grande. They expected these eight missiles to be operational within a week.

Although they had still spotted no IRBMs, the suppositions of the day before were hardening into a certainty that the two sites near Guanajay were intended for 2,200-mile-range SS-5s. The photos showed permanent construction, for SS-5s were too big and heavy to be fired from mobile launchers. And it was the construction pattern that was the giveaway, for they had not only seen it in photographs of the Soviet Union; they had technical data supplied by the spy Oleg Penkovsky. Seeing evidence of a nuclear warhead storage site in the area, the analysts predicted that the IRBMs would be up and operational in six to eight weeks.[1]

The Joint Chiefs of Staff met at 9:00. Taylor told them about the previous night's meeting and that the President and his advisers were leaning toward a blockade of some kind. He said President Kennedy wanted to see them in a few minutes. The Chiefs agreed to recommend a massive air strike against Cuban military targets with no advance warning. They disagreed on the question of invasion; Taylor resisted this step. They then drove to the White House. McNamara joined them for their meeting with the President.

President Kennedy's view of the Joint Chiefs was respectful but skeptical, with a touch of the former junior Navy officer's attitude toward top brass. His most recent experience with the military in a crisis had angered him—not for the first time. On September 30, only a few weeks earlier, at the peak of the crisis over the admission of a black student, James Meredith, to the University of Mississippi, Kennedy had called on troops to provide security amid violent chaos on the campus. He had felt the military was unresponsive, remarking at one point to an aide (with the tape recorder running) that "They always give you their bullshit about their instant reaction and their split-second timing, but it never works out. No wonder it's so hard to win a war."

The Chiefs filed into the Cabinet Room at 9:45. Taylor was accompanied by Air Force Chief of Staff Curtis LeMay, a formidably competent figure then widely respected in the country for his prowess as a leader and organizer both during World War II and in the creation of the Air Force's Strategic Air Command. With them was Chief of Naval Operations George Anderson, a tall, handsome admiral who looked as if Hollywood had cast him for the part. Anderson was widely admired in the Navy as a "sailor's sailor," and his sermons on clean living had earned him the nickname "Straight Arrow." There was also Army Chief of Staff Earle Wheeler, whose reputation had been earned as a brilliant staff officer and Washington planner. Marine Corps commandant David Shoup had the opposite reputation. Shoup had won the Medal of Honor on the blood-soaked atoll of Tarawa in 1943 but was known, by 1962, as uninformed or erratic in the paper battles of the Pentagon. President Kennedy turned on the recorder in the Cabinet Room as the meeting began.

Maxwell Taylor: Mr. President, as you know, we've been meeting on this subject ever since we discovered the presence of missiles in Cuba. And I would say the debates in our own midst have followed very closely in parallel those that you've heard from your other advisers.

From the outset I would say that we felt we were united on the military requirement: we could not accept Cuba as a missile base; that we should either eliminate or neutralize the missiles there and prevent any others coming in. From a military point of view that meant three things.

First, attack with the benefit of surprise those known missiles and offensive weapons that we knew about. Secondly, continued surveillance then to see what the effect would be. And third, a blockade to prevent the others from coming in.

I would say, again, from a military point of view, that seemed clear. We were united on that.

There has been one point, the importance of which we recognize, where we have never really firmed up our own position. Namely, the political requirements and the measures to offset the obvious political disabilities of this course of action. We know it's not an easy course of action, and it has at least two serious weaknesses.

The first is we're never sure of getting all the missiles and the offensive weapons if we fire a strike. Secondly, we see—all of us, all your advisers—that there would be a very damaging effect of this on our alliances.

To offset that, I have reported back some of the political measures considered. I think most of us would say we recognize that some of those things must be done, although they would be at some loss to our military effectiveness of our strikes. I reported the trend last night which I've detected for a couple of days, to move away from what I would call a straight military solution toward one based on military measures plus blockade. And that has been reported to the Chiefs this morning. I've taken the task Mr. McNamara assigned last night and we're working on that at this time.

I think the benefit this morning, Mr. President, would be for you to hear the other Chiefs' comments either on our basic, what I call the military plan, or how they would see the blockade plan.

President Kennedy: Let me just say a little, first, about what the problem is, from my point of view.

First, I think we ought to think of why the Russians did this. Well, actually, it was a rather dangerous but rather useful play of theirs. If we do nothing, they have a missile base there with all the pressure that brings to bear on the United States and damage to our prestige.

If we attack Cuba, the missiles, or Cuba, in any way then it gives them a clear line to take Berlin, as they were able to do in Hungary under the Anglo war in Egypt. We will have been regarded as—they think we've got this fixation about Cuba anyway—we would be regarded as the trigger-happy Americans who lost Berlin. We would have no support among our allies. We would affect the West Germans' attitude towards us. And [people would believe] that we let Berlin go because we didn't have the guts to endure a situation in Cuba. After all, Cuba is 5[,000] or 6,000 miles from them. They don't give a damn about Cuba. And they do care about Berlin and about their own security. So they would say that we endangered their interests and security and reunification [of Germany] and all the rest, because of the preemptive action that we took in Cuba. So I think they've got . . . I must say I think it's a very satisfactory position from their point of view. If you take the view that what really . . .

And thirdly, if we do nothing then they'll have these missiles and they'll be able to say that any time we ever try to do anything about Cuba, that they'll fire these missiles. So that I think it's dangerous, but rather satisfactory, from their point of view.

If you take the view, really, that what's basic to them is Berlin and there isn't any doubt [about that]. In every conversation we've had with the Russians, that's what . . . Even last night we [Soviet foreign minister Andrei Gromyko and I] talked about Cuba for a while, but Berlin— that's what Khrushchev's committed himself to personally. So, actually, it's a quite desirable situation from their point of view.

Now, that's what makes our problem so difficult. If we go in and take them out on a quick air strike, we neutralize the chance of danger to the United States of these missiles being used, and we prevent a situation from arising, at least within Cuba, where the Cubans themselves have the means of exercising some degree of authority in this hemisphere.

On the other hand, we increase the chance greatly, as I think they— there's bound to be a reprisal from the Soviet Union, there always is—of their just going in and taking Berlin by force at some point. Which leaves me only one alternative, which is to fire nuclear weapons—which is a hell of an alternative—and begin a nuclear exchange, with all this happening.

On the other hand, if we begin the blockade that we're talking about, the chances are they will begin a blockade and say that we started it. And there'll be some question about the attitude of the Europeans. So that, once again, they will say that there will be this feeling in Europe that the Berlin blockade has been commenced by our blockade.

So I don't think we've got any satisfactory alternatives. When we balance off that our problem is not merely Cuba but it is also Berlin and when we recognize the importance of Berlin to Europe, and recognize the importance of our allies to us, that's what has made this thing be a dilemma for three days. Otherwise, our answer would be quite easy.

Curtis LeMay: Mr. President—

President Kennedy: On the other hand, we've got to do something. Because if we do nothing, we're going to have the problem of Berlin anyway. That was very clear last night [in the meeting with Gromyko]. We're going to have this thing stuck right in our guts, in about two months [when the IRBMs are operational]. And so we've got to do something.

· · ·

Taylor: Well, I would just say one thing and then turn it over to General LeMay. We recognize all these things, Mr. President. But I think we'd all be unanimous in saying that really our strength in Berlin, our strength anyplace in the world, is the credibility of our response under certain conditions. And if we don't respond here in Cuba, we think the credibility of our response in Berlin is endangered.

President Kennedy: That's right. That's right. So that's why we've got to respond. Now the question is: What kind of response?

LeMay: Well, I certainly agree with everything General Taylor has said. I'd emphasize, a little strongly perhaps, that we don't have any choice except direct military action. If we do this blockade that's proposed and political action, the first thing that's going to happen is your missiles are going to disappear into the woods, particularly your mobile ones.[2] Now, we can't find them then, regardless of what we do, and then we're going to take some damage if we try to do anything later on.

President Kennedy: Well, can't there be some of these undercover now, in the sense of not having been delivered?

LeMay: There is a possibility of that. But the way they've lined these others up—I would have say that it's a small possibility. If they were going to hide any of them, then I would think they would have hid them all. I don't think there are any hid. So the only danger we have if we haven't picked up some that are setting there in plain sight. This is possible. If we do low-altitude photography over them, this is going to be a tip-off too.

Now, as for the Berlin situation, I don't share your view that if we knock off Cuba, they're going to knock off Berlin. We've got the Berlin problem staring us in the face anyway. If we don't do anything to Cuba, then they're going to push on Berlin and push *real hard* because they've got us on the run. If we take military action against Cuba, then I think that the . . .

President Kennedy: What do you think their reprisal would be?

LeMay: I don't think they're going to make any reprisal if we tell them that the Berlin situation is just like it's always been. If they make a move we're going to fight. Now I don't think this changes the Berlin situation at all, except you've got to make one more statement on it.

So I see no other solution. This blockade and political action, I see leading into war. I don't see any other solution for it. It will lead right into war. This is almost as bad as the appeasement at Munich.

[*Pause.*]

Because if this [*unclear*] blockade comes along, their MiGs are going to fly. The IL-28s are going to fly against us. And we're just going to gradually drift into a war under conditions that are at great disadvantage to us, with missiles staring us in the face, that can knock out our airfields in the southeastern portion [of the United States]. And if they use nuclear weapons, it's the population down there. We just drift into a war under conditions that we don't like. I just don't see any other solution except direct military intervention *right now.*

George Anderson: Well, Mr. President, I feel that the course of action recommended to you by the Chiefs from the military point of view is the right one. I think it's the best one from the political point of view.

I'll address myself to the alternative of the blockade. If we institute a blockade, from a military point of view we can carry it out. It is easier for us and requires less forces if we institute a complete blockade rather than a partial blockade, because instituting a partial blockade involves visit and search of all of these neutral ships, and taking them in, perhaps, to ports, will certainly cause a great deal more concern on the part of the neutrals, than if we go ahead and institute a complete blockade.

If we institute a complete blockade, we are immediately having a confrontation with the Soviet Union because it's the Soviet-bloc ships which are taking the material to Cuba.

The blockade will not affect the equipment that is already in Cuba, and will provide the Russians in Cuba time to assemble all of these missiles, to assemble the IL-28s, to get the MiGs and their command and control system ready to go. And I feel that, as this goes on, I agree with General LeMay that this will escalate and then we will be required to take other military action at greater disadvantage to the United States, to our military forces, and probably would suffer far greater casualties within the United States if these fanatics do indeed intend to fire any missiles.

We certainly cannot guarantee under those circumstances that we could prevent damage and loss of life in the United States itself. I think we have a good chance of greatly minimizing any loss of life within the United States under the present conditions, if we act fairly soon, although we do recognize they're moving very fast. I do not see that, as long as the Soviet Union is supporting Cuba, that there is any solution to the Cuban problem except a military solution.

On the other hand, we recognize fully the relationship to the Berlin situation. The Communists have got in this case a master situation, from their point of view, where every course of action posed to us is characterized by unpleasantries and disadvantages. It's the same thing as Korea all over again, only on a grander scale.

We recognize the great difficulty of a military solution in Berlin. I think, on balance, the taking [of] positive, prompt affirmative action in Berlin demonstrating the confidence, the ability, the resolution of the

United States on balance, I would judge it, would be to deter the Russians from more aggressive acts in Berlin and, if we didn't take anything, they'd feel that we were weak. So I subscribe fully to the concept recommended by the Joint Chiefs.

President Kennedy: It seems to me that we have to assume that just when our two military . . . When we grabbed their two U.N. people [as spies] and they threw two of ours out [of the Moscow embassy], we've got to assume there's going to be—

Anderson: Tit for tat.

President Kennedy: —that they would strike this . . . I mean they can't do it [accept our attack] any more than we can let these go on without doing something. They can't let us just take out, after all their statements, take out their missiles, kill a lot of Russians and not do anything.

It's quite obvious that what they . . . I would think they would do, is try to get Berlin. But that may be a risk we have to take, but it would seem to me . . .

LeMay: Well, history has been, I think, the other way, Mr. President. Where we have taken a strong stand they have backed off. In Lebanon, for instance.[3]

Taylor: I would agree, Mr. President. I think from the point of view of face they'll do something. But I think it will be considerably less, depending on the posture we show here. I can't really see them putting the screws in. The dangers of hitting Berlin are just as great or greater after our action down here, because we have our—

President Kennedy: Right. But I think they're going to wait for three months until they get these things [the IRBMs as well as the MRBMs] all ready, and then squeeze us in Berlin. The only thing, at that point, for what it is worth [and] it may not be worth much, but at least we'd have the support of Europe this way.

Taylor: That is true.

President Kennedy: We have to figure that Europe will regard this action . . . no matter what pictures we show afterwards of [missiles] as having been . . .

Taylor: I think that's right.

Earle Wheeler: Mr. President, in my judgment, from a military point of view, the lowest-risk course of action if we're thinking of protecting the people of the United States against a possible strike on us is to go ahead with a surprise air strike, the blockade, and an invasion because these series of actions progressively will give us increasing assurance that we really have got the offensive capability of the Cuban-Soviets cornered. Now admittedly, we can never be absolutely sure until and unless we actually occupy the island.

Now, I've also taken into consideration a couple of other things at the present time. To date, Khrushchev has not *really* confronted us with *Soviet* power. In other words, he has not declared Cuba a part of the Warsaw Pact. Nor has he made an announcement that this is a Soviet base, although I think that there is a chance that he may do this at any time, particularly later in November when he comes to the United States. And this course of action would then immediately have us confronting the Soviets and not Cuba. And at that time Soviet prestige, world prestige, would be at stake, which it is not at the present time.

The effect of this base in Cuba, it seems to me, has at least two sizable advantages from his point of view and two sizable disadvantages from our point of view.

First, the announcement of a Soviet base in Cuba would immediately have a profound effect in all of Latin America at least and probably worldwide because the question would arise: Is the United States incapable of doing something about it or unwilling to do something about it? In other words, it would attack our prestige.

Not only that. Increasingly, they can achieve a sizable increase in offensive Soviet strike capabilities against the United States, which they do not now have. They do have ICBMs that are targeted on us, but they are in limited numbers. Their air force is not by any manner of means of the magnitude and capability that they probably would desire. And this short-range missile force gives them a sort of a quantum jump in their capability to inflict damage on the United States. And so as I say, from a military point of view, I feel that the lowest risk course of action is the full gamut of military action by us. That's it, sir.

President Kennedy: Thank you, General.

David Shoup, the Marine commandant, offered rambling comments supporting LeMay but also asserting that the Soviet Union already had the capacity to attack the United States without needing missiles in Cuba.

. . .

President Kennedy: Well, it is a fact that the number of missiles there, let's say . . . no matter what they put in there, we could live today under. If they don't have enough ICBMs today, they're going to have them in a year. They obviously are putting in a lot of—

LeMay: This increases their accuracy against the 50 targets that we know that they could hit now.

But the big thing is, if we leave them there, is the blackmail threat against not only us but the other South American countries that they may decide to operate against.

There's one other factor that I didn't mention that's not quite in our field, [which] is the political factor. But you invited us to comment on this at one time. And that is that we have had a talk about Cuba and the SAM sites down there. And you have made some pretty strong statements about their being defensive and that we would take action against offensive weapons. I think that a blockade and political talk would be considered by a lot of our friends and neutrals as being a pretty weak response to this. And I'm sure a lot of our own citizens would feel that way, too.

In other words, you're in a pretty bad fix at the present time.

President Kennedy: What did you say?

LeMay: You're in a pretty bad fix.

President Kennedy: You're in there with me. [*Slight laughter, a bit forced.*] Personally.

Taylor: With regard to the blockade plan, Mr. President, I say we're studying it now to see all the implications. We're not . . . we really haven't gone into it deeply. There are two things that strike us from the outset. One is the difficulty of maintaining surveillance. We just don't see how they can do that without taking losses and getting into some form of air warfare over this island.

.   .   .

President Kennedy: If we were going to do the . . . There's a good deal of difference between taking a strike which strikes just the missiles that are involved—that's one action which has a certain effect, an escalating effect. The other is to do a strike which takes out all the planes, that's very much of an island sweep. Third is the invasion, which takes a period of 14 days or so by the time we get it mounted. Maybe 18 days. Well we have to assume that—I don't know what—the Soviet response to each of these would have to be different. If one were slowly building up to an invasion and fighting our way across the island . . . That's a different situation from taking out these offensive weapons. It seems to you that—

LeMay: I think we have got to do more than take out the missiles, because if you don't take out their air at the same time you're vulnerable down in that section of the world [*unclear*] strikes from their air. They could come in at low altitude and do it. Because we haven't got much of a low altitude capability.

In addition, that air would be used against any other surveillance you have, too. So if you take out the missiles, I think you've got to take out their air along with it, and their radar, and their communications, the whole works. It just doesn't make any sense to do anything but that.

President Kennedy: Well, except that what . . . they've had the air there for some time. And what we've talked about is having ground-to-ground missiles.

There isn't any . . . You know, as I say, the problem is not really some war against Cuba. But the problem is part of this worldwide struggle where we face the Communists, particularly, as I say, over Berlin. And with the loss of Berlin, the effect of that and the responsibility we would bear. As I say, I think the Egyptian and the Hungary thing are the obvious parallels that I'm concerned about.

LeMay: If you lose in Cuba you're going to get more and more pressure right on Berlin. I'm sure of that.

Taylor: This worldwide problem has certainly been before us, Mr. President. We haven't ignored it. For me, it's been a deterrent to my enthusiasm for any invasion of Cuba, as I think you know.

On the other hand, now that we've seen that it's not just going to be a place where they needle us by mobile missiles as I thought perhaps earlier in the week, but really an organized base where the numbers of missile complexes are—

President Kennedy: Of course General Shoup's point, which is also made, is that there isn't any doubt [that] if it isn't today, it's within a year they're going to have enough. . . . when we've talked about the number of ICBMs they have. They may not be quite as accurate. [But] they've got enough, they put them on the cities and you know how soon these casualty figures [mount up]—80 million, whether it's 80 or 100— you're talking about the destruction of a country. So that it . . . just regardless if you begin to duplicate your . . .

Taylor: And we lose our—

President Kennedy: You'll lose it all on cities.

Taylor: And we can never talk about invading again, after they get these missiles, because they've got these pointed at our head.

President Kennedy: Well, the logical argument is that we don't really have to invade Cuba. That's not really . . . That's just one of the difficulties that we live with in life, like we live with the Soviet Union and China.

That problem, however, is after . . . for us not to do anything, then wait until he brings up Berlin. And then we can't do anything about Cuba.

But I do think we ought to be aware of the fact that the existence of these missiles does add to the danger but doesn't create it. The danger is right there now. They've got enough to give us, between submarines and ICBMs, or whatever planes they do have, I mean now they can kill, especially if they concentrate on the cities, I mean they've pretty well got us there anyway.

Taylor: And by logic we ought to be able to say we can deter these missiles as well as the Soviet missiles, the ones from the Soviet Union. I think the thing that worries us, however, is that these [being] in potentially under the control of Castro. Castro would be quite a different fellow to own missiles than Khrushchev. I don't think that's the case now, and perhaps Khrushchev would never willingly do so. But there's always the risk of their falling into Cuban hands.

.   .   .

President Kennedy: Well, let me ask you this. If we go ahead with this air strike, either on the missiles or on the missiles and the planes, I understand the recommendation is to do both. When could that be ready?

LeMay: We can be ready for attack at dawn on the 21st [Sunday], that being the earliest possible date. The optimum date would be Tuesday morning [October 23].

Taylor: Tuesday is the optimum date.

.   .   .

President Kennedy: Then, now the invasion would take . . .

Taylor: Seven days after the air strike you could start the invasion going on for about 11 days.

Unidentified: [*Unclear.*]

President Kennedy: It would go on for 11 days and then we would . . . We would, in other words, be prepared for it, but not necessarily . . . we'd still have seven days to decide whether we want to go in.

Taylor: We have flexibility. Once we strike we would start moving [*unclear*] even though you didn't decide that [*unclear*].

Wheeler: Mr. President, going back to the relationships between Cuba and Berlin. And I certainly feel that the Soviets have concocted what they think is a masterful strategy.

There is no acceptable military solution to the Berlin problem, whereas there is in Cuba. There's no acceptable political-economic solution to the Cuban problem. Conceivably, a solution to the Berlin problem lies in the diplomatic-economic-political field, if we put enough pressure on the Soviet bloc.

Now if we act in Cuba and they respond by making immediately a treaty with the East Germans and surrounding Berlin, denying our access to Berlin, our garrison—the people in Berlin—can survive there for a long time, assuming that the Russians are not just overrunning the city with their own troops. Could we not apply sufficient diplomatic-economic-financial pressures to the entire Soviet bloc and gradually expand this so that we, for a suitable period of time, we're progressively cutting the Soviet bloc off from their access to most of the countries in the free world? And at the same time have some sort of an acceptable, what would appear to be an acceptable long-range political solution to all of Berlin?

Forty-eight seconds excised as classified information.

President Kennedy: In any case, there's no . . . unfortunately. I'm just thinking we come out second-best. So we just . . . I think there's a meeting at eleven. I might as well continue with my tour because [*unclear*] surface all this, and we'll be back in touch tonight. I'm probably [*unclear*].

I appreciate your views. As I said, I'm sure we all understand how rather unsatisfactory our alternatives are. The argument for the blockade was that what we want to do is to avoid, if we can, nuclear war by escalation or imbalance. The Soviets increase; we use [force]; they blockade Berlin. They blockade for military purposes. Then we take an initial action so that . . . We've got to have some degree of control. Those people [the Soviets] last night were so away from reality that there's no telling what the response would be.

Taylor: Did he [Gromyko] give any clue, Mr. President?

President Kennedy: Well, he talked tough about Berlin. On Cuba he really just talked about their defensive aspirations. He said, "We're only sending defensive weapons in." Of course, that's how they define these weapons, as defensive.

Taylor: Well, Mr. President—

President Kennedy: General Shoup, your point is not to argue against action by saying that we've been living with this sort of thing for years.

David Shoup: A lot of people advance that. That is a real question for a reconciliation, for our people, and you and everybody else when . . . We've had a hell of a lot more than this aimed at us, and we didn't attack it. But they're closer, their distance is closer, and as General LeMay pointed out, there are certain areas in which he will certainly get in, if, as I presume, we're going to take him on.

President Kennedy: Well, I think . . . I don't think that it adds particularly to our danger. I think our danger is the use of nuclear weapons [*unclear*] anyway. Particularly on urban sites. With submarines and planes. They've got enough now; they sure will have in a year's [time]. I don't think that's probably the major argument. The major argument is the political effect on United States [*unclear*] Cuba. The certainty is the invasion is key for us.

On the other hand, there are going to be a lot of people that are just going to move away from us, figuring that our . . . I mean, we haven't prepared [*unclear*] existence. There isn't any doubt if we announce evidence of the missile sites, most people, including the Soviets would take a provocative act. Instead, the first announcement may be, under the plan suggested, an act that we took. So that we've got a real problem in maintaining the alliance.

Wheeler: Today . . . am I clear that you are addressing yourself as to whether anything at all should be done?

President Kennedy: That's right.

Wheeler: But that if military action is to be taken, you agree with us.

President Kennedy: Yeah.

Shoup: I question how to reconcile . . . the last thing you really want is [*unclear*] less threat than you've had for a long time.

Taylor: Mr. President, may I mention one thing before you go on because time is running out: the question of the low-level [reconnaissance] flights to get evidence. We discussed [them] last night and we're prepared to do them tomorrow. I'm a little concerned about doing that if there's any likelihood of our following a military course.

President Kennedy: Exactly. Oh, I agree. That's why we've got—

McNamara: No question that we should not undertake those until a decision has been made as to which course of action would—presumably you're ready?

LeMay: Yes, sir. We are.

McNamara: Good.

LeMay: [*Unclear.*]

Taylor: Thank you very much, Mr. President. We appreciate the chance to talk with you.

. . .

President Kennedy left the room. After a while, only the Joint Chiefs remained. The tape recorder continued to run.

Shoup: Well what do you guys [*unclear*]. You, you pulled the rug right out from under him.

LeMay: Jesus Christ. What the hell do you mean?

Shoup: I just agree with that answer, General. I just agree with you. I just agree with you a hundred percent. I just agree with you a hundred percent. That's the only goddamn . . .

He [President Kennedy] finally got around to the word *escalation*. [*Unclear*] I heard him say *escalation*. That's the only goddamn thing that's in the whole trick. It's been there in Laos; it's been in every goddamn one [of these crises]. When he says *escalation*, that's it. [*Pause.*]

If somebody could keep them from doing the goddamn thing piecemeal. That's our problem. You go in there and friggin' around with the missiles. You're screwed. You go in and frig around with anything else, you're screwed.

LeMay: That's right.

Shoup: You're screwed, screwed, screwed. And if some goddamn thing, some way, he could say: "Either do this son of a bitch and do it right, and quit friggin' around." That was my conclusion. Don't frig around and go take a missile out.

Wheeler: Well, maybe I missed the point [*unclear*].

LeMay: [*Unclear*] off any decision, Dave.

Shoup: Well, that wasn't my intention. Goddamn it, if he wants to do it, you can't fiddle around with taking out missiles. You can't fiddle around with hitting the missile sites and then hitting the SAM sites. You got to go in and take out the goddamn thing that's going to stop you from doing your job.

Wheeler: It was very apparent to me, though, from his earlier remarks, that the political action of a blockade is really what he's . . .

Shoup: That's right. His speech about Berlin was the real . . .

Wheeler: He gave his speech about Berlin, and

LeMay: He equates the two.

Shoup: That's right.

Wheeler: If we smear Castro, Khrushchev smears Willy Brandt [in Berlin].

LeMay: Berlin [*unclear*] talk about it. I think our best chance is that we won't have anything happen.

．　．　．

President Kennedy was now less sure that the blockade was the right answer. This might have been because of the weight of arguments he had heard from the Joint Chiefs. He had also talked again to Bundy, probably at the start of his day, before the meeting with the Joint Chiefs. Bundy had changed his mind during the night and had switched from supporting no action (because of concerns about Berlin) to supporting a surprise air strike. Though we can see from the meeting with the Chiefs that President Kennedy continued to favor a blockade, it is possible that Bundy's change of heart gave the President added cause for reflection. After the crisis Bundy privately recorded that Kennedy, just before he left Washington on October 19 (in the few minutes after his meeting with the Joint Chiefs), asked Bundy to keep the air strike option open until he returned. In another brief exchange as he prepared to depart on his campaign trip to Ohio and Illinois, President Kennedy asked his brother, with Sorensen standing by, to "pull the group together."[4]

The President wanted to act soon and said Bobby should call if and and when he should cut short his trip and return to Washington. At 10:35 the presidential helicopter lifted off from the South Lawn of the White House.

Saturday, October 20, 1962

On Friday, October 19, the meetings at the State Department ran all day and into the night. The day started with advisers divided into two camps, one favoring a blockade and the other favoring an air strike. Bundy said that, in the course of a sleepless night, he had decided that an air strike was needed. Decisive action would confront the world with a fait accompli. He said he had spoken with President Kennedy and passed along this advice. Acheson, Dillon, McCone, and Taylor agreed with Bundy.

McNamara disagreed. Ball said he was wavering. Robert Kennedy then said, with a grin, that he too had spoken with the President and that a surprise attack like Pearl Harbor was "not in our traditions." He "favored *action*" but wanted action that gave the Soviets a chance to pull back.[1]

Rusk then suggested that the group divide into working groups to refine the blockade and air strike scenarios. It became plain to all, after hearing from Justice Department and State Department lawyers, that a declaration of war was not needed in order to impose a blockade and that, under the U.N. Charter, the U.S. could obtain authorization for this from the OAS. Martin predicted that OAS approval could be obtained. Robert Kennedy stressed how crucial this judgment was, since a failed attempt to gain approval would be disastrous. Martin stood by his estimate.

After hours of discussion within and among the working groups, McNamara emerged as the chief advocate of a more diplomatic option that envisioned a blockade as a prelude to negotiations. McNamara thought that the United States would at least have to give up its missile bases in Italy and Turkey, probably more.

As the blockade option became dominant, its advocates split again into two factions. One, led by McNamara, emphasized a blockade accompanied by diplomacy and proffered concessions. The other faction would couple the blockade with a stern ultimatum demanding removal of the missiles. The previous day, when this version of the blockade was articulated by Llewellyn Thompson, McNamara had called it "the more dangerous form of the blockade."

During a sobering discussion of the danger of war, Robert Kennedy argued that the time for confrontation had arrived. "[I]n looking into the future it would be better for our children and grandchildren if we decided to face the Soviet threat, stand up to it, and eliminate it, now. The circumstances for doing so at some future time were bound to be more unfavorable, the risks would be greater, the chances of success less good."

As the afternoon waned, Rusk said there needed to be a planned action, then a pause to consider other steps. Advocates of a blockade could not support any military action unless the Soviets were given some chance to back out. Advocates of a strike insisted on doing something about the missiles already in Cuba. Dillon stressed that a blockade could be a first step, effectively conveying an ultimatum, with further pressure or military action following on. To some, this tougher version of the blockade seemed to combine the virtues of both the blockade and the air strike options.

So when McNamara and other military representatives commented that a strike might still be effective after a blockade (though Taylor had his doubts), Robert Kennedy "took particular note of this shift." Toward the end of the day, Robert Kennedy began portraying the blockade as only a first step that would not preclude other action. "He thought it was now pretty clear what the decision should be."

Sorensen had begun to draft a presidential speech. After reviewing the draft on Saturday morning, October 20, Robert Kennedy called his brother and asked him to come back to Washington.[2] Feigning a cold, President Kennedy left Chicago on Saturday morning and arrived back at the White House at about 1:30 P.M. He read the draft speech as his advisers sneaked by various routes into the Oval Room on the second floor of the Executive Mansion. Just as on the night of October 18, the meeting was held in the Mansion rather than in the West Wing business area of the White House. Therefore the meeting could not be tape-recorded. We are dependent therefore on notes taken by a participant.[3]

2:30 P.M.

National Security Council Meeting

Four general approaches had emerged by the time of the meeting. One was that of Taylor and Bundy, who wanted to start with an air strike. A second was that of Robert Kennedy, Dillon, Thompson, and McCone, who preferred to start with a blockade but to treat it as a kind of ultimatum that might soon be followed by a strike. A third approach, advocated by Rusk, was to start with a blockade, try to freeze the Soviet action rather than reverse it, and then decide what to do. A fourth approach, supported chiefly by McNamara and Stevenson, and apparently also by Sorensen, would start with a blockade but treat the blockade as an opening to negotiations, including the offer of a summit meeting, at which trades would be offered to get the Soviet missiles out of Cuba.

It was, officially, a meeting of the National Security Council. McCone led off and asked Ray Cline, deputy director of intelligence at the CIA, to begin the intelligence briefing. Cline followed his marked-up script, which was as follows:[4]

Mr. President: We want to bring you up to date very briefly on the deployment of Soviet military weapons systems to Cuba. You have been briefed many times on the major buildup of equipment in Cuba prior to mid-October.

In the past week we have discovered unmistakable evidence of the deployment to Cuba of medium range ballistic missiles (i.e., 1020 NM range) and intermediate-range ballistic missiles (i.e., 2200 NM range). These ranges imply coverage of targets from Dallas through Cincinnati and Washington, D.C. (by MRBMs) and practically all of the continental United States (by IRBMs).

There are 4 and possibly 5 MRBM sites deployed in field-type installations, 4 launchers at each site. Two of these sites are in a state of at least limited operational readiness at this time. All of the sites are in a state of continuous construction and improvement and we would expect the remaining MRBM sites to become operational in about one week's time.

In addition 2 fixed IRBM sites (with 4 launch pads at each site and permanent storage facilities) are being constructed near Havana. One of these sites appears to be in a stage of construction that leads to an estimate of operational readiness of 6 weeks from now, i.e. about 1 December and the other in a stage indicating operational readiness between 15 December and the end of the year.

We have not seen nuclear warheads for any of these missiles, but we do not rely on ever seeing them in our photography. [*Small excision of classified information.*] We have found what appears to be a nuclear warhead storage facility at one of the IRBM sites at Guanajay, near Havana. It will probably be completed about 1 December along with the missile site itself.

Since the missile systems in question are relatively ineffective without them, we believe warheads either are or will be available. They could be in temporary storage prior to completion of the storage facility we have seen. The *Poltava*, a Soviet ship which we think is the most likely carrier of security-sensitive military cargoes into the tightly guarded port of Mariel, has made 2 trips to Cuba and is due back in about 10 days.

In summary, we believe the evidence indicates the probability that 8 MRBM missiles can be fired from Cuba today. Naturally operational readiness is likely to be degraded by many factors, but if all 8 missiles could be launched with nuclear warheads, they could deliver a total load of 16–24 megatons (2 to 3 MT per warhead). If able to refire, they could theoretically deliver the same load approximately 5 hours later.

When the full installation of missile sites we now see under construction is completed at the end of the year, the initial salvo capability if all missiles on launchers were to reach target would be 56–88 MT. *Lundahl then went through the photographs. When he had finished, he turned to the President and said, "Mr. President, gentlemen, this summarizes the totality of the missile and other threats as we've been able to determine it from aerial photography. During the past week we were able to achieve coverage of over 95 percent of the island and we are convinced that because of the terrain in the remaining 5 percent, no additional threat will be found there."* [5]

Nonverbatim minutes, taken by NSC executive secretary Bromley Smith, pick up at this point. [6]

The President summarized the discussion of the intelligence material as follows. There is something to destroy in Cuba now and, if it is destroyed, a strategic missile capability would be difficult to restore. . . .

Secretary [Robert] McNamara explained to the President that there were differences among his advisers which had resulted in the drafting of alternative courses of action. He added that the military planners are at work on measures to carry out all recommended courses of action in order that, following a presidential decision, fast action could be taken.

Secretary McNamara described his view as the "blockade route." This route is aimed at preventing any addition to the strategic missiles already deployed in Cuba and eventually to eliminate these missiles. He said to do this we should institute a blockade and be prepared to take armed action in specified instances.

(The President was handed a copy of Ted Sorensen's "blockade route" draft of a presidential message, which he read.) [7]

Secretary McNamara concluded by explaining that following the blockade, the United States would negotiate for the removal of the strategic missiles from Turkey and Italy and possibly agreement to limit our use of Guantánamo to a specified limited time. He added that we could obtain the removal of the missiles from Cuba only if we were prepared to offer something in return during negotiations. He opposed as too risky the suggestion that we should issue an ultimatum to the effect that we would order an air attack on Cuba if the missiles were not removed.[8] He said he was prepared to tell Khrushchev we consider the missiles in Cuba as Soviet missiles and that if they were used against us, we would retaliate by launching missiles against the U.S.S.R.

Secretary McNamara pointed out that SNIE 11-19-62, dated October 20, 1962, estimates that the Russians will not use force to push their ships through our blockade.[9] He cited Ambassador [Charles] Bohlen's view that the U.S.S.R. would not take military action, but would limit its reaction to political measures in the United Nations.

Secretary McNamara listed the disadvantages of the blockade route as follows:

1. It would take a long time to achieve the objective of eliminating strategic missiles from Cuba.
2. It would result in serious political trouble in the United States.
3. The world position of the United States might appear to be weakening.

The advantages which Secretary McNamara cited are:

1. It would cause us the least trouble with our allies.
2. It avoids any surprise air attack on Cuba, which is contrary to our tradition.
3. It is the only military course of action compatible with our position as a leader of the free world.
4. It avoids a sudden military move which might provoke a response from the U.S.S.R. which could result in escalating actions leading to general war.

The President pointed out that during a blockade, more missiles would become operational, and upon the completion of sites and launching pads, the threat would increase. He asked General Taylor how many missiles we could destroy by air action on Monday.

General [Maxwell] Taylor reported that the Joint Chiefs of Staff favor an air strike on Tuesday when United States forces could be in a state of readiness. He said he did not share Secretary McNamara's fear that if we used nuclear weapons in Cuba, nuclear weapons would be used against us.

Secretary [Dean] Rusk asked General Taylor whether we dared to attack operational missile sites in Cuba.

General Taylor responded that the risk of these missiles being used against us was less than if we permitted the missiles to remain there.

The President pointed out that on the basis of the intelligence estimate there would be some 50 strategic missiles operational in mid-December, if we went the blockade route and took no action to destroy the sites being developed.

General Taylor said that the principal argument he wished to make was that now was the time to act because this would be the last chance we would have to destroy these missiles. If we did not act now, the missiles would be camouflaged in such a way as to make it impossible for us to find them. Therefore, if they were not destroyed, we would have to live with them with all the consequent problems for the defense of the United States.

The President agreed that the missile threat became worse each day, adding that we might wish, looking back, that we had done earlier what we are now preparing to do.

Secretary Rusk said that a blockade would seriously affect the Cuban missile capability in that the Soviets would be unable to deploy to Cuba any missiles in addition to those now there.

Under Secretary [George] Ball said that if an effective blockade was established, it was possible that our photographic intelligence would reveal that there were no nuclear warheads in Cuba; hence, none of the missiles now there would be made operational.

General Taylor indicated his doubt that it would be possible to prevent the Russians from deploying warheads to Cuba by means of a blockade because of the great difficulty of setting up an effective air blockade.

Secretary McNamara stated that if we knew that a plane was flying nuclear warheads to Cuba, we should immediately shoot it down. Parenthetically, he pointed out that there are now 6,000 to 8,000 Soviet personnel in Cuba.

The President asked whether the institution of a blockade would appear to the free world as a strong response to the Soviet action. He is particularly concerned about whether the Latin American countries would think that the blockade was an appropriate response to the Soviet challenge.

The Attorney General [Robert Kennedy] returned to the point

made by General Taylor, i.e., that now is the last chance we will have to destroy Castro and the Soviet missiles deployed in Cuba.

Mr. [Theodore] Sorensen said he did not agree with the Attorney General or with General Taylor that this was our last chance. He said a missile buildup would end if, as everyone seemed to agree, the Russians would not use force to penetrate the United States blockade.

Air Strike Route

Mr. [McGeorge] Bundy handed to the President the "air strike alternative," which the President read. It was also referred to as the Bundy plan.

The Attorney General told the President that this plan was supported by Mr. Bundy, General Taylor, the Joint Chiefs of Staff, and with minor variations, by Secretary [Douglas] Dillon and Director [John] McCone.

General Taylor emphasized the opportunity available now to take out not only all the missiles, but all the Soviet medium bombers (IL-28) which were neatly lined up in the open on airbases in Cuba.

Mr. McNamara cautioned that an air strike would not destroy all the missiles and launchers in Cuba, and, at best, we could knock out two-thirds of these missiles. Those missiles not destroyed could be fired from mobile launchers not destroyed. General Taylor said he was unable to explain why the IL-28 bombers had been left completely exposed on two airfields. The only way to explain this, he concluded, was on the ground that the Cubans and the Russians did not anticipate [a] United States air strike.

Secretary Rusk said he hesitated to ask the question but he wondered whether these planes were decoys. He also wondered whether the Russians were trying to entice us into a trap. Secretary McNamara stated his strong doubt that these planes were decoys. Director McCone added that the Russians would not have sent one hundred shiploads of equipment to Cuba solely to play a "trick." General Taylor returned to the point he had made earlier, namely, that if we do not destroy the missiles and the bombers, we will have to change our entire military way of dealing with external threats.

The President raised the question of advance warning prior to military action—whether we should give a minimum of two hours notice of an air strike to permit Soviet personnel to leave the area to be attacked.

General Taylor said that the military would be prepared to live with a 24-hour advance notice or grace period if such advance notice was worthwhile politically. The President expressed his doubt that any notice beyond seven hours had any political value.

There was a brief discussion of the usefulness of sending a draft message to Castro, and a copy of such a message was circulated.

The President stated flatly that the Soviet planes in Cuba did not concern him particularly. He said we must be prepared to live with the Soviet threat as represented by Soviet bombers. However, the existence of strategic missiles in Cuba had an entirely different impact throughout Latin America. In his view the existence of 50 planes in Cuba did not affect the balance of power, but the missiles already in Cuba were an entirely different matter.

The Attorney General said that in his opinion a combination of the blockade route and the air strike route was very attractive to him. He felt that we should first institute the blockade. In the event that the Soviets continued to build up the missile capability in Cuba, then we should inform the Russians that we would destroy the missiles, the launchers, and the missile sites. He said he favored a short wait during which time the Russians could react to the blockade. If the Russians did not halt the development of the missile capability, then we would proceed to make an air strike. The advantage of proceeding in this way, he added, was that we would get away from the Pearl Harbor surprise attack aspect of the air strike route.

Mr. Bundy pointed out that there was a risk that we would act in such as way as to get Khrushchev to commit himself fully to the support of Castro.

Secretary Rusk doubted that a delay of 24 hours in initiating an air strike was of any value. He said he now favored proceeding on the blockade track.

Secretary Dillon mentioned 72 hours as the time between instituting the blockade and initiating an air strike in the event we receive no response to our initial action.

Director McCone stated his opposition to an air strike, but admitted that in his view a blockade was not enough. He argued that we should institute the blockade and tell the Russians that if the missiles were not dismantled within 72 hours, the United States would destroy the missiles by air attack. He called attention to the risk involved in a long drawn-out period during which the Cubans could, at will, launch the missiles against the United States. Secretary Dillon said the existence of strategic missiles in Cuba was, in his opinion, not negotiable. He believed that any effort to negotiate the removal of the missiles would involve a price so high that the United States could not accept it. If the missiles are not removed or eliminated, he continued, the United States will lose all of its friends in Latin America, who will become convinced that our fear is such that we cannot act. He admitted that the limited use of force involved in a blockade would make the military task much harder and would involve the great danger of the launching of these missiles by the Cubans.

Sorensen recalled later that these presentations by McCone and Dillon, taking direct issue with McNamara's proposal for negotiations, resulted in "a brief awkward silence," which was then broken by Gilpatric, "normally a man of few words in meetings with the President when the Defense Secretary was present."[10]

Bromley Smith's minutes continue.

Deputy Secretary [Roswell] Gilpatric saw the choice as involving the use of limited force or of unlimited force. He was prepared to face the prospect of an air strike against Cuba later, but he opposed the initial use of all-out military force such as a surprise air attack. He defined a blockade as being the application of the limited use of force and doubted that such limited use could be combined with an air strike.

General Taylor argued that a blockade would not solve our problem or end the Cuban missile threat. He said that eventually we would have to use military force and, if we waited, the use of military force would be much more costly.

Secretary McNamara noted that the air strike planned by the Joint Chiefs involved 800 sorties. Such a strike would result in several thousand Russians being killed, chaos in Cuba, and efforts to overthrow the Castro government. In his view the probability was high that an air strike would lead inevitably to an invasion. He doubted that the Soviets would take an air strike on Cuba without resorting to a very major response. In such an event, the United States would lose control of the situation which could escalate to general war.

The President agreed that a United States air strike would lead to a major Soviet response, such as blockading Berlin. He agreed that at an appropriate time we would have to acknowledge that we were willing to take strategic missiles out of Turkey and Italy if this issue was raised by the Russians. He felt that implementation of a blockade would also result in Soviet reprisals, possibly the blockade of Berlin. If we instituted a blockade on Sunday, then by Monday or Tuesday we would know whether the missile development had ceased or whether it was continuing. Thus, we would be in a better position to know what move to make next.

Secretary Dillon called attention to the fact that even if the Russians agreed to dismantle the missiles now in Cuba, continuing inspection would be required to ensure that the missiles were not again made ready.

The President said that if it was decided to go the Bundy route, he would favor an air strike which would destroy only missiles. He repeated this view that we would have to live with this threat arising out of the stationing in Cuba of Soviet bombers.

Secretary Rusk referred to an air strike as chapter two. He did not think we should initiate such a strike because of the risk of escalating actions leading to general war. He doubted that we should act without consultation of our allies. He said a sudden air strike had no support in law or morality, and, therefore, must be ruled out. Reading from notes, he urged that we start the blockade and only go on to an air attack when we knew the reaction of the Russians and of our allies.

At this point Director McCone acknowledged that we did not know positively that nuclear warheads for the missiles deployed had actually arrived in Cuba. Although we had evidence of the construction of storage places for nuclear weapons, such weapons may not yet have been sent to Cuba.

The President asked what we would say to those whose reaction to our instituting a blockade now would be to ask why we had not blockaded last July.

Both Mr. Sorensen and Mr. Ball made the point that we did not institute a blockade in July because we did not then know of the existence of strategic missiles in Cuba.

Secretary Rusk suggested that our objective was an immediate freeze of the strategic missile capability in Cuba to be inspected by United Nations observation teams stationed at the missile sites. He referred to our bases in Turkey, Spain and Greece as being involved in any negotiation covering foreign bases. He said a United Nations group might be sent to Cuba to reassure those who might fear that the United States was planning an invasion.

Ambassador Stevenson stated his flat opposition to a surprise air strike, which he felt would ultimately lead to a United States invasion of Cuba. He supported the institution of the blockade and predicted that such action would reduce the chance of Soviet retaliation of a nature which would inevitably escalate. In his view our aim is to end the existing missile threat in Cuba without casualties and without escalation. He urged that we offer the Russians a settlement involving the withdrawal of our missiles from Turkey and our evacuation of Guantánamo base.

The President sharply rejected the thought of surrendering our base at Guantánamo in the present situation. He felt that such action would convey to the world that we had been frightened into abandoning our position. He was not opposed to discussing withdrawal of our missiles from Turkey and Greece [*sic*], but he was firm in saying we should only make such a proposal in the future.

The Attorney General thought we should convey our firm intentions to the Russians clearly and suggested that we might tell the Russians that we were turning over nuclear weapons and missiles to the West Germans.[11]

Ambassador [Llewellyn] Thompson stated his view that our first action should be the institution of a blockade. Following this, he thought we should launch an air strike to destroy the missiles and sites, after giving sufficient warning so that Russian nationals could leave the area to be attacked.

The President said he was ready to go ahead with the blockade and to take actions necessary to put us in a position to undertake an air strike on the missiles and missile sites by Monday or Tuesday.

General Taylor summarized the military actions already under way, including the quiet reinforcement of Guantánamo by infiltrating marines and the positioning of ships to take out United States dependents from Guantánamo on extremely short notice.

The Attorney General said we could implement a blockade very quickly and prepare for an air strike to be launched later if we so decided.

The President said he was prepared to authorize the military to take those preparatory actions which they would have to take in anticipation of the military invasion of Cuba. He suggested that we inform the Turks and the Italians that they should not fire the strategic missiles they have even if attacked. The warheads for missiles in Turkey and Italy could be dismantled. He agreed that we should move to institute a blockade as quickly as we possibly can.

In response to a question about further photographic surveillance of Cuba, Secretary McNamara recommended, and the President agreed, that no low level photographic reconnaissance should be undertaken now because we have decided to institute a blockade.

Secretary Rusk recommended that a blockade not be instituted before Monday in order to provide time required to consult our allies.

Mr. Bundy said the pressure from the press was becoming intense and suggested that one way of dealing with it was to announce shortly that we had obtained photographic evidence of the existence of strategic missiles in Cuba. The announcement would hold the press until the President made his television speech.

The President acknowledged that the domestic political heat following his television appearance would be terrific. He said he had opposed an invasion of Cuba but that now we were confronted with the possibility that by December there would be fifty strategic missiles deployed there. In explanation as to why we have not acted sooner to deal with the threat from Cuba, he pointed out that only now do we have the kind of evidence which we can make available to our allies in order to convince them of the necessity of acting. Only now do we have a way of avoiding a split with our allies.

It is possible that we may have to make an early strike with or without warning next week. He stressed again the difference between the conventional military buildup in Cuba and the psychological impact throughout the world of the Russian deployment of strategic missiles to Cuba. General Taylor repeated his recommendation that any air strike in Cuba included attacks on the MIGs and medium bombers.

The President repeated his view that our world position would be much better if we attack only the missiles. He directed that air strike plans include only missiles and missile sites, preparations to be ready three days from now.

Under Secretary Ball expressed his view that a blockade should include all shipments of POL [petroleum, oil, and lubricants] to Cuba. Secretary Rusk thought that POL should not now be included because such a decision would break down the distinction which we want to make between elimination of strategic missiles and the downfall of the Castro government. Secretary Rusk repeated his view that our objective is to destroy the offensive capability of the missiles in Cuba, not, at this time, seeking to overthrow Castro!

The President acknowledged that the issue was whether POL should be included from the beginning or added at a later time. He preferred to delay possibly as long as a week.

Secretary Rusk called attention to the problem involved in referring to our action as a blockade. He preferred the use of the word *quarantine.*

Parenthetically, the President asked Secretary Rusk to reconsider the present policy of refusing to give nuclear weapons assistance to France. He expressed the view that in light of present circumstances a refusal to help the French was not worthwhile. He thought that in the days ahead we might be able to gain the needed support of France if we stopped refusing to help them with their nuclear weapons project.[12]

There followed a discussion of several sentences in the "blockade route" draft of the President's speech. It was agreed that the President should define our objective in terms of halting "offensive missile preparations in Cuba." Reference to economic pressures on Cuba would not be made in this context.

The President made clear that in the United Nations we should emphasize the subterranean nature of the missile buildup in Cuba. Only if we were asked would we respond that we were prepared to talk about the withdrawal of missiles from Italy and Turkey. In such an eventuality, the President pointed out that we would have to make clear to the Italians and the Turks that withdrawing strategic missiles was not a retreat and that we would be prepared to replace these missiles by providing a more effective deterrent, such as the assignment of Polaris submarines. The President asked Mr. Nitze to study the problems arising out of the withdrawal of missiles from Italy and Turkey, with particular reference to complications which would arise in NATO. The President made clear that our emphasis should be on the missile threat from Cuba.

Ambassador [Adlai] Stevenson reiterated his belief that we must be more forthcoming about giving up our missile bases in Turkey and Italy. He stated again his belief that the present situation required that we offer to give up such bases in order to induce the Russians to remove the strategic missiles from Cuba.

Mr. [Paul] Nitze flatly opposed making any such offer, but said he would not object to discussing this question in the event that negotiations developed from our institution of a blockade.

The President concluded the meeting by stating that we should be ready to meet criticism of our deployment of missiles abroad but we should not initiate negotiations with a base withdrawal proposal.

During the 2 hours and 40 minutes of this meeting, lines had been clearly drawn between the groups that would later be labeled doves and hawks.[13] It is a pity that Kennedy held the meeting outside the reach of his microphones, for not even the anodyne vocabulary of an official note-taker conceals the intensity of the exchanges. McNamara seems even more emphatic than usual in describing the possible consequences of not following a blockade and negotiate strategy. Stevenson pleads for such a strategy even after the President has "sharply rejected" negotiations about Guantánamo and has declared that the United States will not initiate talks about trading away the IRBMs in Turkey and Italy. Nitze has "flatly opposed" Stevenson. Dillon has come down hard in saying that the missiles in Cuba are "not negotiable." Taylor has intervened time and again to argue for an air strike and against a blockade, while Rusk has said categorically that "a sudden air strike had no support in the law or morality, and, therefore, must be ruled out."

President Kennedy has emerged from the meeting midway between the hawks and the doves. He has rejected making any offer to negotiate, at least for the time being. He has come down in favor of a blockade, now to be labeled a quarantine. The blockade is to be coupled with a demand that Khrushchev remove the missiles, with at least an air strike (a narrow one, President Kennedy hopes) readied if Khrushchev does not comply. This was the option pressed by Thompson, Dillon, and McCone, vitally backed by Robert Kennedy. After the meeting McCone followed up with Robert Kennedy to nail down this outcome. Later in the evening President Kennedy called to reassure McCone that "he had made up his mind to pursue the course which I had recommended and he agreed with the views I expressed in the afternoon meeting."[14]

When Taylor returned to the Pentagon, he told the Chiefs, "This was not one of our better days." He added that President Kennedy had said, "I know you and your colleagues are unhappy with the decision, but I trust that you will support me in this decision." Taylor said he had assured the President they would. General Wheeler remarked, "I never thought I'd live to see the day when I would want to go to war."[15]

Monday, October 22, 1962

On Saturday, October 20, 1962, President Kennedy had decided on a course of action for the United States in the Cuban missile crisis. Treating the crisis as being more about Berlin and the United States's world position than about Cuba itself, he had sharply ruled out the blockade-negotiate option proposed by defense secretary Robert McNamara and U.N. ambassador Adlai Stevenson, arguing that such action would convey to the world that the United States had been frightened into negotiating its commitments around the globe. He then ruled out a surprise air strike, advocated by national security adviser McGeorge Bundy and the Joint Chiefs of Staff (JCS), and instead chose a combination of the blockade and air strike options. This combination, supported by Robert Kennedy, John McCone, Douglas Dillon, and Llewellyn Thompson, would start with a blockade as a way of emphasizing the seriousness of a U.S. ultimatum—remove the missiles from Cuba or face attack. The blockade would be followed by an air strike, which was to be ready for implementation as early as October 23. Anxious that Berlin not be blockaded on life-threatening terms, Kennedy also decided that the blockade against Cuba would be narrowly focused only on Soviet arms deliveries to that island rather than on all shipments of vital supplies, such as oil.

There were, though, a few subtle signs that President Kennedy had not decided just what he would do if the ultimatum failed. No fixed time limit was set on the U.S. demand for removal. Earlier in the day, President Kennedy had met with the Air Force's commander for air operations against Cuba, General Walter Sweeney. Sweeney had confirmed Kennedy's conviction that an air strike could not offer 100 percent certainty of getting all the Soviet missiles right away. Robert Kennedy had commented, as McNamara recalled, that they would start with the blockade and then, borrowing a metaphor from billiards, "play for the breaks."[1] The operational questions of the moment would be settled consistently with a planned sequence of ultimatum, then strike. But conscious of the awesome responsibilities he shouldered, President Kennedy held back from any unequivocal statement of just when or how the United States might strike, or negotiate, once his government's firm resolve to get the missiles removed was plain to all.

Though the administration's efforts to preserve secrecy had been remarkably successful for nearly a week, the cover was beginning to crack. The front pages that Sunday morning had headlined a sudden, massive surprise attack by China against India, with Chinese armies' storming across the Indian border on two widely separated fronts. The *Washington Post*, however, confined this story to the left side of its front page and on the right side ran a five-column headline: "Marine Moves in South Linked to Cuban Crisis." Although the piece contained few specifics, it cited the mobilization of troops, planes, and ships around Key West allegedly for a training exercise in waters around Puerto Rico, as one of "numerous indications . . . that a major international development was in the making."

Well-connected Washington columnists such as Walter Lippmann and Joseph Alsop already knew that a focus of the coming crisis would be Soviet nuclear forces in Cuba. So did *Post* reporters. Kennedy, told by White House press secretary Pierre Salinger that the whole press corps would soon have the details, called friends at the *Times* and *Post* to ask that they hold off through Monday. (The *Times* actually learned of the story through this phone call.)[2] Clearly, the President was going to have to make a public statement no later than Monday evening.

After meeting with Air Force General Sweeney, President Kennedy talked privately with his old friend, David Ormsby-Gore, the British ambassador in Washington. It was the first time he disclosed the news of the coming crisis to a foreigner. After describing the situation and his choices, including a detailed discussion of how the situation related to the renewed crisis over Berlin, he asked Ormsby-Gore's opinion. The ambassador spoke in favor of the blockade, making almost exactly the arguments that Kennedy himself had made when meeting with the Joint Chiefs of Staff on the morning of October 19. As he had before, Kennedy acknowledged "that he could not help admiring the Soviet strategy. They offered this deliberate and provocative challenge to the United States in the knowledge that if the Americans reacted violently to it, the Russians would be given an ideal opportunity to move against West Berlin. If, on the other hand, he did nothing, the Latin Americans and the United States' other allies would feel that the Americans had no real will to resist the encroachments of communism and would hedge their bets accordingly."[3]

Musing more broadly, President Kennedy remarked that he doubted whether he would ever again have an equally good excuse to invade Cuba. "He, therefore, did his devil's advocate act even at that stage," Ormsby-Gore wryly recalled.[4] Kennedy then commented that the existence of nuclear weapons was making a secure and rational world impossible. The

President groused that the intermediate-range ballistic missiles (IRBM) bases in Turkey and elsewhere were more or less worthless and probably had not been a good idea in the first place. He also worried that the West Germans were refusing to face up to the realities of the situation surrounding Berlin. Returning to the business at hand, President Kennedy arranged for a message to be delivered in London a few hours later for British prime minister Harold Macmillan, giving him early warning of the breaking crisis and the impending U.S. moves.

Shortly after seeing Ormsby-Gore, President Kennedy convened another meeting of the National Security Council (NSC) at the White House, at 2:30 P.M. Again, to avoid press questions about the after-hours gathering, he held the meeting in the mansion, not in the Cabinet Room. It was therefore not taped.

Advocates of using the blockade as an ultimatum were suspicious that the proponents of negotiation would still try to win the day, as the battlefield turned to the speech being drafted by one of the supporters of negotiation, Theodore Sorensen. The argument indeed reopened at the afternoon NSC meeting. The secretary of state, Dean Rusk, had not given up either on a different diplomatic approach, one that asked only for a standstill on Soviet construction in Cuba and international inspection of the missile sites, rather than a demand that Moscow remove the missiles already there.

President Kennedy rebuffed Rusk, though he conceded that perhaps later, once U.S. resolve was clear, he might consider a move through the United Nations to remove the missiles in Cuba along with the obsolete U.S. missiles in Turkey and Italy. Turning to the arguments over his draft speech, Kennedy gave comfort once more to the blockade-ultimatum faction. He removed language on the horrors of war that could have fueled public panic. Backed by Thompson, McCone, and Dillon, he omitted Stevenson's proposed passage inviting Soviet premier Khrushchev for a summit meeting. First he would see how Khrushchev dealt with the missiles in Cuba. He mused, though, that as soon as he finished his speech the Russians would speed up their buildup in Cuba; announce that if the United States attacked Cuba, Soviet missiles would fly; and possibly make a move to squeeze the West out of Berlin.

The chief of naval operations, Admiral George Anderson, came to the NSC meeting and for the first time briefed the President on how the blockade would operate. He explained that 40 ships were already in position. He outlined the method for intercepting a Soviet ship, following international rules. The ship would be asked to stop. If it refused, shots would be fired to disable it; then it would be boarded and towed, if necessary, back to a U.S. port. Anderson suggested giving Moscow a brief grace period after the blockade was announced to instruct merchant ship captains on what they should do.

Anderson then turned to his rules of engagement. If any Soviet warship or aircraft in Cuba took hostile action against a U.S. ship, the offending vessel or plane could be destroyed. If a Soviet submarine tried to evade the blockade and make its way underwater to Cuba, Anderson said he would seek permission to destroy it. McNamara agreed.

Earlier in the discussion President Kennedy had reviewed the circumstances of the U.S. and NATO decision in 1957 to send Jupiter missiles to Turkey and Italy, observing that this had been a response to Soviet deployments of medium-range ballistic missiles (MRBMs) aimed at Europe. But Douglas Dillon had remarked more cynically that they had been sent there because the United States had nothing better to do with these questionable liquid-fueled systems.[5] Toward the end of the meeting Kennedy asked Assistant Secretary of Defense Paul Nitze to study the problem of withdrawing U.S. missiles from Turkey and Italy. Nitze said this would be complicated and might give the Europeans the feeling the United States was willing to take all its nuclear weapons out of Europe. Kennedy explained that he wanted to start with a demand for the unconditional removal of Soviet missiles from Cuba. If at a later time we wanted to negotiate for a less favorable settlement, we could then decide to do that. Kennedy added that the United States should reverse its prior policy and offer help to France's nuclear program to reassure them and secure their support in this crisis.[6]

Stevenson used this opening to press again for a summit meeting with Khrushchev. Kennedy again rebuffed him. An offer to trade Soviet missiles in Cuba for U.S. missiles or bases elsewhere would, Kennedy thought, signal to Khrushchev that "we were in a state of panic." We "should be clear that we would accept nothing less than the ending of the missile capability now in Cuba" as well as stopping further construction.[7]

McNamara dissented. To achieve that result, he warned, the United States would have to invade Cuba. Kennedy held his ground. He repeated that he was talking about the dismantlement of the missiles now in Cuba.

After the meeting, President Kennedy passed along a request that special precautions be taken to be sure that, if the Soviets launched a reprisal attack at any point, the Jupiter missiles in Turkey and Italy would not be fired without express presidential authorization. The Chiefs took umbrage at this request and sent back word that they opposed issuing any such special instruction, since doing so would imply lack of confidence in the effectiveness of standing orders.

The entire apparatus of the U.S. government was now moving into action. This included an immensely complicated program to send letters to foreign leaders and prepare U.S. embassies around the world for what was to come.[8]

As he had on October 17, McCone again briefed former president Dwight D. Eisenhower, this time at McCone's home in Washington. Eisenhower thought a surprise attack would be best, militarily. From a broader point of view, however, he agreed that the United States should forfeit the advantages of a surprise attack, and he therefore endorsed the proposed blockade.[9]

Briefing teams were readied, armed with photos, to travel to Europe and talk personally with Macmillan, de Gaulle, and West German chancellor Konrad Adenauer. Congressional leaders dispersed around the country were mysteriously fetched by soldiers and transported back to Washington for a meeting the next day with the President.

10:40 A.M.

Conversation with Dwight Eisenhower

President Kennedy had taken pains to be sure Eisenhower was briefed on the crisis by John McCone, first on October 17 to give him the news of the deployment and then again on October 21 to tell the former president about the blockade-ultimatum decision. Having already heard from McCone about Eisenhower's supportive reaction, President Kennedy wants to discuss his dilemma directly with one of the few living men who will truly understand what he faces. Despite the distance between the two men in age, experience, and political stance, it is not the first time they have confided in each other, and it will not be the last.

President Kennedy: Ike, I've got the [congressional] leadership coming back at five this afternoon.

Dwight Eisenhower: Yes.

President Kennedy: Then we begin this blockade. Then we'll continue the surveillance. I would anticipate two or three things. First, that Khrushchev will make a statement that any attack upon Cuba will be— the same as he made at the time of the Suez business [in 1956]—will be regarded as an attack upon the Soviet Union and be responded to by all the weapons at their command. Number one.

Number two is, I—we have to assume that, as this surveillance continues with the U-2s, that these SAM sites may shoot one down. At that point, then, we were just discussing what action we would take in attacking the SAM sites. So I would assume that this will only be the first of a rather increasing number of steps. We're not going to be in any position to carry out an invasion for some days because we have to move those troops around from—

Eisenhower: Yeah.

President Kennedy: —San Diego.[10] But we're going to do all those things and we'll just stay in touch with you this week, [during] which, as I say, we anticipate that it will be getting more intense.

Eisenhower: As I understand it. Now, John [McCone] talked to me about three possibilities.[11]

President Kennedy: Right.

Eisenhower: The first one [an air strike alone] I told him—the only way to deal with the thing—I said: "I thought that was completely wrong." And apparently everybody else had the same opinion on it.

President Kennedy: [*assuming Eisenhower is referring to the surprise air strike option*] That's right. And for the reasons, one is we didn't think we could get them all. As well as, we'd have all of the disadvantages without finishing the job.

Eisenhower: That's correct.

President Kennedy: Yeah.

Eisenhower: And the second one [air strike plus simultaneous invasion], the difficulty was of course here between determining—between the second and third [a blockade that gave the Russians a chance to leave Cuba]—I thought there were a number of reasons on both sides. And, of course, I couldn't tell about the understandings that the government had had with the Latin American companies [countries], with NATO, and so on and so on.

President Kennedy: Right.

Eisenhower: But, so there I just . . . my thought was, well, no matter what you're trying to do, have to do, why I will certainly stand it and I'll be doing my best—

President Kennedy: Right. Right.

Eisenhower: —to support it.

Now, the one thing I didn't quite understand [is] that you'd suspected the third program [the blockade] would require a number of increasingly serious steps.

President Kennedy: Well, what we anticipate is, first, his statement—

Eisenhower: Yeah.

President Kennedy:—of, you know, the sort of usual one.

Eisenhower: Yeah.

President Kennedy: But then of course the surveillance will continue. Now, we have to assume that they perhaps will shoot down one of these U-2s. Then in that case . . . and therefore make our surveillance impossible. In that case, of course, we will then have to judge what action to take. But I think that we probably [launch air attacks] . . . , as I don't expect they're going to discontinue work on these things. I don't expect that they're going to withdraw them. And, I would think that we'd probably have that danger [of Soviet retaliation], in any case.

Eisenhower: I should think, Mr. President, that what probably will be bothering you the most after this first statement will be the . . . some outcries from all around the world—probably including Latin America and so on and so on. This will . . . There will of course be a lot of talk about the United Nations and so on.

President Kennedy: Right.

Eisenhower: The only thing that I said to John is something, that even if you don't get as many people in South America, as many governments to go along, that once you have taken this first step in force, then you will have to, if necessary, make all these things unilateral decisions and not—

President Kennedy: Right. That's right.

Eisenhower: That's the big thing. And when, if you see it becomes time to do something, why you yourself, of course, will have to make that decision.

President Kennedy: Right, well, [that depends on the] two-thirds, if we get the two-thirds [support from the Organization of American States (OAS)] we'll operate under the Rio Treaty. If we don't get the two-thirds, then we'll do it under our own act of—

Eisenhower: Yeah, I see.

President Kennedy:—self-defense. Then—

Eisenhower: Your speech will be seven, this evening.

President Kennedy: Seven? Then we're going to go to the U.N. with a . . . And our position will be the withdrawal of these.

[McCloy] up there to assist Adlai, so that we get somebody who's had some experience.

Eisenhower: Well, Jack [McCloy] is a very good man.

President Kennedy: Yeah.

Eisenhower: Well, I thank you for telling me. And I will, I personally, I think you're really making the only move you can.

President Kennedy: Yeah. It's tough to . . . As I say, we will, I don't know, we may get into the invasion business before many days are out.

Eisenhower: Yeah.

President Kennedy: But . . .

Eisenhower: Of course, from the military standpoint that's the clean-cut thing to do, now.

President Kennedy: That's right. That's right.

Eisenhower: Because you've made up your mind you've *got* to get rid of this thing.

President Kennedy: Right.

Eisenhower: The only real way to get rid of it, of course, is the other thing [military attack]. But, having to be concerned with world opinion and—

President Kennedy: And Berlin.

Eisenhower: —of others, why you've got to do it a little slower.

President Kennedy: Well, Berlin is the . . . I suppose, that may be the . . . what they're going to try to trade off.

Eisenhower: Well, they might. But I, personally, I just don't quite go along, you know, with that thinking, Mr. President. My idea is this: The damn Soviets will do whatever they want, what they figure is good for them.

President Kennedy: Yeah.

Eisenhower: And I don't believe they relate one situation with another.

President Kennedy: Uh-huh.

Eisenhower: Just what they find out they can do here and there and the other place.

President Kennedy: Yeah. Yeah.

Eisenhower: And, we're already standing as a unit with NATO, that if they go into Berlin, that's all of it.

President Kennedy: Right.

Eisenhower: That means they've got to look out that they don't get a terrific blow to themselves.

President Kennedy: Right. Right.

Eisenhower: And I don't . . . It might be, I could be all wrong. But my own conviction is that you will not find a great deal of relationship between the two.[12]

President Kennedy: Let me ask—

Eisenhower: They'll try to *make* it that way.

President Kennedy: Yeah.

General, what about if the Soviet Union—Khrushchev—announces tomorrow, which I think he will, that if we attack Cuba that it's going to be nuclear war? And what's your judgment as to the chances they'll fire these things off if we invade Cuba?

Eisenhower: Oh, I don't believe that they will.

President Kennedy: You don't think they will?

Eisenhower: No.

President Kennedy: In other words you would take that risk if the situation seemed desirable?

Eisenhower: Well, as a matter of fact, what can you do?

President Kennedy: Yeah.

Eisenhower: If this thing is such a serious thing, here on our flank, that we're going to be uneasy and we know what thing is happening now. All right, you've got to use something.

President Kennedy: Yeah.

Eisenhower: Something *may* make these people [the Soviets] shoot them [their nuclear missiles] off. I just don't believe this will.

President Kennedy: Yeah, right. [*Chuckles resignedly.*]

Eisenhower: In any event, of course, I'll say this: I'd want to keep my own people very alert.

President Kennedy: Yeah. [*Chuckles some more.*] Well, we'll hang on tight.

Eisenhower: [*also chuckling a bit*] Yes, sir.

President Kennedy: Thanks a lot, General.

Eisenhower: All right. Thank you.

11:00 A.M.

Meeting on Diplomatic Plans

This informal session of a small group of officials in the Oval Office concerned plans for presenting the U.S. position at the United Nations in New York. Arthur Schlesinger, Jr., a renowned historian then serving as a special assistant to Kennedy, had been asked to draft the address that would be delivered by Adlai Stevenson announcing and explaining the U.S. position to the United Nations. It is a statement second in importance only to the speech Kennedy himself would make that night to the U.S. people. In this meeting President Kennedy went over Schlesinger's draft before Schlesinger flew to New York to hand the speech to Stevenson. Schlesinger then stayed in New York as yet more support to the U.N. ambassador in whom Kennedy had so little confidence.

The discussion started with a proposal that Dean Rusk developed for freezing the status quo under U.N. supervision. In part this was a new idea, one that would trade U.N. supervision of U.S. missiles in Turkey and Italy for U.N. intervention into Cuba. But Rusk also found yet another way to renew the argument he had made repeatedly over the weekend, urging Kennedy to moderate his objective and try just to freeze the status quo, rather than demand removal of the missiles. The President remained unmoved.

It was a few minutes into the 11:00 meeting and Kennedy had already begun reviewing the draft address to the United Nations. He turned on the tape recorder in the Oval Office as Rusk made his suggestion. The audio quality is poor.

Dean Rusk: [*Unclear*] to read that.

President Kennedy: All right, [*unclear*] read that. Oh, is that your handwriting [on Schlesinger's draft statement]?

Rusk: That's my handwriting.

President Kennedy: OK. Who would make this suggestion? [U.N. secretary-general] U Thant?

Rusk: Our side.

President Kennedy: Tell me that again.

Rusk: U.N. observer forces, that means military forces, would be placed immediately at all MRBM, IRBM, and ICBM [intercontinental ballistic missile] sites in all countries other than those possessing [their own] nuclear weapons.

President Kennedy: [*Unclear*] Bobby?

. . .

Rusk: There are only three places where nuclear missiles are present outside the territory of the nuclear powers: Cuba, Turkey, and Italy. And this would mean putting U.N. forces right in there immediately.

. . .

President Kennedy: This would be: Take them out of any country that is not a nuclear power.

Rusk: That's right.

President Kennedy: That would leave, definitely—

Rusk: Well, not "take them out" at this phase. Just sit on them. Stop them in their tracks. See that they are not operational. No further work moves forward.

President Kennedy: In preparation for their removal, I would think. Wouldn't we, why don't we go the whole way?

Rusk: Well, without any reference to Turkey and Italy . . . whether you want to do that at this stage.

President Kennedy: Well, actually, this I suppose—

McGeorge Bundy: We can get someone else—

President Kennedy: This gives us an excuse to get them out of Turkey and Italy. As long as they're not connected with it [the proposal], let's try to get them out of both places. We tried to get them out of that other place anyway.[13] We're much better off.

Rusk: But, you see, if we get this removal business turned down, then the removal point is not a very workable point at that stage.

George Ball: Well, except that this is removal on a bilateral basis.

President Kennedy: It's not just them; it's both sides that would remove them.

Rusk: See, the point of removal may take more time. I'm thinking of something, if the other side is interested, that you can do instantaneously.

Bundy: But that would be the presence of inspection teams?

Rusk: The presence of U.N. observer forces at all such sites, to see that they [the missiles] are not operational and that all work on such matters be stopped immediately.

President Kennedy: Well, maybe that's the first stage. But I think we ought to have this—

Rusk: The removal thing is something you could do, say, in Geneva [at the ongoing arms control talks sponsored by the Eighteen-Nation Disarmament Committee]. But the point is to get this whole thing stopped as quickly as possible therefore on the simplest possible basis. I think the removal is a far more difficult thing than to stop in their tracks.

Ball: See, if we go in for withdrawal—

Rusk: We go in for—

President Kennedy: Now, we don't stop the quarantine when this happens, do we? We have to decide that. That's a separate point.

Ball: Yeah, that's correct.

President Kennedy: We have to see how it looks before we . . .

Rusk: I think the quarantine, the removal of the quarantine would be for the United Nations to determine.

President Kennedy: OK. Well, we don't have to commit ourselves to removing the quarantine. This isn't our proposal.

Rusk: And then for the heads of government, the Eighteen, to meet in—

President Kennedy: Yeah, but I think we ought to always keep on this pressure about the removal, because I don't think we're a hell of a lot better off if they're just sitting there, to be honest with you. We're not going to be better off.

Rusk: [Even if the missiles are] in the possession, under the control, of the U.N. forces?

President Kennedy: Well, we don't think they're going to fire them anyway, isn't that right?

I agree we're somewhat better off, because psychologically they cease to become quite the factor they were. So that we are better off. But we're not . . .

I think maybe this is just a political problem. But I think we ought to be looking to the day when they're removed from Cuba, Italy, and Turkey. Now maybe that's two or three days from now, or a week. But that proposal can be made after this one's been accepted [the United States will announce today]. That may be two stages.

Bundy: I don't think there's any harm in having a neutral [country] make a proposal for immediate inspection instead of sanitization, Mr. President. The rest would follow. It gets you . . . you can't have everything in one bite.

President Kennedy: OK. All right.

. . .

11:47 A.M.

Meeting of Berlin Group

The State Department officials joined a few Pentagon officials, led by Roswell Gilpatric, to discuss Berlin contingency planning. Meeting with this Berlin group in the Cabinet Room, President Kennedy turned on the tape recorder as he interrupted Nitze's briefing on Berlin planning. Kennedy wanted to question Nitze. The President had asked, the previous day, that the Joint Chiefs of Staff issue special instructions to make sure the Jupiter missiles in Turkey would not be fired without specific presidential authorization.

. . .

Paul Nitze: McNamara and I wrote out a suggested instruction from him [President Kennedy] to the Chiefs and we took it up with the Chiefs. The Chiefs came back with a paper saying that those instructions are already out.

President Kennedy: Well, why don't we reinforce them because, as I say, we may be attacking the Cubans, and they may . . . a reprisal may come on these. We don't want them firing [nuclear warheads] without our knowing about it.

Dean Rusk: The ones in Turkey are not operational, are they?

Nitze: Yes, they are.

Rusk: Oh, they are.

Roswell Gilpatric: Fifteen of them are on alert right now.

President Kennedy: Can we take care of that then, Paul? We need a new instruction out.

Nitze: All right. I'll go back and tell them.

President Kennedy: They object to sending a new one out?

Nitze: They object to sending it out because it, to their view, compromises their standing instructions. You know you reinforce one standing instruction . . .

McGeorge Bundy: Let's have a look at the existing order and see how definite it is, and then simply say: "The President directs your attention again to umpty-ump section . . . "

Rusk: You can send a personal message to the commander saying: "Be sure you fully understand paragraph so-and-so of your orders."

Bundy: Surely it can be done one way or the other.

Nitze: They did come back with another point, and that is: NATO strategic contact [Soviet nuclear attack] requires the immediate execution of EDP in such events.

President Kennedy: What's EDP?

Nitze: The European Defense Plan, which is nuclear war.

Bundy: So that means an order—

President Kennedy: Now that's why we want to get on that, you see. Now that—

Nitze: No. They said the orders are that nothing can go without the presidential order.

President Kennedy: But you see, but they don't know in Greece and Turkey—ah, Turkey and Italy—what we know. And therefore they don't realize there is a chance there will be a spot reprisal.

And what we've got to do is make sure these fellows *do* know, so that they don't fire them off and think the United States is under attack. I don't think we ought to accept the Chiefs' word on that one, Paul.

Nitze: All right.

President Kennedy: I understand why they did that. These fellows think everybody knows as much as we know. And they don't.

Rusk: They might decide the nuclear war is already on.

Nitze: Well, I'm sure that these fellows are thoroughly indoctrinated not to fire. I mean this is what McNamara and I went over to look into, and they really are indoctrinated on this point.

President Kennedy: Well, let's do it again, Paul.

Nitze: I've got your point and we'll do it again. [*Laughter, joined in by Nitze.*]

Bundy: Send me the documents, and I will show them to a doubting master [presumably Kennedy].[14] [*Laughter.*]

President Kennedy: You were . . . ? You want to go on?

Bundy: Yes, may I? Therefore, many things may need to be done after a Berlin tension is initiated on the Soviet side that we would not want to make too much noise about now.

A quite different thing is the immediate process, which is that we must and will have to find all the ways we can of continuing our regular business on Berlin, and of getting it clear to our allies the context, in which this Cuban action is a reinforcement of their position rather than an extraordinary [*unclear*] fall back.

President Kennedy: I think that's a good point about . . . Because otherwise, the credibility on Berlin, in view of my statement . . .

Bundy: Well, there are two points. There's credibility and there is the fact that, if this buildup [in Cuba] continues, their fundamental guarantee [of U.S. nuclear protection] might be endangered.

President Kennedy: Those are really good points. I don't think we've thought enough about them in our communications to these heads of state. We ought to remind [Dean] Acheson of that.

. . .

After this meeting Kennedy went back to the Executive Mansion and had lunch with his wife. After lunch, still in the Mansion, he worked with a few aides (including Robert Kennedy) to prepare and sign a National Security Action Memorandum (Number 196) establishing "for the current crisis" an Executive Committee of the National Security Council that he himself would chair. It would meet each day at 10:00 A.M., in the Cabinet Room, until further notice. Its regular members would be Vice President Johnson, Rusk, McNamara, Dillon, Robert Kennedy, McCone, Ball, Gilpatric, Taylor, Thompson, Sorensen, and Bundy. Kennedy returned to his office in the West Wing at about 3:00.

3:00 P.M.

National Security Council Meeting

At 3:00 P.M., Kennedy again gathered his chief advisers in a final preparatory session before he began announcing the policy, a process that would begin with his briefing of congressional leaders two hours later. The discussion was convened as a meeting of the National Security Council and included all of the Joint Chiefs of Staff, Kenneth O'Donnell, Henry Fowler from Treasury, Roger Hilsman from State, Ed McDermott from the Office of Emergency Preparedness, and possibly a few other officials who had not been included before.

As Kennedy had explained earlier in the day, a key purpose of this meeting was to establish a common basis of understanding among his top officials about why the U.S. government had made this decision and to give clear guidance on how this decision should be explained to the press and public. President Kennedy did not immediately turn on the tape recorder, but the minutes summarize the opening exchanges and set the scene:[15]

> In response to a suggestion by Mr. Bundy, the President outlined the manner in which he expected Council members to deal with the domestic aspects of the current situation. He said everyone should sing one song in order to make clear there was now no difference among his advisers as to the proper course to follow. He pointed out the importance of fully supporting the course of action chosen which, in his view, represented a reasonable consensus. Any course is extremely troublesome and, as in the case of the Berlin wall, we are once again confronted with a difficult choice. If we undertake a tricky and unsatisfactory course, we do not even have the satisfaction of knowing what would have happened if we had acted differently. He mentioned that former presidents Eisenhower, Truman, and Hoover had supported his decision during telephone conversations with each of them earlier in the day.
>
> The President then summarized the arguments as to why we must act. We must reply to those whose reaction to the blockade would be to ask what had changed in view of the fact that we had been living in the past years under a threat of a missile nuclear attack by the U.S.S.R.
>
> A. In September we had said we would react if certain actions were taken in Cuba. We have to carry out commitments which we had made publicly at that time.

B. The secret deployment by the Russians of strategic missiles to Cuba was such a complete change in their previous policy of not deploying such missiles outside the U.S.S.R. that if we took no action in this case, we would convey to the Russians an impression that we would never act, no matter what they did anywhere.

C. Gromyko had left the impression that the Soviets were going to act in Berlin in the next few months. Therefore, if they acted now in response to our blockade action, we would only have brought on their Berlin squeeze earlier than expected.

At this point in his explanation, President Kennedy turned on the tape recorder. We hear him continuing.

President Kennedy: . . . Khrushchev if we completely failed to react in the case of Cuba.

In addition, seeing that we failed to react, the effect in Latin America [would be] the feeling that perhaps the balance of power really had shifted and that it's just a question of time. There was a feeling of inevitability, that the Soviet advance would have been marked. So we decided to do something. And then we start here.

Now, it may end up with our having to invade Cuba. We should be in a position to do so. There obviously is going to . . . Khrushchev will not take this without a response, maybe in Berlin or maybe here. But we have done, I think, the choices being one of all second best. I think we've done the best thing, at least as far as you can tell in advance.

We haven't settled two or three matters which are going to have to be settled in the coming days. What are we going to do when one of our U-2s is shot down, which we have to anticipate maybe in the next few days, over a SAM site? What will be our response there? Number one.

And, secondly, what will we do if the work continues on these sites, which we assume it will? I think we've got to begin to meet tomorrow and begin to consider what action we take in those cases. Do we intensify the blockade? Or do we begin . . . If they shoot down one of our U-2s, do we attack that SAM site or all SAM sites? These are matters I think we ought to be all thinking about in the next 24 hours and, meeting tomorrow, begin to decide exactly what we will do in that case.

But I think that, as I said, for the press, those who are abroad, and others, those arguments about doing nothing, I think the reasons why we have to do something are quite clear. I don't think there was anybody ever who didn't think we shouldn't respond.

There was a variety of different actions. At least I've attempted to communicate why we took the course we did, even though, as I've said from the beginning, the idea of a quick strike was very tempting and I really didn't give up on that until yesterday morning. So I may have to . . . After talking to General Sweeney and after talking to others, it looked like we would have all of the difficulties of Pearl Harbor and not have finished the job. The job can only be finished by an invasion.

As I understand, we are moving those forces which will be necessary in case, at the end of the week, it looks like that would be the only course left to us, even though I recognize we have to do the air strikes with all the disadvantages we'll now have. And I want to say this very clearly to the military, that I recognize we increase your problems in any military action we have to take in Cuba by the warning we're now giving.

But I did want you to know that the reason we followed the course we have was because, while we would have been able to take out more planes and missiles without warning, as we *are* involved all around the world and not just in Cuba, I think the shock to the alliance might have been nearly fatal. Particularly as it would have excused very drastic action by Khrushchev.

But we still have some pretty basic decisions to make about the two points I've just said: Whatever happens when surveillance ceases. And second, what happens if work on the bases goes on.

Dean Rusk: Mr. President, may I just add one sentence on that. That if there are any of our colleagues who think that this is, in any sense, a weak action, I think we can be quite sure that in a number of hours we'll have a flaming crisis on our hands. This is going to go very far, and possibly very fast.

Robert Kennedy: Mr. President, did you want to go in at all into the questions that are bound to arise and what the answers are to those? For instance, why we didn't put a blockade in a month ago? Why we just detected it a week ago? Or why we didn't—of course, we handled [that]—why we didn't take more forceful action?

President Kennedy: Oh yeah, we'll get some of these questions which, as I say, we have around the government.

The first question [Rusk raised, whether the action was strong enough], as I say, everybody has to follow their own judgment in these matters. But this seems to me to be the appropriate answer. But I'm not . . . Everybody has to decide for themselves the question.

The first question [Robert Kennedy raised]: Why was action not taken earlier? Well, we still are not sure we're going to get the 14 votes in the OAS. If we'd begun the quarantine six months ago. . . . Let's say we'd begun it in August, when there was no evidence that the Soviet military buildup was going to be offensive [with nuclear missiles that could strike the United States]. We obviously would have had difficulty getting 14 votes for a blockade. We wouldn't have had any support by any of the countries, really, of Western Europe as the hazards then began on Berlin, which they inevitably would have, it would have appeared that we had thrown Berlin into jeopardy, and perhaps lost it because of a, rather almost, a fixation on the subject of Cuba, which up to quite recently most of us never, did not, assume would be turned into an offensive base. So we would have to probably . . . If we didn't get an OAS resolution, we would have had to get a declaration of war. And a declaration of war on Cuba at that point would have placed us in an isolated position.

The whole foreign policy of the United States since 1947 has been to develop and maintain alliances in this hemisphere as well as around the world. It would have done for Castro a good deal in rebuilding a very fading prestige in Latin America. And from that point of view would have also endangered our interests.

And, of course, no one at that time was certain that Khrushchev would make such a far-reaching step, which is wholly a departure from Soviet foreign policy, really since, I would say, the Berlin blockade. And, as I say, we might have borne responsibility for the loss of Berlin, without having any justification for our action.

Now, (b) [Robert Kennedy's second question]: The surveillance of the island did not disclose any buildup of offensive capabilities at least until Tuesday [October 16]. We heard rumors of the—from refugees. But when those were borne out, Mr. [Roger] Hilsman, who's in charge of that [intelligence for the State Department], says that most of them were . . . They were all talking about the SAM sites, the ground-air missiles. Is that correct?

Roger Hilsman: Yes, sir. I wouldn't say I was in charge.

President Kennedy: What?

Hilsman: I wouldn't say I was in charge of the whole thing.

President Kennedy: Well, whoever. At least from the refugee interrogation. What about the refugee interrogation?

Hilsman: Well, yes sir, well, the situation here is that Mr. McCone probably would like to speak to it.

Actually, this particular site is the first one [that] was covered by Air Force photography on August 29th and there was nothing there. It has been rechecked again. There was nothing there, August 29th.

We began to be more, began to be suspicious in general as the ships kept coming in, big crates there, and sharply suspicious when, on the 28th of September, when we saw the IL-28 crates. We then began to get a few reports, collateral reports, about this particular site.

We were precluded from flying over that particular site by a cloud cover for a long period of time there, days on end, but I'll let Mr. McCone correct me on that. Then, when finally the weather broke, it was a Sunday [October 14]. We got a flight over it, and we then saw the beginnings of the deployment there. And you can show in photographs, between Sunday and Monday, the dramatic progress in only 24 hours.

President Kennedy: Well, I want to have those available to the [congressional] leadership, Mr. Hilsman.

John McCone: I think we have to be careful at this point because there were some refugee reports. I think this is what [Senator Kenneth] Keating has been basing his position on. I wouldn't be too categoric that we had no information because, as a matter of fact, there were some 15, I think, various refugee reports that circulated around that were indicative that something was going on.

But we had no surveillance, I think, from August the 29th till the 14th of October, that gave us positive information. Therefore we were dealing during that period with conjecture and assumptions, rather than hard intelligence.

But I would be a little bit careful on this because I think this Keating performance, he has made quite a number of speeches on this, and has received some information through refugees, on which he has based his claim that he knew there were missiles there and all the rest.

Robert Kennedy: Mr. President, of course we get the refugees reports which frequently prove inaccurate.

I think the second point, which is extremely important, is the fact that you couldn't really tell—even if we had had photography, it would be difficult on these nonpermanent sites to tell, up until a week or ten days ago, even if we had a flight across there. So I don't think we have to say that it goes back into September, the middle of September or early September, or the end of August. Even if we had had a flight in the middle of September, the chances are we wouldn't have been able to tell up until the last ten days or two weeks. [*Unclear.*]

President Kennedy: There is, of course . . . I don't think any Soviet expert assumed that they would engage in this radical alteration, in view of the fact that no Eastern European satellite, for example, has such [nuclear] weapons on their territory. This would be the first time the Soviet Union has moved these weapons outside their own [*unclear*].

Robert Kennedy: The other thing, of course, is that the Russian ambassador [Dobrynin] has told officials within the government, continuously up until just last week as well as Gromyko's conversation with you, that this was not being done.

President Kennedy: It should be understood that the media . . . Then, of course, we issued our statements on September 4th and 13th and secured OAS approval of stepped-up surveillance. We understood that the medium-range missiles are a field type that can be moved in and out. The intermediate-range missile sites are excavations, so they're going to be developing.

Now, the second question [actually Robert Kennedy's third question] I've already referred to: Why not take stronger action now, such as an air strike or an invasion? I think I've already answered that.

McGeorge Bundy: Mr. President, I think it may be quite important *not* to get into too much public discussion as to the difficulty of hitting these targets. I was out of the room when you discussed this, but I don't think we want to . . . We may be doing this in a few days.

President Kennedy: All right.

Bundy: [*Unclear*] we can't do it, is not the perfect prelude to that.

President Kennedy: No.

Robert Kennedy: I think the Pearl Harbor thing is the . . .

Rusk: And what we say about it doesn't want to tie our hands to the future at this time. I think we say we have obligations to bring such threats to the OAS, to the United Nations. We can be sure our own people fully understand, and give the other side a chance to rethink what it's doing and to take another course.

Bundy: Point out the position of the government is to deal with this matter firmly and resolutely with the minimum necessary force to make the result.

President Kennedy: But it is a fact that even with the air strike we didn't, we couldn't, have gotten . . . We couldn't, perhaps, get all the missiles that are in sight.

Bundy: Entirely true, Mr. President. But I don't think the next few days is the time to talk about it.

President Kennedy: [*annoyed*] I know, but I want everybody [here] to understand it, Mac, if you don't mind. The fact of the matter is there are missiles on the island which are not in sight.

Now, you mentioned Pearl Harbor. Is this action justified, what we're now doing? This is one of the problems which are going to be most troublesome in our discussions with our allies. Inasmuch as the Soviet missiles are already pointed at the U.S., and U.S. missiles are [pointed] at the U.S.S.R., particularly those—the most obvious example is in Turkey and Italy. In other words, what is the distinction between these missiles and the missiles which we sent to Turkey and Italy, which the Soviets put up with, which are operational, and have been for two to three years? My understanding is that the State Department is preparing a brief on that matter.

George Ball: We have prepared that, Mr. President.

President Kennedy: Could you get that? I'd like to take a look at it afterward.

Ball: We've prepared the factual statement.

Rusk: That's labeled "Secret." We've got to have something we can make . . .

Mr. President, on that, in 1957 this, for example, was a decision by NATO to establish certain of these weapons in Europe. This was in the face of an announcement by the Soviet Union that they were equipping their armed forces with nuclear missiles. In the face of a demand on their part that all forces, all NATO forces in Europe, renounce the use of such weapons. Therefore, in the great Soviet-NATO confrontation, the Soviets were insisting upon having hundreds of these weapons aimed at Europe and none of these weapons pointed the other way. That is the NATO . . . That's the Turkey-Italy situation.

President Kennedy: At the time we sent these missiles to Turkey and to Italy, did we have intercontinental ballistic missiles ourselves? Or did the Soviets—

Rusk: Well, we sent them only in '59, sir. So I doubt that we were—

Bundy: No.

Maxwell Taylor: That was just at the start of our [ICBM] program, as I recall.

George Anderson: We didn't have any operational.

President Kennedy: They did not . . . We didn't know that, did we, after Sputnik.

But, anyway, before the end of the day we'll have in everybody's hand—[by] the end of the evening—a brief on this question of the . . . Because this is going to be one of the matters that are going to be most troublesome for our ambassadors. We ought to get it clear in the American press and others as to why we object to something that the Russians—why the situation doesn't match. I think we've got to get that thing declassified and get it in shape and take a look at that, as soon as this meeting's over.

In any case, the Soviet move was undertaken secretly, accompanied by false Soviet statements in public and private. The departure from the

Soviet position that it has no need or desire to station strategic weapons off the Soviet territory, their statement in TASS in mid-September said that they had the rockets and therefore there was no need to do this.

Our bases abroad are by published agreement to help local people maintain their independence against a threat from abroad. Soviet history is exactly the opposite. Offensive missiles in Cuba have a very different psychological and political effect in this hemisphere than missiles in the U.S.S.R. pointed to us. And had we done nothing, Communism and Castroism are going to be spread through the hemisphere as governments frightened by this new evidence of power have toppled.

D. All this represents a provocative change in the delicate status quo both countries have maintained. If we accepted this one [provocative action]—and he may, anyway—he [Khrushchev] would have tried more. In this sense this is a probing action preceding [renewed confrontation over] Berlin, to see whether we accept it or not.

In another sense, Khrushchev was desperate enough to change his missile policy and take this step for the very reason that we have so long frustrated his design in Berlin. And that's . . . Thompson, is he here?

Bundy: Yes.

President Kennedy: I think that, in talking the other day [October 18], he [Thompson] made this point, that [seeing Thompson] you thought that part of this may be due to the point that he [Khrushchev] has a sense of frustration about Berlin and not a very clear way of getting control of it. Tommy?

Llewellyn Thompson: Yes sir. He [Khrushchev] made it quite clear in my last talk with him, that he was squirming under the problems that he was . . . That he felt he couldn't back down from the position he'd taken. He'd come so far. At the same time he was worried about the fact that he was going forward to it [confrontation over Berlin] and going to lose, and then would have to go on and flip the coin as to whether or not we reacted, [*unclear*] war.

Rusk: Mr. President, I know we talked about this point too. And I wonder what your judgment would be about using it with some of the background [briefing for the press] anyhow. That is, that these missiles do create a special threat for the United States quite apart from the fact that we have been living, we know, under the threat of certain Soviet missiles, because these increase the threat to a country [the United States] which is a principal nuclear support of 41 allies all over the world.

It really comes back a little bit to the military argument we had the other day. But it seems to me that it ought to be pointed out that missiles of this magnitude is not something that we can brush aside, simply because the Soviets have some other missiles that could also reach the United States.

The fact is that, you have this [unclear] here in this room, the number of missiles that launch in these sites would double the known missile strength the Soviet Union has to reach this country.[16] And in that sense our basic nuclear strength of all these alliances is the United States, so this is a matter we can't ignore.

Thompson: In the connection to this point, Mr. President, I don't know whether you want to use it or not—but it seems clear now that Khrushchev's statement about putting all Berlin off until after the [U.S. congressional] election was timed to coincide with this.

President Kennedy: Fine. Does this invite Khrushchev to justify trading off Berlin for Cuba? First, (A) the island is not comparable. We have no strategic weapons moving into Berlin and have offered to have internationally supervised free plebiscites by people [of Berlin], to determine whether they wanted us there. If the Cuban people had that same opportunity, that could produce a different situation.

(B) Gromyko made it very clear last week, as they have in all their conversations, [that] they're getting ready to move on Berlin anyway. This does not increase their determination to move on Berlin, no matter what we do, because he said they're going to do it anyway. This may give them a different way of doing it, but they're going to do it anyway.

(C) Our quarantine will not keep out food or medicine and need not endanger war. In other words, we're not stopping any goods but the shipment of offensive weapons. Even today the Soviets inspect our, they stop our convoys going into Berlin. People get out, don't they? They don't inspect the trucks.

Bundy: No, sir. The people do not get out, and this troop inspection is a complicated one. They have ample means of surveillance, but *inspection* is not the word we want to use.

President Kennedy: What surveillance? What does that mean?

Bundy: Well, they have a checkpoint and they watch the convoys.

Rusk: They have ample means of knowing whether—

Bundy: They know that there are no offensive weapons in Berlin. They have plenty of ways of knowing that.

Unidentified: Sometimes they get out; sometimes they don't. And they do let these people look in through the tailgates in the trucks.

Bundy: That's right.

President Kennedy: They do let them? Yeah, well that's—

Rusk: But the central point here is that we're in Berlin by right as well as by the acknowledgment and agreement of the Soviet Union.

They're bringing these things into Cuba contrary to the Rio Pact. So there's all the difference in the world between these.

President Kennedy: Yes. So I think we want to make . . . What we're trying to do is make a distinction between our actions and a Soviet blockade of Berlin, or the [Soviet] blockade of '47–'48. The degree of surveillance and inspection which they have over the movement of troops and personnel [into Berlin]. And the fact that no weapons, no strategic weapons, have been placed in Berlin. And the fact that we're permitting goods to move into Cuba at this point, food and all the rest. This is not a blockade in that sense. It's merely an attempt to prevent the shipment of weapons there.

Khrushchev's conclusion, his purpose apparently, was to force us into, add to his strategic nuclear power, force us into a choice of initiating an attack on Cuba, which would free his hand, et cetera, and/or appearing to be an irresolute ally. [*Unclear.*]

I want to go back to saying: I think that the talk which we considered [at] any time an air attack. I want to restate that now, and that is a matter which I don't think we ought to discuss under any conditions. We may simply have to do it. In any case, we don't want to look like we were considering it. So I think we ought to just scratch that from all our statements and conversations, and not ever indicate that that was a course of action open to us. I can't say that strongly enough. We don't want to ever have it around that this was one of the alternatives that we considered this week. I think it will be very difficult to keep it quiet, but I think we ought to because it may inhibit us in the future. And, in addition, it will become a propaganda matter, that this was a matter seriously considered by the [U.S.] government. So let's not consider that as one of the alternatives in any discussion.

Anybody else have any thoughts about this?

Rusk: [*Unclear*] one more question, Mr. President.

Robert Kennedy: I think probably the reason, when you compare— when somebody brings up why you didn't have an attack or why you didn't have an air strike, to say that it was just not considered on the basis of the fact that we couldn't have the Pearl Harbor kind of operation, rather than go into all the detail of why it would not . . .

Rusk: It was not done because, rather than it was not considered.

Robert Kennedy: Not done. Yeah. Rather than go into all the details, the military reasons we didn't.

President Kennedy: All right. Well, I think that's fair enough.

Taylor: Mr. President, I should call attention to the fact we're starting moves now which are overt, and will be seen and reported on and commented on. So that movement of armor, for example, to the East Coast. We'll start moving some shipping. We'll start loading some Marines on the West Coast. And you'll be faced with the question: "Are you preparing to invade?" We'll be faced with that question. I think we need guidance on that point.

President Kennedy: What do you suggest saying on that?

Rusk: Mr. President, I would suggest that we urge the press not to come back to each one of these things. We say that, obviously, precautionary moves are going to be taken. That it does not serve the public interest to call attention to each and all of them. We are in a very critical situation, and that we should not be forced to relate each of these moves. That, naturally, with tensions as high as they are at the present time, the President's going to be redisposing forces, but it's not in the public interest to try to explain each one of the moves.

Bundy: One slightly supplementary point. We don't want to look as if we got scared off from anything. There is no current order for invasion.

President Kennedy: Plan for invasion.

Bundy: I think that's very important.

Rusk: Well, if the President's speech talks about what he's going to do, therefore there are a lot of things that you could do that he's not doing at the moment. I wouldn't, at this moment, deny any particular line of action too categorically.

Unidentified: Keep it ambiguous.

President Kennedy: In other words, though, I think we shouldn't have it hanging over us that we're preparing invasion. That isn't strategically or politically useful.

Taylor: We're increasing the range of our possible reactions.

President Kennedy: Yes, that's right.

Bundy: Mr. President, we've told the Department of Defense to be ready for any eventuality.

. . .

President Kennedy: All right. Now let me just go back once more to this—because I don't want to leave this dangling—about any action, direct action. Invasion—I think we've got an agreement about what our status is *re*invasion. No orders for that have been given. I've only said we'd be prepared for [that] eventuality.

Robert McNamara: Right.

President Kennedy: The question of air action, I think we'll stick just with: It comes to be a question of the Pearl Harbor thing and not go into any military details. I think that's very important, and security's been so well held with this group, that I don't think there'll be any problem with that. But I do think it's vitally important that we not discuss the tactical nature or the strategic nature of it, and stick with the Pearl Harbor explanation.

Bundy: I think that "No orders have been given" is the perfect phrase.

President Kennedy: Thank you very much.

5:30 P.M.

Meeting with the Congressional Leadership

President Kennedy was now ready to address the American people. But first he had to speak privately with their elected representatives, the Democratic and Republican leaders of the U.S. Congress. Then he would deliver his nationally televised address to tens of millions of anxious viewers across the country, a speech that would be rebroadcast and distributed in many languages across the world.

Congress had not been in session. The 20 members that filed into the Cabinet Room had been gathered from all over the country, usually by military officers calling or arriving with an urgent message and offering military transport to bring them back to Washington. The senators included, in alphabetical order: Everett McKinley Dirksen (R-Illinois), the minority leader; J. William Fulbright (D-Arkansas), chairman of the Foreign Relations Committee; Bourke B. Hickenlooper (R-Iowa), chairman of the Republican Policy Committee; Hubert H. Humphrey (D-Minnesota), the majority whip; Thomas Kuchel (R-California), the minority whip; Michael J. Mansfield (D-Montana), the majority leader; Richard Russell (D-Georgia), chairman of the Armed Services Committee; Leverett Saltonstall (R-Massachusetts), the ranking minority member of the Armed Services Committee; and George A. Smathers (D-Florida), a good friend of Kennedy and a person, obviously, with strong interest in Cuba. Members of the House included Hale Boggs (D-Louisiana), the majority whip; Charles A. Halleck (R-Indiana), the minority leader; John Taber (R-New York), ranking minority member of the Appropriations Committee; and Carl Vinson (D-Georgia), chairman of the Armed Services Committee.

John McCormack (D-Massachusetts), who had become Speaker of the House in November 1961 following the death of Sam Rayburn, was listed among those present but said nothing. At the 10:00 A.M. meeting of the Executive Committee on October 23, Vice President Johnson made comments that indicated he had been present, but if so, he, too, remained silent.

Those to whom Kennedy would listen most intently were Russell, Mansfield, Fulbright, Vinson, Dirksen, and perhaps Halleck. Though Russell's power was waning, largely because of his adamant opposition to almost any civil rights legislation, he remained the single most influential member of the Senate. His judgment carried great weight with the whole bloc of southern Democrats and with Republicans as well. Mansfield was also respected by a large number of fellow senators. On foreign policy issues, Fulbright's voice in the Senate was second only to Russell's. Only later would he acquire a reputation as a maverick. Kennedy had wanted him as secretary of state but passed him over because of his open support for racial segregation. "Uncle Carl" Vinson had the dominant voice in the House on defense programs. Also, he and Russell worked closely together. Dirksen and Halleck not only enjoyed influence with fellow Republicans in Congress but regularly appeared on television to state party policy. Because of Dirksen's distinctive bass voice, delivery in the manner of a Shakespearean actor, and talent for producing quotable comments, this so-called Ev and Charlie Show drew a large audience.

All these senators and members of the House knew that something grave was happening. They also knew the President was scheduled to give a nationally televised speech. But beyond that, they had been left, until this moment, with rumors or more or less educated guesses.

Though Kennedy knew precisely what he intended to say to the nation, he needed to approach the congressional leaders as if seeking their wisdom, not just reading them a lesson. This was not easy to manage, and the session turned out to be at least as difficult as the one three days earlier with the Joint Chiefs.

President Kennedy turned on the tape recorder as the intelligence briefing got underway.

John McCone: . . . carrying military personnel not in uniform as well as civilian technicians and military equipment.

At first it was impossible to tell the nature of the military materiel being transported in this unprecedented Soviet move. Evidence initially obtained supported the conclusion that a major deployment of defensive equipment was taking place. We detected delivery of surface-to-air missiles in quantity and, on August the 29th, noted from aerial photography the start of construction of air defense sites with guided missiles of the latest Soviet type.

Late in September, persistent reports came to us from refugee sources from Cuba indicating that defensive deployment was only the initial phase and was to be followed by the delivery of offensive missiles. Aerial reconnaissance, on September the 5th, indicated no offensive weapons. And flights scheduled for September the 17th and September the 22nd aborted because of weather. Flights in late September and early October gave us added information on the surface-to-air defense installations but did not reveal the offensive missiles or sites.

On October the 14th, we received unmistakable proof of the beginning of the installation of offensive missile sites, that is, a flight on October the 14th, the results of which were obtained a day or so later. Since then, during the past week, the deployment of missiles and missile equipment has continued and the construction of missile base complexes has proceeded in an urgent, highly secretive manner.

The deployment is continuing. There are now 25 Soviet-bloc ships on their way to Cuba. There are 18 Soviet-bloc ships in Cuban ports. There are 15 on their return voyage. Some ships have made two or three shuttle trips back and forth. About 175 Soviet bloc shipments to Cuba have been made since mid-July.

What we have seen to date, either completed or under construction in Cuba, are 24 missile-launcher positions for medium-range ballistic missiles of a range of 1,020 miles located at six base complexes, and 12 launch pads for intermediate-range ballistic missiles of 2,200 miles located at three bases. A total of 36 launchers at nine separate bases. Missiles in these categories are capable of delivering warheads in the megaton range [of explosive yield]. We expect deployment of two missiles per launch position, although to date we have actually seen about 30 medium-range missiles. We have not yet seen any intermediate-range missiles, although they may be in Cuba under cover, or on the ship *Poltava*, which is due to arrive in Cuba in about five days and is peculiarly arranged for the carrying of long cylindrical items of cargo.

The sites are in varying degrees of operational readiness. On the basis of latest evidence, we now believe four MRBM sites containing 16 launchers are in full operational readiness as of October the 22nd. We now estimate that the remaining two MRBM sites containing 8 additional launchers will come into full operational readiness on the 25th and 29th of October, respectively.

Everett Dirksen: How many? Eight?

McCone: Eight more, yeah.

The building of these MRBM sites is a rather simple operation and is accomplished in a week or ten days' time. These MRBMs are considered mobile. They are fired from a trailer-bed type launcher, and their location as now established might suddenly shift to a new location difficult to determine by surveillance methods.

The three IRBM sites containing 12 launch pads still seem likely not to reach full operational readiness until December. However, emergency operational readiness for firing some of the IRBM missiles might be reached somewhat earlier.

In addition, there are 24 primary surface-to-air missile sites in Cuba, of which we believe 22 are now operational. There are also, we believe, 3 coastal defense missile installations with surface-to-surface cruise missiles of about 40-mile range, and 12 missile-launching patrol craft, each craft capable of carrying two surface-to-surface missiles with an effective range of 10 to 15 miles.

Finally, we know that about 40 MiG-21s, an advanced model Soviet supersonic interceptor aircraft, and 20 IL-28s, a Soviet jet bomber with a range of about 1,500 miles, have been delivered to Cuba.

Amid all of this buildup of military strength, evidence of the presence of nuclear warheads has been carefully sought, needless to say. We have found one and possibly three of what appear to be nuclear weapon storage sites. We cannot produce evidence to show that nuclear warheads for these missiles are in Cuba, but we are afraid firm evidence on this point may never become available from intelligence resources at our command. The warheads could be in Cuba, in concealment or temporary storage, without our discovering them. Nevertheless, since the medium-range and intermediate-range ballistic missiles are relatively ineffective weapons without nuclear warheads, we think it prudent to assume that nuclear weapons are now or shortly will be available in Cuba.

.   .   .

McCone: I have only one thing to add, Mr. President. And that is that from a variety of intelligence sources we have concluded that these bases, both the ground-to-air SAM sites as well as the missile sites, are manned by Soviets and, for the most part, put the Soviet guards to keep the Cubans out. We don't think that there are very many Cubans on these bases.

Richard Russell: Mr. McCone, one question. I am sure you are monitoring this. Do you think they have in their complex any electronics installed yet?

McCone: We do on the MRBMs, the more advanced. We do, yes.

Russell: Well, they'd be ready to fire now? And that's true as to the surface-to-air sites?

McCone: Yes. On the surface-to-air we have found that their radars have been latching onto our U-2s [for] the last couple of days, and, while they have not fired a missile at us, we think that they will within a short time.

Russell: My God.

Thomas Kuchel: Are these pictures taken with a U-2?

McCone: They are taken with a U-2. And, incidentally, Mr. President, I would just like to say for the . . . Everybody knows we have to brief a number of people. We're just referring these to pictures taken from military reconnaissance planes. We're making no reference to the U-2 at all. And I think it would be well to—

President Kennedy: The other thing was the numbers. We're not using the precise numbers.

McCone: Yeah, we're not using the precise numbers publicly, nor are we making any reference to the U-2s. Just military reconnaissance.

That's all I have, sir.

Unidentified: Thank you very much.

Bourke Hickenlooper: May I ask—

President Kennedy: Yes, Senator, you go ahead.

Hickenlooper: May I ask, Mr. President, as to the timetable of your estimates, now, when they could really mount an extensive attack against the United States? I mean, I know some of the missiles are ready to go at the moment.

President Kennedy: Perhaps Mr. McCone would want to respond to that.

Hickenlooper: Six weeks, five weeks, four—three months, two months, one month?

McCone: Yes, well we think that at the present time they have two-thirds of their MRBMs in place, which would mean 16 launchers ready to go at the present time. We think that 2 more will be operational by the end of this month. So that you could say, by October the 30th there would be 5 times 4, [that] would be 20 launchers in place. We think the 8—or 12, rather, IRBMs will come into operational status in December with the possibility that some of the pads might be operational in a couple of weeks in advance of that.

Now, we do not know the condition of the warheads because we are unable to detect that from photography. And we have no clandestine sources on the warheads.

Kuchel: Wouldn't that be suicide if they did that?

McCone: Yes, it would be suicide all right—because we could respond.

Dean Rusk: That's as part of the general nuclear exchange. That would be part of the general nuclear exchange. [*Unclear*] at this country and everybody else, in spite of—

. . .

President Kennedy: Perhaps a word from Ambassador Thompson. He has had a lot of conversation with Khrushchev. Perhaps he might want to say something about his evaluation of the purposes.

Llewellyn Thompson: Mr. President, I had my farewell talk with Khrushchev at the end of July. He made very clear then that he was . . . He gave an indication that time was running out on his stalling any further on the Berlin issue. And that at the same time he felt that he had gone too far out on a limb to go back, and he was concerned that if he went forward, he would either lose or he'd start a war.

It also seems subsequently that his timing—his indications that he didn't want to talk until the end of November—was related to this buildup. Of course, a concern has been that—what would you do about it is to . . . The effect on our alliances is that if, in fact, one of his purposes, or perhaps his main one, was the showdown on Berlin. In my view that's the main thing that he had in mind.

Russell: I'm sorry, I didn't get that last.

Thompson: That that was the main thing he had in mind. The purpose was to have a showdown on Berlin and he thought that this would help him in that.

Russell: You mean the buildup in Cuba?

Leverett Saltonstall: Mr. President, Mr. Thompson, then you tie this, what we've just heard, into Berlin?

Thompson: That's right.

Rusk: Mr. President, I might make just one or two comments on that, if I may, because I think that this does mean a major and radical move in Soviet policy and Soviet action. This is the first time these missiles are known to be outside the Soviet Union. They are not even in the satellite countries of Eastern Europe.

We have had some impression over the past few months that they have been going through a reappraisal of policy and, we've had the impression that they're coming out of it with a toughness which was not as visible, say, a year ago. Indications from Peiping [Beijing], for example, is they are somewhat more satisfied with Soviet policy than they were, things of that sort.

I want to emphasize that this is the most major development from the Soviet point of view since the Berlin blockade of 1947 and '48 [actually 1948–49]. Why they choose to pursue such a reckless and hazardous course at this point is, of course, speculation. This has both military and, of course, political ramifications.

But I think we ought not, in any sense, to underestimate the gravity of this development in terms of what it means to the Soviet point of view. They are taking risks here which are very heavy indeed and—

Russell: Very heavy, what?

Rusk: Risks which are very heavy indeed.

I think there is real reason to think there has been quite a debate going on in the Soviet Union about the course of action. The peaceful coexistence theme was not getting them very far, and maybe the—it seems clear now that the hard line boys have moved into the ascendancy. So one of the things that we have to be concerned about is not just the missiles, but the entire development of Soviet policy as it affects the situation right around the globe.

Russell: Mr. Secretary, do you see any chance that it'll get any better? If they keep on establishing new bases and dividing our space more and more?

Rusk: No, Senator.

Russell: You see, how can we gain by waiting? If they're establishing new bases.

Rusk: I'm not suggesting that things are getting any better.

President Kennedy: As I say, this information became available Tuesday morning. Mobile bases can be moved very quickly so we don't know . . . we assume we have all the ones that are there now. But the CIA thinks there may be a number of others that are there on the island that have not been set up which can be set up quite quickly because of the mobility.

Intermediate-range ballistic missile, of course, because of its nature, can take a longer time. We'll be able to spot those. The others might be set up in the space of a very few days.

Beginning Tuesday morning after we saw these first ones, we ordered, we did intensive surveillance of the island, a number of U-2 flights flew Wednesday and Thursday. I talked with—asked Mr. McCone to go up and brief General [Dwight] Eisenhower on Wednesday [October 17].

We decided, the Vice President and I, to continue our travels around the country in order not to alert this—until we had gotten all the available information we could. The last information came in on Sunday morning giving us this last site [Remedios IRBM site] which we mentioned.

We are presented with a very difficult problem because of Berlin as well as other reasons, but mostly because of Berlin. This is rather a . . . It has many advantages from Khrushchev's point of view. He takes a great chance but there is quite some rewards to it. If we move into Cuba, he sees the difficulty I think we face. If we invade Cuba, we have a chance that these missiles will be fired on us.

In addition, Khrushchev will seize Berlin and that Europe will regard Berlin's loss, which is of such symbolic importance to Berlin [he means to say *Europe*], as having been the fault of the United States by acting in a precipitous way. After all, they are 5[,000] or 6,000 miles from Cuba and much closer to the Soviet Union. So these missiles don't bother them and maybe they should think it should not bother us. So that whatever we do in regard to Cuba gives him a chance to do the same in regard to Berlin.

On the other hand, to not do anything is to argue that these missile bases really extend only what we had to live under for a number of years—from submarines which are getting more and more intense, from the Soviet intercontinental ballistic missile system which is in a rapid buildup, has a good deal of destruction which it could bring on us, as well as their bombers—that this adds to our hazards but does not create a new military hazard. And that we should keep our eye on the main site, which would be Berlin.

Our feeling, however, is that that would be a mistake. So that, beginning tonight, we're going to blockade Cuba carrying out the [action] under the Rio Treaty. We called for a meeting of the Rio Pact countries and hope to get a two-thirds vote for them to give the blockade legality. If we don't get it, then we'll have to carry it out illegally or have a declaration of war, which is not as advantageous to us. We don't know what Khrushchev will—

Dirksen: A complete blockade?

President Kennedy: What?

Dirksen: Complete blockade?

President Kennedy: A blockade as it will be announced will be for the movement of weapons into Cuba. But we don't know what the [Soviet-] bloc ships will do. In order not to give Mr. Khrushchev the justification for imposing a complete blockade on Berlin, we are going to start with a blockade on the shipment of offensive weapons into Cuba but stop all ships.

Now, we don't know what the bloc ships will do. We assume that they will probably . . . We don't know what they'll do, whether they'll try to send one through, make us fire on it, and use that as a justification on Berlin or whether he'll have them all turn back. In any case we're going to start on offensive weapons.

We will then consider extending it as the days go on to other—petroleum, oil, lubricants, and other matters, except food and medicine. These are matters we will reach a judgment on as the days go on.

Now, in the meanwhile, we are making military preparations in regard to Cuba so that if the situation deteriorates further, we will have the flexibility. Though the invasion is—it's the only way to get rid of these weapons—the other way to get rid of them. They'll fire so that it's a . . . going to be . . . going to just have to, it seems to me, watch with great care.

As I say, if we invade Cuba, there's a chance these weapons will be fired at the United States. If we attempt to strike them from the air, then we will not get them all because they're mobile. And we know where the sites are, but there isn't much to destroy at the site. And they can move them and set them up in another three days someplace else so that we have not got a very easy situation.

As for the choice between doing nothing, we felt that that would imperil Berlin rather than help it, and imperil Latin America.

So after a good deal of searching we decided this was the place to start. Now we don't know what their response will be. We've got two, three, or four problems. One will be if we continue to surveil them and they shoot down one of our planes. We will then have the problem of taking action against part of Cuba.

So I think that, I'm going to ask Secretary McNamara to detail what we're doing militarily. If there's any strong disagreement with what at least we have set out to do, I want to hear it. Otherwise, I think what we ought to do is try to keep in very close contact before anything that is done of a major kind differently, and it may have to be done in the next 24 to 48 hours, because I assume the Soviet response will be very strong. Then we'll all have to meet again. Needless to say, the Vice President and I have concluded our campaigns.

J. William Fulbright: Mr. President, do I understand that you have decided, and will announce tonight, the blockade?

President Kennedy: That's correct. The quarantine. That's right.

Rusk: Mr. President, may I add one point to what you just said on these matters?

We do think this first step provides a brief pause for the people on the other side to have another thought before we get into an utterly crashing crisis, because the prospects that are ahead of us at this moment are very serious. Now, if the Soviets have underestimated what the United States is likely to do here, then they've got to consider whether they revise their judgment quick and fast.

The same thing with respect to the Cubans. Quite apart from the OAS and the U.N. aspects of it, a brief pause here is very important in order to give the Soviets a chance to pull back from the brink here. But I do want to say, Mr. President, I think the prospects here are for a rapid development of the situation . . . could be a very grave matter indeed.

Russell: Mr. President, I could not stay silent under these circumstances and live with myself. I think that our responsibilities to our people demand stronger steps than that in view of this buildup there, and I must say that in all honesty to myself.

I don't see how we are going to get any stronger or get into any better position to meet this threat. It seems to me that we're at the crossroads. We're either a first-class power or we're not. You have warned these people time and again, in the most eloquent speeches I have read since Woodrow Wilson, as to what would happen if there was an offensive capability created in Cuba. They can't say they're not on notice.

The Secretary of State says: "Give them time to pause and think." They'll use that time to pause and think, to get better prepared. And if we temporize with this situation, I don't see how we can ever hope to find a place where . . . We have a complete justification by law for carrying out the announced foreign policy of the United States if . . . You have announced time and again—that if there was an offensive capability there, that we would take any steps that were necessary to see that certain things which should . . . Transit, for example. They can stop transit through the Windward Passage, the Leeward Passage, easily with these missiles and with these ships. They could blow Guantánamo off the map. And you have told them not to do this thing. They've done it. And I think that you should assemble as speedily as possible an adequate force and clean out that situation.

The time is going to come, Mr. President, when we're going to have to take this gamble in Berlin, in Korea, and in Washington, D.C., and Winder, Georgia, for the nuclear war. I don't know whether Khrushchev will launch a nuclear war over Cuba or not. I don't believe he will. But I think that the more that we temporize, the more surely he is to convince himself that we are afraid to make any real movement and to really fight.

President Kennedy: Well, perhaps, Mr. Senator, if you could just hear Secretary McNamara . . . what we're doing, then we could . . .

Russell: Pardon me. You had said, if anybody disagrees, and I couldn't sit here, feeling as I do . . .

President Kennedy: I understand. Let me just say [*unclear*]—and then we can have a roundtable.

Robert McNamara: The President has asked that we initiate a quarantine. We are redeploying our vessels into position to start those operations. They'll become effective as promptly as the initial political moves are completed. Sometime tomorrow or the next day.

. . .

Russell: Mr. President, I don't want to make a nuisance of myself but I would like to complete my statement.

My position is that these people have been warned. They've had all the warning they could expect. And they're here. And our Secretary of State speaks about the pause. When you enforce this blockade, Khrushchev's never said up to now that he wouldn't fight over Cuba. He is going to start rattling his missiles, and making firmer and firmer and firmer statements about what he's going to do about Cuba. And you will only make it sure that when that day comes, when if they do use these MiGs to attack our shipping or to drop a few bombs around Miami or some other place, and we do go in there, that we'll lose a great many more men than we would right now and—

President Kennedy: But, Senator, we can't invade Cuba. For instance, it takes us some while to assemble our force to invade Cuba. That's one of the problems we've got. We haven't wanted to surface the movement of troops beyond what has been surfaced in the last 48 hours. But we have to bring some troops from the West Coast, and to assemble the force which would give us the 90,000-odd men who might participate in an invasion will take some days. That's why I wanted Secretary McNamara [to be here]. We are now assembling that force, but it is not in a position to invade Cuba in the next 24 or 48 hours.

Now, I think it may very well come to that before the end of the week. But we are moving all of the forces that we have, that will be necessary for an invasion, to the area around Cuba as quickly as we possibly can.

Unidentified: I think if it were a fait accompli we'd—

President Kennedy: Exactly. I agree.

Russell: —we'd have much better . . . we'd much narrower escape an all-out war with Russia.

President Kennedy: But we don't have the forces to seize Cuba.

Russell: Well, we can assemble them.

President Kennedy: Well, that's what we're doing now.

Russell: How long?

President Kennedy: OK. Secretary McNamara can describe this. As I say, we just don't have forces there.

Russell: This blockade is going to put them on the alert. And it's going to give the Russians . . . Khrushchev will be making incendiary statements—

President Kennedy: Exactly.

Russell: —and he'll get worse everywhere he goes and it'll make it more and more sure that, when we are forced to take action in Cuba, that we will still have to further divide our forces and be weaker at every point around the whole periphery of the free world.

President Kennedy: Well, Senator, perhaps Secretary McNamara can describe what our military problem is and then we can see—

Charles Halleck: Well, I just want to reminisce just a little bit. We were here, Dick [*referring to Russell*]. We were told by somebody in the Pentagon sitting right over there that it would take us three months to take Cuba. Am I right about that? [*Unclear exchange about the date of that meeting.*]

President Kennedy: Mr. McNamara, why don't you make a statement.

McNamara: Perhaps I can throw some light on that.

To carry out an invasion against the substantial buildup that has taken place in Cuba would require use of about 250,000 U.S. military personnel. Now, that covers air, sea, and ground personnel. The invasion force itself, excluding reserve forces that would have to be available, would be on the order of 90,000, depending upon exactly how it was done, what portion would be airborne, what air dropped, and what portion was sea landed. The force would require the gathering together of over 100 merchant ships. It requires the call-up from the reserves of C-119 squadrons. Several hundred aircraft must be assembled for that purpose, in addition to the aircraft on active duty. It requires the movement into the ports, as the President indicated, of units from the West Coast, both Army units which will move across the country with their equipment by rail and Marine units which will move by sea from [Camp] Pendleton and which will be part of the potential invasion force.

These movements have started. It was essential they not be started, however, prior to a certain point ahead of the time when it became possible to surface this operation.

We can be prepared within seven days to start an invasion. It's quite clear that that invasion must be preceded by a substantial air attack. I will mention the figure, I know that I can count on you to keep it in confidence. At least 2,000 bombing sorties must take place prior to the invasion. There are about 8[,000] to 10,000 Soviet personnel, probably military personnel, known as technicians but undoubtedly military personnel, on the island at the present time maintaining the missile bases that were discussed and the surface-to-air missile sites.

Halleck: Bombing sorties with what kind of bombs?

McNamara: Initially iron bombs.

The plans for invasion have been laid out in great detail. The movements preparatory thereto have been started at the direction of the President. As I have suggested, it will take at least seven days to carry out the air strikes necessary to introduce the invasion.

Russell: Mr. Secretary, do you see from your position in the Pentagon where we are getting better prepared militarily vis-à-vis the Soviet forces by delaying and waiting and putting this thing off till next year?

You put these tired old B-49s, -47s, or B-49s, whatever they are—

McNamara: 47s.

Russell: 47s—all of them nearly worn out, now, you put them on 24-hour alert, and that's the bulk of our forces, bomber forces. That's three-fourths of it in number, over two-thirds.[17] You have [*someone coughs and a word or two are lost*]; you won't have anything. And you just can't depend on these missiles, our missiles. Our intermediate missiles won't intercept. But if you think time's running in our favor?

McNamara: I do, in this instance.

Russell: What do you base that on?

McNamara: The B-47s and B-52s we have prepared for airborne alert by procuring, as you know, the additional spares necessary to support an airborne alert. I have no doubt whatsoever that we can maintain an airborne alert indefinitely without degrading our force. And this opinion is shared by [Air Force chief of staff] General [Curtis] LeMay.

I have no question but what with a blockade we can not only stop but eventually attrit, stop the buildup, but also attrit the Cuban force, and do this as the President directs. Moreover, we must have the seven-day period of preparation for an invasion. It would not be possible—

Russell: Well, why didn't you start when you first got these notifications of all these [missiles] down there? It's been over seven days.

McNamara: The first notification came in Tuesday [October 16], and there's been intensive review during the entire week of that. The Tuesday reports were far from conclusive, and it wasn't until Sunday morning [October 21] that the information came in that led to the report [about the Remedios IRBM site] Mr. McCone mentioned today.[18]

Nor has it been possible during this week to carry out more than one to two days worth of the seven-day preparation without breaking the whole story. It's been really remarkable that we've been able to do as much as we have without more speculation in the press.

Carl Vinson: Mr. Secretary, does the Joint Chiefs of Staff approve of all your plans with reference to the invasion, if it gets—

McNamara: Yes, sir. The President ordered us to prepare for an invasion of Cuba months ago. I think it was—Mr. President, perhaps you recall better than I, but I believe it was November of last year. And we have developed plans in great detail. We've developed a series of alternative plans, several of them. We've reviewed them with the President over the past ten months on five different occasions. We're well prepared for an invasion, as well prepared as we could possibly be, facing the situation we do.

I think it's quite remarkable, startlingly so, as a matter of fact, that we can consider an invasion with seven days' preparation. No invasion of this size, that any of my military staff can recall, has ever been prepared with no more than a seven-day lead time.

Dirksen: Mr. Secretary, did this have approval of the National Security Council?

McNamara: The plans? Yes, sir.

Dirksen: Were they unanimous?

President Kennedy: We met yesterday.

Dirksen: Good.

President Kennedy: Let me just say, Senator [Russell], I understand your . . . There's two or three points.

In the first place, in order to invade Cuba, it seems to me we have to have this buildup of force, one of the reasons why we've been concerned this week is we wanted to know all the sites. And we wanted to know the firing position of these missiles.

If we go into Cuba we have to all realize that we are taking a chance that these missiles, which are ready to fire, won't be fired. So that's a gamble we should take. In any case we are preparing to take it. I think that is one hell of a gamble. But I think it's because . . . but we're going to have to assume that . . . When we finally decide whether we're going to do it, I am going to have everybody in this room be here with us because we ought to decide this one together. But that's going to have to be the judgment.

In the meanwhile, we are going to move all of the available forces that we have to be in a position to carry out this invasion as quickly as we possibly can. But the key question is going to be, and we all ought to be thinking about it in the next 48 hours, is two or three key questions. In the first place, if the Russians as a response . . .

.   .   .

So, we may have the war by the next 24 hours.

All I want to say is that we are going to move, with maximum speed, all of our forces to be in a position to invade Cuba within the seven-day period. Number One.

Number Two. This group will meet in the next 48 hours—we probably ought to think of coming back again—to see where we stand two days from now and make a judgment as to whether we should take that risk of going in there, under the conditions we have described.

Number Three. We have the prospect, if the Soviet Union, as a reprisal, should grab Berlin in the morning, which they could do within a couple of hours. Our war plan at that point has been to fire our nuclear weapons at them. So that these are all the matters which are—which we have to be thinking about.

Russell: Excuse me again, but do you see a time ever in the future when Berlin will not be hostage to this kind of circumstance?

President Kennedy: No, I think Berlin is . . . And give it up?

Russell: It matters what they do down there, whether they fire on us or not. Berlin will be hostage to these same circumstances we've got right here.

President Kennedy: There isn't a doubt. There isn't a doubt.

Russell: And if we're going to back up on that, we might as well pull our arms in from Europe and save 15 to 25 billion dollars a year and just prepare to defend this continent. We've got to take a chance somewhere, sometime, if we're going to retain our position as a great world power and . . .

. . .

President Kennedy: Now let me just answer that, Senator. That has been one of the matters which we've been concerned about this week, whether a strike of the kind that you're talking about, unannounced, would be able to knock these out. That was one of the reasons why this matter has been held up.

The difficulty with that is, we're not sure of getting them all. We don't know what their orders are. If there was a sudden strike on Turkey or Italy, where we've got missile bases, the [NATO] commanders might fire. They might think it was part of a general attack. We're not sure of getting them all.

In addition, there are at least as many which are still probably in trailers, we figure, and not at the site. So that you would do the Pearl Harbor attack and you'd only get half . . . [*tape interrupted*] . . . haven't had at all the chance somebody's going to blow that button.

Russell: You said after the Cuban [*unclear*] affair before, I recall it very well because I heard it over the radio, that you hoped that the Organization of American States would stand up with us to meet this menace but that, if it didn't, that we would undertake it alone. Now I understand that we are still waiting while the Secretary of State tries to get them to agree to it.

President Kennedy: I'm not waiting. Now, to make the blockade—

Russell: I think we can die by attrition here. I'm through. Excuse me. I wouldn't have been honest with myself if I hadn't. So I hope you forgive me, but you asked for opinion—

President Kennedy: Yeah, I forgive you. As I said, it's a very difficult problem that we're faced with. I'll just tell you that. It's a very difficult choice that we're faced with together. Now, the—

Russell: Oh, my God, I know that. Our authority, and the world's destiny, will hinge on this decision.

President Kennedy: That's right.

Russell: But it's coming someday, Mr. President. Will it ever be under more auspicious circumstances? . . .

President Kennedy: Well now the Organization of American States, quite obviously we'd do better if we'd gotten the other Latin American countries tied in. It's foolish to just kick the whole Rio Treaty out the window.

Russell: Well, I don't want to do that.

President Kennedy: We're going to do the blockade in any case, Senator. The legality of the blockade depends—if it's a peacetime blockade—upon the endorsement, under the Rio Treaty, of the OAS, which meets tomorrow morning. If they don't give us the 14 votes, the two-thirds vote, then we're going to do it anyway. But in that case we are going to have to have what's legally an illegal blockade or a declaration of war.

Now, we will carry a blockade on in any case. We hope with the endorsement—because it will make it a much more satisfactory position if we had that endorsement. But we're going to do it anyway.

In the meanwhile, we've prepared these troops, and then we'll have to just make the judgment later in the week about what we're going to do about it. I understand the force of your arguments. The only point we all have to consider is, if we invade, we take the risk which we have to be conscious of, that these weapons will be fired.

·   ·   ·

Fulbright: Mr. President, do you interpret the blockade will be considered by Russia as an act of war?

President Kennedy: Well, that's only this report, they may or may not.

Fulbright: Of course, it takes two parties to determine that. They might say it's not an act of war. But you're basing your whole—

President Kennedy: No. But they may or they may not, or they may then put a blockade on Berlin. That would be—I don't think there is any doubt that they are going to threaten us.

.   .   .

Kennedy then read aloud a long letter from British prime minister Harold Macmillan which ended:

While you know how deeply I sympathize with all of your difficulty and how much we will do to help in every way, it would only be right to tell you there are two aspects which give me concern. Many of us in Europe have lived so long in close proximity to the enemy's nuclear weapons of the most devastating kind that we have got accustomed to it. So European opinion will need attention. The second, which is more worrying, is that if Khrushchev comes to a conference he will of course try to trade his Cuba position against his ambitions in Berlin and elsewhere. This we must avoid at all costs, as it will endanger the unity of the Alliance.[19]

Saltonstall: Mr. President, you've twice said that a blockade would be illegal unless the OAS gave us 14 votes. Why is it? My only thought is, why emphasize at all any question of illegality?

President Kennedy: I'm not. No, it is a point. That's right. We can always make it legal, as I say, by declaration of war and, in addition, we will do it anyway. But it would give it a particular sanction if we have the OAS endorsement in the morning. If we don't get it, we'll continue it anyway.

.   .   .

Fulbright: Mr. President, one thing about the blockade that does not appeal to me is that you really do have to confront the Russians directly on the ships, whereas if you invade without the blockade, they are not confronted, I mean legally. I mean it's just between us and Cuba. I think a blockade is the worst of the alternatives because if you're confronted with a Russian ship, you are actually confronting Russia. This way, if you have the invasion against Cuba, this is not actually an affront to Russia. They don't pretend that this is their . . . They're not part of the Warsaw Pact.

President Kennedy: I don't think that after the statements they've made . . . I think you have to assume they would not let us build up over a six-, seven-, or eight-day period an invasion force without making these statements.

In addition, I think the inevitable result would be immediate seizure of Berlin. It may be anyway. But I—

Fulbright: I don't see a blockade as being . . . It seems to me the alternative is either just to go to the U.N. and solve without this, or an invasion. A blockade seems to me the *worst* alternative.

McNamara: Mr. President, may I mention that whether an invasion is a confrontation with the Soviets needs to be considered in light of the fact that it would immediately be preceded by over 2,000 bombing sorties directly against the locations occupied by something on the order of 8,000 Soviet military personnel.

Fulbright: But that's quite different. They're in Cuba. Cuba still is supposed to be a sovereign country. It isn't a member of the Warsaw Pact. It's not even a satellite. It's not considered such. It's just a Communist country.

Russell: Do you think the number of sorties is going to get lower, or the number of Russians get fewer?

Fulbright: I don't like the idea of a blockade at all. It seems to me that it complicates the whole thing.

President Kennedy: What are you in favor of, Bill?

Fulbright: I'm in favor, on the basis of this information, of an invasion, and an all-out one, and as quickly as possible.

President Kennedy: Well, now, we've got the seven-day period, as I say.

Fulbright: Well, then, you just stay; I would do nothing until you're ready to invade. I think a blockade leads you to quibbling and delays among our own people, and especially the probability, certainly, of a confrontation with the Russians themselves. It gives him a better excuse for retaliation than our attack on Cuba.

President Kennedy: I don't think there's any use to it. The fact is you can't have any more of a confrontation [than] an invasion of Cuba. An attack on these sites with all—

Fulbright: But they're Cuban sites. They're not Russian sites, and a Russian ship is a Russian ship. I mean, if they can save face, they can just forget it. They're over there, I guess, in whatever their capacity, it is not part of Russia. . . .

But a blockade seems to me the worst alternative. But I don't see why you can avoid saying an attack on a Russian ship is really an act of war against Russia. It is not an act of war against Russia to attack Cuba.

President Kennedy: Well, no. If we have the [OAS] endorsement, just to talk about the legalities of it, it isn't an act of war if we get the endorsement.

Fulbright: It won't be legal—I'm not making the arguments for legal. This is self-defense.

President Kennedy: No, this is legal. Let's say we get a legal . . . under the Rio Treaty and everything. We've got a legal right to take the action we have in regard to the shipment of offensive weapons in there.

Now, when you talk about the invasion, the first [point], excluding the risk that these missiles will be fired, we do have the 7[,000] or 8,000 Russians there. We are going to have to shoot them up. And I think that it would be foolish to expect that the Russians would not regard that as a far more direct thrust than they're going to even regard [firing] on a ship. And I think that the inevitable end result will be immediately the seizure of Berlin.

Now, as I say, we may have to put up with all that and . . . But, I think, that if we're talking about nuclear war, the escalation ought to be at least with some degree of control.

In addition, we've got this seven-day period.

But you can't . . . I don't think in stopping Russian ships—I know that's offensive to the Russians. When you start talking about the invasion it's infinitely more offensive.

Fulbright: But not to the Russians, it seems to me. They have no right to say that is an attack on Russia. I don't think that they have.

Mike Mansfield: Well, I can't quite agree, Bill.

Dirksen: Mr. President, as this thing moves on, and it will take on acceleration, do you contemplate calling the leadership again?

President Kennedy: Yes, I will.

Dirksen: Very soon?

President Kennedy: That's right.

. . .

Vinson: Mr. Secretary, how long will it take you to bring the Marines from Pendleton to the Canal? If you want to talk on that.

McNamara: We're loading the Marines today. It will take about 11 days between the time they leave Pendleton and the time they land in Cuba. They are not in the first wave. We have alternatives—Mr. Chairman, we have alternative plans. Under one plan we go in with a lighter force, a higher percentage airborne. The other plan we go in with a higher percentage seaborne. It's the second plan that uses those Marines. They come in subsequently in the first plan.

. . .

Vinson: Your decision, Mr. President, is based on the fact that it's a risk whatever we do, and that you hope, with the risk of a blockade, it's less of a risk than actually an invasion now. And this risk—

President Kennedy: Well, there's two things. First, Senator, to assemble the forces, being an open society, unlike the Hungarian example [in 1956]. Quite obviously, if we could throw the forces ashore tonight, that would be a different situation. We're going to have for seven days now the movement of these forces and the question of whether we are going to invade is going to be in public speculation. But before we reach the point where we are physically able to do it, we are going to take *this* action.

Now, this action is not quite as hopeless as it . . . It provides for the beginning of an escalation. I don't know where Khrushchev wants to take us. We've got this obligation on Berlin, which is a very difficult place for us to defend. He may put in a blockade in Berlin. He may grab it, in which case we will be taking action there and also in Cuba.

This is only . . . Let me just say that I said at the beginning that the person whose course of action is not adopted is the best off. Because no matter what you do . . . We can go in there with an air strike and you can have the United States . . . Some people would say, well, let's go in there with an air strike. You'd have those bombs go off and blow up 15 cities in the United States. And they would have been wrong. Then we would have—you can go in there and you can not invade and have a worse situation and encourage Khrushchev. You can invade and have those bombs go off and have him also seize Berlin. We have not got . . . The people who are the best off are the people whose advice is not taken because whatever we do is filled with hazards.

Now, the reason we've embarked on the course we have—I'll say this to Senator Fulbright—is because we don't know where we're going to end up on this matter. Ambassador Thompson has felt very strongly that the Soviet Union would regard, will regard the attack on these SAM sites and missile bases with the killing of 4[,000] or 5,000 Russians as a greater provocation than the stopping of their ships. Now, who knows that? We've talked to Ambassador Bohlen. We've talked to Ambassador Thompson. We just tried to make our judgments about a matter about which everyone is uncertain. But at least that—at least it's the best advice we could get.

So we start here, we don't know where he's going to take us or where we're going to take ourselves. But Cuba is dependent on outside shipping. If we ever tighten—if we ever decided that the chance of these rockets going off . . . And I quite agree with Senator Russell, Khrushchev is going to make the strongest statement, which we are going to have to just ignore, about everything. If we stop one Russian ship, it means war.

If we invade Cuba, it means war. There's no telling—I know all the threats are going to be made.

Russell: There's no use in waiting, Mr. President. The nettle is going to sting anyway. You . . .

President Kennedy: That's correct. Now I just think at least we start here, then we see where we go. And I'll tell you that every alternative is full . . .

I'd better go and make this speech [on television to the country].

· · ·

Afterward, Robert Kennedy wrote of his brother's meeting with the congressmen that it had been "the most difficult meeting. I did not attend, but I know from seeing him afterward that it was a tremendous strain."

Yet Robert Kennedy added that although the President was upset when the meeting ended, when the two men discussed it later, "he was more philosophical, pointing out that the congressional leaders' reaction to what we should do, although more militant than his, was much the same as our first reaction when we first heard about the missiles the previous Tuesday."[20]

Around the world, all U.S. military forces began executing orders to come to Defense Condition 3. Defense Condition 5 was normal peacetime readiness. Defense Condition 1 was general war. Nuclear submarines began leaving ports; aircraft and troops were on alert around the world.

At 7:00 P.M., Eastern time, all normal television programming was preempted, and President Kennedy delivered his address to the nation:

> Good evening, my fellow citizens. This Government, as promised, has maintained the closest surveillance of the Soviet military buildup on the island of Cuba. Within the past week unmistakable evidence has established the fact that a series of offensive missile sites is now in preparation on that imprisoned island. The purposes of these bases can be none other than to provide a nuclear strike capability against the Western Hemisphere.
>
> Upon receiving the first preliminary hard information of this nature last Tuesday morning (October 16) at 9:00 A.M., I directed that our surveillance be stepped up. And having now confirmed and completed our evaluation of the evidence and our decision on a course of action, this Government feels obliged to report this new crisis to you in fullest detail.

The characteristics of these new missile sites indicate two distinct types of installations. Several of them include medium-range ballistic missiles capable of carrying a nuclear warhead for a distance of more than 1,000 nautical miles. Each of these missiles, in short, is capable of striking Washington, D.C., the Panama Canal, Cape Canaveral, Mexico City, or any other city in the southeastern part of the United States, in Central America, or in the Caribbean area.

Additional sites not yet completed appear to be designed for intermediate-range ballistic missiles capable of traveling more than twice as far—and thus capable of striking most of the major cities in the Western Hemisphere, ranging as far north as Hudson Bay, Canada, and as far south as Lima, Peru. In addition, jet bombers, capable of carrying nuclear weapons, are now being uncrated and assembled in Cuba, while the necessary air bases are being prepared.

This urgent transformation of Cuba into an important strategic base—by the presence of these large, long-range, and clearly offensive weapons of sudden mass destruction—constitutes an explicit threat to the peace and security of all the Americas, in flagrant and deliberate defiance of the Rio Pact of 1947, the traditions of this nation and Hemisphere, the Joint Resolution of the 87th Congress, the Charter of the United Nations, and my own public warnings to the Soviets on September 4 and 13.

This action also contradicts the repeated assurances of Soviet spokesmen, both publicly and privately delivered, that the arms buildup in Cuba would retain its original defensive character and that the Soviet Union had no need or desire to station strategic missiles on the territory of any other nation.

The size of this undertaking makes clear that it has been planned for some months. Yet only last month, after I had made clear the distinction between any introduction of ground-to-ground missiles and the existence of defensive antiaircraft missiles, the Soviet Government publicly stated on September 11 that, and I quote, "The armaments and military equipment sent to Cuba are designed exclusively for defensive purposes," and, and I quote the Soviet Government, "There is no need for the Soviet Government to shift its weapons for a retaliatory blow to any other country, for instance Cuba," and that, and I quote the Government, "The Soviet Union has so powerful rockets to carry these nuclear warheads that there is no need to search for sites for them beyond the boundaries of the Soviet Union." That statement was false.

Only last Thursday, as evidence of this rapid offensive buildup was already in my hand, Soviet Foreign Minister Gromyko told me in my office that he was instructed to make it clear once again, as he said his Government had already done, that Soviet assistance to Cuba, and I quote, "pursued solely the purpose of contributing to the defense capabilities of Cuba," that, and I quote him, "training by Soviet specialists of Cuban nationals in handling defensive armaments was by no means offensive," and that "if it were otherwise," Mr. Gromyko went on, "the Soviet Government would never become involved in rendering such assistance." That statement also was false.

Neither the United States of America nor the world community of nations can tolerate deliberate deception and offensive threats on the part of any nation, large or small. We no longer live in a world where only the actual firing of weapons represents a sufficient challenge to a nation's security to constitute maximum peril. Nuclear weapons are so destructive and ballistic missiles are so swift that any substantially increased possibility of their use or any sudden change in their deployment may well be regarded as a definite threat to peace.

For many years both the Soviet Union and the United States, recognizing this fact, have deployed strategic nuclear weapons with great care, never upsetting the precarious status quo which insured that these weapons would not be used in the absence of some vital challenge. Our own strategic missiles have never been transferred to the territory of any other nation under a cloak of secrecy and deception; and our history, unlike that of the Soviets since the end of World War II, demonstrates that we have no desire to dominate or conquer any other nation or impose our system upon its people. Nevertheless, American citizens have become adjusted to living daily on the bull's eye of Soviet missiles located inside the U.S.S.R. or in submarines.

In that sense missiles in Cuba add to an already clear and present danger—although it should be noted the nations of Latin America have never previously been subjected to a potential nuclear threat.

But this secret, swift, and extraordinary buildup of Communist missiles—in an area well known to have a special and historical relationship to the United States and the nations of the Western Hemisphere, in violation of Soviet assurances, and in defiance of American and hemispheric policy—this sudden, clandestine decision to station strategic weapons for the first time outside of Soviet soil— is a deliberately provocative and unjustified change in the status quo which cannot be accepted by this country if our courage and our commitments are ever to be trusted again by either friend or foe.

The 1930s taught us a clear lesson: Aggressive conduct, if allowed to grow unchecked and unchallenged, ultimately leads to war. This nation is opposed to war. We are also true to our word. Our unswerving objective, therefore, must be to prevent the use of these missiles against this or any other country and to secure their withdrawal or elimination from the Western Hemisphere.

Our policy has been one of patience and restraint, as befits a peaceful and powerful nation, which leads a worldwide alliance. We have been determined not to be diverted from our central concerns by mere irritants and fanatics. But now further action is required—and it is underway; and these actions may only be the beginning. We will not prematurely or unnecessarily risk the costs of worldwide nuclear war in which even the fruits of victory would be ashes in our mouth—but neither will we shrink from that risk at any time it must be faced.

Acting, therefore, in the defense of our own security and of the entire Western Hemisphere, and under the authority entrusted to me by the Constitution as endorsed by the resolution of the Congress, I have directed that the following initial steps be taken immediately:

First: To halt this offensive buildup, a strict quarantine on all offensive military equipment under shipment to Cuba is being initiated. All ships of any kind bound for Cuba from whatever nation or port will, if found to contain cargoes of offensive weapons, be turned back. This quarantine will be extended, if needed, to other types of cargo and carriers. We are not at this time, however, denying the necessities of life as the Soviets attempted to do in their Berlin blockade of 1948.

Second: I have directed the continued and increased close surveillance of Cuba and its military buildup. The Foreign Ministers of the Organization of American States in their communiqué of October 3 rejected secrecy on such matters in this Hemisphere. Should these offensive military preparations continue, thus increasing the threat to the Hemisphere, further action will be justified. I have directed the Armed Forces to prepare for any eventualities; and I trust that in the interests of both the Cuban people and the Soviet technicians at the sites, the hazards to all concerned of continuing this threat will be recognized.

Third: It shall be the policy of this nation to regard any nuclear missile launched from Cuba against any nation in the Western Hemisphere as an attack by the Soviet Union on the United States, requiring a full retaliatory response upon the Soviet Union.

Fourth: As a necessary military precaution I have reinforced our

base at Guantánamo, evacuated today the dependents of our personnel there, and ordered additional military units to be on a standby
alert basis.

Fifth: We are calling tonight for an immediate meeting of the
Organ of Consultation, under the Organization of American States,
to consider this threat to hemispheric security and to invoke articles
six and eight of the Rio Treaty in support of all necessary action.
The United Nations Charter allows for regional security arrangements—and the nations of this Hemisphere decided long ago against
the military presence of outside powers. Our other allies around the
world have also been alerted.

Sixth: Under the Charter of the United Nations, we are asking
tonight that an emergency meeting of the Security Council be con-
voked without delay to take action against this latest Soviet threat to
world peace. Our resolution will call for the prompt dismantling and
withdrawal of all offensive weapons in Cuba, under the supervision of
United Nations observers, before the quarantine can be lifted.

Seventh and finally: I call upon Chairman Khrushchev to halt and
eliminate this clandestine, reckless, and provocative threat to world
peace and to stable relations between our two nations. I call upon him
further to abandon this course of world domination and to join in an
historic effort to end the perilous arms race and transform the history
of man. He has an opportunity now to move the world back from the
abyss of destruction—by returning to his Government's own words
that it had no need to station missiles outside its own territory, and
withdrawing these weapons from Cuba—by refraining from any
action which will widen or deepen the present crisis—and then by
participating in a search for peaceful and permanent solutions.

This nation is prepared to present its case against the Soviet
threat to peace, and our own proposals for a peaceful world, at any
time and in any forum in the Organization of American States, in the
United Nations, or in any other meeting that could be useful—without limiting our freedom of action.

We have in the past made strenuous efforts to limit the spread of
nuclear weapons. We have proposed the limitation of all arms and
military bases in a fair and effective disarmament treaty. We are prepared to discuss new proposals for the removal of tensions on both
sides—including the possibilities of a genuinely independent Cuba,
free to determine its own destiny. We have no wish to war with the
Soviet Union, for we are a peaceful people who desire to live in peace
with all other peoples.

But it is difficult to settle or even discuss these problems in an atmosphere of intimidation. That is why this latest Soviet threat—or any other threat which is made either independently or in response to our actions this week—must and will be met with determination. Any hostile move anywhere in the world against the safety and freedom of peoples to whom we are committed—including in particular the brave people of West Berlin—will be met by whatever action is needed.

Finally, I want to say a few words to the captive people of Cuba, to whom this speech is being directly carried by special radio facilities. I speak to you as a friend, as one who knows of your deep attachment to your fatherland, as one who shares your aspirations for liberty and justice for all. And I have watched and the American people have watched with deep sorrow how your nationalist revolution was betrayed and how your fatherland fell under foreign domination. Now your leaders are no longer Cuban leaders inspired by Cuban ideals. They are puppets and agents of an international conspiracy which has turned Cuba against your friends and neighbors in the Americas—and turned it into the first Latin American country to become a target for nuclear war, the first Latin American country to have these weapons on its soil.

These new weapons are not in your interest. They contribute nothing to your peace and well-being. They can only undermine it. But this country has no wish to cause you to suffer or to impose any system upon you. We know that your lives and land are being used as pawns by those who deny you freedom.

Many times in the past Cuban people have risen to throw out tyrants who destroyed their liberty. And I have no doubt that most Cubans today look forward to the time when they will be truly free—free from foreign domination, free to chose their own leaders, free to select their own system, free to own their own land, free to speak and write and worship without fear or degradation. And then shall Cuba be welcomed back to the society of free nations and to the associations of this Hemisphere.

My fellow citizens, let no one doubt that this is a difficult and dangerous effort on which we have set out. No one can foresee precisely what course it will take or what costs or casualties will be incurred. Many months of sacrifice and self-discipline lie ahead—months in which both our patience and our will will be tested, months in which many threats and denunciations will keep us aware of our dangers. But the greatest danger of all would be to do nothing.

The path we have chosen for the present is full of hazards, as all paths are; but it is the one most consistent with our character and courage as a nation and our commitments around the world. The cost of freedom is always high—but Americans have always paid it. And one path we shall never choose, and that is the path of surrender or submission.

Our goal is not the victory of might but the vindication of right—not peace at the expense of freedom, but both peace and freedom, here in this Hemisphere and, we hope, around the world. God willing, that goal will be achieved.

In Moscow, a copy of the address was delivered to the Kremlin, along with a letter from President Kennedy to Chairman Khrushchev.

Dear Mr. Chairman:

A copy of this statement I am making tonight concerning developments in Cuba and the reaction of my Government thereto has been handed to your Ambassador in Washington. In view of the gravity of the developments to which I refer, I want you to know immediately and accurately the position of my Government in this matter.

In our discussions and exchanges on Berlin and other international questions, the one thing that has most concerned me has been the possibility that your Government would not correctly understand the will and determination of the United States in any given situation, since I have not assumed that you or any other sane man would, in this nuclear age, deliberately plunge the world into war which it is crystal clear no country could win and which could only result in catastrophic consequences to the whole world, including the aggressor.

At our meeting in Vienna and subsequently, I expressed our readiness and desire to find, through peaceful negotiation, a solution to any and all problems that divide us. At the same time, I made clear that in view of the objectives of the ideology to which you adhere, the United States could not tolerate any action on your part which in a major way disturbed the existing overall balance of power in the world. I stated that an attempt to force abandonment of our responsibilities and commitments in Berlin would constitute such an action and that the United States would resist with all the power at its command.

It was in order to avoid any incorrect assessment on the part of your Government with respect to Cuba that I publicly stated that if certain developments in Cuba took place, the United States would do whatever must be done to protect its own security and that of its allies.

Moreover, the Congress adopted a resolution expressing its support of this declared policy. Despite this, the rapid development of long-range missile bases and other offensive weapons systems in Cuba has proceeded. I must tell you that the United States is determined that this threat to the security of this hemisphere be removed. At the same time, I wish to point out that the action we are taking is the minimum necessary to remove the threat to the security of the nations of this hemisphere. The fact of this minimum response should not be taken as a basis, however, for any misjudgment on your part.

I hope that your Government will refrain from any action which would widen or deepen this already grave crisis and that we can agree to resume the path of peaceful negotiation.

Sincerely, John F. Kennedy

Shortly after he completed delivering his televised speech, President Kennedy placed a phone call to Prime Minister Harold Macmillan. During the afternoon he had approved the dispatch of a reply to Macmillan's letter (the one he had read to the congressional leaders). Part of his letter replied to Macmillan's concerns with the argument that:

I fully recognize the hazards which you rightly point out, but I have had to take account also of the effect of inaction in the face of so obvious and deep a Soviet challenge. This is not simply or mainly a matter of American public opinion, and as for living under a missile threat, we too have been doing that for some time. But this is so deep a breach in the conventions of the international stalemate that if unchallenged it would deeply shake confidence in the United States, especially in the light of my repeated warnings. It would persuade Khrushchev and others that our determination is low, that we are unable to meet our commitments, and it would invite further and still more dangerous moves.

I recognize the particular hazard of a riposte in Berlin, but in the wider sense I believe that inaction would be still more dangerous to our position in that outpost.

I assure you most solemnly that this is not simply a matter of aroused public opinion or of private passion against Cuba. As I am sure you know, I have regularly resisted pressure for unreasonable or excessive action, and I am not interested in a squabble with Castro. But this is something different: the first step in a major showdown with Khrushchev, whose action in this case is so at variance with what all the Soviet experts have predicted that it is necessary to revise our whole estimate of his level of desperation or ambition, or both.

Kennedy concluded: "Our best basic course is firmness, now. I look forward to our talk."

President Kennedy and Prime Minister Macmillan began their conversation at about 7:30 P.M. (Washington time; it was 12:30 A.M. in London). Some excerpts from that conversation provide further insight into Kennedy's thinking. Macmillan asked: "How do you see the way out of this? What are you going to do with the blockade? Are you going to occupy Cuba and have done with it or is it going to just drag on?"

Kennedy answered: "We could not occupy Cuba for some days, and we are preparing a potential for that kind of action if it's necessary. But we didn't start off with that action for two reasons. First, because there has to be a gap of some days to assemble the forces, which of course will always be public information. And, secondly, because we want to see a little where we begin to go on this road. We don't know what's going to happen in Berlin. We don't know what's going to happen anyplace else. This seemed to be the action we could take which would lessen the chance of an immediate escalation into war, though of course it could bring that result."

Macmillan agreed and asked if the blockade would extend "beyond the military and arms into things like oil and all the rest of it in order to bring down the Castro government?"

Kennedy said the United States would confine the blockade to "offensive weapons of war in order not to give him a complete justification for Berlin. In other words, we're not shipping offensive weapons of war into Berlin, so we're just confining it [the blockade of Cuba] to that. But it may be that within the next few days we may need to move it to petroleum, oils, lubricants, and other things. But we don't want to do that just now because it gives him an obvious tit for tat in Berlin."

As for Khrushchev's likely response, Macmillan's next topic, Kennedy agreed Khrushchev might "make us stop one of his ships by force and then take some action in Berlin. He could seize Berlin, or he could put on a blockade there, and there are any number of things he could do. We just have to expect that whatever it's going to be, it's going to be unpleasant. But I don't think anybody is able to predict with certainty what he will do right now. But I would suspect that he will do something unpleasant to us in Berlin, which I think he is going to do anyway."

Contrary to his earlier letter, Macmillan now hinted at a need for definitive action. "What worries me, I'll be quite frank with you, [is] having a sort of dragging-on position. If you occupied Cuba that's one thing. In my long experience we've always found that our weakness has been when we've not acted with sufficient strength to start with."

Macmillan asked about contacting Khrushchev. Kennedy mentioned his letter to the Soviet leader and then returned to Khrushchev's motives. Khrushchev, Kennedy thought, had "played a double game. You remember that he kept saying he was coming over here after the election and would do nothing to disturb the situation until after the election. He said that the weapons were defensive, that they weren't moving any missiles there and all the rest. And obviously he has been building this up in order to face us with a bad situation in November at the time he was going to squeeze us on Berlin. So I didn't feel there was much point in phoning him up, so I just sent him a letter telling him what we're going to do."

Kennedy decided he should stress the military significance of the Soviet missiles in Cuba. The Soviet buildup, he explained,

> will double the number of missiles which the Soviet Union could bring to bear upon the United States.[21] It would also overcome our warning systems because they come from the south, and we don't have an adequate warning. And it comes from so close by that there's always a temptation for them to engage in a first strike or to face us with such a dangerous situation over Berlin that we would have had to quit. That's obviously his purpose. And that's why we feel that we have to take some action.
>
> Now, our action is obviously moderated by the realization that we could move very quickly into a world war over this, or to a nuclear war, or to lose Berlin, and that's why we've taken the course we've taken. Even though, as I say, it doesn't represent any final answer.
>
> The invasion itself, as I said, requires seven days for us to mobilize our forces, which we cannot do under any cloak of secrecy. We may find we have to come to that. But we are preparing for that in the meanwhile. But I won't do anything about that until I've discussed this with you again. But what we're attempting to do is to warn Khrushchev that this action he's taken constitutes a very hazardous threat, which may lead to a great number of courses which would be unpleasant for us, but awful unpleasant for him.

Macmillan, having prodded Kennedy gently about negotiating with Khrushchev, now expressed his worries about engaging in any summit meeting. "If we are forced to a conference all the cards are in this man's hand. But, however, you explained to me what are the possible develop-ments you may have to take. And if we do have to talk to him, and meet him, in the last resort the more cards in our hands the better, in my view. You may say that's rather tough, and perhaps rather cynical, but I think the more cards in our hands the better, and I would be very happy to see them in your hands."[22]

Tuesday, October 23, 1962

Having lived so long with knowledge of nuclear peril, Americans reacted to Kennedy's speech with alarm but not panic. Everywhere, families stocked up on food, gasoline, and other emergency supplies. Reservists prepared for a call-up. In homes and in bars, television watchers saw footage of airplanes taking off and troop trains moving tanks and soldiers. An atmosphere of tension was pervasive. Kennedy's transition adviser, Richard Neustadt, a professor at Columbia University in New York, wrote Theodore Sorensen: "The reaction among students here was qualitatively different from anything I've ever witnessed. . . . [T]hese kids were literally scared for their lives."[1]

All through the night, lights had burned in Washington. At the National Photographic Interpretation Center (NPIC) and elsewhere in the intelligence community, analysts anxiously scrutinized every intelligence indicator of any Soviet military activity. While they saw Soviet (and Cuban) forces being brought to a higher state of readiness, they detected no evident deployments of field units for action against Berlin or Turkey.

At 9:00 A.M. the representatives of the Organization of American States began meeting to consider the U.S. proposal for endorsement of U.S. goals and U.S. actions against Cuba and the Soviet Union, presented by Dean Rusk. The U.N. Security Council would begin its meeting later in the day.

10:00 A.M.

Executive Committee Meeting of the National Security Council

At 10:00 A.M. President Kennedy gathered his chosen advisers, now convened for the first time as the Executive Committee of the National Security Council. He turned on the tape recorder as the intelligence briefing began.

. . .

John McCone: [*Unclear*] one of those downstairs. This is one matter that would interest you. This shows, in last night's photographs, three of the missiles at the M[R]-1 site, the most advanced medium-range type, have disappeared. We can't detect where they are, from yesterday's photography. Also, at other sites, there's evidence of extensive camouflage. I'd like you to see those pictures, when you get there.

Robert Kennedy: The question that I've heard raised rather extensively is why this was not uncovered sooner, when there were some reports about it, to why we didn't know about it, and therefore why a blockade of some kind was not instituted earlier.

And so that this is the second question, [whether] what we are doing now is, in fact, closing the barn door after the horse is gone. And those questions that will be raised. . . .

President Kennedy: Well that ties into Senator Keating's frequent statements. I'm having Senator Keating's statements analyzed. Actually they are quite inaccurate. He made a statement two days ago that it was being built there, pads, which would be ready for fire at the United States in six months. So his information was from . . . He had a piece of it, but it was not precise. But nevertheless that is going to be. . . .

Now it seems to me that somebody in a responsible position ought to take up this question. I don't think that it's realized how quickly these mobile bases can be set up and how quickly they can be moved. So that I'm just wondering now what is the judgment—the question is getting this point over, in view of the next 24 hours. There will be some spraying all around. Arthur Krock's just beginning to say.[2] Then we'll just have that problem of . . .

·   ·   ·

President Kennedy: Did we ever put out my letter to Khrushchev? He'll probably—

McGeorge Bundy: No, sir. We told Khrushchev that we would not do so.

President Kennedy: All right.

Llewellyn Thompson: We told [Soviet ambassador to Washington Anatoly] Dobrynin.

Bundy: What?

President Kennedy: Now, the. . . .

Thompson: The first Soviet reaction was cautious, including on Cuba. In both the TASS statement and Dobrynin's reaction, and the fact that it was the Cubans that raised this in the Security Council.

Bundy: The first two pages of this [just-released TASS statement] are a rehash of stuff we've heard before. I think Tommy [*unclear*].

President Kennedy: What's your second point, Bobby?

Robert Kennedy: Just this. On the second, the fact that they're doing this. We've taken this action after they've got their missiles already there, unopposed. I think probably we get by with this answer for about 24 hours. But we're going to have difficulty after that.

· · ·

Robert McNamara: Mr. President, the critical action we need to take is a determination of when the proclamation will be effective, the proclamation of the quarantine, the time it will be issued, the time it will become effective, and the time for the first intercept of a ship under the terms of that proclamation. We would propose that it be issued as soon as possible today following OAS action. We had hoped that that would be before six tonight. If it is issued before six tonight, we propose that the quarantine be effective at dawn tomorrow. This is a lesser grace period of—approximately 12-hour grace period—instead of the 24 hours that we have discussed previously.

· · ·

President Kennedy: May I just say that one of the answers to this problem that Bobby raised, which you may not want to put on the record, but off the record, is that we're not saying that there's any action that actually we're taking necessarily, that this action alone because of the blockade, results in the elimination of these. Because quite obviously, they're already there.

On the other hand there's no action we ever could have taken, unless we'd have invaded Cuba a year ago, to prevent them being there, because they could have come in, the missiles themselves could have come in by submarines and personnel in separately; particularly the mobile kind that they could set up in the week. And there's just no way, unless you were going to invade Cuba six months ago, really. You might say, no, we could have perhaps found them two weeks before, but you still wouldn't have found any until they were there.

So there's no answer to this unless you were going to invade Cuba six months ago, or a year ago, or two years ago, or three years ago. That's the—and the fact of the matter is there wasn't anybody suggesting an invasion of Cuba *at a time when they necessarily could have stopped these things coming onto the island.* It's possible they could have come on in July on the first ship, before the other technicians came on—particularly the mobile kind. So that what *we* are doing is throwing down a card on the table in a game which we don't know the ending of. But it's not, at least, at the beginning.

We recognize that the missiles are already there. But we also recognize there's not a damn thing anybody could do about the missiles being there unless we had invaded Cuba at the Bay of Pigs or a previous Cuban invasion the year before. That's part of your problem. Some of that you can't put on the record, but it's a very legitimate point. There was no way we could have stopped this happening. We could have stopped this four months ago, what with the SAM sites and all the rest, by an invasion last July. But you see they're going to put up mobile missiles, without an, unless we could have invaded some months ago you couldn't have stopped it. [*Unclear.*]

. . .

McNamara: Then I will leave this executive order with you, Mr. President, and Mac . . . today. [*Bundy agrees.*]

Now, you asked me yesterday to consider the reaction to a U-2 accident and we would recommend this: That SAC [Strategic Air Command] be instructed to immediately inform the Joint Chiefs, as far as myself and yourself, upon any deviation from course of a U-2 aircraft that is unexplained.[3] They maintain a minute-by-minute check on the U-2s as they proceed through their flight pattern. They will be able to tell us when the U-2 moves off course and, we believe, why, particularly if it's shot down. That information can be in here in a matter of minutes, literally 15 minutes after the incident.

We are maintaining aircraft on alert that have the capability, if you decide to instruct it to do so, to go in and shoot the SAM site that shot down the U-2. There would be approximately eight aircraft required to destroy the SAM site. We would recommend the information on the U-2 accident to come in here and that we present recommendations to you at the time as to action required. I believe we would recommend that we send the eight aircraft out to destroy the SAM site. If that is your decision, those aircraft can move out, destroy the SAM site, and have it destroyed within two hours of the time the U-2 itself was struck, so that we could announce almost simultaneously the loss of the U-2 and the destruction of the SAM site that allegedly destroyed it.

. . .

President Kennedy: Now, there are two things. First, do we want to indicate that in advance, number one? Or, number two, if we lose one of our officers in a plane, then the next fellow we send up . . .

I suppose what we do is, when we take out that SAM site, we announce that if any U-2 is shot down, we'll take out every SAM site.

McNamara: Exactly.

             . . .

President Kennedy: Then I would think what we would do is, if the first one [is shot down], we have to take it out [the offending SAM site], and then announce what's happened. And then we would announce that any further reconnaissance planes which are authorized by the OAS are done, then all these SAM sites are . . . [*Bundy and Ball agree.*] We would have to do a SAM site and a U-2 a day.

Maxwell Taylor: One point I might make, Mr. President, I think it's highly unlikely we can really identify the guilty SAM site.

President Kennedy: I understand.

Taylor: It doesn't really matter, I don't think, however.

And secondly, the Secretary mentions eight planes. I would like to reserve judgment on the total . . . approval on the total, because I think if we go in we send in . . .

President Kennedy: Good. OK. Anybody have any question about this?

McCone: A question that we do . . . Would you launch an attack on information received from the plane? Or would you wait until it has returned, so you've got verification on it?

McNamara: We would launch it on information received from the airplane.

Bundy: Wouldn't it depend, how much information?

President Kennedy: Well, I think we can make the . . . We're going to have the chance to . . .

             . . .

President Kennedy: The question is, though, if we're leading up to an invasion, whether we are doing all the things that we would have to do?

McNamara: We believe so. The Reserves would not be used in the invasion, exclusive of the transport aircraft that would be required.

President Kennedy: What about the movement of, like, the 101st [Airborne Division], 82nd [Airborne Division], and all the rest?

Roswell Gilpatric: They're all moving.

President Kennedy: All of their equipment?

Gilpatric: And the Fifth Infantry Division of the Marines is moving from the West Coast and the armored division from Fort Hood is moving to the East Coast.[4]

President Kennedy: The other question is these airfields down in

Florida. Everybody's lived in peace so long that . . . Is everything going to be lined up on those three airports in Florida in a way in which if they come in, if they—obviously they will take a reprisal. I should think one of their planes would strafe us.

Taylor: We're aware of that, Mr. President. It's true, these fields are congested. Unfortunately, a lot of the congestion is necessary. They are dispersing the planes as well as they can on Key West. We've reinforced the air defenses to the extent we're capable of.

We have an officer—General [Curtis] LeMay has been put in charge of representing the Chiefs—of the air defense, to supervise the air defense arrangements down there. He is sending one of his most experienced officers down today on the ground to take a look at the situation.

We have talked to Admiral [Robert] Dennison about these fields. He knows the situation but he feels that he prefers to stay that way because it can help him increase readiness.

President Kennedy: Well, what I'd like to do is, can we have somebody go take a photograph of those fields at about five this afternoon or four this afternoon, and just get an idea of what our . . . ? Because there isn't any doubt. . . . You see these people don't know that we're maybe going to hit a SAM site tomorrow and their reprisal would be to strafe on our fields. And it would be nice to know what our targets are.

Taylor: That's quite true. These are very lush targets; there's no doubt about it. Unfortunately, our fields are so limited, and our requirements are so great, we really can't—

President Kennedy: Well, for example, they're using the West Palm Beach airport, I wonder? That's a hell of a military airport. It hasn't been used much.

Taylor: No, sir. I don't know.

President Kennedy: It seems to me you could close that off because there's not much travel that goes through there. They could go down to Miami and go and they take over that field. There's a lot of barracks there, too. You might check on that.

Unidentified: They're using Opa Locka.

President Kennedy: West Palm is a pretty good field and it was a good base in the war, and it isn't used much now.

Taylor: We just haven't got enough fields in this area to support . . .

President Kennedy: No, but I do think we better . . . We have to figure that if we do execute this plan we just agreed on this morning [for retaliation if a U-2 were shot down], that they're going to strafe our fields, and we don't want them to shoot up 100 planes. We've just got to figure out some other device. [*Unclear exchange.*]

Taylor: This is one of these rather humorous examples of the over-sophistication of our weapons. We have everything, except to deal with a simple aircraft coming in low.

President Kennedy: That's a lot of [*unclear*]. You'll look into West Palm Beach, Ros?

Gilpatric: Yes.

President Kennedy: OK.

.   .   .

Thompson: Mr. President, there are two questions I'd like to raise. One is, if we don't get OAS action today but it appears we're going to get it the next day. Do you want, in fact, to actually stop the Soviet ships beginning tomorrow? The point is that they're much less apt to run a legal blockade than they are an illegal one. And I think you might want to keep that in mind.

President Kennedy: All right. Well, we'll be in touch if we're not going to get it. [*Unclear.*]

Thompson: The second thing is, I'm meeting with the ambassadorial group this afternoon and they'll—we will be discussing what we do about an action in Germany against Berlin. The most likely minimum thing, I think, is that they will insist on inspecting U.S. convoys more than they do now. And what should be our—

President Kennedy: I think we ought to accept that. That's my quick reaction, unless somebody else says that . . . But I don't think we're in very good shape to have a big fight about whether they inspect our trucks or something. I think we ought to—

Taylor: I think we ought to take time out, Mr. President, and not go through until we look it over very hard.

Thompson: Wouldn't it be better to stop any convoys [into Berlin] the next day or so?

President Kennedy: And then we're going to get in the pattern where it's tough to begin again. I would rather have them inspecting them.

Bundy: Mr. President, my suggestion is that we ought to have a second meeting with this committee at the end of the afternoon. We will know about the OAS. We will know about the initial reaction of the ambassadorial group. We will know if the [low-level] pictures came through. We will know about what Kohler's message is [from Moscow].

President Kennedy: Right. Try to keep these meetings as brief as possible. [*The meeting starts to break up. Some fragments of conversations are audible.*]

.   .   .

Unclear exchanges continue. A phone call is being placed to Ambassador Stevenson at the U.S. mission to the United Nations in New York. Meanwhile Rusk arrives, fresh from the OAS session.

. . .

Dean Rusk: There were several [delegates] without instructions. So they're [OAS ministers] meeting again at three.

It looks like we'll have everybody but an abstention with Mexico on one paragraph, unless we can straighten that out before three. López Mateos is on a plane from Hawaii to his home.[5] But we'll have the resolution, with a large majority, shortly after three.

Several: Oh, gee, wonderful!

Rusk: They're really rallying around. Bolivia, who had withdrawn from the OAS pending their settlement with Chile, turned up this morning.

Several: Oh, terrific! Terrific.

U. Alexis Johnson: Now, we can put the question of the timing of the issuance of the [quarantine] proclamation. I should think that we should be ready . . . issue the proclamation [*unclear*].

McNamara: At four. I have it right here. It's all cleared by our lawyers. And I believe by your lawyers.

Rusk: Now, what is the . . . ? Privately I've been telling two or three of these fellows in order to . . . that there could be contact this afternoon. Therefore it's very important for us to have this resolution.

McNamara: We would propose having it [the quarantine] at dawn tomorrow.

Bundy: Daylight tomorrow.

Rusk: Yeah, but don't tell them that.

McCone: This will be very important for what we've been talking about [referring to the United Nations].

McNamara: Oh, very important.

Alexis Johnson: If the OAS were to act, it would help the—

McCone: This will relieve our problems here.

Alexis Johnson: The meeting in the Security Council is set for four this afternoon, if they should act—

Rusk: I understand a long TASS statement is on the wire. Have you been getting that in here?

Unidentified: Not yet.

Rusk: Let's don't howl too soon here, boys.

Alexis Johnson: If the OAS has acted before the Security Council, oh that's going to be a big help. Mmmm. Our diplomacy is working.

Rusk: [*reading the report on the TASS statement*] No demobilization of forces. Meeting of the Warsaw Pact. Well, my God.

Well, as a matter of fact, I said to somebody . . . I don't know what John McCone thinks of this, but I think it was very significant that we were here this morning. We've passed the one contingency: an immediate, sudden, irrational strike.

. . .

George Ball: Well, I just talked to Stevenson, and he says, and Stevenson says, he [Zorin] is dragging his feet because the Russians are getting up a request for a resolution of their own. And there's going to be a countercomplaint filed. And this is what they're dragging their feet for. So that they're meeting at four.

Thompson: It's significant they let the Cubans bring the first one [proposal in the U.N.] and not themselves.

Alexis Johnson: Well, we caught them [the Soviets]. We caught them without their contingency [plan].

McNamara: Tell the Security Council we would be happy to evacuate them to Seattle or someplace. [*Laughter.*][6]

Alexis Johnson: Well, I think we planned that. . . .

Rusk: I'll go on back. [*Unclear.*]

Alexis Johnson: That's great. That's terrific. Oh that's great news. We really caught them with their contingencies down.

. . .

12:25 P.M.

Conversation with Lucius Clay

. . .

President Kennedy: Can you get General Clay on the phone?

Evelyn Lincoln: OK. [*Office noises.*] The President would like to speak to General Lucius Clay.

The Dictaphone machine was briefly turned off. General Clay had headed the U.S. military government in its occupation zone of Germany after World War II, until the creation of the Federal Republic. Clay remained greatly respected in Germany and in 1961 had helped Kennedy as a special representative to Berlin, serving in that post until the spring of 1962. Clay was still a consultant to the Joint Chiefs of Staff.

In the few minutes while the call was being put through to Clay, Ambassador Foy Kohler's cable arrived from Moscow, carrying a letter from Khrushchev to Kennedy. It was the Soviet leader's initial reply to Kennedy's address to the world. When Clay came on the line, Kennedy turned on the Dictaphone and began the conversation by reading the message from Khrushchev to the retired general. Khrushchev's message was reported in the telegraphic style then used in most cables from posts overseas, but Kennedy adds in some of the *the*'s left out of the original cable.

President Kennedy: [*reading the letter from Nikita Khrushchev, dated Tuesday, October 23*]

[I have just received your letter, and have also acquainted myself with] text of your speech of October 22nd regarding Cuba.

I should say frankly that measures outlined in your statement represent serious threat to peace and security of peoples. United States has openly taken the path of gross violation of the Charter of United Nations, the path of violation of international norms of freedom of navigation on high seas, the path of aggressive actions both against Cuba and against the Soviet Union.

The statement of the Government of the United States of America cannot be evaluated in any other way than as naked interference in the domestic affairs of the Cuban Republic, the Soviet Union, and other states. The Charter of the United Nations and international norms do not give right to any state whatsoever to establish in international waters controls of vessels bound for the shores of the Cuban Republic.

It is self-understood that we also cannot recognize the right of the United States to establish control over armaments essential to the Republic of Cuba for strengthening of its defensive capacity.

We confirm that armaments now on Cuba, regardless of classification to which they belong, are destined exclusively for defensive purposes, in order to secure the Cuban Republic from attack of aggressor.

I hope that Government of United States will show prudence and renounce actions pursued by you, which could lead to catastrophic consequences for peace throughout the world.

The viewpoint of the Soviet Government with regard to your statement of October 22nd is set forth in the statement of the Soviet Government, which is being conveyed to you through your ambassador in Moscow.

Signed Khrushchev. [7]

[Kennedy, continuing with Clay] So I suppose, General, we can anticipate difficulties in Berlin as well as other places, and I thought that we would keep you informed. Perhaps, as this situation became more intense there, [I hoped] that you might be willing to come down later in the week.

Lucius Clay: I'm available at anytime for anything, Mr. President.

President Kennedy: Good. Fine. Do you . . . ?

Clay: This is more important than anything else. So, anytime and anything if I'm called on and can do, I'm available and at your service.

President Kennedy: Fine. Well, if you get any, also, thoughts on any of these matters I hope you call General Taylor or me because, as I said, it seems to me Berlin is a key problem, as it has been from the beginning in this whole matter. But I'll be in touch with you later in the week as we get . . . the situation evolves in Berlin.

Clay: Yes, sir.

President Kennedy: Good. Thanks, General.

Clay: Thank you, Mr. President.

President Kennedy: Righto.

Soon after this conversation President Kennedy took a swim in the pool. Dean Rusk tried to reach him while he was swimming. He then asked if he could come over and see the President. Evelyn Lincoln said she would ask. Kennedy went back to the Mansion and rested for a while. At about 3:45 he returned to the office and spoke on the phone with Deputy Secretary of Defense Roswell Gilpatric.

3:52 P.M.

Conversation with Roswell Gilpatric

The initial diplomatic news was good. At the OAS the U.S. resolution had passed without any no votes and with only two abstentions, and those were soon changed so that the support from Latin America was unanimous. At the United Nations Stevenson led a heated attack on Soviet policy in the Security Council and effectively used the photos and other intelligence supplied by the CIA in his briefings for the delegates. The Soviet ambassador claimed the U.S. charges were false and argued that only defensive weapons had been supplied to Cuba. However, he could neither confirm nor deny the presence of Soviet ballistic missiles on the island.

The F8U Crusader aircraft conducting low-level reconnaissance flashed across Cuba, a few hundred feet above the ground, high-speed cameras running. They encountered no enemy fire.

Talking to Gilpatric, Kennedy previewed the concerns he hoped the Pentagon would be ready to address when the ExComm reconvened later in the day. He also returned to a couple of matters he had raised earlier in the day.

President Kennedy: That, as I understood, there's some report that the Russian ships were not going to stop and that we were going to have to sink them [*sighs*] in order to stop them. I thought that . . . or are we going to have to fire on them. I was wondering whether the instructions [are ready] on how that's to be done, or where they're to be shot at and so on to cause the minimum of damage. And in addition, if they're boarded it's very possible the Russians will fire at them as they board, and we'll have to fire back and have quite a slaughter.

I would think we'd want two or three things. First, I'd think we'd want to have some control over cameras aboard these boats so that we don't have a lot of people shooting a lot of pictures, which, in the press might be embarrassing to us—

Roswell Gilpatric: We'll control all the picture taking.

President Kennedy: On the boats?

Gilpatric: Yeah.

President Kennedy: They'll [the sailors will] all turn in their cameras.

Secondly, I don't know enough about the ships, but where they ought to fire or whether they ought to go through three or four steps such as asking them to stop. If they don't stop, asking them to have their crew come above deck so that they don't be damaged. And three, so that we have this record made. Maybe you can talk to someone about that.

Gilpatric: Yes, we've got instructions to CINCLANT [Commander in Chief, Atlantic Fleet] which start with those steps. Shot across the bow, shot through the rudder—

President Kennedy: Shot through the rudder.

Gilpatric: Then a boarding party. And then order the crews to come on deck and the *minimum* amount of force at each stage. Now, maybe we haven't thought of everything, but we'll take another look at it.

President Kennedy: OK, fine.

How did those photographic expeditions [low-level reconnaissance flights] go this morning, do you know?

Gilpatric: No incident. They were back a couple of hours ago. We'll see the pictures later.

President Kennedy: I see. You're getting that one for me, aren't you, of those Florida bases?[8]

Gilpatric: That's right.

President Kennedy: OK. Have you taken a look at West Palm Beach?

Gilpatric: Yeah, the Air Force is doing that. We can look at all the [aircraft] dispersal possibilities down there.

President Kennedy: OK, good.

.   .   .

6:00 P.M.

Executive Committee Meeting of the National Security Council

President Kennedy turned on the tape recorder as his advisers took their seats in the Cabinet Room. President Kennedy can be heard asking about the photography taken by the low-level reconnaissance missions flown earlier in the day and is told the negatives are being worked on now. The mixed conversations soon subside as the meeting begins.

McGeorge Bundy: Mr. President, the first thing we ought to do is to get this [quarantine] proclamation approved, because it needs to be on its way just as soon as possible for the convenience of the naval forces. I think the Secretary of Defense and the Secretary of State have had their joint legal experts working on it.

.   .   .

Robert McNamara: The question is: Can we search a vessel which was proceeding toward Cuba, was hailed, requested to stop, did not do so, but turned around and proceeded to reverse direction away from

Cuba? It's both a legal question and a practical question. The legal foundation of such an act is confused [with the issue of evasive action]. But as a practical matter, I don't believe we should undertake such an operation.

President Kennedy: Not right now.

McNamara: Not immediately. That's right. So my instruction to the Navy was: Don't do it.

President Kennedy: That's right, because if he grabs the stuff, they might be heading home. Then, we change that . . .

Robert Kennedy: Now there is a possibility that this one vessel, that we think is carrying these missiles, that it would be a *hell* of an advantage to be able to come in and have pictures of the missiles. And also, I would raise the point that there possibly would be an intelligence advantage to be able to examine some of this material.

The way you can do it is to set out a zone, and then pick up any vessels within that zone and say you don't know whether, when they turn around, whether they're going to try to come into Cuba in a different fashion. Maybe you don't want to do it for the first 48 hours.

President Kennedy: Well, I think if we got a vessel that we were suspicious of, we ought to try to grab it. But my guess is that anything that's really that suspicious at this point, they're not going to choose this to have the test case. They're going to turn that thing around.

Bundy: We could always get an exception, if we get one that's hot. Can't we?

McNamara: Well, this particular vessel is 1,800 miles out [from Cuba]. That's one of our major problems.

President Kennedy: So why don't you grab it there?

McNamara: We'd have to grab it there, which—

President Kennedy: [*Unclear*] they're going to turn it around. Do we want to grab it if they turned it around, at 1,800 miles away?

Robert Kennedy: I don't think that's too far. If it keeps coming . . . do we know whether it's still coming?

McNamara: It's still coming. It has not yet turned around.

.   .   .

McNamara: I recommend that we not, tonight, decide this issue on that particular ship that's 1,800 miles out. We ought to follow it tonight and see what happens.

Robert Kennedy: As I say, I don't see any problem with the . . . and I think it would be damn helpful to come in with that kind of evidence.

McNamara: This ought to be our primary objective, early after the effective date of the blockade, to grab a vessel obviously loaded with offensive weapons.

Robert Kennedy: It would be a hell of a lot of help.

McNamara: So our prime target at the moment is the *Kimovsk*, which is within our range tomorrow and which we hope we can get around eleven or twelve tomorrow morning. But we haven't yet pinpointed it this afternoon. They're still searching for it.

President Kennedy: They haven't found it yet?

McNamara: No, they know about what area of the ocean it's in, but I remember the Portuguese ship [*unclear*].

Dean Rusk: Mr. President, the direction of the ship is pretty important, particularly if it's going to be a ship with missiles and warheads and things like that on it. I don't know whether the Navy has a capability of giving a surveillance or tailing such a ship. But how do you distinguish between a ship that, in fact, is turning around from one that is going to play cats and mice with you?

McNamara: Oh, we have ample ability to tail them. As a matter of fact—

Rusk: I would think that if you could get them in as far as possible initially, and then, if they do seem to be turning around, give them the chance to turn around and get on their way.

McNamara: Oh, any ship that we stop or hail and request to stop, which then deviates from course, we will follow. This is in the instructions.

But the suggestion of the Attorney General, and I think it's an excellent suggestion, but not to apply the first day, is that even if it turns around and proceeds indefinitely away from Cuba, [*brief repetition as tape reels are changed*] we would nonetheless stop it and search it, because it very probably would have offensive weapons on board. And I think that's very likely the case.

Rusk: So if it's going away from Cuba with offensive weapons on board, what is your plan to do with it?

McNamara: Well, the suggestion was that we stop it, search it, and if it has—

Robert Kennedy: Our argument is that this particular ship is—has been—has made trips to Cuba, it's been destined to Cuba. You don't know when it turns around what direction it's actually going.

I think that the hullabaloo that would be created by the fact that if it deviated from our course . . . We can always say we didn't know where it was going to go, and the advantage—

Bundy: [We can say it was] taking evasive action.

Robert Kennedy: Yes. The advantage of being able to come in ultimately with the pictures and the equipment would, I mean, that would take all their complaints.

Rusk: Well I think I can see that, Bob. The problem here is that, from the Soviet point of view, they're going to be as sensitive as a boil. The question is whether they think we're really trying to capture, and seize, and analyze, and examine their missiles and their warheads and things.

Now, the purpose is to keep them out of Cuba. This adds a very important element into it, you see? This is—

President Kennedy: Well, isn't this a matter that we're going to know in the next 24 hours? I would think we could cross it. They just keep coming into Cuba, obviously, probably tomorrow morning is going to be when they'll refuse to haul to, and we'll have to shoot at them. So that's really our problem tomorrow. Then it seems to me, later we can decide, when we know what they're going to do, whether we start grabbing them as they leave. So I think we're going to have all our troubles tomorrow morning.

McNamara: I think so too. I've tried to simplify tomorrow as much as we possibly can.

President Kennedy: Let's see. Let's get on with this thing now. [*Pause.*]

They're actually faced with the same problem we were faced with in the Berlin blockade [of 1948–49]. [*Unclear*] and we could always go up that autobahn and they could fire if we did [challenge the blockade]. There was always the feeling afterwards that they wouldn't have if they [the Truman administration] had really pushed it.

Now, that's about what they're going to do next. We've given them as clear notice as they gave us. Even in '47 and '48, when we had an atomic monopoly, we didn't push it.

Looks like they're going to.

. . .

Bundy: Mr. President, there's one other item that I think is of some urgency. There is a proposal which has been prepositioned without an approval, because you were not enthusiastic about it earlier in the day, to send an additional message to Chairman Khrushchev. This is the language. [*Unclear.*]

Llewellyn Thompson: We have an alternative draft here.

President Kennedy: [*Pauses to read the draft.*] What does Tommy think?

Rusk: This is the final. We've had the final sentence on that.

Thompson: I think it would be useful if we kicked this off a little earlier.

The idea was that they will, tonight, all be deciding on what instructions are going to these ships. If there is any doubt in their minds, or debate, this would show that there is an alternative to going ahead with forcing this thing, which makes us fire on them, and therefore kicks off probably reaction, then retaliation in Berlin.

The second point, which you already . . . You have a letter [now in from Khrushchev] to answer. This is an answer to put the ball in his court.

President Kennedy: [*addressing others*] Is everybody familiar with this proposed letter?

Unidentified: No, sir.

Rusk: Can I read it?

President Kennedy: Yeah. Now this ends a little . . . which is the preferred draft?

Bundy: [*Mixed voices.*] Do you want to read it, Mr. Secretary?

Rusk: Yes. This draft. [*reading the draft letter*]

I have received your letter of October 23rd. I think you will recognize that the steps which started the current chain of events was the action of your government in secretly furnishing offensive weapons to Cuba. We will be discussing this—we *are* discussing this matter in the Security Council. In the meantime I am concerned that we both show prudence and do nothing to allow events to make the situation more difficult to control than it already is.

I hope that you will issue immediately the necessary instructions to your ships to observe the terms of the quarantine, established by the order of the Organization of American States this afternoon. You may or may not have sent this. We have no desire to seize or fire upon your vessels.

Now, this depends a good deal on intelligence. And we've had no indications of any Soviet instructions or reactions in any way to pull away, or narrow, or widen the gap, and that sort of thing.

John McCone: None at all, no.

Rusk: Just the converse.

McCone: That's right, yeah.

Rusk: I think this is an important point to make.

McCone: The only thing with such intelligence that we've gotten is gossip around the United Nations, in the halls and so forth, to indicate the contrary, that the instructions are [for the Soviet ships] to go through. But we have nothing very hard.

Thompson: The Soviet Embassy this afternoon gave a copy of

Khrushchev's letter to you to the Soviet affairs section [of the State Department], which I take indicates they probably will rely on this exchange. [*Unclear*] a little out of the record books.

Paul Nitze: Isn't there one problem in this, and that is that they might come back in reply, saying: "We will not send our ships in. But we would expect from you comparable observance in the criterion you've set, and you won't attack anything in Cuba or extend the blockade." In other words, set up a situation in which they freeze the status quo with the missiles there.

Bundy: Very unlikely. It's possible.

President Kennedy: Well, we can always come back and say that's unacceptable.

But he just . . . [*unclear*] one last effort before he goes to act tomorrow morning. I don't . . . Anybody have any objection to sending this? [*to Thompson*] Your judgment is that it's a good thing to do?

Thompson: I think so. I don't feel strongly about it. I think it could be helpful in their last-minute decision.

President Kennedy: OK. Well, let's send it then. Hell, I don't see that we're giving away much.

I don't think we want to have that last sentence, do we?

Thompson: No. It's covered by the proclamation, I would think.

President Kennedy: OK. Well, let's send that then.

Bundy: Will you do that, George, or—

President Kennedy: Can you do it right now?

George Ball: It's this draft that we're agreed upon, without the last sentence. [*Exchange, handing off the draft. Bundy agrees.*]

President Kennedy: [*continues speaking while Ball is arranging matters*] I think they'll have that just before it [*unclear*] anyway. Are we telling them when this quarantine begins, that it's starting tomorrow morning?

Ball: Well, we say it was legally established this afternoon. Now, this was the basis for it was legally established. I suppose it won't have—

President Kennedy: Don't we want to say: "which commences tomorrow morning" [Washington time]?

Bundy: Yeah. Be "the basis" [in the wording of the letter to Khrushchev].

Ball: It [the last sentence of the letter] really ought to be "the basis for which was legally established this afternoon."

President Kennedy: "Which commences" . . . Have you told them it's going to commence tomorrow morning?

Ball: Well, that's what this present proclamation [says]; it will be delivered to them by our embassy.

Unidentified: I think it might be well . . . You know, that's going to be a little time getting to them.

President Kennedy: This letter may have a little priority.

Ball and **McNamara** and **Bundy:** [*together redrafting last sentence of letter*] "and which will go into effect at 1400 hours Greenwich time, October 24."

Within an hour the letter was sent to the U.S. Embassy in Moscow for delivery to Khrushchev. Its text was as agreed, ending with the following last sentence: "I hope that you will issue immediately the necessary instructions to your ships to observe the terms of the quarantine, the basis of which was established by the vote of the Organization of American States this afternoon, and which will go into effect at 1400 hours Greenwich time October 24."

Rusk: The mobs [of protesters] that we stimulated turned up in London instead of Havana. Two thousand people stormed the—

President Kennedy: The American Embassy?

Rusk: Bertrand Russell's [British peace movement] people stormed the embassy there. We haven't had any reports of any disorder happening in Cuba.

McCone: No, no.

Robert Kennedy: Americas or something?

Bundy: Some in South America.

McCone: In Chile the Communist-dominated union is bringing a nationwide strike. That's probably the most serious that we've [*unclear*].

President Kennedy: OK, now what do we do tomorrow morning when these eight [Soviet] vessels continue to sail on? We're all clear about how we handle it?

Maxwell Taylor: Shoot the rudders off of them, don't you?

McNamara: Well, if you . . . Max, this is the problem. We want to be very careful. I think we should wait until early in the morning to say exactly what instructions we'll give to [CINCLANT Admiral Robert] Dennison. We ought to try to avoid shooting a ship, a Soviet ship carrying wheat to Cuba or medicine or something of that kind. [*President Kennedy makes some wry comment.*] And therefore, I would propose to try to pick a ship which almost certainly carries offensive weapons as the first ship. And not allow any other Soviet ship to be hailed until that particular ship has been hailed. Now, this is going to be difficult because it means we have to try to see in advance what the ships have.

President Kennedy: Doesn't it mean, though, that by the end of the day, Thursday [October 25], there will be ships arriving in Cuba—

McNamara: Oh yes.

President Kennedy: —which will make it appear as if, but that would remove . . . perhaps we just say that they all went through before the blockade.

The only problem I see, Bob, I would think that the Soviets, if there is a vessel among them [carrying offensive weapons], that's the one vessel I would think they would turn around.

· · ·

McNamara: . . . There's been no change in course that we have yet detected.

Rusk: Well, that could well be the baby food ships. [*Laughter.*]

Bundy: They're all going on course, aren't they?

McNamara: They're all going on course. That's right. As best we can tell.

· · ·

Rusk: I would think that there would be some advantage in testing out on any other kind of ship.

Robert Kennedy: Moving out of Washington. [*Chuckles.*]

McNamara: You mean a British ship and so on?

Rusk: No. I mean a Soviet ship that didn't have food and then [*unclear*].

McNamara: But the instruction from Khrushchev is very likely to be: "Don't stop under any circumstances." So the baby food ship comes out and we hail it. If they don't stop, we shoot it. [*Chuckles.*]

Bundy: We shoot three nurses!

President Kennedy: That's what could happen. They're going to keep going. And we're going to try to shoot the rudder off, or the boiler. And then we're going to try to board it. And they're going to fire a gun, then machine guns. And we're going to have one hell of a time getting aboard that thing and getting control of it, because they're pretty tough, and I suppose there may be armed soldiers or marines aboard their ships. They certainly may have technicians who are military. So I would think that the taking of those ships are going to be a major operation. You may have to sink it rather than just take it.

Robert Kennedy: Or they might give orders to blow it up or something.

President Kennedy: I think that's less likely than having a real fight to try to board it, because they may have 5[00] or 6[00] or 700 people aboard there with guns. And a destroyer . . .

Thompson: That might happen in the morning [*unclear*].

McNamara: Most of these [Soviet] ships, Mr. President, are not likely to have that kind of a crew on board. The crews are relatively small in the type of ships that we wish to stop.

Rusk: What do we do now about a ship that has been disabled, and it's not going to sink. It just can't go anywhere? Do we—

McNamara: We have tows to take them—

Rusk: To tow it to Dakar?

McNamara: We tow it to a prize port.

Rusk: I see.

Ball: Which means a United States port.

Roswell Gilpatric: Yes. Charleston. Jacksonville.

President Kennedy: Well, when we take it back to that port and we find out it's got baby food on it . . . ?

McNamara: Well, we inspect it before we take it—

President Kennedy: They let us aboard?

Unidentified: They don't.

McNamara: That's right. It's this baby food shipment that worries me.

Unidentified: A wheat ship or a nonoffensive weapons ship.

President Kennedy: I'll tell you, for those who considered the blockade course to be the easy way, I told them not to do it! [*Loud laughter, breaking the tension.*]

Bundy: We in fact are in broad consensus today, everybody fell forward! [*More laughter.*]

President Kennedy: Well, that's what we're going to have to do.

Now, the only thing is, these fellows need as detailed instructions as possible, from those who are knowledgeable about the sea and know just how to proceed on this.

But say they shoot, and the boat stops. Then they try a signal for a boarding party, and they say they're not going to permit a boarding party aboard. The ship is drifting. Then I don't think we can probably get aboard if we don't want to go through a machine gun operation. The destroyers aren't equipped. We haven't got . . . The other ship may be tough to get aboard. You have a real fight aboard there.

Gilpatric: Well, the cruisers have helicopters. [*Unclear.*] Can try a helicopter.

McNamara: Unless these freighters are carrying substantial security guards—and I don't believe we have evidence they are—it shouldn't be too difficult. I suppose that under some circumstances there may be a firefight but it ought to be a small one. The normal crew—

Bundy: We're not [*unclear*] a PT boat.

McNamara: Something of that kind.

McCone: It won't be easy.

McNamara: It could be difficult.

Rusk: It's a good reason to send this letter to Mr. Khrushchev and tell him to turn them around.

. . .

President Kennedy: I think at the beginning it would be better if this situation happened, to let that boat lie there disabled for a day or so, not to try to board it and have them [*unclear*] with machine gunning with 30–40 people killed on each side. That would be . . .

McNamara: I think there's some problem with submarines, Mr. President. If there are submarines in the area or are moving in the area, we ought to board it, and inspect it, and get out of there if necessary, towing the ship or leaving the ship there. If the [Soviet] submarines are really moving in, we have some serious problems. This is one of the difficulties we face here. [Chief of Naval Operations] Admiral [George] Anderson is somewhat concerned about the possibility that they'll try to sink one of our major vessels, such as a [aircraft] carrier.

Gilpatric: You see, submarines just fueled yesterday in the Azores and may be moving west.[9]

McNamara: In fact, they sent a ship under high speed, to fuel a submarine yesterday which did fuel and was observed fueling. And it's obviously going to move into the Cuba area. There may well be others that we're not aware of. I think we're going to have to allow the commander on the scene a certain amount of latitude to . . .

President Kennedy: Have we got the *Enterprise* in this area?

McNamara: We have the [aircraft carrier USS] *Enterprise* in the area, that's right, and the [aircraft carrier USS] *Independence*.

President Kennedy: Do we want to keep the *Enterprise* there? Do you think . . . we don't want to lose a carrier right away. [*Chuckles.*]

McNamara: Well, the *Enterprise* is not at this moment anywhere close to the area of the *Kimovsk*.

Gilpatric: We need our aircraft for the surveillance of the area.

President Kennedy: But a submarine could really—as I say, these aircraft carriers—could do a lot of damage.

Bundy: Well, we expect to know reasonably well where the submarines are. Am I not right?

Taylor: Oh yes. We think we can keep tabs on the submarines.

Bundy: That's what I think.

President Kennedy: All right. Well. Mr. Secretary, I think I'd like to make sure that you have reviewed these instructions that go out to the Navy, having in mind this conversation that we've just had.

McNamara: I have, and I will do so again tonight, Mr. President.

. . .

The reel of tape comes to an end. During the interval while the tape is being replaced, President Kennedy urges that General Lauris Norstad be retained as NATO supreme commander in Europe during the crisis, putting off the scheduled change of command over to General Lyman Lemnitzer. President Kennedy had been particularly impressed by a cable that Norstad had sent, received earlier that day, describing how he had tempered the possible alert of NATO defense forces in order to keep from inflaming international sensitivities.[10]

Then Assistant Secretary of Defense for Civil Defense Steuart Pittman begins a briefing on U.S. readiness to withstand a Soviet nuclear attack. The tape recording resumes at this point, but the audio quality is poor.

Steuart Pittman: . . . from Cuba, or the possibility of using nuclear weapons, [unclear] casualties [unclear] defense. [Unclear] miles from Cuba they are somewhat . . . if it's limited to conventional weapons, I'm not sure I'd [unclear].

The local civil defense organizations have been preparing for that kind of event through the years. And most of our efforts in the last years have been to redirect their attention to the problems of nuclear warfare, and Florida is particularly strong in civil defense. They have more training than anyplace in the country and more organization, especially work training police and firefighting, mass casualty care, and so on. They're imperfect, but there's something there in the cities and in the rural areas.

If nuclear weapons are used, we can draw an arc and try and assess the civil defense capabilities at [a possible missile strike radius of] around 1,100 nautical miles [from Cuba], and make a little allowance for [radioactive] fallout on the outer fringe. That takes in 92 million people [in the United States], 58 cities of over 100,000 population. A light, relatively light, nuclear attack of this type, we would lower the protection factors we'd use in deciding whether existing buildings would serve as adequate protection [against blast, heat, and direct exposure to radiation from the nuclear detonation]. We'd be going against, going down to a 40 protection factor. We now set a limit of a 100 protection factor. That would be [buildings that are] cutting the radiation by 40 times instead of a 100 times.

To do this, we'd have the information in hand, and in the hands of local civil-defense directors of states, in buildings that will take care of 40 million people of the 92 million in this area. The spaces now are stocked, and in the process of being stocked, for the 100-protection factor or above. But sometimes it's bound to be a lower-protection-factor space. The [*unclear*] spaces had intended to be stocked by now. But, in fact, we can do a little accelerated [*unclear*].[11]

President Kennedy: OK. Well, let me just ask you this. It seems to me the most likely problem we're going to have in the next ten days is if we decide to invade Cuba. They may fire these weapons. Or at least we've got to go under the assumption that some of them may be fired.

Now, what is it we could do in this [1,100 mile] arc to evacuate these communities so that, after all, people living out in the country, we can take care of them, to the extent that is possible, against radiation. We can take the various steps. And then you've got the problem of blast. Can we, say before we invade, evacuate these cities?

Pittman: Well, if we knew that there would be no nuclear response, it might make some sense. If there will be fallout, the only protection that exists today is in the cities, and there's little or no protection in the rural areas.

President Kennedy: Well, we have to assume that there isn't going to be very much, and on the assumption [*unclear*], we're not going to have an all-out nuclear exchange. If we were going to have an all-out nuclear exchange, then we'd have a different problem.

Let's say we're going into Cuba, and there's maybe some bombs back, 10 or 15 [missiles launched against the United States]. That kind of fallout. Not the usual—I don't know how many megatons. Now, what is it we do, before we go in, by the time we say we're going to invade Cuba, if we give you, say, five or six or seven days' notice? What can we do during this period of a week in which this risk will be with us, or three or four days? What is it that we ought to do with the population of the affected areas, in case some bombs go off? I just don't see [*unclear*] how you can [*unclear*] effectively.

At this point the recording is obscured by background noise for about 13 minutes. McCone summarized the ensuing discussion as follows: "The President asked what emergency steps could be taken. Replied that many arrangements could be made without too much publicity, such as repositioning food, actually obtaining space, putting up shelter signs, etc. I got the conclusion that not very much could or would be done; that whatever was done would involve a great deal of publicity and public alarm."[12]

The recording becomes slightly more audible, with fragments of con-

*versation referring to SAM sites and to Nitze's assignment as chairman
of a subcommittee that would examine Berlin issues. In this capacity
Nitze was invited to sit in regularly on Executive Committee meetings.
The meeting can be heard breaking up, with people leaving. It is just
after 7:00.*

.   .   .

7:10 P.M.

Discussion between President Kennedy and Robert Kennedy

As the recording becomes slightly more audible, in the lull after the just-
concluded meeting, only a few people are left in the Cabinet Room. It is
about 7:10. They are discussing the possible use of General Lucius Clay
to go to Berlin to help deal with the possible escalation of the crisis.
President Kennedy returned to the Cabinet Room while this conversation was going on, having finished the formal, photographed signing of
the quarantine proclamation in the Oval Office.

President Kennedy had been working for days on Berlin contingency
plans and had instructed the Pentagon to prepare a military column, in
battalion strength, to be ready on two hours' notice to move on the
Autobahn toward Berlin if the Soviets and East Germans attempted to
cut off traffic and blockade West Berlin.

.   .   .

Robert Kennedy: Jack, General Clay indicated that he would go to
Berlin, and that he would be glad to go and go in an official or unofficial
capacity. I guess the general agreement is that it would be bad to focus
attention on Berlin right at the moment by him going there and that,
perhaps, General Taylor could tell him that we appreciate the offer and
that [unclear].

President Kennedy: I phoned him today, just to have a chat.

Maxwell Taylor: Mr. President, this was at 5:55, he [Clay] tried to
get me.

President Kennedy: Well, we don't want a . . . If you can call him,
General, and just say: "Well we don't want to . . . There may be Berlin
squeezed and we may want you to go [there] over the next two or
three days."

McGeorge Bundy: [*Unclear*] on standby.
President Kennedy: Have him on standby, yeah.

. . .

The room falls silent as the remaining people leave, but Robert Kennedy remains behind. President Kennedy returns from talking on the phone to his wife.
Robert Kennedy: What was that?
President Kennedy: [*annoyed*] Oh Christ, about the dinner tonight.
Robert Kennedy: What?
President Kennedy: About a dinner tonight. She's [Jacqueline Kennedy] invited somebody and I invited somebody.[13]
  Robert Kennedy: [*switching back to the oncoming confrontation at the blockade line the next morning*] How does it look?
  President Kennedy: Ah, looks like hell—looks real mean, doesn't it?
  But, on the other hand, there is no other choice. If they get this mean on this one, it's just a question of where they go about it next. No choice. I don't think there was a choice.
  Robert Kennedy: Well, there isn't any choice. I mean, you would have been, you would have been impeached.
  President Kennedy: That's what I think. I would have been impeached.[14] I think they would have moved to impeach. I wouldn't be surprised if they didn't move to impeach right after this election, on the grounds that I said . . . and didn't do it and let . . . I mean, I'd be . . .
  Robert Kennedy: I don't think that [*unclear*]. You know that's a . . . If we'd gone in and done something else, or taken some other step that wasn't necessary, and then you'd be . . .
  President Kennedy: Yeah.
  Robert Kennedy: Yeah. But now, the fact is that you couldn't have done any less. The fact that you got all those South American countries and Central American countries to vote unanimously [in the OAS]. When they've been kicking us in the ass for two years, and they vote unanimously for this. And then to get the reaction from the rest of the allies, you know like [British ambassador] David Ormsby-Gore and everybody else. Saying that you had to do it. You calculate . . . I mean, if it's going to come at you, it was going to come as something you couldn't have avoided.
  I think, I just probably had—could get somebody that kept in communication with them [the Soviets]. It's too bad [*unclear*].
  President Kennedy: What is?

Robert Kennedy: You know.

President Kennedy: Take Georgi [Bolshakov]?[15]

Robert Kennedy: No, he had lunch today with— [16]

President Kennedy: What's he [Bolshakov] saying?

Robert Kennedy: He said they are going to go through [the blockade].

President Kennedy: The ships are going through?

Robert Kennedy: He [Bolshakov] says this is [*chuckles slightly*], this is a defensive base for the Russians. It's got nothing to do with Cuba.

President Kennedy: Why are they lying about that? Khrushchev's horseshit about the election. In any event, it's the sickening thing that [*unclear*] to be getting very mad about . . . they revealed about [*sarcastically*] this *horror* that [this] would embarrass me in the election.

Who saw Georgi? Holeman? While we were there? But he's not with us in this.[17]

Robert Kennedy: Well, as you know, he [Bolshakov] is very hurt about the fact that I hadn't seen him. And then he came back to see me, and he said Khrushchev had a message for you. And I followed it up.

The ambassador [Anatoly Dobrynin] kept telling me: "Don't pay attention to Georgi." So I don't know if there's something going on.

President Kennedy: But did any of them tell you that they were going to put missiles there?

Robert Kennedy: No. Remember when I told you that.[18]

President Kennedy: Yeah.

Robert Kennedy: I said to tell Chuck, tell Charlie Bartlett to get hold of Georgi.[19]

President Kennedy: Today?

Robert Kennedy: And let's just say that, you know, it was based a good deal [on this guidance]: "The President had great confidence in the ambassador [Dobrynin]. We [Robert Kennedy and Dobrynin] had this exchange. The ambassador said that they weren't going to put the missiles there. And the President went on television [on September 13], took his position based on a lot of these personal assurances because he thought that he could believe the ambassador and all the rest." [*quieter*] "You see," I said smiling, "I'm not making this approach."

President Kennedy: You said this [for Bartlett] to tell Georgi?

Robert Kennedy: I told him so.[20]

President Kennedy: [*Brief unclear comment.*]

[*changing subject*] What does Charlie Bartlett say about Arthur Krock?[21]

Robert Kennedy: To me? Oh, that he's sore as hell.

I think it's been pretty good. You know, the press reaction is pretty good.

President Kennedy: Until tomorrow morning.

Robert Kennedy: Oh, it's going to be, it's going to end. They all recognize it's going to get unpleasant.

President Kennedy: But as I say and you say on that, I mean, what is he going to do?

Robert Kennedy: I mean that's the thing.

President Kennedy: But who's going to ask him . . . if we give—

Robert Kennedy: The luckiest thing in the world.

President Kennedy: What?

Robert Kennedy: I'll tell you what. Number one, we kept . . . you had to have a decision—we didn't want out. Or facts you didn't want out. You really [would have] had to make up your mind on Thursday [October 18]. I mean, if the facts got out, and you had to make up your mind and were forced to move, and couldn't get hold of the South American countries and Central America, and get this thing set up, that would've been awful tough. I think we wouldn't have just known. . . .

President Kennedy: Isn't that . . . we could . . . likely we would do that by an air strike?

Robert Kennedy: Yeah.

President Kennedy: I mean, you look at the . . . Saturday [strike possibility]. You didn't see a missile and they would have been over there. Shooting up everything. Then the Russians *really* would tense. This way they have to [now] . . . against the united thing of the whole hemisphere, and go in and they know we'd have to—

Robert Kennedy: I don't know whether you could get . . . You know, [we] talked about the ship. I don't know whether we could pursue that a little bit. But if you get a group from the OAS, they disable the ship, or stay with the ship. Then they fire guns, a thing, across the bow. Then they send for representatives from OAS or something. Not just the United States doing it. And then they come out. I don't know what they do when they get there, but then they request to board or request the ship to stop. In the name of the OAS.

President Kennedy: Instead of taking it to the United States? They take it—[*unclear, talking over each other*]. Ought to have a committee to oversee the blockade.

Robert Kennedy: Yeah, not have the United States be doing it. But the OAS.

President Kennedy: [*Unclear*] have that exposure.

Robert Kennedy: Let's say, once they locate the ship, have the OAS . . .

When you know which ship it's going to be, have the OAS fly the group out to board our ship or whatever.

President Kennedy: But what if they are [*unclear*] miles out? How do you land?

Robert Kennedy: Well, I think they can land, I don't know, with a helicopter or . . . I don't know.

[*Unclear reply from President Kennedy.*] Yeah, but what about when they, they're . . .

President Kennedy: Bob [McNamara], you want to talk to him about that? Fine.

Robert Kennedy: But what if I talk to Bundy now?

After a brief, inaudible exchange, the two men leave the Cabinet Room at about 7:20.

Having already used the Holeman-Bolshakov and Bartlett-Bolshakov channels to the Soviets that day, Robert Kennedy made yet another effort. According to Robert Kennedy's memoir, the President suggested that his brother meet privately with Dobrynin. Whoever had the idea, President Kennedy certainly knew about this approach, even though Robert Kennedy told Dobrynin he had come on his own, without any express instructions. The "agitated" Robert Kennedy confronted Dobrynin with strident, emotional accusations of deceit. Dobrynin said he only had known what his government had told him. Interestingly, in this approach undertaken personally, with the clear knowledge of his brother, Robert Kennedy said nothing at all about U.S. missiles in Turkey. Asked if Soviet ships would challenge the quarantine, Dobrynin said that those were the captains' instructions and he knew of no changes. Leaving, Robert Kennedy replied, "I don't know how all this will end, but we intend to stop your ships."[22]

Meanwhile, after the private dinner his wife had arranged, President Kennedy discussed the crisis and the day's diplomatic activities at length with British ambassador David Ormsby-Gore. Robert Kennedy joined them at the White House at about 10:15 and reported on his meeting with Dobrynin. Both Americans asked Ormsby-Gore how he thought the matter would end. He thought that there would either be war or a negotiated settlement and that everyone in his right mind would prefer the latter alternative. However, before Kennedy met Khrushchev, the Soviet leader should have no doubt about the United States's resolution and that the United States would make no unilateral concessions. Otherwise the results would be disastrous. Ormsby-Gore reported that both Kennedys agreed "with this summing up."

President Kennedy had also reviewed with Ormsby-Gore the ideas that had been discussed earlier in the evening for intercepting the first Soviet ships. Ormsby-Gore urged that instead of attempting an interception 800 miles from Cuba, as McNamara had recommended at the meeting, the Americans shorten the radius to 500 miles and give the Russians more time to consider their options. Kennedy promptly phoned McNamara and passed along this suggestion. Again McNamara urged the need to stay out of range of Cuban aircraft. President Kennedy was unimpressed by this argument, and they agreed that a line 500 miles out made more sense, though the application might vary and would depend on the circumstances of the interception.[23]

As the day ended, military forces across the world moved into states of higher readiness. That evening Castro delivered a televised address ordering a full mobilization and placing Cuban armed forces on the highest stage of alert.

Wednesday, October 24, 1962

Executive Committee Meeting of the National Security Council

The Executive Committee of the National Security Council gathered, on a schedule that was becoming routine, at 10:00. As they convened, the quarantine proclamation entered into full legal effect.

At the same time the quarantine became effective, the Strategic Air Command moved from the general Defense Condition 3 that applied to all U.S. armed forces to the higher Defense Condition 2, the level just below readiness for imminent general war. In addition to ICBMs and submarine-based ballistic missiles, every available bomber—more than 1,400 aircraft—went on alert. Scores of bombers, each loaded with several nuclear weapons and carrying folders for preassigned targets in the Soviet Union, were kept continuously in the air around the clock, with shifts refueled by aerial tankers taking turns hovering over northern Canada, Greenland, and the Mediterranean Sea. The Soviet government was presumed to be aware of these movements.[1]

President Kennedy turned on the tape recorder as McCone proceeded with his briefing on the intelligence that had come in through the night.

John McCone: . . . The Intelligence Community does not believe the measures to achieve a higher degree of action readiness for Soviet and bloc forces are being taken on a crash basis.

Communist reaction to the U.S. quarantine against Cuba has not gone beyond the highly critical but [*unclear*] yesterday by the Soviet government.

Surveillance of Cuba indicates the continued rapid progress in completion of the IRBM and MRBM sites. No new sites have been discovered. On the U-2 flight yesterday, where apparently [*unclear*] one of them had 40 percent cloud coverage. Another had only 15 percent cloud coverage. [*Unclear.*] Buildings believed to afford nuclear storage are being assembled with great rapidity. Cuban naval vessels have been ordered to blocking positions at Banes and Santiago Bays.

A survey of Soviet shipping shows 19 [16?] dry-cargo and 6 tanker ships en route to arrive in Cuba. Of these 22, 9 are in position to begin arrival by the end of October. Three ships have hatches suitable for carrying missiles, and two of these are among the ships that have been receiving urgent coded traffic from Moscow. [*Unclear*] substantially is coded traffic. The situation is this: At 1:00 A.M. Moscow time, yesterday, there were seven ships, that received urgent messages, including the *Poltava* but not the *Kimovsk*. Then at 2:30 A.M. this morning, all ships, including the *Kimovsk*, received urgent messages. Then, shortly afterwards, those came out of Odessa control [station for Soviet shipping]. Shortly after that, the Odessa control station notified all ships that, hereafter, all orders would come from Moscow.

The official world reaction showed generally favorable response to the U.S. action, particularly in Latin America. [*Unclear.*] OAS action.

There are no indications of any Soviet aircraft [*unclear*] Cuba. Additional information reported a [Soviet] submarine is tracking the *Kimovsk*. However, the latest position report indicates they're about 200 miles from [*unclear*]. There are three, or possibly four, [Soviet] submarines in the Atlantic, [*unclear*].

A Cuban airliner left Goose Bay this morning, from Dakar, bound for Havana, and had aboard 75 people and 9,000 pounds of cargo. . . .

I have ordered the [interagency intelligence] Watch Committee to meet every morning at 8:00. They will report [*unclear*]. They met with me this morning, and they concluded that the Soviet Union, for the past several days, has taken steps to bring its military forces into a complete state of readiness. [*Unclear exchange with Bundy.*] There are indications of preparations for the deployment of some long-range aircraft to Arctic bases. We have so far noted no major redeployment of other Soviet-bloc forces. However, there are tentative indications of the possible extension of Soviet [*unclear*] in the European area. Bloc military forces [*unclear*] in the European area are in a higher state of readiness. [*Unclear interjection by President Kennedy.*]

I think that's all of the . . .

· · ·

Dean Rusk: We had one intercept indicating that the Cuban armed forces have been given instructions not to shoot at overflying aircraft, except in self-defense.

McGeorge Bundy: How clear is that intelligence?

McCone: I haven't got that.

Maxwell Taylor: It was from a naval communications intercept.[2]

. . .

Robert McNamara: Mr. President, first [*unclear*] yesterday about our own [*unclear*]. Here are these. Pictures. These are our own aircraft; that's 150 of them in that position. [*Photos of U.S. aircraft on airfields in Florida are being displayed.*]

President Kennedy: Where?

McNamara: Homestead [Air Force Base]. I think General Taylor can speak to the implications of this and provide alternatives.

Taylor: The Chiefs are studying this, this morning, Mr. President. Whether we can accept that [the concentration of aircraft at a few fields in Florida] or whether some adjustments should be made. We're having [commander in chief of the Atlantic Theater] Admiral [Robert] Dennison [*unclear*] talk this afternoon and talk about [*unclear*] performance.

What we have done is [*unclear*] in a very high state of readiness in anticipation of a possible sudden order to implement. [*Unclear*], I would say, beyond the level which is now necessary.[3]

And the question is, if we backtrack somewhat, and we at least move the planes out, and perhaps leaving their [*unclear*] in place or moving onto several fields. We don't think the latter would make a good policy. The other question about moving onto the other fields is whether that would degrade our readiness below the level which we are now maintaining, which is [being able to launch strike aircraft within] four hours.

President Kennedy: There's no way to disperse these planes . . . maybe a little more?

Taylor: There can be a certain amount out on the dirt, but you're still going to have [*unclear*].

President Kennedy: But you figure that, well, our orders are if one of our U-2s are shot down, then we're going to then take out the [SAM] site. Were [*unclear*] 50 to 60 MiGs to come over, they're going to shoot up a lot of them, they'll [*unclear*]. And what about that?

Taylor: Of course, we're making every preparation against that that we can and that would include the low-level surprise attack.

. . .

President Kennedy: How many fields are we using there?

Taylor: Four big ones, but only two really big ones, Homestead and Key West, are in serious danger. If the MiGs run out and come in low level, they can't reach the northern [Florida] bases. If they came high, then I don't think there's any problem being able to take them out.

President Kennedy: This is yesterday?

McNamara: Yes.

I think the conclusions, Mr. President, are that, as General Taylor has suggested, we should maintain a substantially smaller alert force than has been maintained, ready to go after a SAM site or a limited target in Cuba with 1 or 2 hours' notice. We should go back to the original plan of 12 hours' notice for any sizable strike.

If we were to do that, the great bulk of those aircraft would move back to their home fields. And the remaining force deployed on these four bases would be much, much smaller. We'd leave the logistical support at the bases, in most cases. Simply move the aircraft back. This will shift our lead time from 1 to 2 hours for the bulk of the force to 12 hours. But I think this is an acceptable reduction in lead time.

President Kennedy: Well, all right.

Roswell Gilpatric: You make the decision the night before.

Taylor: Our problem is to create minimum confusion in a change of this order, and that's what the Chiefs are looking at this morning.

. . .

McNamara: The second point, Mr. President, is the present position of the Soviet vessels, and our plans for intercepting them. There are two vessels that I'll be discussing. One is the *Gagarin*, and the other is the *Kimovsk*, of which these are pictures.

Both of these will be approaching the barrier, by which I mean, they are about 500 miles from Cuba at approximately noon today, roughly the present time, eastern daylight time. I say they will be approaching it— they will be approaching it if our dead reckoning is correct....

Twenty-two seconds excised as classified information.

The *Gagarin* appears to be about 30 to 50 miles behind the *Kimovsk*....

The *Gagarin* declared [its cargo as being] technical material at Conakry. This is a typical declaration of an offensive weapons–carrying ship from the Soviet Union. We have checked back the records, and this appears to be a typical way by which they propose to deceive. Both of these ships, therefore, are good targets for our first intercept. Admiral Anderson's plan is to try to intercept one or both of them today.

There is a submarine very close, we believe, to each of them. Between. One submarine relatively close to both of them. The submarine will be at the barrier tonight, late today. It's traveling 8 knots an hour, and therefore it should be 20 to 30 miles from these ships at the time of intercept.

And hence it's a very dangerous situation. The Navy recognizes this, is fully prepared to meet it. Undoubtedly we'll declare radio silence. And therefore neither we nor the Soviets will know where our Navy ships are for much of today.

And that, I think, summarizes our plan.

President Kennedy: Which one are they going to try to get? Both of them?

McNamara: They are concentrating on the *Kimovsk*, but we'll try to get both. The *Kimovsk* has the 7-foot hatches and is the most likely target.

President Kennedy: If the . . . one of our ships . . . what kind of ship is going to try to intercept? A destroyer?

McNamara: Last night, at about midnight, the plan was to try to intercept the *Kimovsk* with a destroyer. Previously it had been thought it would be wise to use a cruiser. But, because of the Soviet submarine, at the time of intercept, it's believed that it would be less dangerous to our forces to use a destroyer. The [aircraft carrier] *Essex*, with antisubmarine equipped helicopters, will be in the vicinity, and those helicopters will attempt to divert the submarine from the intercept point.[4]

McCone: Mr. President, I have a note just handed to me from . . . [*unclear*]. It says that we've just received information through ONI that all six Soviet ships currently identified in Cuban waters—and I don't know what that means—have either stopped, or reversed course.[5]

Rusk: What do you mean, Cuban waters?

McCone: Dean, I don't know at the moment.

McNamara: Most of these ships [in Cuban waters] are outbound from Cuba to the Soviet Union. There are several, and I presume that that's what that refers to. There are only—

President Kennedy: [*interrupting*] Why don't we find out whether they're talking about the ships leaving Cuba or the ones coming in?

McCone: I'll find out what this guy [*unclear*]. [*He leaves the room.*]

Rusk: [*drily*] Makes some difference. [*A few people laugh.*]

Bundy: It sure does.

McNamara: There were a number of ships so close to the harbors in Cuba this morning that we anticipate their entering the harbors at the present time, inbound from the Soviet Union. There were a number of ships outbound also relatively close to the harbors.

Gilpatric: There is one other ship, a tanker, which is now passing through one of the straits, one of the channels through the islands, a tanker. . . .

President Kennedy: If this submarine should sink our destroyer, then what is our proposed reply?

Taylor: Well, our destroyer, first, will be moving around all the time and the submarine is going to be covered by our antisubmarine warfare patrols. Now, we have a signaling arrangement with that submarine to surface, which has been communicated I am told by . . . to—

U. Alexis Johnson: I sent it [to the Soviets] last night, yes.

Unidentified: But is that . . . ?

Taylor: Could you describe this, I just—

Alexis Johnson: I sent the identification procedures for a submarine. I sent a message to Moscow last night saying that, in accordance with the President's proclamation, the Secretary of Defense has issued the following procedures for identification of submarines, and asked the embassy to communicate this to the Soviet government, and said this is also being communicated to other governments, this would be a general regulation. Whether they . . . I have not got acknowledgment of receipt of that.

As far as our proclamation is concerned, it was delivered to the Soviet foreign office last night and very promptly returned.

Rusk: I presume they took a look at it.

Alexis Johnson: It was also delivered to the embassy here last night. We have not yet received it back. But these identification procedures should be in their hands.

They are standard. . . . I understand they are an addition to standard international practice accepted by the Soviets?

McNamara: No. This is a new procedure I asked them to set up yesterday, Alex.

Alexis Johnson: It is a new procedure.

McNamara: Here is the exact situation. We have depth charges that have such a small charge that they can be dropped and they can actually hit the submarine, without damaging the submarine.

Taylor: They're practice depth charges.

McNamara: Practice depth charges. We propose to use those as warning depth charges. The message that Alex is talking about states that, when our forces come upon an unidentified submarine we will ask it to come to the surface for inspection by transmitting the following signals, using a depth charge of this type and also using certain sonar signals which they may not be able to accept and interpret. Therefore, it is the depth charge that is the warning notice and the instruction to surface.

It was after McNamara made this point in the discussion, Robert Kennedy jotted down later that day, that he thought "these few minutes were the time of greatest worry by the President. His hand went up to his face & covered his mouth and he closed his fist. His eyes were tense, almost gray, and we just stared at each other across the table."[6]

Taylor: I believe it's the second step, Mr. Secretary, as [Admiral George] Anderson described it.

McNamara: Yes.

Taylor: First the signals and then after—

McNamara: Right. The sonar signal very probably will not accomplish its purpose.

Alexis Johnson: The time element being what it has been, I am not sure that we could assume . . .

McNamara: I think it's almost certain they didn't. [*Unclear*] didn't see ours, but you and I were working on it at 1:30 [*unclear*]. I'm sure that it got to the Soviet Union back to the submarine. Now—

Alexis Johnson: That's what I mean. Yes.

McNamara: I neglected to mention one thing about the submarine, however.

. . .

President Kennedy: Kenny?

Kenneth O'Donnell: What if he doesn't surface, then it gets hot?

President Kennedy: If he doesn't surface or if he takes some action— takes some action to assist the merchant ship, are we just going to attack him anyway? At what point are we going to attack him?

I think we ought to wait on that today. We don't want to have the first thing we attack as a Soviet submarine. I'd much rather have a merchant ship.

Taylor: Well, we won't get to that unless the submarine is really in a position to attack our ship in the course of an intercept. This is not pursuing [*unclear*] on the high seas.

McNamara: I think it would be extremely dangerous, Mr. President, to try to defer attack on this submarine in the situation we're in. We could easily lose an American ship by that means. The range of our sonar in relation to the range of his torpedo, and the inaccuracy, as you well know, of antisubmarine warfare is such that I don't have any—

President Kennedy: [*Unclear*] imagine it would.

McNamara: —great confidence that we can push him away from our ships and make the intercept securely. Particularly, I don't have confidence we could do that if we restrict the commander on the site in any way. I've looked into this in great detail last night because of your interest in the question.

Rusk: Can you interpose the Soviet merchant vessel between the submarine and yourself? Or does he have torpedoes that can go around and come in from the other side?

Taylor: He can maneuver anyway he wants to.

Rusk: I know. But I mean, suppose that you have air observation, you keep the Soviet ship—

Unidentified: Right underneath.

Unidentified: I don't think—

McNamara: What the plan is, Dean, is to send antisubmarine helicopters out to harass the submarine. And they have weapons and devices that can damage the submarine. And the plan, therefore, is to put pressure on the submarine, move it out of the area by that pressure, by the pressure of potential destruction, and then make the intercept. But this is only a plan and there are many, many uncertainties.

Rusk: Yeah.

President Kennedy: OK. Let's proceed.

Rusk: Mr. President, I do think it is important in our present procedures—of course, these may change later—but for us to make it, to be quite clear what the object of this present exercise is. And that is to stop these weapons from going to Cuba. It is not to capture them for ourselves at this stage. It is not to do anything other than keep them from going to Cuba. I take it that we all understand the present purpose.

· · ·

President Kennedy: Yes, I want to. . . . I would think that, pending of course on what we learn when Mr. McCone gets back, I would think that if we have this confrontation and we sink this ship, then we would assume there would be a blockade then and possibly one of the responses in Berlin which would be completely . . . which they would say that there's no movement in and out of Berlin—a blockade. Then we would be faced with ordering in air in there, which is probably going to be shot down, which is . . . What is then our situation? What do we do then?

Paul Nitze: What we do then is to . . . We've got our fighters up in the corridor [from West Germany to Berlin] and we try to shoot down their planes, and keep the air corridor open up to the point where it looks as though this is militarily no use, in which event, if they've firmly resolved to demonstrate it, then they're going to put in overpowering air force in the air corridor.

Then we have a decision to be taken by NATO as to whether or not to proceed with attacks on the SAM sites and on the bases from which the planes come. Or whether we want to go into phase two, then regroup, and produce more force before we go further.

McCone returns to the Cabinet Room.

President Kennedy: What have you got, John?

McCone: These ships are all westbound, all inbound for Cuba.

Soviet waters, [*correcting himself*] Cuban waters is considered as west of 30 degrees [west longitude]. I just don't know where that is.

Bundy: [*to an aide*] Get a map.

McCone: Now the ships are the *Poltava,* the *Gagarin,* the *Kimovsk,* the *Dolmatovo,* the *Moscow Festival,* and the *Metallurg Kursk.*

McNamara: The *Metallurg Kursk* is close to the barrier, but to the east of it, if I recall correctly. The *Kimovsk* and the *Gagarin* are the two I mentioned. They are roughly 500 to 550 miles from Cuba at the present time. The other ship I believe is one of the tankers we mentioned which is closer to Cuba, so that at least two of those ships are 500 miles from Cuba.

President Kennedy: Now, what do they say they're doing with those, John?

McCone: Well, they either stopped them [the ships heading toward Cuba] or reversed direction. They reversed at—[*unclear interjection*]. I don't know. I assume this is a communication intercept.

President Kennedy: Well, where did you hear this?

McCone: It's from ONI. It's on its way over to you now. It's on the way over here.

President Kennedy: Now is this all the Russian ships, or would this be just selected ones?

McCone: This apparently is a selected bunch, because there's 24 of them. And . . .

McNamara: It looks as though these are the group of ships that are relatively close to our barrier. There's another group of ships very close to the Cuban shore, a substantial number. So close, I'm sure they wouldn't turn them around. And there might be one in between there. This tanker, the *Raznitch,* which appears to us to be about a hundred miles from Cuba this morning. I'll see if I can get more information.

President Kennedy: Well, let's just say that, if this report is accurate, then we're not going to do anything about these ships close in to Cuba.

Bundy: The ships further in, we would not wish to stop, would we? *Rusk makes some unclear remark in the background and Bundy appears to laugh. This might have been the moment when Rusk whispered to Bundy:* "We are eyeball to eyeball, and I think the other fellow just blinked."[7]

President Kennedy: Now, if these have turned, that would mean that it isn't just they're picking out the ones that might have these weapons on. That sounds like every ship that's within . . . at that certain distance. Now we won't . . . we're not planning to grab any of those, are we?

McNamara: We're not planning to grab any ship that is not proceeding toward Cuba.

. . .

Rusk: This possibly could fit a remark made by the Cuban ambassador to the Brazilian yesterday, at the Security Council, that if we would hold off on the blockade for a day or so or until the Security Council votes, that his government was disposed to accept U.N. inspection. Now, we can't rely on that at all. That's just a remark that the Cuban ambassador was alleged to have made to the Brazilian ambassador.

Robert Kennedy: [*referring to the news that Soviet ships have stopped or are turning back*] Well, will that information get to the Navy?

Rusk: Yeah, we better be sure the Navy knows that they're not supposed to pursue these ships.

. . .

Someone begins whispering information to President Kennedy.

Bundy: Max is talking to Admiral Anderson. [*Unclear exchange.*]

McNamara: That's exactly . . . we also have search planes in the area on that.

President Kennedy: Simultaneously?

Bundy: No, it's one way or the other.

President Kennedy: Well, the question, it seems to me, is: They're going to start to turn them around . . . [*Inaudible reply.*] So I would think you ought to check first: How do we find out if six [ships] are simultaneously turning? Whether we're going to . . . we ought to maybe wait an hour on the *Kimovsk*. To see whether . . . [*Inaudible.*]

General [Taylor], what is the . . . how do we get . . .? What does the Navy say about this report?

. . .

Taylor: Three ships are definitely turning back. One is the *Poltava*, [which] we are most interested in. They did not give an additional number that may leave, but they say certain others are showing indications that they may be turning back. Admiral Anderson is making every effort now to get planes out into the area, to have patrols there that will be vectored into this area.

. . .

President Kennedy: [*after a pause*] It seems to me we want to give that specific ship a chance to turn around. You don't want to have word going out from Moscow: "Turn around," and suddenly we sink a ship. So I would think that we ought to be in touch with the *Essex*, and just tell them to wait an hour and see whether that ship continues on its course in view of this other intelligence.

Wouldn't that be your judgment?

Brief, inaudible exchange. Someone asks McNamara, "Did you talk to [Admiral] George [Anderson]?"

President Kennedy: We have to move quickly because they're going to intercept between 10:30 and 11:00 and we may be in a [*unclear*].[8]

McNamara: Five hundred miles. This particular ship that we are scheduling for an intercept between 10:30 and 11:00 our time, which is right now, is about 500 miles from Cuba.

Robert Kennedy: Isn't that one of the ones that—

McNamara: It is the *Kimovsk*, which has 7-foot hatches.

. . .

After a discussion of crisis communications capabilities in the Western Hemisphere, President Kennedy turned off the tape recorder. He did, however, succeed in eventually getting the discussion back to Berlin. Bundy, in his later summary, wrote that in the remainder of the meeting, "the President directed that State and USIA should give immediate attention to increasing understanding in Europe of the fact that any Berlin crisis would be fundamentally the result of Soviet ambition and pressure, and that inaction by the United States in the face of the challenge in Cuba would have been more and not less dangerous for Berlin.[9] . . . The President directed that a senior representative of USIA should regularly be present at meetings of the Executive Committee."

5:05 P.M.

Meetings with Staff and Congressional Leadership

During the afternoon the U.S. government digested the information about Soviet ship movements and continued to pursue its diplomatic efforts. Bundy phoned Ball with news that the most significant Soviet ships had definitely turned around. Officials met in the afternoon, including Robert Kennedy and President Kennedy's informal adviser, Robert Lovett, and concentrated on one of the problems that had concerned President Kennedy that morning: what to do about the Soviet ships, some of which were turning around and some of which were not.

As President Kennedy had wished, they agreed that the Soviet vessels that were turning around might be trailed and photographed, but the Navy should take care not to interfere with them.[10]

Keeping the promise he had made two days earlier in his meeting with congressional leaders, President Kennedy was again meeting with top congressmen from both parties. McCone, Rusk, and Lovett are there with him from the start (about 5:15); McNamara joined the meeting too, probably after it was already in progress.

President Kennedy turned the tape recorder on during this meeting after it was already underway, with the assembled senators and representatives. McCone had delivered his intelligence update. Rusk is reviewing the diplomatic situation.

. . .

Dean Rusk: . . . to the [U.N.] General Assembly where all this vast mutual opinion has much more weight than it does in the Security Council. But our friends in the U.N., our allies, have been very helpful during this situation.

In general there is still, to be noted, some elements of caution in the Soviet attitudes. In their speech at the U.N., although it was bitter and as violent as ever, it did seem to us to go to some pains to keep the finger on the Cuban-U.S. aspects of the matter, rather than the U.S.S.R.-U.S. aspects of the matter.[11]

So far as we know, the Soviets have not told their own people that they have missiles in Cuba, which indicates that this is not something . . . that they think that their own people may be very disturbed, and create war scares there if they were to give that information.

We do think that, although the situation is highly critical and dangerous, that it is not frozen in any inevitable way at this point, and that we can continue to watch the activity of the other side and their reactions to see what is likely to happen. Now there are a variety of rumors, gossip, contacts, and reports. But I don't think I can give a definitive view today as to what the real attitude of the Soviet Union is on this matter. Our best judgment is that they are scratching their brains very hard at the present time and deciding just exactly how they want to play this, what they want to do about it.

. . .

Everett Dirksen: I've been informed, Mr. President, that just a moment ago somebody overheard on the radio that Khrushchev, indirectly through Bertrand Russell, suggested a summit conference. Is there any . . . ?

President Kennedy: Perhaps the Secretary can read that?

Rusk: The full statement that he [Khrushchev] gave to Bertrand Russell: "The Soviet government will not take any decisions which will be reckless, will not allow itself to be provoked by unwarranted actions of the United States of America. We shall do everything in our power to prevent war from breaking out. We would consider a top-level meeting useful." Noting that the U.S. government must display reserve and stay the realization of its piratical threats, which have brought on the most serious consequences.

And he [Khrushchev] did say that: "As long as the rocket nuclear weapons have not been used, there is a possibility of averting war. When the Americans launch aggression, a meeting at the highest level will become impossible and useless." So he said quite a variety of things in there.

Dirksen: That was no direct invitation to you.

President Kennedy: No.

Dirksen: Do you want any comment on a summit meeting?

President Kennedy: I think it would be useless.

Dirksen: I would too. Absolutely useless.

Hubert Humphrey: Mr. President, has there been any official information at all from the Soviet Union to either you or the Secretary of State?

President Kennedy: No. As you know I wrote them a letter.

Humphrey: Yes.

President Kennedy: And then they sent me back a letter which was a condensation of the statement the government put out, objecting to all the things that we were talking about doing and sending . . .

So we're right now in the position of waiting to see whether these ships are going to, whether they're going to turn back some ships which might be carrying weapons. Or continuing with others. And whether those ships will be stopped when we . . . for example, tankers, which obviously couldn't carry weapons.

I don't know what ship they may choose for a test case, either to have us sink it, or disable it and have a fight about it, or whether they are going to submit to the quarantine those ships which are obviously not carrying any of these offensive weapons. And we ought to know that within the next 24 hours. Until we know that, we don't know much. When we know that, then we'll know where, at least we'll have some indication of where we're going.

.   .   .

Dirksen: Are you surprised by the slow uptake in the Soviet Union?

Rusk: We thought, and I defer to Ambassador [Llewellyn] Thompson, who's my chief adviser on this sort of thing, that this would catch them off timing.

Really, their timing, as we look back on it now, was for Khrushchev to come to the U.N. in late November, prepared to lay on a real crisis over Berlin, in direct talks with the President. He wanted to have all this in his pocket when he had that talk.

And our impression so far is that we have not caught them with a lot of contingency plans all laid out and ready to go. This has upset their timing at some point.

Carl Vinson: May I ask a question of Mr. McCone?

President Kennedy: Yes.

Vinson: Mr. McCone, what was your latest estimate on the number of MiG-21s in Cuba?

John McCone: Our original estimate was 1, which we saw, and 12 possible which were in crates, that we have suspected to be MiG-21s. The next real target we had was when we saw 39, which I believe was on the 17th of October.

Vinson: Thirty-nine—

McCone: Thirty-nine MiG-21s.

Vinson: Do we have any monitoring that would indicate, by pilot chatter or otherwise, whether these are being flown by Cubans or by Russians?

McCone: Yes, we have some information on the MiG-21s that were airborne here a few days ago. About half of them were [piloted] by Russians. One, we suspect, was by a Czech, and the balance by Cubans.

George Smathers: Mr. McCone, may I ask this question? You stated at the outset that something about, "Don't shoot unless attacked." Now, is that the order to the Cubans, not to shoot unless attacked?

McCone: That's the information that we received today.

Smathers: But the other day [October 22], you said the Cubans were not in on these missiles at all, they were not in there. So . . .

McCone: That's right. As far as we know, with the information we have, Senator, they are not in on the missile sites. Except that maybe in a very moderate way, in connection with construction of camps, or things of that kind. And in those circumstances, our information that we have developed is that the Cubans that are on-site are under very careful surveillance.

.   .   .

Bourke Hickenlooper: Well, I was looking at a television this afternoon. A newspaperman reported that Khrushchev had said that he had asked you, or sent a message through, to have a summit conference. And I wondered if that is true?

President Kennedy: No. But I hear that there's such a—

Hickenlooper: What?

President Kennedy: I heard that such a report was on the television, but that isn't true. We've received no message from him about it. [*Unclear*] the other message [*unclear*].

Hickenlooper: If it does come through, what's going to be the answer?

President Kennedy: Well, why don't we wait till the message comes through? But there's no such message as yet. The only message, I think they probably referred to the one of Lord [Bertrand] Russell. But we received no message. And I think, until we do receive one and see what it says, I think it would probably be . . .

Hickenlooper: Have you any type of information as to whether the Russian ships are proceeding toward Cuba?

President Kennedy: Not with precision, no. Some seem to be. Some may not be. But I don't think we'll know for 12 hours.

Hickenlooper: Well, yesterday it was stated that, at least it came over the radio that, Khrushchev had said that he'd ordered his Russian people to resist [the quarantine]. Now if that happens, then we're in it, aren't we?

President Kennedy: Well, we'll have to wait and see, Senator. I think within the next 24 hours we can tell what our problems are going to be on the quarantine itself.

. . .

The meeting then breaks up and everyone begins leaving. It is about five minutes to six. The noise continues for about six minutes while everyone leaves and mills around, talking. Then the tape recorder is turned off, presumably by President Kennedy.

A short time later, the tape recorder is turned on again. This time only a few people are talking, probably having regrouped in the Oval Office. President Kennedy, Bundy, Lovett, and a few others are present.

Robert Lovett: . . . folks asked a direct question, which seemed to make sense to you. Bill [Fulbright] went quite a lot further. And I gather from what he said that he's convinced himself that this is the proper course of action.

President Kennedy: That's what he told me tonight.[12] He thought that Monday he was basing his opposition to it [the blockade] on the grounds that the OAS wouldn't meet.

Lovett: And, I gather, on the same [subject], that Senator Russell seems to be a little more belligerent, or prepared for further action. And I think the answer that I made to him is perhaps the one . . .

It seems to me that the wisdom, that the basic wisdom here, is to regard Cuba really as an extension of Berlin, and to consider the Berlin reaction as the one at which this Cuban affair was, at least in part, aimed. Therefore we have to avoid in the case of Cuba, a diversion of attention and the troops involved in the affair, at this stage.

The primary, one of the primary benefits, dividends, from this form of action which the President has decided on is that it ought to develop, rather quickly, the *intentions* of the Russians. We've had some faint indications they seem to be off balance. It seems to me that it would not be unreasonable to expect them to stay off balance for a couple of days while they make up their *own* minds what their intentions are.

Therefore any invasion, [*unclear*] any strike, any air strike which to me tends to be a result of a congenital habit of overstating the ease as well as the results of an air strike—

McGeorge Bundy: Do you want Paul [Nitze] and Bobby [Kennedy] to come over?

President Kennedy: No, I don't want to take them away from their work. I just want to get a . . . I'm thinking about what we're . . .

Lovett: I don't think there's any such thing as one of these quick and easy, sanitary routes. There's no such thing as a small military action, I don't think. And the moment we start *anything* in this field, we have to be prepared to do *everything*.

So in those circumstances, it seems to me that the decision as to what step is taken, if there is a continuing acceleration of buildup down there, would depend on the intentions which Russia has shown at that point. And I don't think a decision can be made now. It has to be made in the light of what happens within these next few days.

· · ·

President Kennedy: Well, I think then they've their neck [out] just like we've got it there [in Berlin].

Well in any case we've got to think, and we can see in the next 24 hours more, but . . . what we've got to be thinking about is this problem, of our blockade being successful and this work going on, and being faced in November with 50 or 60 of these missiles. Well, we're faced with 30 of them now, so it's . . . but anyway faced with 60 of them. Under what conditions would the Russians fire them? They might be more reluctant to fire them if they've already grabbed Berlin than they would be if we suddenly go in, there. But anyway these are the . . . that's what we've got to make a judgment on.

Let's see. U Thant's [proposal says] [*begins reading quickly, aloud, a copy of U Thant's statement from New York*]:

> The following message is being sent to the President of the United States:
>
> I have been asked by the permanent representatives of a large number of member countries of the UN to address an urgent appeal to you in the present critical situation. These representatives feel in the interests of international peace and security that all concerned should refrain from any action which may aggravate the situation and bring with it the risk of war. In their view it is important that time should be given to enable the parties to get together to resolve the situation the present crisis presented and normalize the situation in the Caribbean.
>
> This involves on the one hand the voluntary suspension of all armed shipments to Cuba and also the voluntary suspension of the quarantine measures involving the searching of ships bound for Cuba. [*Kennedy initially reads "re-searching," and Bundy interjects that this has been read in over the telephone.*]
>
> I believe the voluntary suspension for a period of two or three weeks will greatly ease the situation and give time to the parties to [get together to resolve the situation the present crisis presented and normalize the situation in the Caribbean].[13]

It seems to me, we make—

Bundy: Mr. Secretary, did you discuss this with—

President Kennedy: Well, I did. I talked to Stevenson.[14] We walked through this. To make it equal, you'd have to . . . first they would send no shipments into Cuba if we can't search them. The bloc would send no ships to Cuba. That would have to be the guarantee.

Bundy: Stevenson's proposal is, U.S. ships with U.N. inspectors.

President Kennedy: To do what?

Bundy: Maintain the search, to make sure that they weren't sending arms.

McCone: I would go one step further, in that they stop—

President Kennedy: The work on the sites.

McCone: —that they stop all work on the sites; that they place no missiles on their launchers—

Lovett: And have U.N. observers.

McCone: And that they have U.N. observers.

Bundy: At the sites.

McCone: For verification at the sites, yes.

President Kennedy: We're rather clear, I think, on what we want to say.

Bundy: All right. [*Unclear interjection from President Kennedy.*] I'll check with the Secretary [Rusk] and get a piece of paper for you.

Do you want to answer it [U Thant's proposal] tonight? Stevenson thinks it's an advantage to make a quick answer.

President Kennedy: Yeah, so do I. We ought to welcome his efforts.

. . .

After visiting the White House Situation Room to learn about naval developments, President Kennedy again spoke on the telephone with Prime Minister Macmillan. A British notetaker transcribed the conversation in London.[15]

President Kennedy reported that the critical Soviet ships had turned around, but that others were still coming. "We ought to know in the next 12 hours whether they're going to try to run it or whether they're going to submit to be searched. So we'll be wiser by tomorrow night, but maybe not happier."

Macmillan thought this was a great triumph for the American president and wondered how to exploit it. Kennedy disagreed, since other ships, not carrying sensitive military equipment, were still coming. Macmillan wondered if Khrushchev was frightened. Kennedy thought not, judging that the Soviets were more worried that the Americans might seize and reveal their Cuba-bound missiles in front of the world.

Macmillan turned then to the problem of how to deal with the missiles that were already in Cuba. Kennedy answered that, once the quarantine was firmly in place, "we're going to have to make the judgment as to whether we're going to invade Cuba, taking our chances, or whether we hold off and use Cuba as a sort of hostage in the matter of Berlin. Then any time he takes an action against Berlin, we take an action against Cuba. That's really the choice that we now have." He asked Macmillan point-blank: "What's your judgment?"

Macmillan wanted to think about it. He expected some sort of negotiation, but hopefully not one where Khrushchev "has all these cards in his hands." Kennedy commented that he might have Cuba, but not Berlin. "If he takes Berlin, then we will take Cuba. If we take Cuba now, we have the problem of course of these missiles being fired, or a general missile firing, and we certainly will have the problem of Berlin being seized." Macmillan agreed, and promised to consider Kennedy's question.

After some brief commentary on the diplomatic moves during the day, with Macmillan remarking that Khrushchev "is a bit wondering what to do," Kennedy reiterated his question for Macmillan even more precisely: "If they respect the quarantine, then we get the second stage of this problem, and work continues on the missiles. Do we then tell them that if they don't get the missiles out, that we're going to invade Cuba? He will then say that if we invade Cuba that there's going to be a general nuclear assault, and he will in any case grab Berlin. Or do we just let the nuclear work go on, figuring he won't ever dare fire them, and when he tries to grab Berlin, we then go into Cuba. That's what I'd like to have you think about." Macmillan acknowledged that that was "very well put, if I may say so," and promised to send along an answer.

They exchanged views on U Thant's proposal at the United Nations. Macmillan found it "rather tiresome of him, because it looks sensible and yet it's very bad." But Macmillan wondered aloud whether Kennedy should accept a summit meeting with Khrushchev in order to do a deal. Kennedy wanted to wait before making a judgment on that. Instead he stressed that "part of that answer, Prime Minister, seems to me to depend on the answer to the question that we were originally discussing, which was whether we ought to wait and let this buildup continue in Cuba. Because otherwise we risk war and equally important, at least of some importance, we risk the loss of Berlin. Otherwise we can keep on the quarantine, the buildup of missiles will continue, and then we would threaten to take action in Cuba if they go into Berlin."

Kennedy drew the link to a summit. "Until we have really reached a judgment on that question, which is now what we're thinking about, it's hard to answer the point about whether we ought to have a meeting with him. I don't know quite what we will discuss at the meeting, because he'll be back with his same old position on Berlin, probably offer to dismantle the missiles if we'll neutralize Berlin."

After this conversation, work continued around the government. President Kennedy had a late night. At about 9:30 P.M., a long, new message arrived from Moscow, from Khrushchev.

> Dear Mr. President:
> I have received your letter of October 23, familiarized myself with it and am answering you.
> Imagine, Mr. President, that we had posed to you those ultimative conditions which you have posed to us by your action. How would you have reacted to this? I think that you would have been indignant at such a step on our part. And that would have been comprehensible to us. . . .

You, Mr. President, are not declaring quarantines, but advancing an ultimatum and threatening that unless we subordinate ourselves to your demands, you will use force. Consider what you are saying! And you wish to convince me to agree to this! What does agreement with such demands mean? This would mean to guide oneself in one's relations and other countries not by reason but to indulge arbitrariness. You are no longer appealing to reason, but wish to intimidate us.

And, Mr. President, I cannot agree with this and think that in your heart you recognize that I am correct. I am convinced that in my place you would act the same way.

Reference to the decision of the Organization of American States cannot in any way substantiate the demands now advanced by the United States. This organization has absolutely no authority or basis to make decisions like that of which you speak in your letter.

Consequently, we do not recognize these decisions. International law exists, generally recognized norms of conduct exist. We firmly support the principles of international law, strictly observe the norms regulating navigation on the high seas and in international waters. We observe these norms and enjoy the rights recognized by all states. . . .

The Soviet Government considers that violation of freedom of the use of international waters and international airspace is an act of aggression, pushing mankind towards the abyss of a world missile-nuclear war. Consequently, the Soviet Government cannot give instructions to the captains of Soviet vessels bound for Cuba to observe the instructions of the American naval forces blockading that island. Our instructions to Soviet mariners are strictly to observe the generally recognized norms of navigation in international waters and not to retreat from them by even one step. And if the American side violates these rules, it must realize what sort of responsibility will rest on it in that case. Of course, we shall not be simply observers of piratical actions of American ships on the high seas. We will then be forced for our part to take the measures which we deem necessary and adequate in order to protect our rights. For this we have all that is necessary.

Respectfully yours,

N. Khrushchev[16]

President Kennedy and his advisers studied the letter. Kennedy called Ball at State. Ball focused on the last paragraph, which seemed to threaten a challenge to the quarantine. He advised Kennedy that the United States had no option "but to go ahead and test this thing out, in the morning."[17] Kennedy and the others were concentrating on whether to stop a Soviet tanker, the *Bucharest*, which was approaching the quarantine zone.

Turning to U Thant's message, now made public, Ball conveyed Stevenson's dismay about Kennedy's instruction to give a stern and negative reply that night. According to Ball, Stevenson thought the United States might look like it was blocking a negotiated solution. Stevenson, in Ball's words, was "kicking like a steer" about knocking U Thant's proposal down so quickly. Kennedy brushed aside these complaints.

As he had told Macmillan, Kennedy said the Soviets were still trying to test the blockade; they had only turned around the ships with sensitive military equipment, the ones they could not risk.

A reply to U Thant was prepared. After more discussions, Kennedy phoned Ball again with a new idea. Perhaps, he suggested, U Thant "ought to give out a message in a way that gives them enough of an out to stop their shipments without looking like they completely crawled down." So they would ask U Thant to put aside his original proposal and instead appeal to the Soviets to stop their ships for a few days, while preliminary talks took place in New York. The President and his advisers still thought they might need to set an example by stopping the *Bucharest*, but no one thought Khrushchev would have enough time to recall the tanker and no one was anxious for a confrontation. McNamara preferred just to have the Navy hail the tanker and ask for identification.

Since Khrushchev's letter had threatened a military confrontation when Soviet ships were stopped the next day, a quick reply to that message was also considered necessary. At about 2:00 A.M. on October 25th, as one message was being sent to New York, President Kennedy's terse reply to Khrushchev was sent to Moscow.[18]

Thursday, October 25, 1962

10:00 A.M.

Executive Committee Meeting of the National Security Council

As the sun rose in Washington on October 25th, a message from Macmillan arrived at the White House. In it, Macmillan offered his answer to the big question of what to do next which President Kennedy had posed when the two men had talked the previous evening. In Britain, large peace demonstrations had protested U.S. policy, and even comparatively moderate commentators were questioning the wisdom of Kennedy's stance. The *Evening Standard* published a cartoon with one panel showing Eisenhower holding Eden's coattails to prevent his going over a brink labeled "Suez"; in the other panel, Macmillan merely looks on as Kennedy starts to step across a brink labeled "Cuba."

Macmillan's message shows the influence of this drift in British public opinion. He wrote that he had been "thinking over the 64,000 dollar question which you posed on the telephone. After much reflection, I think that events have gone too far.

"While circumstances may arise in which such action would be right and necessary," Macmillan wrote, "I think that we are now all in a phase where you must try to obtain your objectives by other means." He urged the United States to propose a system of U.N. inspection in Cuba "to stop work on the major military installations so long as the negotiation lasts" about the removal of the missiles. "This would enable you to say that you had in fact obtained your objectives."

Macmillan was urging Kennedy to call off the blockade if he could just get this standstill, even though it would leave the existing missiles still in place. "In other words, such an approach as I suggest fits in with the answer to last night's questions which I feel I must give," which was his advice to avoid a military confrontation. In a final gesture to military bluster, Macmillan did conclude that: "At the same time you will no doubt continue with your military buildup for any emergency. This may be as important a factor for persuading the Cubans to accept inspection as in other directions."[1]

There had been little sleep for those watching the quarantine line and shipping in the Atlantic. McNamara's close scrutiny and constant questions had sparked more tense exchanges with Admiral Anderson, especially over where and how the Navy was monitoring Soviet submarines. The Soviet tanker *Bucharest* approached the quarantine line at 7:15 A.M. and identified itself. President Kennedy directed that the ship be trailed but allowed to proceed for the time being.

The military preparations and troop movements were so rapid, peremptory, and extensive that they inevitably attracted great attention in and out of the U.S. press. In that morning's *Washington Post*, well-known columnist and reputed Kennedy administration insider Walter Lippmann suggested that the crisis be resolved by exchanging the withdrawal of Soviet missiles in Cuba for the removal of U.S. missiles in Turkey.

· · ·

John McCone: Mr. President, according to our reports, there's been no change that's been noted in the scope or pace of the construction of the IRBMs and MRBM missile sites in Cuba. The recent construction is continuing as has been denoted for the last several days.

Cuban armed forces continue their alert, with military aircraft on standdowns since the morning of 23d of October. There are indications that known and suspected dissidents are being rounded up in Cuba at the present time.

Twenty-seven seconds excised as national security information, probably a reference to the 14 of 22 Soviet ships bound for Cuba that had turned back.[2]

Five of the remaining eight are tankers. Two of the dry-cargo ships not known to have reversed course may be carrying nonmilitary cargo.

President Kennedy: [*to someone else*] Why don't you sit up here?

McCone: [*Thirty-seven seconds excised as classified information, probably a reference to the* Belovodsk, *a dry-cargo ship still on course that did have military cargo.*]—carrying 12 MI-4 armed helicopters.

We still see no signs of any crash procedure in measures to increase the readiness of the Soviet armed forces. The Watch Committee concludes in their report this morning as follows: "We conclude that Soviet bloc armed forces are continuing to increase their state of readiness and some units are on alert. We have, however, noted no significant redeployments. So that [*unclear*] crash program, although there is a high level of alert."

Bloc media are playing up Khrushchev's 24 October statement that he would consider a top-level meeting as "useful."

There is, as yet, no reaction to the widely known turnaround of Soviet shipping, which had not become known to the public at the time of the issuance of this report except through this morning's article that appeared in some of the papers. Attention remains centered on the neutralist efforts in the United Nations to find machinery for easing tension, as well as the efforts of U Thant.

. . .

McGeorge Bundy: I think, next, probably, Mr. President, you ought to know the overnight military situation clearly.

Robert McNamara: Mr. President, early this morning, on the order of seven local time, which could have perhaps been six Eastern daylight time, the naval ships, a destroyer in particular, intercepted the *Bucharest*, which is a Soviet tanker, moving in the range of the barrier, queried it as to its name, destination, point of origin, and type of cargo. The *Bucharest* responded it's from the Black Sea. It was bound for Havana. It was carrying petroleum products. To the best of our knowledge, no other words passed between the ships. The destroyer was instructed to maintain surveillance of the *Bucharest*, and that is presently being done.

There are, I think, a series of actions related to this that we might undertake today. At the present time our naval craft participating in the quarantine are under instructions not to board, because they are instructed to board only designated ships, and those ships have been designated.

I believe we should today instruct them to selectively query and subsequently inspect by boarding, certain nonbloc ships. This can be done very quickly. This will establish boarding as a pattern of operation in the quarantine zone.

We could then follow this, later today, by boarding the *Bucharest*, if that seems desirable. But whether it seems desirable or not, I believe we should establish a pattern of boarding as a quarantine technique, and do it immediately.

President Kennedy: Have we got any other ships we can board now?

McNamara: There will . . . Non-Soviet ships, there are many. But in order to allow Admiral Dennison to lay on a plan for doing that, we should give the instructions, and do so very promptly. I think that would be highly desirable.

President Kennedy: Now, why don't you do that right now.

McNamara: Ros [Gilpatric], would you issue the instructions for nonbloc ship boarding, and have them keep us informed on the procedure, and if they say there aren't any [ships?] in range, suggest this helicopter . . . the problem we talked about or the use of the Florida forces we've discussed.

That's one action.

The second action, as to whether we should board the *Bucharest,* I think we ought to talk here further, and I'll pass over that for the moment because there is time to—

President Kennedy: What would be the next ship? And what time would we have a—

McNamara: The next Soviet ship?

President Kennedy: Yeah.

McNamara: The next Soviet ship of real interest to us . . . I say "of interest," because this passenger ship's location is not specifically known. By dead reckoning we calculate it's within the barrier area plus or minus 100 miles or so. But I don't believe we would wish to touch that. It appears to be a passenger ship. Undoubtedly it has cargo on board, but it gets us mixed up with hundreds of people. I think it would be wise to avoid that.

The next ship that would be of particular interest to us would be the *Grozny,* which is a tanker and has behaved rather peculiarly in the last 24 to 36 hours. There is some reason to believe that it may have received an instruction about 36 hours ago to deviate from its established course to Cuba. And instead of moving directly east by turning around completely, it appears that it might have moved northwest. I say "might have" because some of our direction-finding fixes and other information as to how it behaved are not accurate to closer tolerances than about a 90-mile radius. And we're not absolutely sure, therefore, what happened to it. But it looks as though it might have deviated from its established course and then resumed course during the night. And it appears to be moving now toward Cuba. And it's of great interest to us because it's not only a tanker, but it has a deck load. And it declared a deck load of, as I recall, of ammonia tanks. But these could very possibly be, and as a matter of fact probably are, missile fuel tanks on deck. In any case, it will come to the barrier at 2000 hours, eight eastern daylight time, the day after tomorrow night.

President Kennedy: Wait a minute, that would be—

McNamara: Eight P.M.

President Kennedy: Friday night?

McNamara: Friday night [October 26]. Now that's the only other Soviet ship and there's no [*unclear*].

President Kennedy: . . . that could [*unclear*] until Saturday morning, so that would be really like 48 hours.

McNamara: Or, alternatively, we could go further than the barrier on

Friday daylight and intercept it. But that's the only Soviet ship moving in at the moment that we think is attractive.

There are some other actions I think we can take that relate to this, however, Mr. President, that I'd like to mention now. I believe that we should establish a low-level surveillance pattern that is consistent with an air attack.

There is much evidence that the Soviets have instructed the Cubans to act very cautiously. I'd like to run down that because it relates to this low-level surveillance and possible further escalation of our military force. It appears that they've given instructions to Cuban MiGs not to fire on U.S. aircraft. And more than that, it appears that, in a separate instruction, they gave orders to Cuban MiGs not to take off from the airfields. I'm not certain of this, but there's some evidence to believe that.

It's quite clear they have camouflaged the SAM sites, surface-to-air missile sites, thereby reducing their readiness, because they have to pull these covers off in order to fire effectively.

McCone: There's no question about that.

McNamara: If the photographs demonstrate—

McCone: The photographs demonstrate that—

McNamara: Exactly.

Forty-three seconds excised as classified information. Vice President Johnson jotted down at this point that the Soviets or Cubans have "instructed planes not to fire & subs instructed not to attack."[3]

McNamara: We have pictures of the KOMAR craft [missile boats] moored in port, with covers on the missiles.

. . .

McNamara: . . . and therefore, I think that we can conduct low-level surveillance with very little risk of an incident that we did not wish to incite ourselves.

President Kennedy: What's the advantage of the low-level [*unclear*]?

McNamara: Two advantages. Three advantages, really.

One, it will give us some intelligence we can use, benefit from.

Two, it will establish a pattern of operation that is consistent with an attack, and cannot be differentiated from an attack, and therefore reduces the warning of an attack, and may make it possible to attack with lesser forces because we reduced the warning. And this, I think, is an extremely important point we can discuss later.

And three, it demonstrates to the public and the world that we are not only interested in stopping the flow of offensive weapons to Cuba, but also definitely have as our objective the removal of the weapons that are there.

Why are we justified in conducting low-level surveillance under these circumstances? We're justified doing so because there's evidence that the Soviets are camouflaging their sites. There is tremendous evidence of this. You can see the camouflage nets drying on the ground. It's been raining and it's wet and they're drying them out. They're under instructions to camouflage immediately. And they'll camouflage not just the weapons, but various buildings, trucks—

President Kennedy: [*Unclear*] explain to me this whole Russian thing someday. Why they didn't camouflage them before? And why they do it now? And at what point they thought we were going to find it out? I don't see this. That was one of the most [*unclear*].[4]

McNamara: It's an amazing thing. But now I think we're beginning to read their minds much more clearly than was true—

Bundy: Maybe their minds . . .

McNamara: —72 hours ago.

And there's absolutely no question but what they're under orders to camouflage and do it fast. And because the camouflage equipment is wet and spread out on the ground, it's drying. As soon as it dries they put it on everything in sight. They're camouflaging trucks; they're camouflaging erectors; they're camouflaging missiles. It's really a fantastic sequence of action.

And I think this gives us justification to go in and check on what's going on. And be sure we identify these things so we know whether they removed them or haven't removed them. Furthermore, I think we're justified in determining whether they're proceeding to install further offensive weapons.

And therefore I would recommend that, today, for all these reasons, we carry out a low-altitude surveillance pattern that is directed to use approximately eight F8U aircraft, that are now on one-half hour to an hour alert, to go in and cover the IL-28 airfields, and the major airfields, all nine missile sites, and selected SAM sites—not the whole island, but selected SAM sites, the KOMAR bases, and the coastal missile bases— the coastal defense missile bases. I think we can do this.

Roswell Gilpatric: And the nuclear storage areas.

McNamara: I beg your pardon, Ros. Exactly: the nuclear storage areas, which they are working on with great speed and effort.

I think we can do this safely. I think it will give us valuable information that we would need and benefit from if we subsequently decide to carry out an attack. And I think it will establish a pattern of operations consistent with an attack, and therefore it will camouflage an attack.

I would suggest we do it by announcing to the Cubans that we are going to carry out unarmed surveillance today, for the reasons I've outlined, consistent with the OAS requirement and consistent with our own objectives, that these planes are unarmed, but if they are attacked we will attack the attacker.

President Kennedy: If we want to . . . It seems to me we negate one of the purposes, which is to make it possible someday to make this an attack. Why do we even bother to announce it? Why don't we just do it?

McNamara: Well, we may not [announce]. We might say we're going to carry it on not just today, we're going to carry on unarmed surveillance to determine whether they are removing the weapons or whether they are proceeding to continue to install them. We're going to continue surveillance.

McCone: You said that in your speech.

President Kennedy: Yeah.

Unidentified: That's right.

McCone: Why say it again?

McNamara: Well, because if we want to continue this pattern of low-level surveillance or close surveillance, frequent surveillance, I think it would be very useful if we could announce that it's unarmed and get it clear that it's unarmed. And they would think of it as unarmed.

Unidentified: Some day you may want to arm it.

McNamara: Pardon me?

Unidentified: Some day you may want to arm it.

McNamara: Well, we don't have to say that every day hereafter it's going to be unarmed. We simply say we're going to carry out surveillance. Well, let me put that [issue of the announcement] aside. That's a very minor facet of this whole problem.

President Kennedy: OK.

. . .

McNamara: —the missile sites. This as a prelude to a possible subsequent attack on those sites.

There is some possibility that we're moving to the position now, where we could attack those missiles and have a fair chance of destroying them with very few aircraft. I don't wish to emphasize this.

Well, this is exactly the kind of situation we visualized and hoped we could move to here. And I say there's a possibility of that because—and Max doesn't completely agree with me on this yet with certainty—but you have to watch the situation develop hour by hour.

If we get this low-level surveillance in here, we can have interpretation of it within three to four hours, I hope, from now. And if it shows that every single missile site is eight hours from launch, which the pictures I looked at this morning indicated, then we have very little risk of going in within that eight-hour period.

And, secondly, if at the same time that that condition exists, all the Cuban forces, to the best of our knowledge, are under orders not to attack, we know at the very least there will be confusion if we come over there with a few aircraft and shoot it up.

And thirdly, if we have been going in with low-level surveillance for a day or two and that's the pattern of our operation, we send in the same number of ships, but now they're armed instead of unarmed.

And if the Security Council has turned down by veto our proposal— that we send in U.N. inspectors—this might set up the circumstances in which we can go in and take those missiles out.

Robert Kennedy: Bob, do you think that maybe they've gotten the instructions to . . . nonfiring or nonoffensive action, might be based on the expectation or the wish that we fire the first shot and then they'll all be loose?

McNamara: Possibly, Bobby, I don't know.

Robert Kennedy: But that would play a role in the fact that maybe we would want to do this in the next 48 hours.

McNamara: It would. And all I'm suggesting at the minute is that we take the steps that will give us the option to do it if we later choose to. And one of those steps is getting this Security Council veto. And the other step is carrying out this low-level surveillance. We certainly don't have to do anything more today.

Robert Kennedy: I agree.

President Kennedy: Then we come back then to whether the political situation at the U.N. and everyplace else is such that we want to let this *Bucharest* pass today without making the inspection. That's really the question. What is the political effect of our letting that pass? Are we better off to make this issue come to a head today, or is there some advantage in putting it off till tomorrow?

Robert Kennedy: When will it arrive in Cuba?

McNamara: The *Bucharest*, as best we can tell, is traveling about 17 knots, is around 500 miles from Cuba and should arrive therefore sometime tomorrow. And if we're going to [unclear interjection]. Yeah. [Unclear], we have about eight hours left, because it is now 11:35 [in the area at sea, not Washington, which is on daylight saving time] and we wouldn't want to do it tonight.

Dean Rusk: Mr. President, the fact that we have already hailed it [the *Bucharest*], asked it questions. It's answered. We've already passed it through.

McNamara: We haven't passed it. We just hailed it; it replied; and then we're shadowing it. And that is, to the best of my knowledge, the only words that were passed.

Llewellyn Thompson: By the time this arrives in port you will almost then be ready to tackle the other ships, and there wouldn't be much interval between its arrival and the fact that you make [*unclear*].

McNamara: That's approximately correct, Tommy.

President Kennedy: You want to put this . . . Is this any reason to put it off, or not put it off for 24 hours, the searching of a Soviet ship?

McNamara: It actually could be put off possibly for 48 hours, Mr. President.

Rusk: From my point of view, a tanker is not the best example. I mean, we haven't got POL [petroleum, oil, and lubricants] on the [prohibited materials] list, and if there's no visible suspicious cargo on deck there's not much room for anything under, beneath the deck. This is a tanker that left home before all this fracas developed.

President Kennedy: And it kept going. All right, it's obvious [*unclear*] and that's a restraining factor. We wouldn't turn it around. The question really is, if it arrives in Havana tomorrow or wherever it arrives, and it states that the United States—and it states what happened—does that then indicate [that the United States has wavered from the blockade and adopted] a separate pattern?

McNamara: Well, I think that we could say that Khrushchev's message to you stated he had instructed his ship captains not to deviate from the norm of sea practice. He used the word *norm* in his message. We consider this a deviation from the norm of sea practice. It is not customary practice to ask what cargo you're carrying and to get a response. It is done sometimes; but it, I understand, it is not customary. Therefore, we could say—

President Kennedy: Well, we wouldn't want to probably emphasize that it deviates as much as we . . . It seems to me the only . . .

If we decide not to, the only reason for doing it is because we wanted to give sufficient grace to the Soviet Union to get these instructions clear or for the U.N. to have a chance to operate. That seems to be the best grounds to put it on if we decide this isn't our best, our clearest case.

Rusk: Well, couldn't we truthfully say that we . . . ?

President Kennedy: In view of U Thant.[5] I think the only grounds to put it on is that we looked at the vessel. It was obvious what it was carrying. It was not carrying offensive weapons. It responded, and we permitted [*unclear*]. At this point, in view of U Thant's appeal, we let this go. But then, well, we couldn't . . . they're voting in the Security Council.

We've got to give some explanation. Because everybody else was going to have to start the practice of stopping and boarding. I don't think we could ever let it go, and say that all they have to do is hail us.

Rusk: It's important that during the day we board some other ships, some other flag's ships.

. . .

Theodore Sorensen: If it's important to board a Russian ship, and it seems to me it is, this may be the *best* chance you'll have with them. They'll never let you board a ship that really has something serious on it.

President Kennedy: Well, they're not sending anything serious right now. It seems the serious ones [Soviet ships] were turned around. Quite obviously the most [*unclear*].

I think the whole problem is to make a judgment of Khrushchev's message to me last night combined with—in which he said they're not going to do it—they're going to take action if we do—combined with what is happening at the U.N. and so on. Now, unless there is something . . . Unless more time is going to make it more likely that we're going to get something out of either the U.N. or Khrushchev, then I suppose you have to grasp the nettle. I don't know whether 48 hours, having let this go through, having this [ship arrive in Cuba] tomorrow, then announce in Cuba that we've let it go through. An American ship accosted . . .

McNamara: But I think it's such an obvious reason for letting it go through that it would not weaken our position to have them announce it went through, Mr. President.

. . .

President Kennedy: [*Unclear, amid several people speaking*] I just don't want a sense of euphoria to get around. That message of Khrushchev is much tougher than that.

McCone: I thought the statement last night was pretty good. They've altered their course. We don't know the significance of it. You don't have to make any additional statement. Why don't you just say [*unclear*].

McNamara: I would just stay away and simply stand on that, stay away from any statement of what the Soviet ships are doing, and simply report on the day's activities: We applied the quarantine. We stopped ships that we had any reason to believe might have been carrying prohibited cargo. We queried other ships.

President Kennedy: Once we get the principle, once we stop the ship and see what happens then, then it seems to me, if we then, about a day or so later, put POL on the [quarantine] list on the grounds that the missile sites are continuing, as you say . . .

McNamara: Yes, and that the Il-28s are being assembled. And we put aviation gas on the list, therefore.

President Kennedy: Therefore all tankers we'll seize.

McNamara: Right.

. . .

President Kennedy: We're not going to grab any other tankers today. And then I think the Defense Department ought to be thinking about what our explanation will be. We've got some credit on our side, the 14 ships that may have turned around.

And we've got the question of whether this procedure is a little flat. That won't become really a major problem until tomorrow night when it [the *Bucharest*] arrives [in Havana]. By then, as I assume, we may have another Russian ship [the *Grozny*].

Is there a political advantage in stretching this thing out? That's really the question. Are we going to get anything out of the U.N. or Khrushchev?

. . .

Bundy: Well, that is the question then. Because the real problem is whether a three-week standstill which does not move toward removal tends to be self-perpetuating, and unsatisfactory.

Rusk: Well, we've got three time periods here.

Bundy: That's right.

Rusk: We talked about our stance in the Security Council. We reaffirmed that: That's the permanent solution: removal, et cetera. The preliminary talks, no change in the quarantine for a two- to three-week period. If the U.N. can provide effective alternatives, then for that period there would be a U.N. quarantine, discontinuance of development work, and U.N. observers to insure that offensive weapons were not operational.

That's for the two- to three-week period. But during that two- to three-week period, the thing that you're talking about and insisting upon is getting the weapons out of there.

Bundy: Well, the question I raised, and I think is on the Secretary's mind, is whether, when you get into a tangle of this kind, the status quo doesn't come to have a momentum of its own. Is that or isn't it acceptable? That's my question.

McNamara: Could I start back a bit here and say, I don't see any way to get those weapons out of Cuba. I never have thought we'd get them out of Cuba without the application of substantial force.

Now, the force we can apply is of several kinds. It's economic force and it's military force. The insurance rates are rising today. This is gradually going to reduce the amount of trade moving into Cuba. This is a very important element of our force. I wouldn't want to remove the quarantine, no matter kind of inspection we had there, unless they agreed to take the weapons out. Because we could never impose it again, so long as they said they had adequate procedures to insure no more weapons moved in.

Bundy: Suppose we were to add "and an understanding on the part of the U.N. that the object is the removal of the weapons"?

McNamara: Yes, something, or the agreement that that's to be done, or something like that.

Bundy: Something one stage further. So that the status quo moves in our direction. Create some weight. That's what your quarantine is for, is to have weight on.

McNamara: This is my point, exactly.

· · ·

The message was worked on, discussed again with Stevenson, and simplified further after the meeting ended and then sent to New York at about 2:00 P.M. President Kennedy's final reply to U Thant read as follows:[6]

I deeply appreciate the spirit which prompted your message of yesterday.

As we made clear in the Security Council, the existing threat was created by the secret introduction of offensive weapons into Cuba, and the answer lies in the removal of such weapons.

In your message and your statement to the Security Council last night, you have made certain suggestions and have invited preliminary talks to determine whether satisfactory arrangements can be assured.

Ambassador Stevenson is prepared to discuss these arrangements with you.

I can assure you of our desire to reach a satisfactory and a peaceful solution of the matter.

The Executive Committee then turned to other diplomatic issues.

· · ·

Bundy: We checked this around last night, and perhaps the most interesting comment was Ambassador Thompson's. Tommy, would you speak for a moment as to how you interpret that [Khrushchev's most recent letter].

Thompson: Well, I thought the incoming [letter] indicated preparation for resistance by force—that is, forcing us to take forcible action.

Unidentified: But for local reasons?

Thompson: Yeah.

Bundy: Last night we sent this answer—the President did. "Dear Mr. Chairman . . . " It was delivered at 1:30 Moscow time, which was early this morning.

I have received your letter of October 24th and I regret very much that you still do not appear to understand what it is that has moved us in this matter. The sequence of events is clear.

In August there were reports of important shipments of military equipment and technicians from the Soviet Union to Cuba. In early September I indicated quite plainly that the United States would regard any shipment of offensive weapons as presenting the gravest issues. After that time, this government received the most explicit assurances from your government and its representatives, both publicly and privately, that no offensive weapons were being sent to Cuba. If you will review the statement issued by TASS in September, you will see how clearly this assurance was given.

In reliance on these solemn assurances, I urged restraint upon those in this country who were urging action in this matter at that time. And then I learned beyond doubt what you have not denied—namely, that all these public assurances were false and that your military people had set out recently to establish a set of missile bases in Cuba. [*Bundy adds the comment that* "it should have been secret," *meaning that the letter should have said "secret missile bases."*] I ask you to recognize clearly, Mr. Chairman, that it was not I who issued the first challenge in this case, and that in the light of this record these activities in Cuba required the responses I have announced.

I repeat my regret that these events should cause a deterioration in our relations. I hope that your government will take the necessary action to permit a restoration of the earlier situation.

President Kennedy: There you are.

Nitze: Doesn't that suggest, though, that what he intends is to not let his ships be put in a position where they can be held captive, boarded and searched?

President Kennedy: Except he just put one in there, yesterday, with . . .

Unidentified: Some ships . . .

Nitze: But if we hadn't put any . . . I think he'd [*unclear*].

Bundy: It's possible, it seems to me, Paul, that what you're saying is that we may be moving into some kind of de facto, unclarified quarantine.

McNamara: I'd like to assume that that's the case. I think our problem of the minute is to look ahead at least 24 hours here.

For the minute, let's make these assumptions, that:

(a) The Security Council does not accept our proposal or the United Nations does not;

(b) That we have no Soviet ship to intercept tomorrow, or that if we do intercept one it carries no prohibited weapons and submits to whatever action we apply to it;

(c) That the development of offensive missiles continues in Cuba, and we have evidence of that today from our low-level surveillance.

What do we do?

George Ball: I think we escalate to the—

President Kennedy: Well, we first stop a Soviet ship someplace and have [*unclear*] what they're going to do.

McNamara: I'm just speaking of 24 hours now. The possibility is we won't be able to do that, Mr. President. Maybe we can, but let's assume for the minute that we can't.

Or alternatively assume we do, and it wasn't carrying prohibited weapons, and it submitted to our quarantine procedure in any way we choose to apply it, indicating that the Soviet Union, for the time being, is going to prohibit the movement of offensive weapons to Cuba. What do we do under these circumstances?

It seems to me at least, George implied, we have to escalate. And if that's the case, how are we going to escalate?

Now, we have a number of alternatives. And I would like to suggest we consider those today, and at least some of us, perhaps the same group, get together before the end of the day and consider how we would escalate because we . . .

Bundy: May I suggest that we have a meeting of this committee without the President, for some examination of these alternatives?

McNamara: It might well be the thing to do, but later in the day.

President Kennedy: The obvious escalation is POL, isn't it?

McNamara: No, sir, I don't think that is necessarily . . . And as a matter of fact, it is going to be difficult to put POL in on this. There's one way to do it, and that . . . it seems to me, and that is to say that today we found they were accelerating work on the preparation of the IL-28s for operation. And therefore it became essential that we add aviation gas—not POL, but just the select kind of POL to the list, aviation gas—which would be the—or jet fuel, whatever it is—for the bombers.

Now, we could do that, but that's not much of an escalation, because . . .

Paul Nitze: That means then that they can't send any tankers. POL.

McNamara: But I was going to say it's not much of an escalation, because there aren't any tankers immediately within our grasp here. So I'm just wondering about time. It would seem to me that the timing is important. We don't want to allow any particular period of time to go by that starts to freeze the situation. We want to continue to move towards this ultimate objective of removing the missiles. And in order to do that we have to keep this situation moving without being frozen at any particular point.

Bundy: Could we get a consensus on that, and especially the President's own view? I share that view, very much, that a plateau here is the most dangerous thing. [*General agreement.*]

. . .

President Kennedy: All right, well, in any case, I'll tell you what let's do. Let's wait. . . . We got to . . . Let's come back this afternoon and take the ship. I think we can always . . . Your point about we can act . . . "eyeball to eyeball" . . . We could say: "Well, we're waiting for Khrushchev. We're waiting for U Thant. . . . We don't want to precipitate an incident." Which may be [*unclear*].

Bundy: I was thinking about it tomorrow morning, if [*unclear*].

President Kennedy: OK, well, we still have then [tomorrow morning] another six or seven hours [to board the *Bucharest*]. I think the only arguments for not taking it [*unclear*]. I don't think it makes a hell of a lot of difference what ship it is, whether it's a tanker or . . .

Bundy: We can . . .

President Kennedy: I would think the only argument would be that, with U Thant and the U.N. asking us for—

Bundy: We've given them a letter.

President Kennedy: —this is not the appropriate time to blow up a ship. So that maybe, and, if I wrote back to Khrushchev, we could justify withholding the action until about five this afternoon, if that's the way. Let's think a little more about it.

Bundy: Right.

Robert Kennedy: Can you take a tanker without blowing it up, Bob?

McNamara: Yes.

Bundy: Do we know when the Security Council comes to a vote?

Rusk: They meet at four this afternoon. They might come before that.

Robert Kennedy: Could we have a meeting of our group without the President, at least the two of—

Bundy: We can.

At this point President Kennedy turned off the tape recorder.

5:25 P.M.

Executive Committee Meeting of the National Security Council

After the Executive Committee meeting broke up in the morning, a Pentagon spokesman announced, as planned, that at least a dozen Soviet vessels had turned back from the quarantine. The passage of the *Bucharest* was handled by saying that the ship had been intercepted and permitted to proceed without boarding.

During the day in New York, U Thant issued a new statement. Prompted by the suggestion Stevenson had made, on instructions, U Thant's October 25 statement appealed to Khrushchev to order his ships to stay away from the interception area for a limited time and asked Kennedy to order his ships to avoid any direct confrontation with Soviet ships.

The U.N. Security Council began its meeting at 4:00 P.M. During the evening Stevenson delivered a spirited defense of the U.S. position, at one point dramatically pinning the Soviet ambassador, Zorin, with a direct, televised, challenge to state plainly whether the missiles were in Cuba or not. "Yes or no—," said Stevenson, "don't wait for the translation—yes or no." When Zorin said Stevenson would have to wait for his answer, Stevenson declared, "I am prepared to wait for my answer until hell freezes over." President Kennedy, watching the confrontation, said, "Terrific. I never knew Adlai had it in him."[7]

Meanwhile the Executive Committee reconvened at 5:00, at first without President Kennedy, who may have been staying back to keep watching the live coverage of the U.N. meeting on television.[8] The meeting began with an intelligence briefing in which McCone listed 15 ships still en route to Cuba, one of which was the *Grozny*. There were no unusual developments in Europe, though Dillon then observed that there had been a run on gold in Germany and, to a lesser extent, in London. He thought buyers were hedging against the uncertainties of the crisis.

McNamara called attention to the *Marucla*, a Lebanese dry-cargo ship but under Soviet charter. The Pentagon considered it a good candidate for boarding. Ships had been dispatched to meet it, but the *Marucla* appeared to be turning back from Cuba. An East German passenger ship, the *Völkerfreundschaft*, was approaching the quarantine line, perhaps with Soviet missile technicians aboard. This development troubled Taylor and Dillon.

McNamara outlined a plan for more low-level reconnaissance flights. His plan won support in the group, but he would present it again when the President joined them. As he had that morning, McNamara worried that if talks dragged on, new actions against the missiles in Cuba would become more difficult. He mentioned several ways of increasing military pressure, including expanding the quarantine.

Robert Kennedy thought it might be better to go ahead and knock out the missiles with an air attack rather than confront the Soviets at sea. Various other measures to throttle Cuban trade were also considered.

Then President Kennedy joined the meeting and turned on the tape recorder, probably at around 5:25, just as McNamara was returning to the issue of what to do with the East German passenger ship that was approaching the quarantine line.

Robert McNamara: . . . all we liked about the ship. And what we know is that this [*unclear*] is the *Völkerfreundschaft* [which] appears to have left Rostock on the 11th of October, stopping at Leningrad and departing there on the 13th. It is said to be a passenger ship of 12,000 tons, 525 feet long, two cargo holds forward, three aft, and said to have a 6[,000]- or 7,000-ton cargo capacity. Normally a passenger capacity of 392 tourist-type passengers, but [*unclear*] said there are 1,500 industrial workers on board including 550 Czech technicians, plus 25 East German students—

. . .

This should pass through the barrier today, and we have the destroyer, the [USS] *Pierce*, following it.

The question is, should we ask it to halt and submit to inspection? If it did not halt, should we pass it without forcing it to halt, or should we force it to halt? If we were to force it to halt, should we use fire, or should we put a Navy ship in front of it? If we use fire and we damage the ship, with 1,500 people on board, and we find that the cargo [*unclear*], does not include items on the prohibited list, have we not weakened our position? And these considerations led me to conclude this afternoon that I should recommend to this group and to you that we not ask that ship to stop.

President Kennedy: Yeah. I think the only problem really is this U Thant second message where he's saying to us that we not, that we avoid an incident if Khrushchev keeps his ships out. But now, we don't think Khrushchev is going to agree to that but I—

McGeorge Bundy: But I want to point this out, Mr. President. That U Thant's message doesn't cover this ship. He's talking about Soviet ships.

C. Douglas Dillon: Soviet ships.

Theodore Sorensen: This some ways shows that our response to U Thant's message is not a soft one at all. An East German ship came up, so we stopped it. And at the same time, we did not engage the prestige of the Soviets directly.

President Kennedy: What time is the latest we can take—

McNamara: The latest we can make a decision is probably one or two this morning, tomorrow morning—

President Kennedy: We have to stop—

McNamara: We have to give orders to the Navy and it's moving in—

Unidentified: At 22 knots, in fact.

McNamara: Yes, we ought to be positioning our ships early in the morning so they could stop it. We must assume that there is some elapsed time between the time of the decision here and the time of the intercept. It's moved through the barrier already. We estimate very roughly it'll make landfall sometime late tomorrow.

Dean Rusk: When did it leave Leningrad? Do we have—

McNamara: Allegedly the 13th of October.

Maxwell Taylor: May I really question the accuracy of this intelligence we've been talking about? Does John have anything on the source of this?

John McCone: I have nothing on . . .

One minute and 22 seconds excised as classified information.

Taylor: But we have no positive information that these technicians were on board before [*unclear*]?

Unidentified: We do not.

Unidentified: That'll be fine. If it doesn't have anything on board, we let it through.

Sorensen: How do you tell a missile technician from an agricultural technician?

McNamara: What do we gain by stopping it? Let's put it that way. I can see some possible loss. But what do we gain if we stop it?

Dillon: What do you lose? What you lose. Well, I think you do lose something if you let it go through without . . . if it comes out that they . . . you've . . .

Bundy: It's not only what you lose. I think the most dangerous thing you lose is the evidence to the bloc that you're not stopping. That suggests . . .

President Kennedy: Well, I think the only argument for not stopping it, actually, is this U Thant thing, where we have an incident of a kind tomorrow morning on a ship at a time when supposedly he's asking the Russians to stay out of the area, before we've got an answer. Then if we get an answer from them, or not an answer, I would think then we have to pick up some ship tomorrow, after the shoe drops.

What do you think, Bob?

McNamara: I hate to start with a passenger ship, Mr. President. I think there's great problems.

President Kennedy: It might be sunk, you mean.

McNamara: Yes, or seriously disabled and loss of life, under circumstances that would indicate we'd acted irresponsibly. This, I think, would be a serious . . .

President Kennedy: The only reason for picking this ship up is we've got to prove sooner or later that the blockade works.

McNamara: Right. Now, there is the possibility—that's the second point—of picking the *Grozny* up, which is a Soviet tanker with a deck cargo.

President Kennedy: Right. I remember that.

McNamara: It is now we think, about 1,000 miles from Cuba. There's some question as to whether it's continuing to move forward to Cuba. SAC aircraft reported it dead in the water. But it may well be moving in.

In any event, we can send a ship out tonight to meet it tomorrow. We can maintain radar surveillance of it tonight with aircraft and, unless it turns tail, we can intercept that tomorrow. It will be at that point 7[00] to 800 miles from Cuba. And I would strongly recommend we do just that.

President Kennedy: Tomorrow afternoon, though.

McNamara: Afternoon.

President Kennedy: We'll have seen what's happening with his answer [to U Thant's appeal]. Either Khrushchev's accepted it or denied it.

McNamara: That is correct.

. . .

President Kennedy: Well, then, if we followed your point, Bobby, we'd let the East German ship go on the grounds that it's a passenger [ship]. We'd announce tomorrow that the Soviets . . . Tomorrow afternoon we ought to have a Soviet response to U Thant which will affect this *Grozny*. And in any case, we can announce that all the ships are being suspended at that point. If he [Khrushchev] doesn't announce his ships are being suspended—and I don't think he will, probably—then we would announce that in view of the fact that he hasn't, we're putting the . . . POL.

. . .

Robert Kennedy: I don't know that it gets . . . The only weakness, in my judgment, is the idea to the Russians that we are backing off and that we're weak and . . . I'd like to get Tommy on that.

If you did some of these other things quickly, and then the fact that you've announced it. It's a hell of a thing, really, when you think of it, that 15 ships have turned back. And I don't think we really have any apologies to make.

Sorensen: What about the combination, Bobby, of letting the *Grozny* go through, and stopping the East German ship?

Robert Kennedy: I don't have the feeling on the East German, taking and removing . . . That I don't think plays a role in the idea I . . . you know, which we all . . . But I just think that Bob's point, about the fact that it has got 1,500 people on it . . .

Rusk: Mr. President, since I recommended a blockade. I haven't been very helpful about applying it in particular instances, but I suppose we make our best case with a Russian ship that had deck cargo that was highly suspicious, or a blind ship that hadn't—you just had to look at because you couldn't tell what the dry cargo was.

I said the other day that I thought the tanker was not the best case for the first instance of confrontation. I think even less is the big passenger ship. If we fire into that ship or we have to disable it, or if we in some way sink it or anything of that sort, with 1,500 people, I think we're just in a hell of a shape.

Sorensen: I assume we don't have to sink it.

Walt Rostow: On the other hand, if we get a negative from the Russians on . . . , aside from generalized pressure we have two forks in the road. One of them is to build up the line of going in directly. And the other is to pick up [the expanded quarantine list idea] from the IL-14s [meaning IL-28s] and in effect put a POL blockade on, which is another drastic way of [*unclear*] moving ahead.

Robert Kennedy: Then you get what the Secretary said you're going to be doing tonight, anyway.

Rostow: That would be another round. It would be a round against a background. The POL thing is very serious for them [the Cubans]. They have a 100 percent reliance on it, very short supply, and the clock would be ticking on, absolutely grinding that economy to a halt from the moment that you clamped that on.

Rusk: Mr. President, I would point out . . .

McCone: I think it would be quite a long time [to have that effect on Cuba]. You're talking about a few months, anyway.

Robert Kennedy: Yes. I don't think we can rely on it.

Rostow: The effects . . . We had this argument about the Germans in the war [World War II].

George Ball: I'll never forget—

Rostow: As soon as it was cut, it had the most drastic effects.

Ball: You know what happened. As soon as they hit the hydrogenation plants, the German Air Force fell apart because they couldn't do any training because there was such tight rationing that they would put a pilot in the air with [only] eight hours [of flying experience], and this was a major factor . . .

President Kennedy: Have we got a good analysis of what a POL blockade would do to them?

Rostow: I have a general paper and a supplementary one, in detail on the POL point.

Mixed voices. Though we cannot hear McNamara mentioning it, his civilian analysts in the Pentagon had prepared their own analysis of a POL blockade. They thought Rostow was wrong and that such a blockade would be ineffective or worse.[9]

President Kennedy: I think that, it seems to me that, given the U Thant thing that's going to be published to the world, where it looks like a chance of easing this, I think it's probably a mistake when we combine that with the East German cargo [and passenger] ship, which I think . . . You know, you try to disable it. You're apt to sink it. There are no guarantees when you try to shoot a rudder off, because you either sink it or have it catch fire. I would think that the combination of that, with negotiation with U Thant, really we don't want it tomorrow morning. We don't want to sink that ship tomorrow. So I think we can let that one go.

Now, I would think tomorrow afternoon we ought to get an answer from Khrushchev—that he's going through [the quarantine line] or not. Then we have . . . That he's not going to do what U Thant says. Then it would seem to me we then make up our judgment whether we grab—it's an obvious thing—whether we grab this *Grozny*. We've got two days. So I think all we're really doing is holding our hand on this East German one, because we don't want the incident tomorrow morning at a time when we are involved in this back and forth.

Then I think we have to decide whether we take this, or whether we are going to put POL on. Because I think if the work continues, we either have to do this air business or we have to put POL on. Because we've got to begin to bring a kind of pressure. Because otherwise the work's going on and we're not really doing anything about it.

Robert Kennedy: No. And we've got to show the people we mean it.

Dillon: I would think this night reconnaissance tomorrow would be very important, because it would show you whether they were working secretly.

Ball: Bob, are these the same kind of flares you use in night bombing? Are these pathfinder kind of flare?

McNamara: They're basically pathfinder flares, but they're not—

Ball: Could this be regarded by the people seeing it as though they were probably a bombing operation?

McNamara: No, I don't believe so. If we wish to, we could give warning ahead of time—simply say we're going on regular reconnaissance missions night and day.

Robert Kennedy: If they hear that explosion plus the night flares, I think that they'll think something— [*Mixed voices.*]

Robert Kennedy: Although it's probably a good idea.

Unidentified: We want to be sure these missiles aren't on their launchers.

Robert Kennedy: I know.

· · ·

President Kennedy: Well, I'm just trying to think about whether it appears, if we let this ship go, that we've relaxed on them.

As I say, we still could pick up beginning tomorrow night. We'll know a little more of Khrushchev's response. We can still get this

Grozny. So all we really have to decide is the East Germans. Let's let that go. [*Others agree.*]

What do you think, Tommy?

Llewellyn Thompson: I think you've really considered it right. I'm a little troubled by Khrushchev's strong letter of yesterday. That we don't just soon show him that we're not backing away because of a threat. On the other hand, he *is* backing away and that [*unclear*]. We'll just have to [*unclear*]. [*Unclear exchanges.*]

Robert Kennedy: He definitely has, though, when he says: "We're not going to retreat an inch," and we retreat an inch. And he says: "Six feet to go."

Thompson: [*Unclear.*] I talked to the Yugoslav ambassador after the briefing the other day, and he volunteered, without my bringing it up, he said: "I just want to tell you one thing. I don't agree with your [*unclear*] in your papers, that Khrushchev thinks you're afraid to act, or are weak." And he said: "I've had a lot of private conversations with him. And he [Khrushchev] said he doesn't think that." Just to throw that in.

Rusk: However, Mr. President, [Soviet-] bloc shipping is acting normally, except on the Cuban trade.

President Kennedy: That's that . . . You, before this, stated your view that that isn't what has caused him to do this. It's frustration over Berlin. [In contrast with] this idea that Reston advanced, that they think that they're going to do this because they think we're [weak]. I know you can take your choice on these [*unclear*].

Thompson: Yeah.

The taping then stopped; we do not know why. The formal meeting soon ended, with McCone reporting ominously that some of the MRBMs deployed in Cuba were now operational. It was then 5:46.

A short time after he left the ExComm meeting, at about 6:30 P.M. in Washington and 11:30 P.M. in London, President Kennedy got back on the telephone with Prime Minister Macmillan, as promised the previous evening. It was President Kennedy's first opportunity to respond directly to the message he had received that morning from Macmillan. Macmillan had warned Kennedy to avoid a military confrontation. Kennedy chose not to discuss it.[10]

Instead Kennedy reviewed the diplomatic moves at the United Nations and the military moves at the quarantine line, reporting how they had hailed the *Bucharest* but let it pass and were still deciding what to do about the East German passenger ship. He said he would try to avoid any confrontation with Soviet ships while they were waiting for Khrushchev's reply to U Thant's latest appeal. He added the news about the strident, defiant message they had received from Khrushchev the night before.

Macmillan returned to the issue of, as he put it, "immobilizing the weapons in Cuba, which is your major point, isn't it?" Kennedy agreed but repeated that the confrontation at sea would be the first problem. If Russian shipments could be suspended, that would avoid an immediate clash. "Then, if we satisfactorily get through that problem, then when these conversations begin, we are going to begin to emphasize that work on these sites is continuing, and that unless it is discontinued, we must tighten the blockade and possibly take other action. That would probably begin to be emphasized if the talks begin, but even if the talks don't begin we are going to begin to say it on Saturday [October 27] anyway." Macmillan understood, and they said good night.

Friday, October 26, 1962

During the previous evening, surveillance aircraft over the Atlantic Ocean successfully pinpointed the location of the *Marucla*, a Lebanese ship carrying dry cargo to Cuba under Soviet charter. This ship was an ideal answer to the dilemmas that the White House had wrestled with on October 25. The destroyers *Pierce* and *Kennedy* trailed the *Marucla* during the night and boarded her after sunrise on the morning of October 26.[1] The Greek crew of the ship complied with all requests. President Kennedy was awake and, from the Mansion, followed these developments. Later in the morning, at 9:20, he came into his office in the West Wing of the White House.

10:10 A.M.

Executive Committee Meeting of the National Security Council

President Kennedy's attention on October 25 had focused almost exclusively on the operation of the quarantine and the related diplomacy involving U Thant. After the immediate crisis on the quarantine line had passed, by the morning of October 26, his attention began to turn uneasily to the missiles still in Cuba, some already ready for action and others being readied. This was the time when Robert Kennedy remembered a growing private worry that "this cup was not going to pass and that a direct military confrontation between the two great military powers was inevitable. Both 'hawks' and 'doves' sensed that our combination of limited force and diplomatic efforts had been unsuccessful. If the Russians continued to be adamant and continued to build up their missile strength, military force would be the only alternative."[2]

Kennedy's advisers had been working on what to do next to obtain the removal of the Soviet missiles already in Cuba. These issues had been broached on the evening of October 25 and, as advisers gathered on the morning of October 26, all were armed with folders of papers prepared by their staffs. Before the ExComm meeting, Bundy told Ball that McNamara and Robert Kennedy were "all steamed up about getting a think tank going like the ones we had last week" in order to work out alternative plans.[3] As in the previous week, they wanted to hold those meetings in the State Department around midday.

The advisers this morning included Adlai Stevenson and John J. McCloy, both of whom had come down from New York. Back on October 22, Kennedy had tracked down McCloy in Europe and flown him back to the United States to act as Stevenson's assistant. Ostensibly, the aim was to make the U.S. delegation at the United Nations more bipartisan, since McCloy was a prominent Republican. In reality it was done, at Lovett's suggestion, because of fear that Stevenson might be too weak a negotiator. McCloy, a Wall Street lawyer with extensive government service, had the reputation of being very tough. Just before the ExComm meeting Ball (who had breakfast with McCloy that morning) stressed to Bundy how "clear and strong" McCloy was. Ball hoped the President would find ways of making it clear to Stevenson that McCloy should be in on all the talks in New York. Bundy promised to get the word to the President.[4]

The Security Council had had its debate and reached a dead end, given the Soviet veto power. Yet Stevenson's staff would be seeing U Thant that morning; Stevenson would see him in the afternoon. So one key task for the Kennedy administration that day was to work out the instructions to guide Stevenson and McCloy in their talks at the United Nations, where U Thant would be trying to broker a deal.

The military track had also advanced. The largest concentration of U.S. armed forces since the Korean War was massing in the southeastern United States. Several different options for air strikes were readied. Under the contingency plan prepared and preferred by the Joint Chiefs of Staff, designated Operation Scabbards, a massive air strike would hit Cuba 12 hours after the President gave the order. Strikes would continue for seven days, then troops would begin going ashore. These preparations fueled speculation about an imminent invasion, speculation that was featured prominently in the newspapers delivered to the White House on Friday morning, October 26.

Intelligence analysts worked in shifts around the clock to comprehend the miles of film delivered by the U-2 and low-level reconnaissance flights. Castro had also delivered another speech on the evening of October 25, denouncing the U.S. actions and warning that the U.S. reconnaissance flights would not be tolerated.

When the meeting began, at 9:59, President Kennedy did not immediately turn on the tape recorder. McCone began with a substantial intelligence briefing.

McCone then distributed and summarized another intelligence memorandum, and provided a bit more detail on the status of the missiles in Cuba. He reviewed the latest interagency appraisal, which emphasized that "rapid construction activity" was continuing. The "activity apparently continues to be directed toward achieving a full operational capability as soon as possible. Camouflage and canvas covering of critical equipment is also continuing. As yet there is *no* evidence indicating any intention to move or dismantle these sites."[5]

McCone then went over the movements of nonbloc ships to Cuba, emphasizing the possibility that such ships could also be used as arms carriers by the Soviets. As requested the previous day, he also reviewed intelligence analysis of Cuban internal reaction to the crisis. He reported on the celebration that took place in Havana when the *Bucharest* arrived. While on the subject of Cuban internal opinion, McCone turned to the status of Operation Mongoose.

Early in the crisis the CIA had been pressured, especially by Robert Kennedy, to do more with Operation Mongoose against Castro. A plan was developed to land ten 5-man teams of Cuban exiles, by submarine, in Cuba to collect intelligence and conduct sabotage operations, perhaps even using these agents to try to destroy the Soviet missile sites. The project was prepared hastily, with the apparent support of McNamara and civilian officials at the Pentagon, outside of the normal Mongoose supervision channels. By October 25 the idea had become tangled in disagreements between the CIA operators (including Edward Lansdale, who was supposed to be running Mongoose) and the Pentagon.

McCone decided that the CIA would not be prodded into launching this intelligence and sabotage mission on its own. He ordered that the planned operation be suspended and told the ExComm what he had done. If there was a military requirement, he said, then that requirement should be established by McNamara and by the Joint Chiefs of Staff. In other words (perhaps with keen memories of the Bay of Pigs), McCone was telling the administration that if the President and the Pentagon wanted to go after military targets in Cuba with the CIA, then the administration—and the military—would have to take clear responsibility for it. A meeting to decide how to proceed was arranged to take place in the Pentagon that afternoon, a meeting which would now include the hitherto bypassed Mr. Lansdale.

This was the point, about ten minutes into the meeting (10:10), when President Kennedy flipped on the tape recorder.

John McCone: . . . unilaterally, and this is what we're gonna do, and get this thing on track.

President Kennedy: I think as long as . . . This afternoon, it seems to me, we ought to get it arranged as to how, what those areas, where CIA functions without any . . .

McGeorge Bundy: Mr. President, my suggestion is that we should reconstitute Mongoose as a subcommittee of this committee in the appropriate way, and I think we can work that out this afternoon.

McCone: I think that's good because this matter you called me about last night, you see, which is as to what kind of a government [there should be in Cuba]. And have this all part of Mongoose.

President Kennedy: Yes. I called Mr. McCone last night and I then told Mr. [Edwin] Martin that I thought we ought to be making a crash program on . . . The problem becomes, then, what if [there is an] invasion? What kind of people—how many Cubans we'll have, what would be the civil government arrangement and all that?

Bundy: These are very important matters.

President Kennedy: Well, now, who will take on that?

Bundy: Mr. President, I think if we could make that a part of the discussion at the Mongoose meeting this afternoon, because it really is . . . the paramilitary, the civil government, the correlated activities to the main show that we need to reorganize.

President Kennedy: We need to get somebody in charge at State, CIA, and Defense, on this question of—

McCone: There's a meeting going on . . .

Bundy: Post–Castro's Cuba is the most complex landscape.

McCone: There's a meeting going on right now, of a working group. And we put that in operation this morning, in order to meet your requirement of having something at six tonight.

President Kennedy: Fine.

McCone: However, this is a subject that we're going to take up at this meeting this afternoon.

President Kennedy: And the other thing is an analysis, unless we may [already] have it, of the Cuban community in greater Miami—of those Cubans who would be doctors, and all the rest who would be useful, if we have an invasion of Cuba, [could] be useful during the immediate invasion period in various functions. I would think probably the CIA. But this would all be part of the matter which I hope we can discuss today.

McCone: I don't think that . . . I think we ought to have a plan under which the Lansdale organization, the Mongoose organization, is utilized in the interior. Because it's got a lot of knowledge now. It's well organized—[*nine seconds excised as classified information*].

The problem there is if we have to get within 12 miles and we intercept their high-frequency communications.[6] If it gets out [beyond 12 miles, reception] [*unclear*] it deteriorates pretty rapidly. The question is whether there is too great a risk for it to go in [so close to Cuba]. Maybe you have [*unclear*].

Robert McNamara: I think, Mr. President, this is an operational matter and we ought to watch very carefully. I have by frequent contacts between Defense and CIA. The Navy was very much concerned about the vulnerability of this ship and the loss of security if its personnel were captured.

It's been standing 10 miles off of the island of Cuba in the midst of the possible operations, and it seemed wise to draw it out 20, 30 miles to take it out of the range of capture, at least temporarily. I think perhaps we should put it back in if the activity quiets down. But I think this is an operational problem.

Unidentified: I agree, Mr. President.

Twenty-two seconds excised as classified information.

There is an unclear exchange between President Kennedy and Bundy; the President uses the word speaker; *then he appears to leave the room.*

. . .

McNamara: I would suggest that we consider announcing late today that we are continuing surveillance of the buildup of offensive weapons in Cuba. Based on that surveillance we find that the assembly of IL-28s [bombers] has continued at an accelerated pace. Therefore, acting under your authority, I am adding to the prohibited list bomber fuel, and the materials from which it is manufactured.

President Kennedy: We couldn't . . . What we're trying to get at now is tankers?

Bundy: Does that bring in POL [petroleum, oil, and lubricants]?

McNamara: This is POL.

President Kennedy: What about tying it in . . . The missiles are the more dramatic offensive weapons. Because everybody has bombers everyplace. So is there some way that we could tie it into the construction of these missile sites, rather than just the bombers?

McNamara: Well, we could do bomber fuel and associated petroleum products that are used for . . . [*Unclear exchange.*]

Bundy: [*Unclear*] is whether you want at the end to have the bombers there. If you want to get them out, this is as good a time as any to tie them into . . .

President Kennedy: No, I'd rather . . . What we're dealing with once again is the same problem, of stopping tankers, and I would rather tie as much as we could to the missiles.

McNamara: Can't we do it to both?

President Kennedy: Yeah, that's what I [*unclear interjection*]. The missiles . . . I would say that we ought to have . . . It seems to me, that in view of the fact that the missile work is going on, the sites are going on, we are tying up that fuel which contributes to that work. And, in view of the fact that the work on the missile sites is going on, we are also tying up aviation [fuel] because of the bombers. So that we—I think the missiles are the dramatic one. Bombers—hell, they might say: "We can just [*unclear*] your bombers every place."

Dean Rusk: Mr. President, can we break that into two pieces? I think that there would be some advantage in our having a real shot at the U Thant talks for 24 hours before we consider putting on the POL. We really need to have a round there, to see if—

President Kennedy: Wouldn't we be better then to say something about, that the work is going on, and that this must come to a stop, and then tomorrow say it isn't stopped, and therefore move to POL?

Bundy: Well, the 24 hours, I think that doesn't bother the Secretary very much. The point of not losing the momentum is of concern here, and that's a timing problem.

Maxwell Taylor: Mr. President, should we announce every day that when we have evidence that work has continued, that we view the fact with mounting indignation?

McCone: Yes, this is an awfully important point.

President Kennedy: Yeah. Well, that's why it seems to me what we're going to do is really give them a 24-hour notice that if they don't stop the work or assurances, then we're going to start . . .

Bundy: Perhaps, Mr. President, the consideration here we might . . . If we agree that this is the next step on the line of pressure, we might leave the timing until we've talked about the U Thant thing, and see just what— [*Unclear exchange.*]

McNamara: —will report on that.

C. Douglas Dillon: I'd like to raise one thing about agreeing that this is the next step on the line of pressure.

I think we've got to decide very quickly whether we want to proceed down this area, or this track, or not. Because I think it leads to quite different consequences. If we follow this track [moving to blockade POL] we'll be sort of caught up in events, not of our own control. We will have to stop a Soviet ship with what appears to be peaceful cargo on it. We will run into Soviet reactions around the world, which could be similar. I mean they might shoot at an American ship. We might wind up in some sort of a naval encounter all around the world with the Soviet

Union which would have nothing to do with the buildup of the missile bases in Cuba.

The end result of that would be, we either go on to a possible general war, or pressures get so extreme that we have to stop, both sides, doing this sort of thing. Meanwhile the missiles continue in Cuba.

This is the problem of this alternative track, of getting back onto the basic thing, that this work does not stop. This [missile work in Cuba] is not stopping. That [should be] our primary effort of acceleration, instead of increasing confrontation direct with the Soviet Union at sea, which is not as clearly connected with these missile bases. It's difficult to do, what you said, to connect this [confrontation at sea] with the missile bases.

If we put the confrontation there by preparing for air action to hit these bases if there is no . . . if they continue working. This decision would mean that we consider this seriously that it would color the way we handle the U Thant negotiations, we put great pressure on to do something to get inspectors in there to stop this thing. It also would allow us, if we wanted to, to be more relaxed in stopping one of these Soviet ships, if we knew that we were going to do this other action if nothing stops. So if we could . . .

Rusk: That's right. I think we ought to go to the political track before you come to a decision on the attack now.

Dillon: So, I think this is a very major decision, whether you want to build up the blockade, which puts the confrontation, U.S.-U.S.S.R., at sea, or whether you want to divert the confrontation, the escalation . . .

Bundy: I'm not sure it's as sharp as you make it, but this is the range of choices.

McNamara: Nor am I. I don't believe . . . There are alternative courses.

Let me go to another subject then. We conducted daylight surveillance yesterday with approximately ten aircraft of missile sites and the IL-28 airfield. There's no question but what—construction work is continuing. We can measure it. And we can show it.

I would suggest that today we do two things. One, announce that it is our policy to continue surveillance day and night.

Secondly, that we send out immediately, and issue orders from here to do so, eight to ten aircraft to go on daylight surveillance today. They are on alert status. They can be off and over the targets by noon time, Cuban time.

And thirdly, that following our announcement that we are carrying out daylight and nighttime surveillance, that we send out four aircraft tonight on nighttime surveillance. These would be using flares, roughly ten flares per target. It's thrown out of the airplane at about 5,000 feet, opening and becoming, operating at about 2,000 feet, illuminating the target area and the surrounding territory and serving as the basis for photographs.

And further I would suggest that we state that it is our intention to continue surveillance in order to determine the extent to which development of the offensive weapon systems is continuing.

Rusk: Mr. President, I wonder really again, on the nighttime reconnaissance, whether we ought to start that tonight, until we've had a crack at the U Thant discussions.

Dillon: Why is that provocative?

Rusk: Well, these flares are pathfinder flares, typically. They are frequently used with bombs right behind them. And we don't . . . We're not sure what the interpretation of the other side would be.

Dillon: There won't be any bombs now.

McNamara: There won't be any bombs behind [them]. We would tell them in advance that they were for—

Roswell Gilpatric: By telling them in advance that you're . . . if that's the point you're making.

President Kennedy: I don't see anything wrong with saying: "Day and nighttime surveillance."

Adlai Stevenson: Is it necessary to announce it at all?

Bundy: It's very important to announce it, because otherwise the danger the Secretary speaks of is real.

Rusk: They might think there was something big behind it.

Stevenson: No, I say it's unnecessary to announce any surveillance. Continue it, but why announce it?

President Kennedy: So what we're trying to do is to build up this case that they're continuing the work. Because sooner or later we're going to have to do something about that. So that's all we're trying to do here.

McCone: Yeah. On the other hand, by announcing it, it destroys one part of this thing, and that is to simulate an attack.

Bundy: They'll never believe it until it happens. Once they understand—

Stevenson: I don't see any point in announcing it, Mr. President. I should think that would be the last thing you would want to do—

President Kennedy: All right.

Stevenson: I would continue it and then make your announcements, from time to time, as to what the status was.

. . .

President Kennedy: Why don't we wait on this surveillance until we get the political talks, because what . . . It really depends on whether we're going to issue a statement this morning saying work is going on and must cease and so on. Look, you want to put the day ones on . . . Just get them going. We can announce it later.

. . .

Rusk: Mr. President. The political track. We've moved three, possibly four, moves beyond the ones actually in the Security Council at the present time. The first would be discussions with U Thant. Stevenson and McCloy will be having [discussions] with the [acting] secretary-general [U Thant] in the next day or two beginning this afternoon, I believe.

John McCloy: Beginning at 11:30 this morning. [Diplomat Charles] Yost is attending for him [referring to Stevenson].

Rusk: Oh, I see. So we need instructions on that quite urgently. Now we—

President Kennedy: I asked about this. [*speaking to Stevenson*] I said you're going to see him at four? Is that correct?

Stevenson: I'm going to go back and see him, but meanwhile he had sent for us at 11:30 and I didn't want to appear to be indifferent to his request, so I'm sending someone else.

Rusk: The objective of these talks, preliminary talks, would be to set up a situation in which further discussion could occur. But it is absolutely essential, that there be minimum requirements before any further talks can go forward.

These would be: no more offensive arms delivered to Cuba; no further buildup of missile sites or long-range bomber facilities; and any existing Cuban nuclear strike capability would be rendered inoperable. In other words, there has to be a U.N. takeover of the, assurance on the sites, that they are not in operating condition. Now we have to insist upon that very hard, because the whole object here has to be to get rid of this nuclear threat in Cuba.

Now, this is going to be very difficult to achieve because the other side is going to be very resistant to U.N. inspectors coming into Cuba. So we have to make the issue, I think, at that point.

Otherwise, what will happen is that the Soviets will go down the path of talking, talking indefinitely, while the missile sites come into full operation, including the intermediate range. And then we are nowhere. And we are faced with an even more difficult problem on the facts than we are at the present time.

Now, this will involve a considerable effort on the part of the secretary-general, even if the Soviets and the Cubans accept it. He would have to have an observer corps in Cuba. It would have to include up to 300 personnel as a minimum, drawn from countries that have a capacity, a technical capacity, to know what they're looking at and what measures have to be taken to insure inoperability. That would mean countries like Sweden, Switzerland, perhaps Austria, and a limited number of, perhaps Brazil, countries of that sort. That's Canada. We can't have Burmese or Cambodians going in there, or other countries, in the face of three regiments of Soviet missile technicians, being led down the garden path on the operational problem.

Further, on the quarantine itself, we think that the U.N. could put a quarantine into operation. But that ours must remain in position until the U.N. has an effective one in position. Now they could do this in several ways. They could establish, at the designated Havana port, inspection personnel to inspect every incoming ship (these come in about two a day at different ports). We ourselves would maintain complete Navy surveillance of the area and insure that no ships come through any other port, and that we have full information on what is on board each ship.

There are a lot of detailed arrangements on both these items that will have to be considered. But we would have to keep our forces in the immediate background, and move promptly if the U.N. arrangements are not trustworthy.

An alternative would be to have this inspection occur offshore. But the Defense Department and my colleagues have been talking about that, and that doesn't seem to be as feasible as insisting upon a port inspection.

But this is the general nature of the instructions that we have in mind for Ambassador Stevenson. We'll have a detailed draft prepared by State and Defense for you to see just a little later today. But I think we ought to talk about the general policy questions involved now.

First, that the arrangements must include no further arms shipments; no continued buildup; and a defanging of the sites that are already there.

Dillon: That latter is the key thing because if they refuse that consistently, that gives you your excuse to take further action.

Paul Nitze: The most immediate thing one could do, or they could do, would be to move the missiles from the missile sites. That is: they could take the missiles and put them on the IL-28 fields, separated from the erectors, and then move the fuel trucks and the fueling nitric acid trucks to some other place distant from the field. And get them out into an open field where we could get a view of them, we can have an immediate defusing, prior to the time that the inspectors arrive. Because it will take some time for the inspectors to arrive.

McCone: I think that's correct. I think that *inoperable* could be just having a switch turned off or something. I think if you actually dismantle these sites, you can do it very quickly and very easily, because they are—

Unidentified: We can do it from the air [*unclear*] . . . reassemble them?

McCloy: I feel very strongly, Mr. President, that that's the thing to stress. I wouldn't put it in the order that the Secretary's put it. I'd put it in just the reverse order.

The critical thing—I think that all the signs for this thing was for a sinister purpose. The speed with which it was built up makes it look to me as if it was in accordance with a time schedule, and perhaps with an adventure in some other area.

And I think we know we can't reintroduce the blockade once we let it drop. They [the diplomats] won't get the OAS back of us again, and this is the one thing that the country's behind, everybody's behind. I mean there's a growing momentum of opinion developing, perhaps a little slowly, but right now crystallizing. But this is the danger. This has got the—

Rusk: I think one thing that U Thant must understand is that the quarantine is related to the presence of the missiles, the missile sites. And not just to the shipment of new, additional arms.

President Kennedy: Yes, because the . . . McCloy's [point], even if the quarantine's 100 percent effective, it isn't any good because the missile sites go on being constructed. So it's only a first step.

McCloy: And have a pistol at your hip, tomorrow.

President Kennedy: . . . a first step. The quarantine, it isn't going . . .

Rusk: The actual removal of these things from Cuba is something to be worked out in the two to three weeks [negotiating period after a verified standstill].

President Kennedy: Obviously we can't expect them to remove them at this point without a long negotiation. Of course you won't get them ever out unless you take them out. But at least, for the purposes of negotiation . . .

· · ·

President Kennedy: But I thought the proposal was that they would remove these weapons if we guaranteed the territorial integrity of Cuba. [*Unclear exchange.*]

Well, I mean we're . . . obviously we're going to have to pay a price in order to get those missiles out without fighting to get them out or . . .

Rusk: Well, Mr. President, unless there is some violent action by Cuba, along the lines of these offensive weapons, Cuba has all sorts of existing guarantees of territorial integrity. We've got that problem here if we had in mind the violent overthrow of the regime. They've got the U.N. Charter; they've got the Rio Pact; they've got [*unclear*] . . .

President Kennedy: Obviously, this is a [*unclear*]. The quarantine appeals to everybody and if that's one of the prices that has to be paid to get these out of there, then we commit ourselves not to invade Cuba.

・ ・ ・

McCone: One thing I don't like about this, and that is that it would sort of insulate Castro from further actions. Long before these missiles were there, his link with the Soviet Union and the use of Cuba as a base of operations to communize all of Latin America was a matter of great concern to us. Now what this does is more or less leave him in that position. The missiles aren't there, but still this situation that has worried us so much for the last two or three years goes on.

I bring that up because I think there's two things we have to consider here. One is to get rid of these missiles. And the other is to have the Cuban people take over Cuba, and take it away from Castro. This does not involve a break between Castro and the Soviet Union.

・ ・ ・

Bundy: Mr. President, I believe myself that all of these things need to be measured in terms of the very simple, basic structural purpose of this whole enterprise, which is to get these missiles out. Castro is a problem. If we can bring Castro down in the process, dandy. If we can turn him in on other people, dandy. But if we can get the missiles out . . .

President Kennedy: I wouldn't worry yet. If we can get the missiles out, we can take care of Castro. My God, if they do something in Berlin, we can always say "Well, this changes our commitments." So I think we ought to concentrate on the missiles right now.

・ ・ ・

Llewellyn Thompson: One part, I think, has a bearing on this whole strategy. That is that, in my opinion, the Soviets will find it far easier to remove these weapons, or to move them to port for a removal, than they would to accept inspections, I think. Putting Soviet technicians under U.N. people would . . . I think they would resist.

Bundy: If we could verify their disappearance . . .

Rusk: Well, you go on with the alternatives. Mr. Stevenson . . .

・ ・ ・

President Kennedy: We've got to keep saying that work has to cease which we're verifying every day, during these negotiations. We have to keep saying that to U Thant, [to] the Brazilians. We can't screw around for two weeks and wait for them [the Soviets] to finish these [the missile bases].

Governor, do you want to talk a little and give us your thoughts?

Stevenson: Well, sir, I've just seen this proposed track on the political procedures since I came here. I think it's well for you all to bear in mind that the concept of this proposal [from U Thant] is a standstill. That is to say, no one was to take further action for—we could work out the modalities—for two or three weeks while we negotiated a final settlement.

This includes in the immediate modalities as one of the objectives of the final negotiations, which is to make the weapons inoperable. I would be very much troubled by trying to get that included in the original 24-, 48-, 36-hour negotiation, because it includes something that is not a standstill. It includes a reverse, a reversal of something that has already taken place.

I think it would be quite proper to include in our original demands that the weapons be *kept* inoperable.

President Kennedy: Would the work on the sites be ceased?

Stevenson: Work on the sites, of course. Now, the three points that we've talked about are suspending the quarantine—

Bundy: Excuse me, Governor, to be clear. Are we talking now about the first two days or about two or three weeks?

Stevenson: We're talking about the first two days. I'll outline to you the first two days and the subsequent days, if you wish.

The first two days the objectives were, on our side, that no ships go to Cuba carrying arms. This included all arms, not just offensive arms. This is what U Thant said. That's the one place that we have to determine whether we're willing to apply this only to offensive weapons or whether we want to insist, as he put it, in his [*unclear*] all arms.

The second point is how that's to be done. The second point is that there should be no further construction on the bases, and how that is to be policed.

The third point is that we would then suspend our quarantine, pending the two or three weeks' negotiation.

Rusk: The work on the bases [*unclear*] includes the inoperability of the missiles.

McCone: That cannot go on indefinitely.

Nitze: No.

Stevenson: I think it would be quite proper to attempt to include that, to *keep* them inoperable rather than to say that they should be *rendered* inoperable, because that requires the possible—

Rusk: "Keep them inoperable," then.

McNamara: Well, when did they become inoperable? They're operable now.

Bundy: Ensure that they *are* inoperable.

Stevenson: Well, that . . . You see, I'm trying to make clear to you that this is a standstill. This is what I meant. There would be no more construction, no more quarantine, no more arms shipments.

Now, when you say "make them inoperable," that's not a standstill.

George Ball: You can insure that they are inoperable, and that leaves open whether it's a standstill.

Rusk: If they turn out to be operable, then that is really something rather different.

Stevenson: I'm suggesting that we might include in the initial modalities of the negotiation that all the weapons be kept inoperable, and find out what that elicits in response from the other side. But I don't think that there should be any misunderstanding about what was intended here, which was a standstill and only a standstill.

Rusk: Well they should remain inoperable. [*Mixed voices. Someone says* "The two days."]

Stevenson: The next point is for the . . .

Rusk: We're talking about the two days now.

Stevenson: Well then comes the long-term negotiation. What we wanted to obtain in the long-term negotiation, I assume—this is the two-week negotiation—is the withdrawal from the hemisphere of these weapons, and the dismantling of the existing sites for these weapons.

And what they will want in return is, I anticipate, a new guarantee of the territorial integrity of Cuba. Indeed, that's what they've said these weapons were for. The territorial integrity of Cuba.

It is possible that the price that might be asked of us in the long-term negotiation, two-week negotiation, might include dismantling bases of ours, such as Italy and Turkey, that we have talked about. . . .

We might include, you might attempt to include, something like defanging Cuba for subversion and penetration. I'm not sure how we could do that, or whether we could do that, or should do that. That certainly is open for discussion.

But I want to conclude by making it very clear that the intention here was a standstill, not positive acts. And the standstill was to include the discontinuance of construction, discontinuance of shipping, discontinuance of the quarantine which we, we'd have to agree how to do that in 48 hours.

After that, we'd negotiate a final settlement which would relate to the withdrawal of the weapons, or the inoperability of weapons already operable. I would think *inoperable* becomes meaningless, because during the long-term negotiations we're concerned with the withdrawal of the weapons from the hemisphere.

McCone: I don't believe, I don't agree with that, Mr. President. I feel very strongly about it. And I think that the real crux of this matter is the fact that he's got these pointed, for all you know, right now at our hearts. And this is going to produce I think, it may produce, a situation when we get to [the promised confrontation on] Berlin after the [congressional] elections, which changes the entire balance of world power.

It puts us under a very great handicap in carrying out our obligations, not only to our western European allies, but to the hemisphere. And I think that we've got the momentum now. We've got the feeling that these things are serious and that they must be . . .

That threat must be removed before we can drop the quarantine. If we drop that quarantine once, we're never going to be able to put it in effect again. And I feel that we *must* say that the quarantine goes on until we are satisfied that these are inoperable. [*He hits the table.*]

President Kennedy: Well, now the quarantine itself won't remove the weapons. So we've only got two ways of removing the weapons. One is to negotiate them out—in other words, trade them out. Or the other is to go in and take them out. I don't see any other way you're going to get the weapons out.

McCone: I say that we have to send inspections down there to see at what stage they are. I feel that if we lose that . . . But this is the security of the United States! I believe the strategic situation has greatly changed with the presence of these weapons in Cuba.

President Kennedy: That's right. The only thing that I am saying is, that we're not going to get them out with the quarantine. I'm not saying we should lift the quarantine or what we should do about the quarantine. But we have to all now realize that we're not going to get them out. We're either going to trade them out, or we're going to have to go in and get them out ourselves. I don't know of any other way to do it.

. . .

Bundy: No, sir, but we are on a course in which we intend to get them out of there, and if we adopt a course at the U.N. which presumes that they might stay there, we've had it.

Unidentified: Right.

President Kennedy: But I mean . . . As I understand the Governor's proposal, what he's suggesting is that we give this thing the time to try to negotiate them out of there. Now maybe we're not going to be able to negotiate them out of there. But otherwise I don't see how we're going to get them out of there unless we go in and get them out.

Unidentified: That's right.

Stevenson: Simply [*unclear*] take two weeks to determine that.

Rusk: Mr. President, I'm not too optimistic that we will get these necessary preconditions in these first two days of talks. I think we will . . . If the Soviets were to come that far, I think, this would be a major backdown.

Dillon: Well, they can't back down that much.

McCone: The difficulty, it seems to me, is even during these two days, within any eight-hour period, that they could put these things on their stands, and you'd be looking at them. And they're mobile.

Stevenson: But the quarantine isn't going to prevent that.

McCone: No. But I think we ought to have freedom of action that, if we detect any such move during the two-day period or any time during the two-week period, we can take such action as necessary.

Stevenson: If there is any violation of the standstill during the two-week period that we negotiate before a settlement, then of course we would have to . . . it serves them right . . . all bets are off. We're back to status quo.

Rusk: We are taking some risks on that for the next day or two. No question on that.

Nitze: Disassembly would really give you some security during the period while these negotiations go on.

President Kennedy: What did you say, Paul?

Nitze: Disassembly—separating the missiles from the erectors.

U. Alexis Johnson: I think we're entitled to that.

·   ·   ·

Dillon: I just don't see how you can negotiate for two weeks with these things sitting on, right next to the launchers.

McCone: And the IRBMs becoming operational.

Dillon: They've got to be made inoperable or you're going back on our statement that we wouldn't negotiate under threat.

McCloy: And all work is stopped.

Rusk: Well, I do think if you have U.N. personnel at the sites, with regular reporting, so that if there is any change into an actual operating condition, you would know about it.

President Kennedy: Ambassador, does Mr. Yost know what he's supposed to say at 11:30 [in his meeting with U Thant]?

Stevenson: He's going to say I'll be back at 4:30.

President Kennedy: That's all he's going to say?

Stevenson: Yeah.

Unclear exchange. By some remarkable coincidence, Yost was phoning in from New York.

President Kennedy: Excuse me, Mr. Secretary.

Stevenson: Could I be excused, sir? I did want to say one other thing to him for a moment.

President Kennedy: OK, sure. Why don't you go in my office?

Stevenson leaves and talks on the phone to Yost. Stevenson does not know it, but Kennedy has also gotten up, just for a moment, possibly to make sure that his secretary turns on the tape machine in order to record Stevenson's call from his office. The Stevenson-Yost conversation was taped. Stevenson complained to Yost that "there's a lot of flap down here" about adding a new condition for lifting the quarantine, which was that the missiles already in Cuba be rendered inoperable. He told Yost that this went beyond a standstill, but they would now have to insist on that condition. Stevenson speculated though that if the United States could not get that as part of the immediate negotiation to suspend arms shipments and the quarantine, "we'll have to settle for something less." Yost says he'll try, not really understanding, and they agree that Stevenson will go into this matter more carefully with U Thant when he returns to New York that afternoon.[7]

. . .

President Kennedy: We really haven't gotten into this thing, what we haven't *gotten* to is . . . At least Governor Stevenson has this proposal for dealing with . . . which nobody is very much interested in.

But the point is that the blockade is not going to accomplish the job either. So we've got to have some other alternatives to accomplish what Governor Stevenson suggests may or may not be accomplished by negotiations. We don't have any proposal on the other side except to continue the blockade, which isn't going to accomplish it, except it's going to bring the conflagration closer, which may or may not be desirable, but—

Dillon: It may bring it [the conflagration] in the wrong place.

President Kennedy: Well, I think we have to be thinking, what are we going to do on the other track, if we're not going to do the negotiating track. What other devices are we going to use to get them out of there?

McNamara: Mr. President, can't we negotiate *and* keep the blockade? As I understood Secretary Rusk's proposal—

Rusk: Well we don't relax the blockade until . . . Our thought is that we don't relax the blockade in any way, until we get the modalities that [unclear] is talking about, which include: no more arms delivered to Cuba;

no further buildup of missile sites or long-range bomber facilities; any existing Cuban nuclear strike capabilities must be rendered inoperable.

McNamara: Now, and you could define that as separating the missiles from the sites, and having inspectors there.

Rusk: That's right.

President Kennedy: They won't agree to that, but the only thing is—

McNamara: Just to start with.

Bundy: But it's the *inoperable* that's very important, that the Governor must [*McNamara agrees*] get these things clearly in his head.

McCone: Separate the launchers from the sites too.

McNamara: Separate the missiles from the launchers.

In any case, if we could link together, in the initial proposal, U.N. inspection and separation of the . . .

President Kennedy: Then it seems to me we go through 48 hours and a lot of people agree with that, and then he won't agree to that.

Bundy: Then we have a double choice, Mr. President, unless we propose to go up and do nothing. One is to expand the blockade, and the other is to remove the missiles by force.

President Kennedy: Right. OK. Well let's . . . It seems to me this provides some direction to the Governor this afternoon. And then he can come back, and tell us that they won't agree to this, and then we continue with the blockade.

                              .   .   .

Taylor: During any negotiation, Mr. President, shouldn't we be raising the noise level of our indignation over this?

President Kennedy: That comes to the next . . . Let's move on then to the next question, which is whether we ought to sometime today say that photographic evidence taken yesterday indicates that work is going on. And that therefore this is unsatisfactory, some [*unclear*] [statement] like that. Do you have the photographs of this thing?

McNamara: They do indeed. I have the evidence here.

President Kennedy: In the last four days, work has been going on, and we can't accept that.

Then I would think that tomorrow, we would then be in the position of deciding if we're going to go with [expanding the blockade to include] POL or if we're going to decide to go the other route, the force route.

Taylor: We can do a lot of things in the air also, Mr. President, to increase our activity. We could have fighters. We could have night photography of Havana, for example. A great many things that would show mounting activity—

Bundy: Like the problems of last week, Mr. President. The more we even begin to look under these things, the less absolutely clear it is that they're sharply separated.

But we need to work on that today. And with your permission we would constitute a working group, working in the State Department, of this committee on this problem.

Rusk: Mr. President, I do think it would be important to explore the political thing, to be sure that the Soviets have turned down these three conditions before we put on the night photography.

President Kennedy: That's fair enough. I wouldn't be making any concessions now. Now, the Governor will go with this. Now, do we today put out for the world opinion, which is getting an idea this thing is—

Bundy: The work continues. Yes, indeed, we do.

President Kennedy: [*Unclear*] [the statement] about the work continuing? And that comes out of, I would think, the White House, rather than the Defense Department, because otherwise it looks sort of ridiculous. It's like we look to the Defense Department [*unclear*] to State [to speak for the President].

Bundy: That's right. There is stuff on the wires that the Soviets are saying the U.S. military have taken over at this point. It may be even advantageous for the State Department to put that out.

President Kennedy: No, let's give that to Pierre. Let's this afternoon have a statement which Ros and Sylvester and Mac can work on, saying about the work going on, and indicating—we'll have to draw this with care, and clear it with the State Department and Tommy—what severity with which we judge this.

Because this way we start the . . . We perfected the blockade but that's only half the job. This will lead us then to the [expanded blockade on] POL or to the . . .

Bundy: My suggestion would be, Mr. President, that we have a White House spokesman simply say that there are problems—

President Kennedy: OK, why don't you get that out.

Bundy: —that the work is going on, and we call attention to the President's speech [*unclear*].

President Kennedy: Something like that.

. . .

President Kennedy: Now, let me just say the only other question here is a matter which, Doug, you brought up yesterday. I thought that we ought to get somebody . . . I don't know whether we ought to get maybe a presentation tomorrow by the Defense Department on the air action again, whether that is, Bobby is getting . . .

Bundy: Let us work some more on that, Mr. President, and have something ready for you tomorrow.

President Kennedy: In some ways that [air strike option] is more advantageous than it was even a week ago. I'd like to have us to take a look now at whether that can even be [*unclear*].

. . .

After the members of the Executive Committee departed, President Kennedy returned a phone call from David Ormsby-Gore. The British ambassador asked how long President Kennedy felt he could wait for U Thant to try for an adequate, verified standstill. President Kennedy told him that the Soviets were pushing ahead to finish the missile sites. The United States could not, therefore, wait much longer.

As planned, a number of the advisers moved to the State Department to brainstorm about alternative plans, the way they had the week before. They discussed the instructions that would go to New York on U.S. conditions for ending the quarantine. They also worked on a possible air strike against Cuba. Taylor reported back to the Chiefs that a consensus seemed to be emerging in favor of starting with a limited strike just against the missile sites and the IL-28s. The air defenses in Florida were now so strong that fears of a retaliatory air strike by the MiGs had apparently diminished. Taylor and the Chiefs continued to favor a larger air strike, at least extending to the SAM sites as well.

12:00 P.M.

Meeting with Intelligence Officials

As President Kennedy's other advisers were thinking harder about plans for an air strike against Cuba, more ominous intelligence news was being digested, especially from the low-level photography mission flown on October 25. The photos gave new evidence about the pace of Soviet preparations to ready the MRBM sites for firing, and the possible deployment of tactical nuclear weapons. Intelligence analysts concluded that the MRBMs were becoming fully operational, readied for imminent possible use. McCone, with top photo analyst Arthur Lundahl, sought and received a private meeting with President Kennedy to brief him on this information. Robert Kennedy was also present.[8]

We know this meeting occurred at about midday, and before President Kennedy left the office at 1:00, but the exact time is a conjecture. It is in the Oval Office.

Unidentified: [*Unclear*] fields with the trucks that go back there [*unclear*].

John McCone: Yeah, and—

President Kennedy: [*looking at imagery*] Well, if we hadn't . . . ? [*exclaiming*] Isn't this peculiar? If we hadn't gotten those early pictures, we might have missed these. Wonder why they didn't put a cover over it.[9]

McCone: I don't know. I don't know.

President Kennedy: We always think they're so smart that . . .

McCone: Here's another similar . . . This is the missile stand. There's the blocks. Here are the two missile shelter tents. There are two missiles and a third one.

President Kennedy: Those are missiles?

McCone: Yeah.

President Kennedy: Did you see the *New York* or *London Times* where it said we've misread the pictures?

Unidentified: Yeah.

. . .

President Kennedy: This photography is [*unclear*]. We took more pictures today, did we?

McCone: Yes, we sent planes out today. Here are the missile shelters. Here are tanks camouflaged here. You see here they're even covered with netting. Here's an erector covered with netting. Here's trucks camouflaged again over here. Here's something; we don't know what they're doing.

President Kennedy: Yeah, they're really getting [*unclear*].

McCone: Here's something.

President Kennedy: It's just a question of how much [*unclear*]?

McCone: Yeah.

Unidentified: I don't see any people. There's a fellow.

Arthur Lundahl: The ground is so wet they have to lay their cables above ground on little stanchions. And they have to put catwalks around it because there's all kind of water. There's been lots of rain in there in just the last couple of days. Here's some of their advanced equipment, sir.

Unidentified: Now this is another interesting—

Thirty-eight seconds excised as classified information. From the context this appears to be a briefing about the discovery of possible Soviet tactical nuclear weapons, in the form of a short-range nuclear missile called the FROG.[10]

President Kennedy: But you couldn't shoot those up much. Could you just . . . ?

McCone: No, you couldn't shoot these up.

President Kennedy: It shows there. Is this the only place we've got that's sort of an armory?

Lundahl: So far, sir. We have others but we haven't made—

President Kennedy: It would indicate that.

Lundahl: There's a real concentration of effort now.

McCone: Here's an interesting one. Now, here's your launcher. There's those two pads for the wheel chocks. Here's the missile. There's another erector here. Now, here's your cable that comes through some kind of a cutout switch here and then over to a launch-control building and a generator. So there—in addition to the launchers and the missile, there are a number of trucks and trailers and interrelated equipment, much of which is quite sensitive but would go to make this installation a workable installation.

President Kennedy: We don't know how many people there are in each one of these, guards, do we?

McCone: No, we don't. No we don't. We have some information that on some sites there are as many as 500 personnel on-site with 300 additional Soviet guards, but you'll probably find this in a very large restricted area.

· · ·

McCone: It appears to me that there's a very great deal of concern about this thing. I'm getting more concerned all the time, in terms of [*unclear*]. I think that they've got a substantial number of these, that they could start at dark and have missiles pointing at us the following morning.

For that reason, I'm growing increasingly concerned about following a political route which, unless the initial and immediate step is to ensure that these missiles are immobilized by the physical separation of the missile which is on a truck and trailer from the launcher, which is itself a truck and trailer. One of them can be hauled one way and one hauled the other. This, I think, would be—

President Kennedy: Well now, the only problem is . . . I agree, that that's what we want. What other way . . . ? The alternative, of course, is to do the air strike or an invasion. We still are going to face the fact that, if we invade, by the time we get to these sites after a very bloody fight, we will have . . . they will be pointing at us. So it still comes down to a question of whether they're going to fire the missiles.

McCone: That's correct. That's correct.

President Kennedy: I mean, there's no action that, other than diplomatic, that we can take, which does not immediately get rid of these. There are only two ways to do this, as I said this morning. One is the diplomatic way. Which I doubt, I don't think it will be successful. The other way is, I would think, a combination of an air strike and probably invasion, which means that we would have to carry out both of those with the prospect that they [the missiles] might be fired.

McCone: Invading is going to be a much more serious undertaking than most people realize.

President Kennedy: Because of the equipment they are getting [unclear].

McCone: Because of the equipment; because they had a hell of a lot equipment before they got these things that you just saw pictures of, now. It's very evil stuff they've got there. Rocket launchers and self-propelled gun carriers, half-tracks, and all such things as that. If they're equipped to handle them, which I presume these technicians, at least the Russians, can handle, then they'll give an invading force a pretty bad time. It would be no cinch by any manner of means.

President Kennedy: Of course, if you had control of the air, could you chew those up?

McCone: Oh, you could chew them up. But you know how it is. It's damn hard to knock out these field pieces. That was the experience we had in World War II and then Korea.

President Kennedy: We had complete air [superiority].

McCone: Well, you had complete air and bombed the hell out of these gun sites and they're still there. But the . . .

President Kennedy: We're getting in touch with the Pentagon? Who's in charge, sort of, of the . . . with respect to the invasion? Do we have a fellow? Is [Army chief of staff General Earle] Wheeler the one who is working on that?

McCone: Yes, I think Wheeler is working on that just now. And there's a General Trimmer who I don't know, who I think is the man under Wheeler, . . . [Admiral George] Anderson, has set up as the man who is responsible for preparing the invasion forces.

President Kennedy: What about the air strike?

McCone: I don't know who has that.

President Kennedy: Well, but I mean, what about the—what course of action does this lead you to?

McCone: Well, this would lead me . . . This would lead me to moving quickly on an air strike if we—

At this point the recording stopped.

At 1:00 P.M. President Kennedy left the office, took a swim, and went to the Mansion for lunch. From there (where he could not tape his calls) he kept up to date as more details came in about the diplomacy in New York and the operation of the quarantine.

In the Atlantic Ocean, two Soviet submarines had finally been obliged to surface under the scrutiny of watching U.S. sailors. A Swedish dry cargo ship, the *Coalangatta*, that had docked in the Soviet Union and was en route to Cuba under Soviet charter, proceeded to the quarantine line and then refused to stop when it was intercepted by a U.S. destroyer. Faced with this curiously defiant behavior by a ship that had not been on the list of suspect vessels and despite Khrushchev's pledge to U Thant that Soviet ships would avoid the quarantine area, the destroyer asked for instructions. The matter was bumped up to Washington. Ultimately the signal came back: Don't fire. Let the Swedish ship pass. The matter seemed odd, even troubling.

At 4:15 in the afternoon President Kennedy returned to his West Wing office. The diplomacy was intensifying, as was the Soviet military activity in Cuba.

4:30 P.M.

Conversation with Dean Rusk

The diplomacy in New York had become very active. In Stevenson's absence, his deputy, Charles Yost, met with U Thant at about 11:30. U Thant thought the Soviets might be amenable to a deal that withdrew the missiles in exchange for a U.S. pledge not to invade Cuba. Rusk phoned President Kennedy to mention this possibility.[11]

Dean Rusk: The Cubans may want to resolve this by getting their weapons out in exchange for some sort of assurance about their territorial integrity.

President Kennedy: Yeah.

Rusk: We'll be working on the idea here, and the various forms which such [an] assurance might take. But—

President Kennedy: How does it [this information] come to you? How does this come to you?

Rusk: Well, first, U Thant's first discussion with our people this morning.

President Kennedy: Yeah.

Rusk: And it looks as though [removing] the threat of an invasion may be a quid pro quo for getting the missiles out.

President Kennedy: Yeah.

Rusk: Now this would involve some problems. But at least we were not intending to invade, before the missiles got there.

President Kennedy: Yeah, yeah.

Rusk: So I just wanted to let [you know] . . . And then we also have something through the Canadians, to the same effect.

President Kennedy: Yeah.

Rusk: So it's just possible that this may move faster than we had expected.

President Kennedy [*still reacting to the idea*] No. I think we'd have to do that, because we weren't going to invade them anyway.

Rusk: That's right.

President Kennedy: Right.

Rusk: OK.

During the afternoon Rusk (and then Kennedy) had heard more evidence about Soviet interest in trading the removal of the missiles for a noninvasion pledge from an informal source. The ABC News journalist John Scali had been approached by a Soviet KGB officer based in Washington under cover as a journalist, Alexander Fomin. Fomin told Scali that he thought his government would be interested in a deal in which Soviet bases would be dismantled under U.N. supervision, Castro would promise not to accept offensive weapons of any kind, and the United States would pledge not to invade Cuba. Scali promptly reported this to the State Department and to Rusk. Thinking that the Soviet government might be using Fomin as an informal channel to feel out U.S. interest in this bargain, Rusk encouraged Scali to pursue the matter further with Fomin and indicate U.S. interest in such a settlement.[12]

The new intelligence information prompted President Kennedy and Bundy to rework the White House announcement that had been planned at the morning Executive Committee meeting. The final statement, the one Kennedy was mentioning to Stevenson, was read out by White House press secretary Pierre Salinger at 6:15 P.M. It said:

> The development of ballistic missile sites in Cuba continues at a rapid pace. Through the process of continued surveillance, directed by the President, additional evidence has been acquired which clearly reflects that as of Thursday, October 25, defense buildups in these offensive missile sites continued to be made. The activity at these sites apparently is directed at achieving a full operational capability as soon as possible.
>
> There is evidence that, as of yesterday, October 25, considerable construction activity was being engaged in at the intermediate range ballistic missile sites. Bulldozers and cranes were observed as late as Thursday actively clearing new areas within the sites and improving the approach roads to the launch pads.
>
> Since Tuesday, October 23, missile-related activities have continued at the medium range ballistic missile sites resulting in progressive refinements at these facilities. For example, missiles were observed parked in the open on October 23. Surveillance on October 25 revealed that some of these missiles have now moved from their original parked positions. Cabling can be seen running from missile-ready tents to powered generators nearby.
>
> In summary, there is no evidence to date indicating that there is any intention to dismantle or discontinue work on these missile sites. On the contrary the Soviets are rapidly continuing their construction of missile support and launch facilities and serious attempts are underway to camouflage their efforts.

While Salinger was reading this statement to the press corps, President Kennedy was in another meeting, in the Oval Office, with India's ambassador to the United States, B. K. Nehru.

The meeting with Nehru ended at 6:19. Immediately afterward, Kennedy put through his daily call to Prime Minister Macmillan.[13] He debriefed Macmillan on the diplomacy during the day involving U Thant and mentioned his press statement, emphasizing that "unless in the next 48 hours we get some political suggestions as to dismantling the base, we're then going to be faced with a problem of what to do about this buildup." As for the possible Soviet offer to remove missiles in exchange for a pledge not to invade Cuba, Kennedy described this as "a couple of hints, not enough to go on yet."

As he had the previous day, Macmillan then urged Kennedy to avoid any U.S. military action. "At this stage any movement by you may produce a result in Berlin which would be very bad for us all. That's the danger now."

Kennedy replied that "if at the end of 48 hours we are getting no place, and the missile sites continue to be constructed, then we are going to be faced with some hard decisions."

Macmillan pushed back. "Of course, in making those decisions one has to realize that they will have their effect on Berlin, as well as on Cuba."

Kennedy answered: "Correct. And that is really why we have not done more than we have done, up till now." The President then stressed the point he had explained to others a week earlier: "But of course, on the other hand, if the missile sites continue, and get constructed, and we don't do anything about it, then I would suppose that it would have quite an effect on Berlin anyway."

Macmillan conceded that was the difficulty. He said he would send a message outlining the political options. Kennedy promised to keep Macmillan informed about diplomatic developments and said that "we will not take any further action until I have talked to you, in any case." He also asked Macmillan to agree to General Lauris Norstad's retaining his post as NATO's military commander through the end of the crisis.

Very soon after this conversation, Macmillan sent off the promised message to Kennedy to clarify the British position and itemizing three main diplomatic options: a pledge not to invade Cuba, a U.N. mission to Cuba to secure the immobilization of the Soviet missiles and verify that new work had stopped, and his offer to accept reciprocal U.N. supervision of the Thor missiles stationed in Great Britain.

7:31 P.M.

Conversation with Lincoln White

Lincoln White was in trouble. Press spokesman of the State Department, White had delivered the daily press briefing earlier in the day. Kennedy's press secretary, Pierre Salinger, told Kennedy that reporters were writing stories saying that, in his briefing White had hinted that the administration was ready for "further action" if a peaceful solution to the crisis could not be found.

Lincoln White: Well, Mr. President, what I . . . I never said anything about further action. What I did was to cite the sentence in your Monday night speech.

President Kennedy: Yeah.

White: In which, you know, you had—I don't have the text in front of me—the essence of it being—that if this threat . . .

President Kennedy: [*angrily*] Yeah, I understand that. But that's the sort of stuff that's got to come from me and the White House.

Christ, we're meeting every morning on this to control this, the escalation. I don't want to just be . . . The fact that you refer back to my speech, that then gives them a lead headline saying "The United States Is Planning Further Action." And we had a long talk about it this morning and it was agreed that the talk about the statement on the buildup would come from the White House and that we wouldn't say anything about what action we're going to take. And we don't want to . . . When you make a reference back to my speech it then gives them a lead that further action is going to be taken.

Now we got to get this under control, Linc, cause it's too important. I want it to be running out of the White House—

White: Sure.

President Kennedy: —under me, to Salinger, to you people and to [Defense Department spokesman Arthur] Sylvester.

White: Yeah.

President Kennedy: And nothing dealing with the Cuban crisis of any importance is to go out until it goes through Salinger and comes to me. Because I'm not—I don't want to be critical. But the problem is when you say further action's going to be taken, then they all say: "What action?" And it moves this escalation up a couple of days, when we're not ready for it.

White: Yeah. I, I'm sorry, sir.

President Kennedy: So therefore you have to be goddamn careful! You just can't make references to past speeches, because that gives them a new headline—and they've now got it. And every reporter in town is going to be putting together Pierre Salinger's [6:15 P.M.] release about the missile thing with your thing that further action . . . and we're going to find ourselves getting out of control. OK.

White: Well I'm terribly sorry, sir.

President Kennedy: OK.

. . .

At 7:40, shortly after this call, Kennedy went back to the Mansion. Meanwhile, a cable began arriving from the U.S. Embassy in Moscow, divided into four sections that were received between 6:00 and 9:00 P.M. It was a long message from Khrushchev.

This message from Khrushchev was not being made public. It was instead quite confidential and had taken more than six hours to make its way to Washington via the cable circuit running out of Moscow. The copy of the letter given to the embassy appeared to still have Khrushchev's handwritten notations on it, and it certainly appeared to be a very personal message directly from the Soviet leader to the U.S. President. The highlights are quoted below:

Dear Mr. President,

I have received your letter of October 25. From your letter, I got the feeling that you have some understanding of the situation which has developed and (some) sense of responsibility. I value this. . . .

I see, Mr. President, that you are not devoid of a sense of anxiety for the fate of the world, of understanding, and of what war entails. What would war give you? You are threatening us with war. But you well know that the very least which you would receive in reply would be that you would experience the same consequences as those which you send us. And that must be clear to us, people invested with authority, trust, and responsibilities. We must not succumb to intoxication and petty passions, regardless of whether elections are impending in this or that country, or not impending. These are all transient things, but if indeed war should break out, then it would not be in our power to stop it, for such is the logic of war. I have participated in two wars and I know that war ends when it has rolled through cities and villages, everywhere sowing death and destruction.

In the name of the Soviet Government and the Soviet people, I assure you that your conclusions regarding offensive weapons in Cuba are groundless. It is apparent from what you have written me that our conceptions are different on this score, or rather, we have different estimates of these or those military means. Indeed, in reality, the same forms of weapons can have different interpretations. . . .

This indicated that we are normal people, that we correctly understand and evaluate the situation. Consequently, how can we permit the incorrect actions that you ascribe to us? Only lunatics or suicides, who themselves want to perish and to destroy the whole world before they die, could do this. We, however, want to live and do not at all want to destroy your country. We want something quite different: to compete with your country on a peaceful basis. We quarrel with you; we have differences on ideological questions. But our view of the world consists in this, that ideological questions, as well as economic problems, should be solved not by military means, they must be solved on the basis of peaceful competition, i.e., as this is understood in capitalist society, on the basis of competition. We have proceeded and are proceeding from the fact that the peaceful coexistence of the two different social-political systems, now existing in the world, is necessary, that it is necessary to assure a stable peace. That is the sort of principle we hold.

You have now proclaimed piratical measures, which were employed in the Middle Ages, when ships proceeding in international waters were attacked, and you have called this 'a quarantine' around Cuba. Our vessels, apparently will soon enter the zone which your Navy is patrolling. I assure you that these vessels, now bound for Cuba, are carrying the most innocent peaceful cargoes. Do you really think that we only occupy ourselves with the carriage of so-called offensive weapons, atomic and hydrogen bombs? Although perhaps your military people imagine that these (cargoes) are some sort of special type of weapon, I assure you that they are the most ordinary peaceful products.

Consequently, Mr. President, let us show good sense. I assure you that on those ships, which are bound for Cuba, there are no weapons at all. The weapons which were necessary for the defense of Cuba are already there. I do not want to say that there were no shipments of any weapons at all. No, there were such shipments. But now Cuba has already received the necessary means of defense. . . .

You once said that the United States was not preparing an invasion. But you also declared that you sympathized with the Cuban counterrevolutionary emigrants, that you support them and would help them to realize their plans against the present government of Cuba. It is also not a secret to anyone that the threat of armed attack, aggression, has constantly hung, and continues to hang over Cuba. It is only this which impelled us to respond to the request of the Cuban government to furnish it aid for the strengthening of the defensive capacity of this country.

If assurances were given by the President and the government of the United States that the USA itself would not participate in an attack on Cuba and would restrain others from actions of this sort, if you would recall your fleet, this would immediately change everything. I am not speaking for Fidel Castro, but I think that he and the Government of Cuba, evidently, would declare demobilization and would appeal to the people to get down to peaceful labor. Then, too, the question of armaments would disappear, since, if there is no threat, then armaments are a burden for every people. Then, too, the question of the destruction, not only of the armaments which you call offensive, but of all other armaments as well, would look different. . . .

Let us therefore show statesmanlike wisdom. I propose: we, for our part, will declare that our ships, bound for Cuba, will not carry any kind of armaments. You would declare that the United States will not invade Cuba with its forces and will not support any sort of forces which might intend to carry out an invasion of Cuba. Then the necessity for the presence of our military specialists in Cuba would disappear.

Mr. President, I appeal to you to weigh well what the aggressive, piratical actions, which you have declared the USA intends to carry out in international waters, would lead to. You yourself know that any sensible man simply cannot agree with this, cannot recognize your right to such actions.

If you did this as the first step towards the unleashing of war, well then, it is evident that nothing else is left to us but to accept this challenge of yours. If, however, you have not lost your self-control and sensibly conceive what this might lead to, then, Mr. President, we and you ought not now to pull on the ends of the rope in which you have tied the knots of war, because the more the two of us pull, the tighter this knot will be tied. And a moment may come when that knot will be tied so tight that even he who tied will not have the strength to untie it, and then it will be necessary to cut that knot. And what that would mean is not for me to explain to you, because you yourself understand perfectly of what terrible forces our countries dispose.

Consequently, if there is no intention to tighten that knot and thereby to doom the world to the catastrophe of thermonuclear war, then let us not only relax the forces pulling on the ends of the rope, let us take measures to untie that knot. We are ready for this. . . .

These, Mr. President, are my thoughts, which, if you agreed with them, could put an end to that tense situation which is disturbing all peoples.

These thoughts are dictated by a sincere desire to relieve the situation, to remove the threat of war.

Respectfully yours, N. Khrushchev.[14]

After this message arrived, several of Kennedy's advisers gathered informally to analyze it. Taken together with U Thant's initiative earlier in the day, which possibly had been prompted behind the scenes by the Soviets, and combined with the Fomin approach to Scali, Khrushchev's letter seemed to suggest, vaguely, the same idea of a bargain that would exchange a noninvasion pledge for the Soviet withdrawal of their missiles from Cuba. To the Americans, this was a very encouraging development. With this sense of cautious optimism, they retired for the night. The Executive Committee would meet the next morning to consider how the United States should respond to the letter and explore the apparent Soviet proposal.

Saturday, October 27, 1962

10:05 A.M.

Executive Committee Meeting of the National Security Council

The Executive Committee began what would become the longest day of the crisis with an intelligence briefing. McCone emphasized again the rapid pace of continuing work at the missile sites as well as the fact that almost all of the MRBMs were now ready for action. Analysts were worried by the observation of tracks that seemed to indicate that missiles were being moved into the ready position for firing and had been checked out during the night. We do not know, however, whether McCone mentioned these concerns in his briefing. He did highlight the key points from that morning's Watch Committee report, which were:[1]

> Based on the latest low-level reconnaissance mission, 3 of the 4 MRBM sites at San Cristobal and the 2 sites at Sagua La Grande appear to be fully operational. No further sites or missiles have been identified.[2]
>
> The mobilization of Cuban military forces continues at a high rate. However, they remain under orders not to take any hostile action unless attacked.
>
> Steps toward establishing an integrated air defense system are under way. On the diplomatic front, Cuban representatives are trying to plant the idea that Havana would be receptive to U.N. mediation. They indicate, however, that a prerequisite must be "proof" that the U.S. does not intend to attack Cuba.
>
> Despite Khrushchev's declaration to U Thant that Soviet ships would temporarily avoid the quarantine area, we have no information as yet that the six Soviet and three satellite ships en route have changed course. A Swedish vessel, believed to be under charter to the U.S.S.R. [the *Coalangatta*], refused to stop yesterday when intercepted by a U.S. destroyer and was allowed to continue to Havana.
>
> No significant redeployment of Soviet ground, air, or naval forces have been noted. However, there are continuing indications of increased

readiness among some units. Three F-class submarines have been identified on the surface or near the quarantine line.

There has been no distinct shift in the pattern of reaction. In Western Europe, further support for the U.S. has come from several quarters and unfavorable reactions are decidedly in the minority.

Official London seems intent on checking premature optimism which is showing up in widely scattered parts of the world, particularly among the neutrals. French support for the U.S. is hardening.

There are reports that anti-U.S. demonstrations have broken out in several Latin American capitals, including Buenos Aires, Caracas, and La Paz.

After the briefing from McCone, McNamara reported on the status of the quarantine and the positions of Soviet-bloc ships moving toward Cuba. The *Grozny*, about 600 miles from Cuba, was finally approaching the quarantine line.[3] The secretary of defense recommended that U.S. ships be readied to board that vessel.

Undersecretary of State George Ball wondered if the Soviets knew where the quarantine line had been drawn. The group agreed that a message should be sent quickly to U Thant, asking him to be sure to tell the Soviet representatives at the United Nations, in New York, just where the line was drawn, to be sure Moscow could decide whether to turn the *Grozny* around. Toward the end of the discussion of this message, President Kennedy turned on the tape recorder.

President Kennedy: —both of these points to U Thant as soon as we've got them in a position to put it out.

Robert McNamara: We could be in position in an hour.

President Kennedy: OK. Put it out. Send it over to him.

McGeorge Bundy: [Know of] any other ships [besides] the *Grozny*, Bob?

McNamara: No, I don't. I believe we'll find the *Grozny* does not carry prohibited material.

John McCone: That's what I think too. It's scheduled—

McNamara: But I think we ought to stop it anyhow, and use force if necessary.

U. Alexis Johnson: Will you give me the information we should give to U Thant on it, where it was at such time and where it will be?

McNamara: Yes. Yes, I will do so, Alex.

Now, on other forms of action, Mr. President, we would recommend two [low-level] daylight surveillance missions today. We're prepared to send one flight out of approximately eight aircraft—I say approximately— it might be seven or nine—immediately and have it over the target at about 11:30 Cuban time, and send another flight out this afternoon about 4:00.

President Kennedy: To a different place?

McNamara: Same targets. Missile sites.

President Kennedy: Well, let me ask my two questions, Bob. First, are we sending different pilots, to gather experience?

McNamara: Yes. We've got our . . . As a matter of fact we instructed them last night to try to rotate some fighter pilots through this reconnaissance mission, so we'll get some people . . .

President Kennedy: Now, the other thing, are we going to do this, [having the pilots] eyeball [the sites] for this? And then we're going to have them interrogated afterwards and see what they saw? Will they take one turn around there, to see how much they can pick up as they would have if—

Maxwell Taylor: I'd leave it to the pilot. He'll know what the purpose of it is and, if he needs to be able to make a swing around, take another look, he will.

President Kennedy: [*reading from news ticker copy handed him by Theodore Sorensen*] "Premier Khrushchev told President Kennedy yesterday he would withdraw offensive weapons from Cuba if the United States withdrew its rockets from Turkey."

Bundy: Hmm. He didn't.

Theodore Sorensen: That's how it is read by both of the associations that have put it out so far. Reuters has the same thing.

Bundy: He didn't . . .

Sorensen: He didn't really say that, did he?

Bundy: No, no . . .

President Kennedy: They may not be . . . He may be putting out another letter.

Bundy: —another paper.

Unidentified: [*to Bundy*] Most of this thing is Metro/City.

President Kennedy: What is our . . . ? Well our . . . But anyway, they've got this clear about how this . . .

Let's just go on then. Are you finished, Mr. Secretary?

Unidentified: [*Unclear*] to U Thant.

President Kennedy: [*calling out*] Pierre [Salinger]? Pierre?

That wasn't in the letter we received, was it?

Sorensen: No. I read it pretty carefully. It doesn't read that way to me either.

President Kennedy: Well therefore, is he supposed to be putting out a letter he's written to me or putting out a statement?

Sorensen: Putting out a letter he wrote to you.

President Kennedy: Well, let's just sit tight on it. We just have nothing to go on.

Bundy: Is it a different statement?

Dean Rusk: You know I think we'd better get [the text].

[*speaking to an aide*] Would you check and be sure that the letter that's coming in on the ticker is the letter that we were seeing last night?

McNamara: OK. Can we issue the orders, then, for the two [surveillance] missions [*unclear*]? Max, would you do that?

Taylor: [*Unclear.*]

McNamara: [*to Taylor*] Yeah, but that we don't have to issue orders for.

President Kennedy: What's the advantage of the second mission?

McNamara: It creates a pattern of increasing intensity of surveillance, Mr. President. We believe that we should do this.

President Kennedy: OK.

McNamara: Now, further, I would recommend, although we don't need—

Bundy: Are these two 8s [two missions of eight planes each]?

McNamara: Yes, two 8s, on the missile sites from up in the air.

Bundy: Oh sure, sure.

McNamara: And I would also recommend, although we don't have to decide now, that we conduct a night surveillance mission tonight. There appears increasing evidence that they're working night and day on these sites.

President Kennedy: OK.

McNamara: All right, sir. Two in daylight, one at night.

Unidentified: One tonight?

Bundy: The night is laid on but not finally authorized?

President Kennedy: You don't have to come back to me, but if you want to do it, then go ahead.

Bundy: Well, then we believe there ought to be an announcement of that or at least as of yesterday.

Rusk: I really think we ought to have a talk about the political part of this thing, because if we prolong this, after two days on the basis of the withdrawal of these missiles—

President Kennedy: From Turkey?

Rusk: No, not from Turkey, from Cuba. The Turkish thing hasn't been injected into this conversation in New York and it wasn't in the letter last night. This appears to be something quite new.

McNamara: This is what worries me about the whole deal. If you go through that letter, to a layman it looks to be full of holes. I think my proposal would be to keep—

Bundy: Keeping the heat on . . . it's a very important matter.

McNamara: —keep the heat on. This is why I would recommend the two daylight and the one night mission. And I fully agree we ought to put out an announcement that we *are* going to send the night mission over.

Bundy: Well, which way do you want it to stand? That we approved it [the night reconnaissance mission], Mr. President, subject to appeal or do you want to hold it?

McNamara: We can hold it, Mr. President.

President Kennedy: All right. I tell you what I'd like to do is I . . . think we ought to go ahead if they want it. So it's all right with me. I think we might have one more conversation about it, however, at about 6:00, just in case during the day we get something important.

McNamara: There's plenty of time. We'll keep it on alert.

President Kennedy: But otherwise let's just plan to put it on unless there's something in the daytime that . . .

Bundy: Well, the announcement can . . . That is a complication. We can't very well make the announcement and not do it [the night reconnaissance].

McNamara: We won't make the announcement. But at that time we'll make it.

Bundy: Well, I would suggest we review it at four and make the announcement.

McNamara: Or we'll have the announcement prepared, and how we're going to get it out.

Bundy: If you make the announcement late it's not much good. So have the announcement all ready to go from the Pentagon at four.

McNamara: And we'll have some time to chat over it.

Bundy: We'll have to make sure the President gets that in time.

President Kennedy: OK.

Vice President Johnson: Does that involve these flares dropping and so forth?

McNamara: Yes, it does, Mr. Vice President.

Unidentified: [*checking on news about the possible Khrushchev statement*] Will you be ready to beam it in?

Unidentified: Yes sir, if I get the word on the radio.

President Kennedy: You finished, Mr. Secretary?

McNamara: Yes I am.

President Kennedy: Getting to this, in case this [newly reported Khrushchev proposal] *is* an accurate statement, where are we with our conversations with the Turks about the withdrawal of these . . . ?

Paul Nitze: Hare says that this is absolutely anathema and as a matter of prestige and politics, but George [Ball] has read the [*unclear*] reports from Finletter.[4]

George Ball: We have a report from Finletter, and we've also gotten a report from Rome on the Italians which would indicate that that would be relatively easy.[5]

Turkey creates more of a problem. We would have to work it out with the Turks on the basis of putting a Polaris [ballistic missile submarine] in the water, and even that might not be enough according to the judgment that we've had on the spot. We've got one paper on it already and we're having more work done right now.[6] It is a complicated problem because these [Jupiter missiles] were put in under a NATO decision and to the extent that they really now are . . .

Nitze: The NATO requirement involves the whole question of whether we are going to denuclearize NATO. I would suggest that what you do is to say that we're prepared only to discuss *Cuba* at this time. After the Cuban thing is settled and these things are out, we're prepared to discuss anything.

President Kennedy: No, I don't think we can . . . If this is an accurate [story] and this is the whole deal, we'll just have to wait. I don't think we can take the position—

Bundy: No. It's very odd, Mr. President. If he's changed his terms from a long letter to you and an urgent appeal from the counselor [Alexander Fomin] only last night, set in the purely Cuban context, it seems to me we're well within our . . . There's nothing wrong with our posture in sticking to that line.

President Kennedy: But let's wait, and let's assume that this is an accurate report of what he's now proposing this morning. There may be some changes over there.

Bundy: I still think he's in a difficult position to change it overnight, having sent you a personal communication on the other line.

President Kennedy: Well now, let's say he has changed it. This is his latest position.

Bundy: Well, I would answer back saying I would prefer to deal with your, you know, with your interesting proposals of last night.

President Kennedy: Well now, that's just what we ought to be thinking about.

We're going to be in an insupportable position on this matter if this becomes his proposal. In the first place, we last year tried to get the missiles out of there because they're not militarily useful, number one.

Number two, it's going to—to any man at the United Nations or any other rational man, it will look like a very fair trade.

Nitze: I don't think so. I think you would get support from the United Nations on the proposition: "Deal with this Cuban thing. We'll talk about other things later." But I think everybody else is worried that they'll be included in this great big trade if it goes beyond Cuba.

Rusk: That's true of the allies. It would not be true of the neutrals.

Bundy: No.

Rusk: But later. I think we can leave those off for the moment, to think about this. One possibility would be to, if this is persistent—

Unidentified: [*bringing in new information*] Entirely new stuff, Mr. Secretary.

Rusk: Entirely new stuff?

President Kennedy: [*apparently reading from a news ticker*] "In a special message he appeared to call for negotiations on the parts of both nations, Cuba and Turkey, to give their consent to the United Nations to visit their territories. Mr. Khrushchev said that, in the Security Council, the Soviet Union would solemnly pledge not to use its territory as a bridgehead for any attack on Turkey, and called for a similar pledge from the United States not to let its territory be used as a bridgehead for an attack on Cuba. A broadcast shortly after said it was out of the question for the United States to abandon its Turkish military bases. . . ."

Now, we've known this has been, might be coming for a week. We can't . . . It's going to be hung up here now. This is their proposal.

Unidentified: It might just—

President Kennedy: How much negotiations have we had with the Turks this week? Who's done it?

Unidentified: No, we have not.

Rusk: We haven't talked with the Turks. The Turks have talked with us.

President Kennedy: Where have they talked with us?

Rusk: In NATO.

President Kennedy: Yeah, but have we gone to the Turkish government before this came out this week? I've talked about it now for a week. Have we had any conversations in Turkey, with the Turks?

Rusk: Well we've asked Finletter and Hare to give us their judgments on it. We've not actually talked with the Turks.

Ball: We did it on a basis where, if we talked to the Turks, I mean, this would be an extremely unsettling business.

President Kennedy: Well, *this* is unsettling *now*, George, because he's got us in a pretty good spot here. Because most people would regard this as not an unreasonable proposal. I'll just tell you that. In fact, in many ways—

Bundy: But what "most people," Mr. President?

President Kennedy: I think you're going to have it very difficult to explain why we are going to take hostile military action in Cuba, against these sites, what we're here thinking about, when he's saying, "If you'll get yours out of Turkey, we'll get ours out of Cuba." I think you've got a very touchy point here.

Bundy: I don't see why we pick that track when he's offered us the other track within the last 24 hours.

President Kennedy: But that offer is a new one.

Llewellyn Thompson: I hear you. And you think the public one is serious, when we have the private one. . . .

President Kennedy: Yes! I think we have to assume that this is their new and latest position, and it's a public one.

Rusk: What would you think of releasing the letter of yesterday?

Bundy: I think it has a good deal of virtue.

President Kennedy: Yeah, but I think we have to be now thinking about what our position is going to be on *this* one, because this is the one that's before us, and before the world.

Sorensen: Well as between the two, I think it's clear that practically everyone here would favor the private proposal.

Rusk: We're not being offered a choice. We *may* not be offered a choice.

President Kennedy: There are serious disadvantages also to the private one, which is this guarantee of Cuba.

But in any case, this is now his official one. We can release this other one, and it's different, but this is the one that the Soviet government obviously is going on.

Nitze: Isn't it possible that they're going on a dual track, one a public track and the other a private track? The private track is related solely to Cuba and the public track is one that's in order to confuse the public scene and divide us with additional pressures.

President Kennedy: It's possible.

Taylor: I think, personally, that that statement is one that the Soviets take seriously.

Rusk: Well, I think, yes. I think that the NATO-Warsaw Pact arms problem is a separate problem and ought to be discussed between NATO and the Warsaw Pact. They've got hundreds of missiles looking down the throat of every NATO country. And I think this is—we have to get it into *that context*. The Cuba thing is a Western Hemisphere problem, an intrusion into the Western Hemisphere.

Nitze: I think we ought to stand as much as we can on a separate basis.

Bundy: Absolutely.

Nitze: And fight the Turkish one with the best arguments we can. I'd handle this thing so that we can continue on the real track, which is to try to get the missiles out of Cuba pursuant to the private negotiations.

Bundy: The other way, it seems to me, is if we accept the notion of the trade at this stage, our position will come apart very fast.

We are in a very difficult position. It isn't as if we'd got the [Jupiter] missiles out, Mr. President. It would be different. Or if we had any understanding with the Turks that they ought to come out, it would be different. Neither of these is the case.

President Kennedy: Well, I'd just like to know how much we've done about it and, as I say, we talked about it—

Bundy: We decided *not* to, Mr. President. We decided *not* to play this directly with the Turks.

Rusk: Our own representative is—

Ball: If we talked to the Turks, they would bring it up in NATO. This thing would be all over western Europe, and our position would have been undermined.

Bundy: That's right.

Ball: Because immediately the Soviet Union would know that this thing was being discussed. The Turks feel very strongly about this. We persuaded them that this was an essential requirement, and they feel that it's a matter of prestige and a matter of real—

Bundy: If we had talked to the Turks, it would already be clear that we were trying to sell our allies for our interests. That would be the view in all of NATO. Now it's irrational and it's crazy, but it's a *terribly* powerful fact.

Thompson: Particularly in the case that this is a message to you and to U Thant.

Alexis Johnson: It seems to me we ought to get word to [Adlai] Stevenson that, if this is put out up there, he should immediately say we will not discuss the Turkish bases.

Bundy: The problem is Cuba. The Turks are not a threat to the peace. Nobody smells the Turks as—

President Kennedy: I think it would be better, rather than saying that, until we get time to think about it, just saying: "Well, the fact of the matter is that we received a letter last night from Khrushchev and it's an entirely different proposal." So, therefore, we first ought to get clarification from the Soviet Union of what they're talking, at least to give us a . . .

As I say, you're going to find a lot of people who will find this is a rather reasonable position.

Bundy: That's true.

President Kennedy: Let's not kid ourselves.

Unclear exchange. President Kennedy is either handed a document or begins scanning one that is a summary of a part of Khrushchev's broadcast statement.

President Kennedy: [*reading occasional words from the document*] "Literally . . . the sides . . . guarantee not to infringe . . . in Turkey . . . must do the same for Cuba. This means of offense . . . this means if it's disturbing the [*unclear*] . . . the accidental use of . . . "

Well, all right, we know what the problem is now.

Rusk: Well, I take it that it's relevant here to be able to say that we supported the declaration of Iran that they would not accept foreign missiles in Iran. The Turkish problem is a NATO–Warsaw Pact problem. And it's an arms problem between these two groups that is something for these two groups to talk about with *each other* as a problem of disarmament with respect to NATO and Warsaw Pact.

C. Douglas Dillon: Well, there's also this thing of upsetting the status quo, and we did not upset it in Iran and [*unclear*] it's not being upset there, and they did in Cuba.

President Kennedy: He's put this out in a way to cause maximum tension and embarrassment. It's not as if it was a private proposal, which would give us an opportunity to negotiate with the Turks. He has put it out in a way in which the Turks are bound to say that they won't agree to this. And therefore we're at the mercy of these others. They're not American proposals.

Dillon: There's another military thing to it. It may be preparations for counteraction against those particular [kind of] bases we warned Cuba against. The ones he's talking about. Could be that. [*Pause. Unclear aside.*]

President Kennedy: Until we have gotten our position a little clearer, we ought to go with this last night's business, so that that gives us about an hour or two—we don't have Khrushchev.

Rusk: There's nothing coming in yet on our tickers.

·   ·   ·

President Kennedy, along with Sorensen, leaves the room, with Kennedy's making some faint suggestion to Rusk about continuing the discussion. There is a short lull in the discussion with a few quiet asides from Rusk and others.

. . .

Robert Kennedy: Can I throw out some ideas?

Rusk: [*Unclear, referring to the President.*]

Robert Kennedy: [*replying to Rusk, discussing a possible U.S. position*] The first point being that this is a question of Cuba and the bases and must be resolved within the next few days. This can't wait. The negotiations and discussions must get on, and the work that is continuing despite our protests has been going on. So therefore it's got to be resolved, and quickly. This action that has been taken is not an action just by the United States but it is an action by all of the Latin American countries plus the United States.

This has nothing to do with the security of the countries of Europe, which do have their own problems. We would obviously consider negotiating the giving up of bases in Turkey if we can assure the Turks and the other European countries for whom these bases were emplaced, if there can be some assurances given to them for their own security. This will entail inspection, as we anticipate that there will be some inspection in Cuba and in the United States at the time that these bases are withdrawn from Cuba, and we give assurances that we are not going to invade Cuba. Something along those lines.

. . .

The group, or at least Rusk, finally appears to get some copies of the text of Khrushchev's message to President Kennedy, being broadcast and carried by the press. The text of the message, as the Executive Committee received it, was:

Dear Mr. President:

It is with great satisfaction that I studied your reply to Mr. U Thant on the adoption of measures in order to avoid contact by our ships and thus avoid irreparable fatal consequences. This reasonable step on your part persuades me that you are showing solicitude for the preservation of peace, and I note this with satisfaction. . . .

In your statement, you said that the main aim lies not only in reaching agreement and adopting measures to avert contact of our ships, and, consequently a deepening of the crisis, which because of this contact can spark off the fire of military conflict after which any talks would be superfluous because other forces and other laws would begin to operate—the laws of war. I agree with you that this is only a first step. The main thing is to normalize and stabilize the situation in the world between states and between people.

I understand your concern for the security of the United States, Mr. President, because this is the first duty of the president. However, these questions are also uppermost in our minds. The same duties rest with me as chairman of the U.S.S.R. Council of Ministers. You have been worried over our assisting Cuba with arms designed to strengthen its defensive potential—precisely defensive potential—because Cuba, no matter what weapons it had, could not compare with you since these are different dimensions, the more so given up-to-date means of extermination.

Our purpose has been and is to help Cuba, and no one can challenge the humanity of our motives aimed at allowing Cuba to live peacefully and develop as its people desire. You want to relieve your country from danger and this is understandable. However, Cuba also wants this. All countries want to relieve themselves from danger. But how can we, the Soviet Union and our government, assess your actions which, in effect, mean that you have surrounded the Soviet Union with military bases, surrounded our allies with military bases, set up military bases literally around our country, and stationed your rocket weapons at them? This is no secret. High-placed American officials demonstratively declare this. Your rockets are stationed in Britain and in Italy and pointed at us. Your rockets are stationed in Turkey.

You are worried over Cuba. You say that it worries you because it lies at a distance of 90 miles across the sea from the shores of the United States. However, Turkey lies next to us. Our sentinels are pacing up and down and watching each other. Do you believe that you have the right to demand security for your country and the removal of such weapons that you qualify as offensive, while not recognizing this right for us?

You have stationed devastating rocket weapons, which you call offensive, in Turkey literally right next to us. How then does recognition of our equal military possibilities tally with such unequal relations between our great states? This does not tally at all.

It is good, Mr. President, that you agreed for our representatives to meet and begin talks, apparently with the participation of U.N. Acting Secretary General U Thant. Consequently, to some extent, he assumes the role of intermediary, and we believe that he can cope with the responsible mission if, of course, every side that is drawn into this conflict shows good will.

I think that one could rapidly eliminate this conflict and normalize the situation. Then people would heave a sigh of relief, considering that the statesmen who bear the responsibility have sober minds, an awareness of their responsibility, and an ability to solve complicated problems and not allow matters to slide to the disaster of war.

This is why I make this proposal: We agree to remove those weapons from Cuba which you regard as offensive weapons. We agree to do this and to state this commitment in the United Nations. Your representatives will make a statement to the effect that the United States, on its part, bearing in mind the anxiety and concern of the Soviet state, will evacuate its analogous weapons from Turkey. Let us reach an understanding on what time you and we need to put this into effect.

After this, representatives of the U.N. Security Council could control on-the-spot the fulfillment of these commitments. Of course, it is necessary that the Governments of Cuba and Turkey would allow these representatives to come to their countries and check fulfillment of this commitment, which each side undertakes. Apparently, it would be better if these representatives enjoyed the trust of the Security Council and our—the United States and the Soviet Union—as well as of Turkey and Cuba. I think that it will not be difficult to find such people who enjoy the trust and respect of all interested sides.

We, having assumed this commitment in order to give satisfaction and hope to the peoples of Cuba and Turkey and to increase their confidence in their security, will make a statement in the Security Council to the effect that the Soviet Government gives a solemn pledge to respect the integrity of the frontiers and the sovereignty of Turkey, not to intervene in its domestic affairs, not to invade Turkey, not to make available its territory as a *place d'armes* for such invasion, and also will restrain those who would think of launching an aggression against Turkey either from Soviet territory or from the territory of other states bordering on Turkey.

The U.S. Government will make the same statement in the Security Council with regard to Cuba. It will declare that the United States will respect the integrity of the frontiers of Cuba, its sovereignty, undertakes not to intervene in its domestic affairs, not to invade and not to make its territory available as [a] *place d'armes* for the invasion of Cuba, and also will restrain those who would think of launching an aggression against Cuba either from U.S. territory or from the territory of other states bordering on Cuba.

Of course, for this we would have to reach agreement with you and to arrange for some deadline. Let us agree to give some time, but not to delay, two or three weeks, not more than a month.

The weapons on Cuba, that you have mentioned and which, as you say, alarm you, are in the hands of Soviet officers. Therefore any accidental use of them whatsoever to the detriment of the United States of America is excluded. These means are stationed in Cuba at the request of the Cuban Government and only in defensive aims. Therefore, if there is no invasion of Cuba, or an attack on the Soviet Union, or other of our allies then, of course, these means do not threaten anyone and will not threaten. For they do not pursue offensive aims.

If you accept my proposal, Mr. President, we would send our representatives to New York, to the United Nations, and would give them exhaustive instructions to order to come to terms sooner. If you would also appoint your men and give them appropriate instructions, this problem could be solved soon. . . .

All this, possibly, would serve as a good impetus to searching for mutually acceptable agreements on other disputed issues, too, on which there is an exchange of opinion between us. These problems have not yet been solved, but they wait for an urgent solution which would clear the international atmosphere. We are ready for this.

These are my proposals, Mr. President.

Respectfully yours, Nikita Khrushchev[7]

. . .

McNamara: How do you interpret the addition of still another condition over and above the letter that came in last night. We had one deal in the letter; now we've got a different deal. And why shouldn't we say—

Rusk: And most important, what if Moscow decides this is too much of a setback for them?

Unidentified: Shouldn't we point this out in a letter?

McNamara: How can we negotiate with somebody who changes his deal before we even get a chance to reply, and announces publicly the deal before we receive it?

Bundy: I think there must have been an overruling in Moscow. What does Tommy say?

Unidentified: We've got three changes going outside, Bob. We've got three changes, three positions.

Unidentified: My bet is that the letter, the long letter last night, he wrote himself.

Rusk: And sent out without clearance.

Ball: Without clearance there, yes.

Thompson: The Politburo intended this one.

McNamara: You see, this completely changes the character of the deal we're likely to be able to make, and also, therefore, our action in the interim, in [*unclear*] has got to really keep the pressure on them, in this [*unclear*] situation.

Bundy: I agree. This should be knocked down publicly. A private . . .

Let me suggest this scenario. We knock this down publicly in the way we have just described, separating the issues, keeping attention on Cuba, with a four-point requirement involved, as expressed.

Privately, we say to Khrushchev: Look, your public statement is a very dangerous one because it makes impossible immediate discussion of your private proposals and requires us to proceed urgently with the things that we have in mind. You'd better get straightened out.

Dillon: This is exactly what I think.

Unidentified: Yeah.

Unidentified: And that's exactly right.

Unidentified: And we release the fact that there was the other letter?

Bundy: No, we don't. We say we are reluctant to release this letter which displayed the inconsistency in your position, but we don't have very much time.

At about this time, President Kennedy returned to the Cabinet Room.

McNamara: Our point, Bobby, is he's changed the deal. Well, almost before we even got the first letter translated, he added a completely new deal and he released it publicly. And under these circumstances we've . . .

Unidentified: What is the day he changed the deal?

McCone: What is the timing on this?

Robert Kennedy: What is the advantage? I don't know which, where you are 24 hours from now. So we win that argument. But before 24 hours—

McNamara: We incorporate a new deal in our letter.

Robert Kennedy: We give him four steps that he has to take: Stop construction; [*unclear*] his missiles so they can't be made alert . . .

McNamara: Remove the missiles.

Robert Kennedy: . . . have inspection sites and then have the inspections. Now the problem is going to be, not the fact that we have this exchange with him, in my judgment, but the fact that he's going to have a ploy publicly that's going to look rather satisfactory at the present. How are we going to have him do anything but take the ball away from us publicly, if we don't agree, if we just write him a [*unclear*] letter.

Bundy: In the letter, Bobby, should we surface his earlier message?

Robert Kennedy: Well, I think all of that. I think we're going to have to, in the next three or four hours, not just put the ball completely in his hands and allow him to do whatever he wants. We can have an exchange with him and say: You double-crossed us, and you—and we don't know which deal to accept. And then he writes back in the meantime. He's got all the play throughout the world on the fact that he—

McNamara: Just turn him down publicly.

Robert Kennedy: Yeah, but I think that's awful tough.

Bundy: But I think we *have* to do that.

McCone: I don't think you can turn that down publicly without referring publicly to his letter of yesterday.

Robert Kennedy: I'd like to have a consideration of my thought [*someone else is also talking, explaining, possibly to the President, the willingness to accept some inspections*] about saying that he made this arrangement, he offered this deal—Now, I haven't refined it at all—but that he's offered this arrangement in Cuba—that he will withdraw the bases in Cuba for assurances that we don't intend to invade Cuba. We've always given those assurances. We will be glad to give them again. He said, in his letter to me, you said that you would permit inspection. Obviously that entails inspection not only of Cuba but entails inspection of the United States to ensure that we're not—by United Nations observers—to ensure that we're not getting ready to invade. Now this is one of the things U Thant said.

The bases in Cuba involve the security of the Western Hemisphere. This is not just a question of the United States. This is a question of all the Latin American countries which have all joined together in this effort. Time is running out on us. This must be brought to fruition.

The question of the Turkish bases—we think that's excellent that you brought that up, in that there should be disarmament of the Turkish bases. But that has nothing to do with the security of the Western Hemisphere. It does have to do with the security of Turkey, and we would be happy, as we are sure the Turks would be, about making a similar arrangement in Turkey. That we will withdraw the bases from Turkey if—and allow inspection of Turkey to make sure that we've done that. And you withdraw your invasion bases of the Soviet Union and permit inspection there.

Bundy: I think it's too complicated, Bobby.

Robert Kennedy: Well, I don't think it is.

President Kennedy: Well wait, just it seems to me the first thing we ought to try to do is not let the Turks issue some statement that this is totally unacceptable, so that before we've even had a chance to get our own diplomacy, we're . . .

The first thing, it seems to me, that you want to emphasize before you go over some details is that they've given us several different proposals in 24 hours, and that work's got to stop today before we talk about anything. At least then we're in a defensible position.

The other thing is to not have the Turks make any statement so that this thing . . . Khrushchev puts it out and the next thing the Turks say they won't accept it. Then whatever we do in Cuba [possible attack], it seems to me he has set the groundwork for doing something in Turkey.

So I think we ought to have the Turks . . . We've got to have a talk with the Turks, because I think they've got to understand the peril that they are going to move into next week if we take some action in Cuba. The chances are that he'll take some action in Turkey. They ought to understand that. And in fact he may even come out and say that once the Turks turn this down. [*Unclear*] any more that he's tried to be fair and if we do any more about Cuba then he's going to do it to Turkey. So I think the Turks ought to think a little. I think we ought to try to get them not to respond to this until we've had a chance to consider what action we'll take. Now, how long will it take for us to get in touch with the Turks?

Unidentified: I'll find out [*unclear*], Mr. President. We'll see.

Ball: I think it's going to be awfully hard to get the Turks not to say this.

Rusk: They'll have to say something.

Ball: They'll have to say something.

Unidentified: And this is a NATO problem, after all.

Rusk: I think this is the thing the Turks ought to say: That the military assistance and the security of Turkey and military arrangements in Turkey are part of the NATO problem, are part of the NATO.

Bundy: Part of the Atlantic, part of the Western Alliance, and have no . . . with NATO and have nothing to do with Cuba. They ought to— they can certainly make a statement disassociating this.

Taylor: It should be discussed in a different context.

Bundy: It seems to me it's important that they *should*. If anyone pulls them in, it will be us. And they *can't* be expected to do that.

President Kennedy: No, but we want to give them some guidance. These are American missiles, not Turkish missiles. They are under American control, not Turkish control.

Unidentified: But the missiles aren't, Sir, don't the missiles belong—

McNamara: Yes, the missiles belong to Turkey and they're manned by Turks, but the warheads are under U.S. custody.

Taylor: And committed to NATO.

McNamara: And they're committed to NATO.

President Kennedy: In other words, we couldn't destroy the missiles anyway, could we? They belong to the Turks.

McNamara: They belong to Turkey.

President Kennedy: All we can destroy is the warheads.

Unidentified: That is correct.

McNamara: And we can't even really withdraw the warheads. We simply are custodians of the warheads for the account of the Turks, in recognition that you [President Kennedy] must release them [under NATO nuclear release procedures].

President Kennedy: Well now, what we have to do first is get, I would think, is just act very quickly until we get a chance to think a little more about it.

But what we ought to say is that we have had several publicly and privately different proposals, or differing proposals from the Soviet Union. They all are complicated matters and involve some discussion to get their true meaning. We cannot permit ourselves to be impaled on a long negotiating hook while the work goes on on these bases. I therefore suggest that work, that the United Nations immediately, with the cooperation of the Soviet Union, take steps to provide for cessation of the work, and then we can talk about all these matters, which are very complicated.

Bundy: I think it will be very important to say at least that the current threat to peace is not in Turkey; it is in Cuba. There's no pain in saying that, even if you're going to make a trade later on.

I think also that we ought to say that we have an immediate threat. What is going on in Cuba and that is what has got to stop. Then I think we *should* say that the public Soviet, the broadcast, message is at variance with other proposals which have been put forward.

President Kennedy: Within the last 12 hours.

Bundy: Within the last 12 hours. And I get to surface those for background.

President Kennedy: That being so, until we find out what is really being suggested and what can really be discussed, we have to get something on [stopping] work. Their weakness is, the work's going on.

Bundy: That's right.

President Kennedy: There isn't any doubt. Let's not kid ourselves. They've got a very good proposal, which is the reason they've made it public—

Bundy: The work's going on.

While you were out of the room, Mr. President, we reached an informal consensus that—I don't know whether Tommy agrees—that this last night's message was Khrushchev. And this one is his own hard-nosed people overruling him, this public one. That they didn't like what he said to you last night. Nor would I, if I were a Soviet hardnose.

. . .

President Kennedy: The only thing is, Tommy, why would they say it privately if they were serious? The fact they gave it to us publicly, I think they know the kind of complexities that are—

Thompson: Well, they're building up pressure on us this way.

Bundy: And it's a way of pinning themselves down.

President Kennedy: Now let's . . . I would think the first thing we have to do is, as I say, rather than get into the details, the fact that work is going on is the one defensible public position we've got.

They've got a very good product. This one is going to be very tough, I think, for us. It's going to be tough in England, I'm sure, as well as other places on the Continent. If we then are forced to take action, this will be, in my opinion, not a blank check but a pretty good check [for the Soviets] to take action in Berlin on the grounds that we are wholly unreasonable. Emotionally, people will think this is a rather even trade and we ought to take advantage of it. Therefore, it makes it much more difficult for us to move [against Cuba] with world support. These are all the things that—why this is a pretty good play of his.

That being so, I think that the only thing we've got him on is the fact that, while they put forward varying proposals in short periods of time, all of which are complicated, under that shield this work goes on. Until we can get somewhat of an agreement on the cessation of work, how can we possibly negotiate with proposals coming as fast as the wires will carry?

Bundy: And the ships are still moving, in spite of his assurances to U Thant. His ships still—

President Kennedy: Well we ought to emphasize the ships, but that is certainly not . . .

Dillon: There is one other very—might be a very dangerous sentence in this thing that no one has particularly mentioned. But it's a thing I've been afraid of all along on the Cuban trade. And it's where he says: "How are we to react when you have surrounded our country with bases about which your military speaks demonstratively." That will affect our whole base system.

President Kennedy: He has only intended this for Turkey though, hasn't he?

Dillon: Well, no. Then he goes on and says that. But he's left it open to be able to say it's—

President Kennedy: That is propaganda. But the direct trade is suggested with Turkey.

Thompson: Mr. President, it's far beyond the missiles, because he says "the means which you consider aggressive." This would include planes, the presence of technicians, and everything else. This means the real abandonment of our base in Turkey is what he's looking for here.

Bundy: Obviously that's subject to various shades. See, he could take missile for missile, which wouldn't be good enough from our point of view with due respect to Cuba. It would be tough, anyway.

President Kennedy: Well, we could talk for three weeks on that message, couldn't we?

Bundy: That's right.

President Kennedy: But the problem is, at least, work on their bases to stop. And that, in my opinion, is what our defensible position is.

· · ·

Officials are working while they wait for Kennedy's call to be put through to Stevenson in New York. A few fragments of quiet side conversations can barely be heard.

President Kennedy: Do you have any idea how many bases, missiles may be facing Turkey—those [Soviet] intermediate[-range ballistic missiles]?

Taylor: I don't know offhand, Mr. President. I could . . .

Unidentified: I would guess it is at the order of at least 100, that are within range. [*Unclear interjection.*]

Unidentified: We have 15 Jupiters.

President Kennedy: We have 15 Jupiters in Turkey?

McNamara: Yeah but we have a lot of planes with nuclear weapons.

Unidentified: F-100 bombers.

McNamara: Those are the "analogous weapons" that he's speaking of here. If you take the bombers out of Cuba, we could get the nuclear-weapon-equipped planes out of Turkey.

· · ·

President Kennedy: Hello? Oh, Governor, we're here, I got your message. What? No, the letter that I received last night was different than this. What's your judgment? [*Long pause.*] Right. [*Long pause.*] Good. [*Long pause.*] All right. [*Long pause.*] Yes. [*Long pause.*]—and to act against Cuba—[*Long pause.*] Last night's letter. Yeah, they threw that in addition. [*Long pause.*] [*Unclear comment by Kennedy.*] [*Pause.*]

I think we have been around and around too much on that. Oh, fine. Well, I think the only . . . What we've got to do is get them to agree to stop work while we talk about all these proposals, all these propositions. [*Long pause.*] OK, good. Fine, thank you.

Kennedy hangs up and turns to the group.

President Kennedy: What about our putting something in about Berlin?

Dillon: Well, that's the trade, if you stop talking about Cuba, and about Turkey, then you've got—

President Kennedy: Once you get it out of this problem, then you might as well—I mean, just to try to put some sand in his gears for a few minutes.

Bundy: In what way?

President Kennedy: [*a bit whimsically*] Put satisfactory guarantees for Berlin.

Which he's not going to give. I'm just trying to think of what the public problem is, because everybody is going to think this is very reasonable.

Dillon: This Turkish thing has got to be thrown—you are quite right, Mr. President—into the overall European context. That you can bring in Berlin, I think it's fine, because it's not only going to be Turks that are going to be answering here. The Germans are going to be making statements in the next few hours. And various other people about this, when they're asked. And they're going to take a very strong position.

President Kennedy: They're getting a call into [Ambassador to Turkey Raymond] Hare there [at the State Department], aren't we?

Dillon: [*still on the previous point*] I mean you can have statements out of Bonn.

Alexis Johnson: I'm trying to find out where he [Ambassador Hare, in Ankara] is, Mr. President, and I'll put the—do you want to put the call in right away, sir?

President Kennedy: Who has talked to the Turks? Has Finletter talked to them?

Alexis Johnson: No.

Rusk: The [Turkish] prime minister talked on his own yesterday, to Hare.

President Kennedy: What have we heard from him?

Dillon: I would say that the Turkish proposal opens the way to a major discussion of relaxed tensions in Europe, including Berlin.

Unidentified: I think if we mention Berlin—

Nitze: Oh, no, no, no! If you mention that, you've lost the Germans.

Unidentified: That's right.

Nitze: Right then and there. If we start [bringing in Berlin], if we are the first ones . . .

At this point in the meeting the tape recording stops, possibly because the reel of tape had been exhausted and no one was standing by at the moment, ready to replace it.

From other notes of the meeting, it appears that the group turned to drafting the press statement that would offer a public reaction to Khrushchev's public letter. Bundy and Gilpatric read drafts that they had prepared. Alexis Johnson reported that, as President Kennedy had expected, the Turkish government had quickly issued a public statement that sharply rejected the Soviet proposal.

Sorensen then described his own draft for the U.S. statement. The group chose to concentrate, however, on the Gilpatric draft. As revised, that draft became the following statement, which was promptly released by the White House press office to the world media. It read:

> Several inconsistent and conflicting proposals have been made by the U.S.S.R. within the last 24 hours, including the one just made public by Moscow. The proposal broadcast this morning involves the security of nations outside the Western Hemisphere. But it is the Western Hemisphere countries and they alone that are subject to the threat that has produced the current crisis—the action of the Soviet Government in secretly introducing offensive weapons into Cuba. Work on these offensive weapons is still proceeding at a rapid pace. The first imperative must be to deal with this immediate threat, under which no sensible negotiations can proceed.
>
> It is therefore the position of the United States that as an urgent preliminary to consideration of any proposals work on the Cuban bases must stop; offensive weapons must be rendered inoperable; and further shipment of offensive weapons to Cuba must cease—all under effective international verification.
>
> As to proposals concerning the security of nations outside this hemisphere, the United States and its allies have long taken the lead in seeking properly inspected arms limitation, on both sides. These efforts can continue as soon as the present Soviet-created threat is ended.

As discussion in the Executive Committee continued, both Robert Kennedy and Gilpatric emphasized that the Cuba and Turkey problems had to be kept separate and dealt with separately. Negotiations on other issues could not proceed until the missile threat in Cuba was removed.

President Kennedy did not quite agree. He reminded the group how, in the spring of 1961, the U.S. government had wanted to get the Jupiter missiles out of Turkey because they had become obsolete and had little military value. While the missiles in Cuba added perhaps 50 percent to the entire Soviet nuclear missile strike capability against the United States, the missiles in Turkey added almost nothing to the U.S. strike capability against the Soviet Union. So the United States was now in the position of risking war in Cuba and in Berlin over missiles in Turkey that had little military value.

Kennedy added that, from the political point of view, it would be hard to get allied support for an air strike against Cuba because many would think the Cuba-Turkey trade was a good deal. The United States would be in a bad position if it appeared to be attacking Cuba in order to keep useless missiles in Turkey.

President Kennedy also elaborated the point he had made earlier (on tape) that the United States could not propose to withdraw Turkish missiles from Turkey, but the Turks could offer to do it. This was why the Turks should be informed of the great danger in which they would live during the coming week and urged to face up to the possibility of some kind of a trade over missiles.

Then, at about noon, President Kennedy left the meeting to meet a group of state governors that had already been waiting about half an hour to see him. These governors, including Nelson Rockefeller of New York and Pat Brown of California, had been brought to Washington to be briefed on the crisis and on their states' role in the necessary civil defense preparations. McCone and Gilpatric had briefed the governors earlier in the morning at the Pentagon. Now President Kennedy talked briefly with them at the White House.

While President Kennedy saw the governors, the Executive Committee continued to work. The study of Khrushchev's message created more uncertainty about whether his proposal included all NATO bases or was confined only to Turkey. Robert Kennedy wondered what would happen if the United States got bogged down in negotiations with the Soviets while the missiles in Cuba had not been rendered inoperable. Others answered that the United States could then decide to attack the Cuban bases with an air strike. The possibility of another press release to be put out by the White House was considered and rejected.

Thompson, meanwhile, had drafted a possible reply from President

Kennedy directly to Khrushchev. This was discussed with a view to later presenting it to the President. The group then broke up, agreeing to reconvene at 2:30 at the State Department without President Kennedy, then return to the White House at 4:00 to again begin discussions with the President.

4:00 P.M.

Executive Committee Meeting of the National Security Council

McNamara returned to the Defense Department at about 1:30 and asked the Joint Staff of the JCS to prepare two additional military plans. One would involve moving a Polaris ballistic missile submarine into firing position off the Turkish coast before the United States attacked Cuba. If the Jupiters were attacked, the United States would still then have 16 invulnerable missiles offshore. The other plan he requested was a detailed U.S. response if the Soviets attacked Jupiter bases in Turkey with conventional weapons.

Meanwhile the Joint Chiefs of Staff (absent Taylor) had decided, mindful of their previous views and that morning's intelligence, to draft a formal, written recommendation to the President urging him promptly to order a massive air strike against Cuba to begin the next day, Sunday, October 28, or Monday, October 29, and also to prepare to invade the island. Probably over the phone, McNamara discussed this recommendation with President Kennedy.

In the early afternoon, news arrived that a U-2 on a mission to collect air samples from Soviet nuclear tests near the North Pole had been lost near Alaska. Expressing sharp alarm about the danger of war, McNamara left the Pentagon briefly to tell Rusk. They learned that, as a result of navigation difficulties, the U-2 had gone off course into Soviet airspace. Soviet MiG fighters had tried to intercept the aircraft. Then U.S. fighters based in Alaska had been sent aloft to protect the U-2 once it reentered U.S. airspace, which it did.[8] The Soviet leaders, already aware of the constant patrolling of U.S. strategic bombers on flight paths that would lead into the Soviet Union, could be presumed to have noticed this incident.

When McNamara returned to the Pentagon, he learned that another U-2, overflying Cuba for that day's photography, was 30 to 40 minutes overdue. He then went to the State Department for the scheduled 2:30 meeting. The Chiefs completed their war recommendation to the

President. Taylor would present it when the Executive Committee reconvened.

The session at the State Department reached no consensus on next steps. Discussion dwelled more and more on the plans for an air strike against Cuba.

While the advisers deliberated at State, worrisome news came in from the Navy. The *Grozny* continued to move toward the interception zone. At the State Department, Robert Kennedy argued for avoiding a clash over the *Grozny*. Rather than trigger a confrontation immediately, at sea, he thought the government should try to buy time in order to launch its prepared air attack against Cuba on Monday, October 29, or Tuesday, October 30.

The next news to arrive, as the State meeting continued, was even worse. The assumption that air defenses in Cuba would not shoot at the unarmed U.S. reconnaissance aircraft was shattered. Intelligence analysts had already noticed that Soviet officers appeared to be taking control of the command network for all Cuban air defenses. The U-2 that had flown over Cuba that morning was still overdue. As Washington frantically tried to figure out what had happened to it, the pilots returning from the low-level reconnaissance flights reported that gunners in Cuba had tried to shoot them down. The Pentagon press statement defending the legal basis of the Jupiter deployment in Turkey was now amended to add that any interference with U.S. surveillance would meet counteraction. That statement was released at about 3:30.

The Executive Committee resumed work in the Cabinet Room at 4:00, discussing a draft reply to Khrushchev.

. . .

President Kennedy: Now, this last paragraph [in the draft letter to Khrushchev], Mr. Secretary, I think we ought to say: "As I was preparing this letter, which was prepared in response to your private letter of last night, I learned of your . . . " Then I would say, " . . . this immediate crisis in Cuba" and so forth. "When we get action there, I shall certainly be ready to discuss the matters you mentioned in your public message."

You see, that's more forthcoming because we're not . . . What we are saying here is, we are rejecting his public message. We might as well—

C. Douglas Dillon: Certainly be prepared to discuss the actions that—the detailed thinking—

President Kennedy: Well, we would be prepared to discuss your [Khrushchev's] public message, the matters in your public message or the issues in your public message.

This is not going to be successful. We might as well realize *that*. That's why I am just wondering whether he's going to come back to us. And that way we will have rejected his deal, and then where are we going to be? Tomorrow he will come back and say that the United States has rejected this proposal he made.

So I think that we ought to be thinking also of saying that we are going to discuss all these matters if he'll cease work. That is the only place where we have got him.

So I think we ought to be able to say that the matter of Turkey and so on, in fact all these matters, can be discussed if he'll cease work. Otherwise, he's going to announce that we've rejected his proposal. And then where are we?

We're all right, if he would cease work and dismantle the missiles. Then we could talk for another two weeks. But until we get that . . .

Well I think we ought to put that in. Just say: "I learned of your public message attempting to connect the NATO bases and Cuba" and then say it's no good. [There is an] immediate need in the crisis. "Contact is necessary," period. "You must realize that these other matters involving NATO and the Warsaw Pact countries will require time for discussion."

Unless we want him to [*unclear*]. Unless we want him to announce that we've rejected it [a possible Turkey deal], I don't think we ought to leave it this way. I think we ought to say, if we're going to discuss this, then we're going to have a cessation of work. We're not going to get a cessation of work probably, and therefore the burden is on him.

That is our only, it seems to me, defense against the appeal of his trade. I think that our message ought to be that we're glad to discuss this and other matters but we've got to get a cessation of work.

McGeorge Bundy: And the bases [*unclear*] that are already there.

President Kennedy: And then in your public message you attempt to connect it to their missile bases in Cuba.

Llewellyn Thompson: This proposal's come down from New York.

U. Alexis Johnson: Mr. [Valerian] Zorin has been to U Thant. And one of the people who were there just came out and said that the position that Zorin had taken was that the first letter [from Khrushchev on October 26] was confidential and it was designed to reduce tension but, so far as he was concerned, the second letter [of October 27] contained the substantive proposal.

Unidentified: The second letter was the public letter.

Alexis Johnson: Yes.

President Kennedy: I think we ought to say to U Thant this afternoon that: "Can he give us any assurances, can he get any assurances from the Soviet Union that work has ceased?"

We ought to get that, it seems to me, before the end of the afternoon. Just that simple message to U Thant. He ought to call Zorin in before we discuss these other matters.

Alexis Johnson: Oh, I think that's a good idea.

Robert Kennedy: And the missiles may come, too.

President Kennedy: Why don't we send that up to U Thant right now, before we discuss these other matters which are complicated and involve other countries and which are bound to take time, and everybody will recognize take time.

. . .

Maxwell Taylor: We have some more information on the afternoon [low-level reconnaissance] flight, Mr. Secretary.

These planes took off at 15:41. [*Unclear*] were part of the afternoon flight. The planes took off at 15:41. Eight [planes] out. One developed mechanical trouble, so the pair [the affected plane and its wing plane] turned back. So six approached the Cuban coast in three flight plans. One of the flight plans was fired on, so following instructions the boys turned back, leaving four planes who presumably have completed the mission. They will be back on base at 16:58, 17:38, and 17:14. I would expect that it's around six before [*unclear*] field [*unclear*].

Dean Rusk: It indicated fired on by what?

Taylor: It did not say. Presumably low-level ack ack [antiaircraft artillery], that's the only thing could have fired.

Robert Kennedy: Seventeen hundred, what time?

Taylor: Eastern Daylight Savings. I remind you it will be at least six before we wrap this thing up and find out what they recommend, sir.

President Kennedy: This is the night we want to put on [*unclear*]. [*Unclear exchange.*]

Rusk: How many U-2s were going today?

Unidentified: Just one, I believe.

Unidentified: Just one.

Bundy: They put out the public statement yesterday. [*Unclear, referring to the statement*] They could still, perhaps, stop it. [*Unclear exchange.*]

President Kennedy: Just have it ready and then we will call up the Secretary to verify.

Roswell Gilpatric: Night flights [*unclear*]. It doesn't say that there were 12.

President Kennedy: I just think we might have one more conversation about the details of this firing on.

Gilpatric: Do you want to hold it [the proposed announcement of night surveillance flights] up, Mr. President?

President Kennedy: Yeah I think we've got to do that now, until I talk to . . . I just want to talk to the Secretary a little more about it before we put it out. He may want to do something else. [*Unclear exchange between Taylor and Rusk.*]

Rusk: [*Unclear.*] Looks like the U-2 flight into Russia [referring to U-2 that strayed into Soviet airspace near Alaska]. They will probably be making a big blast out of that in the next day or so.

The question will be whether there will be any advantage in our saying that an Alaska-based U-2 flight was engaged in routine air sampling operations in an area, assigned to an area normally 100 miles from the Soviet Union. It had an instrument failure and went off course. Efforts by ground stations and our aircraft to recall it to its course did not succeed in time to prevent it from overflying a portion of the Soviet Union. Now whether we should use—

President Kennedy: I think we are better off not to do it [reveal the accidental U.S. overflight] if we can get away with not having some leak. Because I think our problem is to maintain our credibility with Khrushchev.

.   .   .

Robert McNamara: Mr. President, may I say in relation to that, I think that if we haven't announced already, and I know we haven't, we shouldn't do it now.

One of our afternoon [low-level reconnaissance] aircraft was hit by a 37-millimeter shell. It's coming back. It's all right but it simply indicates that there's quite a change in the character of the orders given to the Cuban defenders. I don't think we ought to confuse the issue by issuing a White House—

President Kennedy: I agree. Let's let it go.

Dillon: I know that's an—

Rusk: Mr. President, here's a [draft] letter, this letter, to Mr. Khrushchev that would follow on, just the U Thant issues.

President Kennedy: [*after looking at the draft*] I think we've got two questions [for the letter to Khrushchev]. One is, do we want to have these conversations go on about Turkey and these other matters while there's a sort of standstill in Cuba. Or do we want to say that we won't talk about Turkey and these other matters until they've settled the Cuban crisis. I think these are two separate positions.

And I don't think we're going to get there. They are not going to announce that [once] they have taken a public position. Obviously, they're not going to settle the Cuban question until they get some compensation on Cuba.

That being true, I think the best position now, with him and publicly, is to say we're glad to discuss this matter [Turkey], and this whole question of verification, and all the rest once we get a positive indication that they have ceased their work in Cuba.

Otherwise, what we're really saying is: We won't discuss Turkey until they settle Cuba. And I think that he will then come back and say that the United States has refused his offer. Now I don't think that is as good a position as saying that we'd be glad to discuss his offer, if we can get a standstill in Cuba. Because that puts us in a much stronger world position because most people will think his offer is rather reasonable.

I think we ought to put our emphasis, right now, on the fact that we want an indication from him in the next 24 hours that he's going to stand still, and disarm these weapons. Then we will say that under those conditions, we'll be *glad* to discuss these matters. But I think that if we don't say that, he's going to say that we rejected his offer and, therefore, he's going to have public opinion with him. So, I think our only hope to escape from that is to say that, we should insist that, he should stand still now.

We don't think he'll do that. Therefore, we're in a much better shape to put our case on that, than rather that Turkey is irrelevant.

. . .

Alexis Johnson: The only question I would like to raise about that is that it really injects Turkey as a quid pro quo for—

Bundy: That's my worry about it.

President Kennedy: No, but negotiations . . . The point is that we are not in a position today to make a trade; that is number one. And we won't be. The trade may be made in three or four days. I don't know. We have to wait and see what the Turks say.

We don't want the Soviet Union or the United Nations to be able to say that the United States rejected it. So I think we're better off to stick on the question of a freeze [of Soviet missiles in Cuba], and *then* we'll discuss it [the Cuba-Turkey trade].

Bundy: Well, there are two different audiences here, Mr. President. There really are. And I think that if we sound as if we wanted to make this trade, to our NATO people and to all the people who are tied to us by alliance, we are in *real* trouble. I think that, we'll all join in doing this if it is the decision. But I think we should tell you that that's the universal assessment of everyone in the government that's connected with these alliance problems.

Robert Kennedy: Now what report did you get from Chip Bohlen saying that what—

Bundy: That the knockdown [of Khrushchev's public message] in this White House statement this morning was well received.

Finletter's report is in. [Ambassador to Turkey Raymond] Hare's long telegram is in.[9] They all make the same proposition, that if we appear to be trading the defense of Turkey for a threat to Cuba, we'll just have to face a radical decline in the effectiveness [of the alliance].

President Kennedy: Yes, but I should say that also, as the situation is moving there, Mac. And if we don't [accept it]—if for the next 24 or 48 hours—this trade has appeal. Now, if we reject it out of hand, and then have to take military action against Cuba, then we'll also face a decline [in the alliance].

Now, the only thing that we've got, [with] which I would think we'd be able to hold general support, would be [demanding a standstill in Cuba while keeping the door open to subsequent discussion of Turkey] . . .

Well, let's try to word it so that we don't harm anyone in NATO. But the thing that I think everybody would agree to is that while these matters, which are complicated, are discussed, there should be a cessation of work. Then I think we can hold general support for that. If they won't agree to that—the Soviet Union—then *we* retain the initiative. That's my response.

· · ·

Bundy: General [Lauris] Norstad [U.S. supreme military commander in NATO] is on the secret wire. Would you like to talk with him?

President Kennedy: That phone? Yeah, I'd like that.

See if you can get this [the message to U Thant]. Let it go.

President Kennedy then left the Cabinet Room for a telephone conversation with General Norstad over a secure line.

· · ·

With President Kennedy out of the room, the discussion subsides into a period of collective drafting work with mixed conversations going on.

· · ·

Robert Kennedy: I think that he [President Kennedy] almost said that he would be willing to discuss Turkish bases or anything that they want to discuss.

McNamara: Yeah, but the point was he wanted to appear reasonable. He didn't want to appear to turn down the proposal that some people in the world would think was a reasonable proposal. He wanted to turn it down. He wanted to defer consideration of it, but do it with a good excuse, which was that they hadn't yet given us this assurance.

Dillon: Why can't you just start with the first sentence that Dean has and then follow with the second paragraph without the *therefore* of our original statement, this morning's statement? "It is the position of the United States . . . ," and so forth. And then finish up: "If this is accomplished, we will be prepared to discuss all these other things."

Robert Kennedy: Tommy [Llewellyn Thompson] brings up the point about whether this—if he [Khrushchev] sends this kind of a telegram, a wire, or whatever to get that message across—whether it [the second, public, message] blows the whole other operation on Cuba contained in this other letter [the first, private, message] that he's sent. The idea of trying to get this whole matter . . .

Bundy: How do you mean, Tommy?

Thompson: Well, he's [Robert Kennedy's] speaking of this letter of last night.

He [Khrushchev] made this proposal that the whole problem is raised by our threat to Cuba. And we're prepared to remove that threat. This point [in the second, public letter involving Turkey], this undercuts that effort entirely.

If they're talking about this, that's . . .

Dillon: Ignoring this. It's spoiling the downstairs [*unclear*].

Bundy: If we start talking about what?

Thompson: About that we are willing to discuss this question of bases with only a freeze in Cuba.

Bundy: Yeah.

Thompson: You see, then, this other thing—

Bundy: What did Zorin say this morning?

Dillon: That the first one was for public consumption and wasn't the real Soviet position.

McNamara: To reduce tensions.

Dillon: Public relations. Totally different.

Thompson: For one or two reasons they changed their minds on this. One was that they may have picked up this [Austrian foreign minister Bruno] Kreisky thing [suggesting the trade with Turkey], and thought they could get more.

The other is Khrushchev may have been overruled.

But in either case, we have got to change that. That means we have to take this other line. If he starts this wobbly . . .

Rusk: Why don't we go back to the original idea of putting a final paragraph [suggesting other matters can be negotiated if there is a standstill in Cuba] on this letter [to Khrushchev] that we have drafted?

Unidentified: That's what I think, because—

McNamara: That's what I propose.

Rusk: Because we really ought to leave U Thant a chance to work on the original track if possible. I think that we heat up the situation a bit in Cuba. Because Khrushchev may find that he wins out again. It looks more dangerous then.

Dillon: Well, the way the situation is going in Cuba with this fellow [in the low-level reconnaissance flight] being shot at? We haven't got but one more day.

Bundy: That's right.

McNamara: That's right.

Thompson: I'd much prefer the track of this letter [to Khrushchev] in beefing up the last part of it.

Paul Nitze: The real question is whether its target is Khrushchev or whether it's the U.N.

Bundy: That's the point. It seems to me that Turkey and Cuba is all very well for us to [unclear]. Turkey and Cuba is not workable for us except in the context of our doing a violent thing. And after we've done a violent thing we, none of us, know where it will go.

The one chance of avoiding that is to impress Khrushchev and get him back where he was last night.

Alexis Johnson: We have to operate on Khrushchev's public warning using a carrot and a stick. [Unclear.] Certainly have something of a carrot. Can't we afford to put it in the paragraph?

Thompson: That's the last paragraph, in terms of an enlargement of the last paragraph [offering to discuss other matters after the missiles in Cuba have been addressed]. [Unclear exchange.]

Bundy: I'm not worried about that and the quarantine. I don't think that proves very much.

Thompson: You can beef up this last paragraph and get this in there.

Unidentified: [Unclear] can do that on his own.

Nitze: The position, there isn't any significance, except to indicate that we're prepared to start with something.

Thompson: The point of changing our whole policy for a public relations aspect is that if we have decided definitely that we are going in [to attack Cuba], then this might be [unclear] . . . Otherwise, it is—

Rusk: What about *this?* Look at the last paragraph of the proposed letter [to Khrushchev] that we are working on:

> As I was preparing this letter, I read over your important broadcast message of this morning. That message raises problems affecting many countries and complicated issues unrelated to the existing tensions imposed by Soviet intentions to have the bases in Cuba. They can be fully resolved only in relation to NATO defense arrangements as well as the strength and deployment of Soviet forces. The United States will be glad to discuss these matters with you and others— after consultation with other interested governments.

Vice President Johnson: I don't see why you don't take the last paragraph—after the first sentence, the last paragraph here on page three— just add the last paragraph of your statement this morning. That's what you're ready to say:

> As I was preparing this letter, which was prepared in response to your letter of last night, I learned of your public message attempting to connect NATO with bases in Cuba. As this proposal affects the security of nations outside this hemisphere, the United States and its allies have long taken the lead to see that these problems are discussed on both sides. These efforts can continue as soon as the present Soviet [*unclear*] threat has ended.

There it is! That's a proposal to them saying we can and will just as soon as you get rid of these bases and make them—

Bundy: Well, I see no reason why a private message to the Chairman shouldn't be a touch more forthcoming. I think that is the . . . Again, I don't see any reason why we can't say: "We understand your sensitivity on this matter but we can't get at this until we get past the Cuba problem."

Robert Kennedy: Well, I think here what Bob says is what concerns the President. The fact that this [public Soviet offer], to the average person, is very reasonable, and we just turned it down. And people are going to start thinking about the two things: Turkey and Cuba. And we just turned it down. And suddenly we drop the bomb on Cuba.

Vice President Johnson: Well, we didn't turn it down. This says we'll continue just as soon as you stop work.

Theodore Sorensen: Why don't we see if we can agree on this language for the secretary-general's appeal and maybe that will give us some idea of the language [for the letter to Khrushchev].

President Kennedy returns to the Cabinet Room. He is accompanied by General Lyman Lemnitzer, who has just completed his term as Chairman of the JCS (replaced by Taylor) and is waiting to take General Lauris Norstad's place at NATO.

Robert Kennedy: We really cut it up while you've been out of the room. Let's look at it.

President Kennedy: Is this the new draft?

Lyman Lemnitzer: I want to read it.

President Kennedy begins looking at some pages, with Robert Kennedy and McNamara pointing out material.

Lemnitzer: If anybody has one, I want to read it.

Dillon: This is the latest.

Unidentified: The latest. [*Brief, unclear exchanges.*]

Bundy: The real question, of course, is—turns, comes back to the action in question. The justification for this message is that we expect it to be turned down, and expect to be acting [against Cuba] tomorrow or the next day. That's what it's for, and it's not good unless that's what happens.

Rusk: I think we've got to make a judgment here as to whether—Tommy and everybody else—whether the Soviet Union, in putting this further demand forward this morning, is putting it forward as a real sticking point up to the point of shooting, or whether it is an attempt at the last minute to try to get something more. After they had indicated last night that they would settle for something less.

· · ·

Dillon: Is this letter to Khrushchev going to be public, Bobby?

Rusk: It's likely to become public.

Dillon: It shouldn't be, I mean—

Rusk: Because U Thant is likely to make that letter of last night public, along with our reply.

Unidentified: He should make it public. We shouldn't make it public.

Dillon: Well, what I'm thinking of is some public longer letter from us than this thing, that would counteract the Soviet propaganda in the press about Turkey. [*Unclear, mixed conversation, partly about completing and sending out the message to U Thant, lasts for about two minutes.*]

Bundy: What's our military plan?

McNamara: Well, the military plan now is very clear. A limited strike is out. We can't go on a limited strike without the reconnaissance aircraft.

So the military plan now is basically invasion, because we've set a large strike to lead to invasion. We might try a large strike without starting the invasion, or without any plan to get started with the invasion at the time of the strike, because we can't carry it out anyhow for a period of x days. So we have time to cancel invasion plans. But they should be put on. We should start the strike; call up the reserves. We need the air units for the invasion in any case. We need the army units in reserve and our strategic reserve in relation to actions elsewhere in the world.

But we shouldn't start this until we do two things: One, until we minimize the Soviet response against NATO, and there is a possible way to do that. And two, until we know how we are going to respond to a Soviet response against NATO.

I would suggest that to minimize the Soviet response against NATO following a U.S. attack on Cuba, we get those Jupiters out of Turkey before the Cuban attack. I say out of Turkey; I mean inoperable. And let the Soviets know that before the Cuban attack.

Now, on that basis, I don't believe the Soviets would strike Turkey. They might take other actions but I don't think they'd take that action.

Then we have—

Rusk: They might then take some other action in Berlin.

McNamara: They might.

Thompson: Isn't it possible that this . . . You know, the fact that one [low-level reconnaissance] plane was fired on and the others weren't. This doesn't indicate necessarily that they're generally going to fire on our reconnaissance.

Bundy: Well I would say it gets awfully close, Bob.

McNamara: I am not prepared at this moment to recommend air attacks on Cuba. I'm just saying that I think we must now begin to look at it more realistically than we have before.

Dillon: You might say, "with these Jupiters" just to indicate the fact that we have no intention of doing anything else—that we have rendered these Jupiters inoperable.

McNamara: Well, I could do this in only by replacing—

Dillon: Temporarily inoperable.

McNamara: Well I could do it only by replacing with Polaris.

Thompson: Well you can't replace them by Polaris.

McNamara: Oh yes, Tommy. Oh yes we can.

Thompson: In 24 hours?

McNamara: Well, we can say . . . we've done it. We say we've got a Polaris in the Mediterranean we're deploying immediately to key places off the coast of Turkey at x time.

Unidentified: You can get air to cover the targets.

Thompson: There is a dilemma in that formula, and that is that if you advertise the Polaris publicly as the substitute, then from the point of view of the Soviet Union they have achieved nothing by getting rid of the Jupiters.

McNamara: Well they haven't achieved anything, but they surely have less of a basis for striking Turkey.

Taylor: That's right. You minimize Turkey as a target.

McNamara: Well, I would hate . . .What I would try to avoid, if I could, is an immediate Soviet military response to a U.S. attack on Cuba.

Thompson: Well we have no better reply.

McNamara: That's right.

.   .   .

The message to U Thant was passed along to be phoned to Stevenson, in New York. The Executive Committee then turned to alliance issues, and President Kennedy's telephone conversation with General Norstad.

President Kennedy: I just talked to General Norstad. He thinks that we ought to have a meeting of the NATO Council tomorrow morning to present this to them so that they all have a piece of it. Otherwise, no matter what we do . . . If we don't take it [the Cuba-Turkey deal], we're going to be blamed. If we do take it, we'll be blamed. Very right.

Bundy: I talked to Finletter and asked him to present it individually [to each country's representative at NATO]. Would you prefer to have a meeting?

President Kennedy: Yes, I think we ought to have one. And I think the United States's position ought to be that here it is [the proposed deal, and the consequences of rejecting it]. And we ought to have the . . . If we don't take up what the prospects will be, as well as what we do . . . Otherwise it's too easy to say: "Well, let's not take it then."

We ought get up a message to Finletter of instructions, and we ought to call for a meeting at nine or ten in the morning.

Robert Kennedy: You don't think—It blows the possibility of this other one, of course, doesn't it?

President Kennedy: What?

Robert Kennedy: It blows the possibility in your first letter.

President Kennedy: Of what?

Robert Kennedy: Of getting an acceptance of the proposal that goes up in your letter now, which is that Paris [NATO headquarters] has nothing to do with that [Cuba]. I think that if they understand you have a meeting in NATO on this—

Bundy: That's the disadvantage of the [North Atlantic] council meeting.

Rusk: Why just a report . . . ? It doesn't have to be known that that is the only purpose of the discussion. The whole situation—

Robert Kennedy: They are going to know that.

Dillon: Well it's perfectly obvious that, since they [the Soviets] made the suggestion about Turkey, the NATO Council would be interested in meeting about that.

Bundy: Yeah. I don't think that there is any pain in the meeting. Why don't we get the meeting called?

President Kennedy: The advantage of the meeting is that, if we reject it [Khrushchev's Cuba-Turkey deal], they participate in it. And, if we accept it, they participate in it.

Bundy: [*quietly to the side, while the President is talking*] The Department [of State] should call Finletter to call a meeting.

President Kennedy: I think he ought to . . .

Robert Kennedy: But what if they await instructions. . . . The other possibility is that, if you wait 24 hours and see if they accept this other thing [Kennedy's draft reply that would promise not to invade Cuba]. But they won't—they're not going to accept it. Yeah.

President Kennedy: You mean the word *ceasing?*

Robert Kennedy: Well no. The proposal—

Bundy: The trade of last night.

Robert Kennedy: The trade, you know, the letter that he offered [the private letter of October 26] which we accepted today. We wrote him this [draft] letter, that you've approved, where we say that we won't invade Cuba in return for . . .

George Ball: You see, the way the record would stand, Mr. President, is this.

That we got out a blast this morning in which we said: "Look, we don't think that this [Turkish issue] is really relevant." Then you send a query [to U Thant] this afternoon as to whether they're going to stop work.

Then, if we send a letter this afternoon, along the lines of the letter we were proposing, which ties it back to his message of last night . . . If this [public offer of a Cuba-Turkey deal] was simply a kind of fishing expedition in Moscow to see if they could get beyond what he'd put in his last night's letter, they may get the impression that they can't do it [get more], in which case we—

Bundy: That's what I think.

Ball: —we might get something. Otherwise we can then go forward along the other track with the, you know, take the [military action] . . .

Thompson: If you have a NATO meeting, I gather from some word we've had from Italy, the Italians are likely to come up with a proposal to withdraw the bases there, the missiles there. I don't know if we [the others members of the ExCom] ever got that message, did we?

Nitze: We have a letter—a telegram—from [ambassador to Italy] Freddy Reinhardt saying that the Italians really don't care at all about . . .

Thompson: There was supposed to be a message coming through from [unclear].

Nitze: Oh I don't know.

Rusk: Well now, in view of that message just gone up to U Thant, [how do] we wind up this letter [to Khrushchev]? [reading] "As I was preparing this letter, I learned of your broadcast message today. That message raises problems affecting many countries and complicated issues not related to Cuba or the Western Hemisphere. The United States would be glad to discuss these matters with you and the other governments concerned. The immediate crisis is in Cuba and it is there that very prompt action is necessary. With that behind us, we can make progress on other, wider issues."

We still don't have any other suggestions.

President Kennedy: Well isn't that really rejecting their proposal of this morning?

Bundy: I don't think so. It is rejecting—

Rusk: I wouldn't think so.

Dillon: It is rejecting the immediate tie-in [to Turkey], but we've got to do that.

President Kennedy: Well, don't we just have to ask? We're not rejecting the tie-in. If we're going to reject it, I think we ought to have all of NATO rejecting it.

What we want to insist on now is a cessation of work et cetera while we *discuss* it. Then we may reject it, but NATO ought to reject it because I think the reprisal is going to be on all NATO. And I don't want them around saying, well . . . that's the problem.

It's just a question of timing, isn't it?

Ball: I would suggest this, Mr. President. If you have a NATO Council meeting in the morning, I think you are going to get a flat rejection of this [deal involving Turkey], which then ties our hands. I mean, then you can't go forward very easily in the face of this, because the NATO ambassadors [to the U.N.] met this afternoon in New York, and they took a *very* strong line against any discussion of this.[10]

President Kennedy: I don't think the alternative has been explained to them. You see, they just think it's sort of a continuation of the quarantine. They don't have any notion that we're about to do something [militarily]. And that's going to be on them. You see that hasn't been explained to NATO, and I'd like to have them get into *that* before they reject it [the Cuba-Turkey trade].

Dillon: Tomorrow morning. That's what . . . If you have the [North Atlantic] council meeting, you'll probably get a strong reaction from a great many of the members of NATO against our taking any action in Cuba. Doubtless they'd say: "Don't trade." But they'd also say: "Don't do anything in Cuba."

Robert Kennedy: Exactly. [*Unclear interjection.*]

McNamara: Mr. President, I wonder if we should not take certain actions with respect to the Jupiters in Turkey and Italy before we act in Cuba. And if we decided to take that action with respect to the Jupiters in Turkey and Italy before we acted in Cuba, then we could tell NATO that, at the time we talked to them about this proposal from Khrushchev and our response to it.

If we act in Cuba, the only way we can act now is with a full attack. I don't think we can take any of these limited attacks when they are shooting at our reconnaissance aircraft because we would—we would not dare go in with the kind of limited attack that we've been thinking about the last 24 hours without taking out their SAM sites.

The moment we take out the SAM sites and the MiG airfields we're up to the 500-sortie program. If we send 500 sorties in against Cuba we must be prepared to follow up with an invasion in about seven days. If we start out on that kind of a program, it seems to me that the Soviets are very likely to feel forced to reply with military action someplace, particularly if these missiles—Jupiter missiles—are still in Turkey.

We might be able to either shift the area in which they would apply their military force, or give them no excuse to apply military force, by taking out the Turkish Jupiters and the Italian Jupiters before we attack Cuba.

One way to take them out would be to simply develop a program with bilateral negotiations between Turkey, Italy, and the U.S. saying that we are today defusing the Jupiters in those two countries and replacing them with Polaris submarines stationed off the shores of those nations to carry the same targets the Jupiters were directed to, in order to reduce the risk to those two nations but maintain the full defense of NATO.

Now, if we were willing to undertake . . . In the first place, I think that kind of action is desirable prior to an invasion of Cuba. In the second place, if we are willing to decide to do that, we're in a much better position to present this whole thing to NATO.

Nitze: What would be the reaction if the Soviet Union was to reply that they were going to maintain three atomic [missile] submarines off the United States coast?

McNamara: We would say they're doing it anyway. We have already detected three submarines off the U.S. coast in the last 48 hours. Now they, as far as we know, they don't carry missiles, but that's just happenstance.

President Kennedy: The Turks won't take them [the Jupiters] out, will they? Isn't that . . . ?

McNamara: I think, I think we could. In the first place, we can tell the Turks—

President Kennedy: Well, I don't . . . except if we took them out, we'd get the trade the Russians have offered us. If we take them out, they'll take them out [of Cuba].

McNamara: Well, I think we have to say to the Turks we're going to cover the targets with Polaris missiles.

President Kennedy: Yes, but I think, if we're going to take them out of Turkey, they say they will take them out of—

Bundy: It's one thing to stand them down, Mr. President, in political terms. It is one thing to stand them down as a favor to the Turks, while we hit Cuba, and it's quite another thing to trade them out.

McNamara: But what we could do is unilaterally, unilaterally . . . Bilaterally with Turkey, we would agree to defuse them [the Jupiters] and replace them with Polaris.

Then we would go back to the Soviet Union and say: "Now, [you said] the threat is there. The threat is gone. You don't have to worry about that. We're going back to your letter of last night, and this is the proposal we make. We agree not to invade. You agree to take your—"

Bundy: But the incentive to them is to go back to Italy, and . . .

McNamara: But Turkey is gone.

Bundy: It could lead the Soviet Union to just come back to the next problem.

Dillon: Then they say Italy, and then they say England.

President Kennedy: I just said Turkey. I just said Turkey.

Robert Kennedy: You made an offer, up there now, and you also asked U Thant to find an answer to this. Now if U Thant could come back and say, number one, that they are going to continue the work on the bases, in which case, I suppose we have to move in some way.

Or they are going to say that they are going to discontinue the work on the bases. If they say they are going to discontinue the work on the bases, they can either accept our proposal, or they can reject the proposal and say we still want Turkey for Cuba.

If they reject the proposal and say they want Turkey for Cuba but they are going to discontinue the work on the bases, then, I would think, would be the time to bring NATO in and say: "This is the proposal, do you want to consider it?" We haven't lost anything and they have discontinued the work on the bases.

If they say they are going to continue the work on the bases, I think then we've got to decide whether, if they have said by tomorrow morning that they are going to continue the work on the bases, whether we are going to have a military strike.

But I don't think if you have a meeting of NATO tomorrow morning, I don't see that that is going to—I think it's going to shoot this other possibility which U Thant has suggested [the previous day, October 26], of going forward with this letter [from Khrushchev the previous night], and see if we can trade the noninvasion of Cuba for this, and I think we are keeping the pressure on. We don't look like we're weakening on the whole Turkey complex. I mean I don't see that you are losing anything by not having the meeting tomorrow morning. Except that perhaps, then I think you are risking something because some of the allies are going to say that you're out of your mind, or . . .

Alexis Johnson: I would prefer to let Finletter find out for a day what people think.

President Kennedy: It's going to be . . . You see, they haven't had the alternatives presented to them. They'll say: "Well God! We don't want to trade them off." They don't realize that in two or three days we may have a military strike which would bring perhaps the seizure of Berlin or a strike on Turkey. And then they'll say: "My God! We should have taken it."

So when the time, the crucial time, comes, obviously we want it [the NATO meeting]. Now the question is, whether it's tomorrow morning [October 28] or Monday morning [October 29].

McNamara: I think in part it's going to be related to the strike. If tomorrow we don't have a favorable answer from U Thant or Khrushchev to this message that's going out now, is it important to strike tomorrow? Or do we have some more time?

If we have some more time, then you can still have the NATO meeting. It would seem to me the NATO meeting ought to be held before the strike. If it's necessary to strike tomorrow, there ought to be a NATO meeting tomorrow morning.

Robert Kennedy: Can I just say something? What if he says: "We're going to discontinue the work on the bases, now we are going to make the missiles inoperative, and we'll work out with you United Nations provisions." That could take three weeks to just work that problem out, couldn't it? And then what are we doing for the . . . ?

McNamara: If he said he was going to discontinue work on the bases and he's willing to make them inoperable, we carry on surveillance.

Robert Kennedy: And we would continue the—

McNamara: The blockade.

Robert Kennedy: —the blockade, until the United Nations observers get in.

McNamara: That's a good course of action.

Robert Kennedy: We're not in bad shape.

McNamara: No, that's an *excellent* course of action, which I don't believe he is going to accept. The probability is, he won't *say* he'll stop work on the bases. And we're faced with a decision tomorrow of what to do.

Robert Kennedy: Yeah, but of course we're, before the world, we're in much better shape.

Thompson: Not only that but it seems to me we ought to surface all of this correspondence with him, including this [private] letter [of October 26]. He broke his [new] proposal [to the press] before you got it. And I'd do the same thing [to his previous proposal]. Then you've got the rest of the world's focus back on Cuba and Latin America and the fact that we're prepared not to invade. And this makes it, I think, much tougher for him to go ahead and—

Bundy: That's right.

Unidentified: Good point.

President Kennedy: What I'm concerned about is that NATO . . . Norstad said the BBC radio or TV to say that there's no connection [between Cuba and Turkey]. There's going to be a lot of tough talk in New York saying that they [the NATO ambassadors at the U.N.] all said it. And they are going to say [at NATO headquarters] in Paris, that there is no connection. They don't realize that's what's coming up.

Rusk: Mr. President, if NATO seems solid on this, this has a chance of shaking Khrushchev off this point.

Ball: Now suppose that we give him [Khrushchev] a letter which is addressed to his letter of yesterday, and ask U Thant to release them both. He's the fellow who releases it. Then he releases correspondence which consists really of an offer from Khrushchev, and we come back and say—

Bundy: "Why thank you, yes."

Ball: We'll practically say: "Thank you, yes." And it doesn't mention Turkey. Then it seems to me that—

Bundy: He is in a difficult position.

Taylor: How much will Finletter be allowed to tell the NATO people what [*unclear*] in view of the alternatives? So they can see the point of view you referred to, Mr. President.

President Kennedy: Well, I think that he would probably just say that: "The work is going on. If you are not going to take these, if you are not interested in this deal, then I think we are going to have to do something." I don't think that he has to say what it is, but the escalation is going to go on and we think this is very likely that there will be some reply against, possibly, Turkey and, possibly, against Berlin. They should be aware of that.

What we don't want is for the cheap turndown by them without realizing that the turndown puts us in the position of then having to do something. What we are going to be in there faced with is, because we wouldn't take the missiles out of Turkey, we are either going to have to invade or have a massive strike on Cuba which may lose *Berlin*. That's what concerns me.

Rusk: Mr. President, there's one other variation here, that Mr. Foster has been giving some thought to, is that we say the missiles in Cuba and the missiles in Turkey be turned over to the U.N. for destruction.[11] And that the nuclear defense of NATO, including Turkey, is provided by other means. An actual disarmament step. Turn them over for destruction, on both sides.

Thompson: The Soviets don't want to let anybody get at their missiles and see what their technology is.

President Kennedy: They'll have to take them out.

I think the real problem is what we do with the Turks first.

Rusk: Yeah.

President Kennedy: If we follow Secretary McNamara, what we are going to do is say to the Turks, which they are bound to think is under Soviet pressure: "We want to get your missiles out of there."

McNamara: Well what I would say to the Turks: "Look here, we're going to have to invade Cuba. You are in mortal danger. We want to reduce your danger while at the same time maintaining your defense. We propose that you defuse those missiles tonight. We're putting Polaris submarines along your coast. We'll cover the same targets that your Jupiter missiles did, and we'll announce this to the world before we invade Cuba and thereby would reduce the pressure on the Soviet Union to attack you, Turkey, as a response to our invasion of Cuba." This is what I would say to the Turks.

Robert Kennedy: All right, now. And they say: "What if the Soviet Union attacks us anyway? Will you use the missiles on the nuclear submarines?" they're going to ask us.

McNamara: Before we attack Cuba I think we've got to decide how we'll respond to Soviet military pressure on NATO. And I'm not prepared to answer that question.

President Kennedy: Aren't the Soviets going to take their missiles out if we take them out of Turkey? If they don't, they're in an impossible position.

McNamara: Well, I don't know. What we'd do would be to work this out with Turkey first, then we announce it to the world, and then say to the Soviets: "Now we accept, well yeah, now we accept your deal of last night [only trading for a pledge not to invade Cuba]."

President Kennedy: The question is whether we can get the Turks to do it.

McNamara: Well, I think it would be important to them.

Taylor: You're deeply in trouble with NATO by [taking] this bilateral kind of approach.

McNamara: Well, the other course of action is not to have the bilateral course of approach, to invade Cuba, and have Turkey . . .

Bundy: Well we haven't tried the enlargement of the blockade. We haven't even thought about it for some hours, and it's been on my mind a good deal. I think POL [petroleum, oil, and lubricants] we still have to—

Rusk: If we get a negative answer to this message that has just gone up to U Thant, I think we really ought to consider whether in a fashion as low key as is possible—although there'll be a tremendous flap about it—in order to give you the necessary authority to call up additional units beyond those provided by the 150,000 legislation, you'd declare a state of national emergency.

McNamara: I'd call a requisition of 29 ships.

Rusk: I think some mobilization measures, not only here but in other NATO countries, might be very timely here in shaking Khrushchev off this position at this point. His change in position in a matter of hours here means either that . . .

Bundy: Ted [Sorensen] points out that his message of last night is not categorical about taking the missiles out. It says the specialists would go out.

Unidentified: That's right.

Thompson: It's a very loose, loose term.

President Kennedy: This morning's [public message from Khrushchev] is more precise, isn't it?

Unidentified: Yeah.

Unidentified: That was not in exchange for a hard . . . That was a different bargaining position.

Thompson: Mr. President, if we go on the basis of a trade, which I gather is somewhat in your mind, we end up, it seems to me, with the Soviets still in Cuba though, with planes and technicians and so on, even though the missiles are out. And that would surely be unacceptable and put you in a worse position.

President Kennedy: Yeah, but our technicians and planes and guarantees would still exist for Turkey. I'm just thinking about what we're going to have to do in a day or so, which is 500 sorties, and seven days, and possibly an invasion, all because we wouldn't take missiles out of Turkey.

We all know how quickly everybody's courage goes when the blood starts to flow, and that's what is going to happen to NATO. When they start these things and they grab Berlin, everybody's going to say: "Well, that was a pretty good proposition."

Let's not kid ourselves that we've got . . . That's the difficulty. Today it sounds great to reject it, but it's not going to, after we do something.

Nitze: I think there are alternatives. One of them is to plan that we're going to make this 500 sorties which I think is going to result in an attack by them someplace, even if you do this about Turkey. In someplace or other. The other alternative is to make the blockade total [including POL and everything else], and live with the missiles. They're not going to let you conduct reconnaissance over them. You're going to have planes that are shot down. [*Unclear*], same as the 500 attack.

Unclear exchange; McNamara says something about "every hour on the hour." Someone whispers something to President Kennedy about the call that was placed to Adlai Stevenson at the United Nations.

President Kennedy: I think we're in pretty good shape [at the U.N.] with this morning's message [the White House statement] about the work ceasing. So I think, if he feels that strongly, we better . . .

Does he mind our sending the message [to U Thant]?

Bundy: No, he thought the message is good. He says it's a yes. But he said that this is what U Thant's been trying to do.

President Kennedy: Well, what I'm concerned [about] is that the NATO groups will all take a hard position on this before they've understood what our . . . They've met already in New York. They're going to be talking in Paris. And the word's going to be coming out that this is unacceptable. Pretty soon, before they've had a chance to realize that the—

Nitze: Yesterday, I had a meeting with the Four and brought them right up to the point of seeing how serious this was, and I think Dean talked to them about the alternatives they face.[12] If a message was to go to NATO, to Finletter, giving him the same information so that he could use it to [*unclear*], then it would, I think—

President Kennedy: Do you think that we ought to call the meeting if we have it, or Stikker?[13]

Unidentified: Stikker's absent.

Unidentified: He's in the hospital.

Bundy: No, Finletter can get the meeting called. His own advice is against having them in a group, but he may not be as shrewd as Norstad about it.

Taylor: Mac, would you say that his advice would be to get a decision, or to paint the picture?

Bundy: We don't know.

President Kennedy: Norstad just feels that no matter what we do, it's going to be . . . We've got to have NATO have a hand on this thing, or otherwise we'll find no matter [what], if we take no action or if we take action, they're all going to be saying we should have done the reverse. And we've got to get them in on some of this.

Now, the question really is—two questions: First, whether we go immediately to the Turks and see if we can work out some, see if they are receptive to the kind of deal which the Secretary [McNamara] talked about. If they are not receptive, then we ought to go to the general NATO meeting because the NATO meeting may put enough pressure on them.

I just tell you, I think we're better off to get those missiles out of Turkey and out of Cuba. Because I think the way of getting them out of Turkey and out of Cuba is going to be very, very difficult and very bloody, in one place or another.

Nitze: I'm sure that the Turks will not take them out, will not agree to take them out, except under NATO pressure.

Dillon: I don't see any point in talking to the Turks in the White House. I think you have to do it through NATO.

Bundy: Well, I'm not sure. Let's speculate with this, Mr. President. If you have that conviction, and you are yourself sure that this is the way we want . . . the best way out, then I would say that an immediate personal telegram of acceptance [of Khrushchev's public offer] was the best thing to do.

President Kennedy: Well, I don't think we accept it. Because I think then . . . What I think we have to do is get the Turks to agree. Accepting it over their opposition and over NATO opposition, I think *would* be . . .

I'd rather go the total blockade route, which is a lesser step than the military action. What I'd like to do is have the Turks and NATO equally feel that this is the wise move.

Sorensen: I wonder, Mr. President, inasmuch as your statement this morning does give some answer to the public statement of the Soviets, whether we can't defer this for 24 or 48 hours while we try the private letter route in answer to his private letter of last night. There's always a chance that he will still accept that.

The problems will be deferred [if we go ahead with the planned NATO consultation]. We meanwhile won't have broken up NATO over something that never would have come to NATO.

.   .   .

President Kennedy: [*impatiently*] The point of the matter is Khrushchev is going to come back and refer to his thing this morning on Turkey. And then we're going to be screwing around for another 48 hours.

I think what we've got to do is say that we've got to make the key of this letter the cessation of work. That we're *all* in agreement on. There's no *question* about that.

Then the question is whether Turkey's in or just Cuba. Otherwise he'll come back and say, "Well, we're glad to settle the Cuban matter. What is your opinion of our proposal about Turkey." So then we're on to Monday afternoon, and the work goes on, and we haven't had a chance to specifically get his good faith on the cessation of work. We haven't got an answer to *that* question. So I think that we ought to make *that* the key question—the cessation of work. Then if we get the cessation of work, we can settle the Cuban question and we can do other things. Otherwise he can hang us up for three days while he goes on with the work.

Dillon: For three weeks.

.   .   .

President Kennedy: Well, now if, number 1, you'd [Khrushchev] undertake immediately to cease work on offensive missile bases in Cuba and promptly to render inoperable all weapons system in Cuba and permit U.N. verification of this action. That would be number 1.

McNamara: Right.

President Kennedy: Then we would get into discussion of all these matters.

McNamara: Right.

Bundy: But I think that that ought to just be made as a separate matter in the letter.

Sorensen: I just raise the question to make sure that we do insist on U.N. verification, because I understand from the Defense Department that we could verify it by ourselves, and even, they say . . .

President Kennedy: If we can't let the U.N. in?

Sorensen: Yeah.

Robert Kennedy: Well, now, can you actually? If they put them under trees and what we were discussing a week ago, or ten days . . . ?

Ball: Well then we'd know that the work has stopped . . . [*Unclear exchange.*]

Nitze: The key here is whether they shoot at our reconnaissance planes.

Robert Kennedy: Well can't they just stick them under the trees, [*unclear*] on another base?

Unidentified: If the Cubans would agree not to interfere with reconnaissance.

Unidentified: He said "under international verification" this morning. I think we'd better stick with that.

. . .

President Kennedy: It seems to me what we ought to . . . To be reasonable, we're not going to get these weapons out of Cuba, probably, anyway—but I mean, by negotiation. We're going to have to take our weapons out of Turkey. I don't think there's any doubt he's not going to—now that he made that public.

Tommy, he's not going to take them out of Cuba if we . . . ?

Thompson: I don't agree, Mr. President. I think there's still a chance that we can get this line going.

President Kennedy: That he'll back down?

Thompson: Well, because he's already got this other proposal which he put forward [to remove the missiles for a promise not to invade Cuba].

President Kennedy: Yeah, but now this other public one, it seems to me, has become their public position. Isn't it?

Thompson: This is maybe just pressure on us. I mean, to accept the other. I mean so far he's [*unclear, others interjecting*] to see if we've accepted this noninvasion of Cuba.

John McCone: The important thing for Khrushchev, it seems to me, is to be able to say: "I saved Cuba. I stopped an invasion."

And he can get away with this if he wants to, and he's had a go at this Turkish thing, and that we'll discuss later. And then, in that discussion, he will probably take . . .

President Kennedy: All right, what about, at the end, if we use this letter and say: "It would be a grave risk to peace. I urge that you join us in a rapid settlement of the Cuban crisis as your letter starts to suggest, and then we can go to [*unclear*] which are not insoluble. And then say:

"The first ingredient, let me emphasize, for any solution is a cessation of the work and the inoperability of the missiles under reasonable standards." I mean I want to just come back to that. Otherwise time ticks away on us. [*Unclear.*]

Sorensen: In other words, Mr. President, your position is that once he meets this condition of the halting work and the inoperability, you're then prepared to go ahead on either the specific Cuban track or what we call a general detente track?

President Kennedy: Yeah, now it all comes down . . . I think it's a substantive question because it really depends on whether we believe that we can get a deal on just the Cuban [aspect], or whether we have to agree to his position of tying [Cuba to Turkey]. Tommy doesn't think we do. I think that, having made it public, how can he take these missiles out of Cuba if we just do nothing about Turkey?

Bundy: You give him something else.

Thompson: Why give him something else on the broader thing?

Ball: And the promise that when all this is over there can be a larger, larger discussion.

President Kennedy: He's going to want to have that spelled out a little.

Thompson: His position, even in this public statement, is this is all started by our threat to Cuba. Now he's [able to say he] removed that threat.

Robert Kennedy: He must be a little shaken up, or he wouldn't have sent the message to you in the first place.

President Kennedy: Well, that's last night. But this—

Robert Kennedy: Yeah, but I mean—so that you can—it's certainly conceivable that you could get him back to that. I don't think we should abandon it.

· · ·

President Kennedy: [The current draft pledges no invasion] "upon removal of the weapons in Cuba and peace in the Caribbean" Can't we say that, without going into whether we guarantee Cuba . . . ?

Rusk: They're going to be worried about that, because you're not dealing precisely here with an agreement. We're simply talking about a concrete agenda of peace.

Unidentified: Yes.

President Kennedy: We don't want to put it out until we know whether there's any chance of acceptance. There's going to be a hell of a fight about that [publicly pledging not to invade Cuba]. I don't mind taking it on if we're going to get somewhere. I don't want to take on the fight if we're not going to get . . . He'll just say "assurances of peace."

· · ·

There followed a period of drafting work on the letter to Khrushchev.

Robert Kennedy: But that's not—I think you change that in there. Send this letter and say you're accepting his offer [in his private letter of October 26]. He's *made* an offer and you're in fact *accepting* it. And you state ...

I think that [other draft] letter sounds slightly defensive about the fact. "God, don't bring in Turkey now; we want to settle [Cuba]." I don't know whether it adds anything. And I think this little letter ... He made an offer last night. This letter [the Washington draft] accepts the offer.

The group then resumed work on the draft letter, comparing a Washington draft with a draft suggested from New York by Adlai Stevenson.

. . .

Robert Kennedy: Why do we bother you with it, Mr. President? Why don't you let us work this out?

President Kennedy: I think we ought to move. There's no question of bothering me. I just think we're going to have to decide which letter we send.

Robert Kennedy: Why don't we try to work it out for you without you being there to pick it apart. [*Prolonged laughter.*]

President Kennedy: And then you're going to have to worry about old Adlai, so you might as well work it out with him. [*Louder laughter.*]

Sorensen: Actually, I think Bobby's formula is a good one. It doesn't sound like an ultimatum if we say: "And we are accepting your offer of your letter last night. And therefore there's no need to talk about the these other things." [*Unclear*] your second letter.

Unidentified: What did he say?

Rusk: [*reading*]

I think the mutual explanations in which you and I have been engaged in the past few days, and the discussion in New York, have gone far enough to set forth a concrete agenda for peace, depending upon the removal of the weapons in Cuba and assurance of peace in the Caribbean. I am reading your letter to mean that this is acceptable.

President Kennedy: Your [Khrushchev's] letter of October 26th?

Rusk: "I read your letter of October 26th to mean that this will be acceptable."

Bundy: That's unacceptable.

Rusk: What is? [*Unclear exchange.*]

Unidentified: [*reading from the Washington draft*] "The elements of the proposal which you have put forth seem to me to be as follows."

Unidentified: What does that mean? [*Unclear exchange.*]

Robert Kennedy: Yeah. I think we've got to list all the things which we can accept.

Unidentified: "These are, it seems to me, to be as follows." And write them down.

President Kennedy: As I say, they're not going to . . . he's not going to now [agree just to the terms of his October 26 letter]—Tommy isn't so sure. But anyway, we can try this thing. But he's going to come back, I'm certain.

But the only thing is, I don't want him to. . . . That's why we've got to end with saying, whatever we're going to do, that we've got to get a cessation of work.

Bundy: That's right, Mr. President. But I think that Bobby's notion of a concrete acceptance on our part of how we read last night's telegram is very important.

Taylor: Mr. President—

President Kennedy: In other words, you want to . . . you're suggesting we say: "We accept your proposal of last night."

Robert Kennedy: Spell it out and accept it, and then say: "Now you've made—I just read the last paragraph of the other letter"—however we phrase it.

Taylor: Mr. President, the Chiefs have been in session during the afternoon on studying the same issues we have over here. The recommendation they give is as follows:

That the big [air] strike, that is Oplan [Operations Plan] 312, be executed no later than Monday morning, the 29th, unless there is irrefutable evidence in the meantime that offensive weapons are being dismantled and rendered inoperable.

That the execution of this strike plan be followed by the execution of 316, the invasion plan, seven days later.

Robert Kennedy: Well, I'm surprised. [*Loud laughter.*]

President Kennedy: Well, that's where we need to go. But let's get this letter [to Khrushchev]—

Taylor: I think the Monday morning date now is just something to think about. It does look now, from a military point of view . . .

President Kennedy: What are the reasons why?

Robert Kennedy: Can you find out about that?

Taylor: They just feel that the longer we wait now . . .

President Kennedy: I know, OK. But there's no . . . ? Right. OK.

Dillon: Well, also, we're getting shot at as we go in for our surveillance. The Cubans . . . we're not going to talk about it, we're just . . .

President Kennedy: [*aside, probably to Rusk*] Can you get Adlai [Stevenson] on the phone? Let's get this letter [*unclear*]. [*then louder*] Bobby, you want to go out now and get this letter set with Adlai?

[*louder still*] Now the next question is the Turkish one and NATO. We've got Secretary McNamara's proposal and . . . Did we ever send that message to [ambassador to Turkey Raymond] Hare, Mac, that you and I talked . . . ?

Bundy: No, we have a long message in from Hare, which arrived this afternoon, in which he responds to the message sent to him, on Wednesday, at great length.[14] He concludes that he'll do his damnedest, but it's very difficult, which is in essence what he—the way it comes out.

President Kennedy: Well, now we have the question of a choice between the bilateral arrangements with Turkey—in which we more or less do it [McNamara's proposal]. Or, whether we go through NATO and let NATO put the pressure on, and also explain to the Turks what's going to happen to them if it doesn't—if they end up slowing things down.

Dillon: All of this is going to take an awful lot more time than Monday morning.

Bundy: Yeah, yeah.

McNamara: There is a way to shorten it. If you're going to deal directly with the Turks, the President simply sends a message to the prime minister and says: "This is the problem, and this is the way I think it ought to be solved, and I'm prepared to do it tonight. And I need an answer from you within six hours, or eight hours," or something like that. That's one way to do this.

Now, let me tell you about my conversation with [Giulio] Andreotti because it bears on this.

President Kennedy: Who's Andreotti?

McNamara: Andreotti's the defense minister of Italy. I talked to him just two weeks ago about these Jupiters in Italy, and the Italians would be happy to get rid of them if we want them out of there.

Bundy: The difference between Reinhardt's report [from Rome] and Hare's [from Ankara] is between night and day.

McNamara: I realize that. But there are . . . What I'm suggesting is, we can do this with both Italy and Turkey, and we can get Italy to go along with us, I think. And this will put some additional pressure on Turkey.

Dillon: [*Unclear*] by Monday?

McNamara: No, but the aftereffects of the case in which . . . [the U.S. attacks Cuba].

President Kennedy: We want to do it—if we're going to do that, Bob, and that may be the way we ought to do it. The effect of that, of course . . . I don't know how . . . Not having had it explained to NATO what's going to be the effects of continuing the [Jupiter] missiles, it's going to look like we're caving in. Now, do we want to go through NATO to do that, or do we want to do it bilaterally?

To get it done, probably you have to do it bilaterally, to take all the political effects of the cave-in of NATO. Whether we want to have a meeting, in the morning, of NATO and say: "If we don't do it, here's the problem."

Unidentified: I think you have to do it simultaneously.

McNamara: I think you have to do it simultaneously.

Bundy: I think the disadvantage of having a NATO meeting and going to the Turks tonight and tomorrow, is that you don't give this track a fair run that you just tried out on us.

McNamara: Yes, I agree, Mac. I really don't think we have to move immediately on a Turkish track, but I think we have to get—

Bundy: Ground up [prepared] to do so.

McNamara: We have to get ground up to do it, and we have to look at some of the actions in between.

Now, are we going to stop surveillance while these discussions go on on the deal of last night? We have intense ground fire against our air.

Taylor: I wouldn't worry. I wouldn't pay any attention.

McNamara: Well, I asked Ros [Gilpatric] to talk to Curt LeMay and—

Taylor: No, I wouldn't. Flak came up in front of the flight, and they veered away.

President Kennedy: Was this the—

McNamara: What about the hit?

Taylor: That has not been confirmed.

Bundy: No.

Unidentified: Did you talk later?

Gilpatric: Well I heard his conversation. I talked to Captain [*unclear*], but there's some difference [in what the pilots said]. I think you'd have to wait until a little later.

McNamara: Let me just put it this way. We had fire on the surveillance.

Now, the first question we have to face tomorrow morning is: Are we going to send surveillance flights in? And I think we have basically two alternatives. Either we decide not to send them in at all, or we decide to send them in with proper cover. If we send them in with proper cover and they're attacked, we must attack back, either the SAMs and/or MiG aircraft that would come against them or the ground fire that comes up.

We have another problem tomorrow. The *Grozny* is approaching the zone. We sent out a message today outlining the interception zone.

President Kennedy: Was this publicly released?

McNamara: We sent it to U Thant and it's released publicly. The *Grozny* will be coming into this zone. Khrushchev has said he is ordering his ships to stay out of the zone. If a Russian ship moves into the zone after he says that publicly, we have two choices: Stop it and board it, or don't. Now, when you—

Bundy: Stop it.

McNamara: —when you put the two of these together—the question of stopping surveillance and [the question of] not stopping the ship—it seems to me we're too weak.

Unidentified: Yeah.

Bundy: Yeah.

Taylor: I'd say we must continue surveillance. That's far more important than the ships.

McNamara: Well, what my main point is: I don't think at this particular point we should show a weakness to Khrushchev. And I think we *would* show a weakness if we failed on both of these actions.

Unidentified: Yes.

Taylor: And we mustn't fail on surveillance. We can't give up 24 hours at this stage.

McNamara: I fully agree, Max. I was just trying to lay out the problem.

Therefore, I would recommend that tomorrow we carry on surveillance but that we defer the decision as late as possible in the day to give a little more time. Because if we go in with surveillance, we have to put a cover on, and if we start shooting back we have escalated substantially.

President Kennedy: [*Unclear*] with the shoot—

Dillon: Why cover on it? I don't understand that.

McNamara: Well, we can't send these low-altitude aircraft in.

Dillon: And the cover, they'll attack that?

President Kennedy: If you're going to take a reprisal, the cover isn't much good because you've got the antiaircraft guns. You've got somebody up there at 10,000 feet and actually they can't give much more cover.

What you'd really, it seems to me, have is a justification for more elaborate action, wouldn't you? Do we want to worry about whether we're going to shoot up that one gun or do we want to just use this as a reason for doing a lot of other shooting at the SAMs?

Taylor: The main thing is to assure effective reconnaissance—whatever that implies. We won't know, really, till we . . .

President Kennedy: I would think we ought to just take a chance on reconnaissance tomorrow, without the cover, because I don't think the cover is really going to do you much good. You can't protect, hide it, from ground fire, and if they're shooting tomorrow, and if we don't get an answer from U Thant, then we ought to consider whether Monday morning [October 29] we [go ahead with the air attack on Cuba]. I'm not convinced yet of an invasion, because I think that's a much . . . I think we may . . .

Taylor: I agree with that. My personal view is that we should be ready to go in Monday [with the strike] and also ready to invade, but make no advance decisions.

President Kennedy: What do you think? [*turning to McNamara*]

McNamara: Well, I doubt—

President Kennedy: I don't think your cover's going to do much good.

McNamara: No. I . . .

My point is, I don't think we should stop the surveillance tomorrow. That I want to underline.

Point number two is, if we do carry on a surveillance tomorrow and they fire on it—

President Kennedy: That's a signal then. Then we know. . . .

McNamara: Then I think we ought to either do one of two things. We ought to decide at that moment that we're either going to return that fire, tomorrow, in a limited fashion against the things that fired against us or against their air defenses.

Or, alternatively, if we don't return the fire tomorrow, we ought to go in the next day with the recommended sorties [for the large strike]. One or the other.

President Kennedy: That's right. That's right. I'm rather inclined to take the more general response.

However, why don't we wait. Let's be prepared for either one tomorrow. Let's wait and see if they fire on us tomorrow and meanwhile we've got this message to U Thant, and we're . . . So let's be fully prepared.

What?

Dillon: We've got to be very clear then that, if we're doing this tomorrow, and then they do shoot weapons, then we do need to have the general response. There's no time to do what you're talking about with Turkey, and then we do that.

President Kennedy: Well no, but that's why I think we ought to go to that. I think what we ought to do is not worry too much about the cover.

Do the reconnaissance tomorrow. If we get fired on, then we meet here and we decide whether to do a much more general [strike]. I [would] announce that we've been fired on and announce that the work is going ahead. Announce that we haven't gotten an answer from the Soviets. Then we decide that we're going to do a much more general one than just shooting up some gun down there.

. . .

Robert Kennedy: What is the rush about this, other than the fact of when we have to make the strike?

McNamara: I think the rush is what do we do.

President Kennedy: The U-2.

McNamara: The U-2 was shot down. The fire against our low-altitude surveillance.

President Kennedy: A U-2 was shot down?

McNamara: [*Unclear*] [Defense Intelligence Agency official Colonel John] Wright just said it was found shot down.

Robert Kennedy: Was the pilot killed?

Taylor: This was shot down over Banes, which is right near a U-2 site in eastern Cuba.

Unidentified: A SAM site [*correcting Taylor's slip*].

Taylor: The pilot's body is in the plane. Apparently, this was a SAM site that had actually had the Fruitcake radar. It all ties in in a very plausible manner.[15]

President Kennedy: Well now, this is much of an escalation by them, isn't it?

McNamara: Yes, exactly. And this, this relates to the timing.

I think we can defer an air attack on Cuba until Wednesday [October 31] or Thursday [November 1] but *only* if we continue our surveillance, and fire against anything that fires against a surveillance aircraft, and only if we maintain a tight blockade in this interim period. If we're willing to do those two things, I think we can defer the air attack until Wednesday or Thursday and take time to go to NATO.

President Kennedy: How do we explain the effect of this Khrushchev message of last night and their decision [to shoot down U.S. planes], in view of their previous orders [to fire only if attacked], the change in orders? We've both had flak and a SAM site operation. How do we . . . I mean, that must be—

McNamara: How do we interpret this? I don't know how to interpret it.

President Kennedy: What?

Taylor: They feel they must respond now. The whole world knows where we're flying.

That raises the question of retaliation against the SAM sites. We think we—we have various other reasons to believe that we know the SAM sites [that shot down the U-2]. Two days ago—

President Kennedy: How can we send a U-2 fellow over there tomorrow unless we take out all the SAM sites?

McNamara: This is exactly the problem. I don't think we can.

President Kennedy: Did anyone see the pilot?

Taylor: Yes, sir.

Rusk: And it's on the ground?

Taylor: It's on the ground. The wreckage is on the ground and the pilot's dead.

McNamara: It's in the water, isn't it?

Taylor: I didn't get the water part.

Bundy: If we know it, it obviously must be either on friendly land or on the water.

Gilpatric: It is on Cuban land at this point, isn't it? I don't know [*unclear*] the pilot was [*unclear*].

Taylor: That's why I've got [*unclear*].

McCone: I wonder if this shouldn't cause a most violent protest. Write a letter, following up your letter, right to Khrushchev. Here's, here's an action they've taken against us, a new order in defiance of a public statement he made. I think that—

McNamara: I think we ought to.

Nitze: They've fired the first shot.

McCone: If there's any continuation of this, we've got to take those SAM sites out of there.

Taylor: We should retaliate against the SAM site, and announce that if any other planes—if we have any other planes fired on we will come back and [*unclear*]. [*Mixed voices.*]

Dillon: Only this one sentence?

Taylor: It's what we agreed to do two days ago.[16]

Unidentified: It looked good then and it still looks good to me.

Unidentified: Isn't this what we told the NATO people we'd do—or the Quadripartite Group?

Rusk: Yes. We told the Quadripartite Group. [*Unclear.*]

Bundy: You can go against one [SAM site], can you? Now? Tonight?

McNamara: No, it's too late. This is why it gets into tomorrow, and I . . . Without thinking about retaliation today, what are we going to do if we want to defer the air attack until Wednesday or Thursday, given the situation?

Taylor: It will be very dangerous, I would say, Mr. Secretary, unless we can reconnoiter each day—reconnoiter each day, having difficulty with reconnaissance.

McNamara: And if we're going to reconnaissance, carry out surveillance each day, we must be prepared to fire each day.

Taylor: That's correct.

President Kennedy: We can't very well send a U-2 over there, can we now, and have a guy killed again tomorrow?

Taylor: We certainly shouldn't do it until we retaliate and say that if they fire again on one of our planes that we will come back with great force.

Nitze: I think you've just got to take out that SAM site. You can't continue surveillance.

President Kennedy: Well, except that we've still got the problem of . . . even if we take out this SAM site, the fellow still is going to be awfully vulnerable tomorrow from all the others, isn't he?

Taylor: Next time, we go in—

Bundy: If you take one out, you've got to—

McNamara: I think we can forget the U-2 for the moment.

Rusk: It builds up, though, on a somewhat different track than the all-out attack track.

McNamara: Yeah. We can carry out low-altitude surveillance tomorrow, take out this SAM site, and take out more SAM sites tomorrow and MiG aircraft if the low-altitude—

President Kennedy: Well, now, do we want to announce tonight that this U-2 was shot down?

McNamara: I think we should. I mean, if we're going in to fight, we can [*unclear*] now or—

Gilpatric: Earlier today we announced, Mr. President, we said any interference with such surveillance will meet counteraction and surveillance will be—[17]

President Kennedy: Do we want to announce that we're going to take counteraction, or just take it tomorrow morning?

Gilpatric: Just take it.

Unidentified: Well this is the statement that was announced, wasn't it?

President Kennedy: That the U-2 was shot down?

Gilpatric: No, no. This is a general statement that we would enforce surveillance.

President Kennedy: Well now, do we want to just announce that an American plane was shot down—a surveillance plane was shot down in Cuba? It seems to me that then—

Ball: I would announce it after you've taken further action.

Taylor: I understand Havana's announced it. That's where we—

President Kennedy: Well, I think that we ought to announce it because it throws off Khrushchev's protestations about—

Taylor: This came in a cable from over there.

Bundy: This about the pilot is from Havana?

Nitze: Oh, that's Havana radio!

President Kennedy: We haven't confirmed that.

There are so goddamn many. . . . We could stay here all day if we . . .

Well now, let's say if we're sure the U-2 has been shot down, it seems to me we've got to announce it or it's going to dribble out. Havana's announced it anyway. We ought to announce it.

Bundy: We don't know that yet, Mr. President.

President Kennedy: Then we ought to not say anything, don't you think? And just take the reprisal without making any announcement? We don't want to announce that we're going to take a reprisal against that SAM site tomorrow, or would that make our reprisal more difficult?

McNamara: It would certainly make it more difficult.

President Kennedy: I think we ought to announce that, and that action is being taken—action will be taken to protect our various aircraft.

McNamara: Exactly. Then we ought to go in at dawn and take out that SAM site. And we ought to send a surveillance aircraft in tomorrow with the regular flights early in the morning and we ought to be prepared to take out more SAM sites and knock out the . . .

President Kennedy: Well, what we want to do then is get this announcement written.

Ros, why don't you write this out, plus this thing about what we're going to do. And then we'll get back to what we're going to do about the Turks. [*amid overlapping voices*] his proposal this morning.

McNamara: This was the point. [*Unclear exchange.*] Well, I think he was shot coming in.

Robert Kennedy: If he came in—

Rusk: The map I have showed him the other way around.

McNamara: Now, he was to go up here.

President Kennedy: Well, can we take that SAM site out?

Rusk: Here's the chart that was just handed us. It shows he was on his way out.

McCone: . . . because that's the Banes site.

Robert Kennedy: In addition, there was one other Cuban shooting at the low level too.

Unidentified: Yes.

McCone: Where was that, Bob, do you know?

McNamara: I haven't the detail.

McCone: Who has the most [*unclear*]?

Rusk: We'll look if I can place, [*unclear*], they started the shooting.

President Kennedy: Well now, we're going to get out an announcement once we have confirmed this thing, and we're going to say that . . .

McNamara: We're going to say that it was shot down, and we're going to continue our surveillance protected by U.S. fighter aircraft.

Gilpatric: With suitable protection. The assumption is—

McNamara: I'd just say U.S. fighter aircraft so you don't leave any doubt about it.

Robert Kennedy: Then tomorrow morning, add POL [to the quarantine]?

McNamara: I wouldn't do it tonight, Bobby. I'd just announce this one.

I think tomorrow morning we ought to go in and take out that SAM site, and send our surveillance in with proper protection immediately following it or on top of it, or whatever way they—

Taylor: [*Three seconds excised as classified information.*] The plane is on the ground. It is not in the water.

Bundy: In Cuba?

Taylor: [*to an aide*] Thank you.

President Kennedy: Well, we don't—we have no—

Bundy: Well, let's put it out. Otherwise, they will put it out.

President Kennedy: We don't know. It's overdue anyway, isn't it? So we can assume it's quite . . .

Taylor: Hours overdue now.

President Kennedy: Do we want to say it was shot down? We don't know whether . . . They say they shot it down, the Cubans?

Well, why doesn't Ros, and you, General, get a statement which would cover whatever. It may be . . . We don't know if it was shot down.

McCone: We don't know it.

McNamara: I think . . . well I think I'd say it was shot down. Because the probabilities are that it was shot down, and we want an excuse to go in tomorrow and shoot up that SAM site and send in around—

Dillon: If the plane's on the ground there, it was shot down. I mean, it didn't just come down and land.

McNamara: Well, it might have had mechanical failure problems.

Dillon: Well, no, he would have been—

President Kennedy: The only point is—the only thing that troubles us—is the other plane was shot at.

McNamara: That's right. Exactly.

President Kennedy: They say . . . that's why I'd like to find out whether Havana says they did shoot it down.

Bundy: We haven't heard anything from Havana yet, do we?

Gilpatric: We assume these SAM sites are manned by Soviets.

McCone: Yes.

Gilpatric: That's the significant part of it, if the SAM fired. You might have . . .

Unidentified: [*Unclear*] that small, you might have a Cuban that just—

Unidentified: No, but they wouldn't operate it.

McNamara: Well, but they . . . You had antiaircraft there against the other [low-level reconaissance aircraft]. This is a change of pattern. Now why it's a change of pattern, I don't know.

Robert Kennedy: Yeah.

. . .

After leaving the room for some minutes, President Kennedy returns to his seat and the meeting starts again. Robert Kennedy and Sorensen are still out of the room, where they have taken over and are completing the redrafting of the message to Khrushchev.

President Kennedy: What we got to do is—let's just see if we can get this. Castro just announced that any plane that intruded over the airspace of Cuba would be fired upon.

Let's see if . . . Gentlemen, come up and sit here now. Gentlemen.

Let's talk a little more about the Turks, how we're going to handle that. NATO and the Turks, that's the one matter we haven't settled today.

Dillon: I am really very much concerned about this. It's going to be very difficult with this Castro announcement [and] what's happened, if we wait until Wednesday or Thursday on this thing [taking action against the Soviet missiles in Cuba]. Therefore, if we want to do something—

President Kennedy: I think we ought to . . . Why don't we send an instruction to Hare to have a conversation [with the Turks], but also have the NATO meeting? We need to explain to them what's happening over here. Otherwise, we're going to be carrying a hell of a bag.

Dillon: I think you're going to have such pressure internally, in the

United States too, to act quickly. You have . . . things are all shot down and I just don't quite see what we're going to do. Sit around . . .

President Kennedy: Therefore, we've got to move. That's why I think we'd better have a NATO meeting tomorrow.

Dillon: Then the fact that something's shot down is the reason to have a NATO meeting tomorrow morning. It's to explain the whole—

President Kennedy: We'll explain to them where we are. I think it's a . . . I'm just afraid of what's going to happen in NATO, to Europe, when we get into this thing more and more, and I think they ought to feel that they were part of it. Even if we don't do anything about the Turks, they ought to feel that they know what the . . .

What do you think?

McNamara: I would agree, but I think we ought to know what we want NATO to do tomorrow, which means that we have to have a proposition. NATO itself won't initiate anything. There will be 15 voices without—

Ball: Instructions.

McNamara: —without instructions from the governments, so that . . .

Ball: Actually, what we should do tonight, Mr. President, is not only get a message to NATO but get a message to the capitals, to our ambassadors so they can talk to the governments, because these permanent representatives won't be able to do anything.

President Kennedy: We're not sending a night [reconnaissance] mission tonight, are we?

McNamara: No, we're not.

Alexis Johnson: I would suppose that what we might do would be to send a, get a NIACT message off to these governments—to the embassies in the capitals.[18] And get hold of Finletter and tell him to call a NATO meeting for the end of the afternoon tomorrow which would enable, hopefully, at least for some of them to have some instructions.

Dillon: And then the message to the capitals saying we are doing this, and that we want the representatives to be instructed.

President Kennedy: Of course, it would be relatively easy if we wanted to get NATO to reject this rejoinder [the Soviet proposal for a Cuba-Turkey trade]. But that isn't necessarily what we want right now, is it?

Ball: Well, if they rejected it—

President Kennedy: What kind of a briefing?

McNamara: I don't think you can go to NATO. I don't think you can send any messages out to the capitals until we decide what we want to do.

Unidentified: That's right.

McNamara: When we decide that, I think we can force them, and I think we can do it in such a way that the aftereffects will not—not be too severe. But I think we've got to decide ahead of time what it is we want to do, and what I would suggest we decide is, we want those missiles taken out of Turkey. And we simply say that we believe this is, as I do believe, in the interest of the alliance, and that we will replace those missiles with other fire.

President Kennedy: But they're going to say is we're seeking the trade with the Russians, aren't they?

McNamara: But I would say: "We may have to attack Cuba. If we attack Cuba, they're holding Turkey as a hostage and they're likely to attack Turkey and this . . ."

Bundy: "To free our hands in Cuba, we must get these missiles out of Turkey," is what we say.

McNamara: Yeah. Without endangering you, the alliance. This is the theme we give to them.

Unidentified: And the point that always has to be made to these countries is that: After all, the menace of these missiles like these in Cuba is a menace to the retaliatory power of the United States, which is the central defense of the whole free world, including yourselves.

McNamara: Yeah, well, I would put it like this. "We're not trading Turkish missiles for Cuban missiles."

Bundy: No, no.

McNamara: Not a bit. We're relieving the alliance of a threat that is presently upon them.

Bundy: Of a local threat—

President Kennedy: But they will say, it's going to be regarded in the NATO meeting as a trade, isn't it? They're going to say: "Well now, do you have a deal with the Russians if we take them out of Turkey?"

Bundy: It will be seen as a trade by a great many people, Mr. President. There's no doubt about that. We've looked that one in the eye. If you don't buy that, then it seems to me Bob has the best way of dealing with it.

President Kennedy: Of course, what we would like to do is have the Turks come and offer this, wouldn't we?

Unidentified: Yeah.

McNamara: Given time, we might work that out, but you can't work it out with the Turks in a short time. I'm certain of that.

Unidentified: That's right.

McNamara: They are a terribly stubborn people to talk to on this kind of a point.

Robert Kennedy and Sorensen return to the Cabinet Room. Sorensen approaches President Kennedy with the now completed redraft of the message to Khrushchev.

. . .

After some additional discussion of what to say to the United States's NATO allies, President Kennedy leaves the room. The discussion continues, more informally.

Unidentified: I really don't think we're very clear on that.

Vice President Johnson: What you're saying is that you're willing to give them up, as McNamara proposes. Why not trade?

Unidentified: No, that isn't—that's what he said.

McNamara: Let me start my proposition over again.

Ball: And then save a few hundred thousand lives.

McNamara: Let me start my proposition over again.

We must be in a position to attack quickly. We've been fired on today. We're going to send surveillance aircraft in tomorrow. Those are going to be fired on without question. We're going to respond. You can't do this very long. We're going to lose airplanes. We'll be shooting up Cuba bit by bit, but we're going to lose airplanes every day. You just *can't* maintain this position very long. So we must be prepared to attack Cuba quickly. That's the first proposition.

Now, the second proposition. When we attack Cuba, we are going to have to attack with an all-out attack, and that means 500 sorties at a minimum the first day, and it means sorties every day thereafter, and I personally believe that this is almost certain to lead to an invasion. I won't say certain to, but *almost* certain to, lead to an invasion.

Dillon: Unless you get a cease-fire around the world.

McNamara: That's the second proposition.

Bundy: Or a general war.

McNamara: The third proposition is that if we do this and leave those missiles in Turkey, the Soviet Union may, and I think probably will, attack the Turkish missiles.

Now the fourth proposition is, if the Soviet Union attacks the Turkish missiles, we *must* respond. We cannot allow a Soviet attack on the Jupiter missiles in Turkey without a military response by NATO.

Dillon: Somewhere.

McNamara: Somewhere. That's right. Now, that's the next proposition. . . .

Ball: Well, the next—go ahead, go down the track. Because I think we—

McNamara: Why don't I get through. Then let's go back and attack each one of my propositions.

Now, the minimum military response by NATO to a Soviet attack on the Turkish Jupiter missiles would be a response with conventional weapons by NATO forces in Turkey. That is to say, Turkish and U.S. aircraft against Soviet warships and/or naval bases in the Black Sea area. Now that to me is the absolute minimum. And I would say that it is *damn dangerous* to have had a Soviet attack on Turkey and a NATO response on the Soviet Union. This is *extremely* dangerous.

Now, I'm not sure we can avoid anything like that if we attack Cuba. But I think we should make every effort to avoid it. And one way to avoid it is to defuse the Turkish missiles before we attack Cuba. Now, this is the sequence of thought.

McCone: I don't see why we don't make the trade then. [*Mixed voices.*]

Ball: I would say that is in the assumption that if you defuse the Turkish missiles, this saves you from a reprisal. It may mean a reprisal elsewhere.

McNamara: Oh—

Ball: It doesn't save you from a reprisal. In Berlin or somewhere.

McNamara: No, no! [*Other voices raised.*]

Ball: Then you're in a position where you've gotten rid of your missiles for nothing.

McNamara: Well, wait a minute. Now, I didn't say it saves you from a reprisal. I simply said it reduces the chances of military action against Turkey.

Ball: But what good does that do you if you get action against Berlin or somewhere else?

McNamara: Well in the meantime . . . Wait a minute, you have to go back to my proposition and say: "If there aren't Jupiter missiles in Turkey to attack, they're going to apply military force elsewhere." I'm not at all certain of that.

Taylor: Oh, I am.

Vice President Johnson: Bob, if you're willing to give up your missiles in Turkey, you think you ought to defuse them, why don't you say that to him and say we're cutting a trade, make the trade then. Save all the invasion, lives, and everything else?

Walt Rostow: We've been going around this at the State Department, and day and night we've talked about this. And we said we'd be *delighted* to trade those missiles in Turkey for the thing in Cuba.

McNamara: I said I thought it was the realistic solution to the problem.

Rostow: Sure. Right. Last week what we were afraid of was he would never offer this, but what he would want to do is trade something for *Berlin!*

Unidentified: Right.

Rostow: Last week we regarded this as just the kind of thing that—

McNamara: I'm not opposed to it now. All I'm suggesting is, don't push us into a position where we *haven't* traded it, and we *are* forced to attack Cuba and the missiles remain in Turkey. That's all I'm suggesting. Let's avoid that position. And we're fast moving into that.

Unidentified: Well, I mean, we're now back at the point where I wanted—

Bundy: We were going to *let* him have his strike in Turkey, as I understood it last week. At one point, at least, that was the way we thought about it.

McNamara: That's right. That was one alternative.

Ball: Actually, what we were thinking last week was that what he [Khrushchev] was doing was going to trade this against Berlin—or nothing. We thought that if we could trade it out for Turkey this would be an easy trade and a very advantageous deal. Now we've made that offer to him.

Bundy: And it doesn't look so good.

Ball: And we don't want it. And we're talking about a course of action which involves military action with enormous casualties and a great, grave risk of escalation. Now I really don't think this is . . . we ought to *shift* this one.

McNamara: Well, why don't we look at two courses of action?

Bundy: Why don't you just see what consequences George draws.

Ball: Well, I would far rather, if we're going to get the damn missiles out of Turkey anyway, say: "We'll trade you [Khrushchev] the missiles. We're going to put Jupiters—I mean we're going to put Polarises in there. You [Khrushchev] are not going to benefit by this. But we will— if this is a matter of real concern to you, to have these on your borders, all right—we'll get rid of them. You get rid of them in Cuba."

These things [the Jupiters] are obsolete anyway. I mean, you are not going to reduce the retaliatory power of the NATO alliance.

Unidentified: If we're going to put a Polaris in there, it's going to be a lot bigger.

Ball: Yeah.

Unidentified: Effective deterrent against you.

Ball: And I'd tell him.

McNamara: Well, I think you have two alternatives.

Bundy: I missed George's statement. I have to ask you to say it again.

Ball: I'd say: "Sure, we'll accept your offer. If this is a matter of grave concern to you and you equate these things—which we don't, but if you do, OK—we can work it out. We're going to put Polarises in the Mediterranean because you've got the whole sea to range in, and we can't keep you out of the ocean."

Bundy: And what's left of NATO?

Ball: I don't think NATO is going to be wrecked. And if NATO isn't any better than that, it isn't that good to us.

Dillon: What happens, though, to the missiles in Cuba over the next three weeks while this is going on?

Ball: Well, I mean, if you do this, you do it on the basis of an immediate trade and they immediately—

Bundy: And surveillance.

Ball: And surveillance, which is one of the conditions.

Gilpatric: What you do, you go with the Turks and NATO . . . you go through the propositions that Bob has outlined here.

McNamara: Let me suggest this. Let's get the message [to NATO capitals] written on the assumption that either the Soviets don't want to trade or we don't want to trade, one or the other. And hence the trade route of Jupiters in Turkey for missiles in Cuba is not acceptable and therefore we're going to attack Cuba.

Now, let's follow that [path of making the Jupiters in Turkey inoperable], and get a message written on that basis. Before we attack Cuba we're going to reduce the danger to Turkey to a minimum.

Bundy: I'd like to see both of these messages written.

Unidentified: I think they both need to be written.

McNamara: But, Mac, this other course will, in a sense, be that other one. So let's get first the message written on the assumption that it does—

Ball: Why don't you write that and I'll go write the other one, because—

· · ·

Robert Kennedy: I don't know if there's a chance to do it openly like that [working it out with the Turks]. I mean I think it's worthwhile.

Bundy: All right. You write it—

Robert Kennedy: Write it up anyway?

Unidentified: Yeah.

Bundy: Yeah. Do you want to write one? Or do you want me to draft it, or what do you want to do? All right. I'll get a draft.

Unidentified: Have you got a piece of paper?

Unidentified: Who's it to, Bob?

McNamara: Well, it's going to go to three parties. It's going to go to the Turks, to the heads of government of NATO countries, and to the North Atlantic Council. Same message, in effect.

Bundy: Do people want dinner downstairs, do they want trays, or do they want to wait?

McNamara: Well let's wait. Don't have to worry . . . eating is the least of my worries.

We probably ought to think about the course of action in the next two or three days. What alternatives we have here.

Max is going back to work out the surveillance plan for tomorrow with the Chiefs, as to how much cover we need and so on. But we're just going to get shot up, sure as hell. There's just no question about it. Then we're going to have to go in and shoot. Now we can carry this on, I would think, a couple of days, maybe three days, possibly four, but we're going to lose planes.

We had eight [low-level reconnaissance] planes that went out today. Two aborted for mechanical reasons. Two went through safely and returned, and four ran into fire—

Taylor: And had to abort.

McNamara: And had to abort.

Dillon: What was it before, they just saw . . . ?

McNamara: Low-altitude fire.

McCone: You know, it seems to me we're missing a bet here. I think that we ought to take this occasion to send directly to Khrushchev, by fast wire, the most violent protest, and demand that he stop this business and stop it right away, or we're going to take those SAM sites out immediately. This is what I'd tell him. I'd tell him this is a . . . I'd just use one of the messages that he's sent to us, and I'd send it right off. And if he won't . . .

And I would trade these Turkish things out right now. I wouldn't be talking to anybody about it. We sat for a *week* and there was . . . everybody was in favor of doing it. And I would make that part of the message. Tell him we're going to conduct surveillance as announced by the President, and *one shot* and in we come. And he can expect it. If he wants to sit around and talk about this thing, he can call off his gunfire and do it right away.

McNamara: Well, I think that we can assume that that kind of an approach will be made against the . . . I mean I think we can assume an approach to trade the missiles will be made one way or another. He'll know that. But now let's assume that that's made. And time goes by and nothing happens and we're losing airplanes. What do we do here?

Dillon: Well, I mean, this is what John said.

McCone: That's what I said.

McNamara: I know. Let's assume that the approach [for a Cuba-Turkey trade] is made.

Dillon: And he doesn't do it.

McNamara: And either he doesn't do it or he comes back . . .

Let me go back a second. When I read that [Khrushchev] message of last night this morning, I thought, my God! I'd never sell, I would never base a transaction on that contract. Hell, that's no offer! There's not a damn thing in it that's an offer. You read that message carefully. He didn't propose to take the missiles out. Not once is there a single word in it that proposes to take the missiles out. It's 12 pages of fluff.

McCone: Well, his message this morning wasn't that way—his public message.

McNamara: Well, no. I'm speaking of the last night message. The last night message was 12 pages of fluff. That's no contract. You couldn't sign that and say we know what we signed.

And *before* [*he slaps his hand*] we got the damn thing read, the whole deal changed—*completely* changed! All of which leads me to conclude that the probabilities are that nothing is going to be signed quickly.

Now, my question is, assuming nothing is signed quickly, what do we do? Well, I don't think attack is the only answer. I think we ought to be prepared for attack, all-out attack. And I think we ought to know how far we can postpone that. But I don't think that's the only answer, and we ought to think of some other answers here.

Now John's suggestion, I think, is obviously one, to try to negotiate a deal.

McCone: I wouldn't try to negotiate a deal. I would send him a threatening letter.

I'd say: "You have made public an offer. Now, we'll accept that offer. But you shot down a plane today before we even had a chance to send you a letter, despite the fact that you knew that we were sending unarmed planes on a publicly announced surveillance.

"Now, we're telling you, Mr. Khrushchev, this is just one thing, that we are sending unarmed planes over Cuba. If one of them is shot up, we're going to take your installations out, and you can expect it. And therefore, you issue an order *immediately.*"

McNamara: Right.

McCone: And be prepared to follow that up.

McNamara: But what I'd do is disassociate that from the Turkish missiles, John. That's part of your message that I would—

McCone: No, I wouldn't, because then the pressure gets easier, you'll get another proposal. You'll have Berlin thrown in it tomorrow. [*He pauses as someone gives an instruction to an aide about giving a paper to a secretary.*] Bob, you'll get something else thrown in tomorrow. You'll get Berlin.

McNamara: Oh, I think that's possible. I think that's exactly possible. That's why I think we have to be prepared for attack.

· · ·

Vice President Johnson: Generally, trading a Polaris for the Jupiters wouldn't necessarily imply that we would not come [to the aid of Turkey], would it? It would indicate that we would come with more, quicker, wouldn't it?

Why, if you were prime minister of Turkey, say that we're going to hit Cuba but he's got this big fuse here, all advertised, with a big red light on each one of these Jupiters. We want to take them out. We are going to give you more protection than ever—with Polaris. And less advertising. And it's going to make it less likely that you'll get hit. Why wouldn't he buy that?

Nitze: I'm not sure why he wouldn't buy it, but the whole proposition hasn't been made to him, as far as I know.

Vice President Johnson: But suppose you were prime minister. What would you do about it? Wouldn't you rather have Polaris?

I think the reason he wouldn't buy it would be a fear that that meant that we were through and that we wouldn't come [to his defense].

Rostow (?): That would be one of his worries.

Unidentified: If we give him the assurance, it certainly wouldn't be a valid reason.

Vice President Johnson: If we gave him assurance that we're hitting Cuba at the same time, why have we got to be there with him? It's a big problem. [*Pause.*] I think if we showed them; we send that tomorrow, take the time out before [we strike Cuba] . . . We might as well pull our planes and end up pretty well [*unclear*]. At least radio and TV reports will give the impression . . . [*Unclear reply.*]

That we're having to retreat. We're backing down. I think we've been [backing down] gradually from the President's speech. It's not like this. They [*unclear who he means*] don't know what the hell I'm talking about. They [the people] are concerned. They're [*unclear*]. In this country, just like every one of these damn places you go. When you walk into

Turkey they are probably insecure, [*unclear*]. They might have thought Berlin, [*unclear*].

I mean, people feel it. They don't know why they feel it and how. They just—

Robert Kennedy: [*as he is perhaps drifting back in the room*] [*Unclear*] feels we're backing down?

Vice President Johnson: We've got a blockade and we're doing them, and do this and that and the [Soviet] ships are coming through.

Robert Kennedy: [*annoyed*] No, the ships aren't coming through. They all turned back. [*Unclear*] 90 percent of them, they haven't been running for 24 hours, those that can get through.

Vice President Johnson: [*Unclear.*] I'm not debating the justification.

Robert Kennedy: No, but I would think that they would think, quite to the contrary, the Russians [*unclear*] and all of their own ships back.

Vice President Johnson: [*more quietly*] I don't think we can justify, at this moment, [the argument] that it looks like we are as strong as we were the day of the President's announcement. [*Unclear.*]

This exchange subsides. Robert Kennedy probably leaves the Cabinet Room again. There is a mostly inaudible exchange about the U-2 warning.

• • •

Vice President Johnson: Well then, to summarize it, . . . what went out this morning? What has been done today? Let's just see how he [Khrushchev] is looking at our performance today before he shot down this plane.

Rusk: Well we—

Vice President Johnson: Last night he [Khrushchev] sent us a long letter. Before we could read it, he made the public trade proposal, didn't he? That was his move. Those were the last two things we heard from him before the shot, right?

Rusk: Right.

Vice President Johnson: Right. First thing we did to him was send this proposal to U Thant, saying: "Find out if he will stop the work and disable the missiles."

Rusk: Well, in the meantime we . . . [*Vice President Johnson starts speaking.*] And we announced [in the afternoon Pentagon announcement] that we would enforce surveillance.

Vice President Johnson: That's right. And we made the [White House] announcement this morning and called attention again to the necessity of his stopping his missile work. That announcement, that's the first thing.

And the second thing, we sent U Thant a very short message, that paragraph of Bobby's. Wasn't that the second thing we did?

Rusk: Well, the first thing was the comment that—the first comment on the broadcast message [in the morning White House statement].

The second thing was an announcement [in the afternoon at the Pentagon] that we would enforce surveillance and take counteraction if they shot at us.

The third thing was the short message to U Thant.

The fourth thing was the longer message to Khrushchev.

Vice President Johnson: The letter.

Rusk: The letter.

Vice President Johnson: With the points. Which went to U Thant. I've lost the second one. I don't remember it.

Rusk: I think tomorrow, we—

Vice President Johnson: Is this what you called the second one? [*reading from the morning White House press statement*] "Several inconsistent and conflicting proposals have been made by the U.S.S.R. here in the last 24 hours . . . ?"

Rusk: That's right.[19] And then this [*unclear*] surveillance, with the instruction [to Stevenson for U Thant] and the presidential letter [to Khrushchev].

Now, in the morning we've got to try to shake him back on to last night's track—to concentrate on Cuba.

Thompson: If this ship [the *Grozny*] comes in, I think we should stop it.

Unidentified: Is the ship still proceeding as far as we know?

Rusk: I don't know.

And of course surveillance.

Unidentified: He also notes—the announcement about the surveillance—didn't we also mention night surveillance?

Rusk: Yeah. [*Unclear exchange.*]

Dillon: Make an announcement that we might do night surveillance?

Vice President Johnson: No, I don't . . . hope he hasn't. I've been afraid of those damned flares [for night reconnaissance] ever since they mentioned them. Just an ordinary plane going in there at 2[00] or 300 feet without arms or an announcement. There was four of them had to turn back because of fire.

Imagine some crazy Russian captain doing it. The damn thing [the flare] goes "blooey" and lights up the skies. He might just pull a trigger. Looks like we're playing Fourth of July over there or something.

I'm scared of that, and I don't see what you get with that photograph that's so much more important than what you . . . You know they're working at night, and you can see them working at night. Now what do you do?

Psychologically, you scare them [the Soviets]. Well, hell, it's always like the fellow telling me in Congress, "Go on and put the monkey on his back." Every time I tried to put a monkey on somebody else's back, I got one. If you're going to try to psychologically scare them with a flare, you're liable to get your bottom shot at.

Unidentified: What is George Ball doing?

Rusk: George is—

Vice President Johnson: He's drafting his view of the trade with the Turks. He says that if you're going to [make the Jupiters inoperable], you ought to accept the trade. If you're going to give up the Turkish bases, that you ought to say: "OK, we'll give them up for Cuba."

McNamara says: "Tell them we'll give them up for nothing." That's the way I see it, the two of them. That there are two sides. McNamara says: "If we're going to hit Cuba, we've got to say to the Turks that we want you to give up your Jupiters, and we'll give you Polaris instead." Ball says: "Well, if you're going to do that, just say to Mr. Khrushchev: Yes to your proposal today." So he's drafting that. So to take the two proposals. McNamara's drafting one; Ball drafting the other; both of them coming back with the two.

Dillon: Here is the third thing, which is really the Ball line, plus McCone's ultimatum idea about surveillance, which is: [*reading*]

> Mr. Chairman:
> We have reached a moment of utmost gravity. Your forces in Cuba have fired on one of our unarmed planes conducting surveillance in accordance with the resolution of the OAS. You have done this before I had an opportunity to reply to your letter of this morning, offering to remove your offensive weapons in Cuba in return for the removal of similar weapons from Turkey. This suggestion of yours requires consultations with our NATO allies. I am undertaking such consultation and recommending that our allies agree to the removal of the Jupiter missiles from Turkey at the same time that your missiles are removed from Cuba. Meanwhile, it is essential that these weapons [in Cuba] be made inoperable immediately. Until this is done—

Rusk: The weapons in Cuba.

Dillon: Yeah. "these weapons in Cuba be made inoperable immediately. Until this is done, subject to reasonable international control, we must continue our unarmed aerial surveillance of Cuba. If these planes," or again, "if these unarmed planes"—we keep saying that—"If these unarmed planes are again fired upon, we will be required to respond with all the necessary force.

"The decision, Mr. Chairman, is yours. If you give orders to your forces in Cuba to cease interference with our unarmed planes and if you agree to immediately render the offensive weapons in Cuba inoperable, the way to peace is open. Otherwise, we will be forced to act."

Rusk: What do you think?

Vice President Johnson: I think you've got a point.

I think you're going to have a big problem right here, internally, in a few more hours in this country. This ought to start the wires [telegrams from citizens] in now from all over the country, the states of the Union, [saying]: "Where have you been? What are you doing? The President made a fine speech. What else have you done?"

Rusk: What, you mean about more action?

Vice President Johnson: They want to know what we're doing. They see that there's some ships coming through [the quarantine]. There's a great feeling of insecurity. I told you the other day, before these fellows [congressional leaders] came in here [on October 24]. They're reflecting it. They're going to be saying: "I told you so." Tomorrow or the next day.

Rusk: What would be the effect in the country of accepting the Turkish thing?

Vice President Johnson: I don't know.

Brief gap in recording, as tape reels were changed. Tape 42 begins here.

What would [Ismet] Inonu say if you said: "Now you've got these Jupiters, and they're lighted up there. The searchlights [are] on them, and everybody knows about them. They're not worth a damn. And we'll take that old T-Model out, and we'll give you a Polaris, a much better job." And how will he feel?

Well, he might feel that we wouldn't come to [aid] him [in a crisis].

Rusk: But we've got 17,000 men there [in Turkey].

Vice President Johnson: We've got 20,000 in there.

So we could say: "Now, we're going to come. But we've got to hit Cuba, and we think that you're in less danger by pulling down these Jupiters and getting them out of here and having the Polaris than you are the other way. Now, what do you think about it?" I think he *might* . . .

Dillon: If you do this, if you at the same time send that message to everybody, you see, just explaining why, which is the message that's being drafted . . .

Vice President Johnson: [*musing*] I think governments are old and tired and sick, don't you think?

Thompson: There may be one angle to it, Mr. Vice President, that may bother him a little bit. A Polaris submarine would be strictly a U.S. organization.

Vice President Johnson: I think what will bother them is that this man in the United States is not coming [to his aid in a crisis].

Rusk: Well, that would be . . . The point is, the point there, is that we're there. Our NATO [*unclear*] includes the nuclear aircraft there. Those are our planes?

Unidentified: Yes. Always. There are both U.S.—there are both U.S. aircraft and [other NATO].[20]

Vice President Johnson: Well, then, if we're going to do it, why don't we try to sell them on that, Mr. Secretary? Have Hare talk to him and just say: "Now, you're more likely to get hit this way than you are the other way."

Isn't that true, Tommy?

Thompson: Yeah. Actually, we'd give them better protection. The Jupiters are totally obsolete. But, which I think we can . . .

The trouble with all this is that, unless we're absolutely decided we're going to hit Cuba, bomb them, then this would leave us in a very difficult position. They'll take their guided missiles, but they'll leave their technicians in Cuba, and their bombing planes in Cuba, and we're in a hell of a mess.

Unidentified: Say [in U.S. demands to the Soviets]: "nuclear weapons, nuclear delivery systems."

Dillon: Well, now, we're just talking about missiles. Because we can't talk about planes, because then we have to take our planes out of Turkey, you see, and we don't want to do that.

Thompson: The only possible, it seems to me, justification for this [approach to Turkey] is if they know you're going to bomb.

Vice President Johnson: Look, the weakness of the whole thing is, you say: "Well they [the Soviets] shot down one plane, and they [the Americans] gave up Turkey." Then they [the Soviets] shoot down another, and they [the Americans] give up Berlin. You know, like a mad dog—he tastes a little blood, he . . .

Thompson: You see, I think they've been put up by the Lippmann piece.[21] It occurs to me that we really aren't prepared to talk Turkey for Cuba.

Dillon: Well, we had something of the basic thing. All this talk—this was less than a week ago—we all said that was fine, and we would . . .

Thompson: Not the base [in Turkey].

Dillon: Well not the base, just the missiles.

Thompson: He's now gotten on the idea that he can get a lot more. His proposal is that whatever you want out of Cuba, you take out of Turkey.

Dillon: Oh, I see what you were talking about. A week ago, it was that they'd take everything out of Cuba and we'd just take the missiles out of Turkey whereas now he's saying: "I'll take the missiles out of Cuba. You take missiles out of here. I take aeroplanes out. You take aeroplanes out."

Thompson: That's right.

Unidentified: Technicians for technicians.

Unidentified: Well, those are different things. They are not alike.

Dillon: There's everything in Turkey.

Unidentified: They don't match. They are not alike.

Thompson: That's why I think any suggestion that we're willing to accept this, unless we have made an irrevocable decision that we're to take these out by bombing, is very dangerous. Because then we're really getting nothing on this thing, insofar as . . . I don't know.

I can't believe it's [the Cuba-Turkey trade] necessary. You know, the night before he was willing to take this other line [asking only for a U.S. pledge not to invade Cuba].

Vice President Johnson: So what happened? Is somebody forcing him to up his ante? Or did he try to just say: "Well, maybe they'll give up more. Let's try it; and I can always come back to my original position."

Thompson: Well, I think it's one of two things. Either Khrushchev was overruled and . . . Or Khrushchev and/or his colleagues were deceived by the Lippmann piece and the fact that [Austrian foreign minister Bruno] Kreisky put this out, in which he made him [Khrushchev] think that we were putting this out—that we were willing to make the trade.

Dillon: Well let me veer at this thing differently, because we ought to say: "Unless you agree not to shoot at our unarmed planes until these things of yours are inoperable in Cuba, then we're going to have to hit you. The choice is yours."

Vice President Johnson: What did Lippmann's piece say now?

Dillon: Doesn't say anything about Turkey.

Vice President Johnson: Turkey and Cuba offset each other?

Thompson: He said at least it is negotiated on this basis. . . . Turkey out. He suggests—

Vice President Johnson: We're getting a feeling now where he's at all the time. This was what—

Dillon: Well, he [Khrushchev] made the Turkey-Cuba trade [proposal] right after Lippmann did. So he thought that was, again, what inspired [*unclear*] to do, just to see [*unclear*].

Thompson: And too, he [Lippmann] has a close relationship with Mac. [Khrushchev is saying:] "These boys are beginning to give way. Let's push harder."

I think they'll change their minds when we take any forceful action, stopping their ship or taking out a SAM site or killing a Russian somewhere. But if we . . . Other than that, I'd rather shoot at any planes that come up or shoot [at] some of our [reconnaissance aircraft] . . .

Dillon: Or would you rather send them a thing like this which says: "If they shoot at all, you're going to take them all out." Or would you rather just go in and take one SAM site out?

Thompson: I'm inclined to take one site. I don't think, given an ultimatum of this kind . . . I don't necessarily—

Dillon: If he's given an ultimatum—

Thompson: We ought to take some action that makes him realize there is going to be . . . [*Unclear exchange.*]

Vice President Johnson: You war hawks ought to get together. [*Laughter.*]

Well, what if he's . . . If he was motivated by Lippmann's message, why? Is it your theory that he got it after he sent his letter last night and before this one this morning?

Thompson: No. I think the decision was made after he sent that first letter. In the first letter he was wobbling around and going on about Cuba. Everybody was [*unclear*]. [*Unclear*] is not to be ignored. We can get . . . if we state this publicly.

McCone: I want to go somewhere where we can dictate something.

Dillon: Try downstairs.

McCone: I propose that—

Unidentified: Who's got a secretary?

Unidentified: They're down in the Situation Room, aren't they? [*Unclear exchange.*]

McCone: [*reading*]

I think that it is the responsibility of the United States to make the necessary provisions to order surveillance of the missile sites you have been secretly installing in Cuba. This I announced to the world on last Monday night in a statement with which you are familiar.

As a result, unarmed United States planes have conducted regular surveillance flights over Cuba, and from them I have learned and informed the American public that you are persisting in the construction of these missile bases. Today your forces have fired on our planes, damaging some of them, including—

Dillon and **Rusk:** Unarmed planes.
McCone: Yes.

—unarmed planes, damaging some of them and shooting down one, killing a pilot. This shocking further provocation on your part, coming to my attention as I was drafting a response to your recent messages, causes me to advise you that further attacks on our unarmed reconnaissance planes cannot be tolerated and that, if they occur again, there is no course open to me than to order such action as is necessary to ensure the safety of United States planes.

Obviously you cannot expect me, in view of the highly secret nature of your Cuban operation, to do other than to learn, by all means available to me, the nature of the threat against my country you have secretly created—

Unidentified: The nations of this hemisphere.
McCone: Yeah, I have that.
Rusk: The nations of this hemisphere.
McCone: [*continuing*]

—if I am to discharge my responsibility, which you so clearly recognize.

Yesterday, Secretary General U Thant received one proposal from you. In the evening I received another quite different one. And this morning I received through public channels a communication, still a third proposal, this one introducing a new and wholly unrelated matter. All are worthy of serious consideration and discussion, and I am prepared to make such arrangements from my side.

However, I must know that during both the preliminary talks, and the more extended ones you intimate, that the work on your offensive bases in Cuba is halted, the missiles are made inoperable and ultimately are to be removed.

Until the United Nations or other agreed means of verification are established, no course is open to me [other] than aerial surveillance as publicly announced, and any action on your part to halt this will necessitate such actions by the United States as I deem necessary.

Rusk: That's very good. Can we get it back?

Dillon: Well, that's very good but you don't talk about giving up [missiles in Turkey] . . .

McCone: No. I do say that all three of them [Khrushchev's proposals] are worthy of talking about.

Unidentified: There's someplace for having them do that too.

McCone: Yeah, that's someplace to start from.

Now I think we ought to send him . . . I don't think we ought to let this one go by.

Mixed voices, there may be some people entering or leaving the room.

Rusk: The shooting starts around Cuba. Again, I'll say it once further, that the Cubans are beginning to realize that something serious is up.

Vice President Johnson: I'm surprised that they have been allowing these planes to go in all these days anyway without any action. That's what . . .

Unidentified: They've stepped up.

Vice President Johnson: I'm concerned with how gleeful our people have been for the last couple of days in the papers. I mean how the whole appearance is. And I don't think that's good for us. He's [Khrushchev] looking at it, he's in behind the eight ball a little bit, and he's got to get a little blood. And he's *got* it.

Now, when they realize that they shot down one of our pilots, we're letting this ship go through and that ship go through, and we've had a hell of a . . . They'll want to know what we are going to be doing.

[*quietly*] I guess it will be done tomorrow. I guess we'll be doing something tomorrow. Put the blanket [surveillance] down. And they'll shoot and we'll shoot and that's . . .

. . .

Vice President Johnson: Actually, the Russians are doing it, but you have to give them hell.

Dillon: We know the Russians are doing it, but we don't want to kill the Russians. Don't we have to change it [*perhaps referring to McCone's draft message to Khrushchev*] and say: "Unless you prevail upon your Cuban . . ."

Thompson: The only thing that bothers me at all about is the . . . You can see that we have two conflicting things here. One is to prepare for an attack on Cuba, and the other is to get a peaceful solution along the lines which we have proposed. And the purposes are conflicting. If you want to get him to accept this thing that he put in his letter last night, then we shouldn't give any indication we're ready to talk about the Turkish thing. Because if we do, and put it forward, then we have to take one of those two courses.

Rusk: Is that [message to Khrushchev] now being translated?

Unidentified: Yes, they are going to deliver it in English. They called the messenger into the local embassy here.[22]

Rusk: I see.

Unidentified: The whole problem is to make those operational.

Unidentified: Can we send it on the wire from here?

Unclear exchange; two conversations are going on at once, one culminating in brief laughter.

Vice President Johnson: —those damn planes that he has going.

Thompson: They've [the Soviets have] done two things. They've put up the price and they have escalated the action.

Vice President Johnson: The action?

Thompson: The action. And I think to mention, as McCone does [in his new draft message to Khrushchev], that we can discuss these other things may be to give them a further ground for attack, but it certainly is bad from the perspective of Khrushchev. I think this is a further sign of weakness.

Unidentified: The Turks?

Thompson: It's a further sign of weakness to indicate a willingness to talk about this thing which he put up which was, I think, comparatively unacceptable to us. This is missiles for missiles, and technicians for technicians, and planes for planes.

Vice President Johnson: I guess what he's [Khrushchev is] really saying: "I'm going to dismantle the foreign policy of the United States for the last 15 years in order to get these missiles out of Cuba." [*Pause.*] Then we say we're glad, and we appreciate it, and we want to discuss it with you.

Thompson: How is it left about this last letter to U Thant—after Khrushchev has talked to U Thant? Is that not to be made public? Is that entirely consistent? Because if we get that [President Kennedy's letter to Khrushchev] out in public, I think that offsets a lot of things. I think we're worried here at present about the public posture. It would make the Cuban thing—I mean the Turkish deal—look good. And this thing was put forward by Khrushchev, and that weakens his position. I mean he's put this forward, then suddenly he shifts. The public will realize this, that he's suddenly stepped up the ante.

Vice President Johnson: Yes if he's looking last night [*unclear*], thinking this morning they were going to have much less. They shoot down this plane; it won't make the folks too anxious to trade anyway.

Dillon: Well, I think that it's very good that this letter be sent to [both] Khrushchev and U Thant [effectively making it public]. If it's not out tomorrow, it looks like we haven't even answered, sat around for 24 hours, and done nothing.

Unidentified: The letter we need . . . We have to have this letter [to Khrushchev]; the thing leaves at 7:30.

Dillon: It is. The one you just sent?

Unidentified: The one we've just sent to him just now.

Unidentified: The one to Khrushchev leaves at 7:30.

And the answer to the inevitable questions about it: "Are you going to tell us what was in the letter Mr. Khrushchev sent to Mr. Kennedy [referred to in Kennedy's letter]?" The President instructed Pierre to say that: "You can draw your own conclusions from the letter President Kennedy wrote."

Thompson: Do you suppose that's [*unclear*], because Khrushchev put his last letter on the wire before we got it.

Vice President Johnson: Mr. Khrushchev's letter of last night still is—[*Mixed voices.*]

Dillon: I don't think you should publish his private letter. If you *ever* want to keep the channel that way.

Unidentified: Well, I think the whole thing actually—

Rusk: What time do you think we ought to reassemble, Mac? Or should we just stay here? I was just thinking about getting off [*unclear*].

Vice President Johnson: We should ask Mr. McNamara how far along he is with his draft. He and Ros ought to be over with the different one they did. [*Unclear exchange; people are moving around.*]

Dillon: . . . may be one or the other, if we're serious about [*unclear*] reconaissance. It's just to go in and take aim at the SAM site tomorrow.

Unidentified: We've already told them.

Dillon: Well then, also, it just isn't an ultimatum unless you do so.

Thompson: It's not an ultimatum to them, if it was announced in advance that we would do it. [*Unclear exchange.*]

Vice President Johnson: You just ask yourself what made the greatest impression on you today, whether it was his letter last night, or whether it was his letter this morning, or whether it was that U-2 boy going down.

Dillon: The U-2 boy.

Vice President Johnson: That's exactly right; that's what did it.

That's when everybody started to change, and that [attacking a SAM site] is what's going to make an impression on him—not all these signals that each one of us write. He [Khrushchev] is an expert at that palaver.

There is a pause. At this point, at about 7:20 P.M., President Kennedy returned to the Cabinet Room. During the approximately fifty minutes that President Kennedy was away, Robert Kennedy and Sorensen had hammered out the final version of the letter to Khrushchev. The President approved it. Perhaps while it was being typed and prepared for transmission to the U.S. Embassy in Moscow, President Kennedy and his brother talked about the death of the U-2 pilot. President Kennedy commented, his brother remembered, on how it is always the brave and the best who die.

President Kennedy and his brother also decided that Robert Kennedy would arrange to see Soviet ambassador Dobrynin and personally deliver a copy of the letter to Khrushchev. Robert Kennedy called Dobrynin at about 7:15 and arranged to see him at the Attorney General's Justice Department office in half an hour. They then rejoined the meeting in the Cabinet Room. President Kennedy is ready now to wrap up the Executive Committee meeting that has been going on for about three and a half hours.

President Kennedy: I'm sorry. I didn't mean to keep you. I think we ought to go, Mr. Secretary, go back to this problem. And then when we get these messages to the Turks, the British, and the NATO messages . . .

Bundy: We have to [send] to the NATO . . . We have to instruct Finletter. We have really to agree on the track, you see, Mr. President, and I think that there is a very substantial difference between us.

Vice President Johnson: Secretary McNamara is drafting that message. [*Unclear exchange.*]

President Kennedy: Let's see what the difference is, and then we can think about that. What is the difference?

Bundy: Well, I haven't been in as much of the discussion as some others, Mr. President, to back them up at this stage.

Thompson: Well, I can't express his view better than Bob McNamara could do, but I think we clearly have a choice here, that either we go on the line that we've decided to attack Cuba and therefore are set to prepare the ground for that.

Or we try to get Khrushchev back on a peaceful solution, in which case we shouldn't give any indication that we're going to accept anything on Turkey because the Turkish proposal is, I should think, clearly unacceptable. It's missile for missile, plane for plane, technician for technician, and it leaves, if it worked out, it would leave the Russians installed in Cuba. And I think that should be . . . something we couldn't accept.

It seems to me there are many indications that they suddenly thought they could get it and upped the price. They've upped the price, and they've upped the action. And I think that we have to bring them back by upping our action, and by getting them back to this other thing [the no-invasion pledge proposal] without any mention of Turkey. Because this is bad, maybe, from the point of view that you said . . . it seems to me we have to . . . we have to cover that [the Jupiters] later.

But [in your current letter to Khrushchev] we're going to surface his first proposal [of October 26], which gets it off the public position and gets them back centered on Cuba, and our willingness to accept it. And that somewhat diminishes the need for any talk about Turkey. It seems to me the public will be pretty solid on that, and that we ought to keep the heat on him and get him back on the line which he obviously was on the night before.

That message [of October 26] was almost incoherent, and showed that they were quite worried. And the Lippmann article and maybe the Kreisky speech has made them think they can get more, and they backed away from it.

President Kennedy: When did Kreisky make his suggestions about Turkey?

Thompson: In a public speech to a party group, we think.

President Kennedy: And Lippmann had it when?

Bundy: Two days ago.

President Kennedy: Two days ago?

Sorensen: It was in the *Washington Post*, [*unclear*] on Wednesday.

Unidentified: It's been around; can't avoid it.

President Kennedy: Still I think we ought to—[*unclear aside*]—I'm just saying that first we ought to try to go the first route which you suggest. Get him back. That's what our letter's doing. That's what we're going to do by one means or another.

But then it seems to me we ought to have a discussion with NATO about these Turkish missiles, but more generally about sort of an up-to-date briefing about where we're going. So . . .

Vice President Johnson: Well, we have two alternatives. Secretary McNamara suggests that we draft a message to the Turks and to the NATO people, saying that we will give you Polaris for the Jupiters in Turkey. And then we're going to hit Cuba, and therefore we ought to do this because then it means that *you're* safer than you would be. That's what he's drafting.

Ball takes the position that you shouldn't. You should get something for your trade. If you're going to give up the Jupiters, why, you ought to get him to take care of Cuba.

President Kennedy: Well—[*mixed voices*] There's a third view, which is that you take him back to his [October 26 proposal]—

Vice President Johnson: McCone's got one [his new draft message to Khrushchev] that lays down an ultimatum, that just says we're going to [say]: "You shot our man there, and we aren't going to take any more of this."

Rusk: Well, where would you be on Cuba on that one?

Mr. President, I think that the trouble with Ball's track is that their public statements today would mean—plane for plane, man for man, missile for missile—

Unidentified: Who said this?

Rusk: That's Ball's track, a sort of accepting, in effect, the broadcast speech of this morning. It would just get us completely out of Turkey in every respect or leave the Soviets very much in Cuba.

It's the track of last night we want to get them back to. I think if we step up our actions tomorrow against Cuba, not against—not necessarily against the Soviet Union . . .

President Kennedy: Well, we're going to call up some Air [Force] Reserves tonight.

Dillon: Ambassador Thompson has another idea, which was that instead of the ultimatum, a lot of talk about if you shoot any more of our unarmed planes, that it would probably be more effective and make more of an impression on him if we did do what we said we were going to do before, and just go in and knock out this one SAM site.

Bundy: That would be the best way of impressing him.

Dillon: Don't say anything. Just do that.

President Kennedy: And we don't know where that plane was shot there, do we?

Bundy: We know about where it was shot down.

President Kennedy: But we don't know if it was shot down yet, do we?

Four seconds excised as classified information.

Bundy: The Cubans have command of the ground, but they've probably shifted, if I understand it. . . .

Unidentified: That's correct.

Unidentified: The time and the place where he went off our track is where the Cubans say. But there is still no evidence, on our side—

President Kennedy: That he was shot down.

Bundy: We can't get any more evidence than that. That's what the intercepts say.

Unidentified: Havana might announce it, which would be—

Unidentified: Havana *has* announced it, that he *was* shot down by antiaircraft fire.

President Kennedy: Oh, they have? I'm sorry, I didn't know that yet.

Unidentified: Havana radio has announced that.

President Kennedy: Well, we ought to get that, because I'm not sure that Secretary McNamara knows that. Can you get the actual program?

Unidentified: That came from [CIA official Herbert "Pete"] Scoville, and let me double-check the messages.

Thompson: I also think that we ought to . . . If that Soviet ship [the *Grozny*] comes in within this line, we ought to stop it.

Unidentified: Do we have any idea what that ship is carrying?

Unidentified: No.

Unidentified: Has it got deck cargo?

Unidentified: Yeah, but just a [*unclear*].

Thompson: You have to stop and inspect it and let it go through. If you let it . . .

President Kennedy: In his [Khrushchev's] message this morning on Turkey, did he say if we took out the missiles in Turkey, he'd take out the missiles in Cuba?

Dillon: Yes. He said: "*analogous* things." We take out what we considered offensive, and analogous things would have to come out of Turkey. That was the wording.

Thompson: [*reading from his version of Khrushchev's message*] "I therefore make this proposal. We agree to remove from Cuba those means which you regard as offensive means. We agree to see this carried out and make" a pledge in the U.N. "Your representatives will make a declaration to the effect that the U.S., on its part . . . will remove its similar means from Turkey."[23]

That's why I think it's very dangerous to indicate any tentative play on this thing. He's really got us there. As the Secretary says, it's either/or. If we get along this path we either get out of Turkey completely, or we leave the Soviets in Cuba and have only missiles out.

Bundy: Well, we could make a counterproposal—

Thompson: Yes.

Bundy: —obviously, that if he would get everything out of Cuba, we would negotiate with the Turks with the same objective, if he would undertake to do so.

Dillon: Can't do that.

President Kennedy: We can't very well invade Cuba, with all this toil and blood it's going to be, when we could have gotten them [the Soviet missiles] out by making a deal on the same missiles in Turkey. If that's part of the record, then I don't see how we'll have a very good war.

But other than that, it is really a question of what to say to NATO. I don't . . .

Vice President Johnson: It doesn't mean just missiles. He takes his missiles out of Cuba; and takes his men out of Cuba; and takes his planes out of Cuba. Why then your whole foreign policy is gone. You take everything out of Turkey. Twenty thousand men, all your technicians, and all your planes, and all your missiles. And crumble.

Thompson: Especially if [*unclear*].

Vice President Johnson: It won't. It won't.

President Kennedy: How else are we going to get those missiles out of there then? That's the problem.

Rusk: Well, last night, he was prepared to trade them for a promise not to invade. Now he's . . .

Vice President Johnson: Somebody told him to try to get a little more.

McCone: Well maybe you ought to send him a tougher message.

President Kennedy: Well I've already sent him one.

McCone: Well this is a thoughtful one. [*Laughter, unclear exchange.*]

Vice President Johnson: Do you have a copy of it?

McCone: Here it is.

President Kennedy: [*Unclear, reading draft.*] [*Unclear exchange.*]

Thompson: Call them Cuban forces, instead of your forces.

McCone: No. I think they are his forces.

Rusk: No, but I mean we—

President Kennedy: Can we meet here . . . I don't think we can get it.

I think we've got two or three different proposals here. Can we meet at nine [P.M.] and everybody get a bite to eat, and then come back and see whether we send this [McCone's] message.

We'll see about what we do about our plane. We see about our two messages to the U.N.—I mean—this Turkish thing [the McNamara and Ball alternatives], and probably think about that. And I think it would be better at . . . Say nine we meet?

The marathon Executive Committee meeting then broke up. There is some mixed discussion for several minutes as participants leave.

President Kennedy's message to Khrushchev was transmitted to Moscow a few minutes later, at about 8:00 P.M. Robert Kennedy was preparing to deliver it personally to Dobrynin. The message was being simultaneously released to the press. The final message read as follows:

Dear Mr. Chairman:

I have read your letter of October 26 with great care and welcomed the statement of your desire to seek a prompt solution to the problem. The first thing that needs to be done, however, is for work to cease on offensive missile bases in Cuba and for all weapons systems in Cuba capable of offensive use to be rendered inoperable, under effective United Nations arrangements.

Assuming this is done promptly, I have given my representatives in New York instructions that will permit them to work out this week and—in cooperation with the Acting Secretary General and your representative—an arrangement for a permanent solution to the Cuban problem along the lines suggested in your letter of October 26. As I read your letter, the key elements of your proposals—which seem generally acceptable as I understand them—are as follows:

1. You would agree to remove these weapons systems from Cuba under appropriate United Nations observation and supervision; and undertake, with suitable safeguards, to halt the further introduction of such weapons systems into Cuba.

2. We, on our part, would agree—upon the establishment of adequate arrangements through the United Nations to ensure the carrying out and continuation of these commitments—(a) to remove promptly the quarantine measures now in effect and (b) to give assurances against an invasion of Cuba and I am confident that other nations of the Western Hemisphere would be prepared to do likewise.

If you will give your representative similar instructions, there is no reason why we should not be able to complete these arrangements and announce them to the world within a couple of days. The effect of such a settlement on easing world tensions would enable us to work toward a more general arrangement regarding "other armaments," as proposed in your second letter which you made public. I would like to say that the United States is very much interested in reducing tensions and halting the arms race; and if your letter signifies that you are prepared to discuss a detente affecting NATO and the Warsaw Pact, we are quite prepared to consider with our allies any useful proposals.

But the first ingredient, let me emphasize, is the cessation of work on missile sites in Cuba and measures to render such weapons inoperable, under effective international guarantees. The continuation of this threat, or a prolonging of this discussion concerning Cuba by linking these problems to the broader questions of European and world security, would surely lead to an intensification of the Cuban crisis and a grave risk to the peace of the world. For this reason I hope we can quickly agree along the lines outlined in this letter and in your letter of October 26.

/s/ John F. Kennedy

As the members of the Executive Committee filed out of the Cabinet Room, at about 7:45 P.M., some of them were asked to stay behind and join President Kennedy in the Oval Office for another, brief, discussion on just how Robert Kennedy should deliver this letter to Ambassador Dobrynin. Dobrynin would be waiting for Robert Kennedy at the Justice Department. President Kennedy gathered some of his advisers in the Oval Office for this brief discussion about what his brother should say to Dobrynin, to amplify on the contents of the letter to Khrushchev. That meeting was not taped, but Bundy, who refreshed his memory with long hours listening to these recordings, recalled clearly that:[24]

. . . a smaller group moved from the Cabinet Room to the Oval Office to talk over the second means of communication—an oral message to be conveyed to Ambassador Dobrynin. As I remember it, those present in the discussion that followed with the president were Dean Rusk, Robert McNamara, Robert Kennedy, George Ball, Roswell Gilpatric, Llewellyn Thompson, Theodore Sorensen, and I. One part of the oral message we discussed was simple, stern, and quickly decided—that the time had come to agree on the basis set out in the President's new letter: no Soviet missiles in Cuba, and no U.S. invasion. Otherwise further American action was unavoidable. This stern part of the message was implicit in what we had been discussing all day, and I do not recall that we had difficulty in agreeing on it. The president in particular was clear and insistent on this part of the message.

The other part of the oral message was proposed by Dean Rusk: that we should tell Khrushchev that while there could be no deal over the Turkish missiles, the president was determined to get them out and would do so once the Cuban crisis was resolved. The proposal was quickly supported by the rest of us and approved by the president. It was also agreed that knowledge of this assurance would be held among those present and no one else. Concerned as we all were by the cost of a public bargain struck under pressure at the apparent expense of the Turks, and aware as we were from the day's discussion that for some, even in our closest councils, even this unilateral private assurance might appear to betray an ally, we agreed without hesitation that no one not in the room was to be informed of this additional message. Robert Kennedy was instructed to make it plain to Dobrynin that the same secrecy must be observed on the other side, and that any Soviet reference to our assurance would simply make it null and void.

. . . The meeting in the Oval Office lasted perhaps 20 minutes. The moment Dean Rusk made his suggestion it became apparent to all of us that we should agree. It would allow us to respond to Khrushchev's second proposal in a way that he might well regard as helpful, while at the same time it did not require us to engage NATO or the Turks in a public trade of "their" interests for "ours."[25] No one could be sure it would work, but all of us believed it was worth a try.

That it was Rusk who offered the proposal made it easier for the rest of us to support it. None of us could suppose that he was insensitive to the interests of allies, and none could think of him as eager to make unwise concessions to Soviet pressure. . . . If he thought this assurance could properly be offered, it became relatively easy for the rest of us to agree.[26]

The finesse Rusk suggested would not have been new to some officials in the room. In the portion of his message that had arrived early in the afternoon, Ambassador Hare, in Ankara, had suggested a secret deal with the Soviets, if the Soviets could be trusted to keep it secret (which he doubted). From their remarks during the afternoon Executive Committee meeting and other evidence, it is plain that at least Rusk and Bundy had read Hare's cable.

Robert Kennedy immediately left for the Justice Department, where he met with Dobrynin. A few days later, he prepared the following account of his conversation with the Soviet ambassador.[27]

We met in my office. I told him [Dobrynin] first that we understood that the work was continuing on the Soviet missile bases in Cuba. Further, I explained to him that in the last two hours we had found that our planes flying over Cuba had been fired upon and that one of our U-2s had been shot down and the pilot killed. I said these men were flying unarmed planes.

I told him that this was an extremely serious turn in events. We would have to make certain decisions within the next 12 or possibly 24 hours. There was a very little time left. If the Cubans were shooting at our planes, then we were going to shoot back. This could not help but bring on further incidents and that he had better understand the full implications of this matter.

He raised the point that the argument the Cubans were making was that we were violating Cuban air space. I replied that if we had not been violating Cuban air space then we would still be believing what he and Khrushchev had said—that there were no long-range missiles in Cuba. In any case I said that this matter was far more serious than the air space over Cuba and involved peoples all over the world.

I said that he had better understand the situation and he had better communicate that understanding to Mr. Khrushchev. Mr. Khrushchev and he had misled us. The Soviet Union had secretly established missile bases in Cuba while at the same time proclaiming, privately and publicly, that this would never be done. I said those missile bases had to go and they had to go right away. We had to have a commitment by at least tomorrow that those bases would be removed. This was not an ultimatum, I said, but just a statement of fact. He should understand that if they did not remove those bases then we would remove them. His country might take retaliatory action but he should understand that before this was over, while there might be dead Americans there would also be dead Russians.

He asked me then what offer we were making. I said a letter had just been transmitted to the Soviet Embassy [U.S. Embassy in Moscow] which stated in substance that the missile bases should be dismantled and all offensive weapons should be removed from Cuba. In return, if Cuba and Castro and the Communists ended their subversive activities in other Central and Latin-American countries, we would agree to keep peace in the Caribbean and not permit an invasion from American soil.[28]

He then asked me about Khrushchev's other proposal dealing with the removal of the missiles from Turkey. I replied that there could no *quid pro quo*—no deal of this kind could be made. This was a matter that had to be considered by NATO and that it was up to NATO to make the decision. I said it was completely impossible for NATO to take such a step under the present threatening position of the Soviet Union. If some time elapsed—and per your [Rusk's] instructions, I mentioned 4 or 5 months—I said I was sure that these matters could be resolved satisfactorily.[29]

Per your instructions I repeated that there could be no deal of any kind and that any steps toward easing tensions in other parts of the world largely depended on the Soviet Union and Mr. Khrushchev taking action in Cuba and taking it immediately.

I repeated to him that this matter could not wait and that he had better contact Mr. Khrushchev and have a commitment from him by the next day to withdraw the missile bases under United Nations supervision for otherwise, I said, there would be drastic consequences.

9:00 P.M.

Executive Committee Meeting of the National Security Council

When Robert Kennedy returned to the White House at about 8:40 P.M., he found President Kennedy had just finished a brief swim and was having a light dinner with a close aide, Dave Powers, in the Mansion. Powers remembered Robert Kennedy giving a pessimistic account of the meeting with Dobrynin. Powers was gobbling down his food. "God, Dave," President Kennedy said, "the way you're eating up all that chicken and drinking up all my wine, anybody would think it was your last meal."

"The way Bobby's been talking, I thought it was my last meal," Powers answered.[30]

The Defense Department was preoccupied with the question of what to do about the downed U-2 flight and what to say about it to a clamoring press.

At the State Department some additional news had come in, none of it good. As some Soviet ships continued to steam toward the quarantine line, the government wanted to be sure there was no misunderstanding about the location of the line. Stevenson had offered a formal, written clarification of the contours of the interception zone to Zorin. Zorin had refused to accept the document. Castro had publicly answered the previous day's appeal to him from U Thant, asking for a temporary suspension of missile site construction. Washington now received a copy of Castro's message refusing the appeal and demanding an immediate halt to the quarantine.

Castro did, however, invite U Thant to come to Havana for direct talks about the crisis. Castro also delivered another speech to the Cuban people, which was being digested in Washington as the 9:00 meeting of the Executive Committee began.

President Kennedy apparently turned on the tape recorder as Rusk was completing his status report.

Dean Rusk: . . . Certainly he [Khrushchev] has made a public speech on the subject [referring to his public message earlier that day]. But we've also made some public speeches, and I think we're in such a confrontation that he's got to worry very much as his telegram last night, it seemed to me, obviously showed. He's got to worry a great deal about how far he wants to push this thing. He's on a bad footing on his relations with the United States, his relations with you, the actual strategic situation.

I would think that tomorrow we take certain steps to build up the pressure. We have an enforced surveillance. We shoot anybody who gets in our way. We see whether U Thant produces any result tonight, or into the morning. We intercept that Soviet ship [the *Grozny*]. We consider, tomorrow afternoon, putting POL on the blockade.

In the firing that goes on in Cuba, we keep the focus on the Cubans. I had some suggestions in John McCone's draft that would tend to do that—the message to Khrushchev about the necessity for enforced surveillance—that would keep the monkey on Cuba's back with this regard. If we do have to enforce our right to overfly and to have a look, the accidental fact that some Russian technicians may be around at the time we have to shoot, since they've already fired the first shot, is something that is regrettable. But it is not something that we can make a very public issue out of. We are enforcing this with respect to Cuba, not the Soviet Union—the surveillance business.

C. Douglas Dillon: Do anything about the SAM site that shot down our plane?

President Kennedy: We don't know if it did yet, Doug.

Rusk: If we are going in tomorrow with the . . . previously announced that we are going to enforce the right to surveillance—

McGeorge Bundy: If U Thant gets assurances that allow him [U Thant] to proceed to Havana.

Dillon: We probably just go in if nobody . . . without the assurance.

Bundy: Would you like to discuss the surveillance problem?

Maxwell Taylor: Yes.

The Chiefs have been . . . I went back to them [*unclear*] and talked this over with the Chiefs. The problem of low-level surveillance is becoming difficult because in all the flights today around the SAM sites and the certain missile sites there is low-level ack-ack [antiaircraft artillery].

President Kennedy: There was a lot of firing today, wasn't there?

Taylor: Quite a bit. The planes are turning back. Got overused at the first of the missile sites and then, at the second, turned back and cut out. We have some photography.

So I would say by tonight, by the end of the day, we probably have seen some of the [antiaircraft] dispositions around these sites. However, the kind of 20-millimeter flak that's involved is very hard to pick up. It's very hard to know exactly where it is. So that by tomorrow, I would say we're not ready to go back with *armed* reconnaissance preceding the actual photographic missions, with any hope of cleaning out these little air sites.

We think, however, the Chiefs would recommend, that we still go back with about six planes tomorrow, picking out targets which we don't know have this kind of flak around, and verify the work [on the missile sites] is still going ahead, and also prove we're still on the job.

But we're approaching the point I think, Mr. President, where low-level reconnaissance will be entirely impossible. And if we reach that point, and if we're going to continue reconnaissance, without actually taking out the whole works, we're faced with taking out a number of the SAM sites that—say ten—to get a squad coming in again at medium- and high-level reconnaissance. But low-level reconnaissance probably is on its way out, as I think we'll learn at the end of tomorrow.

Robert McNamara: I would add to that, I don't believe we should carry out tomorrow's U-2 mission. The U-2 is just too dangerous [*unclear*].

But I do believe we should carry out the low-level reconnaissance with the necessary fighter escorts and preparations for following the reconnaissance, if it's attacked, with attack on the attackers.

Taylor: We don't think that fighter escort on the low level will help tomorrow. These [fighter] planes are off the coast now, in case they have a cripple [a damaged reconnaissance aircraft] coming out. But this was a case again of us trying to put a rush crew on certain targets that we know, we don't think are . . .

Dillon: I wasn't quite clear. Is the antiaircraft shooting at these things around the missile sites themselves?

Taylor: Either side of these missile sites, they are.

McNamara: I think that the point is, that if our planes are fired on tomorrow, we ought to fire back. That's what I'd have the [*unclear*], we fire back at the best indication of the antiaircraft sites that we have, [which] is around the missile sites—

Rusk: Why fire back at some missiles on the ground on the basis that you're firing back at the antiaircraft [guns]?

Dillon: Because that's where they are, that's what they think.

President Kennedy: Let me say, I think we ought to wait till tomorrow afternoon, to see whether we get any answers if U Thant goes down there [to Havana].

We're rapidly approaching a real . . . I don't think that firing back at a 20 millimeter [gun] coming off the ground is good. I think we ought to figure that Monday [October 29], if tomorrow they fire at us and we don't have any answer from the Russians, then Monday, it seems to me . . . . We ought to, maybe, consider making a statement tomorrow about the firing and that we're going to take action now any place in Cuba on those areas which can fire. And then go in and take *all* the SAM sites out. I don't think that it does any good to take out, to try to fire at a 20 millimeter on the ground. We just hazard our planes, and the people on the ground have the advantage.

On the other hand, I don't want, I don't think we do any good to begin to sort of *half* do it. I think we ought to keep tomorrow clean, do the best we can with the surveillance. If they still fire and we haven't got a satisfactory answer back from the Russians, then I think we ought to put a statement out tomorrow that we are fired upon. We are therefore considering the island of Cuba as an open territory, and then take out all these SAM sites.

Otherwise, what we're going to do is find this buildup of the protection for the SAM sites low [with guns to fire at low-flying planes], and the SAM sites high [missiles for high-flying aircraft], and we'll find ourselves without . . . Our reply will be so limited and we'll find ourselves with all the disadvantages.

I think we ought to, tomorrow, let's get U Thant our messages: If they fire on us, tell them [the reconnaissance pilots] to come on out. And then if we don't get some satisfaction from the Russians or U Thant or Cuba tomorrow night, figure that Monday we're going to do something about the SAM sites. What do you think?

McNamara: I would say only that we ought to keep some kind of pressure on tonight and tomorrow night that indicates we're firm. Now if we call off these air strikes tonight, I think that settles that—

President Kennedy: I [*unclear*] want to do that, I think—

McNamara: I have a paper here that relates . . . we haven't discussed it yet, Mr. President. If I can interrupt now to say I believe we should issue an order tonight calling up the 24 air reserve squadrons, roughly 300 troop carrier transports, which are required for an invasion. And this would both be a preparatory move, and also a strong indication of what lies ahead.

President Kennedy: I think we ought to do that.

McNamara: All right, sir.

Taylor: I might say this, that as a part of the help to cutting the time short of an invasion, shipping is really more important than this, although I'm entirely for this.

President Kennedy: Well, tomorrow, when we talk, Mr. Secretary, I thought tomorrow we'd do the shipping. We ought to break it in two. Because the air is the focus of interest right now, what we're trying to do is get a settlement of this. I thought maybe the first one ought to be the air.

Unidentified: Are you going to alert them or call them up?

Roswell Gilpatric and **McNamara:** Call them up.

President Kennedy: I think you ought to go ahead and do that.

McNamara: I would like to put that out. [*Unclear interjection.*] I can do it under the Executive Order that you signed granting me the authority. [*Unclear comment.*]

I would like this to . . . Let me read this [draft press statement] and see:

> Today, U.S. unarmed reconnaissance aircraft, conducting surveillance of the buildup of offensive weapons secretly introduced into Cuba by the Soviet Union, were fired upon. Such surveillance operations were in accordance with the resolution adopted on October 23rd, by the Organ of Consultation of the inter-American system under the provisions of the Rio Treaty of 1947. To ensure that the nations of the Western Hemisphere continue to be informed of the status of the threat to their security, it is essential that such reconnaissance flights continue. To protect these flights against attack, they will henceforth be accompanied by fighter escorts. The possibility of further attack on our aircraft and the continuous buildup of the offensive weapon systems in Cuba require that we be prepared for any eventuality. Therefore, tonight, acting under the authority granted to me by the Executive Order such and such, I have instructed the Secretary of the Air Force to order to active duty 24 troop carrier squadrons of the Air Force Reserve and their associated support units.

. . .

Rusk: Mr. President, just to remind us of seven things then that will happen today. We need just to see whether they are building up the pressures on Khrushchev with an impact that we can live with.

One was the [White House] statement this morning on the broadcast [message from Moscow].

The second was this business on the intercept for U Thant [formally clarifying the contours of the interception zone].

Third was an announcement [from the Pentagon] on enforced surveillance.

Fourth was our short message to U Thant, diplomatic answer [to Khrushchev's public message] on the two terrific questions.

Five was our answer to K's letter [Khrushchev's letter] of October 26th.

Six was a call-up of air squadrons.

Seven will be a warning to U Thant of an approaching ship.

Now, in general, I think perhaps for one day, that's building up. But I think tomorrow we'll need to be sure that the pressures continue to build up, if we . . .

President Kennedy: Well, we've got two things [we can do]. First place we've got the POL [blockade].

Secondly, we've got the announcement about these [air defense sites].

Whatever happens. if we don't take this ship [the *Grozny*], we announce that the agreement has been broken, and from now on it's POL [being stopped], all ships, and so on.

McNamara: [*having returned from his brief press appearance*] Twenty-nine [reserve] ships ready [to prepare for the invasion]—

President Kennedy: Call up an addition [to] our own ships. So it seems to me we've got two or three things tomorrow left . . .

Rusk: Bob, if you may take this action calling up, how much of the 150,000 [call-up of reservists authorized by Congress] is left?

McNamara: The air squadrons are 14,000 out of a total of 150.

Bundy (?): There are 125,000 now.

McNamara: Fourteen thousand out of 150. We have 135 left.

Taylor: Can't stress too much the shipping, the importance of shipping, Mr. President. That the next step in my judgment ought to be calling up ships.

President Kennedy: I thought tomorrow we'd do that. But if you add ships, it's just a little late tonight and I think probably tomorrow . . .

Unidentified: I think it's a separate action.

Rusk: Are we going to call up the National Guard?

Gilpatric: No.

McNamara: No, I don't think so, Dean.

Gilpatric: We talked to the governors about that today. We may do something—

McNamara: Yeah, let's put that off.

President Kennedy: What we'd better do now is figure out these messages to NATO and Turkey and . . .

The group then worked on drafting a message that would engage NATO allies, meeting in Paris at the North Atlantic Council on the issues that now faced them all.

. . .

President Kennedy: What we want to do. It seems to me, Mr. Secretary, that even if we want them to end up that way, we don't want it to look like that's where we urged them and therefore they have accepted, some reluctantly, some eagerly, the United States's opinion. Then it goes bad, which it may well. Then they say: "Well, we followed you, and you bitched it up."

But so far what's happened really just involves us, the Russians, and Cuba. Beginning with the offer on Turkey, then they're really in it. I don't think we ought to even indicate . . . All we're doing is saying: "This is it. The situation is getting worse, and we're going to have to take some action. And we want you to know. We want you to have an opportunity, and we're consulting with you, [*unclear*]. Is there any merit in this?

And if we don't take it [the proffered Cuba-Turkey trade], then we want everybody to understand that what we think may be the alternative is we're going to have to move. I think that's probably what this first meeting ought to be, and then have a next . . . have another one the next morning.

But I think this . . . Otherwise, I'm afraid they will say, well, we worked with you but . . .

. . .

John McCone: [*returning to his draft message discussed at the end of the previous meeting*] Well, are we going to start any communications with Khrushchev on this provocation?

President Kennedy: The plane going down? The plane going down?

McCone: Yeah.

President Kennedy: That's the next one.

Rusk: There's a [draft] message there that would keep the finger pointed on Cuba on this business of surveillance, but I gather that those points have already been covered.

President Kennedy: What are we going to announce in regard to tomorrow's planes?

McNamara: We shouldn't announce anything.

President Kennedy: Not whether we are continuing or—

Gilpatric: Because we've already announced that we are going to continue.

McNamara: But we didn't say tomorrow. We just said we're going to continue surveillance.

President Kennedy: We've got enough messages right now, John. I think that he knows about the plane. He's announced it. So I think that . . . let me see this, John.

Theodore Sorensen: I think in some ways it's a sign of weakness if we keep responding in messages.

President Kennedy: I think we shouldn't send him one again. I think we ought to just let that one go tonight. The boat [the *Grozny*] is going to be the important thing. Whether he is going to turn that boat around.

·   ·   ·

McNamara: We have two major decisions we have to make quickly at eleven. We can wait on both of those until eleven. [*Unclear exchange, including Taylor, about the next day's surveillance flights.*] Yes, but we don't let it off until we talk to [*unclear*]. [*Mixed voices, the meeting appears to be breaking up.*]

President Kennedy: They say they shot down our U-2. They say they shot it down. [*Unclear exchange. Eleven seconds excised as classified information.*]

. . . if we go with the low-level reconnaissance at this time. And we don't follow with the . . .

Robert Kennedy: Then I think we ought to, when we get shot at tomorrow, then we ought to have these answers out there.

McNamara: Well. Mr. President, if we go in at the low level tomorrow, we ought to be prepared, it seems to me, to attack MiGs if they attack our aircraft.

Taylor: Well we always, I've said that we're always [*unclear*].

McNamara: This time we would make it perfectly clear if they attack our aircraft, we're going in after some of their MiGs.

Taylor: Yeah.

President Kennedy: It won't be the ground. We'll save that [SAMs and antiaircraft guns] for a real operation, which would [get them]. Under this schedule, you wouldn't do it until Tuesday morning [October 30] because we'll have to go back to NATO again Monday, in which we say the situation is getting worse and so on and so forth. Give them that last chance.

Taylor: Tuesday morning looks like the . . . [*Unclear discussion.*]

McNamara: The thing we haven't talked about today, when we get back, is this [interim occupation] government [for Cuba] in case we do shoot up Cuba in the morning or sometime. The Cuban government. We haven't discussed that today. And we have the military holding the civil affairs problem until the proper stage.

President Kennedy: Is anybody in charge of the—

McNamara: There's a task group of some kind working on it. We ought to take some time tomorrow to talk about that. [*Quiet, inaudible, reply from President Kennedy.*]

Gilpatric: How are the [*unclear*] plans?

Taylor: The plan is about the whole thing and it has civil, civil defense activities.

Robert Kennedy: He [the Army] goes from Mississippi to Cuba?

Laughter, unclear discussion as officials begin leaving the room. President Kennedy has apparently left.

Unidentified: What time did we decide on [meeting] tomorrow morning?

McNamara: Eleven in the morning.

Unidentified: I'll be here.

Unclear reply, and laughter. More mixed voices and fragments of conversation as the officials file out. Sorensen can be heard commenting, "We're really just wasting our time to . . . " Robert Kennedy, McNamara, Dillon, and a few others linger.

Robert Kennedy: How are you doing, Bob?

McNamara: Well. How about yourself?

Robert Kennedy: All right.

McNamara: You got any doubts?

Robert Kennedy: No, I think that we're doing the only thing we can do, and so on. You know.

McNamara: I think the one thing, Bobby . . . we ought to seriously do before we attack them, you've got to be *damned sure they* [the Soviets] *understand it's coming.*

Robert Kennedy: Right?

McNamara: In other words, you need to really escalate this.

Robert Kennedy: Yeah.

McNamara: You can't just throw more of what we're now doing, because . . .

And then we need to have two things ready: A government for Cuba, because we're going to need one after we go in with bomber aircraft.

And, secondly, plans for how to respond to the Soviet Union in Europe because sure as hell they're going to do *something* there.

Dillon: So it's your point [we] have to pick out what's the thing there—

McNamara: Well, I think so, yeah, that's right.

Dillon: It might be just the smallest thing that would aggravate—

McNamara: Yeah. I would suggest to have an eye for an eye.

Unidentified: Yeah. That's right. It isn't too serious.

McNamara: In fact . . .

Dillon: That would do it.

Robert Kennedy: I'd like to take Cuba back. That would be nice.

Unidentified: Yeah, and let's take Cuba away from Castro. [*McNamara begins to stammer a reply.*]

Unidentified: Get all of the Mongoose [people].[31]

Unidentified: Yeah! [*Laughter.*]

Unidentified: [*chuckling*] Don't say . . . you ought to see what fools they are. [*Unclear comment.*]

Unidentified: Yeah, how are you going to partition it [Cuba]?

Unidentified: Suppose we make Bobby mayor of Havana?

Dillon: That's something you're going to have to get done tomorrow.

The Executive Committee meeting then broke up for the night. Work went on, however. The first task was to send off the instructions to NATO and selected U.S. ambassadors in allied capitals. The cable that had been discussed was sent out around midnight. It told the envoys that Khrushchev's October 26 message to President Kennedy and other contacts had "seemed to offer real hope solution could be found" but, as a result of Khrushchev's new, public message, "these hopes have been diminished." The United States would "continue to press for solution in Cuban framework alone." Using President Kennedy's language, the cable then added that the situation was "deteriorating." Given the activity at the missile sites and continued movement of Soviet ships into the interception zone, the ambassadors were warned that the United States might find it necessary "within a very short time" to "take whatever military action may be necessary to remove this growing threat to the Hemisphere." So that they could take the temperature of their foreign counterparts, the ambassadors were also cryptically advised to pass along that "U.S. action in Cuba may result in some Soviet moves against NATO."[32]

Macmillan's reply to Bundy's reports came during the night in

Washington, a night made a little longer because clocks were turned back from daylight saving time to standard time. The message was brief:

> Please pass following message from Prime Minister Macmillan to the President.
>
> I have had the report of Bundy's talks through our night.
>
> The trial of wills is now approaching a climax. Khrushchev's first message, unhappily not published to the world, seemed to go a long way to meet you. His second message, widely broadcast and artfully contrived, adding the Turkey proposal, was a recovery on his part. It has made a considerable impact.
>
> We must now wait to see what Khrushchev does. I shall expect to hear from you how things are developing. I agree that the use of any initiative by me is all a matter of timing.[33]

As many officials, in addition to Bundy, spent the night at their offices that night, President Kennedy was restless too. He and Dave Powers stayed up and watched a screening of a movie Kennedy liked, *Roman Holiday*, starring Audrey Hepburn and Gregory Peck.

SAC bombers continued their round-the-clock circling in Arctic skies. Nearly one hundred warships maintained the quarantine, as more ships readied for invasion. U.S. destroyers patrolled constantly over Soviet submarines in the Atlantic. The Fifth Marine Expeditionary Brigade began boarding the ships that would carry it to the invasion staging areas. The 14,000 Air Force reservists that had been called up that night were saying their good-byes and moving to their active duty stations.

Sunday, October 28, 1962

On the morning of October 28 the *Grozny*, en route into the interception zone, stopped dead in the water. At about 9:00 A.M. in Washington, wire services announced that Khrushchev was sending a new message to the world. The message, broadcast over Radio Moscow, soon began coming off the ticker. The Soviet government would dismantle and remove its missiles from Cuba. The full text of the message followed, as translated unofficially by the U.S. agency that monitored foreign broadcasts.[1] Its highlights were:

> Esteemed Mr. President:
>
> I have received your message of October 27, 1962. I express my satisfaction and gratitude for the sense of proportion and understanding of the responsibility borne by you at present for the preservation of peace throughout the world which you have shown. I very well understand your anxiety and the anxiety of the United States people in connection with the fact that the weapons which you describe as "offensive" are, in fact, grim weapons. Both you and I understand what kind of weapon they are.
>
> In order to complete with greater speed the liquidation of the conflict dangerous to the cause of peace, to give confidence to all people longing for peace, and to calm the American people, who, I am certain, want peace as much as the people of the Soviet Union, the Soviet government, in addition to previously issued instructions on the cessation of further work at building sites for the weapons, has issued a new order on the dismantling of the weapons which you describe as "offensive," and their crating and return to the Soviet Union.[2]
>
> Mr. President, I would like to repeat once more what I had already written to you in my preceding letters—that the Soviet government has placed at the disposal of the Cuban government economic aid, as well as arms, inasmuch as Cuba and the Cuban people have constantly been under the continuous danger of an invasion. . . .
>
> I regard with respect and trust your statement in your message of

October 27, 1962 that no attack will be made on Cuba—that no invasion will take place—not only by the United States, but also by other countries of the Western Hemisphere, as your message pointed out. Then the motives which promoted us to give aid of this nature to Cuba cease. They are no longer applicable. Hence we have instructed our officers—and these means, as I have already stated, are in the hands of Soviet officers—to take necessary measures for stopping the building of the said projects and their dismantling and return to the Soviet Union.

As I already told you in my letter of October 27, we both agree to come to an agreement that United Nations representatives could verify the dismantling of these means.

In this way, if one is to rely on your assurances which you have made and on our orders to dismantle, then all necessary conditions for liquidation of the conflict which has arisen appear to exist.

I note with satisfaction that you have responded to my wish that the said dangerous situation should be liquidated and also that conditions should be created for a more thoughtful appraisal of the international situation which is fraught with great dangers in our age of thermonuclear weapons, rocket technology, space ships, global rockets, and other lethal weapons. All people are interested in insuring peace. Therefore, we who are invested with trust and great responsibility must not permit an exacerbation of the situation and must liquidate the breeding grounds where a dangerous situation has been created fraught with serious consequences for the cause of peace. If we succeed along with you and with the aid of other people of good will in liquidating this tense situation, we must also concern ourselves to see that other dangerous conflicts do not arise which might lead to a world thermonuclear catastrophe.

In conclusion, I wish to speak of the regulation of relation[s] between NATO and states of the Warsaw Treaty, which you mention. We have long ago spoken of this and are ready to continue an exchange of opinions with you on this question and find a reasonable solution. I also wish to continue an exchange of opinions on the prohibition of atomic and thermonuclear weapons, general disarmament, and other questions concerning the lessening of international tension. . . .

In connection with negotiations in progress between U.N. Acting Secretary General U Thant and representatives of the Soviet Union, the United States, and the Cuban Republic, the Soviet government

has sent to New York U.S.S.R. First Deputy Minister of Foreign
Affairs [Vasily] Kuznetsov with a view to assisting U Thant in his
noble efforts aimed at liquidation of the present dangerous situation.

    With respect for you,

    Khrushchev. October 28, 1962

At the Pentagon, the Joint Chiefs were skeptical of Khrushchev's offer.
They approved a memorandum to President Kennedy saying: "The JCS
interpret the Khrushchev statement, in conjunction with the [continuing]
buildup, to be efforts to delay direct action by the United States while
preparing the ground for diplomatic blackmail." The Chiefs asked
Kennedy to order a full air strike against Cuba the next day, to be followed
by invasion, unless the United States received "irrefutable evidence" that
dismantling had actually begun. General Taylor forwarded this recommendation to McNamara but noted that he disagreed with his colleagues.[3]

President Kennedy attended mass that Sunday morning at St.
Stephen's Church. He returned to the White House in time for a meeting of the ExComm at 11:00.

11:05 A.M.

Executive Committee Meeting of the National Security Council

The mood at the ExComm meeting was euphoric. As the meeting
started, Rusk began by saying that everyone had helped bring about the
good result. As he was speaking, President Kennedy turned on the tape
recorder.

Rusk: . . . [Earlier in the crisis President Kennedy] remarked that
whichever line of action you adopt, those who were in favor of it were
going to regret it. In this situation, I think there is some gratification for
everyone's line of action, except [those who wanted] to do nothing.

    Those who were in favor of invasion were getting ready for the thing
which turned out to be the major quid pro quo to getting these weapons
out of Cuba. Those who wanted a first strike—

At this point, perhaps finding the self-congratulation tiresome after
hearing only a few seconds of it, President Kennedy switched off the tape
recorder. He left it off for the rest of the meeting.

    After Rusk's comment, Bundy added that some had been hawks and some had been doves, but today was the day of the doves. (This remark may have been the moment when the hawk-dove metaphor entered the world's political vocabulary for the first time.)

The ExComm agreed to suspend further air reconnaissance for the day. They then discussed ways to arrange the planned U.N. inspections of the missile sites in Cuba. President Kennedy thought the United Nations should either carry out reconnaissance or agree that the United States would do it. He authorized U.S. officials to share the necessary intelligence information with U.N. officials. The President mentioned that though he would prefer not to get hung up over also getting the Soviet IL-28 bombers out of Cuba too, the United States should try hard to get them out. Everyone agreed.

President Kennedy asked his advisers to be reserved in their public comments. He cautioned them that no one should be under the illusion that the problem of Soviet weapons in Cuba was now solved. The quarantine/blockade would remain in force while negotiations continued. Much work remained, including efforts to prevent Communist subversion in Latin America. The ExComm meeting broke up at 12:15 P.M.

12:08 P.M.

Conversations with Dwight Eisenhower, Harry Truman, and Herbert Hoover

President Kennedy may have left the ExComm meeting a little early, because the White House phone logs show that at 12:08 he placed the first in this trio of calls to all of the former Presidents.

President Kennedy: Hello?
Operator: Yes, please.
President Kennedy: Oh, is the General on there?
Operator: Yes. I'll put it on here, sir. Ready.
President Kennedy: Hello?
Dwight Eisenhower: General Eisenhower, Mr. President.
President Kennedy: General, how are you?
Eisenhower: Pretty good, thanks.
President Kennedy: Oh, fine.
General, I just wanted to bring you up to date on this matter because I know of your concern about it. We got, Friday night [October 26], got

a message from Khrushchev which said that he would withdraw these missiles and technicians and so on, providing we did not plan to invade Cuba. We then got a message, that public one the next morning, in which he said he would do that if we withdrew our missiles from Turkey. We then, as you know, issued a statement that we couldn't get into that deal. So we then got this message this morning.

So we now have to wait and see how it unfolds and there's a good deal of complexities to it. If the withdrawal of these missiles, technicians, and the cessation of subversive activity by them—

Eisenhower: Yeah.

President Kennedy: —well, we just have to set up satisfactory procedures to determine whether these actions will be carried out. So I would think that, if we can do that, we'll find our interests advanced, even though it may be only one more chapter in a rather long story as far as Cuba is concerned.

Eisenhower: Of course. But, Mr. President, did he put any conditions in whatsoever, in there?

President Kennedy: No, except that we're not going to invade Cuba.

Eisenhower: Yes.

President Kennedy: That's the only one that we've got now. But we don't plan to invade Cuba under these conditions anyway.

Eisenhower: No.

President Kennedy: So if we can get them out, we're better off by far.

Eisenhower: That's correct. I quite agree.

I just wondered whether he was trying to, knowing we would keep our word, whether he would try to engage us in any kind of statement or commitment that would finally, one day, could be very embarrassing. Listen. Suppose they got in . . . suppose they start to bombard Guantánamo?

President Kennedy: Right.

Eisenhower: That's what I'm getting at. I quite agree this is a very, I think, conciliatory move he's made.

President Kennedy: Right.

Eisenhower: Provided that he doesn't say that [unclear].

President Kennedy: Oh, well, I agree. Oh, yes, that's right. I think what we've got to do is keep . . . That's why I don't think the Cuban story can be over yet. I think we will retain sufficient freedom to protect our interests if he—

Eisenhower: That's all I was saying.

President Kennedy: —if he, if they engage in subversion. If they attempt to do any aggressive acts and so on, then all bets are off.

In addition, my guess is that, by the end of next month, we're going to be toe to toe on Berlin, anyway. So that I think this is important for the time being because it requires quite a step down, really, for Khrushchev. On the other hand, I think that, as we all know, they're . . . They just probe, and their word's unreliable. So we just have to stay busy on it.

Eisenhower: As I've averred before, Mr. President, there's one thing about . . . They, these people, do not equate, and it may have been a mistake to equate, Berlin with Cuba or anything else.

President Kennedy: Right. Right.

Eisenhower: They take any spot in the world. They don't care where it is.

President Kennedy: That's right.

Eisenhower: And it's just [that] the question is: Are you in such a place you either can't or won't resist?

President Kennedy: That's right. Yeah.

Eisenhower: When we got into Tibet. What is it with Tibet? Goddamned mountainous country over there, we couldn't even reach it.[4]

President Kennedy: Right.

Eisenhower: And so, well, what we could do then was to [*unclear*] itself, that's all.

President Kennedy: Right. Right.

Eisenhower: Now. So they get you, and they probe when it . . . when you can't do anything. Then if they get another place where they think that you just won't [resist] for some reason or other—

President Kennedy: Yeah.

Eisenhower: —why then they go ahead.

President Kennedy: That's right.

Eisenhower: So I think you're doing exactly right on this one. Go ahead. But just let them know that you won't be the aggressor in there. But, on the other hand, you've always got the right to—

President Kennedy: That's right.

Eisenhower: —to determine whether the other guy has been the aggressor.

President Kennedy: Well, we'll stay right at it and I'll keep in touch with you, General.

Eisenhower: Thank you very much, Mr. President.

President Kennedy: OK. Thank you.

A few minutes later, at 12:16, President Kennedy was connected to Harry Truman. The former President was then 78 years old.

Operator: Yes, sir.

President Kennedy: President Truman, please.

Operator: Thank you. [*Phone connection is made.*] Hello?

Harry Truman: Yes, hello.

Operator: He'll be with you in just one minute, Mr. President.

Truman: All right. All right.

President Kennedy: Hello.

Truman: Hello, this is Harry Truman.

President Kennedy: Hello! How are you, Mr. President?

Truman: Well I'm all right and I'm just pleased to death the way these things came out.

President Kennedy: Well, we'll just stay at it, and I just wanted to bring you up to date on it.

We got a letter from him on Friday night which was rather conciliatory on these withdrawals. Then on Saturday morning, 12 hours after the other letter was received, we got this entirely different letter about the missile bases in Turkey.

Truman: That's the way they do things.

President Kennedy: Then, well then we rejected that. Then they came back with and accepted the earlier proposal. So I think we're going to have a lot of difficulties. But at least we're making some progress about getting these missiles out of there.

In addition, I think that Khrushchev's had some difficulties in maintaining his position. My judgment is that it's going to make things tougher in Berlin because the fact he's had something of a setback in Cuba is going to make him—

Truman: That's right.

President Kennedy: —rougher in Berlin. But at least it's a little better than it was a couple of days ago.

Truman: Well, you're on the right track. Now you just keep after them. That's the language that they understand, just what you gave them.

President Kennedy: Right. Good.

Truman: They've been asking me for comments and I've said the President of the United States is the only man who can comment on it.

President Kennedy: [*Chuckles.*] All right. OK. Good. Take care. I'll be in touch with you.

Truman: All right.

President Kennedy: Thank you, Mr. President.

Truman: I certainly appreciate your call.

President Kennedy: Well, thank you, Mr. President. Bye-bye.

Then, after another few minutes, President Kennedy was connected to former President Herbert Hoover. Hoover had remained active after leaving the presidency in 1933, both as an elder statesman and as a writer. He was 88 years old.

Herbert Hoover: It seems to me these recent events are rather incredible.

President Kennedy: They are incredible. I just . . . We got a message on Friday night which was rather forthcoming from them. And then on Saturday we got the one on Turkey. Then this morning we got the one going back to their more reasonable position. So we're going to stay right on it and see if we can work up satisfactory verification procedures, but I just wanted to bring you up to date on it. We got a lot of problems still to go but I think we've made some progress.

Hoover: That represents a good triumph for you.

President Kennedy: Well, I think we just have to . . . the rhythm of these things . . . we'll see what happens this week. But I just wanted you to know. I'll keep in touch with you and keep you up to date.

Hoover: Thank you.

President Kennedy: Thank you, Mr. President. Bye-bye.

President Kennedy then worked on and signed his response to Khrushchev, which was sent to Moscow that afternoon. It read:

Dear Mr. Chairman:

I am replying at once to your broadcast message of October 28 even though the official text has not yet reached me because of the great importance I attach to moving forward promptly to the settlement of the Cuban crisis. I think that you and I, with our heavy responsibilities for the maintenance of peace, were aware that developments were approaching a point where events could have become unmanageable. So I welcome this message and consider it an important contribution to peace.

The distinguished efforts of Acting Secretary General U Thant have greatly facilitated both our tasks. I consider my letter to you of October 27th and your reply of today as firm undertakings on the part of both our governments which should be promptly carried out. I hope that the necessary measures can at once be taken through the United Nations as your message says, so that the United States in turn can remove the quarantine measures now in effect. I have already made arrangements to report all these matters to the Organization of American States, whose members share a deep interest in a genuine peace in the Caribbean area.

You referred in your letter to a violation of your frontier by an American aircraft in the area of the Chukotsk Peninsula. I have learned that this plane, without arms or photographic equipment, was engaged in an air sampling mission in connection with your nuclear tests. Its course was direct from Eielson Air Force Base in Alaska to the North Pole and return. In turning south, the pilot made a serious navigational error which carried him over Soviet territory. He immediately made an emergency call on open radio for navigational assistance and was guided back to his home base by the most direct route. I regret this incident and will see to it that every precaution is taken to prevent recurrence.

Mr. Chairman, both of our countries have great unfinished tasks and I know that your people as well as those of the United States can ask for nothing better than to pursue them free from the fear of war. Modern science and technology have given us the possibility of making labor fruitful beyond anything that could have been dreamed of a few decades ago.

I agree with you that we must devote urgent attention to the problem of disarmament, as it relates to the whole world and also to critical areas. Perhaps now, as we step back from danger, we can together make real progress in this vital field. I think we should give priority to questions relating to the proliferation of nuclear weapons, on earth and in outer space, and to the great effort for a nuclear test ban. But we should also work hard to see if wider measures of disarmament can be agreed and put into operation at an early date. The United States government will be prepared to discuss these questions urgently, and in a constructive spirit, at Geneva or elsewhere.

John F. Kennedy

President Kennedy then left Washington to join his wife at their home, Glen Ora, in Middleburg, Virginia.

As President Kennedy suspected, the missile crisis had turned a decisive corner but was not over. Weeks of secret, often tense, negotiations followed until a complete Soviet and U.S. understanding and an accompanying end to the U.S. blockade could be announced on November 20. President Kennedy was wrong, though, about having to go toe to toe with Khrushchev over Berlin. For reasons that then remained obscure to the Americans, the end of the missile crisis also became the end of the Berlin crisis. Khrushchev simply dropped, without comment, the ultimatum he had issued in September. The ominous clouds dissipated, bringing an uneasy calm.

Conclusion

Three questions linger. First, after the last tape, what happened? How did the deal work out? Second, what do we know now about Soviet behavior? Kennedy said on the first day of the crisis, "It's a goddamn mystery to me." Is it less so now? Third, what do the tapes tell us? What about the missile crisis do we learn from them that is new, and of what possible use now or in the future is this unique record of concentrated, high-level decision making?

Aftermath

Though anxiety gave way to euphoria after Khrushchev's broadcast of Sunday, October 28, the crisis was not over. Low-level reconnaissance on October 29 appeared to detect continuing construction. The Joint Chiefs suspected Khrushchev of simply trying to buy time. If Kennedy stopped aerial surveillance, as U Thant had requested, how would he know whether the Chiefs were right or wrong?

President Kennedy's position remained awkward through the last days of October. Led to believe that the crisis was essentially over, reporters expected evidence that the missiles were being pulled out. The government had no such evidence to release. Kennedy had little to go on except his own belief that Khrushchev was sincere, a belief reinforced by intelligence of Cuban and Chinese anger at what they seemed to regard as Soviet betrayal.

On October 28 Khrushchev sent a private message to President Kennedy, trying to nail down the deal on withdrawal of the Jupiter missiles. Khrushchev said he understood the need to handle this matter confidentially. He had respected that need in his public message agreeing to withdraw the missiles from Cuba. But the Soviet leader said his concessions "took into account" the U.S. agreement to resolve the Jupiter problem.[1]

Dobrynin delivered this letter to Robert Kennedy on October 29. The next day Robert Kennedy called in Dobrynin and gave the letter back, refusing to accept it. Robert Kennedy's handwritten notes for this meeting say: "No quid pro quo as I told you. The letter makes it appear

411

that there was." The missiles would leave Turkey; "you have my word on this & that is sufficient . . . ; if you should publish any document indicating a deal then it is off." Dobrynin said his government would never publish anything. Robert Kennedy reminded Dobrynin that his government had also said it would never put missiles in Cuba. Dobrynin took the letter back, and the U.S. government kept no record of the letter or its receipt.[2]

On October 30 Khrushchev sent another private letter to President Kennedy congratulating them both on having "in the main liquidated" a "dangerous crisis"; but in the same letter he suggested immediate removal of the quarantine and U.S. abandonment of Guantánamo.[3]

Not surprisingly, President Kennedy remained wary. He continued to review invasion plans, leaving in place forces to execute the air strike and invasion. Though McNamara and others predicted that nothing would come of U Thant's mission to Havana, Kennedy waited on its outcome.

When U Thant met with Castro in Havana on October 30, he found a Cuban leader whose fury covered all points of the compass. U Thant later told the Americans that Castro had been in an "impossible and intractable mood"—"extremely bitter" toward the Soviets, the Americans, and even U Thant himself, whom he seemed to regard as a lackey of the imperialists. U Thant said he had never had a more trying encounter in all his experience. Castro refused any cooperation in verification.[4] Given Castro's mood, U.S. resumption of aerial reconnaissance involved the risk of further shoot-downs and further debates about appropriate forms of reprisal. Nonetheless, Kennedy authorized new U-2 and low-level reconnaissance flights.

Meanwhile in New York the U.S. negotiating team of Adlai Stevenson and John McCloy found that Khrushchev's emissary, Soviet deputy foreign minister Vassily Kuznetsov, did not count the IL-28 bombers as offensive weapons. Kuznetsov was instructed to say that the bombers had no military value, and Khrushchev wrote to Kennedy denying that the bombers could threaten anyone.[5] At the beginning of October, the Kennedy administration had been willing to overlook these aircraft rather than provoke a crisis. Now they had become part of the threat President Kennedy had publicly pledged to erase.

These two problems, lack of verification and the status of the IL-28s, were the principal issues dogging November talks in New York. Khrushchev sent one of his more trusted Presidium colleagues, Anastas Mikoyan, to the talks. He also exchanged further confidential letters with Kennedy. By November 20, Kennedy could announce at a press conference that the outstanding issues had been resolved. The IL-28s would come out of Cuba within 30 days. Though there would be no U.N. inspection, U.S. forces would be allowed to observe the departing Soviet ships. Their cargos of departing missiles would be on deck and could be observed by passing U.S. ships or aircraft. The United States would keep flying reconnaissance planes over Cuba. When the offensive weapons were gone, the quarantine would finally be lifted. The U.S. forces would return to normal peacetime deployments and readiness levels. The Strategic Air Command would stand down its airborne alert.

Left less clear at President Kennedy's press conference, except to those who studied his words with care, was the status of the original October 27–28 deal which traded verified withdrawal of Soviet "offensive weapons" for a U.S. pledge not to invade Cuba. The U.S. government had concluded that if Cuba would not allow verification of the settlement, the Cuban part of the deal was off: There would be no noninvasion pledge beyond the safeguards any country enjoyed under international law. Thus the United States was back to its old precrisis position that if Cuba did not interfere with anyone else's security, it would have nothing to fear from the United States. President Kennedy told Mikoyan directly that if the original agreement with U.N. inspection was not upheld to the letter, the President could "only act in the best way the situation permits."[6]

The U.S. intelligence community thought that it saw hard evidence of Cuban readiness to shoot again at U.S. reconnaissance aircraft. The intelligence was accurate, and the Soviet government bluntly instructed its envoy to tell the Cubans that this time Soviet forces would not help to shoot down any U.S. planes. Periodic U-2 flights continued (invulnerable to the guns controlled by the Cubans) until satellite photography took their place. The Executive Committee agreed to keep forces poised to attack Cuban antiaircraft sites if a U.S. plane was shot down.[7]

Covert harassment of the Castro government resumed, spurred by discoveries of new Cuban attempts to subvert the governments in Venezuela and other South American countries. By the summer of 1963 these operations had returned to about where they had been in the summer of 1962, before the Soviet arms shipments began. Washington was again back to a policy judged to have low risk and low return—petty harassment that was probably not enough to bring down Castro but also not enough to drag the United States into an open or direct intervention in Cuba.

Also left out of President Kennedy's November 20 press conference was any mention of the Jupiter missiles. The matter was not forgotten but was handled in broader reviews of NATO's nuclear force posture, including a meeting in Paris in December 1962 marked, as one delegate put it, by almost "intolerable serenity," spilling over from the satisfying outcome of the Cuban crisis. The Turks agreed to removal of the Jupiters. The missiles were dismantled by the end of April 1963. A Polaris missile submarine took up station in the Mediterranean.[8]

The Soviet Side of the Story

Throughout the crisis, the Americans asked themselves repeatedly why the Soviets had decided to put missiles in Cuba despite Kennedy's explicit and repeated warnings. They differed in their guesses as to how the Soviets would react to U.S. statements and actions and why the Soviets did what they did. Why, for example, did most ships subject to Moscow's orders stop sailing for Cuba while some, particularly the *Grozny,* kept going? Why did Soviet SAM crews in Cuba do nothing about U-2 flights from October 14 through October 26, then shoot one down on October 27? Why did Khrushchev change his terms for withdrawing the missiles? In his long private message received by the United States late on October 26, he seemed to say his only condition was a U.S. promise not to invade Cuba. In his message publicly broadcast on the morning of October 27 (U.S. time), he called in addition for removal of U.S. "offensive means" from Turkey. Why? And why, having publicly adopted this position, did Khrushchev back down on October 28?

Owing to the passage of time, the publication of memoirs by Khrushchev and others, and a study by Aleksandr Fursenko and Timothy Naftali with access to Presidium and KGB files not yet accessible to other scholars, we have information on these questions well beyond that available to Kennedy and his circle.[9] The two main findings are these. First, Kennedy and his advisers did not make any serious misjudgments about the Soviets. Most of what we know now confirms what was surmised by Kennedy's "demonologists," especially Thompson. Second, our best retrospective judgments about the Soviet side still entail guesswork; in all probability, no one will ever be able to answer with complete confidence *any* of the questions about the Soviets that bothered Kennedy and his advisers.

With these caveats, let us summarize what can now be said about each of the major puzzles, beginning with the question of why the Soviets put the missiles into Cuba and thus brought on the crisis. This separates, like a Russian doll, into several parts. Why did Khrushchev order in May 1962 that the Soviet Strategic Rocket Forces set up MRBM and IRBM launchers in Cuba, and why did he make such a secret of it? Had he announced his intentions or even told Kennedy privately that he planned to base IRBMs in Cuba, the crisis would have unfolded differently. Conceivably, there might have been no crisis at all. The tapes of the September 4 meetings show that Kennedy's public warning was crafted to give the appearance of firmness and head off a decision which he thought Khrushchev had not yet made but which some of Kennedy's advisers (including his brother) thought might tempt Khrushchev if the United States did not show a bit of steel. After the Soviet government then announced (on September 11) that no missiles would be sent, Kennedy himself was emboldened to repeat his warning two days later, again trying to show the public (and Congress) that he took Soviet moves in Cuba seriously but at seemingly little risk. It was the fact that Khrushchev lied to Kennedy and tried to surprise him that made the missile deployments such an excruciating test of Kennedy's mettle and the credibility of the United States. Why did Khrushchev not at least *consider* telling Kennedy what he had in mind?

Khrushchev had made his decision in May. But since the missiles were still only en route to Cuba when Kennedy issued his September 4 warning, why did Khrushchev not at least pause to reconsider what he was doing? Since the Soviets understood the U-2's capabilities and knew that the United States conducted reconnaissance over Cuba, what made any of them think the secret could be kept? What did they plan to do if the secret were not kept? And, if the secret were kept, what did they plan to do once the missiles were fully in place?

To explain the original Soviet decision, Kennedy and his advisers considered several hypotheses. Their favorite was that Khrushchev intended the missiles in Cuba as levers to loosen U.S. concessions regarding Berlin. A second hypothesis focused on the strategic balance. The Joint Chiefs of Staff, for example, presumed that Khrushchev had gambled as he did in order to get wider target coverage against the United States and offset the U.S. lead in ICBMs. A third hypothesis was that Khrushchev had acted in order to protect Cuba from invasion. Everyone knew this was Khrushchev's story; no one seemed to believe it. This was why, on October 18, Kennedy told visiting Soviet foreign minister Gromyko that the United States would be happy to promise not to invade Cuba and that the Soviet government could have had such a pledge for months. With this hyperbole he was daring the Soviet foreign minister to name this condition, which seemed quite trivial to Kennedy in comparison to what was at stake with Berlin. Kennedy does not appear to have been the least bit surprised that Gromyko ignored his offer. Thompson argued, in the afternoon meeting of October 27, that the Jupiters in Turkey were of secondary interest to the Soviets. "The important thing for Khrushchev . . . ," he said, "is to be able to say: I saved Cuba. I stopped an invasion." But Thompson was speaking then of how Khrushchev could save face. A fourth hypothesis presumed factional interplay in the Kremlin. Thus, whatever the motive or motives, they might not be Khrushchev's own. To account for the difference in content between Khrushchev's private letter and broadcast message, Bundy hazarded that the former was Khrushchev's, the latter that of "hard-nosed people overruling him."

Since 1962 no other hypotheses have been advanced to supplement the four voiced by Kennedy and his advisers. But the hypotheses have had different fates. Berlin, oddly, dropped from sight. Hardly anyone writing retrospectively about the crisis, except the participants, stresses Berlin as a possible primary factor in Soviet decisions. The strategic balance hypothesis has proved more hardy. Two RAND analysts wrote a book not long after the crisis, developing at length the strategic balance rationale for Khrushchev's actions. This argument has remained an important strain in writings about the crisis by historians and political scientists specializing in international relations or security studies. But the defense-of-Cuba hypothesis has proved the most robust and longest lived, especially among historians. This view has derived its strength and longevity not only from the United States's demonstrated "arrogance of power" (in Senator Fulbright's phrase) before, during, and since the Vietnam War but also from documentary revelations concerning Operation Mongoose and precrisis invasion planning, as well as the subsequent stories offered by Khrushchev and some other Russians.[10]

Kennedy and his advisers understood the reasoning in the Kremlin better than have most scholars writing about the crisis in retrospect. While Khrushchev and his colleagues did indeed care a great deal about Cuba, the thought of deterring a U.S. invasion figured only incidentally in their discussions about the missile deployments. Calculations about the strategic nuclear balance were much more in evidence. Berlin was an omnipresent and dominating concern.

To summarize what we now know about Soviet deliberations in 1962 is not, however, to state a final verdict on the motives guiding Soviet behavior before and during the crisis. The more we learn about Soviet decision making in the Khrushchev era, the less confidence we can feel in any analyses that explain decisions in terms of a hierarchy of interest calculations.

To interpret Soviet decisions is to interpret Khrushchev. He alone decided on policy. Other members of the Soviet elite who favored other policies could have their way only when Khrushchev was not around or not paying attention. No one could overrule him—yet.

Khrushchev made decisions largely on his own. Now and then, he would talk over a question with a fellow member of the Politburo or someone from the bureaucracy, but he did not systematically seek even advice, let alone policy analysis. He looked on other members of the Politburo as potential enemies. He may have had some respect for military leaders; he treasured memories of working with generals on the Ukrainian front in World War II. But he probably heeded military men only with regard to narrowly military issues. Khrushchev never obtained advice and analysis such as Kennedy obtained from his Executive Committee and, given the quality of the rest of the Soviet leadership, he could not have got it if he had tried.

Khrushchev acted more from instinct than from calculation. Whether Berlin or the strategic balance or concern about Cuba was uppermost in his mind at the time he ordered the missiles sent to Cuba, he himself could probably not have said. Having made a decision, however, he tended not to entertain second thoughts unless and until he had no choice. In both foreign and domestic affairs, he behaved like a roulette player who chooses a number and puts chips on the number until it produces a big payoff or the stack of chips has disappeared. Searching for the right adjective with which to characterize him, Fyodor Burlatsky and Georgi Shaknazarov, who had been aides to Khrushchev, agreed on the word *azartnyi*, which means, in Russian, "reckless" or "hotheaded."[11]

Khrushchev's instincts in foreign affairs were disciplined by relatively little experience or knowledge. Sixty-eight in 1962, he had been a coal miner as a youth and then a party functionary for most of his life. He was party boss in Moscow at the time of Stalin's death when, by outmaneuvering better-educated and less plebeian rivals, he became number one in the hierarchy. For practical purposes, he did not think at all about the world outside the Soviet Union until the mid-1950s, when it fell to him to test whether Stalin had been right in prophesying that the capitalist-imperialists would wring the necks of his successors. His first encounter with capitalist-imperialist leaders came when he met Eisenhower at the Geneva summit conference in 1955.

The framework into which Khrushchev fitted what he learned about the outside world was built around a rather simplistic version of Marxism-Leninism. Although he was intelligent, quick, shrewd, and capable of subtlety, his observations of the outside world were influenced by tenets he had absorbed and taught in his decades of party work. When he visited the United States in 1959, he was eager to meet Wall Streeters because he had grown up believing that they called the tunes for U.S. political leaders. He seems to have assumed that U.S. decisions would usually be governed by crass interest. By the same token, although he knew of and had participated in the brutalities of Stalinism, he retained a romantic belief that Soviet-style socialism did ride the wave of the future and did promise eventual happiness for humankind. This viewpoint helps to account for his "secret speech" at the Twentieth Party Congress in 1956, exposing Stalin's crimes, as well as for his boastful prophecies that movements of national liberation would eventually bury the West.

Because of his narrow experience of the outside world, Khrushchev probably misread Kennedy. At Geneva in 1955, he had been a bit awed by Eisenhower. He changed his estimate when he visited the United States in 1959 and saw an Eisenhower weakened by medical problems and on his way out of power. When he saw Kennedy in 1961 at Vienna, Khrushchev was more impressed than he had expected to be by the "young millionaire and . . . son of a millionaire," but whereas he had come away from Geneva crediting Eisenhower with toughness, he came away from Vienna crediting Kennedy with "flexibility." He would later praise Kennedy for being "realistic enough to see that now the might of the socialist world equaled that of the capitalist world."[12]

Khrushchev's thinking about foreign affairs had been molded by the Suez-Hungary crisis of 1956. Prior to that crisis, the United States had treated the Soviet Union on a par with Britain and France. In the course of the crisis, the United States temporarily broke with the British and French, deploring their surprise attack on Egypt and demanding that they desist. Khrushchev joined in this demand. Blustering, he threatened the British that, if they did not pull out of Egypt, the Soviet Union might use its "modern destructive weapons." The British and French did withdraw, largely because of diplomatic and economic pressure from Washington, but Khrushchev credited his threats with having had decisive effect.[13]

Because Britain thereafter abandoned its previous pretensions and France did so until General Charles de Gaulle came to power in 1958, the Soviet Union became by default the other superpower, even at the moment of brutally crushing opposition in Hungary. Thereafter, it became Khrushchev's standard practice to make demands and talk loudly about Soviet rockets. Though he had had to back down more than once when he found the West united with regard to Berlin, and the Americans unflinching, Khrushchev still derived from the Suez experience the lesson that the way to succeed with foreign powers was to rattle rockets in their faces.

Khrushchev's decisions were influenced by Kremlin politics, but not in the way suggested by Bundy's reference to his "hard-nosed people."

Although Khrushchev was in absolute control in Moscow, he knew that he might on almost any day find himself absolutely not in control. After Stalin's death, police head Lavrenti Beria and Premier Georgi Malenkov had formed, along with Khrushchev, a ruling triumvirate. Beria had been removed from power by gunfire, arranged for him by Khrushchev and Malenkov. As indication that Soviet politics were becoming more humane, Malenkov's removal involved mere demotion. Similar things happened to other Khrushchev opponents. Murder went out of fashion. But Khrushchev could never for a single day forget that he, too, might receive the Soviet equivalent of the black spot. In the spring of 1962, forced to admit the failure of his programs to increase croplands and farm output, he had to announce 20 to 30 percent increases in the state-controlled prices of basic foods. This move triggered protests that, in one city near the Black Sea, exploded into a revolt put down only by machine gun fire and mass arrests.[14] Possibly to defend against having the military old guard also regard itself as an injured party, Khrushchev allowed the Presidium to reverse his earlier massive reduction in resources for the military and heavy industry. Thus the period of Khrushchev's crucial decision to send missiles to Cuba was one in which he seriously needed some success to offset a string of losses.[15]

A few years later, as he dictated his memoirs, Khrushchev remembered that during an official visit to Bulgaria, from May 14 to 20, 1962, "[O]ne thought kept hammering at my brain: what will happen if we lose Cuba?"[16] Soviet-Cuban relations were deeper and much more complex than Americans realized. The Soviets had begun providing covert assistance to the Castro government in the spring of 1959 and secretly arranged the first sales of arms that fall, before the U.S. government had decided whether Castro would be a friend or a foe. Some Americans and many Cubans suspected that the Castro regime harbored a secret radical agenda, that the security ministries were being brought under the control of pro-Soviet Communists in order to pursue this revolutionary agenda at home and abroad, and that this faction included Fidel Castro's brother, Raul, and Che Guevara, if not Fidel himself. Evidence from Soviet files shows that these suspicions were well founded.[17]

From 1960 onward Castro repeatedly predicted horrific scenarios involving U.S. action against him, then took actions that made his prophecies self-fulfilling. In March 1960, blaming U.S. agents for the catastrophic explosion of a ship carrying arms into Havana from Belgium (there is no evidence of any U.S. involvement in the event), he denounced Washington and tightened his relations with Moscow. In anticipation of nationalizing U.S. property and liquidating his domestic opponents, he sought further Soviet military, economic, and intelligence assistance to contend with the U.S. intervention that he asserted would surely follow. The Kremlin obliged with a "blank check to buy whatever he needed," including direct cash payments to Fidel.[18] Though Washington did not know all this, Castro's March 1960 attacks did catalyze the Eisenhower administration's decision to begin preparing covert operations to overthrow the Cuban leader.

In June 1960 Castro nationalized U.S. oil refineries (which had refused to refine Soviet crude oil) and again told the Soviets that an invasion was imminent. At about the same time Khrushchev received an intelligence report from a Soviet spy at NATO that the "chiefs at the Pentagon" were hoping to launch a preventive strike against the Soviet Union (the report was untrue). Apparently this report was taken seriously, for in early July Khrushchev gave a speech stressing Soviet capabilities for nuclear attack on the United States. In his best Suez crisis vein, Khrushchev threatened that Soviet rockets might fly if Washington chose to invade Cuba. The speech delighted the Cuban leader, who told the Soviets they had deterred an U.S. attack.[19] Castro then publicized his closer friendship with Moscow.

There was another invasion scare in October 1960, Fursenko and Naftali discovered, based on rumors that Cuban exiles were being trained by the CIA in Guatemala. (Such training was in fact taking place, but the force was still months from being ready.) The Soviet and Cuban governments, genuinely believing an attack to be imminent, mobilized troops and sounded loud public alarms. Moscow again threatened use of its nuclear missiles. When the invasion did not come, the Cubans again believed the Soviet threats had deterred it. In early November, in a private address heard by Cuban Communists and the Soviet KGB resident, Castro extolled Marxism, professed always to have been a Marxist, and said again and again: "Moscow is our brain and our great leader, and we must pay attention to its voice."[20]

Both the Cubans and the Soviets were caught by surprise when the Cuban exiles actually did invade, in April 1961. Khrushchev again thundered support for Castro and warnings to Washington, adding this time the threat that the flames ignited in Cuba could touch off a chain reaction of conflict across the globe.[21] Again the Soviets took credit for deterring Kennedy from providing the military support that might have made the invasion succeed. And the Americans still failed to grasp that the Soviets and Cubans credited Soviet missiles for an apparent series of deterrent successes.

Increasingly, Khrushchev and the Soviet government linked their prestige with Castro's. They held out Cuba as the prime example of success in their newly announced global strategy of undermining capitalism through wars of national liberation in the developing world. It offered the chief proof that the Soviet Union, not China, remained the vanguard of world revolution.[22]

In the fall of 1961 Castro asked for much larger arms shipments and especially for large numbers of the most modern antiaircraft missile, the SA-2. Khrushchev did not immediately act on this costly request. In the interval, Castro purged his government of perceived rivals, criticized the Soviets for revealing insufficient revolutionary boldness, and began talking with China about possible economic assistance. Particularly alarming to Moscow was Castro's ousting of Anibal Escalante, the leader of the Cuban Communist Party, along with practically all of Escalante's pro-Moscow cadres. The March 1962 Escalante affair brought Soviet-Cuban relations to a crisis.[23]

In early April the Soviet government decided to meet Castro's demand for SA-2s. In addition to pacifying Castro and keeping him in their camp, Soviet officials were concerned once again with the possibility of a U.S. invasion. They had inklings of Operation Mongoose and of contingency planning by the U.S. military. Khrushchev's son-in-law, the editor of *Pravda*, claimed to have heard President Kennedy say that he viewed Cuba much as Khrushchev viewed Hungary. Though Cuban intelligence appears to have correctly understood that there was no real danger of a U.S. invasion and said so to their Soviet colleagues and though KGB sources in Washington downplayed chances of an invasion, Khrushchev and other political figures in the Soviet government may have still been worried.[24] Khrushchev later said, "I'm not saying we had any documentary proof that the Americans were preparing a second invasion;" he wrote in his memoirs, "We didn't need documentary proof. We knew the class affiliation, the class blindness of the United States, and that was enough to make us expect the worst."[25] Whether it was this worry or more a desire to firm up relations with Castro in the aftermath of the Escalante affair, on April 12 the Presidium confirmed the delivery of about 180 SA-2 antiaircraft missiles to Cuba as well as a battery of Soviet coastal defense cruise missiles, along with trainers and a regiment of regular Soviet troops. A military mission was to survey additional needs.[26] The United States knew nothing of this.

No new information about threats to Cuba seems to have arrived in Moscow between the Presidium decision in April 1962 on the antiaircraft missiles and May 1962, when the Presidium made the new decision to send an entire Group of Soviet Forces to Cuba, including nuclear-armed ballistic missiles. The military mission sent after the initial decision did receive from Castro on May 18 new requests, certainly for more coastal defense missiles, possibly for more Soviet troops (his own later testimony is vague on this point). But neither Castro nor any other Cuban nor any Soviet representative in Cuba mentioned nuclear weapons.[27] Knowing that the presence of nuclear weapons in his country could both provoke and legitimize a U.S. attack, Castro had stated repeatedly that Cuba had "no intention to offer any part of its territory to any state for the establishment of military bases."[28]

Khrushchev, however, had begun to ponder this quite new possibility not long after the decision on the antiaircraft missiles. Anastas Mikoyan, who had served with Khrushchev under Stalin, had the dacha just next to Khrushchev's in the Lenin Hills. He was probably the member of the Politburo whom Khrushchev came nearest to trusting and in late April, in one of their one-on-one backyard chats, Khrushchev mentioned to Mikoyan that he was thinking of basing ballistic missiles in Cuba. Mikoyan's son, from whom we have the report of this conversation, says that his father reacted negatively. He had been to Cuba and had helped cement relations with Castro, and he predicted that Castro would reject the idea because of fear of the U.S. reaction.[29]

If Mikoyan did try to discourage Khrushchev, he did not succeed. Khrushchev broached his idea to Defense Minister Rodion Malinovsky, who instantly became an enthusiastic supporter. Knowing not only that the Soviet Union was far behind the United States in ICBMs but also that the existing ICBMs (SS-6s) were monstrous weapons of doubtful reliability and that successor models (SS-7s and SS-8s) were stalled in the two missile design bureaus, Malinovsky recognized in Khrushchev's proposal a way of shortcutting the time required to even the strategic balance. And Khrushchev was apparently enthusiastic. "Why not throw a hedgehog at Uncle Sam's pants?" he asked Malinovsky.[30]

The Americans did not fully grasp how deeply, in the spring of 1962, Khrushchev and his colleagues felt that, in Malinovsky's words, "our inferior position was impossible to us."[31] The United States touched the Soviets on this raw nerve by completing the long-delayed deployment of 15 Jupiter IRBMs at five launch sites in Turkey in early 1962. The Soviets had known all about the planned deployment for years. The plan was publicly announced by NATO in 1957, and Moscow had complained loudly, especially during 1958 and 1959. Although there is no evidence that Soviet planners attached any particular strategic significance to these obsolete systems or even to the nuclear-armed U.S. aircraft based in Turkey, which were the more worrisome weapons militarily, the deployment may have made it easier for Khrushchev and others to rationalize the decision concerning the missiles in Cuba.[32]

In March and April 1962 the aspect of the nuclear standoff that most fully engaged both the Soviets and the Americans was their intense negotiations in Geneva about banning further test explosions of nuclear weapons. The Soviets had resumed aboveground testing with a dramatic series of detonations in September 1961. Under constant pressure to reciprocate in kind, Kennedy had held back. The key issue was the verification of a ban. Rusk and Gromyko wrangled over the issue in Geneva and got nowhere. On April 25 the United States resumed test explosions in the Pacific. This was when Khrushchev began privately exploring with Mikoyan and Malinovsky the idea of deploying missiles to Cuba.[33]

Together, the Jupiter deployments and the resumption of testing irritated Khrushchev. He recalled later thinking that "it was high time America learned what it feels like to have her own land and her own people threatened."[34] Since the United States was already threatened by Russian bombers and ICBMs, few or primitive though they might be, Khrushchev was surely thinking of the more visceral sense of threat created by missiles just across one's borders. Yuri Andropov, then a senior adviser to Khrushchev, privately told his boss that the Soviet deployment of missiles to Cuba was a way to "sight them at the soft underbelly of the Americans."[35] Kennedy certainly felt it just that way. "A thing stuck right in our guts," was the metaphor he used to the Joint Chiefs of Staff on the morning of October 19.

What happened after Khrushchev's initial talks with Mikoyan and Malinovsky remains murky. Apparently Khrushchev put together a small group of top officials to consider the idea. Malinovsky's newly appointed deputy and also the new head of the Soviet Strategic Rocket Forces, Marshal Sergei S. Biryuzov, not only supported Malinovsky's view regarding the strategic advantages of missiles in Cuba but ventured the opinion that the missiles could be deployed without being discovered by the Americans. Mikoyan's son says that his father, who knew Cuban geography at first hand, regarded Biryuzov as "a fool" and was amazed that the marshal "thought there were places in the mountains where the Americans would not discover the missiles."[36]

At the end of April the most-trusted Soviet envoy in Havana, Alexander Alexeev (then the KGB resident), was recalled to Moscow, not knowing why. On May 7 Khrushchev told him that he would become the new ambassador to Cuba. On May 20, after returning from his week in Bulgaria, Khrushchev summoned Alexeev and asked him how Castro would respond to a Soviet deployment of nuclear missiles in Cuba. A bit dumbfounded and intimidated, Alexeev said he "could never suppose that Fidel Castro would agree to such a thing." Cuba was relying on its own defenses, built with Soviet aid. If the Soviet government "installed missiles, I thought this would provoke a rejection of the Cuban Revolution from the rest of the hemisphere."[37]

In another sign that Malinovsky was a lead advocate for the missile idea, the defense minister immediately took issue with Alekseev, refusing to believe that "a socialist country could refuse our aid." Khrushchev said nothing, but then informed Alekseev that he and Marshal Biryuzov would be joining a delegation to Havana to explain matters to Castro. The decision had already been made. On May 21 Khrushchev formally presented his plan to the Defense Council, consisting of top civilian and military leaders (no uniformed military men were members of the Presidium), and received its unanimous approval. The initiative was then formally drafted by General Staff officers and presented by Malinovsky at a combined meeting of the Presidium and the Defense Council on May 24. Khrushchev offered his comments. After a pro forma discussion everyone agreed to the proposal. Five days later the delegation was in Havana.

Castro reluctantly agreed to the deployment. Though he was told over and over that the deployment was only for his own good, he and his colleagues always thought, and often said, that they were doing a favor for the Soviets, helping Moscow change the global balance of military power in favor of socialism. Castro expected that the deployment would produce an intense crisis, but "we really trusted that they [the Soviets] were acting with the knowledge of the entire situation."[38]

Several other options were available to the Soviets. They could have signed a defense treaty with Cuba without deploying forces; or deployed purely conventional forces as already planned, forcing U.S. invaders to risk direct conflict with Soviet forces; or deployed conventional forces armed with purely tactical nuclear weapons that could reach offshore targets but not the continental United States; or deployed nuclear-armed bombers presenting a slower-moving and less-nerve-racking challenge to the Americans.[39] But none of these options had been analyzed except the flow of purely conventional arms authorized by the Presidium decision of April 12 and discussed by the subsequent military mission to Cuba. Certainly Khrushchev did not analyze them in any visible way. For the Soviet General Staff, Khrushchev's plan "was like a roll of thunder in a clear sky."[40]

In addition to the deployments of arms and forces envisioned by the earlier decisions to aid Cuba (including the 140 air defense missile launchers), Moscow followed up Castro's agreement with plans, approved in June, to deploy 40 land-based ballistic missile launchers and 60 missiles in 5 missile regiments. These would be part of a full-sized Group of Soviet Forces, more than 45,000 strong, with 4 motorized rifle regiments (and more than 250 armored fighting vehicles), a wing of the latest Soviet fighter aircraft (the MiG-21), about 80 nuclear-capable cruise missiles for coastal defense, and a regiment of more than 40 IL-28 bombers.

After the fact the Americans speculated that the Soviets intended to develop Cuba into a full-scale strategic base. They were correct. The operation also included a plan to build a submarine base that would become the home port for an initial deployment of 11 submarines, including 7 carrying submarine-launched ballistic missiles (SLBMs) with nuclear warheads.[41] Basing Soviet missile submarines in the Caribbean would transform the strategic power of this previously weak and vulnerable arm of Moscow's nuclear forces.

In addition to the nuclear warheads for the ballistic missiles, low-yield nuclear weapons, each with an explosive power comparable to that of the atomic bombs used against Japan in 1945, would be provided for the coastal defense cruise missiles. The Americans did not know and never seriously imagined that the coastal defense cruise missiles were deployed with nuclear warheads. Nor did the Soviets plan to reveal this fact to them.

Khrushchev also checked his judgment, mainly with Biryuzov, on whether the deployment could be concealed, given that U.S. surveillance aircraft frequently overflew Cuba. After traveling to Cuba, Biryuzov and his delegation reported back that the terrain and camouflage efforts would indeed shield the missile sites from U.S. surveillance.[42]

In July 1962 Raul Castro visited Moscow bringing a question for Khrushchev from Fidel: What would happen if the operation was discovered while in progress? Khrushchev answered that there was nothing to worry about; if there were trouble, he would send out the Baltic fleet as a show of support. Castro later acknowledged that the Cubans "did not think that it was the Baltic fleet that would solve the problem. What we were thinking about was Soviet will and determination, about Soviet strength. And we got the statement of the top leader of the Soviet Union that there was nothing to worry about, that he would not allow it. So what was really protecting us was the global strategic might of the USSR, not the rockets here."[43] Castro was presuming that Khrushchev had thought through how he would handle a nuclear confrontation if the missile deployment was discovered before it was complete. As Castro himself later realized, there is no evidence that Khrushchev ever seriously considered this question.

Khrushchev did have an image of what would happen if he succeeded in presenting the United States with his planned fait accompli. The Kennedy administration, he believed, would "swallow this bitter pill. . . . I knew that the United States could knock out some of our installations, but not all of them. If a quarter or even a tenth of our missiles survived—even if only one or two big ones were left—we could still hit New York, and there wouldn't be much of New York left."[44] Viewing Kennedy as a young, inexperienced intellectual presiding over a dangerously bellicose military establishment, Khrushchev apparently thought that Kennedy would let him get away with trickery and that he would end up with both the Soviet Union and Cuba better protected against the "chiefs in the Pentagon."[45]

Khrushchev did not ask whether his ambassador in Washington or any other experts shared his estimate of the United States. Gromyko claimed later that he had warned Khrushchev privately "putting our missiles in Cuba would cause a political explosion in the United States" but that Khrushchev was unmoved by this advice. Commenting that Khrushchev "grossly misunderstood the psychology of his opponents," Ambassador Anatoly Dobrynin complained later: "Had he asked the embassy beforehand, we could have predicted the violent American reaction to his adventure once it became known. It is worth noting that Castro understood this. . . . But Khrushchev wanted to spring a surprise on Washington; it was he who got the surprise in the end when his secret plan was uncovered."[46]

On May 12, on the eve of the key decisions about sending missiles to Cuba, Khrushchev spent about 14 hours with Kennedy's press aide, Pierre Salinger, then visiting Moscow. He barely mentioned Cuba. The central issue, Khrushchev said, was Berlin. Dobrynin, who took up his post at this time, remembered that "Germany and Berlin overshadowed everything."[47] Describing what he expected to be his position when negotiations on Berlin resumed, Khrushchev had written to Kennedy in November 1961: "You have to understand, I have no ground to retreat further, there is a precipice behind."[48]

The expression "precipice behind" vividly conveys the value Khrushchev now attached to success on Berlin.[49] In another letter to Kennedy, Khrushchev protested that Washington's willingness to threaten a nuclear war to protect Berlin "can rest, excuse my harsh judgments, only on the megalomania, on an intention to act from the position of strength."[50] In March 1962 he promised Kennedy that "one way or another" he would force the Western troops out.[51] In late April the negotiations in Geneva between Gromyko and Rusk had reached a stalemate over Berlin. Angering his West German allies, Kennedy was willing to offer a modus vivendi that might allow the status quo to continue. But this had not been good enough for the Soviet government, which denounced the failure of the talks at the end of April.[52]

Thus in late April and early May 1962, when Khrushchev was in the final stages of his decision to send missiles to Cuba, Berlin clearly had a large place in his thinking. Having issued ultimatums in 1958 and again in 1961, demanding Western departure from Berlin by specified deadlines, and having let those deadlines pass with the promise that negotiations would attain this goal, he was being forced to acknowledge failure publicly. East Germans were demanding a tougher Soviet policy.[53] The Americans, relying on their nuclear superiority, were pursuing a "policy of strength."[54] In March 1962 Khrushchev told Dobrynin, just before the new ambassador left for Washington, that Berlin was the principal issue in U.S.-Soviet relations, said the U.S. was acting "particularly arrogant" about their nuclear deterrent, and concluded, "It's high time their long arms were cut shorter." He liked Kennedy and considered him a man of character, yet he also clearly believed "that putting pressure on Kennedy might bring us some success."[55]

In Moscow, Ambassador Thompson, ignorant of Khrushchev's plans to send missiles to Cuba, was puzzled. No American knew Khrushchev better or had followed his positions more closely. Thompson could not understand why Khrushchev was increasing pressure on Berlin. "He must surely know our position is firm," and "it does not seem reasonable that he would wish further to commit his personal prestige which [is] already deeply engaged." And the pressure just kept increasing.[56] The Soviets began telling the Americans that, though they would wait until after the U.S. congressional elections, the Berlin issue would be forced to a conclusion in November.[57]

By the beginning of September 1962 Khrushchev had arranged to unveil the existence of the missiles in Cuba and publicly sign a treaty with Castro in late November, after the congressional elections. He also planned, probably in a speech to the United Nations on the same trip, to renew his ultimatum for final resolution of the Berlin crisis, demanding the withdrawal of Western troops from their sectors. Khrushchev knew the United States would threaten war if he carried out his ultimatum. But by that time Khrushchev would have the missiles, poised in Cuba, to help him call the United States's bluff. He would finally carry his four-year-old Berlin policy to a successful conclusion and permanently transform the striking power of the Soviet Union's land- and sea-based nuclear arsenal.

Khrushchev practically spelled out these plans to a senior U.S. visitor, Stewart Udall, on September 6. On September 28 Khrushchev wrote directly to Kennedy and told him that a settlement of the Berlin issue would come after the U.S. elections, probably "in the second half of November." (This is the letter Kennedy is discussing in the taped meeting of 29 September 1962.) When Khrushchev's foreign minister, Gromyko, met with Kennedy on October 18, the message was the same.

When the missiles were discovered, Llewellyn Thompson (now recalled from Moscow to serve as the State Department's special adviser on the Soviet Union) immediately understood why Khrushchev in July seemed to be staking even more of his prestige on a policy that would meet unaltered U.S. resistance. Thompson solved his puzzle. Circumstances had changed. It remained to be seen whether U.S. policy would change too.[58]

Khrushchev's plans began to go awry at the end of August, when a U-2 overflight discovered the installation of some of the SA-2 air defense missiles. Then, as recounted in the taped conversations that day, President Kennedy issued his September 4 warning to Khrushchev against placing "offensive weapons" in Cuba (an ambiguous term, but the Soviets understood what the Americans meant). Later, after the ballistic missiles had arrived and been discovered, Bundy wondered aloud (preserved on tape) whether Khrushchev had failed to heed the September 4 warning because the decision to deploy the missiles had already been made. Bundy was half right.

The decision had been made, but the nuclear weapons themselves had still not been shipped. Khrushchev now feared that the Americans might attack Cuba before the nuclear deterrent to stop them could be put in place. Rather than abandon his plan, the gambler increased his bet by rushing tactical nuclear weapons to Cuba that could immediately be used against invading ground forces. These rockets were called Lunas by the Soviets and FROGs (Free Rockets Over Ground) in the West. Vacationing at the Black Sea resort at Pitsunda, Khrushchev bullied the U.S. visitor, Stewart Udall, with his threat that he could "swat your [America's] ass" if it chose to fight for Berlin. On the same day he received a visit from Mikoyan, bearing a report on how to get more nuclear weapons to Cuba. On September 7 Khrushchev approved the dispatch of 6 Luna rocket launchers with 12 nuclear-armed rockets, and 6 nuclear bombs for the IL-28s already being sent to Cuba. The Defense Ministry dissuaded Khrushchev from sending these weapons by airplane to Cuba. Instead they would be added to the shipment of MRBM warheads that would leave the Soviet Union on September 15.[59] That ship left on schedule and arrived in Cuba on October 4. Khrushchev's other reaction to Kennedy's warning was to redouble his deception, issuing the September 11 TASS statement that promised to defend Cuba but said there was no need to send any missiles there.

Kennedy's renewed, personal warning on September 13, which was prompted by the discovery of the coastal defense cruise missiles, again did not deter Khrushchev from proceeding with the deployment. Yet Khrushchev did decide to postpone setting up the base for Soviet missile submarines, fearing that the related ship movements and construction would be too visible.[60] Near the end of September 1962, as Khrushchev was getting progress reports on the missile deployment, he turned to an aide, saying, "Soon hell will break loose." The aide replied, "I hope the boat does not capsize, Nikita Sergeyevich." Khrushchev thought for a moment, then answered, "Now it's too late to change anything."[61]

After his October 18 meetings with Kennedy and Rusk, Gromyko reported back that the overall situation on Cuba was "completely satisfactory." Seeing no indications that the Americans knew about the missiles, he concluded his report by saying that "a USA military adventure against Cuba is almost impossible to imagine."[62]

Moscow was caught completely off guard by the U.S. discovery of the missiles and by Kennedy's simultaneous unveiling of both the discovery and the blockade. The reasons for their surprise puzzled U.S. officials at the time and remains puzzling to this day.

To provide a defense against U-2 surveillance, Khrushchev had suggested in July that the SA-2 air defense missiles go in first so they could shoot down U-2s and thwart detection of the missile installation. The vast plan for the shipments was reorganized accordingly, and the SA-2 missiles were in place and operational by late September.[63] The U.S. fears of a U-2 shoot-down had, after some argument, deterred Washington from flying directly over Cuba for more than a month, but the overflights resumed in mid-October.

Soviet troops in Cuba seem to have tracked the U-2 overflights of October 14, 15, and 17. Their standing orders appear to have granted them authority to fire. We do not know why they did not. We can speculate that, with the U.S. warnings in the air, the central authorities in Moscow informally let commanders in Cuba know that they did not want any clash or gave other orders we do not know about.[64] The Soviet forces in Cuba realized at the time of the overflights that the missile sites and IL-28s could well have been discovered. Fingers were pointed about adequate camouflage, though the construction of such complex sites for such large missiles was inherently hard to conceal.[65] Yet, in a further mystery, there is no evidence that the commanders in Cuba ever dared to tell Moscow that the missile sites had been overflown and that the Americans probably knew about the missiles.

The Kremlin plunged into its own crisis deliberations on October 22, with news of the impending Kennedy speech. Unlike Kennedy, Khrushchev continued his usual foreign policy process, consulting a small group of Presidium members aided by the defense and foreign ministers and the leading international expert from the Communist Party's Central Committee. When a formal decision was needed, Khrushchev convened the full Presidium. At this point the 36 MRBMs (for 24 launchers) were in Cuba, with their nuclear warheads. So were nearly 100 other nuclear warheads for the coastal defense missiles, short-range rockets, and IL-28 bombers. Nuclear warheads to be carried on the IRBMs (for the 18 launch sites still under construction) were also in Cuba. The IRBMs themselves were still at sea.[66]

Khrushchev was now very worried that the Americans would attack Cuba. He considered turning the nuclear weapons over to the Cubans and letting them respond. But he assured his colleagues he would not let Castro use the MRBMs against the United States. Perhaps, he wondered, the Cubans could deter an invasion simply by threatening use of the short-range tactical nuclear weapons against an invading force.[67] In such a case, of course, a U.S. air strike, by itself, would in effect be uncontested.

The Presidium first decided that Malinovsky should cable General Issa Pliyev, the commander of Soviet troops in Cuba, ordering him to bring his troops to combat readiness and to use all Cuban and Soviet forces, except the nuclear arms, to meet an attack. Then, changing its mind, it considered a message authorizing use of the tactical nuclear weapons but not the ballistic missiles. Malinovsky was uneasy about this instruction, worrying that the Americans might intercept it and use it as a pretext for striking with their own nuclear weapons. So the Kremlin sent the first draft, withholding final authorization to use the nuclear weapons.[68]

News of Kennedy's speech announcing the quarantine was greeted with relief when it arrived in Moscow in the early morning of October 23. The Americans were not going to attack. Reports also arrived from Soviet envoys. Dobrynin characterized the U.S. move as a general effort to reverse a decline in its world power, partly as a result of fears about Berlin. He warned that the Americans were preparing for a real test of strength, and then recommended that Moscow threaten a move against Berlin, starting with a ground blockade and "leaving out for the time being air routes so as not to give grounds for a quick confrontation." Yet Dobrynin added that Moscow should not be in a hurry to implement a blockade "since an extreme aggravation of the situation, it goes without saying, would not be in our interests." Alexeev meanwhile reported from Havana that the Cubans had mobilized, would not fire on U.S. planes unless the Americans fired first, would await the Soviet response, "and are placing their hopes on the wisdom of our decisions."[69]

Considering the U.S. imposition of a blockade a weaker response that left room for political maneuver, the Kremlin issued its flat, tough response of October 23. Khrushchev and his Presidium did decide to halt most of the 30 ships en route to Cuba, but they directed that the 4 carrying IRBMs and a fifth, loaded with nuclear warheads for these missiles, continue on course. They ordered that the nuclear-armed submarines headed for Cuba also keep going. When Kuznetsov echoed Dobrynin's suggestion of countering the blockade with pressure against West Berlin, Khrushchev answered sharply that he could "do without such advice. . . . [W]e had no intention to add fuel to the conflict."[70] Thus, General Curtis LeMay may have been right when he told Kennedy on October 19 that U.S. nuclear might would continue to safeguard Berlin. Nevertheless, some Soviet officials were ready to consider the option.

Tension increased on October 24. That morning brought Kennedy's brief unyielding demand for strict Soviet observance of the OAS quarantine. It also brought Dobrynin's cable reporting Robert Kennedy's flat statement that "We intend to stop your ships." Replying defiantly to Kennedy, Khrushchev declared that Soviet captains would run the blockade. At the same time, however, the Presidium decision of the previous day was apparently reversed. As McCone reported in the taped meeting on October 24, a fresh burst of signals had gone out to Soviet ships at sea in midmorning (Moscow time). The ships carrying the IRBMs now halted. A few ships with more innocent cargoes, including the *Bucharest* and *Grozny*, became the ones sailing ahead to test the quarantine. (The ship carrying the nuclear warheads for the IRBMs had already made it to a Cuban port.) Since it is extremely unlikely that the IRBM ships acted without Khrushchev's knowledge, it is possible that he was not candid with his own colleagues when he spoke at the Presidium of October 25 as if the missile ships were continuing on their way.[71] Actual Soviet behavior justified Rusk's conclusion that, in the face of American firmness, Khrushchev "blinked."

As in past crises, Khrushchev made an attempt to open prolonged negotiations. Valerian Zorin, his ambassador to the United Nations, had begun such an effort as soon as the crisis broke, and Moscow had done nothing to discourage him. On October 24, Khrushchev supplemented his harsh message to Kennedy with a candid open letter to the philosopher Bertrand Russell, who had been leading anti-American demonstrations in London. In this open letter, as the Americans discussed in their taped meeting that afternoon, Khrushchev suggested a possible summit meeting. Calling in a visiting U.S. businessman, William Knox, Khrushchev made the same proposal. Talking with Knox for more than three hours, Khrushchev had said that if the United States stopped and searched a Soviet merchant ship, he would instruct his submarines to sink the U.S. vessels.

Khrushchev also criticized Kennedy's handling of the crisis, observing that Eisenhower would have handled it in a more mature way. Kennedy, he remarked, was younger than his eldest son. "You cannot now take over Cuba," Khrushchev said. It was true, he admitted, that ballistic missiles with nuclear warheads had been supplied to Cuba. But the Cubans were volatile people and all the weapons were under the control of Soviet officers. They would be used only if Cuba were attacked. If the United States really wanted to know what kind of weapons could defend Cuba, the Americans had only to attack, and they would find out very quickly. He told Knox that he was not interested in the destruction of the world, but if the Americans wanted to meet in hell, it was up to them.

Khrushchev also related an anecdote to Knox: A man came on hard times and found it necessary to live with a goat. Even though the man became used to the smell, he still did not like it. Still, it soon became a way of life. Russians, Khrushchev said, had been living with a goat in the form of certain NATO countries such as Turkey, Greece, and Spain. The Americans had a goat in the form of Cuba. "You are not happy about it and you won't like it, but you'll learn to live with it."[72]

On the morning of October 25 the Soviet leadership had received Kennedy's tough, terse reply to Khrushchev's message. Khrushchev reconvened the Presidium. He told them he did not want to trade "caustic remarks" any longer with Kennedy. Instead he wanted to turn around four ships that were still carrying IRBMs to Cuba and try to resolve the crisis. (Again a puzzle, was Khrushchev only now revealing to his colleagues that he had ordered these ships to turn around the previous day?) Conciliation supplanted the previous day's defiance. Khrushchev announced to the Presidium his readiness to "dismantle the missiles to make Cuba into a zone of peace." He suggested sending a message including the words, "Give us a pledge not to invade Cuba, and we will remove the missiles." He would allow U.N. inspection of the missile sites. First, though, he wanted to be able to "look around" and be sure Kennedy really would not yield.[73]

There is little evidence to explain why Khrushchev had changed his mind and decided to give in. Perhaps the tone of Kennedy's letter under-scored the certainty of a nuclear confrontation and Khrushchev was unwilling to make this threat. In any event, the Presidium approved his plan with the usual unanimous vote.[74]

Later on October 25 the Soviets learned that the *Bucharest* had been allowed to proceed toward Cuba. They may also have received news that the Americans had begun low-level reconnaissance flights over Cuba. On that day U Thant also issued his new appeal for Khrushchev to keep his ships away from the quarantine line and for the United States to avoid a direct confrontation. Khrushchev sent no messages to the U.S. govern-ment. Perhaps he was still "looking around" for evidence of U.S. firmness.

Khrushchev was stirred to action on October 26. That morning he received a series of intelligence reports of increased U.S. military readi-ness and preparations. Among these a KGB report from Washington stood out, saying that, according to a well-connected U.S. journalist, a U.S. attack on Cuba was "prepared to the last detail" and "could begin at any moment." This report was based on conversations with Warren Rogers, a reporter for the *New York Herald Tribune*, who had simply expressed his own free-wheeling, confident personal opinion.[75] His sta-tus as the lead source on Khrushchev's desk that morning speaks vol-umes about the quality of Soviet intelligence and Soviet analysis.

Khrushchev presumably also received a report cabled on October 25 from Alexeev in Havana. Alexeev said that Castro had approved of the Soviet action to avoid a confrontation on the quarantine line. However, Castro now wanted to shoot down "one or two piratic American planes over Cuban territory" (that is, U.S. reconnaissance planes). The Cuban leader did not take rumors of a possible U.S. invasion very seriously.[76]

Khrushchev promptly made several moves. He sent instructions to accept U Thant's proposal for avoiding a confrontation at the quarantine line, thereby promising to keep Soviet ships away from this line. He also dictated the long letter to Kennedy suggesting a peaceful resolution of the crisis: if the US promised not to invade Cuba, "the necessity for the presence of our military specialists in Cuba would disappear." More a hint than a concrete proposal, this message was well within the guide-lines approved by the Presidium the previous day, so Khrushchev did not seek that body's formal approval but merely sent copies of the letter to the members.[77] Khrushchev may also have suggested that a Soviet offi-cial (probably KGB) in New York prompt U Thant to suggest a deal trading a noninvasion pledge for withdrawal of the missiles, though this cannot be confirmed. When the KGB resident in Washington, Feklisov, broached this idea to journalist John Scali that day, he may have heard informally about such probes or he could have been acting on his own initiative, perhaps prompted by his own worries about the ominous signs he had been reporting to Moscow.

There is no evidence of Soviet interest in the United States's boarding of their chartered cargo ship, the *Marucla*. During the day of October 26 Khrushchev might have heard that the Swedish cargo ship under Soviet charter had successfully defied the blockade. That it passed through the line at all seemed to the Americans to contradict Khrushchev's promise to U Thant, but we have no evidence about any Soviet consideration or even awareness of this matter. Nor do we have any evidence about Soviet consideration of the movement of the *Grozny* toward the quarantine line, though this was a continuing concern in Washington.

With his October 26 letter to Kennedy, Khrushchev had moved to defuse the threat of an imminent invasion, but he had still not conceded anything concrete. Moreover, by keeping the correspondence private, he had hidden his tentative move from Castro. The frantic Soviet military activity in Cuba continued. By the next morning, October 27, Khrushchev came to a judgment, for reasons that are still obscure, that the Americans could be pushed harder. Perhaps, as some Americans had feared he might, he interpreted the selective U.S. enforcement of the quarantine as a sign of weakness.[78] In direct contrast to Castro, whose relaxed attitude about a U.S. invasion had switched to alarm on October 26, Khrushchev had switched from alarm on October 26 to a more relaxed attitude on October 27.

The Soviet commander in Cuba, General Issa Pliyev, reported to the Defense Ministry that the Cubans had concluded that a U.S. air strike would begin that night or at dawn on October 27. Castro had ordered air defense units to fire at U.S. aircraft if there was an attack. Pliyev said that he had dispersed nuclear warheads closer to their launchers. The Soviet leaders endorsed Pliyev's plans.[79]

Nevertheless, when Khrushchev convened the Presidium he told them that the United States would not dare to attack Cuba. Five days had passed since Kennedy's speech, and nothing had happened. "To my mind they are not ready to do it now." Since, however, there was no guarantee against a U.S. attack, Khrushchev would make another, more concrete offer that both acknowledged the presence of missiles in Cuba and added the U.S. missiles in Turkey to the bargain. With that, he said, "we would win."[80]

Just as there is little evidence to explain why Khrushchev reversed his assessment of U.S. intentions, there is little evidence to explain why he now chose to add the Turkish missiles as a bargaining point. The missiles in Turkey had not been an important topic in any of the previous Presidium discussions during the crisis.

There are some signs Khrushchev took his cue from a report telling him about Lippmann's column of October 25. Or perhaps he got the idea from some other scattered hints of U.S. willingness to contemplate such an offer, like Robert Kennedy's unauthorized suggestions of the idea through his private emissaries on October 23 (see our notes to the taped conversation that evening between Robert and his brother). Had Khrushchev included the Turkey idea in his private letter of October 26, the U.S. reaction might have been more positive. No one, including Dillon and McCone, had much use for the Jupiter missiles.

Yet introducing the idea at this point and in public raised some obvious questions. Wouldn't the Americans perceive this as a change in the Soviet negotiating position, plainly inconsistent with the October 26 letter (and even more inconsistent with the positions being floated by KGB men in Washington and perhaps New York too)? The Americans might think the Soviet leader had reneged on his previous offer.

Surely any thoughtful analyst would have suggested that there was at least a good chance that therefore Washington would, rather than accepting the new offer, instead doubt that the Soviets were negotiating in good faith or wanted a settlement. The United States might then turn to military action. There is no evidence that the Soviet government considered this danger. One insider simply remembers that Khrushchev's public proposal of October 27 was "advanced in the hope of further bargaining."[81]

Khrushchev also reduced the chance of success for his latest initiative by making his offer public. This move made U.S. acceptance of it extremely unlikely, especially given the implications for NATO of such a public trade. A public deal might save face for Khrushchev, but no face would be saved if the Americans rejected it—which almost any analyst would have predicted. The Turks publicly rejected the trade just as the Americans started to discuss it. Castro certainly expected the Americans to reject such a deal, and Alexeev reported to Moscow that Castro was comforted by that prospect.[82]

There is no evidence that Khrushchev or any member of the Presidium analyzed this point. Apparently the new proposal was broadcast over the radio in order to save time in the interest of reducing transmission time and "nobody foresaw that by making public the Turkish angle of the deal we created additional difficulties to the White House."[83]

Of course, Khrushchev's actions may not have been thoughtless. He could have offered the deal in order to stalemate the negotiations. The position was well designed for public consumption, if not for U.S. acceptance. The Soviets may have hoped that the Americans would in effect back down, by accepting prolonged and fruitless negotiations over the terms of such a formal trade, talks involving Cuba and NATO and extending to bombers and bases – just as Thompson and Lyndon Johnson warned during the taped White House meetings that day.

But if this was Khrushchev's gambit, it was another example of recklessness, for the U.S. reaction could well have been to abandon negotiations and concentrate on military plans. In fact, this was how many of President Kennedy's advisers did react.

Having dictated the message to President Kennedy, Khrushchev and the others had second thoughts about Pliyev's dispersal of nuclear weapons. An order was quickly sent to Pliyev not to employ any nuclear weapons without express authorization from Moscow. Khrushchev also sent a message to Havana urging Alexeev to caution Castro against any rash actions.[84]

Events during October 27 dispelled Khrushchev's complacent mood. A message from Castro, sent from Cuba on October 26, announced that a massive U.S. air strike, and possibly also an invasion, was "almost inevitable" in the next 24 to 72 hours. In the event of invasion, Castro urged Khrushchev to consider the "elimination of such a danger," plainly referring to the use of Soviet nuclear weapons against the United States. "However difficult and horrifying this decision may be," Castro wrote, "there is, I believe, no other recourse."[85]

The same day brought news about the incursion of the U.S. U-2 into Siberian airspace. Aside from a reproach in his October 28 letter to Kennedy, we have no evidence about how Khrushchev viewed that episode.

Then the Cubans shot at unarmed U.S. low-level reconnaissance aircraft. On October 26 Castro had given the order to fire on any aircraft entering Cuban airspace.[86] Alexeev had reported this intention on October 25, but Moscow seems not to have noticed. Castro discussed his order with Soviet commanders on October 26; this fact may have been reported to Moscow too. On October 27 Khrushchev sent instructions to Alexeev to suggest that Castro rescind the order; but by then, of course, it was too late, even if Castro had wished to heed the advice.

When the U-2 came over, it too was apparently, and falsely, perceived as posing a threat. Authority to fire had been delegated in the event of U.S. attack, and the local Soviet commanders (below Pliyev himself, who was temporarily unavailable) chose to interpret their instructions liberally in order to aid their excited Cuban comrades.[87] Although a Soviet missile actually downed the plane, Khrushchev seems not to have fully grasped this fact until some time later.[88]

Late in the afternoon of October 27 Khrushchev would have heard that the Americans had immediately rejected his public proposal with a press statement of their own. Alexeev reported telling Castro that "in the present circumstances it would not be fitting to aggravate the situation and initiate provocations." He said Castro understood, but "considering the rise in the army's martial spirit and the Americans' warning, our friends were compelled to take such a step."[89]

Shaken by the shoot-down of the U-2, Khrushchev was also unnerved by Castro's urging him to prepare for using nuclear weapons against the United States. A few days later, in another message to Castro, Khrushchev referred to this "very alarming" message in which "you proposed that we be the first to carry out a nuclear strike against the enemy's territory." "Naturally," Khrushchev added, "you understand where that would lead us. It would not be a simple strike, but the start of a thermonuclear world war."[90]

Kennedy's message to Khrushchev arrived late that evening, laying out the deal that would entail the verified withdrawal of Soviet "offensive weapons" in exchange for the noninvasion pledge. Khrushchev opened the Presidium session on the morning of October 28 with a very different assessment from the day before. He warned his colleagues that they were "face to face with the danger of war and of nuclear catastrophe, with the possible result of destroying the human race." He went on: "In order to save the world, we must retreat."[91]

The new assessment was *not* apparently based on news of Robert Kennedy's latest (October 27) conversation with Dobrynin, but the news reinforced it. *After* Khrushchev made his declaration to the Politburo, word came in of the cable from Dobrynin reporting on the discussion in bleak, ominous terms. A summary of the cable was read to the Presidium. One of Khrushchev's staff recalled that the "entire tenor of the words by the President's brother, as they were relayed by Anatoly Dobrynin, prompted the conclusion that the time of reckoning had come." Khrushchev later told Castro that his warning of an imminent U.S. attack had been confirmed by other sources and that he had hurried to prevent it.[92]

Khrushchev's resolve to yield was reinforced by Robert Kennedy's reported warning and by his assurance that Jupiters would eventually be withdrawn from Turkey. Reportedly only Khrushchev, Gromyko, and Mikoyan had much to say at this Presidium session. "Others preferred to keep silent as if hinting to Khrushchev that since he had made his bed, he could sleep on it."[93]

The tension was compounded by a report that at 5:00 P.M. Moscow time (9:00 A.M. in Washington), President Kennedy would be making another speech to the U.S. people. In fact this was only going to be a rebroadcast of Kennedy's October 22 speech, but Khrushchev and his advisers feared an imminent announcement of U.S. military action. An urgent, conciliatory reply was prepared and hurriedly broadcast over the radio to be sure it reached Washington in time. Another message was rushed to Dobrynin in Washington, directing him to "quickly get in touch with R. Kennedy" and to pass on the following "urgent response: The thoughts which R. Kennedy expressed at the instruction of the President finds understanding in Moscow. Today, an answer will be given by radio . . . and that response will be the most favorable. The main thing which disturbs the President, precisely the issue of the dismantling under international control of the rocket bases in Cuba, meets no objection and will be explained in detail. . . ." Pliyev received a cable chiding him for having been in such a "hurry" to shoot down the U-2. He was ordered to ground all Soviet jets in Cuba to avoid any further clashes with U.S. reconnaissance aircraft.[94]

There was no time to consult with Castro. He learned of Khrushchev's decision from the radio, along with the rest of the world.

After the missile crisis was over, in January 1963, Khrushchev began walking away from his failed Berlin policy, by simply declaring victory. He began to argue that he had really won because in 1961 he had forced the West to accept the construction of the Berlin Wall and live with a divided Berlin.[95] This had not, of course, been his position in 1962.

Khrushchev still could not stop wondering whether the Americans would really have gone to nuclear war over Berlin. Surely the Americans would not make such a threat unless they were incredibly complacent about their nuclear superiority. His Cuban deployment would have punctured that complacency. It would have vividly demonstrated the vulnerability he wanted the Americans to feel, the vulnerability that he thought would restrain them. After the Cuban venture failed, even after he had then also abandoned his 1962 plan of action on Berlin, Khrushchev still wanted to know: Had Washington been bluffing? In August 1963 Khrushchev asked Rusk point-blank: "Why should I believe that you Americans would fight a nuclear war over Berlin?" Rusk remembered, "That was quite a question. . . . So I stared back at him and said, 'Mr. Chairman, you will have to take into account the possibility that we Americans are just goddamn fools.' We glared at each other, unblinking, and then he changed the subject and gave me three gold watches to take home to my children."[96]

In November 1963 President Kennedy was murdered by a gunman who had long harbored grievances about Kennedy's hostility toward Castro's Cuba. In October 1964 Khrushchev was ousted from power by his Presidium colleagues. "You insisted that we deploy our missiles in Cuba," one of his Presidium accusers thundered. "This provoked the deepest crisis, carried the world to the brink of nuclear war, and even frightened terribly the organizer of this very danger."[97]

Further Reflections on the Tapes

The material in this book offers the most complete set of data available on how a modern government actually made a set of important decisions. President Kennedy certainly had discussions that he did not record. Yet much of the analysis lying behind all the major policy choices can be reconstructed from the recordings and other available material. The most secret move, Rusk's idea of providing a unilateral assurance on the withdrawal of the Jupiters from Turkey, emerged from deliberations that had already covered the range of possibilities. Kennedy did not make any impulsive decisions during the crisis. He invariably opened up much of his reasoning about the pros, cons, and likely consequences of his choices before he made them. He exposed his thinking to a range of analyses and critiques from formal advisers, informal advisers, and representatives of the British government.

There are some large revelations in the recordings. One is the close connection between the crisis and the stalemated East-West struggle over Berlin. We believe, with Thompson and the experts in London, that the key to Khrushchev's strategy for Berlin in 1962 was missiles in Cuba. The Cuban gamble can thus be seen as a climax in the Cold War. Khrushchev had embarked on a risky Soviet effort to change the way the world perceived the balance of power and then ride that achievement to victory on the great diplomatic issue of the time. Instead Khrushchev failed in both the immediate gamble and in his plans for Berlin. It is not too far-fetched to characterize the missile crisis as the Pearl Harbor *and* Midway of the Cold War. Never again, even in the crisis years of 1979 to 1983, would the Soviet challenge or the Western response be so direct and so intense.

Certainly Berlin was never far from President Kennedy's thoughts. He refers to it constantly, calculating every move in light of its probable impact there. After the crisis he voiced his frustration with the ways

Berlin had constrained his freedom of action at every turn. The creative solution Kennedy sought to this problem never really emerged. During the crisis Walt Rostow had suggested moving tactical nuclear weapons into Berlin to deter a Soviet countermove, but the idea was quashed before it reached the White House. After the crisis Nitze suggested (perhaps remembering a similar idea that George Kennan had developed and Nitze had supported in 1948) that the United States propose a unified but demilitarized Germany. This idea, too, was quashed before it reached the White House.[98]

Another revelation is the extent of President Kennedy's own role in the management of the crisis. Naturally this role is enhanced by the fact of recordings made at the White House, with the President selectively choosing what to record for posterity. Kennedy is also reticent during the first day of the crisis, mostly letting others reason through the problems. Yet by the meeting of October 18 he is plainly shaping the discussion and thinking ahead, and the results of this are apparent in his October 19 meeting with the Joint Chiefs of Staff in which, alone, he takes on the combined weight of their arguments and has apparently gone far toward making up his mind. From October 22 onward Kennedy is dominating the meetings.

Saturday, October 27, may well have been the finest hours of John F. Kennedy's public life. To us he seems more alive to the possibilities and consequences of each new development than anyone else. He remains calm, lucid, and is constantly a step, or several steps, ahead of his advisers. He is the only one in the room who is determined not to go to war over obsolete missiles in Turkey. Having seen and thought about this issue earlier in the crisis, he fully understands and is trying to work around the large consequences of appearing to sell out the Turks. We can understand why, in a taped conversation on October 29 (not in this volume), Kennedy kept Rusk behind after a meeting and privately but witheringly dressed him down for not having better planned to cope with Khrushchev's predictable move.

The recordings subtly but significantly alter our understanding of practically every major question about U.S. policy during the crisis, sometimes by validating one interpretation over another, sometimes by spotlighting overlooked aspects of the deliberations. We think the material largely speaks for itself, but we can note a few examples.

The decision not to launch an air strike during the first few days was restrained, in substantial part, by the belief that such a strike had to include a wide attack on Cuban airfields as well as SAM sites. The reasoning behind such a wider strike plan was careful. It derived less from reflexive routine than from reasonable fear of MiG strikes against Florida, at a time when air defenses in the U.S. Southeast were flimsy, and from the need to suppress air defenses to make U.S. bombing raids more accurate and less dangerous. Concern about Berlin also weighed on Kennedy as he considered the air strike, for he had to worry about how U.S. allies would behave if called on to deal with a Soviet response against Berlin.

The concentration on military moves and countermoves during the crisis is natural. Yet diplomatic maneuvers are equally central. U Thant played an important role that was largely forgotten by participants and has never received much attention from historians. It is also obvious from these records that Macmillan and Ormsby-Gore became de facto members of Kennedy's Executive Committee, though we suspect that by October 26 Kennedy had become skeptical about the quality of Macmillan's advice.

Classification restrictions are almost entirely gone, and the general content of material that remains restricted can be readily imagined. So we now have a much clearer picture of the role of military plans and intelligence concerns in the deliberations. The military discussions range from Kennedy's grimly amusing October 22 exchange with Nitze about the standing orders for use of the Jupiter missiles in Turkey, to the timing and detailed preparation of plans for managing the blockade or attacking Cuba or preparing an occupation government, to the horrific talk of how to protect Americans against fallout after U.S. cities have been devastated by a Soviet nuclear strike.

The intelligence issues are everywhere, often interlocked with dilemmas about military plans. The bad news about the missiles in Cuba did not come all at once but broke in waves, and the wave of news about the IRBMs, disseminated on October 18, strengthened the momentum favoring military action. The yield from intelligence gathering and organizations such as the National Photographic Interpretation Center is impressive. Enlarged, one day's U-2 mission produced "100 miles of film, 20 feet wide," McCone noted at one session. "Quite a job" to analyze that in a day, he laconically added. We agree.

But the policy challenges involved in gathering such data were a constant problem too. There is the argument about how to place the electronic surveillance ship, the USS *Oxford*. There is the argument about use and coordination of Cuban exiles to gather intelligence, and the fate of the Mongoose program. There are regular discussions about whether to risk U-2 flights, and what to do if one were shot down, then about what to do when one was shot down. There is the question of low-level reconnaissance, then the question of low-level reconnaissance at night aided by explosive flares. We keep remembering Lyndon Johnson's pithy summary: "Blooey!"

Collecting intelligence only began the problem of analyzing what it meant and what to do about it. We come to know Kennedy better in these recordings, and his advisers too. Robert Kennedy, whether alone with his brother or in a group, is quick and insightful. Sorensen usually stays in the background. Bundy is unsettled during the first week about what to do, offering many questions and few answers, but seems to become stronger and more focused as the crisis develops. Yet Bundy never seems to do enough to help President Kennedy prepare for these meetings or organize what will happen in them.

Rusk too seems to offer clearer advice later in the crisis. He is often the voice of caution. Though at the outset McNamara slows the rush toward military action with his pointed questions and forceful presentations, he becomes increasingly consumed as the crisis wears on by the task of managing the spiraling military preparations and he becomes more expectant of the need to use them. Referring to the Soviet missiles, he comments on October 25, "I never have thought we'd get them out of Cuba without the application of substantial force."[99]

Taylor and McCone have a consistent stand which President Kennedy understands and for which he always has some sympathy. Kennedy respects their professional opinion. He apparently has little faith in the judgment of Taylor's colleagues who, unlike Taylor, appear to make little effort to understand the President's problems. This quality of empathy was one that President Kennedy valued highly and often practiced in his clinical, ironic way.

Once the blockade is securely in place, after October 24, the crisis moves toward the climactic issue of whether Khrushchev will agree to stop construction and pull out the "offensive weapons" he has already deployed in Cuba. The Americans are plainly feeling time pressure to resolve the matter, with the military's planning for a strike before the end of the month. The pressure seems to be related to the missile buildup.

Why the rush? It is still hard to know. At first, of course, they are concerned about when the MRBMs will become operational. But by October 26 and 27 it is too late; the MRBMs are judged to be ready for action. The IRBMs are still projected to be weeks away from completion, and (unknown to the Americans) the missiles to go on those launch pads have been kept out by the blockade. Nuclear warheads, though not yet found, are always assumed to be already on the island.

This question, "Why the rush?" will probably never have a complete answer. Some officials think that the missiles are becoming more elusive, harder to hit, as hurried Soviet efforts belie some of Lundahl's early optimism about the futility of camouflage. There also seems to be a strong sense that if the momentum relaxes, and negotiations string out, then the world might realize that the MRBMs really were a fait accompli. That fact was obscured only by the lack of general knowledge that the missiles were complete, and by the Americans' robust exercise of diplomatic initiative. Yet, as time passed, U.S. insistence that the finished missiles be removed might become increasingly hollow and incredible. Bundy, McNamara, and others warn about letting the situation "freeze" or reach a "plateau," constantly urging that momentum be sustained.

President Kennedy and the advisers who had favored starting with a blockade may have sensed, consciously or semiconsciously, that perhaps they had already waited too long. Lyndon Johnson actually voices this concern in one of the taped meetings on October 27, at one point sparking a defensive reply from Robert Kennedy. By that time the Soviet MRBMs were plainly deployed and ready. The country was galvanized by the crisis, anxious and expectant, and congressional elections were only ten days away.

The turning point of the crisis may have been October 25, the day that Khrushchev decided that he would withdraw the missiles on terms that would abandon his most important original goals for the deployment. At that moment Khrushchev had made the fundamental decision that he could not so readily change the strategic balance of missile power; nor would he be able to use this new position to break the stalemate over Berlin. Even during the tense hours on October 27 the Americans commented on how much better it was to talk about trading useless Jupiters instead of talking about losing Berlin. What would have happened, had Khrushchev not made this bitter choice, is awful to contemplate.

Even having made the choice, Khrushchev hesitated. He did nothing on October 25 and little on the day following. When no invasion materialized, he hardened his stance, constantly holding open the possibility of keeping the missiles in Cuba until he was convinced—again—that U.S. military action might really be imminent.[100]

From the evidence of these recordings, we feel confident that the White House would have continued to escalate pressure on the Soviets. Kennedy would have chosen either a direct strike against the missiles, possibly followed by an invasion, or he would have tightened the blockade to include POL, the oil that made Cuba run. If Khrushchev had continued to condition withdrawal of the missiles on a deal in Turkey, Kennedy would probably have worked with the Turks and NATO to acquiesce, but in some way that put withdrawals from Cuba first and strengthened or spotlighted the new, replacement deterrent forces. A more intransigent stance by Khrushchev would have made U.S. military action against the missiles very likely.

All these steps would have carried grave dangers of further escalation, as Kennedy knew. The shoot-down of the U-2 on October 27 should, according to the agreed plan, have prompted an immediate U.S. air strike, but Kennedy overrode the contingency plan and held back the planes. Had Khrushchev's acceptance of Kennedy's offer not come through, President Kennedy probably would have authorized more reconnaissance flights on October 28 and would have had a renewed readiness to respond to another shoot-down with a retaliatory strike.

The Americans were also already worried about an encounter with the *Grozny* at the quarantine line on October 28. A total blockade would have extended the issue from the missiles to the whole survival of the Castro government, and Soviet officials could then have been expected to renew suggestions that Khrushchev counter with a blockade of Berlin. We doubt that the weary, impatient U.S. officials, already pressed by the sense that time was against them, would have waited long for a tighter blockade of Cuba to produce results, if they had bothered with it at all. McNamara's civilian experts at the Pentagon had already told him such a blockade would be inadequate and would even make matters worse.

On the other hand, President Kennedy would certainly have paused and talked through the original military plan to follow a strike with an invasion of Cuba. Intelligence had discovered the tactical nuclear arms on October 25, and Kennedy was briefed about them the next day. On October 28 the JCS formally asked Admiral Dennison to revise his invasion planning accordingly, though they turned down his request to provide the invasion force with counterpart tactical nuclear missiles of its own. Reviewing military contingency plans on October 29, Kennedy was already diverted, we think, by the question of how to deal with this tactical nuclear danger.

In any case an invasion would be preceded by seven days of air strikes, and McNamara had become more confident about the efficacy of the strikes (if continued air reconnaissance could be maintained). So it seems likely that President Kennedy would have ordered the air strikes and withheld final judgment on the invasion until the last possible moment, seeing first what damage the air strikes had done, how the Soviets reacted worldwide, and how the diplomatic picture had changed.

The outcome of Khrushchev's gambit would in all likelihood have been very different—perhaps inconceivably different—if someone else had been president of the United States. But to speculate about such possibilities seems to us idle. We can content ourselves with the observation that Khrushchev might also have adopted quite different policies if he had had a different president to deal with or had gauged Kennedy's character differently. Given the circumstances that existed on October 16, though, it is hard to imagine that any president (in a list of those who could imaginably have been elected) would have adopted a more peaceful course than the one Kennedy chose. It seems fortunate that, given the circumstances he had helped create, Kennedy was the president charged with managing the crisis.

Given what we now know, Soviet processes seem to offer a model of how not to make sensible decisions. Kennedy was right to treat Khrushchev as if he was in complete charge of his government. Khrushchev *was* in complete charge. Yet if a government or a leader consistently relies on false intelligence reports, makes little effort to assess other governments, does not analyze policy alternatives, and has little open debate among senior officials who are overawed by an insecure and impulsive risk taker, we would not expect very good results unless the other relevant actors are weak, equally incompetent, or extraordinarily unlucky.

We therefore close with some broader remarks on U.S. decision making. Both authors can call on some direct experience to observe that White House deliberations during the Cuban missile crisis were unique in some respect but by no means in all. This record captures the feel of such discussions, so obvious to those who have participated in many of them, so difficult to describe to those who have not.

First, critical meetings have an inherently disorderly character. Rarely do they fall neatly into place around an "options paper." In this volume, by editing the meeting transcripts, we have made what happened seem somewhat more orderly and less cluttered than was actually the case. Yet there is more structure to these 1962 meetings than might meet the eye at first glance. They ordinarily begin with an intelligence briefing. Kennedy turns to Rusk, then to McNamara, or in reverse order, for reports on developments and issues needing decision in their areas of responsibility. Then, especially as the crisis wears on, he draws the participants toward questions that seem most salient to him in preparing for the next phase, all the while digressing to handle various specific action items.

The disorderly quality arises as much from the surfeit of issues and associated judgments as from any defect in the formal organization of the meeting. This source of disarray can be suppressed only by suppressing analysis or by delegating the analysis to others, in another place. Yet at the point when he chooses to go to the meeting, in this crisis Kennedy judges, rightly we think, that he should not be too quick to suppress analysis or to delegate it. Still, the meetings cover a lot of ground and do so in surprisingly little time. On these occasions Kennedy does not encourage much superfluous talk. He himself rarely says ten words if he thinks he has made his point in eight.

One way to try to trace the many threads of analysis that interweave in the meetings transcribed here is to imagine for a moment that you are a notetaker at the meeting, jotting down summaries in real time. Consider the problem of summarizing, for someone who was not there, what has happened—not just what was decided, but the contrasting chains of reasoning and clash of personalities. Think too about the information and analysis provided (or not provided) before people came to these meetings and presented in the reports or recommendations that you read. Think finally about the analytical problems and action issues that arise from what has been raised, that should be addressed before the next meeting or action-forcing event.[101]

There are countless details and bits of information affecting the plans for action. The details require someone to take time to master them or to work them out or to act on them, often by drafting a letter or paper, making a call, or talking with someone not present at the meeting. Someone usually assumes the responsibility for that action. People go off, sometimes during a meeting, to take the action. Bohlen, publicly expected to appear in New York and Paris, leaves the deliberations completely. On Thursday night, October 18, Rusk and Thompson miss the White House meeting because they must attend a dinner with Gromyko. On October 27, Robert Kennedy and Sorensen go off to complete a draft of a message to Khrushchev and see that it is typed up properly. That night McNamara goes off to make a press announcement at the Pentagon, then he comes back. And so on.

People with action responsibility have greater control, greater influence, over "their" issue. They may be influenced by agendas of their own. State Department officials, challenged to think about the Turkish problem, sought a solution that would advance their long-standing project for a NATO multilateral nuclear force, though such a scheme could not possibly be readied within the time frame of the crisis.[102] One result was that little useful analytical help was available to Kennedy when the Turkish issue arose on October 27.

Yet action responsibility also takes people out of meetings, takes them "out of the loop," takes them away from other issues or information, tiring them and tying them down. McNamara is vital to Kennedy's management of the crisis. The Defense Secretary voraciously takes on responsibilities. To us, one result is that by the end of the crisis his analyses and judgments seem narrower, less helpful to President Kennedy, than they were when the crisis began.

Perhaps, above all, we observe in this record—more clearly than in any other documents we have ever seen—the contrary pulls of detail on the one hand and belief (or conviction or ideology) on the other. Almost from minute to minute, new information or recognition of some previously unperceived implication in information already at hand or a new argument will change in subtle or sometimes not subtle ways the form or even the character of the issue being addressed. When Kennedy and his advisers learn that the Soviets are putting in IRBMs as well as MRBMs, their understanding of what is at stake clearly changes, though they might have been hard put to explain how or why. Similarly, though they have talked about the possibility of a U-2's being attacked, they have to take stock anew when they face the reality that Major Anderson's plane has been shot down.

These are large examples of how details drive debate. The records here are particularly rich because they show the extent to which this is a constant process, with even small bits of information or slight alterations in atmosphere affecting the delicate processes of issue definition and decision making. Nothing is harder to relate about experience in government than this sense of being driven by daily detail, because students or interested citizens removed from the event cannot comprehend all these details, do not have time to know them. They tend much more to see an episode like the Cuban missile crisis as a single event, with a problem, one or two key choices, and an outcome. Such a level of understanding may well be accurate, as far as it goes.

Often it does not go far enough. Participants themselves often remember decision making in a blurred way. They forget how they saw an issue before the details or atmosphere changed. As a result, the world usually learns little or nothing about courses of action that were considered but not pursued. For example, on October 26 and again on October 27, McNamara strongly advocates low-level reconnaissance missions at night, with flares to light up the earth. The reasons for this turn in part on intelligence details, the day's worries about nighttime construction activity or concealments. Other agendas are also engaged. Both the recommendation and the information that prompted it are practically unknown, half-forgotten by the participants themselves. But if the recommendation had been accepted, the activity could have been misread by the Cubans or Soviets as preparations for an imminent attack (which was indeed part of McNamara's agenda), thereby transforming their own assessments and responses in ways that are nearly incalculable.

Or, for another example, recall the care taken on the afternoon of October 27 to draft a particular kind of letter to Khrushchev. It is not quite the draft letter suggested by Stevenson (a lengthy discussion thread we pared away in our edits for this volume) or the one suggested by McCone, and the manner of its delivery—through Robert Kennedy— is a deliberate choice. At the same time McNamara is sent out to announce a call-up of Air Force reservists. This complex combination of judgments resulted in a particular set of signals sent to Khrushchev, inadequately captured by the conventional assertion "Kennedy chose to accept Khrushchev's initial offer of October 26." We know that the particular set of signals sent from the White House helped drive Khrushchev to a particular action. He had decided to give in *before* the report came in of Robert Kennedy's talk with Dobrynin. The actual terms of the subsequent settlement were driven, too, by the particular way the U.S. position had been crafted in Kennedy's letter of October 27.

But the constant flow of detail, with continual pressure to act, works on the conscious and unconscious minds of decision makers, who see facts and form presumptions within frameworks of understanding shaped both by their personal interests and by their accumulated experience. Thus Kennedy probably never forgets about the impending congressional election, even though he seldom alludes to it and even though only sophomoric analysis would suppose that it dominated his thinking. Nor did Rusk or McNamara ever entirely lose sight of their parochial concerns as heads of cabinet departments.

Auxiliary interests, political, bureaucratic, or personal, probably had less to do with how the decision makers acted than did filters in their minds formed by their own past experiences. Intellect and conscience alike tell Kennedy and Rusk and others that they cannot be—or seem to be—"appeasers." Kennedy, however, is not unsettled, as someone else might have been, when LeMay says to him on the morning of October 19 regarding the quarantine option, "This is almost as bad as the appeasement at Munich." The author of *Why England Slept* knows that the quarantine is not *Munich.* The son of Joe Kennedy also probably feels some empathy when he reads Adlai Stevenson's agonized plea that *everything* be considered negotiable. And Stevenson probably felt steeled to give such advice because he, after all, had been an arch antiappeaser back when Munich had been news, not shibboleth.

The Kennedy tapes are instructive not only for what they contain but also for what they do not contain. Listening to the tapes or reading the transcripts, one is struck by the decreasing frequency with which Kennedy and his advisers refer to historical landmarks. In the first day or two, such references abound. Participants try to make sense of the crisis by likening it to the Berlin blockade or Suez-Hungary or by invoking Pearl Harbor. This is a natural tendency when busy persons of active temperament confront unfamiliar circumstances. The more Kennedy and his advisers become immersed in the details of the particular crisis before them, the less they resort to such intellectual shortcutting; the more they apply to the unique problems at hand, general rules—a sense of possibilities— derived from and informed by many such experiences.[103]

In Rusk's remarks one can detect implicit lessons drawn from painful but proud recollections of both Pearl Harbor and the Korean War. Don't presume too heavily on the adversary's acting rationally, according to *our* standards of rationality, he cautions. Recall that at the very first White House meeting, he comments: "I'm beginning to wonder whether maybe Mr. Khrushchev is entirely rational about Berlin." Don't lose patience, Rusk also advises; and don't yield to temptation to solve one problem by making it a larger problem. Thus he cautions against stopping a tanker just for the sake of stopping some Soviet ship, and he picks up the formula for offering up the Jupiters by sleight of hand. In Taylor's remarks, one can see enduring effects of his analysis of the Korean War as one in which the United States forgot that military and diplomatic measures need not be alternatives but could complement one another. And one is tempted to attribute McNamara's shifts back and forth from urging caution to urging action in part to lack of moorings such as those in the minds of Kennedy, Rusk, or Taylor. McNamara's long preoccupation with the problems of financial control and with the management of the Ford Motor Company had equipped him with few precepts applicable to the missile crisis.

Someone who wants to learn all that can be learned from this extraordinary record of decision making needs not only to notice how the process stutters and veers amid barrages of detail but also to infer how individuals of different backgrounds and temperaments are sorting the detail, discerning choices, and selecting among them, often guided by inner beacons of which they themselves may be incompletely aware. These tapes and transcripts, especially the complete versions provided in the reference volumes produced by the Presidential Recordings Project, form an almost inexhaustible resource for analyzing not only the mechanics but also the psychology of decision making.

We come away from this study convinced that major policymaking episodes repay the closest possible examination. Only such examination can reconstruct key judgments within the little worlds in which they are made. Only by penetrating these worlds can we truly understand and evaluate that extraordinary human faculty that we label "judgment." And only by doing that, can we learn to do better. Reconstruction that oversimplifies or ignores the incessant tension between realities and beliefs makes us no wiser. By coming fully to grips with the particulars of past moments of choice, we may become better able to handle our own.

Notes

Introduction

1.   On the Kennedy family, see Richard J. Whalen, *The Founding Father: The Story of Joseph P. Kennedy* (New York: New American Library, 1964); David E. Koskoff, *Joseph P. Kennedy: A Life and Times* (Englewood Cliffs, NJ: Prentice-Hall, 1974); Ronald Kessler, *The Sins of the Father: Joseph P. Kennedy and the Dynasty He Founded* (New York: Warner Books, 1996); *Hostage to Fortune: The Letters of Joseph P. Kennedy*, ed. Amanda Smith (New York: Viking, 2001); especially Doris Kearns Goodwin, *The Fitzgeralds and the Kennedys, an American Saga* (New York: Simon & Schuster, 1987).

2.   In the enormous literature on John Kennedy, the fullest account of the early years is Nigel Hamilton, *JFK: Reckless Youth* (New York: Random House, 1992); the most balanced is Herbert Parmet, *Jack: The Struggles of John F. Kennedy* (New York: Dial Press, 1980). The first part of Seymour M. Hersh, *The Dark Side of Camelot* (Boston: Little, Brown, 1997) adds lurid gossip to that collected by Hamilton.

3.   David Halberstam, *The Best and the Brightest* (New York: Random House, 1972), p. 9.

4.   George W. Ball, *The Past Has Another Pattern* (New York: Norton, 1982), pp. 165–66.

5.   Dean Rusk, *As I Saw It: As Told to Richard Rusk*, ed. Daniel S. Papp (New York: Norton, 1990), pp. 36–37, 74–83. On Rusk, see also Warren Cohen, *Dean Rusk* (Totowa, NJ: Cooper Square, 1980); Thomas J. Schoenbaum, *Waging Peace and War: Dean Rusk in the Truman, Kennedy, and Johnson Years* (New York: Simon & Schuster, 1988); Thomas W. Zeiler, *Dean Rusk: Defending the American Mission Abroad* (New York: Scholarly Resources, 1999).

6.   Hamilton, *JFK: Reckless Youth*, pp. 424–25.

7.   Joan Blair and Clay Blair, Jr., *The Search for JFK* (New York: Berkley, 1976), p. 114.

8.   John Bartlow Martin, *The Life of Adlai E. Stevenson*, 2 vols. (Garden City, NY: Doubleday, 1976–77), is the best and fullest biography, but see also Jeff Broadwater, *Adlai Stevenson and American Politics: The Odyssey of a Cold War Liberal* (New York: Twayne, 1994).

9.   On Ball, besides his own *The Past Has Another Pattern*, see James A. Bill, *George Ball: Behind the Scenes in U.S. Foreign Policy* (New Haven, CT: Yale University Press, 1997). On Robert Kennedy, see Arthur M. Schlesinger, Jr.,

Robert Kennedy and His Times (New York: Random House, 1978); Evan Thomas, *Robert Kennedy: His Life* (New York: Simon & Schuster, 2000).

10.   Peter Collier and David Horowitz, *The Kennedys, an American Drama* (New York: Simon & Schuster, 1984), p. 155.

11.   Hamilton, *JFK: Reckless Youth*, pp. 694–96.

12.   Ibid.

13.   Deborah Shapley, *Promise and Power: The Life and Times of Robert McNamara* (Boston: Little, Brown, 1993), pp. 3ff.

14.   Curtis E. LeMay with MacKinlay Kantor, *Mission with LeMay: My Story* (Garden City, NY: Doubleday, 1965), p. 10.

15.   Ibid., pp. 380–81.

16.   On the Cold War, see various works by John Lewis Gaddis, particularly *We Now Know: Rewriting Cold War History* (New York: Oxford University Press, 1997); Marc Trachtenberg, *A Constructed Peace: The Making of the European Settlement, 1945–1963* (Princeton, NJ: Princeton University Press, 1999).

17.   Winston S. Churchill, speech at Fulton, Missouri, *New York Times*, 6 March 1946.

18.   Hamilton, *JFK: Reckless Youth*, p. 700.

19.   John F. Kennedy, speech of 4 January 1947, quoted from the *Congressional Record* in *The Kennedys*, Collier and Horowitz, p. 196.

20.   Kennedy's understanding of the history of the blockade and airlift was imperfect. As of 1948, the United States had only a few nuclear weapons and very limited capabilities for using them against the Soviet Union. See McGeorge Bundy, *Danger and Survival: Choices about the Bomb in the First Fifty Years* (New York: Random House, 1988), pp. 383–85.

21.   John F. Kennedy, speech of 21 February 1949, quoted from the *Congressional Record* in *Jack*, Parmet, p. 210.

22.   LeMay, *Mission with LeMay*, p. 382.

23.   Maxwell Taylor, *Swords and Plowshares* (New York: Norton, 1972) is an autobiography; John M. Taylor, *General Maxwell Taylor: The Sword and the Pen* (New York: Doubleday, 1989) is a family biography.

24.   This development is surveyed in Michael S. Sherry, *In the Shadow of War: The United States since the 1930s* (New Haven, CT: Yale University Press, 1995).

25.   Richard Reeves, *President Kennedy: Profile of Power* (New York: Simon & Schuster, 1993), p. 305. This work draws on sources not available to previous writers on the Kennedy presidency, but it does not supersede, either in detail or in insight, Theodore Sorensen, *Kennedy* (New York: Harper & Row, 1965), and Arthur M. Schlesinger, Jr., *A Thousand Days: John F. Kennedy in the White House* (Boston: Houghton Mifflin, 1965). A forthcoming biography by Robert Dallek is likely to be more nearly definitive.

26.   The best introduction to this phenomenon is Stephen J. Whitfield, *The Culture of the Cold War* (Baltimore: Johns Hopkins Press, 1991). See also Ellen Schrecker, *The Age of McCarthyism* (Boston: Bedford Books, 1994).

27.   Ball, *The Past Has Another Pattern*, p. 112.

28. Schlesinger, *Robert Kennedy*, p. 135.

29. For the best-informed and coolest analysis of the issues, as well as a firsthand account of the missile crisis, see Bundy, *Danger and Survival.*

30. Details about nuclear weapons can be found in Natural Resources Defense Council, *Nuclear Weapons Databook*, vol. 1; Thomas B. Cochran, William M. Arkin, and Milton M. Hoenig, *U.S. Nuclear Forces and Capabilities* (Cambridge, MA: Ballinger, 1984); and Chuck Hansen, *U.S. Nuclear Weapons: the Secret History* (New York: Orion Books, 1988).

31. Stephen E. Ambrose, *Eisenhower*, vol. 2, *The President* (New York: Simon & Schuster, 1984), p. 494.

32. Robert A. Divine, *Blowing on the Wind: The Nuclear Test Ban Debate, 1954–1960* (New York: Oxford University Press, 1978), p. 267.

33. John F. Kennedy, campaign speech in Detroit, 26 August 1960, John F. Kennedy Library. Kennedy used the same language repeatedly during the campaign. He did so in a swing through Texas in September 1960, and he reminded his listeners of those words in Dallas on 22 November 1963, the day of his assassination.

34. Maxwell Taylor, *The Uncertain Trumpet* (New York: Harper, 1959), p. 142.

35. The most thoughtful general survey is Jorge Dominguez, *Cuba: Order and Revolution* (Cambridge, MA: Harvard University Press, 1978). See also Andres Suarez, *Cuba: Castroism and Communism, 1959–1966* (Cambridge, MA: MIT Press, 1967); Maurice Halperin, *The Rise and Fall of Fidel Castro* (Berkeley: University of California Press, 1972); Tad Szulc, *Fidel: A Critical Portrait* (New York: Morrow, 1986); Robert E. Quirk, *Fidel Castro* (New York: Norton, 1993), pp. 137–52, and 402–3; Thomas M. Leonard, *Castro and the Cuban Revolution* (New York: Greenwood, 1999). More analysis informed by Russian sources appears in Aleksandr Fursenko and Timothy Naftali, *"One Hell of a Gamble": Khrushchev, Castro, and Kennedy* (New York: Norton, 1997).

36. See Ernest R. May, *American Cold War Strategy: Interpreting NSC 68* (New York: Bedford Books, 1993).

37. Schlesinger, *A Thousand Days*, p. 127.

38. Shapley, *Promise and Power*, pp. 31, 53, 70, 83-86.

39. Reeves, *President Kennedy*, p. 33. On the difference between Eisenhower's public and private personae, the landmark work is Fred I. Greenstein, *The Hidden-Hand Presidency: Eisenhower as Leader* (New York: Basic Books, 1982).

40. See, in addition to the works on Cuba mentioned in an earlier note, Peter Wyden, *Bay of Pigs: the Untold Story* (New York: Simon & Schuster, 1979); Philip Zelikow, "American Policy and Cuba, 1961–1963," *Diplomatic History* 24, no. 2 (Summer 2000): 318–21 and the documentary sources cited therein.

41. Reeves, *President Kennedy*, p. 103.

42. John Ranelagh, *The Agency: The Rise and Decline of the CIA* (New York: Simon & Schuster, 1986), pp. 383–90; Lawrence Chang and Peter Kornbluh,

eds., *The Cuban Missile Crisis, 1962: A National Security Archive Documents Reader* (New York: New Press, 1992), nos. 5 and 6.

43. Chang and Kornbluh, *The Cuban Missile Crisis*, pp. 355–59.

44. Reeves, *President Kennedy*, p. 103.

45. Ibid., pp. 102–3, 113–14.

46. Ibid., p. 116.

47. The best account is Michael Beschloss, *Mayday: Eisenhower, Khrushchev, and the U-2 Affair* (New York: HarperCollins, 1986).

48. Reeves, *President Kennedy*, p. 174. Khrushchev dictated his memoirs after his fall from power, and they were smuggled to the West. His reminiscences have been published in three volumes: *Khrushchev Remembers*, trans. and ed. Strobe Talbott (Boston: Little Brown, 1970); *Khrushchev Remembers: The Last Testament*, trans. and ed. Strobe Talbott (Boston: Little, Brown, 1974); *Khrushchev Remembers: The Glasnost Tapes*, trans. and ed. Jerrold Schechter with Vyacheslav Luchkov (Boston: Little, Brown, 1990). The best overview of governance in the Soviet Union during the period of Khrushchev's rise to supreme power is still Merle Fainsod, *How Russia is Ruled* (rev. ed.; Cambridge, MA: Harvard University Press, 1970). On Soviet politics and foreign policy generally, the most important recent works are Vladislav Zubok and Constantine Pleshakov, *Inside the Kremlin's Cold War* (Cambridge, MA: Harvard University Press, 1996), and Fursenko and Naftali, *"One Hell of a Gamble."*

49. Memorandum of Conversation, Vienna, 4 June 1961, in *FRUS*, 14: 87–96.

50. Paper prepared by Thomas C. Schelling, 5 July 1961, ibid., 170–72.

51. Reeves, *President Kennedy*, pp. 193–95.

52. See Jerrold L. Schechter and Peter S. Deriabin, *The Spy Who Saved the World: How a Soviet Colonel Changed the Course of the Cold War* (New York: Scribner's, 1992).

53. Kevin C. Ruffner, *CORONA: America's First Satellite Program* (Washington, DC: History Staff, Center for the Study of Intelligence, Central Intelligence Agency, 1995), pp. 24, 28; NIE 11-8-62, "Soviet Capabilities for Long Range Attack," 6 July 1962, in *FRUS*, 8: 332–42.

54. Reeves, *President Kennedy*, p. 247.

55. Kennedy to Khrushchev, 8 October 1962, in *FRUS*, 6: 163–64.

56. Schlesinger, *Robert Kennedy*, p. 471.

57. Khrushchev to Kennedy, 22 April 1961, in *FRUS*, 6: 10–16.

58. Chang and Kornbluh, *The Cuban Missile Crisis*, p. 350.

59. Ibid., p. 351.

60. Passavoy to Record, "Topics Discussed during Meeting of Dr. Miro Cardona with the President," 25 April 1962, and Goodwin to President Kennedy, 17 April 1963, "Cuba: Subjects, Miro Cardona, Material Sent to Palm Beach," folder, National Security Files, Box 45, John F. Kennedy Library.

61. Memorandum of Conversation, 19 February 1962, 4:30 P.M., in *FRUS*, 14, no. 300.

62. Memorandum of Conference with President Kennedy—Bi-Partisan Congressional Leaders—Off the Record, 21 February 1962, ibid., no. 304.

63. Khrushchev to Kennedy, 10 March 1962, and Khrushchev to Kennedy, undated but received 5 July 1962, in *FRUS*, 6: 118–26, 137–41; Weiss to Alexis Johnson, 11 July 1962, in *FRUS*, 15: 213–14.

64. Michael Beschloss, *The Crisis Years: Kennedy and Khrushchev, 1960–1963* (New York: HarperCollins, 1991), p. 371.

65. Chang and Kornbluh, *The Cuban Missile Crisis*, pp. 350, 352; John McCone, "Memorandum on Cuba," 20 August 1962, in *CIA Documents on the Cuban Missile Crisis, 1962*, ed. Mary McAuliffe (Washington, DC: Central Intelligence Agency, 1992), pp. 19–20.

66. McCone, Memorandum of Meeting with the President, 23 August 1962, ibid., pp. 27–29.

67. Chang and Kornbluh, *The Cuban Missile Crisis*, pp. 354–55; Robert F. Kennedy, *Thirteen Days: A Memoir of the Cuban Missile Crisis* (New York: Norton, 1971), pp. 24–26.

68. David Mayers, *The Ambassadors and America's Soviet Policy* (New York: Oxford University Press, 1995), pp. 200–2.

69. Shapley, *Promise and Power*, p. 78.

70. Paul H. Nitze, *From Hiroshima to Glasnost: At the Center of Decision, a Memoir* (New York: Grove Weidenfeld, 1989); David Callahan, *Dangerous Capabilities: Paul Nitze and the Cold War* (New York: HarperCollins, 1990).

Tuesday, September 4, 1962

1. Lyman B. Kirkpatrick, Memorandum for the Director, "Action Generated by DCI Cables Concerning Cuban Low-Level Photography and Offensive Weapons," in *CIA Documents on the Cuban Missile Crisis, 1962*, ed. Mary McAuliffe (Washington, DC: Central Intelligence Agency, 1992), document 12.

2. Pierre is Pierre Salinger, the President's press secretary.

3. What Robert Kennedy did not know was that indeed his suspicions were correct and Soviet missiles were on their way to Cuba, though they had not arrived there. However, Ambassador Dobrynin was as much in the dark about these missile deployments as the U.S. government.

4. A U-2 photographed the central and eastern portions of Cuba on 5 September. The mission detected three additional SAM sites in the central portion of the island. Heavy cloud cover prevented the U-2 from seeing much along the eastern side of the island. "U-2 Overflights of Cuba, 29 August through 14 October 1962," 27 February 1963, in *CIA Documents*, McAuliffe, pp. 127–37.

5. Vertical photography was taken from directly overhead, rather than at an angle, pointed inland from a flight along Cuba's periphery.

6. The McDonnell RF-101 Voodoo was the world's first supersonic pho-

toreconnaissance aircraft. Originally built as a fighter-interceptor, it was a highly maneuverable, low-altitude reconnaissance plane.

7.   Over previous weeks, Wiley had called publicly for a blockade of Cuba.

8.   Respectively, chairmen of the House and Senate Armed Services Committees.

9.   Senator Everett Dirksen spoke at the Winnebago County (Illinois) Labor Day picnic (*Rockville Register Star*, 4 September 1962). We are grateful for the assistance of the Everett Dirksen Center, University of Illinois, in tracking down this reference.

Saturday, September 29, 1962

1.   Bundy to President Kennedy, "Memorandum on Cuba for the Press Conference," 13 September 1962, National Security Files, John F. Kennedy Library.

2.   SNIE 85-3-62, "The Military Buildup in Cuba," 19 September 1962, in *CIA Documents on the Cuban Missile Crisis, 1962* , ed. Mary McAuliffe (Washington, DC: CIA, 1992), document 33.

3.   Khrushchev to Kennedy, 28 September 1962, in *FRUS*, 6: 152–61.

4.   Editorial Note, in *FRUS*, 15: 336.

5.   Vladislav Zubok and Constantine Pleshakov, *Inside the Kremlin's Cold War: From Stalin to Khrushchev* (Cambridge, MA: Harvard University Press, 1996), pp. 263–65.

6.   Memcon between Udall and Khrushchev, 6 September 1962, in *FRUS*, 15: 308–10.

7.   F. D. Reeve, *Robert Frost in Russia* (Boston: Little, Brown, 1964); Richard Reeves, *President Kennedy: Profile of Power* (New York: Simon & Schuster, 1993), p. 351.

8.   Referring to Khrushchev.

9.   One of Fidel Castro's closest associates, Ernesto "Che" Guevara, visited Moscow in August to discuss the conclusion of a Soviet-Cuban defense agreement. Khrushchev, however, refused to sign the proposed agreement.

10.   *Solution C* was a term thrown around during the Kennedy administration as it tried to devise a negotiating position on the German and Berlin problems. Solution C was to seek negotiations aimed toward an informal, interim agreement to preserve the status quo in Berlin despite a G.D.R.-U.S.S.R. peace treaty. It appeared to offer the most likely chance of success with the least fuss. It was a view favored by State's old Berlin hands.

11.   Dean Rusk had been president of the Rockefeller Foundation.

12.   Bohlen seems to be referring to a draft response from President Kennedy. The actual response, as sent from Washington on 8 October 1962 did not include any reference to the Berlin question (see Kennedy to Khrushchev, 8 October 1962, in *FRUS*, 6: 163–64).

Tuesday, October 16, 1962

1. On 28 September a Navy reconnaissance aircraft in the Atlantic had photographed a Soviet freighter bound for Cuba, carrying ten fuselage crates for IL-28s. The Soviet freighter arrived on 4 October. Due to delay in the Navy's transmission of its photos to CIA interpreters, the IL-28s were not identified until 9 October. See McCone to File, "Memorandum on Donovan Project," 11 October 1962, in *CIA Documents on the Cuban Missile Crisis*, ed. Mary McAuliffe (Washington, DC: Central Intelligence Agency, 1992), p. 124; Dino Brugioni, *Eyeball to Eyeball: The Inside Story of the Cuban Missile Crisis*, ed. Robert F. McCort (New York: Random House, 1991), pp. 172–74.

2. Full details are in Brugioni, *Eyeball to Eyeball*, pp. 187–217. (Brugioni was in NPIC at the time.)

3. McGeorge Bundy, *Danger and Survival: Choices about the Bomb in the First Fifty Years* (New York: Random House, 1988), pp. 395–96.

4. Kenneth P. O'Donnell and David F. Powers, with Joe McCarthy, *"Johnny, We Hardly Knew Ye"* (New York: Pocket Books, 1972), p. 369.

5. An erector launcher trailer can carry a missile and then be secured in place at a designated launch point. The missile launcher is then erected to the firing angle and the missile is fired from it. To say the site is *unrevetted* means that earthworks or fortifications to protect against attack or the blast from the missile have not been constructed.

6. These are references to the Naval Photographic Intelligence Center in Suitland, Maryland, and to the National Photographic Interpretation Center, directed by Lundahl, that was part of the CIA.

7. The acronym COMOR stands for the interagency Committee on Overhead Reconaissance, a committee of the U.S. Intelligence Board. Chaired by James Reber, COMOR set guidelines and priorities for U.S. surveillance overflights of other countries.

8. Low-level reconnaissance overflights went underneath clouds, low and fast, over their targets. These flights were carried out by Air Force or Navy tactical reconnaissance units with aircraft like the F-101 or F8U. In September the CIA had asked McNamara to dispatch low-level flights over Cuba but at that time he declined, preferring to leave the work to the U-2.

9. The Organization of American States (OAS) was created after World War II as a collective organization of states in the Western Hemisphere for several cooperative purposes, including the task of responding (by a two-thirds vote) to aggression from a member or nonmember state, including with economic or political sanctions. The founding documents were signed in Mexico City (1945) and especially the Inter-American Treaty of Reciprocal Assistance, signed in Rio de Janeiro (1947) and usually referred to as the Rio Pact. The OAS, spurred by the United States, had adopted sanctions against Cuba in early 1962.

10. A sortie is one mission by one airplane. If eight airplanes flew against

a target, that would be 8 sorties. If the planes flew two missions in one day, that would be 16 sorties in the day.

11.   Commander in Chief, U.S. Forces, Atlantic. Headquartered in Norfolk, CINCLANT at this time was Admiral Robert Dennison.

12.   On the sources for Keating's allegations, see Max Holland, "A Luce Connection: Senator Keating, William Pawley, and the Cuban Missile Crisis," *Journal of Cold War Studies* 1 (Fall 1999): 139–67.

13.   In this context the word *black* means to keep undercover, covert.

14.   Based on notes taken from transcripts of JCS meetings in October–November 1962. The notes were made in 1976 before these transcripts were apparently destroyed. They have since been declassified and are available from the National Security Archive, in Washington, D.C.

15.   The Guided Missile and Astronautics Intelligence Committee (GMAIC) was another interagency committee of the U.S. Intelligence Board.

16.   The word *IRONBARK* was a codeword for documentation passed to the United States by Colonel Oleg Penkovsky, an officer in Soviet military intelligence. Penkovsky had already fallen under suspicion and was arrested six days later (on 22 October, Washington time). He was later executed by the Soviet government.

17.   Carter was referring to the Special National Intelligence Estimate, "The Military Buildup in Cuba," of 19 September, which had concluded that the Soviet Union "could derive considerable military advantage" from deploying MRBMs and IRBMs in Cuba but that such a development was incompatible with Soviet practice and policy because "it would indicate a far greater willingness to increase the level of risk in U.S.-Soviet relations than the U.S.S.R. has displayed thus far. . . ." in *CIA Documents*, McAuliffe, document 33.

18.   Carter was partly in error. In fact, the estimators thought the deployment would improve the Soviet military position. This was a unanimous view in the intelligence community. Every lower-level expert, whether in State, the Office of the Secretary of Defense, the armed forces, or the CIA, all believed (and separately wrote) that MRBMs and IRBMs in Cuba would materially improve the Soviet position in the strategic balance of power.

19.   In late 1957, in the wake of fears arising from the Soviet Sputnik flight and concerns about Soviet missiles targeted at Europe, the United States had publicly offered to deploy intermediate-range ballistic missiles, Jupiters, on the territory of its European allies. The Jupiters were not actually deployed to Turkey (and Italy) until 1961–62. A similar type of missile, the Thor, was deployed to England; those are the ones Johnson is talking about.

20.   A reference to the mysterious explosion that sank the USS *Maine* while it was visiting Havana harbor during a period of tension between the United States and Spain over the conditions of Spanish rule in Cuba. Robert Kennedy is echoing the belief that this incident precipitated the U.S. declaration of war that began the Spanish-American War in 1898.

Thursday, October 18, 1962

1.   Stevenson letter to President Kennedy, 17 October 1962; reprinted in *The Cuban Missile Crisis, 1962: A National Security Archive Documents Reader*, ed. Laurence Chang and Peter Kornbluh (New York: New Press, 1992), pp. 119–20.

2.   The sortie numbers were derived by examining a target and determining how many individual aim points should be hit in order to destroy it. Then planners used training experience to judge how many bombs would need to be dropped on an aim point to be fairly sure that one would hit it. From that, after incorporating attrition from enemy action or mechanical problems, planners could come up with sortie numbers. These numbers first grew because new targets were identified. They later grew because the staff began incorporating additional requirements for escort, air defense suppression, and poststrike reconnaissance. A few days later, exasperated by the latest revision, Taylor exclaimed to his JCS colleagues: "What! These figures were reported to the White House. You are defeating yourselves with your own cleverness, gentlemen." Notes taken from Transcripts of Meetings of the Joint Chiefs of Staff, p. 6.

3.   These meetings were attended (though not everyone was there all of the time) by Robert Kennedy, Dean Rusk, Robert McNamara, Maxwell Taylor, McGeorge Bundy, John McCone, George Ball, Roswell Gilpatric, U. Alexis Johnson, Charles Bohlen, Llewellyn Thompson, Theodore Sorensen, Edwin Martin, possibly Paul Nitze, and (late in the day for a shorter time) Dean Acheson.

4.   C. Douglas Dillon, "Memorandum for the President," 17 October 1962; reprinted in *The Cuban Missile Crisis*, Chang and Kornbluh, pp. 116–18.

5.   "Position of George W. Ball," 17 October 1962, ibid., pp. 121–22.

6.   In their conversation at dinner on Tuesday night, 16 October, Kennedy had asked Bohlen to postpone his highly publicized departure for Paris and help with the crisis. Bohlen worried about the notice his change of plans would cause but said he would try to come up with a cover story. The next day Bohlen discussed the matter with Rusk, who thought that Bohlen should proceed with his plans and that Thompson could provide the needed advice on the Soviet Union. Rusk called President Kennedy, and Kennedy called Bohlen and told him to go ahead with his departure.

On the morning of 18 October, Kennedy changed his mind, possibly after reading Sorensen's note highlighting Bohlen's advocacy. Just before the 11:00 meeting transcribed here, Bohlen was summoned (from the airport) to come to the White House. On the phone, Bohlen convinced the President to let him go ahead with his travel, since he was now expected at a public event that day in New York. Robert Kennedy later voiced bewilderment and anger about Bohlen's decision.

7.   Sorensen to Kennedy, 18 October 1962, "Cuba—General: 10/15/62–10/23/62" folder, National Security Files, John F. Kennedy

Library. Dillon's approach—an ultimatum and blockade, then a strike—
was thus close to Bohlen's. Ball's suggestion—a blockade followed by political pressure—was different.

8.   Rusk was referring to events that preceded and immediately followed
the outbreak of World War I in 1914, using the title of a well-known book
recently published about this episode, *The Guns of August*, by Barbara
Tuchman.

9.   In fact it is not at all easy to hide even the MRBMs in the woods and of
course not the fixed IRBM sites. But Thompson is relying on the assumption that was then prevalent, if unexamined.

10. The Board of National Estimates at the CIA was then preparing a
Special National Intelligence Estimate, distributed the next day, on "Soviet
Reactions to Certain U.S. Courses of Action on Cuba."

11. The Kennedy administration had considered abandoning the delayed
deployment of Jupiter missiles to Turkey and had discussed the possibility
with Turkish officials in the spring of 1961. The Turks wanted the missiles.
Before top administration officials resolved the problem, the confrontation in
Vienna between Kennedy and Khrushchev over Berlin intervened. After
Khrushchev's intimidating rhetoric in Vienna, the administration agreed that
the Turkish deployment had to proceed, since canceling the deployment
might then be mistaken as a sign of U.S. fear or weakness.

12. The principal idea then being considered for the replacement of
Turkish and other obsolescent land-based ballistic missiles deployed in
Europe was to offer some sea-based substitute for them, possibly linked to
the Polaris nuclear missile submarines then entering service.

13. President Kennedy was referring to the rapid Soviet suppression of
the revolt in Hungary during November 1956 and the perceived Western
inability to organize an effective response, especially because of the simultaneous distraction of the Anglo-French-Israeli military action against
Egypt arising from the Suez crisis.

14. Thompson was referring to the planned Paris summit between
Eisenhower and Khrushchev in May 1960. After the shoot-down of a U.S.
U-2 over Soviet airspace and after Eisenhower took personal responsibility
for authorizing such flights, Khrushchev canceled the summit shortly
before it was to take place. At the time Thompson was the U.S. ambassador
in Moscow.

15. The United States had stockpiled nuclear bombs in Turkey, under U.S.
control, for possible use by Turkish (or U.S.) F-100 aircraft.

16. Quotations are from the full State Department Memorandum of
Conversation for the meeting (A. Akalovsky was the notetaker), in Cuban
Missile Crisis Files, National Security Archive, 1992 Releases Box.

17. These were apparently the participants in the White House meeting
that had just ended. Dean Rusk and Llewellyn Thompson had stayed at the
State Department attending the dinner for Gromyko, which dragged on
until after midnight.

Friday, October 19, 1962

1.   The estimates briefed on 19 October were written down in a joint estimate of GMAIC, JAEIC, and NPIC, "Joint Evaluation of Soviet Missile
Threat in Cuba," 19 October 1962.
2.   In fact the SS-4 MRBMs, the only type which were mobile, were far
too large to move into dense woods, especially with all their associated
equipment. But it took a few more days before U.S. officials comprehended
this limitation. The SS-5 IRBMs were to be deployed at fixed concrete sites.
3.   A landing of thousands of U.S. Marines in Lebanon in 1958 was unopposed, and the bloodless action was believed to have prevented a takeover of
Lebanon by anti-Western dissidents supported by the United Arab
Republic and the Soviet Union.
4.   Bundy's recollection is drawn from notes excerpted from his private
papers by Francis Bator. Bator shared this information in an April 1998
letter to Ernest May and Philip Zelikow. Deputy Under Secretary of
State U. Alexis Johnson, who attended almost all of the meetings during
the crisis, remembered that the apparent consensus that had formed in
favor of the blockade on 18 October "came unstuck" on Friday, 19 October.
Alexis Johnson thought this was because of Dean Acheson's argument for
an air strike [U. Alexis Johnson with Jef Olivarius McAllister, *The Right
Hand of Power* (Englewood Cliffs, NJ: Prentice-Hall, 1984), p. 383]. In fact
Kennedy had already heard Acheson's case on the afternoon of the 18th,
before the consensus formed that night, and had not talked again to
Acheson. On the "pull the group together" exchange, see Theodore C.
Sorensen, *Kennedy* (New York: Harper & Row, 1965), p. 692.

Saturday, October 20, 1962

1.   This account draws on several sources, but these and other quotations
from the 19 October meetings are from minutes drafted by State
Department deputy legal adviser Ralph Meeker, in *FRUS*, 11: 116–22
(Robert Kennedy's emphasis on *action* is in Meeker's notes).
2.   The timing of the call is based on Sorensen's account. Much later, however, Lundahl told Dino Brugioni that Robert Kennedy, worried about the
tone of the 19 October discussions, called his brother on Friday, 19 October,
failed to reach him, then called him again on Saturday, got him, and urged
him to return [Dino Brugioni, *Eyeball to Eyeball: The Inside Story of the
Cuban Missile Crisis*, ed. Robert F. McCort (New York: Random House,
1991), pp. 303–4].
3.   The notetaker of the NSC meeting was Bromley Smith. This was the
first meeting during the missile crisis which Smith was allowed to attend,
because it was the first such meeting styled as a formal meeting of the NSC,
of which Smith was the executive secretary. Smith attended and took notes
at every subsequent major meeting during the crisis, because the next two

meetings were also deemed NSC meetings and then, after that, this crisis management body was formally constituted as the Executive Committee of the National Security Council (or Excomm for short). Smith's notes of this 20 October meeting were more detailed than his notes of subsequent NSC and Excomm meetings during the crisis, perhaps because this growing accumulation of work left Smith less and less time to type up more-detailed summaries. Fortunately Kennedy was able to tape the subsequent NSC and Excomm meetings during the crisis, from 22 October on.

4.   The briefing notes, with Cline's handwritten annotations, are reproduced in *CIA Documents on the Cuban Missile Crisis, 1962*, ed. Mary McAuliffe (Washington, DC: Central Intelligence Agency, 1992), pp. 221–26.

5.   About two hours earlier Robert Kennedy and Robert McNamara had visited NPIC (National Photographic Interpretation Center), escorted by John McCone, and reviewed its operations.

6.   Minutes of the 505th Meeting of the National Security Council, 20 October 1962, in *FRUS*, 11: 126–36.

7.   No copy of this draft has been found: ibid., p. 128, note 3.

8.   Afterward, McNamara recalled in some detail the arguments that he had made at this meeting for and against a blockade, but he appeared to have no recollection of taking this Stevenson-like position with regard to possible negotiations with the Soviets. Interview with Robert McNamara conducted by Arthur M. Schlesinger, Jr., John F. Kennedy Library Oral History Project, 1964, pp. 23–25.

9.   "Major Consequences of Certain U.S. Courses of Action on Cuba," in *CIA Documents*, McAuliffe, pp. 211–20.

10.   Theodore Sorensen, *Kennedy* (New York: Harper & Row, 1965), p. 694.

11.   To reassure the German allies but also to discourage any thoughts on their part of an independent nuclear deterrent, the United States in the late 1950s had begun to equip Luftwaffe aircraft with "tactical" nuclear bombs and missiles. The nuclear devices remained under U.S. control. The proposed multilateral nuclear force [MLF] was supposed to include Germans among the multinational crews whose ships would carry nuclear-armed missiles, but authority for the release of the weapons remained exclusively with the U.S. President. Champions of the MLF in the United States, mostly in the State Department and sometimes referred to as the "cabal," hoped that it would not only dampen any German interest in nuclear weapons but would lead the French and perhaps the British to abandon their own independent nuclear forces [see McGeorge Bundy, *Danger and Survival: Choices about the Bomb in the First Fifty Years* (New York: Random House, 1988), pp. 487–90]. Some Western officials interpreted Khrushchev's position regarding Berlin as traceable chiefly to Soviet concern that Germany acquire nuclear weapons [see Marc Trachtenberg, *History and Strategy* (Princeton, NJ: Princeton University Press, 1991), pp. 169–234]. Robert Kennedy's suggestion here must have been startling to

the State Department contingent, especially to Ball, who was active in the cabal.

12.   Like Eisenhower before him, Kennedy had never been an all-out opponent of France's having independent nuclear forces. He had gone along, however, with the MLF scheme and had approved public statements by McNamara that described such forces as "dangerous, expensive, prone to obsolescence, and lacking in credibility as a deterrent." He had also drawn upon himself strong French criticism because of a loosely worded press conference remark which seemed to single out French nuclear forces, not British, as "inimical to the community interest of the Atlantic alliance" (see Bundy, *Danger and Survival*, pp. 484–86).

13.   The terminology may have been Kennedy's own. It achieved popularity through a postmortem on the crisis: Stewart Alsop and Charles Bartlett, "In Time of Crisis," *Saturday Evening Post*, 8 December 1962, for which Kennedy was a source [see Michael Beschloss, *The Crisis Years: Kennedy and Khrushchev 1960–1963* (New York: HarperCollins, 1991), p. 569].

14.   McCone to File, 20 October 1962, in *FRUS*, 11:137–38.

15.   Notes taken from Transcripts of Meetings of the Joint Chiefs of Staff, October–November 1962, p. 13, National Security Archive. These notes must be used with some caution, but we rely on passages that the original notetaker marked as direct quotations.

Monday, October 22, 1962

1.   The best that Sweeney and Joint Chiefs of Staff Chairman Maxwell Taylor could promise was to destroy 90 percent of the known missiles, and they estimated the known missiles were no more than 60 percent of the total emplaced on the island. See McNamara's notes of the meeting, 21 October 1962, in *FRUS*, 11: 140.

2.   See Montague Kern, Patricia W. Levering, and Ralph B. Levering, *The Kennedy Crises: The Press, the Presidency, and Foreign Policy* (Chapel Hill: University of North Carolina Press, 1983), pp. 123–27.

3.   On what President Kennedy said to Ormsby-Gore, see Washington No. 2636, "Cuba," 22 October 1962, and Washington No. 2650, 23 October 1962, both in Public Record Office (hereinafter PRO), PREM 11/3689, 24020. On the advance message to Macmillan, see Washington 2630, 21 October 1962, and the October 21 message from Kennedy to Macmillan, T488/62, both ibid.

4.   Interview with Lord Harlech (Ormsby-Gore) conducted by Richard Neustadt, transcript approved 12 March 1965, John F. Kennedy Library Oral History Project, p. 15.

5.   The NSC notetaker, Bromley Smith, wrote this down as: "Secretary Dillon recalled that we sent United States missiles to Europe because we had so many of them we did not know where to put them." President Kennedy heard it differently. He jotted down on a notepad (as we interpret

his handwriting) the following: "Sunday afternoon—In course of discussion, on missiles in Turkey & Italy—Douglas Dillon stated that the reason Jupiters were sent was they were flops & this would have been proved if they had not been sent." Kennedy added: "Rusk rather quiet & somewhat fatigued during discussion" [Correspondence—Cuba—Conference Notes and Doodles (in slip for Notes, 10/23/62), President's Office Files, John F. Kennedy Library].

6.   When Nitze pursued this presidential directive a few days later, on 24 October, State officials wedded to their multilateral nuclear force solution to this problem combined to block him. Nitze was, in any case, already too late. No one had attempted to get President Kennedy's offer into the talking points that Dean Acheson, Kennedy's emissary, had already taken with him to Paris (and Acheson had not attended the Sunday meeting where Kennedy had discussed this idea). Once French president Charles de Gaulle had given his strong support to Kennedy anyway, which he did on 22 October, the original presidential impetus behind the offer evaporated.

7.   See the Minutes of the 506th Meeting of the National Security Council, 21 October 1962, in *FRUS*, 11: 141–49.

8.   On the details of this program see U. Alexis Johnson with Jef Olivarius McAllister, *The Right Hand of Power* (Englewood Cliffs, NJ: Prentice-Hall, 1984), pp. 383–87; see also Frank Sieverts, "The Cuban Crisis, 1962," internal State Department history, August 1963, transmitted to the White House in Manning to Bundy, "History of the Cuban Crisis," 22 August 1963, copy obtained at the National Security Archive.

9.   McCone also briefed Vice President Johnson on Sunday evening. Johnson favored the surprise strike, complaining that we are "telegraphing our punch" and were "locking the barn after the horse was gone." Johnson finally agreed reluctantly with the blockade plan, McCone noted, "but only after learning among other things the support indicated by General Eisenhower" [McCone to File, "Meeting with the Vice President on 21 October 1962," 22 October 1962, in *CIA Documents on the Cuban Missile Crisis, 1962*, ed. Mary McAuliffe (Washington, DC: Central Intelligence Agency, 1992), p. 245].

10.   President Kennedy is referring to Marine Corps units based at Camp Pendleton that will embark from San Diego.

11.   As outlined by McCone to Eisenhower the previous day, these were: (1) an air strike, (2) an air strike plus simultaneous invasion, and (3) a blockade that might give the Russians a chance to leave Cuba [Dwight D. Eisenhower Post-Presidential Papers, Augusta-Walter Reed Series, Presidential-National Subseries, Box 1, "Cuba (1) (October 1962–August 1966)," Dwight D. Eisenhower Library, Abilene, Kansas (courtesy of Andrew Erdmann)].

12.   The two men had the same difference of opinion on 22 April 1961, after the failure of the U.S.-backed invasion of Cuba at the Bay of Pigs. Kennedy privately told Eisenhower that he had minimized U.S. military

backing for the invasion because he feared Soviet retaliation against Berlin. Eisenhower then answered, as he recorded in his diary at the time: "Mr. President, that is exactly the opposite of what would really happen. The Soviets follow their own plans, and if they see us show any weakness that is when they press us the hardest. The second they see us show strength and do something on our own, that is when they are very cagey" [from Eisenhower's notes of the meeting in his Post-Presidential Papers, Box 11, at the Dwight D. Eisenhower Library, which are also reproduced in the *FRUS* Microfiche Supplement on Cuba 1961–1963. The conversation is described in Richard Reeves, *President Kennedy: Profile of Power* (New York: Simon & Schuster, 1993), pp. 102–3].

13. Kennedy is referring to the effort made in the spring of 1961 to persuade the Turks to call off the deployment of Jupiter missiles to Turkey, a deployment the United States had promised publicly in 1957.

14. About an hour later Taylor sent a message (JCS 6866) to the commander in chief of U.S. forces in Europe (and the Supreme Allied Commander for NATO), General Norstad, which stated: "Make certain that the Jupiters in Turkey and Italy will not be fired without specific authorization from the President. In the event of an attack, either nuclear or nonnuclear . . . U.S. custodians are to destroy or make inoperable the weapons if any attempt is made to fire them." Norstad was further instructed to keep this order secret from the Turks and Italians.

15. Minutes of the 507th Meeting of the National Security Council, 22 October 1962, in *FRUS*, 11: 152–53.

16. The kind of estimate on which Rusk based this assertion was: "Sites now identified will, when completed, give Soviets total of 36 launchers and 72 missiles. This compares with 60–65 ICBM launchers we now estimate to be operational in the U.S.S.R." (CIA, "Soviet Military Buildup in Cuba," 21 October 1962, in *CIA Documents*, McAuliffe, p. 259). The intelligence community also reported, late in the evening of 21 October, that Soviet deployments would result in a "first salvo potential of 40 missiles with a refire capability of an additional 40 missiles . . . this threat against the U.S. is approximately one-half the currently estimated ICBM missile threat from the U.S.S.R." (GMAIC, JAEIC, and NPIC, "Supplement 2 to Joint Evaluation of Soviet Missile Threat in Cuba," 21 October 1962, ibid., p. 262). Rusk was more accurate than he knew, because the Soviet Union at the time had only 44 operational ICBMs, with another 6 undergoing tests [see Raymond L. Garthoff, *Intelligence Assessment and Policymaking: A Decision Point in the Kennedy Administration* (Washington, DC: Brookings Institution, 1984), p. 30].

17. He is referring to the aging B-47 bombers which still made up the bulk of the aircraft in the Strategic Air Command. They were being replaced by the newer intercontinental-range B-52s.

18. McNamara must have known that this description of the intelligence information was untrue.

19. London 7396, 22 October 1962, in PRO, PREM 11/3689, 24020.

20. Robert F. Kennedy, *Thirteen Days: A Memoir of the Cuban Missile Crisis* (pbk. ed., New York: Norton, 1969), pp. 53, 55.

21. Rusk had made this assertion in the afternoon NSC meeting. Records at the John F. Kennedy Library also indicate that Bundy was sitting in during this conversation with Macmillan and passed Kennedy a note suggesting these arguments about the military significance of the missiles in Cuba (Memorandum of Conversation, 22 October 1962, "Cuba–General–Macmillan Telephone Conversations, 10/62–11/62" folder, National Security Files, Box 37, John F. Kennedy Library).

22. "Record of a Conversation between the Prime Minister and President Kennedy at 12:30 A.M. on Tuesday, October 23, 1962," in PRO, PREM 11/3689, 24020. In quoting from this document, which dovetails with but is much more complete than the comparable U.S. record, we have changed some of the punctuation in the original.

Tuesday, October 23, 1962

1. Montague Kern, Patricia Levering, and Ralph B. Levering, *The Kennedy Crises: The Press, the Presidency, and Foreign Policy* (Chapel Hill: University of North Carolina Press, 1983), p. 126.

2. Arthur Krock, long a reporter covering Washington, was then a member of the editorial board of the *New York Times*. Krock had been a friend of Kennedy's father and a mentor to the young John Kennedy during the 1940s. Like the elder Kennedy, Krock was politically conservative, often sympathetic to the Republican Party, and the relationship between the older columnist and younger president had become wary and ambivalent.

3. At that time the Strategic Air Command (in cooperation with the then-secret National Reconnaissance Office of the U.S. Air Force), not the CIA, was operating the U-2s flying over Cuba. Later SAC would draw on CIA pilots in support of its effort.

4. Actually not the Fifth Infantry but the Fifth Marine Expeditionary Brigade.

5. Because López Mateos was on a plane returning from his visit to the Philippines, he was unable to approve revised instructions for Mexico's representative at the OAS meeting.

6. The context of this bit of gallows humor is that most of these officials had, in recent days or hours, been obliged to review plans for the evacuation of themselves or family members in case of a Soviet nuclear attack.

7. Kennedy read the entire letter. See Kennedy-Khrushchev Exchanges, in *FRUS*, 6: 166–67.

8. Pursuing a topic he had raised at the morning ExComm meeting, President Kennedy asked McNamara and Gilpatric quietly to arrange to have one of the reconnaissance flights take pictures of one or more of the crowded airfields in Florida. All understood how Kennedy's concerns stemmed from memories of the planes crowded on Hickam Field near Pearl

Harbor, caught and destroyed by the Japanese surprise attack in 1941. Kennedy wanted the photos as a way of checking on what the military was doing. Taylor and the senior officers understood Kennedy's concern but had a different judgment on what was required, operationally, which came up again in later ExComm discussions.

9.   Several Soviet F-class (termed "Foxtrot") attack submarines, then the most modern such vessel in their navy, had left Murmansk at the end of September and had moved into the open Atlantic, the first time such submarines had ventured so close to U.S. waters. There they were apparently to rendezvous with a Soviet oiler, the *Terek*, and a supply ship that had been deployed to the same area of the Atlantic. The U.S. Navy endeavored to monitor these movements as closely as possible [see Dino A. Brugioni, *Eyeball to Eyeball: The Inside Story of the Cuban Missile Crisis*, ed. Robert F. McCort (New York: Random House, 1991), pp. 385–86].

10.   See McCone to File, "Executive Committee Meeting on 23 October 1962, 6:00 P.M.," in *CIA Documents on the Cuban Missile Crisis, 1962*, Mary McAuliffe, ed. (Washington, DC: Central Intelligence Agency, 1992), p. 291. Norstad's cable, which so impressed President Kennedy, had explained that he was not putting U.S. forces in Europe into the highest state of preparedness for war but was merely recommending to commanders that "certain precautionary military measures should be taken of a non-provocative and non-public nature" (Paris 1907, 22 October 1962, Record Group 59, National Archives, Washington, DC).

11.   Pittman is referring to stocking spaces with survival supplies. These spaces were civil defense, or fallout, shelters where people would take refuge in order to try to survive a nuclear attack and its aftermath.

12.   McCone to File, "Executive Committee Meeting," p. 291.

13.   Returning a favor of hospitality shown when Jacqueline Kennedy had visited India, President Kennedy had agreed before the crisis to host a dinner on 23 October for the Maharajah and Maharani of Jaipur, staying at the White House guest quarters in Blair House.

14.   Robert Kennedy recalled a part of this exchange in his memoir. In his account President Kennedy said: "'It looks really mean, doesn't it? But then, really there was no other choice. If they get this mean on this one in our part of the world, what will they do on the next?' 'I just don't think there was any choice,' I said, 'and not only that, if you hadn't acted, you would have been impeached.' The President thought for a moment and said, 'That's what I think—I would have been impeached' " [*Thirteen Days: A Memoir of the Cuban Missile Crisis* (New York: Norton, 1969), p. 67]. Robert Kennedy placed this conversation the next morning, 24 October. However, it is clear from the tapes that the conversation occurred at about 7:15 P.M. on 23 October. Robert Kennedy did recall in his memoir that after that evening's group meeting and a smaller informal gathering after the proclamation signing, "the President and I talked for a little while alone. He suggested that I might visit Ambassador [Anatoly] Dobrynin and personally relate to

him the serious implications of the Russians' duplicity . . ." (ibid., p. 63). The origin of that suggestion is apparent later in this taped conversation.

15.   Georgi Bolshakov, a military attaché at the Soviet Embassy, was presumed to be affiliated with Soviet military intelligence or the KGB. Until the summer of 1962, Bolshakov had been the principal channel for special, private communications between the White House and the Kremlin. The channel ran through Robert Kennedy, and the two men had become good friends. The 1962 arrival of the new Soviet ambassador, a talented and seasoned diplomat, Anatoly Dobrynin, displaced Bolshakov as Dobrynin sought successfully to make himself the principal contact in this special channel.

16.   At this point Robert Kennedy is probably referring to an additional channel for secret contacts with Bolshakov—a *New York Daily News* reporter named Frank Holeman. Holeman was the first person to see Bolshakov that day, saying he was doing so on behalf of Robert Kennedy, and the other contacts were office meetings, not a lunch. On Holeman's meeting with Bolshakov and the origins of the Holeman-Bolshakov channel, see Aleksandr Fursenko and Timothy Naftali, *"One Hell of a Gamble": Khrushchev, Castro, and Kennedy, 1958–1964* (New York: Norton, 1997), pp. 110–13, 249–50.

17.   "Not with us in this" could refer either to Bolshakov or to Frank Holeman. In the case of Holeman, it could imply that President Kennedy was uneasy about Holeman's personal loyalty or ties to Republicans. As a reporter Holeman had closely covered Richard Nixon and had first become a private channel between Soviet military intelligence and the U.S. government during the Eisenhower administration.

18.   Robert Kennedy is referring to his own hunches, dating perhaps to 1961 and certainly to the spring of 1962, that Khrushchev might put missiles into Cuba.

19.   Having tried Holeman as a channel, Robert Kennedy had also turned to Charles Bartlett, a nationally syndicated columnist. Unlike Holeman, Bartlett had a personal tie of longstanding friendship directly with President Kennedy (see Fursenko and Naftali, *"One Hell of a Gamble,"* pp. 236–37). So, having heard his brother's reaction to Holeman, Robert Kennedy has dodged the President's question about whether Holeman had met with Bolshakov and is instead emphasizing that he used Bartlett as the channel. Robert Kennedy later acknowledged that he had used Bartlett as a channel to Bolshakov, but he never admitted using Holeman. Yet, we agree with Naftali's conclusion that Holeman was not acting on his own. When Holeman told Bolshakov he was acting for Robert Kennedy, we think he was truthful, and the messages passed by Holeman and by Bartlett had similar content.

20.   Bartlett had met with Bolshakov twice that day, apparently both times during the afternoon. Robert Kennedy had given Bartlett photos of the Soviet missile installations in Cuba to use in talking with Bolshakov. On the basis of Bolshakov's own report of the meetings, both Holeman and

Bartlett had mentioned to Bolshakov that the United States might be willing to settle the crisis by exchanging a withdrawal of missiles from Cuba for a withdrawal of U.S. Jupiter missiles from Turkey. Holeman had added that "the conditions of such a trade can be discussed only in a time of quiet and not when there is the threat of war." All of this was reported to Moscow (ibid., pp. 249–52).

From the way in which we can hear Robert Kennedy describing these matters privately to President Kennedy, it seems apparent that President Kennedy had *not* authorized his brother to cue Holeman and Bartlett to broach the idea of a Cuba-Turkey trade. Had the President approved such a plan, Robert Kennedy would not have had to explain the background as he did; nor did Robert Kennedy allude to the Jupiters in recapitulating the guidance he had given to Bartlett (and presumably Holeman).

To be sure, the idea of such a trade had repeatedly been discussed with President Kennedy who was always sympathetic to it, since he thought the Soviets were playing for far higher stakes. But only the day before the President had again made clear, in rebuffing a suggestion from Rusk, that he was willing to negotiate the withdrawal of the Jupiters from Turkey only *after* the Soviets had agreed to withdraw their missiles from Cuba. Robert Kennedy may or may not have understood this or may have received a different impression of the President's views. It is also possible that Robert Kennedy gave guidance to Holeman about the planned two stages of negotiation and Holeman either garbled the message or was misunderstood by Bolshakov. Bolshakov did not report hearing any qualifiers at all from Bartlett. Whatever Robert Kennedy's intention, there is no evidence that the President knew his brother had asked Holeman and Bartlett to go beyond a simple exploration of Soviet views and float such a major proposal for resolving the crisis in a way that was bound to be reported to Moscow. We think that, in an excess of zeal, Robert Kennedy had gone too far, and did not want to tell his brother.

21. A columnist at the *New York Times*, Arthur Krock had been a friend of Kennedy's father and a mentor to the youthful Kennedy during the 1940s. Yet Krock's politics were quite conservative (like Kennedy's father), and the relationship between the older journalist and the young President was now wary and ambivalent.

22. See Robert Kennedy to President Kennedy, 24 October 1962, in *FRUS*, 11: 175–77. A copy of this report was shared with Rusk. Robert Kennedy's account tracks well with Dobrynin's own report, from which we drew the "agitated" description and the concluding words (Fursenko and Naftali, *"One Hell of a Gamble,"* pp. 252–53).

23. The general content of the meeting with Ormsby-Gore is confirmed in Kennedy, *Thirteen Days*, pp. 66–67; but for details we relied on the ambassador's reports of his talks, both titled "Cuba," Washington 2662 and Washington 2664, and both sent on 24 October 1962, PRO, PREM 11/3690, 24020.

Though the earlier White House discussions on 23 October might have given the Kennedys the impression that there was a quarantine line fixed at a given radius from Cuba, there is in fact little evidence that such a formal line was contemplated by the relevant military planners. Interceptions were being contemplated in a more flexible way, with attention both to danger from aircraft in Cuba (almost all of which were the shorter-range MiGs) and from Soviet submarines, as well as concentration on the specific ships that would be intercepted.

Wednesday, October 24, 1962

1. The enhanced generation of SAC forces was ordered, with McNamara's approval, in JCS 6917 to CINCSAC, 23 October 1962. Notes Taken from Transcripts of Meetings of the Joint Chiefs of Staff, p. 17, October–November 1962, obtained from the National Security Archive, Washington, D.C.; see also Scott D. Sagan, *The Limits of Safety: Organizations, Accidents, and Nuclear Weapons* (Princeton, NJ: Princeton University Press, 1993), pp. 62–67.

2. A U.S. Navy electronic intelligence ship, USS *Oxford*, was then deployed in international waters (according to the U.S. definition of that term) just off the coast of Cuba.

3. The Joint Chiefs of Staff had met earlier that morning. Taylor had explained that McNamara would be bringing photos of crowded Florida airfields to the White House and asked whether the planes should disperse. LeMay thought it was best to stay on the good concrete airfields with the 450 aircraft, 150 on each of three fields. (Notes Taken from Transcripts of Meetings of the Joint Chiefs of Staff, p. 17.)

4. The aircraft carrier USS *Essex*, a lead ship of Navy Task Force 136, commanded by Vice Admiral Alfred Ward, was directly responsible for implementing the quarantine under CINCLANT (Admiral Robert Dennison) and the chief of naval operations (Admiral George Anderson).

5. The ONI was the U.S. Navy's Office of Naval Intelligence.

6. Robert Kennedy's handwritten notes on the meeting, found in the Robert Kennedy Papers, are quoted in Arthur Schlesinger, Jr., *Robert Kennedy and His Times* (New York: Random House, 1978), p. 514. See also Robert Kennedy's own later reconstruction of this part of the meeting in *Thirteen Days: A Memoir of the Cuban Missile Crisis* (New York: Norton, 1971), pp. 69–70.

7. See Dean Rusk, as told to Richard Rusk, *As I Saw It*, ed. Daniel S. Papp (New York: Norton, 1990), p. 237.

8. At that moment, it was about 10:40 A.M. in Washington.

9. The USIA is the U.S. Information Agency, then headed by Edward R. Murrow. Murrow was in ill health at the time, and Donald Wilson was acting in his stead.

10. See Rostow to President Kennedy, 24 October 1962, in *FRUS*, 11: 181.

Walt Rostow, head of policy planning at State, was chairing the planning subcommittee of the ExComm.

11.   The speech was delivered by Soviet ambassador to the United Nations Valerian Zorin on the afternoon of 23 October.

12.   President Kennedy had met alone with Senator J. William Fulbright from 4:58 to 5:05 P.M.

13.   Though this passage is unclear on the tape, we assume that President Kennedy read out the bracketed portion of the final sentence. The full document is reprinted in *The "Cuban Crisis" of 1962: Selected Documents, Chronology, and Bibliography*, ed. David Larson (2d ed.; Lanham, MD: University Press of America, 1986), p. 134.

14.   While in the Mansion earlier in the afternoon, Kennedy had spoken on the phone with Stevenson at about 3:30.

15.   The following is from "Record of telephone message between the Prime Minister and President Kennedy, 24.10.62," in PRO, PREM 11/3690, 24020.

16.   Reprinted in *The "Cuban Crisis*," Larson, document 37.

17.   Memorandum of Telephone Conversation between Ball and President Kennedy at 10:30 P.M., 24 October 1962 (prepared by anonymous State Department note taker), in *FRUS*, 11: 188–89.

18.   The reply was read aloud, in full, to the Executive Committee during its morning meeting on 25 October.

Thursday, October 25, 1962

1.   PRO, PREM 11/3690, 24020.

2.   Other evidence indicates that, at this stage of the briefing, McCone reported: "As of 0600 Eastern Daylight Time, at least 14 of the 22 Soviet ships which were known to be en route to Cuba had turned back" [CIA Watch Committee Memo, "The Crisis U.S.S.R./Cuba," 25 October 1962, in *CIA Documents on the Cuban Missile Crisis 1962*, ed. Mary McAuliffe (Washington, DC: Central Intelligence Agency, 1992), p. 304]. The recorded material may have referred to the intelligence sources of this information, which Vice President Johnson noted as "Turk & Copenhagen & other sources" (Vice President Security Files, Policy Papers and Background Studies on Cuba Affair, document 155a, Lyndon B. Johnson Library).

3.   Vice President Security Files, Policy Papers and Background Studies on Cuba Affair, document 155a, Lyndon B. Johnson Library.

4.   For a possible answer to President Kennedy's question about Soviet camouflage, see Graham Allison and Philip Zelikow, *Essence of Decision: Explaining the Cuban Missile Crisis* (2d ed.; New York: Longman, 1999), pp. 212–14.

5.   Probably a reference to the U.S. suggestion to U Thant, late the previous evening, that he publicly ask Soviet ships not to challenge the U.S. quarantine line in order to allow more time for a peaceful settlement.

6.   State 12974, 25 October 1962, National Security Files, John F. Kennedy Library.

7.   Richard Reeves, *President Kennedy: Profile of Power* (New York: Simon & Schuster, 1993), p. 406.

8.   The following summary is based on Bromley Smith, "Summary Record of NSC Executive Committee Meeting No. 5," 25 October 1962, in John F. Kennedy Library.

9.   Adam Yarmolinsky led the analysis, which concluded that "nothing short of direct attacks on Cuban resources (crop destruction, contamination of raw materials by sabotage, etc.) would produce immediate and drastic results, and all of these measures seem less desirable than direct military action." The POL stoppage would take two to six months to be effective, they thought. "In general, these economic measures would appear to insure only an escalation of our objectives [by undermining Castro's government in Cuba] while reducing the means available to accomplish them" (Yarmolinsky to McNamara, "Possible Economic Measures in the Cuban Situation," 25 October 1962, pp. 1, 4, Cuban Missile Crisis Files, National Security Archive, 1992 Releases Box).

10.   The following is from PRO, PREM 11/3690, 24020.

Friday, October 26, 1962

1. Destroyers are commonly named after war heroes, and these were no exception. The full names of the destroyers were USS *John R. Pierce* (DD 753) and USS *Joseph P. Kennedy, Jr.* (DD 850). The *Kennedy* had been named after President Kennedy's elder brother, a pilot who had lost his life after volunteering to fly an exceptionally dangerous mission in Western Europe during World War II. That a ship so named should be carrying out the first boarding of a vessel was a coincidence, but one that was certainly noticed.

2.   Robert F. Kennedy, *Thirteen Days: A Memoir of the Cuban Missile Crisis* (New York: Norton, 1969), p. 83.

3.   Memo of Telephone Conversation between Ball and Bundy at 9:25 A.M., 26 October 1962, in *FRUS*, 11: 219.

4.   Ibid., p. 220.

5.   GMAIC, JAEIC, NPIC, "Supplement 6 to Joint Evaluation of Soviet Missile Threat in Cuba," 26 October 1962 ("Summary"), in *CIA Documents on the Cuban Missile Crisis, 1962*, Mary McAuliffe (Washington, DC: Central Intelligence Agency, 1992), p. 314.

6.   McCone appears to be referring to the electronic intelligence ship, USS *Oxford*, located in international waters just outside of the 12-mile territorial limit.

7.   Dictabelt 38.1, Cassette K, John F. Kennedy Library, President's Office Files, Presidential Recordings Collection. Yost's lack of understanding is evident in his reaction about trying to make sure that missiles are not removed from their hangars (ballistic missiles are not ordinarily stored in hangars).

8. Robert Kennedy's memoir included an accurate quotation from McCone's briefing, though he places it incorrectly in the morning Executive Committee meeting (*Thirteen Days*, pp. 85–86).

9. The missiles were now being concealed by much more aggressive camouflage efforts, which troubled the analysts. They were now able to spot the missiles only with the aid of the photographs taken of them earlier in October.

10. The FROG missile launchers were discovered by the same low-level photography of 25 October that was a main subject of this briefing. The next day's GMAIC, JAEIC, NPIC joint report included the following: "Photography (Mission 5012 of 25 October) confirmed the presence of a FROG missile launcher in a vehicle park near Remedios. (The FROG is a tactical unguided rocket of 40,000 to 50,000 yard range, and is similar to the U.S. Honest John)" ("Supplement 7 to Joint Evaluation of Soviet Missile Threat in Cuba," 27 October 1962, in *CIA Documents*, McAuliffe, p. 325).

11. A call was logged from Rusk at 4:30. The content of the call makes us a bit uneasy about the accuracy of this logged time, since it sounds like a conversation that might more likely have occurred just before 1:00, when Kennedy left his office.

12. Fomin's real name was Feklisov. The text presents the story as it was then understood by Rusk and others in the U.S. government. The real story is murkier, but it seems that Feklisov was improvising a position of his own and not acting as an agent of his government in this matter. See Alexander Fursenko and Timothy Naftali, "Using KGB Documents: The Scali-Feklisov Channel in the Cuban Missile Crisis," *Cold War International History Project Bulletin*, Issue 5 (Spring 1995), p. 58; Aleksandr Fursenko and Timothy Naftali, *"One Hell of a Gamble": Khrushchev, Castro, and Kennedy, 1958–1964* (New York: Norton, 1997), pp. 263–65.

13. The following relies on both the U.S. and British notes of this conversation. See "Cuba–General–Macmillan Telephone Conversations, 10/62–11/62" folder, National Security Files, Box 37, John F. Kennedy Library; PRO, PREM 11/3690, 24020.

14. Again we use the version of the letter actually read and relied on by the decision makers at the time, in this case the unofficial translation done at the U.S. Embassy in Moscow when they transmitted the letter to Washington. It is reprinted, with some notes about later corrections, in *The "Cuban Crisis" of 1962: Selected Documents, Chronology, and Bibliography*, ed. David L. Larson (2d ed.; Lanham, MD: University Press of America, 1986), pp. 175–80. It differs in various small ways from the official State Department translation, which was prepared later but which appears in many of the documentary compilations

Saturday, October 27, 1962

1. CIA, "The Crisis USSR/Cuba," 27 October 1962, in *CIA Documents on the Cuban Missile Crisis, 1962*, ed. Mary McAuliffe (Washington, DC: Central Intelligence Agency, 1992), p. 328.

2.   The identification of the FROG tactical nuclear rockets had been mentioned prominently in that morning's interagency estimate on missile readiness. The President had already been briefed on them the day before (26 October).

3.   The location of the *Grozny* had been lost for a time; the ship was found again that morning by reconnaissance aircraft of the Strategic Air Command. In these efforts one of the aircraft, an RB-47, crashed at takeoff and its four-man crew was killed.

4.   Raymond Hare was U.S. ambassador to Turkey. A few days earlier the State Department had cabled him to ask how he thought the Turks would react to a possible deal involving the withdrawal of the Jupiter missiles from Turkey. Hare was not instructed to approach the Turks, just to give his opinion. Hare was sure the Turks would object. "Problem would be partly psycho-political, partly substantive; psycho-political, in sense that Turks are proud, courageous people who do not understand concept or process of compromise. . . . Problem is also substantive in sense that Turks, as we well know, set great store on arms which they feel necessary meet their needs and were adamant in refusing our suggestion last year that Jupiter project not be implemented . . . if we insist to contrary, demand for arms to fill vacuum would be specific and sizeable" (Ankara 587, 26 October 1962, in "NATO— Weapons, Cables—Turkey" folder, National Security Files, Box 226, John F. Kennedy Library.)

In the second section of his cable, received in Washington as this meeting of the Executive Committee was getting underway, Hare suggested four alternatives. One, no deal. That would be easiest. Two, unilateral phaseout of Jupiters to be replaced by the long-discussed but still-nonexistent NATO multilateral seaborne deterrent force (MLF) in Polaris submarines. Three, a trade with the Soviets on Turkey and Cuba but one that was kept on a "strictly secret basis with Soviets." Hare wondered if the Soviets could be trusted to keep the secret and noted that the Turks would still need to be placated with other arms. Fourth, a deal that became public. "This would be most difficult of all" (ibid., Section 2 of three).

The initial Turkish reaction to the crisis had been completely supportive, asking only for accelerated deliveries of F-104 fighter aircraft and spare parts for F-100 fighter bombers. A day later the Turkish foreign minister expressed shock about public comparisons between Turkey and Cuba and renewed the request for the military equipment. Two days later the foreign minister's line was the same, and he was "in exceedingly good and confident mood." (See Ankara 576, 23 October 1962; Ankara 581, 24 October 1962; and Ankara 585, 26 October 1962, ibid.)

5.   Thomas Finletter was U.S. permanent representative to NATO's North Atlantic Council, in effect, the U.S. ambassador to NATO, then head-quartered in Paris. In the same 24 October message that asked for Hare's opinion on a Cuba-Turkey trade, the State Department also asked for Finletter's view of the matter. Finletter thought the Turks would attach

great symbolic value to the Jupiter missiles, and he also mentioned the possibility of trying to offer some sort of alternative based on the new Polaris submarines (Paris Polto 506, 25 October 1962, ibid.).

6. Ball was probably referring to a memo from the relevant State officials that used this situation to renew the idea of the sea-based MLF, phasing out Turkish Jupiters once this force—based at sea—could take its place. See (William) Tyler (assistant secretary of state for European affairs), (Walt) Rostow (director of policy planning), and (Phillips) Talbot (assistant secretary of state for Near Eastern and South Asian affairs) to Rusk, "Cuba," 24 October 1962, in Cuban Missile Crisis Files, National Security Archive, 1992 Releases Box.

7. Unofficial translation reprinted in *The "Cuban Crisis" of 1962: Selected Documents, Chronology, and Bibliography*, ed. David L. Larson (2d ed.; Lanham, MD: University Press of America, 1986), pp. 183–86.

8. Because of the state of nuclear alert then prevailing as a result of the crisis, the U.S. fighter aircraft carried fully armed Falcon air-to-air missiles with nuclear warheads [see Scott Sagan, *The Limits of Safety: Organizations, Accidents, and Nuclear Weapons* (Princeton, NJ: Princeton University Press, 1993), pp. 136–38]. And on this and the predelegation of nuclear use authority, see Graham Allison and Philip Zelikow, *Essence of Decision: Explaining the Cuban Missile Crisis* (2d ed.; New York: Longman, 1999), pp. 199–201 and notes 4, 5, and 11.

9. On these telegrams see the initial footnotes in the transcript of the morning meeting (27 October). Hare's "long telegram" (Ankara 587) had arrived in three sections; the third section was received in Washington during the early afternoon of 27 October. This was the cable that first answered the direct question about likely Turkish views of a trade (negative) but then went on to suggest four alternative ways to look at a trade. Hare listed them as: First, don't do it. Second, replace Jupiters with the seaborne multilateral NATO force being considered in State. Third, do a trade but only as a secret understanding with the Soviets, with the danger that this option "would involve good faith of Soviets who would always have option reveal to detriment U.S.-Turkish relations." Fourth, do a public trade.

10. Stevenson had met that afternoon with NATO ambassadors as well as ambassadors from friendly Latin American countries. He said that other matters might be discussed but only after the problem in Cuba had been addressed. He had implied that Turkish bases might be discussed in later talks. The Turkish ambassador rejected this notion so vehemently that, as the British ambassador (Sir Patrick Dean) reported later, Stevenson "drew in his horns a little before the Turkish delegate's obvious unhappiness at any prospect of negotiations over Turkey." The group agreed that the situation was becoming very urgent and that the introduction of Turkey and NATO bases would lead to an intolerable delay in resolving the underlying problem in Cuba (U.K. Mission U.N. 1801, "Cuba," 28 October 1962, in PRO, PREM 11/3691, 24020).

11.   William C. Foster was director of the U.S. Arms Control and
Disarmament Agency. A veteran executive in the steel and chemical industry,
Foster had been deputy secretary of defense in the last two years of the
Truman administration (when Robert Lovett was the secretary).

12.   The Four, also called the Quadripartitite Group, was a group of representatives from Britain, France, West Germany, and the United States that
habitually conferred on Berlin and German issues.

13.   Dirk Stikker, from the Netherlands, was NATO's secretary-general,
the top civilian official.

14.   Bundy is referring to Hare's cable, Ankara 587. The first section of
this message arrived on 26 October; the last two sections came in during
the day on 27 October. Its contents are detailed in note 4, "Executive
Committee Meeting of the National Security Council," 27 October 1962,
10:05 A.M.

15.   The pilot who was killed was Major Rudolph Anderson of South
Carolina.

16.   Taylor is referring to the contingency plan agreed on four days earlier, during the morning meeting on 23 October.

17.   Gilpatric is referring to the statement issued by the Defense
Department's press spokesman at about 3:30 P.M. in reaction to the hostile
fire encountered by the low-level reconnaissance aircraft.

18.   The acronym NIACT stands for "night action." Sending a cable with
this designation sets off procedures in the receiving embassy alerting them
that the message requires immediate action without waiting for the cable to
be read after the normal opening of business in the morning.

19.   It was not right. A moment earlier, Rusk had put the White House
statement first, not second.

20.   Both U.S. and Turkish aircraft capable of carrying nuclear bombs, and
with the U.S. aircraft certified as ready to carry them, were based on land in
Turkey. Nuclear bombs for these aircraft were also stockpiled in Turkey
under U.S. control.

21.   Thompson is referring to a column by Walter Lippmann, suggesting
a Cuba-Turkey trade, that appeared in the *Washington Post* on the morning
of 25 October.

22.   This exchange is probably referring to the message to Khrushchev.
The speaker probably meant to say *Russian* rather than *English*, as the
Soviet Embassy in Washington would translate the message into Russian
and was calling in a messenger (such as one from Western Union) in order
to have the encrypted cable transmitted to Moscow.

23.   Since the message was broadcast, different U.S. officials were using
unofficial translations of the message prepared by assorted press agencies
or wire services. The term *weapons* was also often translated as *means*.
Thompson's version translated *analogous* as *similar*.

24.   McGeorge Bundy, *Danger and Survival: Choices about the Bomb in the
First Fifty Years* (New York: Random House, 1988), pp. 432–33.

25.   Rusk's proposal thus also answered the argument that Thompson, speaking for others, had just voiced so strongly about the danger of accepting Khrushchev's trade. Ball had advocated this approach. Thompson, Vice President Johnson, and others had argued that the trade would become a full-scale negotiated, reciprocal bargain of everything in Cuba and in Turkey—plane for plane, man for man. By offering only a unilateral statement of general intent and expressly ruling out a formal trade, the United States was getting the Jupiter missiles *off* the table, delinking the timing or scope of the U.S. move from the specific and urgent demands about Soviet missiles in Cuba.

26.   Much later, Rusk said that during the evening, President Kennedy had talked privately with him about another diplomatic contingency plan. Rusk would telephone the president of Columbia University, Andrew Cordier. Cordier was very close to U Thant (he later edited U Thant's papers) and would be in a position to suggest discreetly that Washington might be receptive to a proposal involving the Turkish missiles in order to gain removal of the Soviet installations in Cuba. If Khrushchev rejected President Kennedy's offer, then Rusk could call Cordier and give him the go-ahead to prime U Thant to propose the trade. Mark White has argued, using British evidence about an analogous Rusk-Cordier contact, that, 25 years after the event, Rusk forgot that he had talked to Cordier on 24–25 October and that the idea had concerned the possibility of U.N. monitoring of Turkish missile sites in exchange for U.N. monitoring of Cuban missile sites to be sure they were inoperable [Mark J. White, *The Cuban Missile Crisis* (London: Macmillan & Co., 1996), pp. 202–3].

Rusk and the Executive Committee had been much concerned with the modalities of such U.N. supervision at that time, as is evident from the taped discussions. Cordier's intervention with U Thant was not requested, in the event, for any purpose. Indeed, such a U.S. move, under Rusk's version of the story, might have been preceded and certainly would have been followed by prolonged and skeptical discussion in the Executive Committee. If U Thant had made such a proposal, it would have been debated in the ExComm; Kennedy could not have avoided that. His advisers would have stressed the same problem Kennedy himself had repeatedly identified, of (as he put it) "being impaled on a long negotiating hook" while the missiles became a fait accompli.

If Rusk's story is accurate, and we are unsure that it is, Kennedy is likely to have seen it more as a deniable way to buy a little more time, rather than as a move that would present the negotiated and public trade of Turkish and Cuban missiles in a significantly more appealing way. U Thant's proposal, in Rusk's version, was a way of keeping open or reviving the "Ball track" that had already been discussed and apparently rejected by the ExComm and by the President. Against Rusk's account is the fact that the President had finally committed himself, in front of his advisers, to moving toward an air strike against Cuba if Khrushchev did not give a positive reply to his letter, and Robert Kennedy had—with the President's approval—conveyed this warning plainly to Khrushchev's representative.

27.   Robert Kennedy to Rusk, 30 October 1962, in President's Office Files, John F. Kennedy Library. Robert Kennedy relied on this account in preparing his memoir, *Thirteen Days*, but a few sentences in this portion of his draft were edited and rewritten by Sorensen when the book was prepared for its posthumous publication. We consider his original account, declassified in 1991, to be reliable, especially since his description of the meeting is substantively identical to the report of the talk sent back to Moscow that night by Dobrynin. The Dobrynin cable is published in *Bulletin of the Cold War International History Project*, Issue 5 (Spring 1995), pp. 79–80. On the circumstances that prompted Robert Kennedy to write up this account, see Arthur M. Schlesinger, Jr., *Robert Kennedy and His Times* (New York: Random House, 1978), pp. 522–23. Schlesinger's book quotes some of Kennedy's notes on the matter, accurately describing the substance of the Jupiter discussion, although Schlesinger mistakenly presumes that the United States was accepting Khrushchev's proffered trade, not perceiving the difference between the trade option (the "Ball track") and Rusk's finesse.

28.   Note Robert Kennedy's reference to an additional condition, about Cuban subversion. Such a condition was in the original draft letter to Khrushchev discussed in the afternoon, using the phrase "peace in the Caribbean," but the language was dropped in the final editing of the message. Possibly Robert Kennedy had forgotten that the condition had been dropped from the final version of the letter approved by the President. Rusk was later asked by Martin, who had not attended the 4:00 Executive Committee meeting, what had happened to this language, and Rusk said he did not know. As a result an urgent cable was sent to U.S. Embassies in Latin America telling them that the U.S. pledge not to invade in Kennedy's letter (now public) was "subject to Cuba behaving herself as required under Hemisphere treaties to which she is committed" [Edwin McCammon Martin, *Kennedy and Latin America* (Lanham, MD: University Press of America, 1994), pp. 435–36].

29.   In the original of this document, on Justice Department letterhead, a line is drawn through this last sentence. The original is in the President's Office Files, John F. Kennedy Library, not in the Robert Kennedy Papers. Since the memo does not appear in Rusk's files, it seems likely that Robert Kennedy drafted the memo to Rusk and showed it to his brother, who then took it and kept it. The paper was retained in the President's files and never sent to Rusk. We cannot tell who drew the line through this sentence or when or why, but the sentence is certainly accurate, as it was echoed in both Dobrynin's report and in the handwritten notes quoted by Schlesinger.

30.   Kenneth P. O'Donnell and David F. Powers, with Joe McCarthy, *"Johnny, We Hardly Knew Ye"* (New York: Pocket Books, 1972), p. 394.

31.   He is referring to the CIA's covert action program, code-named

Mongoose, created to spy on, harass, and possibly overthrow Castro's government.

32.   State telegram (no Deptel number but ToPol 578 to Finletter at NATO), 28 October 1962 (dated 26 October but actually sent shortly after midnight in the early morning of October 28), in Meetings and Memoranda, "ExComm Meetings 6–10, 10/26/62–10/28/62" folder, National Security Files, John F. Kennedy Library.

33.   From PRO, FO 371/162388, 25000.

Sunday, October 28, 1962

1.   Foreign Broadcast Information Service translation of text broadcast on Moscow Domestic Service; reprinted in Lawrence Chang and Peter Kornbluh, *The Cuban Missile Crisis, 1962: A National Security Archive Documents Reader* (New York: New Press, 1992), pp. 226–29.

2.   However, after studying photography from the reconnaissance flights of October 27, U. S. intelligence analysts judged that activity at the missile sites had been continuing at least during the day of 27 October.

3.   JCS to President Kennedy, "Recommendation for Execution of CIN-CLANT OPLANS 312 and 316," JCSM-844-62, 28 October 1962; Taylor to McNamara, CM-61-62, 28 October 1962, Records of the Office of the Secretary of Defense, 71-A-2896, National Records Center.

4.   China invaded and occupied Tibet in 1950. The Tibetans fought a bloody guerrilla war for years against Chinese rule. While Eisenhower was president, in 1956, the CIA began helping the Tibetans by supplying arms from bases in India and Nepal and, in 1959, also began training groups of Tibetans at a base in the United States.

Conclusion

1.   Khrushchev to Kennedy, 28 October 1962, in *FRUS*, 6: 189–90. A copy of this letter was released from the Russian archives in 1992 and is included in the collection for the sake of completeness. It was never officially received by the Kennedy administration, and no copy exists in the U.S. archives.

2.   See Robert Kennedy to Rusk, 30 October 1962, President's Office Files, John Fitzgerald Kennedy Library. On the circumstances that prompted Kennedy to write this note to Rusk and for the material quoted from Kennedy's handwritten notes of his 30 October meeting with Dobrynin, see Arthur M. Schlesinger, Jr., *Robert Kennedy and His Times* (New York: Random House, 1978), p. 523. We have found no evidence that Kennedy's memo was ever sent to Rusk. From the way the memo was preserved in the archives, it seems more likely that Robert Kennedy showed the memo to his brother, who then just took it and kept it in his own files.

Dobrynin's account of this unpleasant meeting differs from Robert

Kennedy's. In a report to Moscow, Dobrynin described the Attorney General as saying that he could not be party to an exchange of letters because it "could cause irreparable harm to my political career in the future." According to Dobrynin, Robert Kennedy gave assurances that President Kennedy would keep his promise by mentioning that, in connection with the Laos neutralization arrangements of the preceding summer, Kennedy had made and kept a secret promise to pull out U.S. troops deployed to Thailand. Dobrynin to Foreign Ministry, 30 October 1962, in a set of documents obtained by the Woodrow Wilson International Center's Cold War International History Project and translated at Harvard, hereinafter referred to as CWIHP/Harvard Collection. On the troops in Thailand, see Michael Beschloss, *The Crisis Years: Kennedy and Khrushchev, 1960–1963* (New York: HarperCollins, 1991), pp. 397–98.

3.   30 October 1962, in *FRUS*, 6: 190–98.

4.   USUN New York 1585, 1 November 1962, reprinted in Lawrence Chang and Peter Kornbluh, *The Cuban Missile Crisis, 1962: A National Security Archive Documents Reader* (New York: New Press, 1992), pp. 249–51.

5.   14 November 1962, in *FRUS*, 6: 209–12.

6.   See, for example, Martin to Alexis Johnson, "Invasion," 30 October 1962; Ball through Bundy to President Kennedy, "Suggested Policy Line for Cuban Crisis," 10 November 1962; the State briefing papers for the press conference; President Kennedy's explanation on this point to Mikoyan in the Memorandum of Conversation for their meeting, 29 November 1962, all in Cuban Missile Crisis Files, National Security Archive, 1992 Releases Box.

7.   See Bromley Smith to File, "Summary Record of Executive Committee Meeting No. 27," 19 November 1962, in Executive Committee Meetings, vol. 3, Meetings 25–32a, National Security Files, Box 316, John F. Kennedy Library; Gromyko to Mikoyan (then in Havana), 18 November 1962, in CWIHP/Harvard Collection.

8.   See Ankara 619, 13 November 1962, State Department Decimal Central Files, 782.56311/11-1362, National Archives, Washington, DC; Deptel 1151, "Jupiter Missiles," 18 December 1962, in *FRUS*, 13: 460–61. On the "intolerable serenity" see Paris Secto 22 (Eyes Only from Rusk to President Kennedy and Ball), 15 December 1962, pp. 458–59.

9.   Aleksandr Fursenko and Timothy Naftali, *"One Hell of a Gamble": Khrushchev, Castro, and Kennedy, 1958–1964* (New York: Norton, 1997).

10.   For the first, see Arnold L. Horelick and Myron Rush, *Strategic Power and Soviet Policy* (Santa Monica, CA: RAND Corporation, 1963); Alexander George and Richard Smoke, *Deterrence in American Foreign Policy* (New York: Columbia University Press, 1974); Marc Trachtenberg, *History and Strategy* (Princeton, NJ: Princeton University Press, 1991), pp. 253–60. For the second, see Thomas G. Paterson and William G. Brophy, "October Missiles and November Elections: The Cuban Missile Crisis and American Politics, 1962," *Journal of American History* 73, no. 1 (1986): 87–119; Thomas G. Paterson, *Kennedy's Quest for Victory: American Foreign Policy,*

1961–1963 (New York: Oxford University Press, 1989); James G. Blight and David A. Welch, *On the Brink: Americans and Soviets Reexamine the Cuban Missile Crisis* (New York: Hill & Wang, 1989), pp. 294–95; a panel discussion on the missile crisis in *Diplomatic History* 14, no. 2 (1990); Russell D. Buhite, "From Kennedy to Nixon: The End of Consensus," in *American Foreign Relations Reconsidered, 1890–1993,* ed. Gordon Martel (London: Routledge, 1994), pp. 125–44.

11.   Blight and Welch, *On the Brink,* p. 235.

12.   Nikita S. Khrushchev, *Khrushchev Remembers: The Last Testament,* trans. and ed. Strobe Talbott (Boston: Little, Brown, 1974), pp. 513–14.

13.   See Khrushchev, *Khrushchev Remembers,* pp. 434–36. Shakhnazarov said in 1989, in a conversation with Ernest May in Cambridge, Massachusetts, that Khrushchev had been like a German prince in a play whose title he could not remember. Fervently sympathetic with the Americans in their revolution for independence from Britain, the prince had finally declared war on Britain. When he learned soon afterward that Britain had granted independence to the United States, he assumed that his action had been the cause. Thompson may not have been fully conscious of the significance of Suez for Khrushchev. He had been serving in Austria at the time and had not been on top of Soviet affairs. His predecessor, Bohlen, had not been close to Khrushchev and, judging from his cables, was so focused on Soviet relations with Poland and Hungary that he didn't notice much of the larger context. The scholar who has done most to call attention to Suez as a turning point in Soviet foreign policy is Adam B. Ulam, but his writings on the subject did not appear until the late 1960s. See his *Expansion and Coexistence: The History of Soviet Foreign Policy, 1917–1967* (New York: Praeger, 1968), pp. 586–89, and *The Rivals: America & Russia Since World War II* (New York: Viking, 1971), pp. 253–66.

14.   Twenty-three protesters were killed in fighting in the city of Novocherkassk; 87 others were seriously wounded; hundreds were arrested and, of these, at least a dozen were later executed. Massive new internal security measures were secretly put in place throughout the country. Vladislav M. Zubok and Constantine Pleshakov, *Inside the Kremlin's Cold War: From Stalin to Khrushchev* (Cambridge, MA: Harvard University Press, 1996), pp. 263–65. For background see Merle Fainsod, *How Russia Is Ruled* (rev. ed.; Cambridge, MA: Harvard University Press, 1970), pp. 545–58, 611–12 (on developments in agriculture and the significance of the decisions on resource allocation).

15.   Though in not quite the same terms, this point is made in Richard Ned Lebow and Janice Gross Stein, *We All Lost the Cold War* (Princeton, NJ: Princeton University Press, 1994), pp. 19–66.

16.   Khrushchev, *Khrushchev Remembers* [1970], p. 493.

17.   Fursenko and Naftali, *"One Hell of a Gamble,"* pp. 3–38.

18.   Ibid., p. 44.

19.   Ibid., pp. 49–53.

20.   Ibid., p. 70.

21.   Khrushchev to Kennedy, 18 April 1961, in *FRUS*, 6: 7–8.

22.   Khrushchev, *Khrushchev Remembers* [1970], p. 493. Khrushchev's colleague in the Presidium, Mikoyan, later described Soviet interests in Cuba by explaining that "a defeat of the Cuban revolution would mean a two or three times larger defeat of the whole socialist camp. Such a defeat would throw back the revolutionary movement in many countries. Such a defeat would bear witness to the supremacy of imperialist forces in the entire world. That would be an incredible blow which would change the correlation of forces between the two systems." Memcon for Meeting between Castro and Mikoyan, 4 November 1962, in *CWIHP Bulletin*, no. 5 (Spring 1995), p. 96. In other words, this is a Soviet version of what Americans called the domino theory.

23.   Fursenko and Naftali, *"One Hell of a Gamble,"* pp. 158–63. Background and context can be found in two books by Jorge Dominguez: *Cuba: Order and Revolution* (Cambridge, MA: Harvard University Press, 1978), pp. 210–18, and *To Make a World Safe for Revolution: Cuba's Foreign Policy* (Cambridge, MA: Harvard University Press, 1989), pp. 72–77. See also Tad Szulc, *Fidel: A Critical Portrait* (New York: Morrow, 1986), pp. 569–70, 610–13; Maurice Halperin, *The Rise and Decline of Fidel Castro* (Berkeley: University of California Press, 1972), pp. 132–54; Robert E. Quirk, *Fidel Castro* (New York: Norton, 1993), pp. 402–03; Andres Suarez, *Cuba: Castroism and Communism, 1959–1966* (Cambridge, MA: MIT Press, 1967), pp. 137–52.

24.   Domingo Amuchastegui, "Cuban Intelligence and the October Crisis," in *Intelligence and the Cuban Missile Crisis*, ed. James G. Blight and David A. Welch (London: Cass, 1998), pp. 96–97. Amuchastegui writes that Soviet intelligence skewed its assessments to convince Cuban colleagues that the U.S. threat was real, so the Cubans would accept the Soviet missiles. As the essay in the same volume by Aleksandr Fursenko and Timothy Naftali points out, there is little evidence of such dissembling by Soviet intelligence, but we can readily imagine some talk of the U.S. threat coming from the Soviet envoys who (after Khrushchev made his decision) urged the Cubans to take the missiles. Since the Soviet ambassador to Cuba was also the former KGB resident in Havana, the distinction between Soviet political and intelligence judgments might have seemed blurry to Cuban listeners.

25.   Khrushchev, *The Last Testament*, p. 511. See Fursenko and Naftali, *"One Hell of a Gamble,"* pp. 148–63.

26.   Fursenko and Naftali, *"One Hell of a Gamble,"* pp. 167–68.

27.   Ibid., p. 177.

28.   Reprinted, significantly, in *Pravda*, February 26, 1962 and quoted in Yuri Pavlov, *Soviet-Cuban Alliance: 1959–1991* (New Brunswick, NJ: Transaction, 1994), p. 37.

29.   Blight and Welch, *On the Brink*, p. 238.

30.   Dmitri Volkogonov, *Sem Vozhdei* [Seven Leaders], quoted in Fursenko and Naftali, *"One Hell of a Gamble,"* p. 169. At the time, the Soviet ICBM force

totaled about 20. So adding at least 40 more launchers with 60 missiles would double the missile striking power for an initial salvo against the United States. As General Anatoli Gribkov pointed out, "In one stroke he [Khrushchev] could redress the imbalance in strategic nuclear forces" [Anatoli I. Gribkov and William Y. Smith, "The View from Moscow and Havana," in *Operation ANADYR: U.S. and Soviet Generals Recount the Cuban Missile Crisis*, ed. Alfred Friendly, Jr. (Chicago: Edition Q, 1994), p. 13].

31. Malinovsky, quoted in Beschloss, *The Crisis Years*, p. 332.

32. The best study so far of the Jupiter deployment is Philip Nash, *The Other Missiles of October: Eisenhower, Kennedy, and the Jupiters, 1957–1963* (Chapel Hill: University of North Carolina Press, 1997). Nash works on ground that was first cleared in an essay by Barton J. Bernstein, "Reconsidering the Missile Crisis: Dealing with the Problems of the American Jupiters in Turkey," most recently reprinted in *The Cuban Missile Crisis Revisited*, ed. James A. Nathan (New York: St. Martin's Press, 1992), pp. 55–67.

33. For Rusk's report on his talks with Gromyko, see Minutes of Meeting of the National Security Council, 28 March 1962, in *FRUS*, 7: 411; see also Memcon of Meeting between Rusk and Dobrynin, 23 April 1962, in *FRUS*, 7: 443. The nuclear test series, Dominic I, involved 36 detonations in the Pacific, in the vicinity of Christmas Island and Johnston Island, beginning on April 25. The Soviets followed with a further series of their own atmospheric tests, beginning in August 1962.

34. Khrushchev, *Khrushchev Remembers* [1970], p. 494.

35. Andropov, quoted in Oleg Troyanovsky, "The Caribbean Crisis: A View from the Kremlin," *International Affairs (Moscow)*, April–May 1992, pp. 147, 148.

36. Blight and Welch, *On the Brink*, p. 239. Mikoyan's son identifies five people as having been in the group consulted by Khrushchev. In addition to Mikoyan pére, Malinovsky, and Biryuzov, it included Frol Kozlov (the Presidium member responsible for party personnel and organization) and Foreign Minister Gromyko. But Gromyko claims that Khrushchev first informed him about the planned deployment on the flight home from Bulgaria on 20 May (Andrei A. Gromyko, "The Caribbean Crisis: On *Glasnost* Now and Secrecy Then," *Izvestiya*, 15 April 1989, p. 5).

37. This paragraph and the next draw on Fursenko and Naftali, *"One Hell of a Gamble,"* pp. 177–79; Alexeev's recollections in *Back to the Brink: Proceedings of the Moscow Conference on the Cuban Missile Crisis, January 27–28, 1989*, ed. Bruce J. Allyn, James G. Blight, and David Welch. CSIA Occasional Paper No. 9 (Lanham, MD: University Press of America, 1992), pp. 150–51; Alexeev again at a 1992 conference in Havana in *Cuba on the Brink: Castro, the Missile Crisis, and the Soviet Collapse*, ed. James G. Blight, Bruce J. Allyn, and David A. Welch (New York: Pantheon, 1993), pp. 77–78; and Alexeev in *Mezhdunarodnaya Zhiz'n*, July 1992, p. 54. Alexeev has dated his exchange with Khrushchev as 11 May, but Fursenko and Naftali, partly on the basis of their own interviews with Alexeev, date it as 20 May.

38. Castro, quoted in *Fidel*, Szulc, pp. 579–83. For the recollections from the member of Castro's Secretariat, Emilio Aragones, and another Cuban official, Jorge Risquet, see Allyn, Blight, and Welch, *Back to the Brink*, pp. 51, 26. See also Castro's account in *Cuba on the Brink*, Blight, Allyn, and Welch, pp. 197–98; Alexeev, in *Back to the Brink*, pp. 151–52. On Cuban reluctance, see also Pavlov, *Soviet-Cuban Alliance*, pp. 38–40. See also Blight, Allyn, and Welch's discussion of Castro's real motives for accepting the missiles in *Cuba on the Brink*, pp. 345–47.

39. A defense pact, drafted and initialed by Malinovsky and Che Guevara, was to be signed triumphantly by Khrushchev in Cuba in November 1962, at the time the operational missiles were unveiled to the world. The signing ceremony never took place. When Guevara and Emilio Aragones went to Moscow at the end of August to finalize the pact, they asked Khrushchev to publicize the preparation of the treaty and end the attempted deception, hoping the treaty would be enough to deter the United States: they could insist on their right openly to accept a Soviet base, much as the United States had handled its overseas nuclear deployments (for example in Turkey). Khrushchev said no. See Castro in Blight, Allyn, and Welch, *Cuba on the Brink*, pp. 85–86; Emilio Aragones in *Back to the Brink*, Allyn, Blight, and Welch, p. 52; Gribkov, "The View from Moscow and Havana," p. 23.

40. Gribkov, "The View from Moscow and Havana," p. 13.

41. Fursenko and Naftali, *"One Hell of a Gamble,"* pp. 186–87.

42. Gribkov, "The View from Moscow and Havana," pp. 15–16.

43. Castro, in *Cuba on the Brink*, Blight, Allyn, and Welch, pp. 83–84. Alexeev provided a similar account at the same meeting.

44. Khrushchev, *Khrushchev Remembers* [1970], p. 494.

45. The best compilation of this evidence is Beschloss, *The Crisis Years*, e.g., pp. 223–34 (on the Vienna meeting). For more details on Khrushchev's perception of Kennedy see Zubok and Pleshakov, *Inside the Kremlin's Cold War*, pp. 239–48, 257–58.

46. Gromyko, "The Caribbean Crisis"; Anatoly Dobrynin, *In Confidence* (New York: Random House, 1995), pp. 79–80.

47. Fursenko and Naftali, *"One Hell of a Gamble,"* p. 174; Dobrynin, *In Confidence*, p. 63.

48. Khrushchev to Kennedy, 9 November 1961, in *FRUS*, 6: 57; see also Hans S. Kroll, *Lebenserinnerungen eines Botschafters* (Köln: Kiepenheuer & Witsch, 1967), pp. 524–27. For a more elaborate review of explanations for Khrushchev's spring 1962 decisions, see Graham Allison and Philip Zelikow, *Essence of Decision: Explaining the Cuban Missile Crisis* (2d ed.; New York: Longman, 1999), pp. 78–108.

49. For more on Khrushchev's difficult domestic and international position by late 1961, see James G. Richter, *Khrushchev's Double Bind: International Pressures and Domestic Coalition Politics* (Baltimore: Johns Hopkins Press, 1994), pp. 142–47; Michel Tatu, *Power in the Kremlin*, trans. Helen Katel (New York: Viking, 1969), pp. 148–214; Robert M. Slusser, *The*

Berlin Crisis of 1961: Soviet-American Relations and the Struggle for Power in the Kremlin, June–November 1961 (Baltimore: Johns Hopkins Press, 1973).

50.   Khrushchev to Kennedy, 13 December 1961, in *FRUS*, 14: 683–84, 690.

51.   Khrushchev to Kennedy, 10 March 1962. Kennedy sought a conciliatory modus vivendi with Khrushchev. See Kennedy to Rusk, 11 March 1962, both in *FRUS*, 15: 11, 15.

52.   See note 5 on Dobrynin-Rusk meeting of 23 April, in *FRUS*, 15: 119; State 2964, 28 April 1962, in *FRUS*, 15: 121; Marc Trachtenberg, *A Constructed Peace: The Making of the European Settlement, 1945–1963* (Princeton, NJ: Princeton University Press, 1999), esp. pp. 348–51; Richter, *Khrushchev's Double Bind*, p. 148; Tatu, *Power in the Kremlin*, pp. 233–34.

53.   See, based on research in East German archives, Michael Lemke, *Die Berlinkrise 1958 bis 1963: Interessen und Handlungsspielräume der SED im Ost-West Konflikt* (Berlin: Akademie Verlag, 1995), pp. 186–90.

54.   McNamara certainly believed that evident U.S. nuclear superiority was keeping the Soviets from returning to direct confrontation over Berlin. He explained the point to Kennedy in detail. See McNamara to Kennedy, "US and Soviet Military Buildup and Probable Effects on Berlin Situation," 21 June 1962, in *FRUS*, 15: 192–95.

55.   Dobrynin, *In Confidence*, p. 52.

56.   Moscow 187, 20 July 1962, in *FRUS*, 15: 234. By this time the sense of impending crisis was becoming general, and U.S. allies were also anxious to consider contingency plans. See Weiss to Johnson, "Berlin," 11 July 1962, and Secto 13 (Rusk to Kennedy and Ball), 22 July 1962, in *FRUS*, 15: 213–14, 236–37.

57.   See Moscow 225, 25 July 1962; see also Moscow 228, 26 July 1962; and Copenhagen 76 (Thompson to Rusk), in *FRUS*, 15: 252–55; on communications in Washington see Bundy to Sorensen, "Berlin," 23 August 1962, in *FRUS*, 15: 284–85; Dobrynin, *In Confidence*, pp. 67–68.

58.   Thompson set down this analysis, already well understood in Washington, for the benefit of overseas posts in State telegram, 24 October 1962, in *FRUS*, 15: 397–99. British experts in the Foreign Office's Northern Department submitted a very similar opinion. "Yet if Khrushchev was to bring things to a head fairly soon over Berlin something must be done urgently to rectify imbalance if Soviets would be negotiating politically in an inferior military position. Khrushchev may well have calculated that once Cuban missile complex completed he could frighten Americans off taking determined action in Berlin by pointing to their own vulnerability to attack from his Cuban base and thus obtain heavy leverage in negotiations on Berlin which he has been planning for the end of year" (London 1696, 26 October 1962, conveying the estimate that had been provided to the British Cabinet's Joint Intelligence Committee, in Cuban Missile Crisis Files, National Security Archive, 1992 Releases Box.

59.   Fursenko and Naftali, *"One Hell of a Gamble,"* pp. 206–12. Khrushchev did decide, however, to turn down his military's suggestion that he also

send a brigade of 18 other short-range nuclear missiles (the SCUD B, SS-1c). See Raymond L. Garthoff, "New Evidence on the Cuban Missile Crisis: Khrushchev, Nuclear Weapons, and the Cuban Missile Crisis," *CWIHP Bulletin*, no. 11 (Winter 1998), p. 251.

60.   Fursenko and Naftali, *"One Hell of a Gamble,"* pp. 211–12; Garthoff, "New Evidence on the Cuban Missile Crisis," pp. 251–52. This alteration in the plan was apparently made on 25 September. Moscow proceeded with deployment of four diesel attack submarines. On each of these 1 of the 22 torpedoes was armed with a nuclear warhead. These were the four submarines detected by the Americans, tracked near the quarantine area, discussed in the White House meetings, and harassed by U.S. antisubmarine vessels.

61.   Troyanovsky, "The Caribbean Crisis," p. 150.

62.   Gromyko cabled report to the Central Committee of the Communist Party of the Soviet Union, 19 October 1962, in "Russian Foreign Ministry Documents on the Cuban Missile Crisis," *CWIHP Bulletin*, no. 5 (Spring 1995), pp. 66–67; see also the gloating tone and complete misreading of both Kennedy and Rusk apparent in the final paragraph of Gromyko's longer report on his conversation with Rusk (Gromyko to Central Committee, October 20, 1962, ibid., p. 69).

63.   Fursenko and Naftali, *"One Hell of a Gamble,"* p. 190.

64.   One standing order, issued on September 8, was that air defense forces "will not permit incursion of foreign aircraft" into Cuban airspace (Malinovsky and Zakharov to Pliyev, 8 September 1962, document no. 5, in "New Evidence on the Cuban Missile Crisis," Garthoff, p. 260). On the tracking of the earlier American U-2 overflights, see Gribkov, "The View from Moscow and Havana," p. 52. For a fuller discussion of the Soviet air defense behavior, see Allison and Zelikow, *Essence of Decision*, pp. 214–15, but that account must now be qualified by the language in the September 8 order translated and published by Garthoff.

65.   For more on why the missiles were not effectively camouflaged, see Allison and Zelikow, *Essence of Decision*, pp. 211–14.

66.   Gribkov, "The View from Moscow and Havana," pp. 45–46.

67.   Fursenko and Naftali, *"One Hell of a Gamble,"* pp. 238–39.

68.   Ibid., pp. 240–41. This account supersedes the reported instruction in "The View from Moscow and Havana," Gribkov, p. 62, which was apparently prepared for the Presidium but not used.

69.   Dobrynin to Foreign Ministry, 23 October 1962, in "Russian Foreign Ministry Documents," pp. 70–71; Alexeev to Foreign Ministry, 23 October 1962, CWIHP/Harvard Collection.

70.   Fursenko and Naftali, *"One Hell of a Gamble,"* pp. 247–48; Troyanovsky, "The Caribbean Crisis," p. 152.

71.   Fursenko and Naftali, *"One Hell of a Gamble,"* pp. 252–53.

72.   Ibid., p. 253.

73.   Ibid., p. 257.

74.   Ibid., p. 258. The Presidium and KGB files available to the authors apparently shed no light.

75.   Ibid., pp. 255–56, 258–60.

76.   Alexeev to Foreign Ministry, 25 October 1962, in CWIHP/Harvard Collection.

77.   Fursenko and Naftali, *"One Hell of a Gamble,"* p. 261.

78.   See ibid., pp. 273–78; Lebow and Stein, *We All Lost the Cold War,* p. 115; Raymond L. Garthoff, *Reflections on the Cuban Missile Crisis* (rev. ed.; Washington, DC: Brookings Institution, 1989), p. 67, note 107.

79.   Fursenko and Naftali, *"One Hell of a Gamble,"* pp. 269–71.

80.   Ibid., p. 272.

81.   Troyanovsky, "The Caribbean Crisis," p. 153.

82.   Alexeev to Foreign Ministry, 27 October 1962, in CWIHP/Harvard Collection.

83.   Troyanovsky, "The Caribbean Crisis," p. 153.

84.   Gribkov, "The View from Moscow and Havana," p. 63; Fursenko and Naftali, *"One Hell of a Gamble,"* pp. 274–75.

85.   Alexeev to Foreign Ministry, 25 October 1962 and Castro to Khrushchev, 26 October 1962, both in CWIHP/Harvard collection.

86.   Fursenko and Naftali, *"One Hell of a Gamble,"* p. 266.

87.   Alexeev in *Back to the Brink,* Allyn, Blight, and Welch, p. 30; Garthoff, *Reflections on the Cuban Missile Crisis,* pp. 84–85.

88.   The next day Khrushchev sent a message to Castro that said "you shot down" one of the provocative U.S. overflights, and Khrushchev warned Castro that such steps "will be used by aggressors to their advantage, to further their aims." At that time Castro explained that he had mobilized all his antiaircraft batteries "to support the positions of the Soviet forces" and that, "if we wanted to prevent the risk of a surprise attack, the crews had to have orders to shoot." Castro cryptically added that, "The Soviet Forces Command can give you further details on what happened with the plane that was shot down" (Khrushchev to Castro, 28 October 1962 and Castro to Khrushchev, 28 October 1962). This correspondence was published by the Cuban government in 1990, and Soviet sources verified its accuracy. Copies are available from the John F. Kennedy Library.

89.   Alexeev to Foreign Ministry, 27 October 1962, in CWIHP/Harvard Collection. Alexeev's report was oddly ambiguous in describing whether Soviets or Cubans had shot down the U-2.

90.   Khrushchev to Castro, 30 October 1962, in released correspondence at the John F. Kennedy Library.

91.   Fursenko and Naftali, *"One Hell of a Gamble,"* p. 282.

92.   Ibid.; Troyanovsky, "The Caribbean Crisis," p. 154.

93.   Ibid.

94. See ibid.; Foreign Ministry to Washington (handwritten by Gromyko in Soviet archives), 28 October 1962, in "Russian Foreign Ministry Documents," p. 76; Fursenko and Naftali, *"One Hell of a Gamble,"* p. 284.

95.   By April 1963 Khrushchev was explaining to one U.S. visitor, Averell Harriman, that the socialist countries had gained more from the Wall than they would have gained from signing a peace treaty with East Germany. "Berlin," he said, "is no longer a source of any trouble" (Memcon of Meeting between Harriman and Khrushchev, 26 April 1963, in *FRUS*, 15: 510).

96.   Dean Rusk as told to Richard Rusk, *As I Saw It*, ed. Daniel S. Papp (New York: Norton, 1990), p. 228.

97.   Dmitri Polyanski, quoted in Fursenko and Naftali, *"One Hell of a Gamble,"* p. 352.

98.   Rostow raised his idea and saw it rejected at the first meeting of Nitze's subcommittee of the Executive Committee, on 24 October. Nitze made his Germany suggestion at another meeting of his subcommittee on 1 November. The State Department official present reported that the JCS representative was so furious that he "is still in orbit!" and added that it was hard to believe Nitze would advance an idea that was so "unsound, he is too intelligent. . . . At the same time, however, quiet efforts are being made to try and get the Nitze Committee phased out." It was indeed phased out. See Record of Meeting No. 1, NSC/ExCom/BER-NATO, 24 October 1962, in *FRUS*, 15: 395–97; Kitchen to Alexis Johnson, "Nitze Subcommittee," 1 November 1962, in Cuban Missile Crisis Files, National Security Archive, 1992 Releases Box. Nitze sent President Kennedy a memo on "Berlin in Light of Cuba," that contained suggestions for adjusting East-West relations throughout the world, including a dramatic suggestion to reduce all East and West nuclear delivery vehicles to a total of 500 on each side, with warheads of a combined yield of no more than 50 megatons. All other types of nuclear weapons would be banned. Nitze to Kennedy, undated but returned for filing from the President's office on 5 November 1962, in *FRUS*, 15: 411–19.

99.   At the time McNamara said this could mean either military force or economic force, but we think the quotation fairly represents his thinking and helps explain why he urged his colleagues to reevaluate the merits of at least an air strike against Cuba.

100.   On the relative importance of nuclear and conventional forces in persuading Khrushchev, McNamara testified that, "I realize that there is a kind of chicken-and-the-egg debate going on about which was preeminent. To me that is like trying to argue about which blade of the scissors really cut the paper" (McNamara testimony to the House Armed Services Committee, 12 January 1963, in files of the Office of the Secretary of Defense).

101.   A typical list of things to do, jotted down by Gilpatric on 18 October and left in his files, has 13 major sets of needed actions, from legal analysis of a blockade or state of war, to planning responses if Berlin is blockaded, to handling domestic political aspects (assigned to Robert Kennedy and Sorensen).

102.   See Tyler to Rusk, "Nuclear Sharing with France," 25 October 1962, on State's panicked reaction to Nitze's paper "U.S.-French Reconciliation on

Defense Matters," partly because it conflicted with State's multilateral answer for Turkey, described in Tyler, Rostow, and Talbot to Rusk, "Cuba," 24 October 1962, both in Cuban Missile Crisis Files, National Security Archive, 1992 Releases Box.

103.   See also Ernest R. May, *"Lessons" of the Past: The Use and Misuse of History in American Foreign Policy* (New York: Oxford University Press, 1973); Robert Jervis, *Perception and Misperception in International Politics* (Princeton, NJ: Princeton University Press, 1976); Richard E. Neustadt and Ernest R. May, *Thinking in Time: Uses of History for Decision-makers* (New York: Free Press, 1986).

Index

491